Archaic and Classical
Greek Sicily

Archaic and Classical Greek Sicily

A Social and Economic History

FRANCO DE ANGELIS

OXFORD
UNIVERSITY PRESS

OXFORD

UNIVERSITY PRESS

Oxford University Press is a department of the University of Oxford. It furthers
the University's objective of excellence in research, scholarship, and education
by publishing worldwide.Oxford is a registered trade mark of Oxford University
Press in the UK and certain other countries.

Published in the United States of America by Oxford University Press
198 Madison Avenue, New York, NY 10016, United States of America.

Library of Congress Cataloging-in-Publication Data
Names: De Angelis, Franco, author.
Title: Archaic and classical Greek Sicily : a social and economic history /
Franco De Angelis.
Description: New York, NY : Oxford University Press, 2016. | Series: Greeks
overseas | Includes bibliographical references and index.
Identifiers: LCCN 2015030331| ISBN 978-0-19-517047-4 (hardback : alkaline paper) |
ISBN 978-0-19-972155-9 (e-book) | ISBN 978-0-19-046533-9 (online) |
ISBN 978-0-19-088713-1 (paperback : alkaline paper) |
Subjects: LCSH: Sicily (Italy)—History—To 800. |
Greeks—Italy—Sicily—History. | BISAC: HISTORY / Ancient / Greece.
Classification: LCC DG55.S5 D38 2016 | DDC 937/.802—dc23 LC record available at
http://lccn.loc.gov/2015030331

1 3 5 7 9 8 6 4 2

Printed in the United States of America by Sheridan
on acid-free paper

Contents

List of Figures

List of Tables

List of Maps

Acknowledgments

THIS BOOK WOULD not have been possible without the generous support of certain people and institutions. In the first instance I am especially grateful to Ian Morris (Stanford University), who approached me with the initial idea to publish this book, and to Elissa Morris, the then Classics Editor at Oxford University Press in New York, who oversaw the process of taking the book from proposal to contract. Their successors, Robin Osborne (Cambridge University) and Stefan Vranka, have been ever helpful and have seen the book through to completion. Particular key moments allowed the book to take shape. A generous three-year Standard Research Grant from the Social Sciences and Humanities Research Council of Canada made field and library work in Sicily and Italy possible. In 2005, at the invitation of Carla Antonaccio and Barbara Tsakirgis, I delivered a paper at their session "Morgantina at Fifty" (as part of the 106th Archaeological Institute of America Annual Meeting in Boston), which allowed me to lay the preliminary groundwork for the book's introduction. Later that same year, I organized a workshop called "Frontier History: Cross-cultural and Interdisciplinary Perspectives" at the Peter Wall Institute for Advanced Studies, University of British Columbia, which allowed me to bring together several colleagues studying frontiers across time and space and which contributed greatly to my comparative and theoretical understanding of frontiers. I received generous support from the then director of the Institute, Dianne Newell, whom I would like to thank here. The book began to take shape during the 2007–2008 academic year, when I held a Research Fellowship from the Alexander von Humboldt Foundation at the Ludwig-Maximilians-Universität in Munich. Subsequent research talks delivered especially in Berkeley, Cambridge, Göttingen, Leiden, Pisa, and Rome gave me the opportunity to air many of the ideas contained in the book's various chapters. I am most grateful to my hosts for their invitations and to my audiences for their questions and comments. The three anonymous readers for Oxford University Press also supplied me with much valuable feedback on the various drafts of the manuscript. They provided much food for thought which I have taken on board and for which I am most grateful. Deepest thanks must be given to Robin Osborne for being an extraordinary overseer during the revision of the manuscript, for minding the small details with the big picture always in view and offering always the best possible advice. Deepest thanks must also be extended to Carla Antonaccio and Nino Luraghi for their comments and for welcoming this book into their series. Any misjudgments or errors that may result from the feedback of all these readers are entirely my responsibility. For photographs, other than my own or from the Monte Polizzo project with which I have been involved, I would like to thank the British Museum, the Hunterian Museum and Art Gallery of the University of Glasgow, the Museo Mandralisca, the Parco Archeologico di Himera (and its then director Dr. Francesca Spatafora), and Christine Lane. The original maps have been drawn by the talented Eric Leinberger (Department of Geography, University of British Columbia). I am most grateful to him and to my department for helping to subsidize the costs of their production. My students Odessa Cadieux-Rey and Heather Purves have been excellent editorial assistants as the final manuscript approached submission. A big thank-you is also due to them. The final word of thanks is reserved for Tara, Inessa, and Gisela. They have been by my side from start to finish of this book, patiently supporting me in all ways. Without them, this effort would not have been possible.

Abbreviations: Bibliographic

THE ABBREVIATIONS USED in citing ancient authors and their works follow those in the third edition of *The Oxford Classical Dictionary* (1996), edited by S. Hornblower and A. Spawforth, pp. xxix–liv. Abbreviations for journal titles follow the conventions of *L'Année Philologique*. All other bibliographic abbreviations are listed below.

AA.VV.	various authors
AnnalesESC	*Annales. Economies, sociétés, civilisations*
ASAA	*Annuario della Scuola Archeologica di Atene e delle Missioni Italiane in Oriente*
ArchStorSir	*Archivio Storico Siracusano*
ArchStorSic	*Archivio Storico Siciliano*
ArchStorSicO	*Archivio Storico per la Sicilia Orientale*
AWE	*Ancient West and East*
BAR	*British Archaeological Reports*
BdA	*Bollettino d'Arte del Ministero della Pubblica Istruzione*
BEFAR	*Bibliothèque des Écoles Françaises d'Athènes et de Rome*
BSA	*Annual of the British School at Athens*
BTCGI	*Bibliografia Topografica della Colonizzazione Greca in Italia e nelle Isole Tirreniche* (Pisa and Rome 1977–)
CAJ	*Cambridge Archaeological Journal*
CdA	*Cronache di Archeologia* (new series created out of CronASA in 1972)
CRDAC	*Centro di Ricerche e Documentazione sull'Antichità Classica*
CronASA	*Cronache di Archeologia e di Storia dell'Arte*
DdA	*Dialoghi di Archeologia*
FA	*Fasti Archeologici*
FGrH	F. Jacoby, *Die Fragmente der griechischen Historiker* (Berlin and Leiden 1923–58)

IG	*Inscriptiones Graecae* (Berlin 1873–)
IGCH	M. Thompson, O. Mørkholm, and C.M. Kraay (eds.), *An Inventory of Greek Coin Hoards* (New York 1973)
MAL	*Monumenti Antichi dell'Accademia dei Lincei*
NSc	*Notizie degli Scavi di Antichità*
PdP	*La Parola del Passato*
P.Oxy.	B.P. Grenfell, A.S. Hunt, and others (eds.), *The Oxyrhynchus Papyri* (London 1898–)
QuadMess	*Quaderni dell'Istituto di Archeologia della Facoltà di Lettere e Filosofia dell'Università di Messina*
RE	*Paulys Real-Encyclopädie der classischen Altertumswissenschaft*
RSF	*Rivista di Studi Fenici*
RSP	*Rivista di Scienze Preistoriche*
RTA/JAT	*Rivista di Topografia Antica/Journal of Ancient Topography*
Σ	Scholiast or ancient commentator on an ancient author
SEG	*Supplementum Epigraphicum Graecum* (Leiden 1923–)
SicArch	*Sicilia Archeologica*

Abbreviations: Chronological

BF   Black Figure
BG   Black Gloss
EC   Early Corinthian
EIA   Early Iron Age
EPC   Early Protocorinthian
FBA   Final Bronze Age
G   Geometric
LBA   Late Bronze Age
LG   Late Geometric
LPC   Late Protocorinthian
MBA   Middle Bronze Age
MG   Middle Geometric
MPC   Middle Protocorinthian
PG   Protogeometric
RBA   Recent Bronze Age
RF   Red Figure
SG   Subgeometric

*Archaic and Classical
Greek Sicily*

Introduction

THIS BOOK REPRESENTS the first ever systematic and comprehensive endeavor to tackle the social and economic history of Archaic and Classical Greek Sicily. It has two goals: to collect and analyze the evidence in an interdisciplinary and theoretically informed way, and to help shape future research. The chronological parameters embraced here are the more than four hundred years of Sicilian history that began with the initial settlement of Greeks at the start of the Archaic period in the eighth century BC and ended with the Classical period in about 320 BC.[1] The basic patterns of social and economic behavior were developed and set in this period. As for Greek Sicily's spatial parameters, the modern political boundaries of Sicily today occupy a surface area of some 25,800 square kilometers and include several small surrounding islands, like the Aeolians and Aegates (Map 2).[2] In this book, Greek Sicily is taken to mean the main island. However, Greek Sicily's sphere of interaction was much wider (Map 1). Greg Woolf's description of Roman provinces as "simply concatenations of adjacent yet contrasting microregions linked to each other by the light hand of gubernatorial power, and to microregions

---

1. The following early Hellenistic period, the last sixty years of Greek Sicily to the start of the First Punic War in 264 BC, has been excluded from the present discussion. This is a period that has been well trodden in recent years, helped along by the more abundant epigraphic and literary sources, regarded by many scholars, as we will see throughout this book, as the "real stuff" of history. See the extensive bibliography in Braccesi and Millino 2000, 222–26, to which add since then Consolo Langher 2000; Caccamo Caltabiano, Campagna, and Pinzone 2004; Carroccio 2004; Lehmler 2005; Osanna and Torelli 2006; Zambon 2008; Prag 2009; Prag and Crawley Quinn 2013.

2. Beloch 1886, 261–62 is a still useful discussion of Sicily's surface area both today and in antiquity.

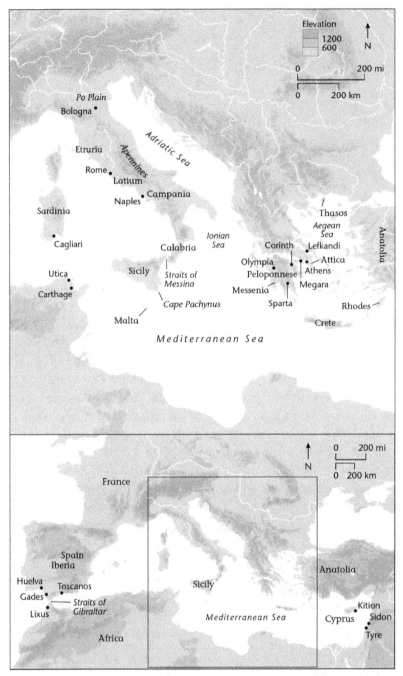

MAP 1 Map of Mediterranean, with major regions and places mentioned in the text.
© Author

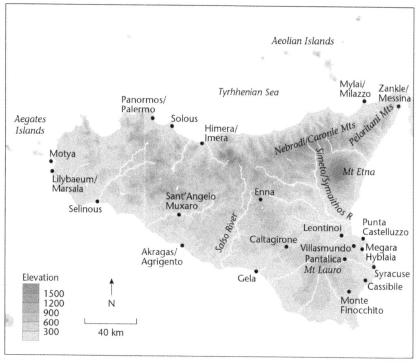

MAP 2 Map of Sicily, showing major geographical features and places mentioned in the text.
© Author

outside the province by more powerful ties of trade and migration, language, ethnicity, and so on" applies equally well to Greek Sicily.[3]

The social and economic history of Archaic and Classical Greek Sicily is a story of remarkable developments. These developments come best into focus when the narrow disciplinary divides and regional specializations that currently characterize the study of Greek Sicily are bridged. Ancient Sicily as a whole must be viewed as a land influenced by the dynamics of multiple cultures and networks, which made the island simultaneously part of frontier and world history, shaped all at once by local, regional, and global phenomena. These are dynamics that go back right to the start of Sicilian Greek history, when Greeks established themselves in Sicily as Greece was rapidly developing in the eighth and seventh

---

3. Woolf 2004, 423–24. In the case of Cyprus, see the thoughtful discussion by Knapp 2008, 14–19.

centuries. Sicily provided both the conditions and opportunities for Greeks to satisfy their growing appetite for a larger share of the Mediterranean's resources and possibilities. Sicily's coasts were little populated and much land needed to be cleared, factors which conditioned the social and economic decisions of the early Greek settlers. The control of labor became central, affecting the possible kinds of economic decision-making. Cities began as frontier establishments, with nascent populations and institutions. But when we combine into a single approach the political, territorial, and urban trajectories of these cities, we see that the first of four economic takeoffs that occurred in Archaic and Classical Greek Sicily was within a century of initial settlement. These fledgling cities were well on their way to becoming very successful states, with larger cosmo-politan populations and more complex institutions. Their impressive physical and spatial developments were spearheaded by elites who organized themselves into clans that tightly controlled the distribution of land and protected their place at the top of the social hierarchy. The initial frontier conditions encoun-tered in Sicily contributed significantly to the elite's ability to shape and hold on to power, and calls for egalitarian and democratic thinking over the course of Sicilian Greek history proved difficult to achieve. Grain exports made consid-erable sense as an early economic activity, given the ideal environmental con-ditions, low labor requirements, and demand in Greece, but Greek Sicily was never a colonial monoculture. Abundant evidence exists today for manufactur-ing, mining, fishing, and other agricultural crops, particularly olive and vine, in the Archaic period, shattering old stereotypes of an unchanging Sicilian Greek economy over four hundred years. Some of these developments mark out Sicily as unique when compared to the history of the Greek homeland from where the settlers came. Local and regional features and dynamics explain these dif-ferences. At the same time, Sicily and Greece maintained enduring diasporic links right from the start of their conjoined histories. Their relationship was not one of center and periphery or of haphazardly overlapping regional trajectories. Instead, the two regions were interconnected and interdependent throughout the Archaic and Classical periods, with Sicily forming an integral and important region of the ancient Greek world.

Many of these conclusions mirror recent trends in ancient historical prac-tice that Woolf alludes to in the quotation above. The history of Greek Sicily, however, has not always been conceived of and studied in this way. From the sixteenth century to the present, the study of Greek Sicily has, like any other historical field, been influenced by a combination of regional, national, and international developments that have shaped its questions and data. We need to outline these developments here and take a stand on what to discard and what to adopt in light of recent evidence.

Between the sixteenth century and the unification of Italy in 1861, four main regional and international developments affected the study of Greek Sicily. The first was Sicily's dependent status as part of a larger kingdom or empire. Sicilians studied their past for models and ideas that could help them better understand the present, and that meant primarily that ancient Rome and its provinces received the lion's share of scholarly attention. In other words, there was a near absence of studies on Greek Sicily. Virtually all of these early Sicilian studies, moreover, belonged to an antiquarian tradition characterized by an extremely strong regional focus (even in discussions of ancient Greek literature) and a usually uncritical, believe-all attitude to ancient sources.[4] The second development was the Grand Tour, which entailed learned and usually foreign travelers seeking firsthand experience with ancient Greece, Hellenism being now regarded as the source of the European spirit. Both southern Italy and Sicily were initially major draws for these travelers, because of these regions' impressive ancient Greek monuments and the fact that the Ottomans ruled Greece, making it less accessible to foreigners. In Sicily the activities of Grand Tour travelers often centered around writing travelogues, studying and illustrating art and architecture (sometimes accomplished through excavation, as it was then conceived), and absorbing as much of Greek antiquity and its survival as possible.[5] The Grand Tour's legacy of foreigners associating Sicily with Hellenism has lived on to the present day, as have the strong regional focus and approach to the ancient sources.[6]

These developments were taking place alongside two other international ones that redefined ancient Hellenism. While ancient Hellenism remained the dominant inspiration for Europeans at home and abroad, some of its branches started to be deemed more important than others. The American Revolution and the creation of the modern Greek nation-state acted as prime stimuli. The lead-up to the American Revolution caused European powers to reassess their settlement and colonization policies and to favor mercantile endeavors and federalist associations.[7] In this light, ancient Greece, rather than Rome, served

---

4. On the Sicilian antiquarian tradition, see generally Pace 1958, 1–100, 551–54; Salmeri 1993; Ceserani 2000; De Francesco 2013, 100–106. On the uncritical uses of sources in this period, see Pace 1958, 55; La Rosa 1987, 708; Pinzone 2000, 113, 130. It is worth stressing that Sicilian antiquarianism was regional in its focus, but that should not be translated into isolation (Brancato 1973).

5. The best discussion on Sicily can be found in Momigliano 1979. For Italy as a whole, see Black 2003.

6. Momigliano 1979, 178.

7. See Urquhart forthcoming.

as the better model. The drive for American independence elicited intense discussions on the relationships between ancient Greek *metropoleis* and their so-called colonies (a translation of the ancient word *apoikia*, technically an independent "home away," that only became more entrenched as a result of these discussions).[8] The independence of the American colonies led to the ancient Greek colonies gaining their independence in the scholarly mindset. But this was only a temporary victory. The creation of the modern Greek nation-state, following liberation from the Ottomans, threw a wrench in the works. Greece naturally became a rallying point for discussions of Hellenism in all its temporal and spatial manifestations. When Athens was chosen as the capital of this new nation-state in 1834, in large part because of Athens' associations with its impressive ancient counterpart, it was a watershed moment. Ancient Athens appealed to Europeans because of the Ottoman Empire, which represented Europe's single biggest political foe. Ancient Athens could be used to distinguish Europeans from the Ottoman Turks. For Athens, in addition to its cultural and historical achievements, had defeated the Persians, another eastern empire. Athens, moreover, was quite uppity about its ethnic and racial purity, something meaningful to Europeans, both at home and in their colonies, as they fought for supremacy of the world and its many peoples. Europeans worried that cultural mixing would submerge them. Ancient Athenian democracy appealed too, as modern fledgling democracies began to emerge; this provided yet another way to distinguish Europeans as politically different from the Ottomans and their stultifying sultans. In Athens, ancient evidence and modern mindsets coalesced, giving rise to a new framework in which to appreciate and study the history of ancient Greece. Within this new paradigm of ancient Hellenism, the long shadow of marginalization inevitably began to be cast on such regions as Sicily.

This new configuration of Hellenism is most clearly seen in the twelve-volume history of ancient Greece by the Englishman George Grote published between 1846 and 1856.[9] Grote solidified the trend of Hellenocentrism, and Athenocentrism in particular. The civilizing mission of England in its colonial possessions was introduced into ancient Greek history through a process of Hellenization of non-Greeks, or "barbarians."[10] Grote allowed for fusion between incoming settlers and existing natives. Such fusion, however, was not between equals and was couched in a racialized discourse,

---

8. Cf. Osborne 1998; De Angelis 1998, 539.

9. Grote 1846–56. See recently Ceserani 2012, 215–19.

10. Grote 1846–56, 3:494–97.

characteristic of the time, of a debased and inferior end product caused through miscegenation.[11] On the one hand, ancient Greeks brought civilization to backward lands and peoples, in which the cultural dominance of the ancient Greeks went unquestioned. On the other hand, this intermixture affected the purity of the ancient Greek settlers, who for this reason were inferior to their Athenian and Aegean brethren and thus secondary in the overall scheme of Grote's history.[12] Sicily, therefore, was not a land of pure Hellenism and consequently deserved less scholarly attention. The conditions were created for cutting Sicily loose from the larger narrative of ancient Greek history, now that the Sicilian "colonies" were regarded as independent of their homeland.

These developments were reinforced and expanded when Italy unified in 1861 to create the modern Italian nation-state with its capital at Rome. Regional asymmetry emerged in the two decades following Italian unification through the development of the so-called "Southern Question" discourse, a form of Orientalism, which emphasized and contrasted Italy's internal differences in contemporary colonial and neocolonial terms.[13] The country was divided into two blocs: an advanced and industrialized North and a backward and peasant South. Sicily was placed in the backward peasant category.[14] Scholarship was impacted in three main ways. First, Sicilian scholars expressed harsh attitudes over the relationship ancient Rome had with the province of Sicily. At the time of unification, Sicily was ruled by a kingdom whose capital was Naples, which self-identified with ancient Rome. While Sicily's negative attitudes to ancient Rome had existed since the eighteenth century as a way to be anti-Naples, in the aftermath of unification these attitudes gained new momentum and spurred on interest in Sicily's pre-Roman past, including the development of prehistoric archaeology.[15] Second, the establishment of a national framework for the study and display of Italy's past also affected Sicily. Antonino Salinas (1841-1914), the director of the Palermo Museum, proposed in 1873 a kind of total history research and museum strategy for Italy, in which classical remains were to appear alongside Byzantine, Arab, and medieval ones, and

---

11. Grote 1846–56, 3:494–97, 494–95, 498–99. See now Macgregor Morris 2008; Challis 2010.

12. Grote 1846–56, 1:ix; 3:369.

13. See in particular Schneider 1998 and Shavit 1994, 322.

14. Mack Smith 1968, 445–52; Dyson 2006, 108–109.

15. Momigliano 1979, 183; 1980, 775; Guidi 1988, 53; Salmeri 1991, 286–93; 1992, 99; Pinzone 2000, 138; Fantasia 2003a, 107; De Francesco 2013, 100–06.

high art beside everyday objects.[16] Italy's central government rejected Salinas' proposal, even though Sicily's very history invited world historical and comparative perspectives. Third, the rejection of Salinas' proposal had much to do with the poor regard the central Italian government had for its southern regions, which, because of the "Southern Question" discourse, were treated as politically insignificant cultural backwaters that were racially inferior. These attitudes were often back-projected into earlier periods of history, including Greek Sicily, by Italian and foreign scholars alike.[17]

World historical and comparative perspectives were nevertheless introduced in a big way to Sicilian history by Edward Freeman (1823–1892), Arthur Evans' father-in-law, in his massive four-volume unfinished universal history.[18] Freeman declared that the main revolution in historical method was the comparative approach, which would eliminate the distinction between the classical and barbarian worlds, and between the ancient and modern worlds.[19] In general, Freeman refused to be confined by traditional scholarly categories: "Nowhere do we better learn than in Sicily the folly of those arbitrary divisions which have made the study of history vain and meaningless."[20] It should cause no surprise, therefore, that Freeman discussed Sicily's native populations and factored them and geography into his history. Freeman's main form of evidence was perforce ancient literary sources, given that archaeology and epigraphy were infant disciplines in Sicily at the time. That meant that he mainly concentrated on the political and military events narrated in these literary sources. He did raise social and economic matters, both when these sources did[21] and when he felt something could be said about, for instance, the reasons for choosing a site for settlement, the sizes of Greek territories, and geographical changes from antiquity to his day.[22] Freeman,

---

16. Bonacasa 1977, 678; La Rosa 1987, 714–16; Barbanera 1998, 14–19; Dyson 2006, 53. Cf. also Giannitrapani's (1998) plea for more prehistoric and medieval archaeology in Sicily, no doubt a distant symptom of the decision not to take up Salinas' proposal.

17. See Gras 1989, 399–400; Barker 1995, 15–16; Gibson 1998; Pandolfi 1998; Rosengarten 1998; Dench 2003, 296–97; De Angelis 2006; Ceserani 2012, 3–5 and throughout; De Francesco 2013, 133–57; cf. also van Wees 2000. Many of the authors note the lingering effects of this thinking on scholarship still today.

18. Cf. Freeman 1891–94, 1:viii, for this description of his work. On Freeman's life and work, see Pace 1958, 75–76; Manni 1977, 22–27; Mazzarino 1977, 8–9, Cracco 1981; Gabba 1981; Momigliano 1981; Salmeri 1992, 121 n. 74; Barlow 2004; Calder 2004; Shepherd 2005a.

19. Cf. Cracco 1981, 350, 353; Momigliano 1979, 185; 1981, 321.

20. Freeman 1891–94, 1:viii.

21. Freeman 1891–94, 2:13–14, 174–75, 390–401; 4:13.

22. Freeman 1891–94, 1:368–69, 394–95, 401, 416, 419, 440; 2:2–3, 22–23, 33.

living in England at the height of the British Empire, was naturally drawn to making parallels between ancient Sicily and modern colonial America.[23] Freeman was careful to distinguish between modern colonies and ancient Greek *apoikiai* and noted that the so-called Greek and Phoenician "colonies" in Sicily were independent of their homelands.[24] The sharing of Sicily by these "colonies" made the island a borderland and a battleground between Semites and Aryans (to use the word then in vogue for what we today call Indo-Europeans).[25] Freeman ascribed ancient Sicily's success, as apparently in colonial America, to outside settlement, and as a result he argued that the true history of Sicily was owed to Greeks.[26] We will return to this point in the Conclusions, where it will be tested against the evidence, which seems to be in favor of it. Nevertheless, Freeman had an open attitude toward the interaction and integration of natives and Greeks, in large part because he rightly viewed them as "near kinsfolk" of Aryan origin and thus unlike the "Red Indians" (again, to use the words then in vogue) of the New World.[27] Natives and Greeks both learned from and taught one another.[28] Even so, he regarded Greeks as the superior of the two groups, with the natives becoming Hellenized without conquest.[29] Freeman's thinking was both characteristic and uncharacteristic of the time in adopting a middle-ground cultural approach that still recognized the dominance of Hellenism, but played down the racial factor.

The world historical and comparative perspectives of both Freeman and Salinas were in some respects ahead of their time. They introduced valuable perspectives that will be adopted and reinvigorated in this book. While their perspectives may seem natural and fully acceptable to us today, this has not always been the case. They have had a limited impact since the nineteenth century, because their perspectives had to compete with nationalism and especially with the Italian government's policies on cultural heritage, formally adopted in 1875.

In that year, the Italian national government officially adopted the German intellectual model on behalf of all state institutions of cultural

---

23. For a recent overview of nineteenth-century settler colonialism, see Belich 2010.

24. Freeman 1891–94, 1:14–15.

25. Freeman 1891–94, 1:v–viii. Cf. also in a similar vein Pais 1894, vii–xvi.

26. Freeman 1891–94, 1:5–8, 10, 45, 319.

27. Freeman 1891–94, 1:19–20, 308; 2:22–23.

28. Freeman 1891–94, 1:103–104, 174.

29. Freeman 1891–94: 1:17, 151–52, 446.

heritage. The professionalization of classical scholarship emerged very early in Germany, at the forefront internationally in this period and very influential until well after World War II. Italy wanted to link itself to this German tradition in order to insert itself into the wider European intellectual community.[30] Association with Germany's classical scholarship carried prestige, but it also brought an arsenal of methods. For ancient history, this entailed a rigorous and positivistic philological approach, largely concerned with *Quellenforschung* ("source research") and political and military history. For classical archaeology, this involved the adoption of an aesthetics and art historical orientation. For both disciplines, the collection of basic sources was the central concern. As a result, German classical scholarship was generally also characterized by an unwillingness to advance interpretations and to synthesize data, the attitude being that more data were needed before any history could be written.[31] From 1875 onward, the Italian government's policies on cultural heritage also excluded Germans and other foreigners from excavating in Italy (Sicily included).[32] Among other things, this resulted in Greece becoming the center of classical archaeology in the Mediterranean, aided by Hellenism and the slow but steady removal of Ottoman control. But this ban also necessitated the creation of another outlet for the dissemination of German classical scholarship in Italy.

This occurred in two ways: Italians, like Salinas, were sent to Germany to study, and Germans came to Italy to fill chairs of ancient history and classical archaeology. Of the Germans who came to Italy to fill chairs, two in particular stand out in regard to the study of ancient Sicily: Adolf Holm (1830–1900) and Karl Julius Beloch (1854–1929).[33] Both men made contributions to social and economic history, but in different ways.

Adolf Holm was among the first Germans who took up professorships in Italy, arriving in Palermo in 1877. He was already a key figure in the study of ancient Sicily while still in his hometown of Lübeck, from where he laid

---

30. Mazzarino 1977, 16; Momigliano 1987, 161–78; Salmeri 1991, 294; Ampolo 1997, 79–80; Dyson 2006, 100, 103. Salvatore Settis (1993) has noted one of the strange situations this adoption of the German model resulted in: Ennio Quirino Visconti, the so-called "Italian Winckelmann," was a prime influence in the formation of German classical archaeology, which, in turn, Italy then went on to adopt.

31. See Härke 1991, 200; Salmeri 1992, 98.

32. Dyson 2006, 98–99, 194.

33. On Holm, see Christ 1996, 144–49; Barbanera 1998, 72; Pinzone 2000; Uggeri 2000; AA.VV. 2003. On Beloch, see Momigliano 1966; Polverini 1990; Christ 1996, 150–51, 157–70; Ampolo 1997, 96.

important groundwork with the publication of several basic works, including a three-volume general history and monographs devoted to historical geography and Catania.[34] A monograph on Sicilian coinage until Augustus followed toward the end of his life.[35] Holm was a product of his time and environment. Like so many German-trained scholars then, he adhered to a positivistic approach, generally avoiding interpretations in favor of collecting evidence. These were immensely useful and pioneering efforts, which some scholars openly acknowledged,[36] and are not without interest to social and economic historians today. Holm made room in his general history for all of Sicily's peoples, not just Greeks and Romans, although, like so many of his contemporaries, he thought that the arrival of Greeks, and not Phoenicians, introduced the genius that "made" the island.[37] Holm also included historical geography in the broadest sense, including speculations about the size of Greek territories and their population. The study of ancient Sicilian coins proceeded, until relatively recently, along the same lines as laid down by Holm, the focus being to attribute coins to their time and place.[38]

Social and economic questions were of central importance to Karl Julius Beloch, the other transplanted German with a strong interest in ancient Sicily. From a young age, ill health brought Beloch to the warmer and sunnier climate of Italy, where he completed his undergraduate studies in Palermo and Rome before going on to Heidelberg for his doctorate.[39] While Beloch should have served as a bridge between Germany and Italy, he fell between two stools, so to speak, having throughout his career critics in both countries.[40] Nevertheless, Beloch pioneered the use of certain basic approaches to ancient history that we take for granted today, namely the use of statistics, comparativism, and a questioning attitude to ancient sources, sometimes verging on the hypercritical.

---

34. Holm's *Geschichte Siciliens im Alterthum* appeared in Leipzig between 1870 and 1898; the Italian edition appeared between 1896 and 1906 and has been regularly reprinted since then. The other two monographs originally appeared as *Antike Geographie Siciliens* (Lübeck 1866) and as *Das alte Catania* (Lübeck 1873). For the Italian versions, see Holm 1871; 1925.

35. This appeared as a monograph within the third volume (on pp. 543–741) of his *Geschichte Siciliens im Alterthum* (Leipzig 1898). For the Italian version, which was published separately, see Holm 1906.

36. Cf. Freeman 1891–94, 1:ix.

37. Holm 1896–1906, 1:105–322, 3:172–80, esp. 1:231 on the Greek genius.

38. Caccamo Caltabiano 2003, 287. Cf. also Finley 1979, 201.

39. Momigliano 1966, 32–33; Bruno Sunseri 1994; Thomson de Grummond 1996, 142–43.

40. Ridley 1975–76, 532; Cagnetta 1994, 211, 213.

Beloch stood out in his time with these approaches and put forward many new interpretations of ancient history.[41]

Holm and Beloch had different visions of ancient Sicily and were thus often critical of each other's work. They were at opposite ends of the spectrum when it came to estimating the demographic and agricultural resources and capacities of Greek Sicily, Holm aiming high and Beloch aiming low.[42] While both Holm and Beloch used wheat yields to estimate ancient Greek agricultural potential in Sicily and to recognize slaves as a significant part of the labor force,[43] Beloch thought Greek Sicily was a precursor to Roman Sicily and thus was structured as a wheat monoculture, with producers and consumers residing in nucleated settlements.[44] Beloch also had a tendency to down-date and deny the validity of certain historical phenomena. The best example of this is his writing the Phoenicians out of early Greek history, not only because he avoided using mythical and legendary source material, but also as a way to quell rumors of his Jewish roots in a world of growing anti-Semitism.[45] Holm and Beloch did much to engineer the structure of ancient Sicilian social and economic history in terms of approaches and interpretations. Nevertheless, many of their conclusions can today be revised, thanks to new evidence and thinking. In the chapters below, we will see in particular that their estimates for population are too high and their estimates for agricultural capacity too low. Beloch's belief in a timeless Sicilian Greek wheat monoculture and nucleated settlement patterns and his downplaying of Phoenicians are also reconsidered.

The creation of a hybrid approach involving the combination of classical and prehistoric studies resulted from the grafting of this imported German tradition of classical scholarship onto Sicily's regional scholarly tradition.[46] Some of the biggest names in Sicilian scholarship—Francesco Saverio Cavallari (1809–1896), Paolo Orsi (1859–1935), and Luigi Bernabò Brea (1910–1999)—were fine practitioners of this approach.[47] They retrieved data not

---

41. See recently Polverini 2009. On the works most relevant to Sicily, see Beloch 1874; 1886, 261–305; 1889; 1895; 1912–1927, 1.1:229–51; 1.2: 17, 218–31, 245–53; 2.1:69–74, 126–37, 322–23, 373, 402–13; 3.1:49–60, 110–31, 263–313, 580–92.

42. For discussion, see De Angelis 2000a, 139 n. 30.

43. See De Angelis 2000a, 118.

44. For discussion, see De Angelis 2000a, 140; 2006, 39.

45. Bernal 1987, 373–77; Ampolo 1997, 96.

46. D'Agostino 1991, 52–54; Guidi 2002.

47. On Cavallari, see La Rosa 1987, 712–13; Pinzone 2000, 119. On Orsi, see Arias 1976, 15–29; Leighton 1986; La Rosa 1987, 719–20; AA.VV. 1991; Barbanera 1998, 80–82; Dyson 2006, 109–10, 195–96. On Bernabò Brea, see La Rosa 1987, 724–25; Guidi 1988, 135–36; D'Agostino 1991, 59–60; Pelagatti and Spadea 2004. In general, see Guidi 1988, 82.

commonly collected (such as faunal remains) and raised issues that would otherwise have fallen between two disciplinary stools.[48] As prehistorians they had broader definitions of material culture, whereas as classicists they tended to view this same material culture through the filter of classical literature and culture. Orsi and Bernabò Brea laid the foundations for the study of prehistoric Sicily against this classically inspired backdrop. The pro-Hellenic values that accompanied this practice ultimately caused the native cultures of Sicily to be placed in an inferior position vis-à-vis the Greeks, whose literature and culture infused themselves into interpretations and terminology, from the labeling of archaeological cultures to the imposition of the "Dark Ages" on the western Mediterranean. We will encounter these and other examples of this practice in this book and test their soundness on each occasion.

By the close of the nineteenth century, certain approaches to Greek Sicily had become rooted. Scholarly infusions from national and international sources were already the norm, leading to various intellectual directions still evident today. Central to all scholarly efforts was the collection of basic evidence in the German academic tradition. This made considerable sense given the infancy of the various disciplines, but entailed a positivistic retrieval and handling of the evidence, wherein historical interpretation was usually a secondary by-product of the main activity. While these practices might be viewed today in a negative manner, in context they were logical and meaningful steps that created the large and indispensable database currently available for study. The task of the social and economic historian today is to navigate between respecting these practices, which are still common, and interpreting the data in light of the latest theoretical and methodological developments. The way forward, in my opinion, was already delineated in the last generation of the nineteenth century through the melding of scholarly disciplines and approaches. The hybrid practices and enlightened perspectives taken by scholars like Karl Julius Beloch, Edward Freeman, and Paolo Orsi have to be more appreciated for their pioneering efforts, which often challenged the scholarly currents of their times. Three of their contributions in particular deserve our attention today: the combination of classical and prehistoric studies (Orsi), the interplay between regional and interregional (world) forces on Sicilian history (Freeman), and the use of comparison from later, better-documented periods of frontier and settler history (Beloch and Freeman). These contributions are to be preferred to their opposites: seeing Sicily as a self-contained region, studying it as either classical or prehistoric in isolation, and treating data without theoretical and methodological input. By the end of the nineteenth century, the main historical interpretations emerging out of the

---

48. For the faunal remains, see Villari 1987; 1995

adoption or rejection of these scholarly practices and perspectives—between, say, Freeman's multicultural middle-ground approach that played down race, Orsi's pro-Hellenic stance of cultural superiority vis-à-vis natives, and Beloch's denial of a Phoenician role—had also taken shape. These practices and viewpoints only became starker in the century that followed.

In the first half of the twentieth century, scholarship on Greek Sicily developed further along two new lines. In the first, Italian nationalism, with its use of ancient Rome as a model of national identity, left its stamp on scholarship in an even greater way. This culminated in a cult of *Romanitas* under the Fascist regime of Benito Mussolini, as part of which was constructed an image of Italian national unity and identity not seen before or since.[49] Revealing the glories of ancient Rome through the spade was modern Italy's way of gaining prestige and importance in the eyes of rival nations. This affected the study of Greek Sicily in two ways. The first was by comparing the merits of ancient Greek and Roman civilization, including how ancient Rome's detractors had gone too far in upholding Hellenism.[50] It was argued that ancient Rome kept Greek civilization alive and made great contributions to the spheres of politics and society in ways that the ancient Greeks did not.[51] Secondly, an anti-classicism trend developed in Italy, in which the autonomy and value of Italic art was promoted vis-à-vis its powerful Greek counterpart.[52] Ancient Greek colonization was in a sense a threat to modern Italians, who at the time wanted instead to be viewed as colonizers in the world, and not as citizens of a country itself colonized and regarded as backward, whether in the present or in the past.[53] This included a reluctance to draw comparisons with New World colonization and a strong reaction to such comparisons when drawn by foreign scholars. Study of the ancient Greeks in Sicily had to swim against these two nationalistic currents.

The other new line of development in the first half of the twentieth century concerned the emergence of synthetic works of scholarship. This was made possible by the growth and publication of archaeological data since the later nineteenth century, thanks in large part to the efforts of Orsi.[54] Two major syntheses were written in this period. While they solidified an archaeological

49. Pandolfi 1998, 287; Dyson 2006, 175–86.

50. Pais 1934. On Pais, see recently Ceserani 2012, 219–29; De Francesco 2013, 165–80.

51. Pais 1934, 11–12.

52. Barbanera 1998, 121–26; De Juliis 2000, 5–7.

53. Cf. Dyson 2006, 194–95; Cusumano 2009, 46.

54. Rizza 1971, 352.

history approach to the study of ancient Sicily, they proceeded from very different bases, and as a result produced radically opposed historical visions, which are still under discussion.

One of the syntheses came from the pen of Sicilian-born Biagio Pace (1889–1955). It consisted of a four-volume history of ancient Sicily in almost 2,500 pages published between 1935 and 1949.[55] Pace wanted to put the study of ancient Sicily on a completely new footing.[56] This required two things: an interpretive outlook that avoided the positivist approach of the German sort,[57] and a unified vision that had been missing before (and even afterwards).[58] Pace was open-minded with his subject matter, studying all peoples and materials, practicing a kind of total history in the way advocated by his teacher Salinas.[59] In Pace's vision, the ancient Greeks were not the main and only player in the island's ancient history, as was sometimes thought, especially by foreigners; there were natives, Carthaginians, and Romans too.[60] Pace also enlisted the nationalist agendas of his day. His own nationalism grew through taking part in Italian archaeological work in the Levant in the years before and after World War I and through his involvement in the upper echelons of Italian fascist politics.[61] Pace's work, in consequence, is also characterized by a softening of anti–ancient Rome attitudes, including the acceptance of the politically useful claims of the ancient literary sources regarding the Roman origins of the Sikels.[62] Pace's acceptance and views of Sicily being under the umbrella of ancient Rome reflected his own place in the world.

Within this larger Italian framework, Pace sought to establish a distinct Sicilian identity. He subsumed the impact of ancient Greek and other cultures coming to

---

55. The first volume was published posthumously in a second edition in 1958.

56. Pace 1958, vii–viii.

57. Pace 1958, 63. Cf. Manni 1977, 22; Mazzarino 1977, 5 n. 7; Salmeri 1992, 98; and Pinzone 2000, 131.

58. Bonacasa 1977, 680–81.

59. Salmeri 1993, 296–97. Some reviewers, like Jean Bérard (1937, 259; 1939, 545) and John Myres (1937, 128), went so far as to describe Pace's work as a "compilation" or "directory," but supporters of Pace have vehemently denied these labels (Caputo 1955, 102).

60. Caputo 1955, 104–107; Momigliano 1979, 185–86; 1980, 768, 773–74; Salmeri 1993, 297 and 298 n. 103.

61. Caputo 1955, 83–85, 92–95; Rizza 1971, 347–48.

62. Pace 1958, 393–97. Cf. Devoto 1957, 9; Rizza 1971, 349; Mazzarino 1977, 5–6. It is extremely revealing to observe that Ettore Pais' overall handling of ancient sources can best be described as hypercritical, yet he too accepted the Roman origins of the Sikels, as he also became more closely associated with the Fascist regime (Salmeri 1992, 104, 109).

Sicily from outside under a strictly Sicilian lens, as Sicilians were generally wont to do, from Tommaso Fazello in the sixteenth century onward.[63] Pace maintained that there was a Sicilian genius at work, quite distinct from the Greek,[64] and he was ready to accept native influences on Greek culture and to see the island as a place of cultural innovation and dynamism. Particularly the first three volumes of Pace's history are of interest to us, for they deal with ethnic and social factors (including, interestingly, modern historiography of ancient Sicily), art, craftworking, engineering, culture, and religious life.[65] As part of his discussion of ethnic and social factors, Pace included an extended foray into native society and economy prior to the arrival of Greeks in Sicily, emphasizing their achievements and the density of their settlements and population.[66] When it came to Greco-Roman antiquity, Pace devoted individual chapters to production and exchange, navigation and roadways, territory sizes, demography (including the little that could be said about disease), weights and measures (including coinage), figurative art, architecture, engineering, and intellectual life (from science through philosophy and law to poetry).[67] The role of manufacturing, from everyday objects to high art, occupied a special place in Pace's work, again not surprisingly, given that Salinas had been his teacher. In particular, Pace sought to challenge the notion that the Sicilian Greeks did not produce any of their own art or at least were not innovative or dynamic in the face of supposedly superior imported models from the Greek homeland. The lack of written sources for Sicilian artists had led others to take their silence at face value, and this was often coupled with modern colonialist attitudes that regarded Sicily as a backward periphery or "provincial" (the term most commonly used then). This is a dilemma still facing current scholarship (see Chapter 4 below), although most of Pace's conclusions in this regard have been upheld and vindicated through later work.[68]

The denial of artistic achievement was quite pronounced in the other major synthesis of this period, Thomas Dunbabin's 1948 book *The Western Greeks*.[69] Dunbabin modeled the historical development of ancient Greek Sicily on the

63. Momigliano 1980; Ceserani 2000, 191; Cusumano 2009, 43–46.

64. Arias 1976, 41–42, 101; Mazzarino 1977, 14–15; Salmeri 1991, 295; Dyson 2006, 196.

65. The fourth volume discusses the Barbarian Invasions and Byzantine Sicily.

66. Pace 1958, 345–87.

67. Pace 1935–49, 2:3–514, 3:1–450; 1958, 389–539.

68. Arias 1976, 33–37.

69. On Dunbabin's life and scholarship, see De Angelis 1998; Zarmati 2004, 266–67; Dyson 2006, 195. Other notable contemporary scholars possessed similar attitudes, including Arthur Dale Trendall (cf. Denoyelle and Iozzo 2009, 24–27) and William Dinsmoor (1927, 75; cf. Dyson 2006, 196).

British Empire of his time, with the result that contemporary colonialist and imperialist thinking shaped his interpretations. This was done in a much more radical way than in the work of Freeman, his English-language predecessor, perhaps because Dunbabin was born and brought up on the colonial and imperial front lines of Australia. In this light, ancient Sicily's natives were regarded, like the Aborigines of Dunbabin's day, as altogether insignificant and certainly not capable of influencing the Greek settlers. While Pace gave much space to native Sicilian societies and economies, Dunbabin devoted under 7 percent of his first chapter to them, and then only as a kind of appendix after the various Greek foundations had been discussed. For native Sicily was considered *terra nullius* in the same way as the phrase was used in modern European colonization. This similarly entailed a superior culture causing the physical destruction or complete acculturation or assimilation of an inferior culture.[70] Therefore, the outsiders (whether ancient Greeks or modern Europeans) gain dominance in all areas over the existing peoples, and local histories get sidelined in favor of the outsiders' bigger ambitions. Consequently, every trace of the outsiders' material culture in a native context can only mean cultural transformation and assimilation, usually labeled "Hellenization," and the frontier's one-sided political, not social, consequences are emphasized.[71] Contemporary racial theory and the fear of miscegenation helped to create these social barriers. They also acted as the backdrop for Dunbabin to play down the role of the Phoenicians in his reconstructions, following the Orientalist and anti-Semitic world views that had developed in the preceding generations. Phoenician-Greek interactions were minimized and given separate spheres that rarely overlapped. So trade relations and Phoenicians resident in Greek settlements were out of the question; instead, a nearly constant state of hostility existed between the two sides.

Dunbabin put ancient Greeks on a pedestal. At the same time, his Hellenocentrism entailed the Sicilian Greeks looking to Greece, the motherland, for all sense of direction in culture and economics. The colonialist and imperialist ideologies of Dunbabin's time were infused with a very strong Hellenism anchored to Greece, which was regarded as the center, with the so-called colonies as the periphery, as we have already seen. This was aided

---

70. Gosden 2004, 114–52.

71. Still today, whether we recognize it or not, versions of these colonialist and imperialist interpretive forces are at work at sites in culture contact situations across the ancient Mediterranean: note Hall's (2003, 24) reminder that sociopolitical interpretations are equally possible when discussing Greek and Greek-style material culture in native contexts. On the more general legacy of modern colonialism in framing questions and interpretations, see Gosden 2004, 20.

by the absence of a strong Italian tradition for studying the western Greeks,[72] which facilitated the use of Greece as the yardstick against which to measure and compare Sicily. For Dunbabin, Sicilian Greek art was at best a pale reflection of a dynamic and innovative Greek homeland. On this line of thinking, it followed that Sicilian Greeks did little or none of their own manufacturing and instead exchanged staple products, like wheat, for luxury goods imported from Greece in ways that Dunbabin thought paralleled the Australia, New Zealand, and Canada of his day. Dunbabin was not the creator or the sole adherent of this kind of powerful Hellenocentrism. Such thinking can be found in other scholarship beyond the British Empire, though generally not in Italian scholarship, making intelligible Pace's very different interpretations.[73]

The historical syntheses of Pace and Dunbabin were masterful achievements, providing frameworks into which to insert the data and shape them with meaning. Their archaeological historical approaches resulted in a more robust view of Sicilian Greek history, allowing the discussion to move beyond the limited written sources and into areas of social, economic, and cultural history that would otherwise be poorly documented. This basic approach remains perhaps the most enduring feature of their work, and it is one adopted in this book. Both scholars, however, were influenced by very different and charged political perspectives and, in consequence, their common approach led to polarized historical interpretations. This meant either the inclusion or exclusion of peoples as historical actors both in terms of Sicilian regional and interregional interaction, and assigning or negating agency and innovation to the ancient peoples they identified with. The guiding principle in navigating between one extreme or another has to be by testing their arguments against current evidence and thinking. When approached in this way, we see that both scholars have their merits and inadequacies. Dunbabin's ideas of a dependent Sicilian Greek colonial economy must be rejected, as they contradict the abundant evidence for manufacturing and other

---

72. Ceserani 2012.

73. Note Bérard (1937, 260), who views Pace's thesis of native influence on Sicilian Greek culture as wrong. It is worth noting that not all the Italians who worked on Sicily shared Pace's vision of Hellenism. The most notable exception was Orsi, as already seen. Most scholars, however, like Emanuele Ciaceri (AA.VV. 1994), were sympathetic to Italy's so-called native cultures and avoided making direct comparisons with New World colonization with their knock-on effects (cf. Ceserani 2012, 257). Eugenio Manni (1977, 19, 27–29), another Italian scholar, was sharply critical of Dunbabin's approach to the natives, concluding that Dunbabin's account of the natives was already insufficient when written (cf. also Dyson 2006, 195). Probably for this reason Manni did not include Dunbabin in his "top-three list" of dominant foreign scholars (made up instead of Holm, Freeman, and Bérard). The proper inclusion of ancient native cultures in a modern account must be regarded as a defining criterion of quality in Italian eyes. Mazza (in La Rosa 1986, 249) has described Pace as being ahead of his time in his attention to and definition of native-Greek relations.

agricultural activities beyond grain. Pace's ideas about the existence of Sicilian Greek art and manufacturing are well founded, whereas he seems to have overstated the native basis of Greek Sicily's society and economy.

Four more important developments followed in the second half of the twentieth century. The first concerns the "data explosion," in terms of both quantity and quality, throughout the Mediterranean and elsewhere connected with the economic and cultural regeneration that followed World War II.[74] In Sicily, more money became available to archaeological and historical studies, with a concomitant expansion in institutional support.[75] For instance, the creation in Palermo of Eugenio Manni's school of interdisciplinary scholarship continued to view identity as important and native-Greek interaction as reciprocal, especially in the sphere of religion.[76] While research tended to continue along the same lines as before World War II, it was classical Greek archaeology and history that gained the upper hand. This came about because of a second development. The first foreign scholarly teams, particularly the French at Megara Hyblaia and the Americans at Morgantina, were given permission to excavate in Sicily. They were interested in investigating the establishment and development of ancient Greek urban sites,[77] but the move toward more classical Greek studies also has to be connected with Italians wanting to distance themselves from their Fascist (and hence their supranationalistic Romanocentric) past.[78] Decolonization was a third important development.[79] As many European nations lost, both willingly and unwillingly, their overseas colonies, efforts turned among many of the former colonizers and colonized to decolonization, to exposing and eliminating colonialism in all its facets, including in scholarship. The main scholarly tools employed were Marxism and postcolonialism, especially the former in Italy.[80] Such studies have generally focused

---

74. The phrase "data explosion" was coined by Broodbank 2000 in the context of the prehistoric Cyclades, but it can be extended to describe the situation in most parts of the Mediterranean (Chapman 2005, 95).

75. For Sicily specifically, see Griffo 1964–65, 135–37; Pelagatti 1968–69, 349–50; Manganaro 1979; cf. also De Angelis 2003a, xvii.

76. E.g., Inglieri 1957, 232–33. On Eugenio Manni, see AA.VV. 1990–91; Cusumano 1994, 40. Manni is also important for the institutional development of Sicilian archaeology and history through the creation of the journal *Kokalos* and a regular conference devoted to ancient Sicily.

77. Bonacasa 1997, 165; Osborne 2004a, 93.

78. Dyson 2006, 216, 228.

79. Cf. Dyson 2006, 215.

80. For Italy, see D'Agostino 1991, 57–59; Barbanera 1998, 164–69; Guidi 2002, 355–56; Dyson 2006, 217–18.

on everything that colonialist and imperialist approaches tended to ignore or downplay, such as local native histories, agency, resistance, synergy, hybridity, and diasporas—in a word, a multi-sided frontier history.[81] Ettore Lepore, based in Naples, was the strongest advocate of such an approach, including the gaining of perspectives and information via comparisons with frontier situations from other historical periods and regions.[82]

Two spinoffs of this third development are worth noting before turning to the fourth development. The first is the consolidation of another model of culture contact, later formally dubbed the middle ground, in which it is recognized that "A third outcome is not just possible, but common: the creation of a working relationship between incomers and locals that formed a new way of living derived from the cultural logics that all parties brought to the encounters."[83] The second concerns the whole series of methodological and theoretical advances around the globe in the study of archaeology and history that have proliferated since the 1960s, driven in large part by the concurrent dissatisfaction with the narrowness of previous approaches.[84] These changes in intellectual outlook have had a very positive effect, resulting in a new barrage of techniques that have been brought to bear on the acquisition, analysis, and interpretation of classical archaeological and historical data.[85] All in all, since the 1960s there has been a gradual and conscious shift away from Hellenocentrism in favor of more balanced approaches to relations between ancient Greek and other cultures, including the decline of racial theory in historical interpretations.[86] Since the 1990s, more and more attention has been paid to studying native Sicilian cultures and their development. Accordingly, prehistoric archaeology has again come into vogue,[87] alongside close readings

---

81. For an overview, see Ashcroft, Griffiths, and Tiffin 1998, and for their applicability in the ancient Greek context, see Malkin 2004.

82. Lepore 1968, 42–43 (note also Moses Finley's applauding agreement on p. 186); 1973, 32; 2000, 62. On Lepore, see Christ 1996, 155–56. On the relationship between classical scholarship and frontier history, see especially Corcella 1999; Purcell 2003a, 21. For a recent statement on the validity of informed comparativism, see D.G. Smith 2011.

83. Gosden 2004, 82. As we have already seen, some scholars, especially Italian, had already been using a form of middle-ground culture contact in the previous generations.

84. Such developments can be followed in, for instance, Johnson 1999; Lemon 2003; Burke 2004; Trigger 2006.

85. For their impact on classical scholarship, see, for example, Potter 1999; Pelling 2000; Morris 2002; Snodgrass 2002.

86. Bernal 1987, 201–204, 239–40; Pontrandolfo 1989, 334–35; Hall 2004. Challis (2010, 120) calls for more work on the impact of racial theory on the formation of classical studies.

87. La Rosa 1997; Giannitrapani 1998; Shepherd 2009, 21–23.

of older scholarly works written within colonialist and imperialist frameworks, in which their problematic dimensions have been revealed.[88] In this century, this has led to new fieldwork projects on native Sicilian sites aimed at testing the Hellenization model.[89] Stock has already been taken of the situation in the form of new syntheses.[90] The role played by ancient Near Eastern cultures on Greece and other regions has also been greatly appreciated since the 1980s, especially as a result of the bombshell dropped by Martin Bernal's book *Black Athena: The Afroasiatic Roots of Classical Civilization.*[91] The old divide between East and West that Hellenism versus Orientalism fostered in such regions as Sicily is under reconsideration. Along with it comes greater appreciation for the Phoenician contribution to Mediterranean history.

The fourth development concerns the search for other ways to explain the operation of worldwide economic and cultural forces on local and regional ones. From the 1980s on, concepts from world systems theory and globalization were introduced into scholarly arsenals. World systems theory holds that states, acting as cores, systematically exploit peripheries for their labor and natural resources. Globalization in the modern world entails the spread of Western lifestyles into non-Western cultures, resulting in the creation of new cultures that are global in reach. World systems theory as such has never been directly applied to the study of ancient Sicily, though the theory has much in common with Eurocentric colonialist and imperialist modes of thinking that, as seen earlier, have had a healthy history in interpretations. Since its inception in the mid-1970s, adherents of world systems theory have modified it in various ways in response to scholarly criticisms, but today the theory has fallen out of favor in most quarters because of its problematic assumptions.[92] Globalization, by contrast, has recently been applied to the study of ancient Sicily. Ian Morris has spoken of the sixth and fifth centuries BC as having been affected by a kind of ancient globalization (which he dubs "Mediterraneanization"), in which cultural and economic forces created common and far-flung traditions that resulted in tensions and conflicts, winners and losers.[93] There has been a clear and decisive move away from "Cold War"

---

88. De Angelis 1998; Shepherd 2009, 15–17.

89. See Morris et al. 2003 on the acropolis of Monte Polizzo in Western Sicily.

90. Leighton 1999; Castellana 2002; Albanese Procelli 2003a.

91. Bernal 1987. For an overview of the issues, see Morris 2000, 45–46, 102–105.

92. For these modifications to world systems theory, and how the theory is too problematic for historical explanation, see Stein 2002, 904–905.

93. Morris 2003.

regional approaches with little or no integration to a world of interconnected-ness involving the interplay of local, regional, and global forces. By extension, the recognition has emerged that the Mediterranean's connectivity was owed to its microregional nature.[94] This, too, can be seen in some recent studies that include Sicily microregionally. For instance, the island's geographical and historical role during the second millennium BC, along with those of the other three large Mediterranean islands (Cyprus, Crete, and Sardinia), has been investigated. Sicily is shown to have played a strategic role in establishing rela-tionships and maintaining contacts between the various, usually differentially structured Bronze Age polities of the eastern and western Mediterranean.[95] Another example involves how Archaic Greek history has been placed in a wider Mediterranean context, and the formation and development of the Greek state is now as much about Greece as it is about other peoples and processes.[96]

The second half of the twentieth century witnessed four new developments and additions to previously existing ones. Granting foreign scholars permis-sion to undertake archaeological projects in Sicily brought their approaches and perspectives into ever closer contact with Italian ones. At first, opposing viewpoints pretty much continued along the lines established in previous gen-erations, but later, as the century neared its end, a new development of bridg-ing this polarized divide was set into motion. Mixed communities and their cultural and social outcomes became more tolerable in historical accounts, as the modern world came to terms with decolonizing its own frontiers and entered an era of globalization. These discussions, however, occurred predom-inately within a regional Sicilian context, without serious integration into the larger narrative of Greek history with its overwhelming center and periphery thinking that assigned importance and insignificance to, respectively, Greece and Sicily. Recent globalization has helped to reinvigorate a macro-perspective in ancient historical studies, something generally sorely lacking in the study of ancient Sicily since the end of World War II.[97] As a result, greater attempts are being made to include the concepts of mobility and connectivity in writ-ing ancient Greek history, and a greater appreciation for the regional variety

---

94. Most notable in this regard is Horden and Purcell 2000. For the prehistoric period, see now Blake and Knapp 2005; Kristiansen and Larsson 2005; Broodbank 2013.

95. Bietti Sestieri 2003.

96. These recent developments are conveniently summarized in Demand 2004, 76–77; 2006; Vlassopoulos 2007a; 2007b; 2007c; 2011; Schulz 2008.

97. See Manganaro 1979, 5–6; Pugliese Carratelli 1980, 13, who are both highly critical of ancient Sicilian history being studied from an isolationist perspective.

of the Greek world has resulted. While some attempt has been made to integrate Sicily into general Greek histories,[98] this remains the exception to the rule. Most scholarship still concentrates primarily on the ancient Greeks of the Aegean Sea basin as being the center of a kind of world system that ultimately places the wider ancient Greek world on the periphery.[99] Such work usually consists of either of two scenarios. The first is outright exclusion of regions outside the Aegean, like Sicily, sometimes accompanied by a lip-service apology that areas beyond Greece are not within the geographic purview and academic competencies of the researcher(s).[100] The second involves Sicily being used only when it is needed to illustrate and explain some larger phenomenon concerning Greece, such as the development of town planning, Doric architecture, or the Athenian invasion of Syracuse in 415–413 BC.[101] While there may be legitimate and practical reasons for treating Sicily in this way, the bottom line is that the island's absence from modern historical narratives creates a distorted picture of the ancient Greeks.[102] To put the spotlight on Aegean Greece is to recognize only part of the bigger stage and ensemble needed to make the whole performance of ancient Greek history possible. The availability of more data after World War II increases the need for historians today more than ever to strike a balance between the collection and interpretation of data, and to make a concerted effort to adopt an interregional perspective, in an effort to test in a more considered manner the various models of historical development that have been advanced since the nineteenth century. This book seeks to pick up the pace on all these recent developments.

These problems are further compounded by the single most cited book on ancient Sicily in recent times, Moses Finley's *Ancient Sicily*, which has been translated into all the major scholarly languages.[103] This book was originally published in 1968. In the preface to the second edition, published eleven years later, Finley himself admitted that "Now Sicilian archaeology is in floodtide, so

---

98. Gras 1995; Hornblower 2002; Belozerskaya and Lapatin 2004; Demand 2006; Morris and Powell 2006; Cartledge 2009; Osborne 2009; Vlassopoulos 2013.

99. Biers 1987; Shapiro 1996; Sparkes 1998; Cartledge 1998; Shipley 2000; Chamoux 2003; Erskine 2003.

100. Whitley (2001, xxi) and Osborne (2004a, 87) acknowledge their limited focus on the Aegean Sea basin.

101. Pomeroy, Burstein, Donlan, and Roberts 1999; Pedley 2002; Étienne, Müller, and Prost 2000, 3–4, who consciously acknowledge the implications of their decision. Barletta (2001) is a laudable recent exception in discussing the origins of both Doric and Ionic architecture.

102. On the need to include ancient Greek "colonies" in our narratives of Greek history, and on how to achieve this, some first thoughts can be found in De Angelis 2009a.

103. Finley 1979.

much so that in places my book, the first attempt by a historian to evaluate and employ the new evidence synoptically, has become out of date."[104] The archaeological developments Finley described have continued unabated since then. However, it is not only that newer data are available, but Finley's approach and interpretive framework also need updating. As has become clear from recent discussions of Finley's economic history,[105] his emphasis on the ancient value system in conceptualizing the ancient economy meant that he had to favor ancient written sources over archaeology and post-antique economic models as a consequence. It can also be added that while Finley did use archaeological evidence, he generally relied on any interpretations advanced by the archaeologists themselves, without necessarily arriving at his own independent conclusions. The most noteworthy example is his treatment of Timoleon and the supposed revival of fourth-century BC Sicily (see Chapters 2–4 for discussion). In any case, many of Finley's ideas regarding the ancient economy are giving way to less monolithic and more nuanced historical pictures. Moreover, Finley's social vision of ancient Greek Sicily is pretty much shaped by Dunbabin's colonialist stance of superior Greeks versus inferior natives. Finley himself noted some exceptions where he differed from Dunbabin in regard to economics and Carthaginian-Greek relations, but it is clear, as we will see further especially in Chapters 1 and 3 below, that Finley's interpretive framework echoed that of Dunbabin when it came to social history. Some of Finley's other ideas about Sicilian Greek social history require either rejection or tempering, particularly those regarding the absence of inequality until the late sixth century and the predominance of democracy in the later fifth century. A new social and economic history of Archaic and Classical Greek Sicily that not only updates the history but also conceives it differently from Finley's forays is more than amply justified.

This outline of the main developments in historical research serves as our point of entry into the complex world of the subject matter of this book. While the relevance of the foregoing outline has already been discussed, and will become clearer in later chapters, it can also be highlighted here in relating it to this book's approach and chapters. If anything, the review should have made clear that the one-sided and isolationist approaches that have characterized some past scholarship cannot do justice to Greek Sicily's social and economic complexities. Instead, a more comprehensive approach would view ancient Greek Sicily as simultaneously part of both frontier and world history, as some other past approaches have held. In other words, people and processes from elsewhere on the island and

---

104. Finley 1979, xii.

105. Morris, Saller, and Scheidel 2007, 2–5.

beyond in the wider Mediterranean require inclusion. Interdisciplinary methods are needed to achieve this. In particular, this entails combining texts and material culture, as well as prehistoric and classical archaeology, in a theoretically up-to-date manner. Although there have been some interdisciplinary practitioners in Sicily since the late nineteenth century, much of the work on ancient Sicily since World War II has been very discipline-based.[106] This means, for instance, that historians usually focus on written sources and on writing political and military history, and archaeologists usually focus on material sources and on writing culture histories.[107] Any attempt to write a social and economic history of Archaic and Classical Greek Sicily has to bridge the disciplinary divides and to provide an account that will complement the numerous political, military, and culture histories in order to establish, among other things, the integrated nature of all these histories.[108] This integration is taken for granted in the very arrangement and contents of this book's chapters.

Social and economic history can potentially encompass a vast array of subjects. A selection of topics has been chosen for discussion, in large part because of the conditioning caused by the nature of the available evidence and the history of research. Each of the chapters begins with an outline of its topics and evidence; the focus here is to provide a basic sketch of their respective arrangement and contents. The chapters, moreover, have been organized in a building-block format, with each chapter placed in a logical position that allows the discussion to build and develop.

Chapter 1 explores Sicily's larger geographical and historical setting in the period spanning ca. 1200 to 600 BC. This chapter sets the stage for the earliest Greek and Phoenician settlement in Sicily, as well as investigating the relationships between natives and newcomers. The overall intent is to examine how far preceding geographical and historical circumstances shaped the societies and economies established by Greeks.

---

106. For the Archaic period, see my comments in De Angelis 2003a, xiv–xv, 206–207.

107. This can be well illustrated with one example of direct relevance to this book. We turn to the words of two reviewers of Brian Caven's book *Dionysius I: War-lord of Sicily*, published in 1990. First, Gordon Shrimpton (1990, 101) observes that "for the study of the Sicilian, narrative history, we are at the mercy of a limited number of not-too-critical, ancient, secondary sources whose primary authorities are lost to us." Second, Richard Talbert (1992, 456) adds that "Despite the visit which Caven made to Sicily and South Italy (ix), an awareness of how post–World War II archaeology has enlarged our understanding of the entire region during the fifth and fourth centuries seems notably lacking." The very nature of ancient Greek historiography for Sicily presents challenges to modern historians, who, insofar as they can, have not made good these deficiencies through recourse to archaeology to sketch out the material backdrop to the ancient written sources.

108. Cf. the still worthwhile observation made a quarter century ago by Austin 1986, 450 on the interconnection between political, military, social, and economic history.

Chapter 2 discusses the interrelated questions of settlement and territory, in order to set the stage for the social and economic questions in the following two chapters. The physical development of town and country can potentially say much about society and economy. Particular attention is devoted to patterns of building and settlement, and the use of space in general in urban settlements, so that subjects like population size can be discussed in later chapters. These physical developments can be related to four key phases in Sicily's Archaic and Classical history, each representing a major turning point in its political and military history and state formation that caused reconfigurations of its social and economic patterns. These four phases will also be the organizing framework in the next two chapters.

Chapter 3 examines Greek Sicily's societies over these four key historical phases. Greek Sicily's societies developed differently from other parts of the Greek world, having a penchant for authoritarian and hierarchical government. Still today, Sicily and other regions of the Italian South are associated with images and stereotypes of sociopolitical (and economic) backwardness as prescribed in the "Southern Question" discourse discussed earlier in this chapter. These modern images and stereotypes are generally characterized by timelessness and have been applied to these regions in antiquity. But Sicilian Greek societies cannot be measured by external yardsticks. Instead, this chapter looks at the nature of the Sicilian frontier, including its dynamic multiethnic environment and conditions of land availability to explain these developments. Emphasis is placed on such issues as sociopolitical structures, administrative and legal institutions, demography, cultural values, and access to the factors of production.

Chapter 4 focuses on economics and the usual trio of production, distribution, and consumption for the four key historical phases. In taking such a broad approach, we avoid the partial pictures presented in the surviving literary sources and employ the more encompassing archaeological evidence, from which emerges a revealingly different picture. At the end of each of the four historical phases, the aim is to take stock of the evidence and to put forth various economic models and scenarios of how these economic systems might have worked.

A concluding chapter unites all of this book's results. It begins by comparing my conclusions to previous ones. It then rounds out these conclusions by suggesting the future prospects for social and economic questions in the history of ancient Greek Sicily, as well as for the history of the wider Greco-Roman Mediterranean.

To sum up, the ancient Greeks in Sicily have been approached in a variety of ways over the past two hundred or so years. At one end of the interpretive spectrum, scholars viewed the ancient Greeks as one of a long line of incomers whom Sicily and its inhabitants shaped. At the other end of the spectrum, the Greeks have been viewed as the dominant group, acting as the source of innovation and achievement in shaping Sicily and its inhabitants. In turn, these Sicilian Greeks are regarded as secondary to Greece, thought to be at the center of their world. Neither of these extremes is completely satisfactory.[109] They require testing through a broadly based approach that must begin by placing the ancient Greeks in Sicily in their original environmental, ethnocultural, and economic contexts, both inside the island and outside it. That is the subject of the next chapter.

---

109. Cusumano 1994, 43.

I

The Geographical and Historical Setting

TO MAKE A good beginning on our social and economic history, we must consider the question of how preexisting geographical and historical conditions in Sicily shaped the societies and economies that Greeks established there. Previous responses have conformed to the interpretive positions just outlined in the Introduction. Traditionally, historians have believed that prevailing conditions had little impact on the arrival of Greeks in Sicily, except that some native Sicilians were a labor resource.[1] More recently, the middle ground approach has allowed for preceding conditions to play a role.[2] Geographical and historical conditions both within and beyond Sicily will be brought into the discussion far more than is usually done, as this will permit us to steer a course between these polarized positions (Map 1).[3] The emphasis here will be placed on the period between about 1200 and 600 BC and on matters that will allow us to set the stage for the discussion that follows in the next three chapters on settlement, society, and economy in Archaic and Classical Greek Sicily. In particular, we will address the organization of Sicily's preexisting native populations and the degree to which this influenced the earliest decisions of the Greek and Phoenician immigrants who settled alongside them.

1. Finley 1979, 13; Manganaro 1979, 9–10.

2. De Angelis 2003b; Anello 2005; Fitzjohn 2007.

3. As in De Angelis 2010.

The Geographical and Historical Setting:
ca. 1200–600 BC
Concepts and Evidence

During the approximately six hundred years of geography and history under discussion, Sicily went from being an important node in Mediterranean inter-regional contact and exchange to playing a secondary role by 1000 BC, before permanent Phoenician and Greek settlement in the eighth century set into motion a process that eventually reversed that. This period of history was one of transformation across the entire Mediterranean basin and lands beyond. For that reason it is enmeshed in concepts and evidence, along with the research traditions of which they are part, that have come under scrutiny over the last two decades. Given their significance in framing and reconstructing these important centuries of history, the present discussion must begin with some prefatory remarks.

As already noted, these centuries of history witnessed the overlapping of various regional trajectories spanning the eastern and western Mediterranean. Hellenocentrism and ideas of "ex oriente lux" ("from the east, light") have traditionally permeated interpretations of east-west relations. Greeks and other eastern Mediterranean peoples spread their superior civilization through "Hellenization" and similar processes of cultural conversion to more passive and inferior cultures, initiating and controlling these relations. When these eastern civilizations experienced a downturn toward the end of the Bronze Age—which modern scholars usually label the "Dark Ages"—this downturn was also extended to regions further to the west assumed to be underdeveloped.[4] The migration of Greeks and Phoenicians to the western Mediterranean in the centuries that followed rescued Sicily out of these "Dark Ages" through a process traditionally described as "colonization." Activity before colonization has, following this logic, been dubbed "precolonization," and further new settlement from an already established "colony" is called "subcolonization." Once again, these are all problematic terms, for they are part of the same civilizing narrative, in which directionality, agency, and power are all ascribed to the incoming superior easterners.[5] A further corollary of this thinking is the essentialist definitions of identity, in which "Greeks," "Phoenicians," "natives," and other cultures are represented as monolithic blocs, often in

---

4. Thus Bernabò Brea 1957, 136, who was followed by many scholars into the 1990s.

5. See in particular the works by R.M. Albanese Procelli, C. Antonaccio, J.M. Hall, I. Malkin, and M. Torelli cited in the References. Cf. in general Stein 2002.

opposition to one another. Because of the problematic nature of these terms and concepts and the grand historical narrative around which they have been molded, many scholars have either avoided them by creating new ones or have used the traditional ones with quotation marks.[6]

The existence and pervasiveness of some of these concepts help explain the strengths and weaknesses of the current evidence and research traditions. It will be most effective to illustrate how by turning to the main cultures discussed in this book, natives, Phoenicians, and Greeks.

For Sicily's native populations, it was common until recently to base archaeological interpretations, where possible, on classical literature because of its perceived centrality.[7] This practice is dubious for its essentialist definitions and etic perspectives and need not distract us from our aims, on which they arguably have little effect.[8] Archaeology on its own supplies the main and most reliable form of evidence (Map 2). For the EIA, during the Cassibile-Pantalica II phase (so called after the two most important sites), the evidence mostly consists of tomb groups from southeastern Sicily.[9] This phase, however, was delineated before the extent of the links between Sicily and the Aeolian Islands had been fully appreciated. It must be combined with the Ausonian I–II periods delineated for the Aeolian Islands (named after the son of Odysseus, Ausonius, who is reputed in ancient tradition to have settled there).[10] We currently have rather less archaeological evidence for western Sicily. In the center of the island, our knowledge is dominated by two sites, Sant'Angelo Muxaro and Polizello, that are best represented, respectively, by tombs and by tombs and sanctuaries. These sites have long been the type sites for their respective regions, despite the general scarcity of evidence in western Sicily.

---

6. For a recent discussion, see De Angelis 2009a.

7. The practice came to a head with Bernabò Brea's (1957) important synthesis and later adopted and amplified by others (e.g., La Rosa 1989; S. Tusa 1992; Anello 1997; Nicoletti 1997, 529; AA.VV. 2012). For the challenges, see especially Leighton 1999, 215–17; 2000a, 18; Castellana 2002, 4; Albanese Procelli 2003a, 18–27; Hodos 2005.

8. For an illustration of the problem in the context of IA Calabria, see Pacciarelli 2004, 449–51. For Sicily, see recently Albanese Procelli 2003a, 7, whose synthesis is very effectively structured around themes ("settlement," "territory," "funerary practices," and so on) that transcend archaeological cultures and the ethnic labels taken from classical literature. Nonetheless, she too could not avoid altogether previous scholarly practices, most evident in her book's title.

9. Frasca 1996a, 139–42; Leighton 2011.

10. The term "Ausonian" was coined by Luigi Bernabò Brea (1957, 137–39), who drew inspiration from Diodorus Siculus (5.7) to name the new culture of the LBA/EIA that he excavated in the Aeolian Islands. Cf. Albanese Procelli 2003a, 31–34.

In addition to these imbalances in the material record, EIA chronologies all across the Mediterranean are presently under revision. The challenges derive from the radiometric and dendrochronological dates obtained from sites in the Mediterranean and especially north of the Alps, which are at odds with traditional Greek pottery chronology and the Greek literary sources on which they are ultimately based. The absolute dates for layers containing early Greek pottery and Etruscan metalwork derived from these scientific methods are higher than previously thought.[11] Accordingly, it has been proposed to raise the absolute dates for Greek Geometric and early Protocorinthian pottery sequences by a generation or more. This would lengthen Greek involvement in the central Mediterranean to as early as 850 BC, a century before the "Dark Ages" in Greece were previously thought to have ended.[12]

For Sicily, independent dating deriving from radiometric and dendrochronological methods is still rare.[13] Nevertheless, the fact that the chronologies of the BA and IA Mediterranean are made up of a series of interlocking pieces means that direct changes in one can necessitate indirect changes in others.[14] The Cassibile-Pantalica II phase, usually dated to 1000–850 BC, could be shifted to 925–750 BC,[15] to 1000–800 BC,[16] or even to 1000–750 BC.[17] The succeeding Pantalica III-South phase, traditionally dated to 850–750/730 BC on the basis of the serpentine fibula, now seems to have continued for a century longer than usually thought (descending down into the early seventh century). The still rather coarse-grained nature of EIA Sicilian chronology, which obviously requires future fine-tuning, means that material during the crucial centuries before and

---

11. For overviews, see Nijboer 2005a; 2005b; Brandherm 2006; Brandherm and Trachsel 2008.

12. See Nijboer 2005a, 541 for these new absolute dates, which are as follows: EG = 925 (from 900) BC–875 BC; MG 900/875 (from 850) BC–825/800 BC; LG 825 (from 770) BC–750/700 BC; EPCor 750/740 (from 725) BC–700/675 BC. For a review of the whole debate now surrounding early Greek pottery chronology, see Tsetskhladze 2006, xxxiv–xxxviii.

13. See Albanese Procelli 2005a.

14. In view of such interregional connections, Albanese Procelli (2005a, 521–23) has urged that discussions of Sicily's EIA chronology adopt the system presently used in the Italian peninsula and integrate the two systems as much as possible. Four phases are distinguished in this mainland chronology (I Fe, II Fe, III Fe, and IV Fe), with the beginning of the Italian IA placed at ca. 1020–950 and not at 900 BC, as envisaged by this Greek pottery chronology (Bietti Sestieri 1997b, 473–74; Pacciarelli 2000, 67–69; Ridgway 2004, 19–21). Albanese Procelli associates the traditional Greek Geometric pottery chronology phases with each of these four phases, even though, as she recognizes, this traditional chronology is also now under revision.

15. Leighton 1993; 2000b.

16. Frasca 2001a, 53–54.

17. Turco 2000, 6.

just after the arrival of Phoenicians and Greeks can only be dated within a broad range, which can make drawing firm historical conclusions difficult.

Even though more written evidence exists for Phoenicians in Sicily and elsewhere in the western Mediterranean, we must still rely on archaeological evidence. It is true that Near Eastern and classical sources have much to say about Phoenicians, but these sources are generally highly focused (such as belonging to diplomatic and military annals) and, in the case of classical sources, generally not contemporary with the events they discuss.[18] All these sources, moreover, are far from unbiased, given the often rocky relationship Greeks and Romans had with the Phoenicians from Homer on.[19] The question of reliability and representation must always be considered in a contextualized manner and, where possible, set against archaeological evidence. To take a prime example, earlier scholarship overemphasized the Phoenicians and Greeks as two distinct entities with their own distinct motivations. Evidence steadily grows to suggest that political discontent and agricultural motives could have also played parts in Phoenician overseas settlement.[20] In the last generation, as the Phoenicians have become an object of study in their own right, archaeology has sought to redress this imbalance and to throw more light in general on their earliest exploration and settlement activities throughout the Mediterranean.

More written sources exist for Greeks in the western Mediterranean than for Phoenicians. All the same, there is no cause-and-effect relationship between quantity and reliability; the sources must be handled equally carefully and critically to extract the valuable historical information (not always truthful of course) that they contain. Earlier generations of scholars would have accepted at face value the tales recorded in ancient Greek literature about Trojan War heroes wandering all across the Mediterranean, including Italy, following the destruction of Troy as being ultimately evidence of LBA/EIA contacts. That kind of approach, however, has rightly fallen out of favor in recent decades, with such stories now being viewed as creative storytelling, if not charter myths, on the part of later Greeks.[21] For the Archaic period, it has

18. On the sources, and their problems, for Phoenician history, see Gras, Rouillard and Teixidor 1995, 58; Krings 1994; Markoe 2000, 10–13; Aubet 2001, 1–5; Niemeyer 2006, 143–44.

19. So Dougherty 2001, 102–21 about the representation of the Phoenicians in Homer's *Odyssey*.

20. López Castro 2006; Neville 2007, 105–34; van Dommelen and Gómez Bellard 2008, 202–30.

21. For a convenient overview of these tales, see Woodhead 1962, 20–30; Vanschoonwinkel 2006, 83–90. For arguments against their historical reliability, see Ridgway 1990, 69; Dench 1995, 33–38; Leighton 1999, 184–86; Vanschoonwinkel 2006, 91–93; Lane Fox 2008, 180.

sometimes been thought that accurate historical traditions about the earliest permanent settlements could have survived until committed to writing from the fifth century on through annual festivals celebrating the establishment of the various Greek foundations.[22] That seems unlikely. Our written sources are not straightforward, often depicting conditions, thinking, and practices more representative of their own time, from the late fifth century BC to the Roman period, than of the periods they profess to illuminate. The historian must navigate between the complete rejection and the complete acceptance of these written sources.[23] For Sicily, the picture derived from ancient writings (including inscriptions) that Euboeans were largely responsible for founding Zankle, Naxos, Leontinoi, Katane; Corinth for Syracuse; Megara for Megara Hyblaia and Selinous; and Rhodes and Crete for Gela and Akragas seems very likely.[24] Foundation stories and dates, however, can conceal deeper historical complexities and dynamics. The ways in which these stories and dates might be remembered and invented to suit the identity and claims of founders and later inhabitants vis-à-vis their place in the wider community must be borne in mind. The limitations of the written sources become apparent when combined with archaeological evidence, which has grown and developed considerably since especially the end of World War II, as discussed in the Introduction. This evidence both complements and expands the written picture, and in doing so it provides insights that challenge and fill it out.[25]

Despite the hurdles presented by current evidence, which will always be fragmentary given that we are dealing with protohistory,[26] much of relevance still can be said about Sicily in the LBA and EIA.

Geographical and Historical Settings

During the fifteenth to thirteenth centuries, a network formed between four of the Mediterranean's large islands—Cyprus, Crete, Sicily (including the Aeolian Islands), and Sardinia. This network established relationships and maintained contacts between the various, usually differentially structured polities of the eastern and western Mediterranean (Map 1).[27] These islands

---

22. For a recent example, see Parisi Presicce 2003, 269. Compare now Morakis 2011, 465.

23. Thus also Hall 2007b, 18–19.

24. See my discussion in De Angelis 2003a.

25. Leighton 1999, 235–68; Albanese Procelli 2003a, 137–45; De Angelis 2003b.

26. As Boardman 2001, 38, and Dickinson 2006, 258 have emphasized.

27. Bietti Sestieri 2003.

were open to external contacts and often incorporated foreigners into their own local societies.[28] Within Italy, the Sicily-Aeolian Islands and the Palafitte-Terramare (based in the central Po Plain of northeast Italy) were the two most important cores.[29]

This changed at the end of the thirteenth century BC, when "radical change in the overall system of political gravitation and in the organization of long distance trade emerged, and was firmly established by the beginning of the Early Iron Age."[30] The Palafitte-Terramare system may have collapsed because of stress placed on its political and organizational structures, which could not deal effectively with the Po Plain's specific environmental conditions. The breakdown of the core status of Sicily and the Aeolian Islands is attributed to the so-called Ausonian invasion, an organized and archaeologically visible movement from southern Calabria. It appears to be echoed in classical Greek sources and is thought to have entailed the hostile takeover of eastern Sicily and, with it, the breakdown of Sicily's core status.[31] The motivation for such an invasion could have been long-standing hostilities between the two regions, Sicily becoming the core to the detriment of southern Calabria. Whether or not these hypotheses regarding the downfall of the Palafitte-Terramare and particularly Sicily–Aeolian Islands cores are correct, archaeological evidence leaves little doubt that these two areas underwent a significant transformation in the EIA that rearranged dynamics away from them toward metal-rich Etruria and Sardinia (Map 1). In unison, Etruria and Sardinia stood out in EIA Italy for their sociopolitical complexity and interregional connections.

Etruria comprised both Etruria proper (largely synonymous with modern Tuscany and northern Lazio) and "Etruria padana" (Emilia Romagna, from

---

28. For a recent discussion, see Russell 2011.

29. Bietti Sestieri 2005.

30. Bietti Sestieri 2005, 17.

31. Bietti Sestieri 2005, 17. Diodorus Siculus (5.6), Thucydides (6.2), and Dionysius of Halicarnassus (1.22) speak of population movements by Sikels and the Morgetes from mainland Italy to Sicily, information which has encouraged Bernabò Brea (1964–65; 1971) to speak of invasion. Even prehistorians who have disavowed the uncritical use of much later ancient sources in this way to reconstruct earlier epochs have accepted the existence of the so-called "Ausonian invasion" and the archaeological data used to support it (besides Bietti Sestieri, see also La Rosa 1989, 13–18; Leighton 1999, 216; Castellana 2002, 4, 150–51; Albanese Procelli 2003a, 28–29; acceptance of this invasion can also be found in works which are not as explicit in their comments about sources: Manni 1969; S. Tusa 1992, 457–508). The basic idea of a movement of people to Sicily in this period, however much it has been constructed with such a questionable use of ancient sources, has been followed here.

Bologna to the Adriatic Sea) (Map 1).[32] Etruria emerged as the most articulated sociopolitical region in the whole of EIA Italy, starting in the Villanovan period (so named after Villanova near Bologna in northern Italy, where the first finds were made in 1853). There emerged large "proto-urban" centers that measured between 100 and 200 hectares in size and possibly controlling surrounding territories of between 1,000 and 2,000 square kilometers.[33] These polities were home to populations estimated to have been in the several thousands and to have had differentiated hierarchy, judging from burial evidence. Their leaders have been described as chiefs, who, whether or not this terminology is appropriate, headed up powerful systems of production and exchange that were transitioning into early states in the course of the tenth and ninth centuries BC. Etruscan elites are also thought to have settled and ruled parts of the Po Plain, Latium (including early regal Rome), and southern Campania, tapping into the main routes of long-distance exchange.[34]

The other EIA core was the island of Sardinia (Map 1). Its greater remoteness from any mainland became less of a factor as Sardinia developed into the center of east-west traffic, superseding Sicily in this respect.[35] Outsiders were attracted to Sardinia's extensive metal resources, and this may have coincided (although the dating is still imprecise) with the further development of the preexisting nuraghi into fortresses with several towers encircled and interconnected by external bastions.[36] Excavations in the Santu Antine nuraghe revealed very clear evidence of metal production contained within its walls.[37] Hierarchy is most evident in the so-called "Giants' Tombs," made up of slab-lined rectangular funerary chambers enclosed in a long apsidal mound of earth.[38] The elites interred in them almost certainly controlled metal production and distribution and may have possibly arranged themselves as chiefdoms[39] in territorial entities averaging 200 square kilometers.[40] Sardinia's impact on other parts of Italy

---

32. Bietti Sestieri 2005, 20. Bietti Sestieri (1997a) contains the fullest discussion of her case for Etruria's status as core in the EIA. See also Guidi 1998; Barker and Rasmussen 1998, 53–75.

33. For a recent discussion, see Riva 2010, 11–38.

34. Bietti Sestieri 1997a, 396–98. Cf. also Barker and Rasmussen 1998, 139–40.

35. Bietti Sestieri 2005, 12, 21–22.

36. Webster 1996, 117; Dyson and Rowlands 2007, 63.

37. Dyson and Rowlands 2007, 65.

38. Webster 1996, 144; Dyson and Rowlands 2007, 79.

39. Webster 1996, 130, 153; Dyson and Rowlands 2007, 67.

40. Webster 1996, 130–31.

seems to have been negligible, but a special relationship with Etruria developed. As the late David Ridgway hypothesized, Sardinia may have helped to bring out Etruria's metallurgical potential.[41] Certainly, Sardinia was the most important metalworking center in all of EIA Italy,[42] eloquently exemplified via the anthropomorphic and zoomorphic bronze figurines produced in their hundreds.[43]

These recent developments in the study of Early Iron Age Italy have caused the validity of the "Dark Ages" concept for the central Mediterranean to be questioned and have raised the possibility of Italian impact in the eastern Mediterranean.[44] While the lack of sophistication in the Italian EIA assumed by earlier generations of scholarship can easily be refuted, the extent and chronology of the contact between the eastern and western Mediterranean during this period still remain to be firmly established.

Cyprus maintained a very close relationship with Sardinia. It began in the LBA with the trade in oxhide ingots, when Cyprus was in all likelihood a single unified state-level polity (Map 1).[45] Cyprus certainly experienced collapse in the twelfth century, but the degree to which it did so is debated. Some scholars argue for the continuation of state society, now subdivided into several "kingdoms" as documented in Neo-Assyrian records from the late eighth century,[46] while other scholars maintain that Cyprus reverted to chiefdom and/or Big Man societies.[47] What is agreed on is more important for our purposes. Cyprus continued trading copper, made important contributions to iron technology, and played an extremely active role in the international metals market.[48] This is all very evident with regard to Sardinia, where Cypriot imports and imitations are known and provide solid support for interregional contacts between Sardinia and Cyprus.[49]

The Phoenicians may have been operating in the central Mediterranean during this same time (Map 1). Ancient sources claim dates for the foundation of Lixus, Gades, and Utica at the end of the twelfth century BC, and in the Old Testament, cargoes of precious items coming from Tarshish (perhaps the Spanish Tartessos

---

41. Ridgway 2006a, 304.

42. Ridgway 2006a, 303.

43. Webster 1996, 198–206; Dyson and Rowlands 2007, 76.

44. Riva and Vella 2006, 10.

45. Lo Schiavo, Macnamara and Vagnetti 1985; Kassianidou 2001; Lo Schiavo 2001. For Cyprus in the LBA, see Iacovou 2008, 225; Knapp 2008, 335–40.

46. For a recent discussion of this position, see Iacovou 2008, 247, 257–60.

47. For a recent discussion of this position, see Knapp 2008, 294–96, 346.

48. Kassianidou 2001, 100–01; Iacovou 2008, 249–50; Knapp 2008, 366–67.

49. Lo Schiavo, Macnamara, and Vagnetti 1985; Matthäus 2001.

of later Greek sources) to the courts of King Solomon and Hiram are recorded.[50] While Phoenician activity in Greece in the tenth century BC seems well established, at Lefkandi in particular,[51] the material data for similar Phoenician activity in the central and western Mediterranean between the twelfth and tenth centuries are shakier.[52] Nonetheless, that has not stopped some scholars from seeing, on theoretical grounds, continuous contact between Phoenicia and the central and western Mediterranean during the twelfth to tenth centuries.[53]

More recent finds from Huelva in southwestern Spain and Carthage in northern Africa provide fresh fodder for this position (Map 1). At Huelva, carefully executed rescue excavations uncovered local handmade pottery alongside considerable evidence of Phoenician pottery (some 3,233 items out of a total of 8,009 identifiable items) and craft production (metallurgy, pottery, carpentry, and ivory carving), as well as much smaller quantities of Greek, Cypriot, Sardinian, and Etruscan (Villanovan) pottery.[54] Radiocarbon dates obtained from cattle bone from a secondary deposit belong to the first half of the ninth century, if not older still.[55] That we might sometimes place greater confidence in surviving ancient traditions has been recently reaffirmed in connection with the foundation of Carthage in the later ninth century, now likewise supported by radiocarbon dates.[56] There can no longer be any serious doubt that Phoenicians were settling in Iberia and northern Africa in the ninth century BC and operating more generally in the central and western Mediterranean. It may be only a matter of time before more solid evidence for a tenth-century presence becomes available. Phoenician settlement abroad clearly occurred even before the Neo-Assyrian Empire put pressure on the homeland from around the mid-eighth century,[57] when the imposition of direct rule and hefty

---

50. See the discussion in Gras, Rouillard, and Teixidor 1995, 69–71; Nijboer and van der Plicht 2006, 35–36; Lane Fox 2008, 26.

51. Lemos 2002, 226–29.

52. The best collection and discussion of this evidence is that of Aubet 2001, 194–211, to which can be added the *Aegyptiaca* from Torre Galli in Calabria (Pacciarelli 1999, 213–17) and Thapsos III in Sicily (see De Angelis 2003a, 4 with n. 23). Even these two possible additions are not conclusive enough to provide concrete material evidence of Phoenician presence. Pacciarelli thinks it also possible that Cypriots or Syrians could have brought these Egyptian items west, and native Sicilians are likelier candidates behind Thapsos III.

53. Bernardini 2000, 28–29; Bietti Sestieri, Cazzella, and Schnapp 2002, 424; Niemeyer 2006, 146–52.

54. González de Canales, Serrano, and Llompart 2006.

55. Nijboer and van der Plicht 2006, 35.

56. Docter et al. 2005.

57. So, recently, Lane Fox 2008, 24–27; Fletcher 2012.

tribute led Tyre and perhaps Sidon into an active program of exploration and colonization in points west.[58]

The Greeks themselves are not to be excluded from this discussion, although the evidence is much less reliable than the Cypriot and Phoenician material just discussed.[59] Influences of Greek PG pottery on the ceramic traditions of parts of southern Italy and Sicily have been claimed,[60] but such attempts are still at best vague. A stronger case for continuity has recently been made for LG and Archaic Achaean plain banded and monochrome *kantharoi* found at a number of sites in both southern Italy and Sicily.[61] They are argued to provide evidence for the continuing bonds and links between Greece and Italy. Overall, the evidence is extremely unreliable.

This discussion of east-west contact would not be complete without also considering the western and central Mediterranean goods that are increasingly being recognized in Greek and Near Eastern contexts of this date.[62] The dominant interpretive line has been that Greeks could only have brought this material home through their settlement and trade as booty and luxury goods.[63] Italian initiative was never seriously entertained as an option. Winds of change, however, are starting to blow, and such one-sided perspectives are currently under reconsideration. More Sardinian and Etruscan involvement and initiative in maintaining contacts with Greece, Cyprus, and the eastern Mediterranean as a whole have been envisioned.[64] Also aiding this case are the numerous Etruscan and especially Sardinian ship representations in bronze and clay known from this very same period.[65]

---

58. Sidon was perhaps part of a northern Syrian network, at least until Sidon's destruction in the mid-seventh century (Fletcher 2004, 59–66).

59. Cf. Nijboer and van der Plicht 2006, 33.

60. Palermo 1996; Herring 1998. This matter is not discussed in Lemos 2002.

61. Papadopoulos 2001.

62. Mederos Martín 1996; Naso 2000; 2006 (cf. also Ridgway 2006a, 306–07); Kassianidou 2001, 110; Matthäus 2001, 176; Lane Fox 2008, 127. It is likely that, as in the case of Huelva (González de Canales, Serrano, and Llompart 2006, 26), Phoenicians later carried Sardinian material to Iberia and eventually supplanted the Sardinians in bringing material from the Atlantic-Iberian network to Sardinia and from there further east (see the recent discussion in Riva 2010, 50–51).

63. As recently in Lane Fox 2008, 134.

64. Lo Schiavo 2001, 141–42; Bietti Sestieri, Cazzella, and Schnapp 2002, 425–26. Some Greek scholars consider this very likely (Ridgway 2006a, 307; Osborne 2009, 121), while others seem unaware of this issue (Lemos 2002) or continue to uphold the role of the eastern Mediterranean (Dickinson 2006, 196).

65. Lo Schiavo 2000; Höckmann 2001.

We are on the verge of a highly interesting period in the study of east-west EIA contacts. Only time will tell whether Italian archaeological developments will garner the kind of general support they must have to become part of the standard picture of this period.[66] For the time being, it is safe to conclude that the western Mediterranean did not rely entirely on the eastern Mediterranean to survive and flourish, and that in fact movement from west to east may have played a significant role in ways until recently unappreciated. Overall, regional systems developed across the Mediterranean that could exist without one another, but that of course were mutually enriched and challenged when they overlapped.

Where was Sicily in all this? Sicily has been little mentioned, because it was very much secondary in the earliest IA interregional history (Maps 1–3).[67] Arguments in favor of Phoenician "precolonization" in Sicily have declined in recent years.[68] Earlier attempts to find concrete evidence of Phoenicians in Sicily were spurred on because of Thucydides, who claims that the Phoenicians lived all around the island before the Greeks.[69] However, new approaches to Thucydides have gained ground in recent years, resulting in his status as a highly reliable writer being questioned, especially for the early contact period.[70] Moreover, the supposedly "precolonization" archaeological data to support Thucydides have been discounted on various grounds.[71] The earliest material remains for Phoenicians in Sicily can only be securely associated with their permanent settlements. The same holds for Greek "precolonization" in Sicily.[72] The earliest Greek pottery in Sicily can similarly only be associated with the arrival of permanent Greek settlements.[73] By contrast, the earliest Greek pottery in the central Mediterranean is generally made up of MG II drinking cups and some wine jugs and craters and comes from Etruscan and Sardinia contexts. Only one historical conclusion emerges: Sicily was not the main attraction for all these metal-hungry easterners, but rather Sardinia and Etruria, as indicated by archaeological data, which are earlier in date than

---

66. Cf. the intermediate position of Riva 2010, 3.

67. Coldstream 2003, 233; Lane Fox 2008, 125.

68. Spanò Giammellaro 2001, 183–85.

69. Thuc. 6.2.6.

70. Bonnet 2009.

71. Ciasca 1988–89, 76; Guzzardi 1991, 942–52; Leighton 1999, 225–29; Albanese Procelli 2003a, 133–34; De Angelis 2003a, 115–17.

72. De Angelis 2003a, 10–11, 122–23.

73. Albanese Procelli 2003a, 131–36; Hodos 2006, 95–96.

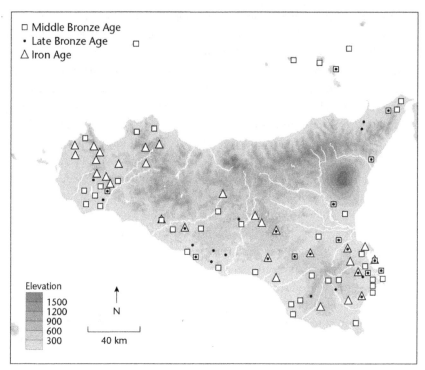

MAP 3 Native Settlement Patterns in Later Prehistory.
© Author

those in Sicily.[74] A strong desire to forge exchange relationships with Etruscan and Sardinian elites for metals preceded Greek settlement in Sicily.[75]

Nevertheless it seems very likely that the Phoenicians and Greeks would have frequented Sicily before establishing their permanent settlements there, since the island would have been an important bridgehead for the east-west and north-south traffic that we know was happening in the later ninth and early eighth centuries BC. Northwest Sicily lies closest to the metal resources of Sardinia and Etruria, leaving little doubt about the earlier uses and subsequent securing of this part of the island.[76] At least a century of such undocumented activity can be posited in view of the alterations to absolute chronology discussed earlier.[77] It is not unimaginable that Phoenician and Greek ships

---

74. Albanese Procelli 2005a, 520.

75. Hall 2002, 109–10; Coldstream 2003, 395; d'Agostino 2006, 208–17; Ridgway 2006a, 302–04; Dickinson 2006, 201–02.

76. Markoe 2000, 175.

77. Guzzardi 1991, 950, 952; Falsone 1994, 677–78; Hodos 2006, 98. Cf. Chiai 2002, 133.

would have had to stop in Sicily in times of bad weather or when fresh water was needed. Nor is it unimaginable that Phoenicians and Greeks engaged in information-gathering expeditions there. These and similar actions are the kinds of activities which we should not expect to leave any archaeological traces or to have garnered much attention from ancient writers on account of their mundane, everyday nature. Otherwise, as already said, the silence of the archaeological record suggests that the Phoenicians and Greeks seem to have largely overlooked Sicily at this stage in favor of Sardinia, Etruria, and other destinations deemed more important. Later that decision was reversed for the general reasons just discussed, and any previous sea routes and landings that Phoenicians and Greeks had already established on Sicily simply became more formalized and more tangible.

What impact did this have on the social and economic development of native Sicily in the period between the island losing its status as the core of BA east-west traffic and the early Phoenician and Greek settlements? Notable material changes are discernible (Map 3). Greater cultural, sociopolitical, and economic links were established between Calabria and Sicily in the EIA, including the arrival of settlers.[78] Similarities in architectural and burial practices can be observed. The newcomers either occupied preexisting sites or created new ones in both coastal and inland locations. More importantly, a clear change in these sites, whatever their location, is signaled by rectangular structures, with their pitched roofs supported by wooden beams, themselves sometimes built into the structures' stone foundation bases. Cemeteries contained individual inhumation and cremation burials, whose grave goods stressed social roles within the community, unlike in the previous period in Sicily. The arrival of iron technology in Sicily was another link.[79] It has been suggested that Calabrian groups came to Sicily because of the mineral resources that existed in this northeastern part of the island.[80] If so, there may have been a different form of ownership of these resources than would probably have been the case in LBA Sicily. Some scholars, drawing in particular on burial data, have speculated that the newcomers were more egalitarian. They stressed economic self-sufficiency and communal ownership of wealth centered on the nuclear family, as opposed to the more hierarchical structures they encountered, which put emphasis on individual ownership of wealth centered on larger family lineages.

---

78. Bietti Sestieri 1997b, 490–91; Leighton 1999, 188; Albanese Procelli 2003a, 49–55, 66–76, 122–26. Whether this was because of the "Ausonian invasion" remains difficult to say with any certainty.

79. Albanese Procelli 1995, 39; 2001a; 2003a, 99–103; Leighton 1999, 188. Giardino (2005) is noncommittal on the origins of Sicilian iron technology.

80. Albanese Procelli 1997b, 514. On the mineral resources themselves, see Chapter 4 below.

We may also understand better the newcomers' sociopolitical and economic structures if we turn to the hypotheses advanced in Calabria, where the data are fuller and better interpreted. There, society belonged to "monocentric village communities."[81] These were medium-sized villages, usually ten to twenty hectares in size. They were located on small plateaus, with a view to both defense and the economy. These villages were the main centers of population, with an estimated five hundred to one thousand residents, who controlled a surrounding territory of high-quality agricultural land within a radius of about five to eight kilometers. They were autonomous and self-sufficient economic, social, and political units. Arms buried in tombs were also common. In particular, long spearheads seem to have overtaken short swords as the main form of weapon, presupposing a form of combat made of ranks of warriors with spears. Combat, moreover, seems to have been organized at the community level, with group solidarity and cooperation, and not so much individual prowess, being the guiding principles. This egalitarian community may have been further subdivided into curia-like associations.[82]

That the interpretations derived from Calabrian data can be extended to Sicily is not to be doubted. The idea of the "monocentric village community" lines up with Sicilian settlement data (Figure 1). The same holds for military organization.[83] Whether the warrior leaders had true political prestige and power remains to be determined.[84] For nearby Calabria, the elite appear to have been poorly developed at the time of the Greeks' arrival and lacked distinction.[85] Given the parallels between Calabria and Sicily in this period, a similar impression seems to obtain.

Developments elsewhere in Sicily, where known, also suggest continuity and change (Maps 2–3). Craftwork continued to follow previous traditions for the most part, though with some innovations in the so-called Cassibile fibula and piumata (or "plumed") pottery with painted geometric designs. Several examples of piumata pottery have been found at Pontecagnano in Campania and in Malta, indicating that Sicily's contacts were not restricted to metal finds, but included

---

81. Pacciarelli 2000, 255–59; 2004, 454–60, 468.

82. Riva 2010, 4 cautions against using terms like curia from later Roman literary sources to describe administrative subdivisions for pre-Roman Italian cultures that she agrees must have certainly existed.

83. Albanese Procelli 1992, 35–37; Albanese Procelli and Lo Schiavo 2004, 410.

84. Bietti Sestieri 1997b, 489; Albanese Procelli 2003a, 127–28.

85. Pacciarelli 2000, 278; 2004, 457–58, 468–69.

the movement of people to and from the island (Map 1).[86] Some examples of Nuraghic pottery from Sardinia have also been found in Sicily.[87] The absence of Sicilian finds in Sardinian contexts may suggest, in this case, unidirectional movement, and the same may have been the case with the Iberian workmanship discernible in Sicilian metal finds, in which case Sardinia acted as the conduit. Latial style *olle* have also been noted at Mt. Finocchito and Caltagirone, and again they probably arrived at second hand.

There were also continuities and changes in burial practices. The norm continued to be inhumation in chamber tombs, but now without the monumentality (Figure 2).[88] This development can be best seen in the Cassibile cemetery, with its estimated two thousand tombs, but it is also known from other tomb groups in this part of the island.[89] In western Sicily, cemeteries dating to this period are as a rule not abundant or well explored in terms of extent and quality of investigation.[90] At some sites, there was a continuation of some of the preceding BA traditions of multiple depositions in tholos-like tombs. This can be seen at the hilltop site of Sant'Angelo Muxaro, which in the seventh century becomes the best known and the wealthiest of all western Sicilian native cemeteries, thanks to the impressive gold finds made there.[91] Before then, no signs of elevated status or wealth exist here, or at any other western Sicilian cemetery in this period for that matter.[92] In general across Sicily, locally produced objects comprised the bulk of the goods in circulation, and egalitarianism could only have been the main social outcome.[93]

---

86. Campania: D'Agostino and Gastaldi 1988, 108, 115; Albanese Procelli 1995, 42. Malta: La Rosa 1989, 14. The absence of this pottery in Calabria has been noted: Bietti Sestieri 1997b, 488. Turco 2000, 109 thinks that the absence of *piumata* pottery in much of southern Italy is an indication that southern Italians initiated and maintained contacts with Sicily, and not vice versa.

87. Albanese Procelli 2003a, 90, 105.

88. Leighton 1999, 188; Albanese Procelli 2001b, 56.

89. Orsi 1899, 33–146; Turco 2000, 100–01. Cf. also S. Tusa 1992, 614–16.

90. For an overview, see Spatafora 2001, 145–48, 159. Note how western Sicilian burial data hardly register in the most recent discussion: Albanese Procelli 2003a, 56–76. Most of the known western Sicilian cemeteries have either been poorly excavated, in part because of the stratigraphic challenges presented by their mulitple burials, or long plundered because of their accessibility (as at Mt. Finestrelle di Gibellina and Caltabelotta, for which see Falsone and Mannino 1997, 621–24).

91. The starting point for understanding this site is now Rizza and Palermo 2004.

92. Albanese Procelli 1988–89, 97; Turco 2000, 104.

93. Turco 2000; Albanese Procelli 2001b, 58–59; 2003a, 126–28.

FIGURE 1 Monte Maranfusa: A Typical Native Hilltop Settlement in the Interior of Western Sicily.
© Author

The lack of exotica changed the character of power to a more democratic or middling sort of ideology, with the community, and not individuals, being more important.[94]

The settlements accompanying these cemeteries are by comparison even more poorly known.[95] Nevertheless, it is clear that many of the LBA sites, especially those in the hilly interior, continued to be occupied and acted as the main foci of human activity in the EIA (Map 3; Figure 1).[96] The historical evidence suggests the same for the so-called kingdoms of Xuthia and Hybla mentioned in ancient sources.[97] The dual aims of defense and the exploitation of inland

94. As argued by González-Ruibal 2004, 291–92 for the transition from BA to IA in northwest Iberia, which witnessed a similar historical trajectory to Sicily's.

95. Cf. Frasca 2001a, 47.

96. Frasca 2001a, 48; Spatafora 2001, 159; Albanese Procelli 2003a, 35–36; Leighton 1999, 192; 2005, 281.

97. For example, Diod. Sic. 5.8.2; Thuc. 6.3–4. Xuthia and Hybla are usually identified with particular sites like Leontinoi, Pantalica, and Villasmundo (Bernabò Brea 1968, 163–64; Graham 1988, 314–16; Domínguez 1989, 264; Albanese Procelli 1995, 44). Galvagno (2003), however, argues that they should be regarded as regions rather than single sites.

FIGURE 2 Calascibetta: A Typical Native Cemetery of Rock-cut Tombs in Eastern Central Sicily.
© Author

and coastal resources and opportunities appear to have been the rule. The structures within these settlements were constructed of a combination of stone foundations, mud-brick superstructures, and thatch roofs supported by posts. There is no evidence of fortifications or buildings for specialized purposes, like sanctuaries. As in the LBA, the territories exploited by such settlements must have been small, extending for only tens of kilometers.[98] The techniques of agricultural production appear to have improved with the coming of iron.[99] Along with the appearance of satellite sites in some territories, the accompanying settlements were intended to exploit both cereal and tree crops.[100]

One recent estimate has calculated 40 percent fewer LBA/EIA sites compared to the MBA, suggesting that nucleation, and not a collapse in overall population numbers, explains the difference.[101] Certainly these numbers reflect that deflation of some kind occurred. The placement of the cemeteries in distinct groupings around these settlements suggests that the settlements were also

98. Cf. Leighton 2005, 278.

99. Albanese Procelli 2003a, 78.

100. Albanese Procelli 2001b, 56; 2003a, 48.

101. Leighton 2005, 279–81.

composed of separate nuclei, perhaps in part made up of such hypothesized population influxes, which together formed a single political community.[102] The population of native settlements is difficult to estimate, but they are unlikely to have surpassed the 1,000–2,000 range estimated for the LBA.

With regionalism mattering more than it did in the LBA, it is only to be expected that the pace of social and economic changes varied across the EIA Mediterranean. This was the case in Sicily, which was not the center of the Mediterranean in any geographical or historical sense, as it had been in the LBA and as it was to be in Classical times. The material record reflects this social and economic deflation, which resulted in a more egalitarian society, where social status was based on ability rather than on external connections and exotic goods, whether or not of Aegean origins.[103] Sicily was certainly not isolated, and it entertained relations with the outside world primarily on account of the metals trade.[104] In return, various agricultural products and resources like alum and rock salt in central Sicily have been suggested. These suggestions are at best guesswork, based on probability and limited archaeological finds (such as the presence of millstones in some native settlements).[105] The whole period merits closer attention in future work, on account of this period's importance in Sicily's history, the eve of permanent Phoenician and Greek settlement, which thickened the plot of the island's history.

Phoenician settlements in Sicily are discussed first, since, as seen above, there are good archaeological and historical reasons for thinking that they preceded the Greek settlements in central Mediterranean. What we know of the three Phoenician settlements in Sicily (Solous/Soloeis, Panormos, and Motya) down to 600 BC is still rather limited (Map 2).

Least is known of Solous/Soloeis.[106] The Archaic settlement was established on land previously unoccupied. It was situated on a promontory and had easy access by sea and to movement inland via a number of watercourses. Solous/Soloeis thus conforms to the canonical requirements of Phoenician settlements, including a small hinterland for direct exploitation.[107] It was engaged in

---

102. Frasca 2001, 49; Albanese Procelli 2003a, 48. For Cassibile, Turco (2000, 100) believes that tomb groups belonged to separate villages that did not form a single community.

103. Leighton 1996c; 1999, 188; Russell 2011, 260–66.

104. Hence Albanese Procelli 2003a, 109–10.

105. La Rosa 1989, 9, 42, 47; Battaglia and Alliata 1991; S. Tusa 1992, 589, 646, 648; Malone et al. 1994, 178, 180.

106. See in particular C. Greco 1997.

107. C. Greco 1997, 100–05; Spanò Giammellaro 2001, 193–94.

the production of transport containers and food for export in mostly Tyrrhenian markets.[108] The cemeteries are located northwest of the settlement. Burials came in a variety of forms, but show no great differences between them, suggesting the existence of a population mostly made up of craftsmen.[109]

A little more is known of Panormos, which lies underneath the modern metropolis of Palermo.[110] Although archaeological work is thereby rendered difficult, excavations and historical intuition have made it clear that the Phoenician settlement occupied the four districts that make up central Palermo, crisscrossed by north-south and east-west thoroughfares. The settlement, whose structures remain entirely unknown to us, was later enclosed by a city wall. Hundreds of Phoenicio-Punic burials have been explored outside the settlement to the southwest. The earliest burials date to the mid-seventh century, which has suggested that Panormos was not founded until then.[111] That proposal puts too much weight on the silence of the archaeological record, which for Palermo is unwarranted.[112] Instead, scholars have normally hypothesized a foundation in the second half of the eighth century BC. Much variety exists in the burial ritual, as so far known: there are inhumations in chamber tombs, stone sarcophagi, and large pots, as well as cremations in urns and pits in the earth. The grave goods are equally diverse, consisting of pottery, metalwork (mainly personal adornments, but occasionally weapons), glass beads, and Egyptianizing amulets. A community of diverse fortunes no doubt existed here.

The third settlement, Motya, is presently the best-known Phoenicio-Punic site in Sicily. Located on a forty-five-hectare island just off the Sicilian mainland, Motya seems to have been unoccupied when the Phoenicians settled it. Phoenician residence in the eighth century is indicated above all by sixteen tombs and some settlement remains.[113] The first evidence for buildings and sacred space comes from the seventh century, when the so-called Cappiddazzu sanctuary, the *tophet*, and what appears to be a warehouse were constructed. The necropolis and *tophet* were located on a "ring road" that ran along the island's edge; other such service areas, most notably craftworking quarters for pottery, dyeing, and metallurgy, were also situated on this road.[114] On the

108. C. Greco 1997, 110–11; Bondì 2002, 92.

109. C. Greco 1997, 109.

110. The fullest picture available can be followed in C.A. Di Stefano 1998.

111. Tamburello 1977, 34–35.

112. Cf. in general the warnings of Gras, Rouillard and Teixidor 1995, 58.

113. V. Tusa 1972, 34–55; Isserlin et al. 1974, 53, 73; Isserlin 1982, 114–15.

114. Spanò Giammellaro 2001, 187.

mainland opposite, the dating of the long-known cemetery at Birgi has been pushed back through excavations to the early seventh century, fueling suspicions that a more substantial Phoenician community existed—a "parallel" Motya, possibly along the lines of Phoenician sites elsewhere with a mainland component.[115] The closest fresh water would have been located on this mainland, a coastal plain protected to the east by a low tableland, all ideal for agricultural and pastoral activities.

The Greek settlements that shared Sicily with these Phoenician ones were also established in the eighth and seventh centuries BC. They will be the subject of the next chapter; here our aim is to put these settlements into the wider context of Greek migration across the Mediterranean between the eighth and sixth centuries BC[116] and to embed them in Sicily's existing geographical and historical conditions.

In the eighth century, life in Greece began to change rapidly as existing and new developments merged to bring about a dynamic period (Map 1). A major cultural transformation, according to Morris a "revolution,"[117] was under way, one that laid the basis for Classical Greece.[118] Population in the Greek world may have doubled in the eighth century, which seems reasonable and which, if accepted, would have had several ramifications. In Morris' words, "Unless my estimate that population doubled is very wide of the mark, we must conclude that either (a) the numbers of poor and hungry multiplied dramatically, (b) resources were redistributed, (c) new resources were brought into use, (d) output per capita increased sharply, or (e) massive social dislocations ensued—or some combination of the above." Morris opts for a combination of factors at work and hypothesizes that there would have been three responses to them: intensification of agricultural production, extensification in three ways (internally, such as through the infilling of Attica; externally, such as the Spartan conquest of neighboring Messenia; and long distance, via overseas settlement[119]), and reorganization (especially in terms of efficient property rights and low transaction costs). Among other things, this revolution resulted in increased demand and competition for resources. In Greece there were limited possibilities.[120]

---

115. Spanò Giammellaro 2001, 187–89; Bondì 2002, 89–90.

116. The most recent and fullest treatment of the subject is in Tsetskhladze 2006–2008.

117. Morris 2009a.

118. For summaries of this transformation, see Whitley 2001, 134–94; Coldstream 2003; Morris 2006a; 2006b; Hall 2007b; Osborne 2009, 66–130.

119. So also Purcell 2005a; Dickinson 2006, 111–12.

120. See also recently Morel 2007, 489 for seeing economics as a prime motivator behind overseas settlement.

In the next two and a half centuries, thousands of Greeks left their home-land for greener pastures abroad, conquering and coexisting with the peoples whom they encountered (Map 1).[121] The Greeks are usually thought to have settled purely for agricultural reasons: to obtain land. But the much debated causes of Greek "colonization" were established long before we had the kind of understanding we now have and require of early Greece.[122] Therefore, some of the other causes usually put forward, such as trade and political discontent, must also not be ruled out.[123] In fact, there are good reasons for not thinking of these causes as mutually exclusive. As I have argued elsewhere, the presence of silos at Megara Hyblaia in Sicily suggests that trade and agriculture, per-haps stimulated by political competition, could all have been complementary activities.[124] Such intertwined motivations can be more generally argued. The main patterns of Greek overseas settlement are relatively clear too. Some five hundred or so permanent settlements were established in many regions of the Mediterranean; this number represents somewhere between one-third and one-half of all Greek states on current estimates.[125] The process started first in southern Italy and Sicily and was the most intense there. It was followed in the seventh and sixth centuries by settlement in the Black Sea and its approaches, Libya, southern France, and the Adriatic. Some areas even within and beyond these regions were clearly off limits to the Greeks, most certainly because of strong preexisting populations, such as the Etruscans,[126] while other areas were not deemed attractive enough to settle.

What kinds of early impacts did the conjunction of these Phoenician and Greek settlements in Sicily have on one another, and especially on the native populations alongside whom they established themselves? Phoenicians seem generally to have had good relations with the local populations they encountered throughout the Mediterranean.[127] Research carried out over the last generation is also suggesting amicable relations between Phoenicians and Greeks all across the Mediterranean. These broad patterns also hold

---

121. Morris (2000, 257) puts the figure at 10,000 people in "colonies" by 700 BC, and Scheidel (2003, 134–35) puts the total figure at between 30,000 and 60,000 adult male emi-grants (assuming, of course, that no women and children went overseas).

122. For a recent overview, see Descoeudres 2008, 293–96.

123. On the political, see most recently Bernstein 2004.

124. De Angelis 2002. For further discussion, see Purcell 2005a and Chapter 4 below.

125. Ruschenbusch 1985; Hansen and Nielsen 2004, 53–54.

126. See Snodgrass 1994a, 1–2.

127. Gras, Rouillard and Teixidor 1995, 58; Markoe 2000, 170–89; Aubet 2001, 354–55; Hodos 2006; Neville 2007, 119–22.

for Sicily in particular.[128] Phoenicians appear to have been resident in some Greek sites, as suggested by the presence of Red Slip Ware plates and lamps at Syracuse, Megara Hyblaia, Zankle/Messina, Gela, and Himera.[129] While exchange is the usual motive for explaining Phoenicians in these nascent Greek cities, it has been suggested that they may have been involved in the setting up of early Zankle/Messina.[130] Greek presence in Sicily's Phoenician settlements is first attested only in the sixth century BC.[131] The evidence is strongest for Motya, where there are funerary inscriptions and graves, and in the fifth and fourth centuries these are joined by literary evidence as well. There is no secure evidence for Phoenicians resident in native Sicilian settlements.[132] Nevertheless, some Phoenician, Egyptian, and Near Eastern objects are known from native Sicilian sites in the interior, so that it is beyond reasonable doubt that Phoenician traders went there, or at the very least were in communication with these sites. Native Sicilians were drawn to the opportunities Phoenician Motya offered.[133] They were similarly drawn to the Greek cities on the coast, just as the Greeks were attracted to native communities inland.[134] So there were interactions and residence together from the Archaic period onward.

This raises the question of the nature of the earliest social and economic relations between native Sicilians, Phoenicians, and Greeks in Sicily. It has been generalized that the Phoenicians introduced prestige economies all across the Mediterranean between the ninth and seventh centuries BC.[135] These prestige objects were either made by them or obtained in places like Egypt, in order to forge exchange relationships with local leaders. While this was manifestly the case in Cyprus, the Italian mainland, and the Iberian Peninsula, a prestige economy is not so blatantly obvious in early contact

---

128. Hans 1983, 5–32; Domínguez 1989, 547–69; Anello 1990–91; 1997; Spanò Giammellaro 2001, 194–95.

129. Gras 1985, 303; Ciasca 1988–89, 77–78; Guzzardi 1991, 952–53; Spanò Giammellaro 2001, 189–90; Albanese Procelli 2003a, 134.

130. Rendeli 2005, 175 n. 16.

131. Ciasca 1988–89, 88; Bondì 2005, 22; Galvagno 2005.

132. Ciasca 1988–89, 76. Cf. more recently Vassallo 1999, 73 for the discovery at native Colle Madore of a Western Greek amphora with a Phoenicio-Punic graffito on it.

133. Spanò Giammellaro 2001, 185–86, 190–91; Bondì 2002, 88–89; 2005, 21.

134. For further discussion, see below in this chapter and in Chapter 3.

135. Aubet 2001, 136–38, who actually says the eighth to sixth centuries. But the revised chronologies now suggest moving the upper end back into the ninth century. For Iberia, see now Neville 2007, 119–22.

Sicily.[136] About sixty objects dating between the fourteenth and seventh centuries BC could be cataloged in a survey of the mid-1980s.[137] These objects consist mainly of various kinds of scarabs and alabaster vases found predominantly in cemeteries and sanctuaries in native, Greek, and even Phoenician sites.[138] Apart from a handful of these objects, the rest date safely from the period of Greek settlement in Sicily. Carthage is believed to have been largely responsible for bringing them to the island, and in turn they were circulated by Carthaginians, Greeks, and natives.[139] Archaeological research conducted since then has increased the number of finds, from native sites in particular (not surprising given the increased archaeological attention they have received in recent years; Figures 3–4), without modifying the chronological and depositional patterns previously established.[140]

But how is all this material to be interpreted? What is to be made of potentially the most revealing find, the impressive gold finds from Sant'Angelo Muxaro, which now survive only as four cups and two rings that in all likelihood date to the seventh century BC?[141] They are perhaps the clearest evidence of the general existence of prestige economies in Sicily that emerged only after the arrival of Phoenicians and Greeks, whether or not we accept them as somehow connected with the Phoenicians.[142] It may be that Sicily's prestige

---

136. So Guzzardi 1991, 950, 952. Cf. also Pisano 1999.

137. Guzzardi 1991, 941–42.

138. The sites include Motya, Syracuse, Megara Hyblaia, Selinous, Kamarina, Mt. Finnochito, Villasmundo, and Centuripe.

139. The gold finds from Sant'Angelo Muxaro are not included in Guzzardi's catalog, since he followed the line of interpretation that sees these objects as being of native "Sikan" manufacture drawing on still lingering BA Greek and Levantine inspiration (Guzzardi 1991, 946). These gold finds are discussed immediately below.

140. Seven Egyptianizing scarabs have come to light from a seventh-century tomb at Polizzello: De Miro 1988a, 35, 38 (not mentioned in Gorton 1996). An Egyptian scarab has been found in the settlement at Mt. Finestrelle: de Cesare and Gargini 1997, 372. Some Phoenician pottery, an eye bead, and an Egyptianizing scarab have been found in the native sanctuary at Mt. Polizzo: Morris et al. 2007. We might also add here the discovery of Punic (sixth-century) amphora fragments at two rural sites found during a surface survey around the native site located at Montagnola della Borrania: Lauro 1999, 244. Egyptian scarabs were also found in a house in Syracuse (Coldstream 2003, 396). Excluded from this discussion are the numerous finds made in the Phoenician settlements, especially Panormos, since the focus here is on assessing the social and economic impact Phoenicians had on the other peoples of Sicily.

141. The case has been well argued in Palermo 2004, 198–99.

142. For a note of caution, see Spanò Giammellaro 2001, 185. On their most recent interpretation, the gold objects are thought to have been of native manufacture and commissioning, but executed by an artist who may have been born and brought up in Greek Gela (Amari 2004, 177; Palermo 2004, 210–15). As prestige objects, see Albanese Procelli 2003a, 127.

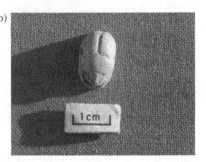

FIGURE 3 Phoenician Scarab Found at Native Site at Monte Polizzo, Western Sicily.
© Author

FIGURE 4 Imported East Greek Cup Found at Native Site at Monte Polizzo, Western Sicily.
© Author

economy was not as well developed as in other parts of the Mediterranean, given the Phoenicians' relatively late arrival on the island (not helped by the uncertainties over when Panormos and Solous were founded), and/or it may be that more surprises await the archaeologist.[143] In any case, there seems no reason to deny in Sicily the existence of a prestige economy introduced in part

---

143. Spatafora 2001, 143–44; cf. also Aubet 2001, 355.

by the Phoenicians and a focus in general on exchange.[144] An initial focus on exchange would have meant that their settlements were accompanied by only small territories and that their relations with native populations were more equal, both in contrast to the Greeks' motivations and accompanying attitudes.

The best place to begin this discussion is with the nature of the landscapes Greeks had to work with, as well as with the native Sicilian settlement pattern, forms of land use, and population distribution that they encountered (Maps 2–3).[145] Both Moses Finley and Giacomo Manganaro believed that Sicily's land had already been cleared and was under cultivation.[146] To a certain degree, this is obviously true,[147] but, on the whole, their views can today be tempered with some contrary paleoecological data that have been accumulating in Sicily over the past fifteen years (see Chapter 4 for full discussion). It can be demonstrated empirically that the amount of land under cultivation had shrunk since the LBA. The landscape was more heavily vegetated and accordingly contained more wild animals at the time of permanent settlement by Greeks than they had thought (Figures 5 and 6). Most major native settlements were situated in the interior away from the coasts[148] and had small territories in the tens of square kilometers—in all likelihood, a day's walk to and from the center to the edge (Figure 1; Map 3).[149] Proprietary rights would have been limited mainly to these small territories.[150] There is evidence for the existence and continuity of some native sites on and close to the coast.[151] At the same time, abandonment of coastal and inland settlements also happened.[152] One has to wonder

---

144. Spanò Giammellaro 2001, 194–95; Bondì 2002, 94; cf. also van Dommelen and Gómez Bellard 2008, 141, 204.

145. Lepore 2000, 69.

146. See note 1 above for references. This is not to deny that Greek settlements sometimes followed their prehistoric predecessors in terms of their topographic placement and configuration and uses (see below Chapters 2 and 4 for further discussion).

147. De Angelis 2003b, 41.

148. For a recent exception from Naxos, see Lentini 2010, 521–25.

149. Cf. Spencer 1998, 7; Bintliff 1999.

150. On prehistoric property rights: Gilman 1998; Earle 2000.

151. Albanese Procelli 2003a, 149.

152. This may have been encouraged, regardless of location, by the synoecism of native settlements, now being seen as a response not just to defense (the traditional answer of modern scholarship working in a conquest-only framework) but also to economic possibilities brought on by these immigrant newcomers (Leighton 1999, 239; 2000a, 21–22; Albanese Procelli 2003a, 146). Coastal abandonment could also have been due to the slave trading and piracy hinted at in Homer's *Odyssey* (*Od.*, 20.383; 24.211; 24.307). For Sicilian

FIGURE 5 Unworked Red Deer Antler Found at Native Site at Monte Polizzo, Western Sicily.

© Author

FIGURE 6 Worked Red Deer Antler Found at Native Site at Monte Polizzo, Western Sicily.

© Author

how much more widespread coastal abandonment was, a question difficult to answer at present because of the current chronology's latitude.[153]

An attempt can be made to estimate native Sicilian population in this period. According to the latest estimates, 41 LBA/EIA settlements are known in Sicily (Map 3).[154] Even if we generously raise this figure to one hundred settlements at the time of Greek and Phoenician settlement in Sicily, making ample allowance for gaps in the archaeological record, and give each settlement a population of 1,000 people and territory of 30 square kilometers, we are still talking about an overall native Sicilian population of 100,000 people exploiting 3,000 square kilometers. These estimates represent about 12 percent of Sicily's surface area and about 3–4 percent of Sicily's carrying capacity.[155] That would work out to about 3 people per square kilometer. On this rough-and-ready picture, Sicily was thinly populated and had much available land to clear and work.

That Greeks had to force their way into Sicily is overstated. The island's coasts were thinly populated and thus attractive to Greeks hungry for land. There was arguably not too much for the Greeks to drive from the coasts into the mountainous interior, as often imagined.[156] Sicily was abundant in land in this period, and even later for that matter.[157] Sicily was also ideally suited from the point of view that it also had much unlived-on and unowned land for the emerging connection among Greeks in the eighth century BC between

---

slaves in Homer, see Lepore 2000, 55; Lane Fox 2008, 121–23. At Thapsos, for instance, our best-explored coastal site, the third phase of occupation spans the Cassibile-Pantalica II period, and even with the chronological extension of this period down to the mid-eighth century discussed earlier, Thapsos appears to have been abandoned at the time the wandering Megarians briefly settled it before going on to establish Megara Hyblaia.

153. Excavations at Thapsos leave little doubt that we are dealing with a permanently occupied settlement. However, evidence elsewhere seems also to suggest that some of the coastal dots usually placed on distribution maps must have belonged to temporary or seasonal settlements. A recent case in point is Punta Castelluzzo, which appears on the distribution maps of standard works without further discussion as to its function (Leighton 1999, 189; Albanese Procelli 2003a, 26–27). Recent survey work in the area failed, despite a concentrated search, to reveal any tombs to accompany this settlement, raising the likely possibility that we are dealing, as with later Greek Leontinoi, with a spot used seasonally for exchange and the exploitation of coastal resources (Russo, Gianino and Lanteri 1996, 13–14; Felici and Buscemi Felici 2004, 37 n. 33).

154. Leighton 2005, 279.

155. Elsewhere I have put Sicily's carrying capacity in the range of 2.4 and 3.2 million people (De Angelis 2000, 138–39).

156. Leighton 1999, 238; Hodos 2006, 99.

157. Isager and Skydsgaard 1992, 122; De Angelis 2000, 138–39; Foxhall 2002, 215.

landowning and citizenship to be satisfied.[158] The ancient literary sources seem to support this picture of land availability.[159] Underpopulated landscapes were an EIA reality.[160] Consequently, "Land abundance and the associated lack of competition for land resources will reduce the need for a military and a legal apparatus aimed at protecting landed property rights and resolving disputes between competing land claimants."[161] Conquest of land was not necessarily always the rule, as usually believed.[162] Original possession of unoccupied land without conquest would have rendered Greeks the de facto owners simply through working and improving it.[163] Ownership could have been thus created, along the lines that we hear about in Homer's *Odyssey*.[164]

To activate production on abundant land requires labor,[165] and scholars have rightly traditionally turned for part of their solution to the question of social relations with the native Sicilian populations. Recursivity must have occurred, in which natives came down, by force or otherwise, from their hilltop villages to take part in the activities of the nascent Greek settlements on the coast, much in the way that Diodorus Siculus suggested.[166] When we join the possibility of recursivity in Sicily, both theoretical and empirical, to the archaeological and written evidence for native presence in these Greek coastal settlements (see Chapter 3 below), native Sicilians were no doubt part of these Greek coastal populations. But on what terms did they live together?

Power relations have traditionally been characterized as comprising conquest, the middle ground, or a combination of middle ground followed by conquest.[167] Relations had to consist of both conquest and the middle ground at one and the same time. Comparative historical evidence suggests that

---

158. See Finley 1980, 89; Snodgrass 1993, 38; Salmon 1999, 147–48.

159. Dion. Hal. 1.22.2; Str. 6.2.2, quoting Ephorus. On both passages, see Cusumano 1994, 70–73, 85. Cf. also Thuc. 6.1–5 with the discussion in Avery 1973, 10.

160. On underpopulation and its effects in EIA Italy, see Bietti Sestieri 1997a, 397.

161. So Pastore 1997, 331 in the context of the comparable early modern Paraguayan frontier.

162. Domínguez 2006, 324.

163. Cf. Earle 2000, 41.

164. Homer, *Od.* 24.205–07, with Hanson 1995, 48–49; Giangiulio 2001, 349.

165. For early Greece, see Osborne 2009, 29–34; Bintliff 2012, 226; cf. also Webster 1990.

166. Diod. Sic. 5.6.5 (supported also by Cusumano 1994, 111–14; Chiai 2002, 136–37; Anello 2005, 155–56; Veronese 2006, 636–37). For a similar process in southern Italy, see de la Genière 1978; Purcell 2005a, 122, 126–27, and for the Black Sea, see Oppermann 2005; Avram 2006, 63.

167. For the combination, see Malkin 1998, 1–61; 2002a, 154; Yntema 2000, 42–44. For the other two positions, see the references in notes 1 and 2 above, as well as De Angelis 2010.

conditions of land abundance are more conducive in the earliest stages of settlement to violence and conflict than is recognized by those scholars who put middle-ground social relations before conquest.[168] People, however, must have been forcefully acquired in the earliest stages too. The point lies at the heart of Robert Allen's discussion of the origins of ancient Egyptian state formation:

> The situation is different when labor is scarce and land abundant. In that case, land does not command a rent, and labor is valuable. The ownership or control of labor—rather than land—is the basis of wealth.... Underpopulation has far reaching implications for social organization because it limits the ability of elites to extract surplus from farmers. When there is "free land," farmers who are dissatisfied with their circumstances can move to other locations to improve their lot.[169]

Similar theoretical and historical conditions can be found in Sicily.[170] Thus for the early Greek *poleis* in Sicily to thrive, it was vital that population movements were minimized, so that economic exploitation could take root. Movements could have been restricted by both conquest and the cooperation of native elites.[171] That something along these lines occurred in early Greek Sicily may also be suspected from a later societal feature that would otherwise be left unexplained: the heavy use of serfs and slaves.[172] This was not due to sociopolitical and economic backwardness, as is sometimes thought, but to land abundance and to the sociopolitical and economic structures of Sicily's prehistoric cultures. Sicily offered the right land conditions (abundant and better-quality land), but also the right social conditions with their weakly developed institutions, all of which together formed ideal circumstances for the making of successful agricultural systems. The notion of conquest of land and people must also be kept among the possibilities of how Sicilian Greeks fueled their societies and economies from the earliest times.

Some material and organizational differences between Greeks and natives existed to command land and labor in these ways. We are certainly much better

---

168. Powelson 1988, 308–10; Drennan and Peterson 2006; Weber 2013, 55, 59–60.

169. Allen 1997, 145–46.

170. Belvedere 2001, 713–14; Fischer-Hansen 2002, 127; De Angelis 2003b, 29–30, 34; 2010.

171. For this general point, see Webster 1990; Barceló, Pelfer, and Mandolesi 2002, 48.

172. Finley 1980, 78 (who observes that the Greek settlements around the Black Sea also shared this feature); Frolov 1986. See also Chapter 3 below.

informed in general about Greek and native Sicilian history today, as well as about the development of power relations through interregional contact and exchange to put matters in better perspective.[173] We have already noted how a local native elite may not have existed as the Greek elite did.[174] Another decisive difference may have been the small size, both demographically and territorially, of native Sicilian communities and their inability to create cohesive political entities to match the newcomers.[175] Resilience against malaria on the part of Greeks could have been another factor that caused native settlements to be located inland and that allowed Greeks to settle the coasts.[176] Demographic and territorial differences imply differences in the organization of people and their activities, including technological, that had no parallels in Sicily at the time of Greek settlement. Such organizational differences must also account for the head start the Greeks generally had over native Sicilians in such areas as the building of ships (probably triremes), warfare, and temples, as well as the use of writing and some facets of craft production.[177] The Greeks had these features first, not necessarily because they had an inherent superiority over native Sicilians, but because they were experiencing the early stages of state formation and interregional integration at home first.

The Greeks, moreover, would have come to Sicily with the motive of establishing permanent settlement, bringing with them important lessons from home to a native Sicilian population that had not yet experienced them. That in itself could have made a crucial initial difference. Military matters, which became an ongoing concern to eighth-century Greeks as compared to native Sicilians, could have also played a role. The Greeks would also have come from a world of cutthroat political and territorial competition, which we know from literary sources that they continued among themselves on arriving in Sicily.[178] Research over the last generation has refined our understanding of early Greek warfare and sketched out a basic picture of native Sicilian warfare.[179] Native Sicilians were certainly more sophisticated militarily than earlier generations

---

173. Stein 2002, 907.

174. On Greek elite in this period, see Alram-Stern and Nightingale 2007.

175. Leighton 2000a, 21–22; Albanese Procelli 2003a, 143; Pacciarelli 2000, 278; 2004, 457–58, 468–69.

176. For discussion, see De Angelis 2010, 39–40.

177. Morris (2000, 257–61) places these developments in the wider context of eighth-century Greek history.

178. De Angelis 2003a, 13, 48; Bintliff 2012, 227.

179. For a recent overview of Greek warfare, see Hall 2007b, 155–77. For Sicilian warfare, see above in this chapter.

of scholars had thought, particularly in the northeast or "Aeolian" parts of Sicily. However, recent scholarship on Greek warfare has only strengthened previous views of the early development of massed fighting, including the hiring of Greek mercenaries by Egyptian and Assyrian monarchs from the seventh century BC onward.[180] It seems likely, therefore, that there were military differences between Greeks and native Sicilians: Sicilians seemingly employing individual or small groups of warriors, which were once common in Greece, versus better-armed and more cohesive groups of nascent Greek hoplites.[181]

A middle-ground form of culture contact should not be ruled out, however. Greeks and natives, besides being unable and unwilling to eliminate one another, would have also realized that benefits could be gained all around (cf. Figure 4).[182] One of the corollaries of middle-ground contact that deserves emphasis here is that ethnic boundaries and belonging were not the only, or indeed main, determinants of relationships in the Archaic Mediterranean.[183] Put another way, society was class-based and defined by wealth and status. Elites and skilled professionals of various ethnic origins readily interacted and integrated.[184] Greeks could have easily integrated with the native leaders and their dependents, since there were no ethnocultural or sociopolitical and economic roadblocks to doing so. Scenarios can easily be conjured up as to why friendly relations had to exist, such as obtaining needed items lacking in the coastal settlements, most notably foodstuffs and other products not yet developed or possessed in sufficient quantities, as well as labor and women to ensure productive capacities in the long term.[185] Intermarriage between Greeks and native Sicilians would have guaranteed full community participation and hereditary rights and the transmission of goods, including land.[186] We should not assume that all was rosy in such cases. The ancient sources, despite their later date, are full of plausible tales of the trickery used by the Greeks in Sicily to get their way.[187] Such trickery could have, for instance, been used to exploit the conflicting modes of

---

180. Luraghi 2006.

181. Leighton 1999, 198; Albanese Procelli 2003a, 142.

182. In discussing Himera, Allegro (1999, 282) has reminded us to avoid thinking of "the natives" as monolithic blocks made up of people of cohesive behavior.

183. Gosden 2004, 65, 70.

184. See, for example, Morel 1984, 135–38; Hall 2004, 43–44. See also Chapter 3 below.

185. So, uncontroversially, Albanese Procelli 2003a, 133, 137.

186. Albanese Procelli 2003a, 235–36.

187. Cusumano 1994, 81–83. Cf. also Davies 2002.

land ownership that seems to have existed between Greeks and natives at this time, between communal ownership with periodic redistribution in some native communities and the Greeks' concept of private ownership of land. Therefore, the Greeks' forging of family and friendly relations with native communities and individuals within them could have at the same time (ab)used and disrupted the latter's practices, creating opportunities for the development of economic strategies that ultimately may have challenged and unraveled preexisting ones.

Three concurrent possibilities fed how early Greeks in Sicily could form their societies and economies. They could occupy unworked land, they could conquer land and labor, and/or they could integrate with native Sicilians to acquire land and labor.[188] This conclusion is more expansive and inclusive than the polarized or stadial theories that currently characterize scholarship.

To conclude this chapter, one can be awash with information about the ancient Greeks as compared to Sicily's native and even Phoenician populations. There certainly exists an "embarrassment of riches," as Robert Leighton put it in talking about the differences in datasets between Greek and native religion in Sicily.[189] As has often been noted throughout this chapter, there is still much that we would like to know on all sides of the equation, in order to have a richer understanding of this period. Nevertheless, the data available today have made clear that the situation in prehistoric Sicily and in the wider central Mediterranean did contribute to the shaping of later Sicilian Greek societies and economies.

Events in prehistory contributed to the material changes that occurred in Sicily between the end of the Bronze Age and the start of the Iron Age, which resulted in a notable drop in the degree of sociopolitical complexity. This impacted native Sicilian settlement patterns (generally moving to the interior on hilltops), land use, and demography, in such a way that much land remained to be cleared and put to productive use in other parts of the island. By extension, events in prehistory contributed to the emergence of state formation in Greece before they did in Sicily. Such geographical and historical conditions allowed the Greek states pretty much unfettered freedom to establish themselves on the coasts and encouraged engagement with local native populations. In general, Greek institutional frameworks were developing faster than native Sicilian ones. That is not to say, however, that native Sicilians were

---

188. So De Angelis 2010.

189. Leighton 1999, 262.

unsophisticated; they had achieved a certain level of cultural, technological, social, and economic attainment when Greeks settled permanently alongside them. In turn, this preexisting platform permitted the subsequent growth and development of native and Greek societies and economies. For this to happen, Greeks first needed to acquire and delineate spaces and resources. That is the subject of the next chapter.

2

Settlement and Territory

RECENT WORK ON Greek state formation has generally emphasized the intimate connection between the *polis'* political, territorial, and urban trajectories: the growth of the town, the formation of a stable political community, and the identification of a certain territory all go together.[1] The scholarly literature for Greek Sicily is especially vast for each of these three topics, let alone in combination.[2] The intention in this chapter is to outline the *poleis'* main urban and rural features and to situate them in their geographic settings, as a first step in understanding the social and economic history of Archaic and Classical Greek Sicily. It will be necessary to take a particular view of the evidence and to emphasize particular details to the detriment of others. A set of specific questions will guide the discussion and help us achieve these aims.

When did the demarcation of different types of space (urban, rural, private, public) and their associated identities occur? How large were the urban centers, so that we can estimate the size and nature of the living community? When did planned towns, city walls, and distinctive urban architecture (private, public, and religious) emerge? How much resource (labor and

---

1. On this point, see in general Hansen 2003, 267, 281–82; 2006a, 101–05, 137–38; for Sicily in particular, see Fischer-Hansen 1996, 350–51; Fischer-Hansen, Nielsen, and Ampolo 2004a, 174–75. The deficiencies of Horden and Purcell's (2000) approach, as noted by their reviewers, in not combining systematically the political, territorial, and urban, are acknowledged and rectified by them (Horden and Purcell 2005, 370; cf. Purcell 2005c). The need for such a combination has only been exceptionally acknowledged for Sicily (Antonini 1996; Carter 1996, 364; Manganaro 1996d, 54). On the importance of politics to the development of Greek cities, see now Morris 2006b.

2. Compare the three very recent big books on Sicilian Greek urbanism and sanctuaries alone: Minà 2005; Mertens 2006; Veronese 2006.

materials) was invested in urban architecture, and what are the social and economic implications of this? How large were the territories of each of the *poleis*, and what sort of resource base did each territory offer? How was this territory organized in terms of settlements? Where did production and exchange take place? In asking these questions, the aim is to trace the development of the social and economic identity of each city through its material remains.

One of the notable features of Sicilian Greek history is the volatility of both settlement pattern and state organization. To reveal and study this to best effect, the following discussion will be arranged diachronically and subdivided into four chronological phases, each representing a major episode in Sicilian Greek state formation: 1) from the *poleis'* foundation between the eighth and sixth centuries BC to the beginning of their incorporation into a fewer larger states beginning in about 500 BC; 2) the generation (ca. 500–465 BC) covering this first attempt at political centralization; 3) the two generations that followed (ca. 465–405 BC),which saw the collapse and return of political centralization at the hands especially of Syracuse and Carthage; and 4) the remainder of the Classical period (ca. 405 to 320 BC), which again witnessed a reinvigorated Syracuse wrestling against Carthage and various other smaller states for, respectively, control and independence. These four chronological phases witness an alternation between the two basic state types: city-states and territorial states. These can be defined as follows, according to the late Bruce Trigger: "City-states were relatively small polities, each consisting of an urban core surrounded by farmland containing smaller units of settlement. In territorial states a ruler governed a larger region through a multilevelled hierarchy of provincial and local administrators in a corresponding hierarchy of administrative centres."[3] Such a basic distinction, which underlines the importance of combining political, territorial, and urban trajectories into a single treatment, has not been previously emphasized in discussions of Greek Sicily.[4] This is unfortunate, because different social and economic features can be associated with each of these two state types.

---

3. Trigger 2003, 92. These definitions are not at variance with current thinking about ancient Greek states (Hansen 2006a, 40, 55). Trigger (2003, 93) has also added that "the long persistence of both types in different regions of the world suggests that territorial states and city-states are stable alternatives rather than sequential stages in the development of more complex societies."

4. The need for more state formation theory has also been noted recently for the study of the Athenian Empire (Ma 2009, 226).

A Diachronic Outline

Sicilian Greek settlement, territory, and politics were all multidimensional historical phenomena. However, the evidence currently available to document them in their every dimension is far from robust.[5]

Archaeology, our best source, is inherently affected by its preservation and research agendas. Some of Greek Sicily's most successful cities have been continuously inhabited since antiquity, thus inhibiting easy access to their remains.[6] This problem is exacerbated by modes of retrieval, particularly the traditional focus of Greek archaeology in Sicily on art history and monuments. This has beneficial effects. Different types of private and public contexts and architecture have been investigated, and in some cases detailed measurements of houses, temples, and city walls are available to be converted into valuable quantifiable data for social and economic history. The archaeological evidence, however, is not yet balanced; it is noticeably absent or weak for such other important matters as urban sanitation and disease[7] and patterns of exploitation in the countryside.

While archaeology can provide evidence of the political choices and outcomes of Greek Sicily's actors, the literary sources supply most of the intricate details of these.[8] The literary sources, as we have already seen, document limited historical episodes in a discontinuous manner and are usually not contemporary with the episodes they claim to represent. This weakness can be partly corrected by recourse to archaeological evidence, which can also allow us to address the reliability of the literary sources, including their sometimes uncritical combination with archaeology.

Despite the evidence's current shortcomings, it will still be worthwhile to consider what can be said of Greek Sicily's political, territorial, and urban trajectories as a first step in understanding its Archaic and Classical societies and economies.

---

5. I have addressed elsewhere some of these matters, especially those connected with rural archaeology (De Angelis 2000a, 113–16). See also subsequently the various contributions in Stazio and Ceccoli (1999), Stazio (2001), and Hansen and Nielsen (2004, esp. 7 for a succinct summary), all of which range across the entire Greek Mediterranean and have many of the same points to make.

6. For Syracuse, note recently Evans 2009, 27.

7. Urban sanitation and disease are important themes in Farris' (2004, 48, 60, 114, 156) social and economic history of Japan to AD 1600.

8. Literary and epigraphic sources can sometimes talk about the kinds of urban and rural matters discussed here—the most prominent examples being Diodorus Siculus (Bejor 1991) and the documentary record for Syracuse (full details in *BTCGI* 19).

1. From Foundation to Political Centralization

Physical Settings. Sicily is best understood as a continent in miniature.[9] It has greater geographical, and hence cultural, variety than neighboring Malta, which is mostly flat and waterless, or the Aeolian Islands, which are mostly mountainous and volcanic. Such one-dimensionality does not apply to Sicily, which since prehistory has consisted of three major subregions (Map 2).[10]

The first subregion spans the north coast and consists of three not very continuous mountain ranges (Peloritani; Nebrodi or Caronie; Madonie) that rise to a maximum height of just under 2,000 meters. This subregion, a continuation of the Apennines on the Italian mainland and part of the Tyrrhenian Sea basin, has been the best forested and watered part of the island since antiquity. It is also the subregion that receives the most rainfall, with annual amounts in the range of 1,000 millimeters common.[11] In many places, the mountains meet the shore, but there are some exceptions where coastal plains are significant enough to attract human settlement, the most notable cases being Milazzo (ancient Mylai), Imera (ancient Himera), and Palermo (ancient Panormos). The Peloritani, the easternmost of the three mountain ranges, also contain mineral resources (copper, iron, and tin) that were exploited in our periods (see Chapter 4).

To the south of these mountains is Sicily's second major subregion, which encompasses the central and southwestern portions of the island between Marsala and the Salso (ancient Himeras) river. This subregion is made up mostly of undulating hills and valleys that are generally under 1,000 meters above sea level and that slope from the interior toward the coast. The topography thus faces North Africa and contributes to this subregion receiving the least amount of rainfall. Annual averages of 500 millimeters are the norm in coastal areas.[12] The region is home to extensive sulfur resources which may have been exploited in antiquity. The sea between this subregion and Africa is not very deep. In some stretches along the coast, the sea is not rough and encourages the stagnation of water, facilitating the exploitation of sea salt.[13]

---

9. Freeman 1891–94, 1:2; Braudel 1972, 148; Finley 1979, xi; Epstein 1992, 26; Leighton 1999, 5; Castellana 2002, 2.

10. Leighton 1999, 11–50. On Sicilian geography since prehistory, see Philippson 1934; Milone 1960; Walker 1967, 215–22; King 1973, 21–37; Bethemont and Pelletier 1983, 184–95; Touring Club Italiano 1989, 20–41; Epstein 1992, 25–74. On ancient toponymy, see Manni 1981.

11. De Angelis 2000a, 121.

12. De Angelis 2000a, 121.

13. Braudel 2001, 24; Epstein 1992, 226.

Sicily's third subregion is formed by the southeastern corner of the island. In the northeastern corner of this subregion stands Mt. Etna, the still active volcano that rises to a height of some 3,300 meters and has had regular additions to its shape and size since prehistory. To the south of Mt. Etna is the Plain of Catania, which, at about 430 square kilometers in size, is the largest in all of Sicily. It is an alluvial plain of volcanic and limestone soils watered by the Simeto (ancient Symaithos) and its affluents, which rise in the western foothills of Mt. Etna. The rest of this subregion consists of the Mt. Iblei, comprised mostly of limestone tablelands eroded by the many watercourses that crisscross its landscape. The highest point is Mt. Lauro at just under 1,000 meters above sea level, from which these tablelands issue. In terms of rainfall and resources, this subregion is, on account of its position, a cross between the other two subregions.

Foundations. *Poleis* were founded by Greeks in Sicily during the Archaic period in all three subregions. Greeks seem first to have become familiar with the eastern coastal side of the second and third subregions. It was only subsequently through their "subcolonization" that other parts of these two subregions and the third subregion were settled. It is notable that these "subcolonies" existed in quite different geographical contexts. Nevertheless, most of the Greek foundations, seven of out of ten,[14] were established in the southern and southeastern subregions (Maps 2 and 4). By contrast, Sicily's Phoenician settlements were not merely on different sorts of sites but in the northern subregion, while native settlements were found in all three subregions but usually in their interior parts, as seen in Chapter 1. A recent discussion of Thucydides' Sicilian archaeology distinguished between private and state initiative behind the Greek foundations, although no such distinction is discernible in choosing where to locate a settlement or in how it developed materially in the generations that followed.[15]

Thucydides tells that Zankle (today Messina) was founded by pirates led by Perieres from Cumae in southern Italy, reinforced by other settlers led by Krataimenes from Chalcis itself in the Euboean homeland, details which

---

14. We know that more than ten *poleis* were founded in this period, but the distinction needs to be made between primary and secondary-order sites. For the known failed primary *poleis* in Sicily by Pentathlos and Dorieus, see Braccesi and Millino (2000, 40–42, 44–47). But there were certainly others, and sometimes archaeology can suggest possibilities like Borgo Bonsignore near Herakleia Minoa (cf. De Angelis 2003a, 197, n. 254), though in such cases it is more difficult to label them either primary or secondary-order sites.

15. Morakis 2011.

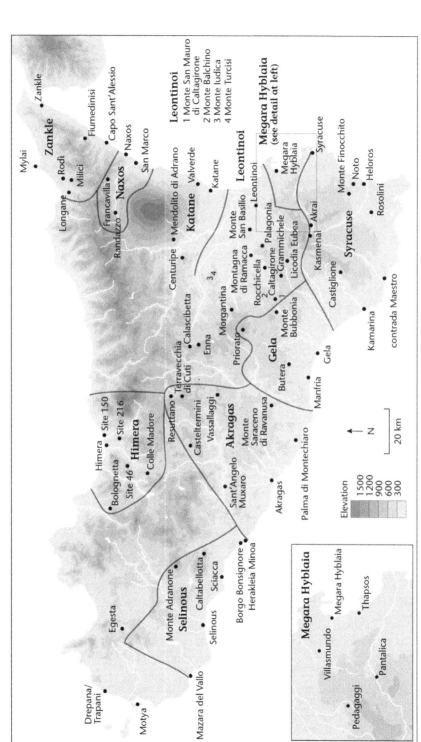

MAP 4 Hypothetical Extent of Archaic Greek Territories in Sicily.

© Author

modern scholars take at face value to mean settlement in two stages.[16] Such a story, however, might simply have been generated by a community that found itself split, as Zankle later did in the Classical and Hellenistic periods. Dates in ancient literature and pottery retrieved from the earliest archaeological layers can be combined to suggest that settlement initially occurred in the third quarter of the eighth century.[17] A hiatus between the BA occupation of the area and the later Greek settlement has been postulated, and no preceding settlement appears to have conditioned Zankle's development.[18] The Greek city's logic and design did take into account, however, preexisting natural features, particularly the steep terrain and numerous watercourses, the result of nearby mountains and a more receded coastline in antiquity.[19] Nature provided, moreover, excellent possibilities for human settlement, especially in terms of abundant water supplies and the sickle-like peninsula that acted as an ideal protected harbor, features taken advantage of from early on.[20]

At Naxos, to the south, Thucydides talks of another Euboean settlement led by the oikist Theokles.[21] The site selected was a low rocky headland today known as Capo Schisò, located to the north of a river. A small bay provided sufficient shelter for ships. Thucydides notes that in his day, all sacred ambassadors leaving Sicily for Delphi sacrificed on the altar of Apollo Archegetes, established on the very spot at which the founding settlers first touched down.[22] This underlines the maritime connectivity of Naxos, located on the route from

16. Thuc. 6.4.5–6. For a full discussion of all the ancient sources, including the suggestion of a foundation in two stages, see Braccesi and Millino 2000, 19–21; Veronese 2006, 136–39. Antonelli (1996, 322) has suggested that, contrary to the ancient tradition, Pithekoussai may have been the initiator of Zankle's foundation.

17. So De Angelis 2003a, 13.

18. Bacci 1999a, 51; Gras 2002b, 20. As is well known (Thuc. 6.4.5), the name Zankle is of native inspiration. Most scholars therefore believe that an EIA native settlement existed here first. There is no evidence for any such settlement; the silence could be due to the patchy archaeological record, but it is equally possible, following the argument made in the previous chapter, that the native toponym refers to a named geographic feature that was not home to a permanent settlement.

19. Bonfiglio 1999.

20. On the evidence of Archaic wells, see Gras 2002b, 22. For occupation of the extreme tip of the peninusla in Archaic times, which may have included a cult (as in later times), see Bacci 1999a, 52; Veronese 2006, 149.

21. Thuc. 6.3.1; Ephoros, FGrH 70 F137. Recent full discussions of all the relevant ancient sources can be found in Braccesi and Millino (2000, 15–18) and Veronese (2006, 151–54). Scholars have rightly rejected Ephoros' high dating and claim of the oikist being of Athenian origin.

22. Thuc. 6.3.1.

Greece, through southern Italy, to Sicily.[23] The literary and archaeological evidence provides chronological markers that Naxos was established in the third quarter of the eighth century BC, with 735 BC becoming the canonical foundation date and thus making Naxos by tradition Sicily's first ever *polis*.[24] Some ancient sources also speak of Ionians, Dorians, and Naxians in the foundation, plausibly suggesting to modern scholars that a contingent from Naxos' namesake in the Cyclades took part.

The Naxian oikist Theokles is also said to have founded Leontinoi a few years later in about 729 BC.[25] The earliest archaeological evidence is compatible with this date, as it is with the ancient claim that natives occupied the site at the time of settlement.[26] Less certain, however, is the ancient claim that these natives were expelled, since coexistence and integration are indicated in various ways. One of them concerns the site's location and logic: it was situated on a hilltop along the San Leonardo river in Sicily's interior and linked to the sea by an outlet at the river's mouth (Figure 7). This system continued to be used in this way until well into the last century, but its origins are to be placed in prehistory before Greek settlement.[27]

The oikist Euarkhos is said to have established Katane soon after Leontinoi, though the ancient sources preserve few other details concerning its foundation.[28] Archaeology has not been able to provide more details to fill out the limited literary evidence, because early settlement evidence has been buried by lava flows from Etna and numerous layers of later occupation on a site with favorable natural conditions for human settlement and communication.

In southeastern Sicily, settlement resulted in the establishment of two *poleis*, Syracuse and Megara Hyblaia (Figure 8). The foundation of Syracuse is usually believed to have come first, in 734 BC.[29] Arkhias of Corinth led a group of settlers who, Thucydides claims, expelled the preexisting native

---

23. Gras 2005, 161.

24. See De Angelis 2003a, 11–12.

25. Thuc. 6.3.3, to be read in conjunction with Braccesi and Millino (2000, 18–19) and Veronese (2006, 151–54).

26. De Angelis 2003a, 12; Frasca 2009, 25–35, 41–44.

27. Caffi 2004.

28. Thuc. 6.3.3. For full discussions of Katane's foundation, see Braccesi and Millino (2000, 18–19) and Veronese (2006, 175–79).

29. Thuc. 6.3.2, which needs to be read with modern accounts, like those of Braccesi and Millino (2000, 24–28) and Veronese (2006, 279–83), to arrive at this date and in general to disentangle fact from fiction in the various literary traditions surrounding Syracuse's foundation.

FIGURE 7 View of Plain between Leontinoi and Megara Hyblaia.
© Author

FIGURE 8 View of Coastal Plain between Megara Hyblaia and Syracuse.
© Author

population. But the picture seems more complicated than that, for at later Syracuse there is evidence for native elements residing among the population and for Euboean-sounding toponyms that have raised reasonable suspicions that Euboeans may have preceded and/or coexisted with the early Corinthian settlers on this very attractive site.[30]

There is both literary and archaeological evidence that success did not come easily to Megara Hyblaia, located north of Syracuse. The ancient sources appear to be reliable in talking about two failed attempts by the Megarian settlers under Lamis to settle down at Leontinoi and Thapsos before doing so successfully through the invitation of the native leader Hyblon.[31] Megara Hyblaia was established on a site previously unoccupied at the time of settlement. Tréziny has recently argued that the later town plan's different orientations reflect this very situation, suggesting that the Insenatura, an area rich in water and good for landings (given its relative flatness and extent), represents the middle of the plan (it divides the settlement into two distinct areas). Through here and from here ran roughly north-south and east-west prehistoric routes that were incorporated into the town plan and given gates in the stone fortification built later, in the last quarter of the sixth century BC.[32]

In the seventh century, Greeks founded more new *poleis* on Sicily's north and south coasts and in new parts of the southeastern and northern subregions, as well in the third southwestern subregion, now settled for the first time.

The earliest of these seventh-century foundations was Gela. Thucydides cites Rhodians and Cretans led, respectively, by Antiphemos and Entimos as responsible for its foundation.[33] A foundation date of 688 BC and the possibility of a contingent of settlers before then can be inferred from statements made by Thucydides; both inferences seem to receive support from archaeological evidence.[34] Gela was established at the head of large and well-watered plain that gave easy access to the interior (Figure 9).

Next in time came Himera on Sicily's northern coast established in the second pocket of good arable land of this geographical subregion (Figure 10). Thucydides speaks of another mixed community, jointly founded by settlers

---

30. For the Euboean-Corinthian connection, see Braccesi and Millino (2000, 25); Cordano (2006, 466–67); Veronese (2006, 279–80). See further Chapter 3 below for these matters.

31. Thuc. 6.4.1; Polyaen. 5.5.1, discussed in full most recently by De Angelis 2003a, 13–14.

32. Tréziny 2002, 267–71.

33. For recent discussions of the literary sources for Gela's foundation, see Braccesi and Millino (2000, 36–39) and Veronese (2006, 257–59).

34. Thuc. 6.4.3, to be read together with the discussion cited in the previous note.

FIGURE 9 View of the Plain of Gela Planted with Grain.
© Author

FIGURE 10 View of Coastal Topography around Himera.
© Author

from Zankle and exiles from Syracuse.[35] Archaeology has made clear that both parts of Himera, the coastal and hilltop plateaus, were occupied in at least the last quarter of the seventh century BC, thus providing support for the foundation date given by Diodorus Siculus. The mixed nature of the community is confirmed by later inscriptions, compatible with the mixed nature of the later community, giving rise to the claims about a mixed origin.

Selinous' foundation in southwest Sicily occurred at about the same time. According to the ancient tradition, Megara Hyblaia requested an oikist from the homeland, whereupon a certain Pammilos and some settlers were sent out to join their Sicilian relatives.[36] There are two foundation dates in the ancient tradition: Diodorus Siculus places it at 651 BC and Thucydides at 628 BC.[37] Both dates can be supported by archaeological evidence, and they may betoken some kind of two-stage settlement process that we have encountered in other Sicilian Greek foundations, or at least some underlying motivation for this divergence.[38] Selinous was situated between two rivers that backed onto a large and relatively flat coastal and fertile plain (Figure 11).

Akragas was the last Archaic Sicilian *polis* to be founded, in about 580 BC. Here, according to the ancient tradition, settlers from Gela, led by Aristonous and Pystilos, are credited with its establishment.[39] The city, which may have at first been restricted to a coastal enclave, developed on a north-south inclined hilltop overlooking the fertile coastal plain (Figure 12).[40]

Regardless of when these *poleis* were established in Sicily, they adhere to the same basic patterns of urban and rural development. The main elements of these patterns can be grouped together for discussion.[41]

---

35. Thuc. 6.5.1 for the settlers' origins and Diod. Sic. 13.62.4 for the chronology. Recent discussions of the literary and archaeological data can be found in Braccesi and Millino (2000, 21) and Veronese (2006, 105–09).

36. Thuc. 6.4.2. For modern discussions of this and other ancient sources, see Braccesi and Millino (2000, 34–36) and Veronese (2006, 497–99).

37. Thuc. 6.4.2; Diod. Sic. 13.59.4.

38. For this whole matter at Selinous, see most recently De Angelis 2003a, 124.

39. Thuc. 6.4.4. For Akragas' foundation, see most recently Adornato (2011, 1–46), who assigns the Rhodian strand of the ancient tradition to Hellenistic fabrication and finds no material support for a Rhodian element at early Akragas as a whole.

40. De Miro 1992, 152; Di Vita 1996, 294; Mertens 2006, 195.

41. As in Crielaard 2009.

FIGURE 11 View of Plain behind Selinous.
© Author

FIGURE 12 View of Salso River Valley Planted with Grain to East of Akragas.
© Author

Town Planning. Some scholars have postulated the existence of temporary camps before the settlers laid out their earliest town plans. The terminology is tendentious. Prolonged residence under canvas is very unlikely. Insubstantial early buildings are almost certain, even if the evidence is either indirect or hypothesized.[42] Within the first and second generations, any such temporary buildings gave way to town planning, according to the archaeological evidence.

The sites best known in this regard include Megara Hyblaia, Naxos, Syracuse, Selinous, Himera, and Akragas (Maps 5–10), whereas Zankle, Katane, and Gela (Map 11) are less known on account of their successive occupation layers. Nevertheless, aside from Katane, all these sites reveal orthogonal planning laid out with an eye to the natural contours of the landscapes in which they were situated.[43] The only exception to this rule is Leontinoi, which was built over several hills and valleys and probably never had an orthogonal town plan.[44] In the case of Syracuse, the plan was not technically orthogonal, since it took account mainly of Ortygia's morphology, which in turn may well have followed pre-contact routes.[45] Otherwise, for the remaining sites, true orthogonal plans are attested which divided the landscape into blocks separated by streets (often paved) ranging anywhere between about 2.5 and 6.5 meters, depending on their purpose in the town plan, with the widest streets serving as major thoroughfares. Megara Hyblaia, Selinous, and Himera have been investigated well enough to reveal details of the sizes of their blocks. At Megara Hyblaia, the blocks measured about 25 meters wide by anywhere from 107 to 116 meters long. They were divided longitudinally into two by a median line. At Selinous, all blocks were 32.8 meters wide (or 100 Doric feet) and subdivided longitudinally, but their lengths and shapes varied considerably depending on their location in the plan.[46] Himera's blocks were 41 meters wide and subdivided longitudinally and latitudinally.

All the town plans covered surface areas that fall within a fairly consistent range (Table 1). Two topographic clues help to determine the sizes of cities. First, the placement of cemeteries is revealing, for in the eighth century the Western Greeks began to separate the world of the living from the world of the dead in a conscious way.[47] Western Greek cities had at least two cemeteries,

---

42. For Megara Hyblaia and Selinous, see the discussion in De Angelis 2003a, 17, 128; Gras, Tréziny, and Broise 2004, 465, 523–24.

43. Bacci 1999a, 52–53; Gras 2002b, 21–22.

44. Frasca 2009, 65.

45. Tréziny 2002, 278 (for the precontact proposal); Mertens 2006, 74.

46. Mertens 2006, 174, 179.

47. Cf. Frederiksen 2011, 60, 76, 89; Bintliff 2012, 269.

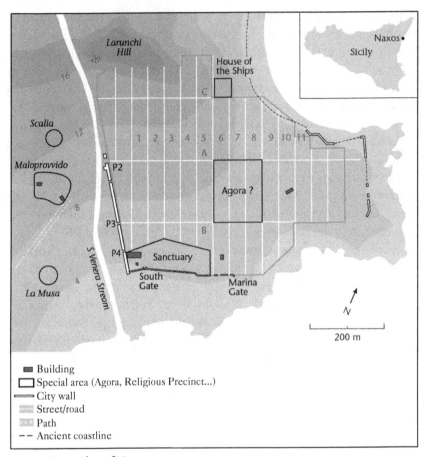

MAP 5 Town Plan of Naxos.
© Author

which were generally spatially segregated between and within them, a matter that can be connected with social choices made by the inhabitants.[48] Second, a city wall was added later (generally between three and six generations from foundation) to demarcate the world of the living from the dead.[49] City walls, discussed separately below, must have been included in planning from earliest

---

48. Zankle: Gras 2002b, 21. Katane: Branciforti and Amari 2005, 52–54. Leontinoi: Frasca 2009, 44–45. Syracuse: Fischer-Hansen, Nielsen, and Ampolo 2004a, 230. Megara Hyblaia: Gras, Tréziny, and Broise 2004; Mertens 2006, 64. Cf. also De Angelis 2003a, 20, 33–34. Gela: Panvini 1996, 32, 69–72. Himera: Fabbri, Schettino, and Vassallo 2006. Selinous: Jackman 2005, 63. Akragas: De Waele 1971; De Miro 1988b, 236–40; Cuomo di Caprio 1992, 71. The possible significance of this spatial segregation will be considered in the next chapter.

49. Frederiksen 2011, 105.

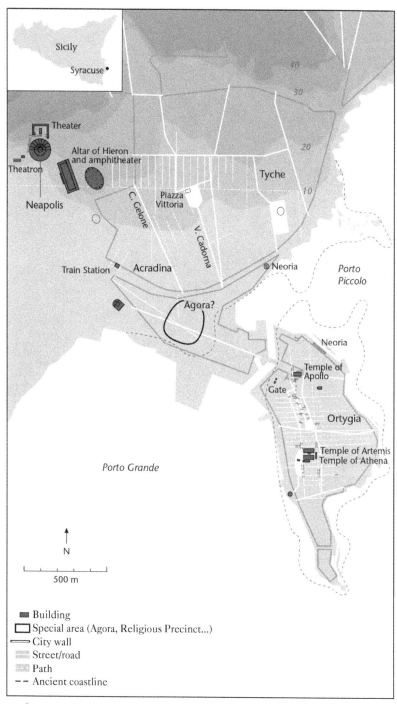

MAP 6 Town Plan of Syracuse.

© Author

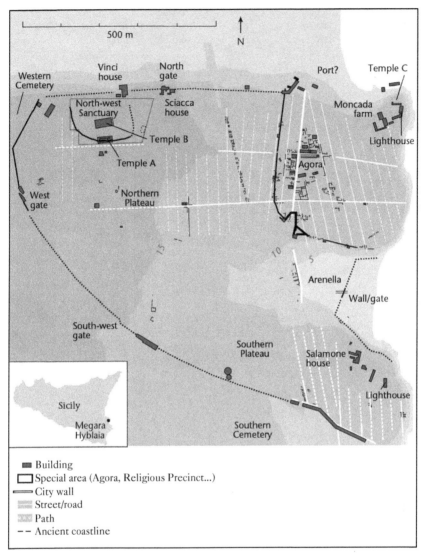

MAP 7 Town Plan of Megara Hyblaia.
© Author

times as well. Sufficient details are known from one or both of these clues for
five of the ten cities to permit quite precise indications of their sizes (Naxos,
Leontinoi, Megara Hyblaia, Himera, and Selinous),[50] whereas in the other five
cases details are such as to allow only general indications (Zankle, Katane,

---

50. Naxos: Tréziny 2002, 273; Mertens 2006, 72–73; Veronese 2006, 154–55. Leontinoi: Frasca
2009, 68. Megara Hyblaia: Tréziny 2002, 273; Mertens 2006, 72–73; Veronese 2006, 154–55.
Himera: Vassallo 2005a, 332; 2006, 316. Selinous: Mertens 2006, 83, 173.

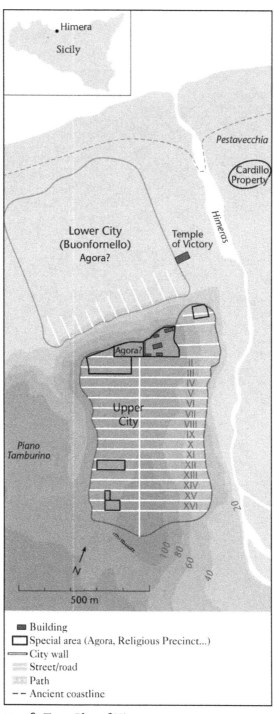

MAP 8 Town Plan of Himera.

© Author

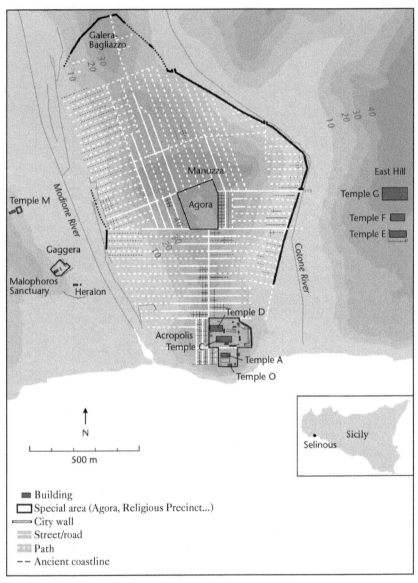

Galera-
Bagliazzo

30
20
10

40
30
20
10

Manuzza

East Hill

Temple G

Temple F

Temple E

Temple M

Modione River

Agora

Gaggera

30
10

Cotone River

Malophoros
Sanctuary

Heraion

Temple D

Acropolis
Temple C

Temple A

Temple O

N

500 m

Sicily

Selinous

■ Building
▢ Special area (Agora, Religious Precinct...)
⇒ City wall
▦ Street/road
▦ Path
– – Ancient coastline

MAP 9 Town Plan of Selinous.
© Author

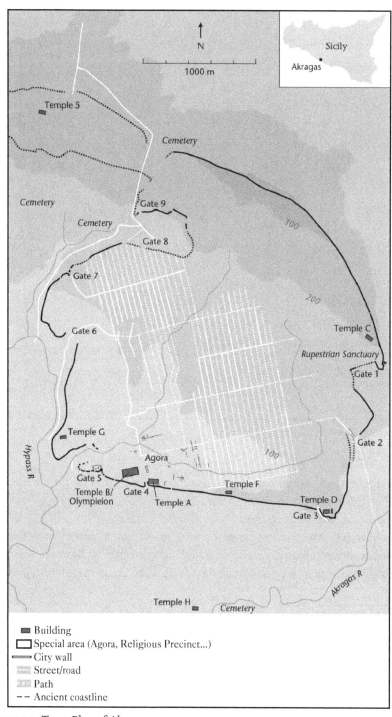

Sicily

Akragas

N

1000 m

Temple 5

Cemetery

Cemetery

Cemetery

Gate 9

Gate 8

Gate 7

Gate 6

300

200

Temple C

Rupestrian Sanctuary

Gate 1

Temple G

100

Gate 2

Hypass R.

Agora

Gate 5

Temple B/
Olympieion

Gate 4

Temple A

Temple F

Temple D

Gate 3

Akragas R.

Temple H

Cemetery

■ Building

☐ Special area (Agora, Religious Precinct...)

═ City wall

▤ Street/road

▥ Path

-- Ancient coastline

MAP 10 Town Plan of Akragas.

© Author

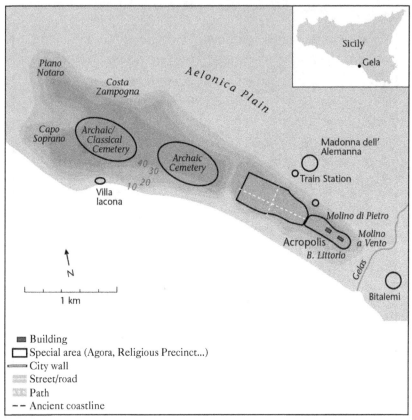

MAP 11 Town Plan of Gela.
© Author

Syracuse, Gela, and Akragas), which are nevertheless still useful for historical reconstruction.[51] In all cases, the cities range in size between 50 and 100
hectares and can thus be classified as agrarian cities.[52]

In at least two cases, two phases of urban growth can be documented, from a
smaller, almost village-like existence into an agrarian city.[53] At Naxos, the earliest
settlement remains suggest that the first settlers had an organized town plan in

---

51. Zankle: Fischer-Hansen, Nielsen, and Ampolo 2004a, 235; Veronese 2000, 244.
Katane: Veronese 2000, 244; Fischer-Hansen, Nielsen, and Ampolo 2004a, 206–
07. Syracuse: Di Vita 1996, 270; Fischer-Hansen, Nielsen, and Ampolo 2004a, 228.
Gela: Fischer-Hansen 1996, 328; Muggia 1997, 76; Fischer-Hansen, Nielsen, and Ampolo
2004a, 194; Mertens 2006, 80. Akragas: Di Vita 1996, 296; Veronese 2000, 244; Mertens
2006, 195, 315–17.

52. Morris 2006b, 28–30; 2013, 145.

53. Cf. Bintliff 2012, 269.

the eastern part of the peninsula over a surface area of about 10 hectares (Map 5). In the seventh and sixth centuries, Naxos grew and developed, and the settlement now covered a surface area of about 40 hectares. Selinous also started modestly, being restricted to the landing area near the river mouths (Map 9).[54] A group of seventh-century graves, enclosed by the later sixth-century city wall, may have been the cemetery of this early settlement still in its planning stages.[55] Selinous became a fully planned and regularly laid out city during the first quarter of the sixth century.[56] Similarly, Akragas' first foothold may have been an emporium at Montelusa at the mouth of the Akragas River.[57] The city later developed further inland and continued to use this area for purposes of exchange and burial.

Within these town plans, areas were also set aside from early on for other public and private activities. The agora was a major locus of such activities.[58] The agora of four cities (Syracuse, Megara Hyblaia, Himera, and Selinous) has been identified with an absolute or a high level of certainty.[59] In the case of Syracuse, Megara Hyblaia, and Selinous, it lay at the center of the town plan. At Himera, this was physically impossible because the city was divided between coastal and hilltop locations, so the inhabitants decide to situate the agora in the lower coastal portion. The dimensions of Megara Hyblaia and Selinous' agoras are similar, given their common heritage, and measure around 0.5 hectares (Maps 7, 9).[60] The dimensions of Himera's agora still require precise definition, but it occupied an area of 120–140 meters east-west by 140 meters.[61] For the remaining six cities, the location of the agora can only be hypothesized, again with varying degrees of certainty.[62] In two of these cases (Zankle and Naxos), the

---

54. Cf. Mertens 2006, 84.

55. The graves continued to be respected in later times (Rallo 2002) and indicate, among other things, that urban space had not been fully planned during Selinous' first generation or so (cf. De Angelis 2003a, 140).

56. Mertens 2006, 173–75.

57. De Miro 1992, 152; Di Vita 1996, 294; Mertens 2006, 195.

58. Kenzler 1999.

59. Syracuse: Di Vita 1996, 269–74; Fischer-Hansen 1996, 334–35; Voza 1999, 77–113; Tréziny 2002, 273–78; Mertens 2006, 73–76, 90, 104–12. Megara Hyblaia: Gras, Tréziny, and Broise 2004; Gras 2006–07. Himera: Vassallo 2005b, 63; Mertens 2006, 192, against Allegro 1999, 285. Selinous: Mertens 2006, 173–75.

60. De Angelis 2003a, 20, 36. On this common heritage, see generally Robu 2014.

61. Vassallo 2012.

62. Zankle: Bacci 1999, 51; Gras 2002b, 23. Naxos: Tréziny 2002, 273; Mertens 2006, 72–73; Veronese 2006, 154–55. Leontinoi: Frasca 2009, 58. Gela: Mertens 2006, 79. Akragas: Mertens 2006, 318. No proposal has been advanced for the location of Katane's agora.

agora may have been situated close to the city's port.[63] We might suspect a similar connection for Katane, whereas for Gela, where we know the location of the port, the agora was likelier situated elsewhere (Map 11).[64] Those agoras located in ports may represent instances in which the city had a close exchange relationship with the outside world. At Himera, this function may have been carried out through an emporium for resident foreign traders identified to the east of the Pestavecchia/Rocca d'Antoni cemeteries in the Cardillo property (Map 8).[65] Gela's port may have also contained an emporium for such purposes.[66] Many of the city's public monuments were located in and around the agora. While most monuments, as will be seen immediately below, took material form only in the seventh and sixth centuries, we can be certain that areas were reserved for them beforehand during the town planning process.

Urban areas were also designated for craft production from early on both inside and just outside the city walls. These areas were located in a variety of settings. On the inside of the city wall, they could be found associated with residences and sacred precincts, and outside the city wall with suburban sanctuaries, cemeteries, and on their own.[67] Scholarly discussions of the various possible political, cultural, social, and economic conditions in which craft production could occur has developed significantly in recent years for both ancient Greek and other historical societies and periods.[68] The social and economic data from Archaic Greek Sicily are enough to allow possible scenarios to be sketched out.[69] The spatial locations of work areas on craft production indicate that production occurred usually associated with a particular household in a residential location or in specially designated quarters, either within or just outside the city. Craft production for religious and ritual purposes is often found in specially designated quarters located next to the sanctuary

63. The case is stronger for Zankle: Bacci 1999, 51; Bacci and Coppolino 2002, 26–27; Bacci, D'Amico, and Ravesi 2002, 19, no. 85; Gras 2002b, 23. For Naxos, see Tréziny 2002, 273.

64. It should be recalled that Leontinoi and Akragas were not located on the coast. Both cities had their emporia on the coast.

65. Allegro 1999, 290; Mertens 2006, 192.

66. Panvini 1996, 54–55.

67. Naxos: Pelagatti 1968–69, 351; Cuomo di Caprio 1971–72, 460; 1992, 73. Megara Hyblaia: De Angelis 2003a, 83–85; Gras, Tréziny, and Broise 2004, 170–92, 481–84. Himera: Vassallo 2005b, 39, 60, 110. Selinous: De Angelis 2003a, 184. Akragas: De Waele 1971; De Miro 1988b, 236–40; Cuomo di Caprio 1992, 71.

68. For convenient summaries, see particularly Tosi 1984; Dark 1995, 135–39; Tanner 1999; Blondé and Muller 2000; M.E. Smith 2004, 82–83; Schortman and Urban 2004.

69. Earlier discussions can be found in particularly D'Agostino 1973; Fischer-Hansen 2000.

which it served. In such cases, production was presumably geared towards a specialized, though intermittent, market. While household production for the consumption of its members would have been common, especially for essential crafts like textiles and other everyday items, there is some possible evidence from Sicily (Himera) and elsewhere in Italy that textile production could also occur in conjunction with ceramic- and metal-working and at the level of the household or workshop industry.[70] In general, we must imagine production occurring in the context of household industry, individual workshops, and nucleated workshops, all in operation in Archaic Sicily and producing at a scale that went beyond the needs of a particular household, supplying more widely the needs of the city to which it belonged and markets outside it.

Town plans represent a first attempt on the ground to delineate the community and to structure it and its institutions internally in a way which the community regarded as rational and meaningful.[71] The Sicilian Greeks were presented with a unique opportunity to organize themselves in landscapes that presented few natural and human hindrances. This is a conclusion that emerges from all the Greek cities, but it is clearest in those cases, like Megara Hyblaia, Gela, and Selinous, for which the evidence is most abundant. In founding these cities, the settlers cleared the land, organized the space in a new way, and had free rein to establish their societies and economies as they saw fit.

Houses. While we know little of the contemporary house architecture of the settlers' homelands, enough evidence exists to show that the newcomers either imported their traditions, as attested at Naxos,[72] or could blend them with the native Sicilian practices they encountered, as at Leontinoi.[73] Archaeological evidence clearly shows that plots of land for housing were reserved at the time of laying out the various town plans; the primacy these settler communities put on allocating individual house plots stands out in comparison with urbanism in Greece.[74] In only three, possibly four, cases is the evidence sufficient enough to determine the absolute and relative sizes of these house plots. Absolute sizes can be determined for Megara Hyblaia, the plots coming in two sizes, 120 and 135 square meters, and for Selinous, the other Megarian settlement in Sicily, where they were larger and ranged between 210 and 225

---

70. Gleba 2008, 197–201.

71. Hansen 2006a, 102. Cf. also Gras, Tréziny, and Broise 2004, 301.

72. Lentini 2006.

73. Fitzjohn 2007, 219–23; Frasca 2009, 71.

74. Gras, Tréziny, and Broise 2004, 566–69.

square meters. These differences are not so significantly large as to allow one to speak confidently of social differences on the ground.[75] Unequal plot sizes have been revealed at Himera and possibly Naxos.[76] In both cases, the evidence currently allows only relative differences to be distinguished. The evidence from Himera is fuller and indicates significant differences between the upper and lower cities: some plots appear to be as much as 50 percent larger in the upper city. It has been suggested that the elite lived there and possessed larger plots, while the lower city with its smaller plots was reserved for merchants and small-scale farmers. A rare inscription from Himera that dates to just before 493 BC gives us tantalizing glimpses of the distribution of house plots to exiles from Zankle seeking refuge there.[77] Among other things, this inscription reveals that there was still undivided space at Himera at this time and that differential values were attached to land, and thus it may provide indirect support for the foregoing explanation.

The earliest eighth-century houses were, as far as we can tell, almost entirely built with local materials, usually gathered from the immediate environs of the city (Figure 13). In plan, these houses were overwhelmingly one-room structures of similar size and design, consisting of a stone foundation on which sat a mud-brick superstructure and a roof of ephemeral material.[78] They were all single-storied dwellings. Square and rectangular plans are known, with dimensions ranging between 3.5 and 8 meters.[79] A one-room house would have had a multifunctional purpose, with household activities taking place both inside and outside it.[80] What the evidence permits us to say confidently is that the construction of private dwellings took place on land demarcated for that purpose; property rights and land ownership are thus presupposed by this very act. The evidence clearly shows, moreover, that not all house plots were simultaneously or contiguously occupied. In some cities (Megara Hyblaia and Zankle), houses were distributed with open spaces between them; at other cities (Naxos and Syracuse), the evidence indicates that they could be closely packed together. These differences in density must have

---

75. Cf. De Angelis 2003a, 50–51; Gras, Tréziny, and Broise 2004, 533–37.

76. Vassallo 2005b; Lentini 2010.

77. Brugnone 1997; Allegro 1999, 292–93; Manganaro 2000. Cf. Lombardo, Aversa, and Frisone 2001, 79–80, 120–21. Fischer-Hansen, Nielsen, and Ampolo (2004a, 200) wrongly attribute this to the period of Theron after 476 BC (for this period, see below).

78. For a recent and extensive discussion of development of Sicilian Greek Archaic houses, see Gras, Tréziny, and Broise 2004, 459–60, 465–66; Mertens 2006, 64–90, 179–214.

79. Lentini 2010.

80. Lang 2002, 16–17.

FIGURE 13 View of Eighth-century House at Megara Hyblaia, with Second Room Added in Seventh-century Renovation.
© Author

represented variant social configurations and dynamics on the ground, involving extensive versus intensive forms of urbanization.[81]

In the seventh and sixth centuries, houses tended to become larger through the addition of other rooms.[82] Renovations could be made to preexisting houses (Figure 13) or new multiroomed houses could be built from scratch; room dimensions fall within the range established in the eighth century. Local building materials appear still to predominate, although the potential for self-expression was now given a mechanism. Some seventh- and sixth-century houses could still stand out above others because of their size, design, and ornamentation. A good example of the new architectural diversification is the so-called *pastas* house, whose front consisted of a courtyard that gave access to the rooms behind it. The rooms and their associated activities buffered the inhabitants, allowing house space to be conceived now with more flexibility. Examples are known from Megara Hyblaia, Naxos, and Selinous.[83]

---

81. For a recent discussion of Zankle and other Sicilian Greek cities, see Ingoglia 2003, 92–93.

82. Zankle: Tigano 1999a, 105–08; Ingoglia 2003, 84–85; Lentini, Vanaria, and Martinelli 2008–09, 376–82. Katane: Frasca 2000a. Himera: Allegro 1999, 287; 2008a; 2008b. At Gela, buildings on the acropolis usually identified as cult structures (Fischer-Hansen 1996, 325–27) may have in fact been houses (Mertens 2006, 79).

83. Naxos: Mertens 2006, 73. Megara Hyblaia: De Angelis 2003a, 55. Selinous: De Angelis 2003a, 128–29, 136–37.

In comparison with before, fewer household activities would have occurred outside the house, and the separation of life into more than a single room allowed for the emergence of functional, social, and economic development.[84] While no house can be associated with certainty with any tyrant or ruler known from the literary sources,[85] elites were certainly active behind the scenes with these grander houses (see next chapter for discussion).

Archaic houses help to document personal and household identities and can tell us a great deal about such socially and economically important things as property rights, ownership, wealth, and status.

Places of Worship. Private and public interests were blurred and blended in Archaic religion.[86] With the development of the *polis*, private cults controlled by families and clans were still in existence that could finance sanctuaries from their own resources.[87] In Sicily, the best-known private cult is that established in the area of the sanctuary of Zeus Meilikhios at Selinous.[88] Another possible instance comes from Megara Hyblaia, where in a single neighborhood two seemingly elite houses were located near a small sanctuary.[89] The state (though rudimentary in early periods) could also contribute to the overlapping of public and private spheres through the establishment of cults for oikists. It remains debated whether these cults were established following the death of the oikist or at the end of the Archaic period as a political tool of the Sicilian tyrants.[90] Possible cult places for oikists at Megara Hyblaia and Selinous have been identified, although one should avoid the circular reasoning involved in regarding them as confirmation of the written sources.[91]

This issue underlines the indivisibility of private and public interests in religion and the difficulty of distinguishing between them solely on the basis of archaeology, without corroborating literary and epigraphic evidence. This

---

84. Lang 2002, 17–18.

85. The identification of the controversial *phrourion* (or fortified citadel) on Selinous' acropolis as an elite residence has recently been followed (Mertens 2006, 184).

86. Lang 2002, 15; Mitchell 2013, 120–21.

87. Hansen 2006a, 118.

88. Robu 2009; Grotta 2010. See also discussion in Chapter 3 below.

89. De Angelis 2003a, 31, 65.

90. For discussion, see De Angelis and Garstad 2006, 219–20.

91. See De Angelis 2003a, 25–29; Mertens 2006, 63–71, 179–83.

private/public dynamic made for fertile ground for the expression of personal and collective identity and prestige through religious structures, which not coincidentally were invariably situated at prominent locations in the town plan. This dynamic seems to have also extended into the domestic sphere, which could provide a logical explanation as to why some houses from Gela have sometimes been mistaken for religious structures (see next chapter for discussion).

Places were set aside for worship from the city's very beginning. This is indicated by ritual deposits, such as that recently discovered at Zankle,[92] and the occasional religious structure, most notably the simple eighth-century temple with altar and possibly *in antis* columns discovered in Syracuse's Piazza Duomo.[93] Religious structures became much more common in Sicily only from the mid-seventh century. These structures were mainly constructed with local materials, as evidenced by numerous quarries found in the cities' environs (and sometimes further afield).[94] The structures were, moreover, modest and uncolonnaded, and their internal space was further subdivided into two or more rooms for cultic purposes (Figure 14).[95]

In the sixth century, some of these structures and other newly constructed ones could achieve monumental dimensions and features, for which skilled labor from other parts of Sicily and beyond was often called upon. This trend toward monumentality is most evident in and around the mid-sixth century.

The phenomenon is especially well represented at Selinous, where the temples are sufficiently preserved to allow for attempts to quantify the amount of stone and man-hours invested in them (Map 9).[96] The seven peripteral temples were constructed in a period of at most ninety years (550–460 BC).[97] Temple C led Selinous' monumentalization in 550 BC. About 5,700 cubic meters of stone, or some 12,800 tons, were used in its construction at a cost

---

92. Bacci, Tigano, Ravesi, and Zavettieri 2010–11, 52–66.

93. Voza 1999, 79.

94. Those of Selinous are best known (De Angelis 2003a, 183–84). For Megara Hyblaia, see De Angelis 2003a, 73–77.

95. Mertens 2006, 64–250; Bacci, Tigano, Ravesi, and Zavettieri 2010–11, 49–52.

96. For full discussion, see De Angelis 2003a, 163–69, where the assumptions, limitations, and methodology behind this exercise are outlined.

97. The chronology of these individual temples is still rather coarse, and they may in fact have been constructed over shorter spans of time, especially in the case of temples A and O. See De Angelis 2003a, 135–39; Mertens 2006, 114–21, 186–89; Veronese 2006, 511–23.

FIGURE 14 View of Sanctuary of Athena at Himera.
© Author

of between 136 and 181 talents. Temple D was started next, in about 540 BC. It was slightly smaller than its predecessor, using about 1,000 less cubic meters of stone and costing between 112 and 149 talents. Temple G was the largest religious structure ever undertaken at Selinous. Work on it began around 525 BC and was broken off around 470 BC (for reasons discussed in the next section). Some 23,700 cubic meters (or about 53,300 tons) of stone were used in its construction and cost somewhere between 567 to 756 talents. Temple F was built next on a scale slightly smaller still. Nevertheless it used some 4,100 cubic meters of stone (or 9,200 tons) at a cost of roughly 98–130 talents. Temples A, O, and E3 were built in the generation spanning 490–460 BC. Of these, Temple E3 was the largest and costliest at 185 to 246 talents (Figure 15). Temples A and O were practically twins: each employed just over 2,100 cubic meters of stone (or about 4,800 tons) and cost between 51 and 68 talents. Altogether Selinous' seven peripteral temples embody just over 50,000 cubic meters (or 113,000 tons) of extracted, moved, and finished stone, which cost between at least 1,200 and 1,600 talents. All these seven temples imply a minimum of 7.3 million man-hours invested in them.

As will be seen in the next section, we know little about salaries and costs of living in the early fifth century, let alone in the late sixth century, in order to put these costs into comparative perspective. Selinous' seven monumental temples cost about three to four times more than the finished Parthenon in

FIGURE 15 View of Temple E3 at Selinous.
© Author

Classical Athens.[98] To take another tack, if we convert the cost in talents (1,200 to 1,600) of Selinous' temples to drachmas, we arrive at totals of 7,200,000 to 9,600,000 drachmas. As assumed below, a hired mercenary infantryman and cavalryman required about 1 drachma per day to maintain. Put another way, Selinous' temples represent a comparable investment of 7,200,000 to 9,600,000 infantry and cavalrymen for a single day. Such hypothetical quantification should make clear that Selinous' temples embody impressive statements about the wealth and aspirations of the city and its people in a way that amazes us still today and make revealing statements about Sicilian Greek social and economic history.[99]

In the countryside, similar factors were at work with places of worship. If these sanctuaries were accompanied by structures, they were always more modest in size and composition when compared with their urban counterparts. The rural environs immediately around cities were regularly implanted

98. Stanier 1953.

99. Polyaenus (5.1.1) speaks of Phalaris establishing his tyranny at Akragas in the 570s BC during the building of the temple of Zeus Polieus on the acropolis. Attempts to locate this structure have proven unsuccessful over the years (Mertens 2006, 197, while Adornato 2011, 47–67, 80 argues that this may be futile because the passage is anachronistic). In any case, the manuscript tradition for this passage records that the temple cost anywhere from 6 to 200 talents. All of this makes this passage unreliable and unusable for the costs of temple building at Archaic Akragas (Tréziny 2001, 376–77).

with places of worship.[100] These were normally associated with agricultural divinities like Demeter and Persephone, whose religious profile suited well the transition between life in the civilized city and the cultivated world beyond it. Rural sanctuaries could also have demarcated the boundaries between the territories of different states.[101]

Public Buildings and City Walls. Public buildings are very poorly represented compared to religious buildings. This has probably more to do with their nonexistence rather than lack of recognition.[102] Public buildings have been identified at Megara Hyblaia and Selinous. From Megara Hyblaia, two stoas and a possible council hall appeared in the agora in the second half of the seventh century, and in the sixth century a *prytaneion* was constructed there too. At Selinous, stoas lining the agora are also known, as well as, on its eastern end, a series of shops and a *hestiatorion* (dining room).[103] The stoas at Megara Hyblaia may have served commercial functions from the mid-seventh century.[104] Limited possibilities for excavation at other Sicilian sites may be partly responsible for this limited picture of public buildings, but it cannot be the whole explanation, because some sites (like Himera and Naxos) have conditions more conducive to excavation. Therefore, because of this gap in the evidence, we are left to speculate on both the location and extent of public activities. The agora would of course have been the likeliest meeting place for political and legal proceedings of both a private and public nature, with any surrounding stoas providing shelter from inclement weather.

City walls are better known, and the most detailed cases are discussed here.[105] While there can be no doubt that space was reserved in the earliest town planning for these city walls, it is only in the seventh and especially sixth centuries that they were physically built. The evolution of city walls in these centuries is documented best by Megara Hyblaia and Leontinoi. At first they consisted of a more ephemeral wall of agger-fossum type of the early to mid-seventh century, and this was replaced by a stone city wall of the last quarter of the sixth century.[106] All the materials employed were local.

---

100. Cf. de Polignac 1995.

101. De Angelis 2000a, 116.

102. Bintliff 2012, 241–42.

103. Mertens 2006, 179–83.

104. De Angelis 2002, 303.

105. For Archaic Greek city walls in general, see now Frederiksen 2011.

106. Megara Hyblaia: Tréziny 1999, 242–43; 2002, 271; 2006, 257–59; 2007, 185; Frederiksen 2011, 162–64. Leontinoi: S. Rizza 2000; Frasca 2009, 67–68; Frederiksen 2011, 159–60.

Whether the city walls of other Sicilian Greek cities followed a similar pattern is unknown. All we can say for certain is that the city walls appeared at Naxos, Katane, Gela, Selinous, and Akragas in the second half of the sixth century (Figure 16).[107]

City walls provide important indications of the social and economic organization and abilities of the community they enclosed. It is only for the third phase of Megara Hyblaia's city wall that we have just enough details to estimate the amount of labor and materials expended in Archaic Greek Sicily. Roughly estimated, the wall itself contained about 58,000 cubic meters of stone and rubble/earth fill, and the ditch in front of this curtain required the movement of another 58,000 cubic meters of earth.[108] These rough-and-ready estimates do seem to support a recent opinion that city walls involved just as much investment of labor and materials as religious monuments, but of course notable differences of skills existed between them.[109] The seven peripteral Archaic temples at Selinous consist altogether of just over 50,000 cubic meters of stone and cost between 1,200 and 1,600 talents.[110] Of course, the construction of a temple requires more ornate and more fine-tuned work than a city wall, but a simple comparison of volume nevertheless supplies a useful indication of a city's overall output in these two spheres of building activity. Besides protecting the community, city walls were important markers for *polis* identity and characteristics, there being no sharp division between city and country in the Greek world as a whole.[111] As we will see in the next

---

107. Naxos: Karlsson 1989, 77; Tréziny 1999, 241–42, 272; 2006, 256, 259; Mertens 2006, 128–29; Frederiksen 2011, 173–74. Katane: Branciforti and Amari 2005, 54–55. Gela: Fischer-Hansen 1996, 331; cf. also Karlsson 1989, 77; Tréziny 1999, 241–42; 2006, 256 (who nevertheless expresses some doubts); Millino 2001, 132 (who presumes that Hippokrates undertook some of this building); Mertens 2006, 209–10; Frederiksen 2011, 143. Selinous: Mertens 2003; cf. also Tréziny's 1999, 241–42, 272; 2006, 256, 259; De Angelis 2003a, 135; Mertens 2006, 175–77; Frederiksen 2011, 185–86. Akragas: see Braccesi and De Miro 1992; Di Vita 1996, 294–96; De Miro 1998; De Angelis 2000a, 135–36; Fischer-Hansen, Nielsen, and Ampolo 2004a, 186–89; Mertens 2006, 195–98; Veronese 2006, 438–96; Fiorentini 2006; 2009a; Adornato 2011, 79–83; Frederiksen 2011, 126–27. Although Akragas' tyrant Phalaris is credited with the construction of the city wall within a decade of the city's foundation, it seems unlikely that he did so, given the anachronistic nature of the literary tradition and the archaeological record, which indicates that the city wall can be dated on stratigraphic grounds to the second half of the sixth century (see recently Adornato 2011, 47–67).

108. Volume has been calculated on the following variables. The wall itself runs for some 3,000 meters and is 2.8 meters wide and 6.5 meters high (cf. recently Frederiksen 2011, 95, 162–64), and the ditch is at least 10 meters wide and 1.9 meters deep (Frederiksen 2011, 88, 162–64). My estimates exclude openings for gates and towers.

109. Frederiksen 2011, 119.

110. De Angelis 2003a, 164–65.

111. Hansen and Nielsen 2004, 135–37.

FIGURE 16 View of Archaic City Wall of Naxos.
© Author

chapter, the size of the urban community enclosed within the city wall can provide crucial clues as to the overall size of *polis* population.

Occupation of the Countryside. The countryside complemented the city with its territory, making the city viable and thus providing the necessary resources to ensure its livelihood. This is without exception the rule.[112] Determining the sizes of these territories is crucial. By delimiting the natural resource base, we can obtain an idea of its extent and features, as well as providing insights into the social and economic organization of both city and country. The general territorial extent of Sicilian Greek cities can be worked out with some certainty in most cases, often by means of informed guesswork based on clues from physical geography, events in political and military history, and the distribution of material cultural remains (Map 4; Table 1).[113] Intensive and extensive

112. It is sometimes thought that the literary tradition maintaining that Zankle was founded by pirates and the appearance of its harbor on its first Archaic coins mean that the city had mainly or solely a maritime vocation, and that lack of evidence for activities in the surrounding territory may reflect accurately the historical situation (Braccesi and Millino 2000, 20; Corretti 2006, 416, 419–21; Veronese 2006, 142). For a recent warning against a solely maritime vocation, and the need for more work in the territory, see Prestianni Giallombardo 2009, 267.

113. For full discussion of the methodology, see De Angelis 2000a, 113–17.

surface survey has occurred in parts of six Sicilian Greek territories, and some other details pertaining to the nature of this occupation can be gleaned from archaeological and written sources.

In the Archaic period, Sicilian Greek territories measured between 400 and 2,500 square kilometers (Table 1).[114] Megara Hyblaia occupied the lower end of this spectrum and Akragas its upper end.[115] We know something of the phases of development for some of the territories. Syracuse's Archaic territory took shape in the seventh century.[116] Expansion southwards around 700 BC is signaled by Heloros' establishment, followed next by a westward thrust with Akrai and Kasmenai in 664 and 643 BC, and wrapping up with Kamarina on Sicily's southwest coast in about 598 BC.[117] It is likely that the tyrant Panaetios was responsible for expanding Leontinoi's territory to its greatest extent in the late seventh century.[118]

Every territory had second-order settlements, which could consist of small towns, villages, fortified outposts, or farmsteads. Not all of these settlement types can be documented for every territory at present, owing to the vagaries of evidence and level of archaeological exploration, as discussed earlier. Nevertheless it is clear that Sicilian Greek territories were not empty of human settlement and unstructured. Examples of towns include Mylai, a dependent *polis* of Zankle, established in the eighth century west of the city at the head of a large patch of fertile land,[119] and Francavilla di Sicilia in Naxos' territory, best known by a small sixth-century sanctuary with numerous clay *pinakes*

---

114. For full discussion, see De Angelis 2000a.

115. In the Sicily chapter of the Copenhagen Polis Centre's Inventory, the territories of Zankle, Naxos, Katane, and Gela are placed in category 4 (territories between 200–500 square kilometres: Fischer-Hansen, Nielsen, and Ampolo 2004a, 192, 206, 218, 233). In my view, the territories of these cities were larger (see Table 1).

116. For recent overviews, see De Angelis 2000a, 122–24; 2000b; Fischer-Hansen, Nielsen, and Ampolo 2004a, 225; Veronese 2006, 284–89.

117. For overviews of these sites, see Voza 1999, 113–20 (Heloros), 129–39 (Akrai), 139–43 (Kasmenai), and Fischer-Hansen, Nielsen, and Ampolo 2004a, 189–90 (Akrai), 195 (Heloros), 202–05 (Kamarina), 205–06 (Kasmenai). For a more recent view of Kasmenai's town plan, see also Tréziny 2002, 278–80.

118. Frasca 2009, 46.

119. The most recent discussion of the status of Mylai is contained in Fischer-Hansen, Nielsen, and Ampolo 2004a, 216–17. Metauros across the Straits of Messina in southern Italy may have been founded by Zankle or Locri in the seventh century BC (Sabbione 2005 has recently argued in favor of Zankle). Later, however, Metauros was under the control of Locri and served as one of the territorial markers between Rhegion and Locri (Cordiano 1996). Metauros' status as a *polis* is also uncertain (Fischer-Hansen, Nielsen, and Ampolo 2004b, 282–83).

Table 1 A Summary of Some Attested and Hypothesized Urban and Rural Features of Archaic Sicilian *Poleis*

Polis	Urban Settlement Size(s) in Hectares	Noteworthy Period(s) of Urban Building	Territory Size in Square Kilometers	Noteworthy Period(s) of Rural Development	Other Noteworthy Urban and Rural Features
Zankle	50–60 or 88	?	1,000 (max.)	550–500 BC?	urban emporium?
Naxos	10 to 40	650–500 BC	600	6th century?	rural sanctuary
Leontinoi	40–60	650–500 BC	830 (max.)	7th–6th centuries?	strategic rural outposts
Katane	50 or 75–100	?	830 (max.)	?	?
Syracuse	50–100	650–500 BC	1,670 (with Kamarina)	700–550 BC	emporia; strategic rural outposts; dispersed farmsteads?
Megara Hyblaia	61	650–500 BC	400		strategic rural outposts; reuse of native tombs in countryside
Gela	200	650–500 BC	1,350	7th–6th centuries	strategic rural outposts; emporium; dispersed farmsteads
Himera	120–130	550–500 BC	1,000–1,300 (max.)	550–500 BC	strategic rural outposts; dispersed farmsteads
Selinous	110	600–500 BC	1,500	600–500 BC	strategic rural outposts; rural sanctuary; emporia; dispersed farmsteads?
Akragas	200?	550–500 BC	2,500	late 6th century	strategic rural outposts; emporia; dispersed farmsteads?
Total:	891–1,089		11,680–11,980		

(or ritual panels).[120] While some of these towns could be fortified, there were also smaller fortified sites in strategic locations whose main purpose appears to have been to secure and protect them. A good illustration of this are the fortified outposts at Rodì and Milici established in the mid-sixth century BC around the mining interests Zankle maintained in the Monti Peloritani.

Farmsteads are attested in the territories of Syracuse, Gela, Himera, Selinous, and possibly Akragas. In Syracuse's territory, rescue excavations along the midpoint of the provincial highway between Noto and Rosolini revealed a wall that could be followed for a length of 30 meters and seems to belong to a large estate.[121] The earliest material recovered dates generically to the sixth century and may possibly represent the estate's first phase of use. Greek pottery of the seventh and sixth centuries has also been retrieved in the river valleys near Heloros and Noto, in areas well suited to agriculture.[122] In Gela's coastal plain there were many farmsteads in the sixth century, as revealed through excavation, topographic survey, and systematic surface survey of some two hundred square kilometers, particularly to the northwest of the city.[123] These farmsteads were sometimes accompanied by burial plots. At Himera, the first permanent settlements belong to about the mid-sixth century BC. The data are most suggestive for sites 46 and 150, whose finds raise the possibility of burial accompanying what have been identified as small farmsteads.[124] Evidence for other possible farmsteads and fortified outposts may also exist.[125] Of these, it is worth singling out site 216, located close to (still used) clay beds, at which ancient wasters plausibly connected with on-site kiln facilities have been found.[126] This provides clear and important evidence that craft production also occurred in the countryside. At Selinous, surveys revealed close to the city itself seven sixth-century farmsteads, possibly accompanied by burial plots in some cases,[127] while the survey around Mazara del Vallo revealed evidence of agricultural and

---

120. Hinz 1998, 156–58; Spigo 2003; Veronese 2006, 156, 172.

121. Guzzardi 2001, 104–05, who connects his finds with ancient sources mentioning the large estate belonging to a certain Polyzelos at the time of the Athenian invasion. For all the literary testimonia for agricultural exploitation in the area, see also A. Curcio 1979, 82–87; Vandermersch 1994, 99; and Chapter 4 below.

122. Guzzardi 2001, 102, 108.

123. Panvini 1996, 32, 64–66; Bergemann and Gans 2004. The evidence is made up of varying quality and quantity, but the overall picture is clear.

124. Alliata et al. 1988, 200–01; Belvedere et al. 2002, 291–93, 383; Vassallo 2005b, 90–93.

125. Alliata et al. 1988, 197–206; Allegro 1999, 291; Belvedere et al. 2002, 85–86, 383.

126. Belvedere et al. 2002, 367–71, 383.

127. Bianchi et al. 1998.

strategic settlements in the sixth and fifth centuries BC.[128] Survey in the water-shed area around Resuttano, at the northern boundary of Akragas' territory, sug-gests the presence of farmsteads (perhaps with a resident population burying on the land) already in the Archaic period.[129] It is also worth noting that two other surveys, one around Sciacca and the other along the coast west of Akragas, revealed no Archaic settlement evidence, which suggests that empty tracts of land still existed in these territories, perhaps left so because they were not ideally suited for agriculture.[130]

Our knowledge of the range of places of production and exchange also expands in considering the countryside, not just as they pertain to agriculture per se. An emporium has been identified at contrada Maestro, at the mouth of the ancient Hyrminos River, in Syracuse's territory.[131] The site covers some ten hectares and is located on the immediate area's highest hill, thus acting as a good vantage point for both land and sea. Excavations have revealed remains of at least three houses, a sanctuary to Demeter, and other as yet unidentifiable structures. Much imported fine-ware pottery and transport amphorae were also recovered. The emporium identification rests on such finds and the site's loca-tion, as well as on a commercial inscription, discussed in Chapter 4. Another possible emporium can be documented at Borgo Bonsignore/Herakleia Minoa and must have acted as the eastern marker of Selinous' territory.[132]

All the material discussed above presents some general noteworthy features and patterns that need to be summed up before closing this section (Table 1).

Patterns of urban development are in line with those observable elsewhere in Sicily and in many other parts of the Mediterranean, both Greek and non-Greek.[133] Sicilian Greek cities, during roughly the first century of their exis-tence, were open-textured in their planning and contained modest domestic architecture and the occasional religious building. Judging from this evidence, communities would seem to have had resources sufficient only for survival.[134]

---

128. Calafato, Tusa, and Mammina 2001.

129. Burgio 2002.

130. Selinous: Tirnetta 1978. Akragas: Di Bella and Santagati 1998.

131. See Di Stefano 1987a; 1987b, 188–96, who places it within Kamarina's jurisdiction (cf. too Fischer-Hansen, Nielsen, and Ampolo 2004a, 202). However, Gras (1993, 107) is right to point out that it lies on the Syracusan side of the river. Any ambiguity should not be pushed, as for a time this was a frontier zone (cf. De Angelis 2000a, 123).

132. Gras 2000, 131.

133. For a recent comparative perspective, see Bintliff 2002a; 2002b; Osborne and Cunliffe 2005; Kolb 2005.

134. Cf. Osborne 2009, 229.

Nevertheless, overall allocations of space occurred from the start; the community clearly maintained control of land, regulating where and how private and public space was used. Space and its associated activities, whether or not it was accompanied by architecture at this stage, was separated, differentiated, and individualized, as elsewhere in the Archaic Greek world.[135] The case that best illustrates this is Megara Hyblaia. The agora, streets, and other public and religious space were distinguished and respected as such from the eighth and into the seventh century. Although the city wall materialized in the first half of the seventh century, its general location seems to have been distinguished from the eighth century, since the cemeteries were simultaneously being placed beyond the future city wall. The pattern best seen at Megara Hyblaia is by no means unique and can be found at other cities, even if they have not been explored to the same degree.

For those *poleis* founded in the eighth century, an important transition involving denser occupation and the appearance of religious and public monuments occurred about 650 BC, usually around the agora. By this point three generations had passed, which allowed for the accumulation of resources in what can be defined as the first economic takeoffs of these communities (see Chapter 4 for further discussion). Such communal investments resulted in these communities taking their first steps toward civic identities in the later seventh century. Private and public spheres both crystallized and became arenas for the expression of individual and collective identities. Those *poleis* founded in the seventh and sixth centuries also picked up this basic pattern within a generation of their existence and were similarly characterized by modest domestic and public architecture. The *poleis* founded in both the eighth and seventh centuries were able to enter another phase of planning and monumentality in and around 550 BC through their building of peripteral temples, city walls, and public buildings. For *poleis* founded in the sixth century, their communities were only in a position to provide these a generation or two later. In the few cases where estimating the costs of such building is possible, they make revealing statements of their cities' social and economic potential that provide much food for thought when we turn to the next two chapters.

Occupation of the countryside is not as well known, because of the biases of archaeological research. The evidence suggests that permanent settlements consisted primarily of agglomerated villages and fortified outposts, as in other parts of the Greek and non-Greek Mediterranean.[136] Some of these villages would certainly have also served as regional markets that connected

---

135. See Lang 2002, 18–19; Gras, Tréziny, and Broise 2004.

136. For the Greek world, see recently Hall 2007b, 240–41; for the non-Greek world, see, for instance, van Dommelen 2006, 12.

city and country.[137] Some late-sixth-century evidence for dispersed settlement (farmsteads) does or may exist for four Sicilian cities (Selinous, Himera, Gela, Syracuse, and possibly Akragas), yet it is still not clear from this limited and often ambiguous evidence whether Greek Sicily fits a change noted elsewhere in the Greek world of increasing residence on and exploitation of the land.[138] If grain was the main crop cultivated (see Chapter 4), we should not necessarily expect any dispersed settlement in the Archaic period.[139] Some places of production and exchange are also attested in the countryside, and they too may have settled on a permanent, or at least seasonal, basis. Known emporia date to the sixth century BC, and their establishment clearly reflects an important development in interregional exchange (see further in Chapter 4).

In any case, developments in the cities doubtless coincided with developments in their respective territories, further underlining the intimate and seamless integration of city and country. For Archaic Sicily, such a connection is so far best attested at Syracuse, where the consolidation of the territory around 650 BC was accompanied by a growth spurt of buildings in the city.[140] The connection is one which new research has the potential to elaborate further. Even so, the relationship between city and country in Archaic Greek Sicily cannot be characterized as one of consumer cities. The city-state context was not conducive to cities forcing their agenda on the countryside in order to support a large number of parasitic individuals who extracted what they needed for their own ambitions.[141] Sicilian Greek cities engaged in little imperialism in the Archaic period to set such a relationship in motion.[142] Many urban dwellers living in city-states, moreover, would have been farmers who commuted to their own fields.

The differences in urban and territorial culture between Archaic Greeks in the Aegean and in Sicily invite comparison. The most glaring difference concerns organized town plans and the allocation of individual house plots within them. Such town plans are first found in Greece only in the early sixth century, arriving there from the Greek West.[143] Within the Sicilian town plans, agoras seem generally to have been larger[144] and to have had an economic function earlier than in

---

137. For the theoretical case, see Bintliff 2002a; 2002b. Cf. also Ampolo 1999.

138. Cf. De Angelis 2000a, 140–41.

139. Osanna 2001, 212.

140. Parisi Presicce 1984, 66.

141. Hansen 2006, 95–97; 2008a, 73.

142. Morris 2006b, 31–32; cf. also Hansen 2008a, 73.

143. Hansen 2003, 274; Crielaard 2009, 362.

144. Greco 1998.

Greece. Possible commercial stoas may have already existed at Megara Hyblaia from the middle of the seventh century, contrasting with the pattern observed in Greece.[145] As will be argued in Chapter 4, the Sicilian Greek *poleis* appear to have been oriented toward external trade from the start. This may be related to another difference: Sicilian Greek territories were bigger and better endowed, in terms of climate and arable land, than in Aegean Greece.[146] Sicilian Greek territories also appear not just to have contained the agricultural branch of their economies, as recently maintained for the Greek homeland.[147] Craft production and exchange did take place in the countryside too. Again, this could in part have been because of their bigger and better-endowed territories (which would have encouraged production closer to, say, materials and markets), as well as perhaps to preexisting native resource use (as in the case of site 216 at Himera) and less need to protect these economic activities within the city walls. Certainly Sicilian Greek *poleis* had urban and territorial features that represented a new phenomenological experience for both their inhabitants and visitors.

2. The First Generation of Political Centralization

Political centralization gained momentum across the Mediterranean in the sixth century BC. While this had always been a feature of Near Eastern political landscapes, more impulse was given to it by the Persian Empire, which laid the groundwork for one of the largest territorial entities then known and which had a knock-on effect on Greeks and other peoples living at its edges. Although it remains debated as to whether or not this political impact extended as far as Sicily,[148] a similar move toward political centralization can be observed at this same time.

Gela seems to have been the first Sicilian Greek city-state to attempt political centralization, in the late sixth century. This was led by two brothers, Kleander and Hippokrates, who ruled the city as tyrants between 505 and 491 BC and who engaged in the conquest of eastern Sicily.[149] On the death of Hippokrates in 491, power passed into the hands of his cavalry commander, Gelon, who initially acted as regent for Hippokrates' sons but then established himself as tyrant in

---

145. For Greece, compare the remarks of Kenzler 1999, 314; Crielaard 2009, 372 n. 57.

146. See in particular De Angelis 2000, 139–40; 2002, 300.

147. Lang 2002, 15–16.

148. For a view that it did, see Luraghi 1994, 169–76, but against it, see Jackman 2005, 174–75.

149. For these individuals and their activities, see Luraghi 1994, 119–86; Braccesi 1998, 21–25; Hofer 2000, 81–83, 101–02.

his own right.[150] Gelon continued the conquests of his predecessors, capturing Syracuse in 485 and making it the capital of his expanding domains. Syracuse developed under Gelon and his two successors, Hieron and Thrasyboulos (the so-called Deinomenid tyrants), in order to accommodate influxes of population from conquered territories and to take on its new role as imperial capital. At Akragas, Theron was the first in a string of tyrants (the so-called Emmenid tyrants) who pursued a similar program of expansion, often working in cooperation with Syracuse.[151] Together, Gelon and Theron had effective control over most of eastern and central Sicily, which caused alarm and provoked reactions not only among the Greek and native communities living there, but also in Carthage with its extensive interests in western Sicily. The result was a showdown between these three major players, with the Syracuse-Akragas alliance inflicting a decisive victory over Carthage at Himera in 480 BC, which led to a first delineation of political spheres between Greek and Carthaginian down roughly the middle of Sicily. Any Sicilian communities that were able to maintain a degree of independence throughout this larger conflict were ones, such as Selinous and Zankle, that allied themselves to one of the major players.

Political centralization in Sicily in the early fifth century, therefore, resulted in power residing in the hands of fewer but bigger states. As elsewhere in the Greek world, such centralized Sicilian Greek landscapes continued to be characterized by *poleis*, though now in some kind of hegemonic or imperial relationship with their new masters.[152] City-states now became part of large territorial states. This affected all spheres of life and thus justifies this episode as our second chronological period, which lasted for about a generation, down to about 465 BC, when the various tyrants who eagerly promoted such centralization were overthrown.

Under Gelon, Syracuse became more monumental and better supplied with infrastructure. The size of the city grew to cover between 100 and 120 hectares, with the new city quarters (Acradina, Tyche, and Neapolis) built both on top of and beyond the preexisting cemeteries (Map 6).[153] Possible traces of the town plan and the structures within them in these areas have been found in excavation, but they are not as abundant or as clear as they could be, thanks

---

150. Cf. Luraghi 1994, 273–373; Braccesi 1998, 25–39; Hofer 2000, 83–89, 97–101.

151. The literary record is poor for these events (Mafodda 1998, 29–30), but see Vassallo (2000), who adduces possible archaeological evidence for these disturbances across western Sicily. In this light, Theron's attempt to gain hold of Motya in Pausanias (5.25.5) may well be trustworthy. For discussion, see Nenci 1988; Adornato 2006, 447, 452.

152. Hansen 2006a, 55, 130.

153. Mertens 2006, 312; Evans 2009, 109.

to their later redevelopment.[154] Nevertheless, they imply continuity with previous practices, in that the city blocks and scale of the public structures are of similar design. On Ortygia, in the oldest part of the city, Gelon also left his mark, constructing a new port with arsenal and possibly the temple of Athena.[155] The temple, later incorporated into the city's cathedral and thus fairly well preserved, was a hexastyle peripteral temple of the Doric order. It is surprising that no attempt has ever been made to estimate the amount of labor and materials employed in it. Nevertheless, an idea can be gained by comparing this temple to temples A and O at Selinous, which are of contemporary date and plan and which have been subjected to such study.[156] Syracuse's Athenaion is almost the twice the size in area at 22.2 by 55.45 meters and thus presumably involved twice the cost and labor of their Selinountine counterparts. Hence it may have cost between at least 100 and 140 talents and embodied at least 600,000 man-hours of labor.

Some of the foregoing physical developments were also intended to support the substantial military that Gelon had built up. Thus it is necessary to combine physical and military expenditures if we would like to get a sense of his overall investment at Syracuse at this time. Gelon's military consisted of a navy, infantry, and cavalry. The navy is more securely attested under Hieron I, Gelon's brother and successor, and a recent discussion has expressed doubts as to whether a navy even existed earlier.[157] At all events, practically nothing is known regarding the number and nature of the ships in the navy under the Deinomenids as a whole, despite the boast that Herodotus puts into Gelon's mouth of being able to supply 200 triremes when addressing the Athenian and Spartan ambassadors seeking aid against the Persians.[158] We are better

---

154. Di Vita 1996, 297; Mertens 2006, 311–13; Veronese 2006, 296–99.

155. For the port and arsenal, see most recently Mertens 2006, 314. For the temple, there are two recent discussions: Mertens 2006, 268–73, 315; Veronese 2006, 307–08; on its dating, see now Adornato (2006, 449, 452) who reminds us that Orsi dated it stratigraphically to the period of Hieron and that the matching of statements in Diodorus Siculus (11.26) with the archaeology is flawed. Instead, Adornato argues that Hieron built the temple with spoils from his victory at Cumae in 474 BC. In a similar vein, aqueducts sometimes attributed to Gelon are better seen in a Hellenistic-Roman context (so Mertens 2006, 313).

156. De Angelis 2003a, 138–39, 163–64, 168, where the roofs of these temples are left out of the discussion for lack of information. Hence the estimates refer to about 80 percent of the total cost of the temples.

157. Corretti 2006, 420–21. On the general context of late Archaic/early Classical naval developments, one can turn to the studies of De Souza 1998 and Davies 2007.

158. Hdt. 7.158.4; see also Hdt. 7.163.1–2 for fifty ships sent with Cadmus to Greece after these ambassadors had returned home. For a recent discussion of the existence or not of Gelon's navy, see Corretti 2006, 417.

informed about the infantry. Perhaps up to 10,000 of them were mercenaries, as more fully discussed in the next chapter. How many citizen soldiers there were alongside them is unknown, but several thousand would not be an unreasonable guess. Gelon continued the cavalry traditions of Gela at Syracuse, where he fielded about 2,000 cavalrymen.[159]

To estimate how much the army and navy of the Deinomenids would have cost, we have to indulge ourselves intellectually and make a few assumptions. We have no idea of how much mercenaries were paid in this period,[160] but let us assume that they were paid 20 drachmas per month, the lower end of the pay scale used by Dionysius I a century later.[161] The mercenaries would have cost 200,000 drachmas (or 33.3 Attic talents) per month, for a yearly grand total of about 400 talents. The cavalry may have cost 1 drachma per day to maintain (or 30 drachmas per month).[162] For 2,000 cavalry, this would work out to 60,000 drachmas (or 100 Attic talents) per month, and a yearly total of 1,200 talents. If we use the figure of 200 triremes recorded in Herodotus (it is the same number of ships as at Salamis), and assume that each trireme cost 1 talent per month to maintain, the figure recorded in the context of the Peloponnesian War,[163] we arrive at a figure of 200 talents per month, or 2,400 Attic talents for the whole year. In summary, these figures add up to 4,000 talents per annum for the mercenaries, cavalry, and navy. Following his victory at Himera in 480 BC, Gelon received 2,000 talents of silver from the Carthaginians.[164] According to Tréziny, this figure is to be considered credible, as it compares to the 2,000 talents he estimates as the cost of Dionysius I's campaign against Motya in 397 BC, which, like the Battle of Himera, did not last a full year.[165] Tréziny argues, moreover, that Gelon, as victor, essentially set his war indemnity at the level needed to recoup the costs he incurred in

159. Frederiksen 1968, 10; Gaebel 2002, 82. As Frederiksen observes, this is "a huge proportion by Greek standards." For the situation in Greece, see, for instance, Spence 1993; Gaebel 2002.

160. Trundle 2004, 80–103.

161. Diodorus Siculus (11.76.2) mentions that in 463 BC each of 600 elite Syracusan soliders was given 1 mina as a prize for their valor and success in battle. This would work out to 100 drachmas per solider and a grand total of 10 talents (E. Boehringer 1929, 76). I am hesitant to use these figures as representing in any way the rate of pay for mercenary and citizen soldiers at Syracuse at this time or for the later fifth century.

162. Gaebel 2002, 23.

163. For previous discussions, see Ampolo 1987, 9; Tréziny 2001, 375.

164. Diod. Sic. 11.26.2.

165. Tréziny's 2001, 376.

his own campaign. These figures provide rough-and-ready, though reliable, estimates of the sort of financial outlays undertaken by Gelon. Moreover, these developments also mean that Syracuse and other cities under its control must have become consumer cities to some degree, supporting a sector of the population, particularly the mercenaries, not directly involved in the production of their own foodstuffs.[166]

Gelon built beyond Syracuse too, seeking the wider projection of his power. This included the Temple of Victory at Himera, whose Doric style was alien to local architectural traditions (where Ionic predominated) and whose design was similar to Syracuse's Athenaion, just discussed.[167] Gelon and his brother Hieron also tapped into Panhellenic networks via the sanctuaries of Delphi and Olympia, dedicating at both sites booty from their victories and setting up a treasury at Olympia.[168] Hieron also established greater presence in his Sicilian territories by rearranging previous patterns of population and establishing new cities.[169] But to appreciate this better, we need first to understand the size of territory controlled by Syracuse under Gelon and his successors.

Syracuse's territory was made up chiefly of the conquered lands of Kamarina, Megara Hyblaia, Leontinoi, Katane, and Naxos.[170] Zankle too was at first part of this conquered territory, owing to Hippokrates' efforts. However, in about 488/87 BC, Anaxilas, tyrant of Rhegion, took the city and renamed it Messana after his homeland, as part of his larger attempt to secure both sides of the Straits of Messina. Hieron later successfully broke this blockade after a naval battle off Cumae in 474 BC.[171] Even so, despite the loss of such a strategically important corner of the island, the Syracusan state now controlled something to the order of 4,330 square kilometers (Map 12a).[172]

---

166. Cf. Morris 2006b, 41–45.

167. Gras 1990; Mertens 2006, 259–60.

168. Mertens 2006, 258–59; Bonanno 2010, 181–86.

169. Mertens 2006, 310; Bonanno 2010, 127–57.

170. Beloch 1886, 298; 1889, 12–14. Fischer-Hansen, Nielsen, and Ampolo 2004a, 225 fail to include Katane in this list.

171. On Anaxilas and his territorial aims, see Luraghi 1994, 187–229; Cordiano 1996; Fischer-Hansen, Nielsen, and Ampolo 2004a, 234. On Hieron's activities in the Straits of Messina and the Tyrrhenian Sea, see Corretti 2006, 417; Bonanno 2010, 159–78.

172. This figure represents the sum total of the estimates reached earlier for the respective territories of Syracuse, Kamarina, Megara Hyblaia, Leontinoi, Katane, and Naxos. This territory size can be located between those of Athens (2,500 square kilometers) and Sparta (8,500 square kilometers), then the Greek homeland's two most powerful states (cf. Hansen and Nielsen 2004; Hansen 2006a).

Within these boundaries, the hands of Gelon and Hieron are in evidence. Gelon forced Megara Hyblaia to be abandoned, and it ceased to be a *polis*. Hieron removed the populations of Naxos and Katane to Leontinoi, which became a kind of "collection basin" for Sicily's Chalcidian populations, although little is known archaeologically of this phase of the city's history.[173] The same holds for Katane, owing to later layers of occupation, but we at least know that Hieron renamed it Aitna.[174] Hieron's intentions are clearest at Naxos, to which he gave a completely new urban look, with a different orientation to the town plan, now with wider streets and possibly grand atrium houses (Map 5).[175] We can only guess at both the financial and personal traumas behind these new foundations and forced abandonments, but they cannot have been insignificant.

Political conditions at Akragas in the early fifth century must have turbulent, for in 488/7 Theron managed to establish himself as tyrant.[176] City and countryside were transformed during Theron's reign.

The most outstanding transformation in the city was the construction of the monumental temple of Zeus Olympios (ca. 56.30 meters by 112.60 meters), with peristasis of seven by fourteen Doric columns (also known as Temple B; Map 10).[177] Recent work has shown that this Olympieion is better placed in the political climate that brought Theron to power and was not conceived as a temple to mark his victory with Gelon over the Carthaginians at Himera.[178] Nevertheless, it is still conceivable that the Carthaginian prisoners from Himera mentioned by Diodorus Siculus as having been used on building projects could have worked on this temple, providing the extra manpower needed to finish it.[179] The sculpture could also have had meaning in the aftermath of the victory of Himera. Each intercolumniation consisted of a lower screen supporting a telamon of 7.5 meters in height (Figure 17). The temple's eastern pediment, moreover, was adorned with a scene from the Gigantomachy, and the western pediment with a scene from the fall of Troy. The Olympieion is

---

173. For Hieron's strategic aims in doing so, see Vanotti 1995, 92. To imagine the trauma, cf. also Hdt. 7.156.

174. Cf. Mertens 2006, 351. This Aitna had soon to be abandoned because of pressure from its original inhabitants, and Hieron founded a second Aitna at Inessa, which is usually located at Cività to the northwest (for full details, see Fischer-Hansen, Nielsen, and Ampolo 2004a, 177, 184).

175. Bell 1997; Mertens 2006, 343–48.

176. On Theron, see Luraghi 1994, 231–72; Braccesi 1998, 51–60; Hofer 2000, 103.

177. For a recent discussion, see Mertens 2006, 261–66.

178. Cf. De Angelis 2001, 180.

179. Diod. Sic. 11.25.2. On the temple's finished state, see Mertens 2006, 266.

FIGURE 17 View of a Telamon to Olympieion at Akragas.
© Author

estimated to have used about 56,000 cubic meters of stone and to have cost about 1,512 talents.[180] This is an amazing sum of money, derived from the monument itself, and which thus provides an important window onto Akragas' social and economic conditions at the time. According to Diodorus Siculus,

180. Martin 1973, 189. On the architectural sculpture produced in this period, as well as free-standing sculpture and other works of art, see Rizza and De Miro 1986, 224, 226, 228–29.

some of the Carthaginian prisoners were also put to work on Phaiax's water supply project.[181] This is an area of infrastructure commonly tackled by tyrants in Sicily and elsewhere to meet the needs of their growing cities,[182] and in the case of Akragas probably involved extracting greater potential out of the pre-existing natural underground water reservoir.[183] There must have been more that Theron did to leave his stamp on the city, but the data remain few.

In the countryside, we know that Theron made considerable territorial gains for Akragas by force. The western boundary with Selinous was extended, with the entire area between the Platani (ancient Halykos) and Verdura Rivers likely acquired during his reign.[184] Recent survey work in the mid and lower parts of the Platani River valley has brought to light Greek pottery of this period on strategic sites tentatively identified as fortified outposts that Theron established.[185] There is no doubt that Himera also came under Akragas' control during Theron's tyranny, indicated, among other ways, by the crabs, Akragas' symbol, on the reverse of Himera's coins (cf. Figure 23).[186] Theron also installed some of his own people at Himera, assigning them the plots of land and houses of those citizens who had gone into exile.[187] Some minor building and modifications may have resulted. Whether other areas were temporarily controlled by Akragas remains difficult to say. If we base ourselves on the more certain boundaries, it can be said that at least some 3,500 square kilometers of land were controlled, making Akragas' territory slightly smaller than Syracuse's but similar enough for an equal political partnership (Map 12a).[188]

Selinous maintained its independence from Akragas and Syracuse throughout this first attempt at political centralization in Sicily (Map 12a). It is likely that Selinous aligned itself with Carthage following the capture of Herakleia Minoa to avoid being taken over completely by Akragas and joined Carthage in war

---

181. Diod. Sic. 11.25.3–4. For the first possible archaeological evidence for this project, see Fiorentini 2009b, 98.

182. Collin Bouffier 2009, 72–73.

183. So Mertens 2006, 319. See also De Miro 1998, 333–34.

184. De Angelis 2000a, 135–36; Veronese 2006, 443–44.

185. Gullì 2000.

186. Cf. Fischer-Hansen, Nielsen, and Ampolo 2004a, 186.

187. Allegro 1999, 293.

188. Cf. De Angelis 2000a, 132, 135–36. Diodorus Siculus (11.20–26) and Deinomenid self-representation confidently proclaim Syracuse as the more powerful force in this relationship, but that seems debatable (for full discussion, see Adornato 2006, 447–48; Harrell 2006, 130).

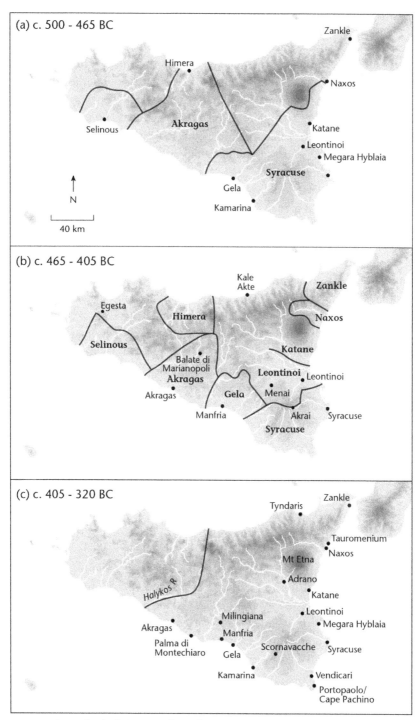

MAP 12 Hypothetical Extent of Greek Territories in Sicily (a) during the First Generation of Political Centralization; (b) from the Collapse to the Return of Political Centralization; and (c) between Political Centralization and Independence.
© Author

against the Akragas-Syracuse coalition.[189] On Carthage's defeat, Selinous too may have had territorial concessions and tribute imposed on it. If so, the impact on Selinous must remain unknown, for lack of evidence and because of the rough dating of most of the known public monuments, which span the years on either side of the Battle of Himera.[190] A freeze in building due to the payment of tribute is a possible scenario, however, with work breaking off on the massive Temple G.[191] Even so, all indications are of a city as flourishing as ever. Some other building occurred in the first half of the fifth century. Temple E3 was adorned with a series of metopes, and apart from a bronze statue dubbed "The Ephebe," dated broadly to the fifth century at best, little else is known of other sculpture and craftwork in general in this period.[192]

Overall, therefore, the carving up of Sicily during this historical phase put the reins of political, territorial, and urban control into fewer but bigger hands (Map 12a; Table 2). Outside of Syracuse, Akragas, and Selinous, the rest of the island was under the control of Carthage and native populations, with Messana controlled by Anaxilas of Rhegion. The tyrants of Syracuse and Akragas embellished their respective cities, with projects that augmented infrastructure and that emphasized the tyrants' power and wealth. Changes in settlement pattern also accompanied these developments and can be related to social and economic developments discussed fully in the next two chapters. The increased sizes of their cities and territories are due to the tyrants' imperial policies, which rearranged the relationship between the two spheres and resulted in Syracuse and Akragas becoming consumer cities, in which individuals, administration, and infrastructure can be presumed to have been supported by surplus production generated by others.

3. From the Collapse to the Return of Political Centralization

The collapse of these first attempts at political centralization resulted in new configurations of urban and rural space all across Sicily over the next two generations (ca. 460–405 BC; Map 12b). Many of the population transfers undertaken by the Archaic tyrants were reversed: exiles returned to their home cities, which, in some cases, lay abandoned and thus required refounding. Alongside this were two native Sicilian attempts at carving out states, those

---

189. De Angelis 2003a, 161–62.

190. Cf. De Angelis 2003a, 138–39.

191. See the discussion in De Angelis 2003a, 162–63.

192. Rizza and De Miro 1986, 224–25 (ephebes), 230–33 (metopes).

Table 2 A Summary of Some Attested and Hypothesized Urban and Rural Features of Sicilian *Poleis* during the First Attempt at Centralization (snapshot ca. 465 BC)

Polis	Urban Settlement Size in Hectares	Territory Size in Square Kilometers	Noteworthy Urban Developments	Noteworthy *Territorial Developments*	Noteworthy Extraterritorial Developments
Syracuse	100–120	4,330	creation of new districts; temple of Athena; port with arsenal	strategic populations transfers; creation of new cities	victory temple at Himera; Panhellenic dedications; victory temple at Himera
Akragas	200?	3,500 (min.)	temple of Zeus; water supply	settlement of population in conquered cities and countryside	victory temple at Himera
Selinous	110	1,500	building freeze?	loss of land?	?
Total:	410–430	8,330			

of Egesta and Ducetius, encouraged in the wake of the breakup of Syracusan and Akragantine power. Ducetius presented a direct challenge to Syracuse, which, for its part, never relinquished entirely its desire to have a larger control of Sicily during these two generations. In general, the political situation remained unstable, as reflected in the Congress of Gela in 424 BC, which attempted to find peaceful solutions to the island's problems. That was not achieved, however, and matters escalated during and after the failed Athenian invasion of Syracuse in 415–413 BC, which caused states, both big and small, either to take sides or remain neutral in this conflict.

The showdown between Syracuse and Carthage came within four years, when smaller cities, like Egesta and Selinous, made appeals to one of these larger states for help in local conflicts, appeals that set into motion a bigger chain of events. Carthage intervened first, resulting in the siege and sacking of Selinous, Himera, and Akragas between 409 and 406 BC. Gela and Kamarina too were threatened and soon abandoned. Carthage took the conflict to Syracuse's doors, which spurred on in 405 BC the rise of another long-lasting tyranny led by Dionysius. Overall, the political landscape was again modified to suit the needs of the larger powers, but before then we have to consider this third and no less interesting phase in Greek Sicily's urban and rural history.

Town Planning and Architecture. In the cities, our knowledge consists of town plans and domestic and religious architecture. No new public buildings are known from this period. This may be due to actual material realities or to the vagaries of the evidence. It is difficult to judge what background factors are at play here, but chance is unlikely to provide the full explanation. Instead, the absence of public building may have something to do with practicality, finances, and necessity at a time when cities were attempting to rebuild themselves.

Exiles returned to Himera, Kamarina, Naxos, Katane, Zankle, and Gela. Something can be said about each of these returns, with the exception of Katane because of later occupation layers.[193] We know most about developments at Kamarina, refounded in 461 following its earlier destruction by Gelon (Map 13).[194] The countryside was completely redesigned (see below) in a way that presupposes similar redesigning in the city. However, urban developments are poorly known by comparison: the late Classical occupation of Kamarina followed the main lines of this fifth-century refoundation, causing the erasure of much evidence.[195] All that can be securely related to this period are two kilns from

---

193. Gentili 1996; Mertens 2006, 351.

194. On Kamarina's history in the first half of the fifth century, see recently Fischer-Hansen, Nielsen, and Ampolo 2004a, 203.

195. So recently Di Stefano 2006, 168; Mertens 2006, 352–53; Pelagatti 2006, 48.

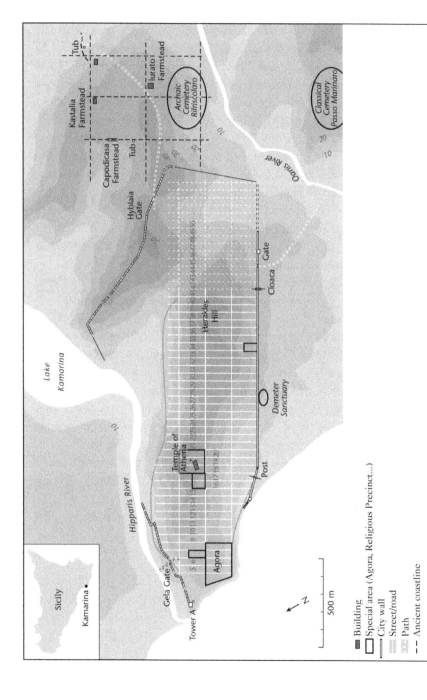

MAP 13 Town Plan of Kamarina.

© Author

a residential area for the production of pottery and terracottas. At Himera, the exiles took up residence again alongside Theron's group of settlers. The city does not appear to have destabilized and seems to have retained its basic look and design from before. At Naxos, the citizens who had been expelled by Hieron returned and resumed their lives as before under an elite regime.[196] The wealthiest from among these exiles may have been responsible for building a series of large atrium houses, although their coarse dating does not preclude a date in the time of the Syracusan tyrant Hieron. At Zankle/Messana, after liberation from Anaxilas, the tyrant of Rhegion, the fifth-century city may have been smaller than its Archaic predecessor, but that impression, as admitted by the site's most recent excavators, is based on limited and perhaps unrepresentative evidence.[197] Recent excavations there have uncovered remains of an ornate house with benches, plastered walls, and courtyard.[198] At Gela the city seems to have continued to use the 200 hectares laid out in the Archaic period,[199] and the few architectural developments that can be traced likewise occurred only in the previously established framework of monuments.[200]

Changing historical circumstances also affected the four other *polis* centers in this period. We know most about Akragas, Selinous, Leontinoi, and Syracuse, in that order.

Akragas experienced a remarkable flourishing in the remaining two-thirds of the fifth century (Map 10).[201] "Monster" monuments such as the Olympieion of the late Archaic/early Classical periods gave way, as elsewhere in the west, to forms of architecture that were influenced by Pythagorean theorizing and that were nevertheless still impressive in their own right.[202] The construction of six temples, all in the Doric order and all situated in prominent topographical positions, was undertaken over the two generations in question.[203]

Just before the middle of the fifth century, the building of temple L added monumentality to the preexisting sanctuary of chthonic divinities.[204] Judging

---

196. Thus Cordano 2003, 124.

197. Bacci 1999, 53.

198. Ingoglia 2003, 87–88.

199. Fischer-Hansen, Nielsen, and Ampolo 2004a, 194.

200. Veronese 2006, 380–401.

201. For an overview, see De Miro 1998.

202. See in general recently Mertens 2006, 381–83.

203. De Miro 1992; De Waele 1992; Mertens 2006 386–99.

204. Mertens 2006, 397–98.

from its surviving architectural members, temple L seems to have been of similar size to the so-called Temple of Juno Lacinia that followed soon after, in the mid-fifth century BC.[205] This temple consists of six by thirteen columns sitting on a stylobate of 16.94 meters by 38.13 meters. The structure inside the colonnade is divided into pronaos, naos, and opisthodomus; a large monumental altar sits outside. Another temple, conventionally attributed to Athena, can be situated in the same building horizon as the latter two and is thus dated on these grounds to about the mid-fifth century BC.[206] This temple is partially incorporated into a church, but enough is known of it to indicate that it too had six columns by thirteen columns on a stylobate of 17.25 meters by 39.43 meters. Around 430 BC, work began on the so-called Temple of Concordia, one of the best surviving examples of Doric architecture anywhere (Figure 18).[207] It is in design and size similar to the latter two temples, and, unlike them, its height can be calculated at about 8.93 meters. Of a similar date to the Temple of Concordia is the so-called Temple of the Dioscuri, of which a partially preserved and reconstructed corner still stands today.[208] The last of the six temples was the so-called Temple of Hephaistos, undertaken in the late fifth century and unfinished at the time of the Carthaginian sack of Akragas in 406 BC.[209] Only two fragmentary columns still stand of this temple, though enough clues can be pieced together to suggest that its design and size paralleled the Temple of Concordia. On any account, this is an impressive monumental output by Akragas, regardless of the frequent similarities between the temples in terms of size and design.

Of the six monumental temples built in this period, it is possible to calculate the amount of stone and cost incurred in the construction of two, the temples of Juno Lacinia and Concordia, because of their good preservation.[210] They required some 5,700 cubic meters and 136 talents to erect. Such estimates provide ample testimony, if any were really needed, that Akragas could muster large amounts of energy and revenue in the later fifth century. The literary sources for Akragas in the later fifth century speak often of the wealth of the city and of particular individuals within it (see Chapter 3 for discussion). However, their residential quarters are by comparison quite poorly known.[211]

---

205. De Miro (1998, 339–40) argues that the temple may have been dedicated to Poseidon.

206. De Miro 1998, 333; Mertens 2006, 398.

207. De Miro 1998, 342–43; Mertens 2006, 391–95.

208. De Miro 1998, 343; Mertens 2006, 395–97.

209. Mertens 2006, 398–99.

210. Martin 1973, 189.

211. De Miro 1998, 334; Mertens 2006, 321–23, 382.

FIGURE 18 View of Temple of Concordia at Akragas.
© Author

Traces of houses have been discovered in the two city blocks sandwiched between the Olympieion to the east and gate V to the west. Their location is interesting, in a very public part of the city, as is their substantial size: between 13 and 13.7 meters in width (north/south) by 17.4 and 17.8 meters in length (east/west). Where identifiable, these houses consist of three rooms which face southwards onto a courtyard.

At Selinous, there was little new public building, and what there was slotted into the already established urban framework (Map 9). A small Hekataion and monumental propylaeum were added to the complex of suburban sanctuaries just west of the city.[212] The elite displayed their status and wealth not through public architecture, as before, or even necessarily in death,[213] but in sumptuous houses strategically located at the heart of the city. These houses were built along the main north-south artery running from the acropolis to the agora and blend public architectural features within a domestic setting, whose full social implications will be discussed in the next chapter. Elsewhere there may have been some structures added to the port, but overall Selinous seems not to have had public infrastructure programs in the fifth century as a

212. Cf. De Angelis 2003a, 139; Mertens 2006, 404–06.

213. Although this is the context where most of the luxury Attic pottery imports are to be found: Meola 1996–98; Kustermann Graf 2002; G. Giudice 2007, 243–76, 355–67.

whole.[214] Whether Selinous also maintained a navy as part of its military commitments is uncertain.[215]

Syracuse also continued to keep a close eye on Leontinoi, a strategically important site for control of southeastern Sicily, although our evidence is weakest for what was happening in that city. Leontinoi knew of Syracuse's ambitions and strengthened its preexisting fortification around 450 BC.[216] Internal problems at Leontinoi led Syracuse to reacquire it; Leontinoi's most powerful became citizens of Syracuse, while the remainder of the population dispersed, for the most part, to perhaps as far away as Chalcis in Greece.[217] The powerful then returned to their lands, although it is unlikely that they were in control of Leontinoi's entire territory.[218]

Occupation of the Countryside. The collapse of attempts at political centralization resulted in three possible scenarios for the development of territory sizes: they could stay the same or become smaller or bigger (Map 12b). This process was often characterized by conflict within and between states, all parties seizing the fluidity of the moment to augment or protect their holdings. As already mentioned, a new development appeared in this period: the first signs of planning principles applied to the Sicilian Greek countryside are attested at Kamarina (Map 13). Dispersed rural settlement was also a feature at Kamarina, as well as at Himera and Syracuse. Little is known of the countryside of Naxos, Katane, Messana, and Gela.[219] By contrast, we are naturally better informed of Syracuse and Akragas, the two imperial powers of the previous period, which stood to lose the most.

While Syracuse never abandoned its imperial desires in this period, loss of territory did nevertheless occur (cf. Maps 12a and b). The regaining of independence by Zankle, Naxos, Katane, Leontinoi, Kamarina, and Gela was in large part responsible for this. To all appearances, each of these cities got back their Archaic territories, with the exception of Kamarina, which acquired Morgantina at the Congress of Gela in 424 BC, adding between 200 and 300 square kilometers to its Archaic predecessor.[220] A threat to Syracuse's territory

---

214. Mertens 2006, 331.

215. De Angelis 2003a, 199 n. 295 has recently summarized the various scholarly views.

216. S. Rizza 2000, 19.

217. Vanotti 1995, 99–100.

218. Vattuone 1994, 87.

219. Katane: Diod. Sic. 11.49.1–2 (Asheri 1980, 147; Berger 1992, 19; Vinci 2010). Gela: Bergemann and Gans 2004.

220. Thuc. 4.65.1. S.M. Thompson 1999, 495; Bell 2000, 295.

was also posed by the state formation pursued by the native leader Ducetius, who operated in the swath of territory from roughly his hometown of Menai in the southeastern interior up to the north coast with his foundation at Kale Akte.[221] The interests of Ducetius and Syracuse overlapped to some degree, especially after Ducetius sought to remove the settlers established by Hieron in the plain of Catania.[222] Syracuse engaged Ducetius militarily, eliminating the threat by 440 BC, and thus obtained his territory.[223] How much territory that entailed is hard to quantify, owing to a paucity of evidence. The same problem holds for the amount of territory Syracuse gained with the takeover of Leontinoi. Some 4,680 to 4,800 square kilometers have reasonably been attributed to Syracuse at the time of Athens' invasion in 415 BC.[224]

Akragas' territory during the last two generations of the fifth century was smaller, primarily on account of Himera's independence (cf. Maps 12a and b).[225] Although our evidence is sparse, Akragas seems not to have had territorial ambitions in this period, not even allowing Athens to cross its territory to join the theater of war elsewhere on Sicily in 415 BC.[226] At this moment Akragas' territory is estimated as having encompassed either 4,285 or 3,100 square kilometers.[227] Of these, the lower estimate seems more plausible in light of what was said earlier about Akragas' territory in the time of Theron.

For Selinous' territory, an emended passage of Diodorus Siculus provides evidence of a border dispute in 454/53 somewhere along the Mazaros River between Selinous and Egesta/Halykiai.[228] This dispute belonged to a larger political context, in which Egesta was forming its own state by taking over smaller neighbors.[229] Victory for Selinous has been presumed on the basis of an inscription found in temple G, but whether or not Selinous' territory size was affected remains unknown.[230]

---

221. On Ducetius, see recently Jackman 2006.

222. Diod. Sic. 11.76; 11.91. Cf. Beloch 1889, 13; Galvagno 2000, 79.

223. Diod. Sic. 12.30.30; Thuc. 6.88. Cf. Beloch 1889, 13–14; Galvagno 2000, 83–98.

224. Beloch 1886, 298; 1889, 19, 60–61.

225. Fischer-Hansen, Nielsen, and Ampolo 2004a, 186. For Himera, see Belvedere 2001, 732–33, 746.

226. Thuc. 7.32. Cf. Beloch 1889, 15.

227. Beloch 1886, 298 (for the higher estimate); 1889, 19, 60–61.

228. Diod. Sic. 11.86.2, to be read in conjunction with De Angelis 2003a, 175–75.

229. For full discussion, see Morris, Jackman, Blake, and Tusa 2002, 187–91; Morris, Jackman, Blake, Garnand, and Tusa 2003, 287–90.

230. IG 14.268. For the presumption of victory in this dispute, see recently De Angelis 2003a, 175; Antonetti and De Vido 2006a, 159.

The permanent settlements established in the Archaic period give every appearance of continued occupation and use as before, but at some cities there are new and additional settlement developments in the countryside.

At Himera there was a simultaneous extension of the agricultural base with the return of the exiled original inhabitants; this may have soothed any potential discord with the Akragantine settlers who remained.[231] Himera's landscapes appear variegated and ample at this time to keep the ambitions of its various sectors of society satisfied enough to avoid conflict.[232] The handful or so known Archaic farmsteads at Himera witnessed a threefold multiplication in the Classical period, suggesting considerable new activity and the reconfiguration of rural space.[233] The new farmsteads are found only in the most immediate parts of Himera's territory, in an area extending about eight kilometers wide by nine kilometers deep. Given their proximity, the farmsteads have been reasonably interpreted as belonging to small and medium property owners. Elite activity in the territory has been postulated in the more labor- and capital-intensive interior, where questions of soil type and vegetation probably put the costs of exploitation beyond the reach of people of lesser means.[234]

At Kamarina, a generation of research in the countryside, particularly within a five-kilometer radius to the east of the city, has established beyond doubt that city and countryside were simultaneously and closely developed (Map 13).[235] The main rural roads are simply continuations of their urban counterparts. Plots of land were oriented in accordance with these and other routes, and their size can accordingly be estimated at about 265 meters by 210 meters (or about 5.8 hectares).[236] On some of these plots of land, farmsteads have been discovered and excavated. The Iurato and Capodicasa farmsteads provide the best and securest fifth-century evidence. Their overall ground plan is never greater than about 25 meters by 25 meters and consists of open central courtyards surrounded on most sides by four to five rooms. Some of the activities that took place in the Capodicasa farmstead can be determined from the finds, namely a wine press and kitchen.[237] The farmsteads are themselves

---

231. Allegro 1999, 296.

232. On the variety of Himera's landscapes, see Belvedere 2001, 710, 712–13.

233. Alliata et al. 1988, 200–05; Allegro 1999, 295; Belvedere 2001, 715–17, 727; Belvedere et al. 2002, 384.

234. Cf. Belvedere 2001, 729–47.

235. For a recent overview, see Di Stefano 2001. According to Mertens (2006, 353), Kamarina is Sicily's clearest example of the relationship between urban and rural planning.

236. Di Stefano 2001, 700–01.

237. On these farmsteads, see Pelagatti 1980–81, 723–29; Di Stefano 2001, 693–94.

aligned with the roads and plots of land, providing further proof that a larger program of planning occurred between city and country. Nuclei of tombs of contemporary date supply indications of residence on the land, which provides the basis for labeling them farmsteads. Pottery production is also attested in Kamarina's countryside, providing evidence of rural production in this part of Sicily in the Classical period and thus reinforcing the observation that this is a phenomenon not just restricted to other parts of Sicily in the Archaic period.

Isolated farmsteads and rural burial are also attested in Syracuse's territory. Five tombs came to light in excavations in contrada Furmica near Akrai (Map 12b). Where datable, they range broadly in date between 450 and 350 BC and consist of four burials in stone-lined pits and one "alla cappucina" in which the burial is covered with tiles arranged in a pup tent–like formation.[238] Later work in the same area uncovered structural and occupational remains of this same century. They provide firm evidence of Classical farmsteads in this part of Syracuse's territory and suggest a mix of small to large landowners, to judge by the range of finds, who were resident on the land to some degree.

This brings to an end our survey of Sicilian Greek settlement and territory during the last two thirds of the fifth century. Some overall summary remarks are in order (Table 3).

The end of the tyrannies at Syracuse and Akragas loosened the political stranglehold these cities had put on Sicily. By extension, Carthage could turn its attention to other matters, particularly extending itself further in its Tunisian hinterland in North Africa.[239] Native Sicilian attempts to establish states were also pursued, with that of Ducetius stopped by Syracuse by 440 BC, whereas that of Egesta, in alliance with Carthage, flourished into the Roman period. Outside Sicily, we have Athens coming to the fore, especially from 460 onwards, whose activities and impact were brought west to southern Italy and Sicily.[240] We have an interconnected world with parallel developments, to which even the evidence of settlement, and not just territory, ought to be related.

This can be seen in the appearance of regular planning principles, farmsteads, and residence on the land, which occurred not only in Sicily but also elsewhere in the Greek and Mediterranean world. Such developments may have more to do with economic factors than with constitutional matters. Although the two are obviously related, and will be discussed further in the following two chapters, there can no doubt that the more intensive cultivation of olive trees and vine, which require more constant attention than grain,

---

238. G. Curcio 1966, 93; A. Curcio 1979, 83–85.

239. Cf. Lancel 1995, 77, 121, 257–302.

240. A point not lost on the ancients: Diod. Sic. 12.30.1 (with Vattuone 1994, 81).

Table 3 A Summary of Some Attested and Hypothesized Urban and Rural Features of Sicilian *Poleis* during the Interlude between Attempts at Political Centralization (ca. 465–405 BC)

Polis	Urban Settlement Size(s) in Hectares	Noteworthy Period(s) of Urban Building	Territory Size in Square Kilometers	Noteworthy Period(s) of Rural Development	Other Noteworthy Urban and Rural Features
Himera	120–130	425 BC	1,000–1,300 (max.)?	ca. 450 BC	strategic rural outposts; expansion of dispersed farmsteads
Kamarina	150?		870–970	ca. 450 BC	planned alignment of urban and rural settlements
Naxos	40?	?	600?	?	?
Zankle/Messana	less than 50–60 or 88?	?	1,000 (max.)	?	?
Katane	50 or 75–100?	?	greater than 830?	?	?
Selinous	110	450–409 BC	1,500?	454–453 BC	development of port?
Gela	200	450–405 BC	1,350?	?	?
Syracuse	100–120	?	4,680–4,800? (incl. Leontinoi)	450–350 BC	dispersed farmsteads and rural burial
Leontinoi	40–53	450 BC	830 (max.)	?	strategic rural outposts (as in Archaic period)
Akragas	200?	450–406 BC	3,100	450–406 BC	strategic rural outposts; emporia; dispersed farmsteads?
Total:	1,060–1,551		15,760–16,280		

will have had something to do residence in farmsteads. While elites may have been the driving forces behind the cultivation of the olive and vine, evidence also exists for the appearance of small and medium properties in this period. This may mean that groups lower down the social ladder gained access to land and resided on it in a way that was new for Greek Sicily.

The building of public monuments, too, could continue after the Archaic monumentalization of the Sicilian Greek city, though in some cases the pace was probably less extensive because of previous efforts. Such was the case at Syracuse and Selinous. Nevertheless, when building did occur, it was not at the hands of tyrants and could be undertaken in equally impressive forms by democratic regimes, as at Akragas in Sicily and Athens in Greece.

4. Between Political Centralization and Independence

The last two generations of the fifth century in Sicily proved to be only a temporary return to city-state culture. The fourth and final phase to be considered lasts from 405 to 320 BC and witnessed the return and expansion of the territorial state phenomenon in Sicily with the recentralization of political power (Map 12c). This began when Carthage's efforts to take over Sicily's Greek portions were brought directly to the doorstep of Syracuse. A certain Dionysius, a soldier who had most recently defended the city in civil strife between democrats and moderate oligarchs, emerged as Syracuse's savior, acquiring power as a tyrant in order to deal with this threat.[241] For thirty-eight years Dionysius ruled Syracuse, during which time his native Syracuse and Carthage sought to gain the upper hand politically and territorially in Sicily. Initially, there were many shifts in these regards, and settlement patterns came to be affected as well, but something of a resolution was reached after Dionysius' defeat at the battle of Cronium in 376 BC. From this point onwards, Carthage was keen to put a proper administrative and defensive apparatus in place in western Sicily to protect its territorial interests, including the garrisoning of several strategic hilltop sites.[242]

On his death in 367 BC, Dionysius was succeeded by his son Dionysius (the two are respectively distinguished as "I" and "II"), who, while less warlike, ruled over the domains established by his father.[243] Dionysius II's reign was mired by disagreement with Dion, Dionysius I's brother-in-law, who had Plato

---

241. Caven 1990; Braccesi 1998, 69–86; Hofer 2000, 190–91, 196–215; Péré-Noguès 2009.

242. See recently Cataldi 2003, 237–38; Helas 2011. For a still valid overview, see Hans 1983.

243. Muccioli 1999.

invited to court to educate Dionysius II on kingship. Plato's visits to Syracuse failed to achieve their intended aims, and soon Dionysius II and Dion fell out, the latter going into exile in Greece. Dion returned in 357 BC with mercenaries and forced Dionysius II into exile, where he remained for a decade. Dion was soon overthrown by his mercenaries out of a fear that his rule was itself nothing more than a tyranny. Anarchy ensued in Syracuse. Dionysius II tried to return to his homeland in 347 BC, but was unsuccessful in reestablishing himself in power. Carthage saw weakness in Syracuse and again threatened invasion, at which point a group of Syracusan exiles appealed for intervention to Corinth, Syracuse's mother city.

Corinth sent one of its citizens, Timoleon, with ten ships and 700 troops to restore order. Timoleon operated in Sicily between 344 and 337 BC, and in these seven years he pushed back the Carthaginian threat and eliminated tyranny altogether from many of the Greek cities by means of force. He also recalled exiles and encouraged upward of 60,000 new settlers to Sicily. As a whole, Timoleon checked Sicily's political and demographic problems and is credited by ancient and modern observers alike with important developments in Sicilian social and economic history.[244] But this was to be a short-lived break from tyranny, for Agathokles of Syracuse set himself up as tyrant in 317 BC and returned to the warfare and centralizing tendencies of Dionysius I. Sicily was plunged into a familiar pattern of behavior, which brought about similar results: the island was once again fought over and divided into Carthaginian and Syracusan spheres. The period before Agathokles' rise to power, therefore, represents a good point to end the present discussion, for it was during the period between Dionysius I and Timoleon that Greek Sicily's social and economic history developed further the previous pattern of political centralization followed by political independence, thus forming a coherent and contained time period that follows naturally upon them.

Some literary sources emphasize extreme volatility of the settlement pattern caused by state organization and state collapse. In Plato's *Seventh Epistle*, Plato and Dion counsel the younger Dionysius (II) to repopulate devastated cities and to undo the amalgamation of the whole of Sicily into Syracuse undertaken by his father.[245] As just seen, Dionysius did not follow their counsel, and that sparked further civic strife until Timoleon restored order.

---

244. As we will see in more detail in this and the following two chapters, this traditional reconstruction of Timoleon has come under criticism since Talbert's (1974) book, which represents its apex of expression, and so needs to be looked at more carefully. While the broad picture seems acceptable, some of the details and methods used to build up the argument are highly questionable. This matter is not noted by Smarczyk 2003, 9–32.

245. Plat. *L* 7.332c–e.

According to Plutarch, because of the ongoing political volatility, Timoleon is said to have encountered an overgrown Syracuse, where wild deer and swine roamed in numbers, and hunters hunted them within the old city limits.[246] While such volatility is theoretically possible, in this case it is not supported by the available archaeological evidence, discussed below. The political and military history of Classical Sicily between Dionysius I and Timoleon can be shown to have occurred against a backdrop of social and economic continuities not emphasized by these literary sources, which are generally anti-tyrant and hagiographic.

Like the Syracusan tyrants before him, Dionysius I focused a considerable amount of his attention on developing the capital city.[247] One of the lessons the Syracusans had learned from the Athenian invasion was that their city's defenses were vulnerable in some respects, and Dionysius I set out to correct these. The old walls of Acradina may have been fixed up,[248] but of itself that would not have been enough. The city's northern flank, known as Epipolae, remained weak, so in 401 BC this area was surrounded with some six kilometers of fortifications enclosing about 1,800 hectares (Figure 19).[249] We know a great deal about this wall and its construction from Diodorus Siculus' long account and recent archaeological investigations led by Mertens.[250] Together they reveal that the limestone was quarried locally and roughly shaped, and that work proceeded by building brief stretches. In all, the fortification had seventeen towers, double gates, garrison posts, and storage areas. Diodorus Siculus says that 60,000 people and 6,000 pairs of oxen completed the work in twenty days, figures which Mertens finds entirely plausible. In any case, there is no doubting that the fortification required an immense amount of human and monetary resources, which Dionysius I's Syracuse was quite capable of amassing (see immediately below for further discussion). Ortygia was another of Dionysius I's focal points at Syracuse. This he made into a fortress for his court and mercenaries. Remains of a gate and towers belonging to this fortress have been found in excavations in Ortygia's northwest corner, but Dionysius I's efforts here are still best known from literary sources, which also speak of a palace.[251] The literary sources talk about other physical developments that are likewise still marginally documented materially, such as

---

246. Plut. *Tim.* 22.3.

247. Evans 2009, 121 with n. 37.

248. Mertens 2006, 431.

249. See in particular Karlsson 1992; Tréziny 1999, 249–55; Mertens 2006, 424–31.

250. Diod. Sic. 14.18.2–5, and for an overview of Mertens' work, see reference in the previous note.

251. For a recent discussion, see Aiosa 2001. Cf. also Mertens 2006, 431–32.

FIGURE 19 View of Epipolae Fortifications at Syracuse.
© Author

the invention of the catapult and the expansion of facilities for a fleet of up to two hundred ships.[252] Other urban developments at Syracuse in this period are difficult to detect because of the well-known problem of later occupation.

These physical developments were in large part stimulated by Dionysius I's military needs. Therefore, as in the case of Gelon, we must combine city development with military expenditure to estimate the kind of financial outlays Dionysius I had at his disposal. For this we can turn again to the study by Tréziny, whose calculations concentrate on the best-known areas—Epipolae fortifications, port installations, and the soldiers and fleet used in the campaign against Punic Motya in 397 BC.[253] Using numbers given in Diodorus Siculus and comparative Greek data for their costs, he arrives at the following costs: 1,700 talents for the Epipolae fortifications, 400 talents for the port installations, and 2,100 talents for the Motya campaign (of which 1,500 talents were for the 60,000 soldiers, 200 talents for their arms, and 400 talents for the fleet of triremes).[254] Costs Dionysius I incurred for other military constructions, siege engines, and his personal bodyguard are harder to gauge, given the patchiness of the sources,

252. Di Vita 2002, 141–42; Mertens 2006, 432.

253. Tréziny 2001, 373–76.

254. Tréziny assumes one drachma per day for the infantry and 200 talents per month for the fleet (Mele 1993, 7, 17 has comparable figures of 20–30 drachmas per month for infantry and one-half talent per month per trireme). Cf. also Trundle 2004, 81, 93, 101.

but these were also big-ticket items.[255] At any rate, if the situation concerning the fleet is anything to go by, the tyrant was clearly able to generate on a recurring basis the necessary funds to meet his military obligations. The fleet of 200 triremes constructed for the siege of Motya was decimated in 396 BC, leaving only 80 ships. In 391 BC, we hear of 120 triremes operating against Rhegion, and in 368 BC this number had risen to 300 triremes. Dionysius I also stockpiled weapons to replenish the spent or lost ones and also because he was unique in providing arms.[256] The expenditures brought on by warfare, therefore, were astronomical. They imply, moreover, that Syracuse and other cities under its control must have become consumer cities to some degree under Dionysius I, supporting a sector of the population, particularly the mercenaries, not directly involved in the production of their own foodstuffs.[257]

The territory under Dionysius I's control extended within and beyond Sicily and experienced notable growth and fluctuations during his reign (Map 12c). In 405, it must have been only somewhat smaller than the 4,680 to 4,800 square kilometers it occupied at the time of the Athenian invasion. In the generation before the battle of Cronium in 376 BC, the territory grew to its largest size ever, reaching a maximum extent of some 21,200 square kilometers.[258] Afterwards, Carthage and Syracuse recognized the Halykos (modern Platani) River as their territorial boundary in Sicily, which gave Dionysius I up to 17,500 square kilometers.[259] Southwestern Italy was important strategically to Syracuse, and unsurprisingly the region became one of Dionysius I's theaters of activity.[260] Here the Greek cities of Locri, Kaulonia, Hipponion, Kroton, and Rhegion came under his orbit in the first quarter of the fourth century, through dynastic marriages in Locri's case and through aggression in the case of the others.[261] The Adriatic was another region where Dionysius I was active, but the settlements implanted there—Issa, Lissos, probably Adria, and possibly Ankon and Pharos—were meant to protect trade, according to Diodorus Siculus.[262] We have a sense of how much dependent territory should

255. Mele 1993, 13; Tréziny 2001, 374, 376.

256. For discussion, see Trundle 2004, 129–30.

257. Morris 2006b, 41–45.

258. Beloch 1889, 20.

259. Beloch 1889, 20; Gulletta 2006, 409–12.

260. See De Sensi Sestito 2002; Sanders 2002; Fischer-Hansen, Nielsen, and Ampolo 2004b, 255.

261. Redfield 2003, 278–90.

262. Diod. Sic. 16.5. Cf. Lombardo, Aversa, and Frisone 2001, 84. For Dionysius I's activities in the Adriatic in general, both within his foundations and beyond, see recently Cambi 2002;

be added to Syracuse's territory from these extra-Sicilian possessions: Kroton, Rhegion, and the Adriatic settlements added about another 1,000 square kilometers.[263] Hipponion and Kaulonia, on the other hand, were given to the loyal ally Locri.[264] However rough and ready all these estimates may be, there is no doubting that Syracuse was the largest territorial state in Europe at the time, at some 18,500 square kilometers (Map 12c; Table 4).

Dionysius I also developed urban settlement outside Syracuse, although on the whole his policies are characterized more by destruction of preexisting urban settlements rather than their creation and renewal. This might explain the general scarceness of evidence, though problems of chronology could also be at stake (see below).[265] Tyndaris on Sicily's north coast is often singled out as the best example of new urbanism under Dionysius I. However, a recent reexamination of the archaeological evidence has convincingly shown that the town plan dates later, to Agathokles, if not later still.[266] Dionysius I's settlement probably consisted of no more than a fortified outpost, whose very name, Tyndaris, has been thought to belong to a wider ideological program too, which Dionysius I used to help hold together his territorial state.[267] The case of Tyndaris underlines the main motivation for Dionysius I's urban decisions, namely that outside Syracuse they centered on strategic concerns and could involve new sites and the revamping of existing ones. The sites selected for attention, moreover, never seem to have become urbanistically flashy, which could well be connected with their limited presence in the archaeological record. This becomes clear at two other sites, Adrano, an entirely new foundation, and Tauromenium, the long-occupied heights above Naxos, both meant to control important areas on either side of Mt. Etna, and so equipped with the urban features needed to do so.[268] An emporium has also been hypothesized around Avola to the south of Syracuse, on the basis of the dozens of coin

Ceka 2002; D'Andria 2002; Gorini 2002; Lombardo 2002; Wilkes and Fischer-Hansen 2004, 323, 325–28, 331–34.

263. Fischer-Hansen, Nielsen, and Ampolo 2004b, 266–70, 290–93; Wilkes and Fischer-Hansen 2004, 323, 325–28, 331–34.

264. See Fischer-Hansen, Nielsen, and Ampolo 2004b, 261–63, 265–66.

265. On Dionysius I's urban policies, see Di Vita 2002, 139. On the scarceness of evidence, see Mertens 2006, 433.

266. For the challenge, see La Torre 2004. For the usual view, see, among others, Di Vita 2002, 142–43; Fischer-Hansen, Nielsen, and Ampolo 2004a, 232–33; Mertens 2006, 433.

267. Musti 2005; Nuss 2010. The ideological strategy also included promoting Sicily as the largest Mediterranean island in terms of land mass (Musti 2004) and ruler cult, for which see the next chapter.

268. For these sites, see recently Fischer-Hansen, Nielsen, and Ampolo 2004a, 183, 231–32.

Table 4 A Summary of Some Attested and Hypothesized Urban and Rural Features of Syracuse's Territorial State between Dionysius I and Timoleon (c. 405–344 BC)

Urban Settlement Size in Hectares	Territory Size in Square Kilometers	Noteworthy Urban Developments	Noteworthy Territorial Developments	Noteworthy Extraterritorial Developments
100–120	18,500	Epipolae fortification; port with arsenal	populations transfers and creation of strategic settlements; development of power ideology; rural intensification	structure and nature of territory acted as a model to others; trade settlements in Adriatic

hoards found outside the inhabited area.[269] Some of Syracuse's mercenaries and other economic traffic may have entered and exited through here, judging from the range of coin types found in these hoards.

The accumulation of territory made a difference to Dionysius I's social and economic base. More people and land not only represented important resources in themselves, they also represented an important source of tax revenue. As will be discussed in Chapter 4, Dionysius I appears to have taxed all agricultural holdings and income; therefore, having more people and land under his control was another way to generate tax revenue for the large expenditures he incurred. It is probably no coincidence that our notions of Sicily's size and centrality in antiquity were forged by Dionysius I, who wanted to emphasize surface area for ideological purposes, as a way to promote his kingdom.[270] Before Dionysius I's reign, the Greeks would have regarded the island of Sardinia as the Mediterranean's largest island on the basis of the length of coastline, which would have constituted an equally valid criterion for ancient Greek maritime culture.[271]

Dionysius I held together his territorial state as best as he could, but his death in 367 BC brought to power his son, Dionysius II, who was less interested in ruling and who was thus susceptible to Dion's intervention. Sicily's history during the time of Dionysius II and Dion is best known to us via the literary sources, which mostly focus, naturally, on the squabbling between these two individuals. The archaeological evidence is thought to be generally limited because of these historical circumstances, which apparently discouraged investments in urban projects.[272] But the problem appears to be deeper and more complicated than that and cannot be separated from historical reconstructions of Timoleon, to whom modern scholars in the postwar generation have overzealously attributed most fourth-century archaeological evidence. The ancient sources claiming that Timoleon revived Sicily from the desert it previously was were slavishly matched to the archaeology.[273] While it

---

269. Cutroni Tusa 1993, 253 n. 43.

270. Musti 2004.

271. Hdt. 1.170, 5.106, 6.2; cf. Rowland 1975; Musti 2004, 36–37; Ridgway 2006b, 250 n. 34. Rowland (1975, 439) was the first to recognize this different method of ancient measurement. Sicily has about 1,039 kilometers of coastline, whereas Sardinia has about 1,385 kilometers of coastline (Maurici 2001, 177–79; Chiai 2002, 145–46; Musti 2004, 36–37; Ridgway 2006b, 250 n. 34 offers slightly different numbers for these coastlines).

272. Di Vita 2002, 139–40; Mertens 2006, 433, 438; Evans 2009, 123.

273. Cf. Di Vita's (2002, 140) admission to this effect. Note in this general regard Lomas' (2006, 111) observation: "Archaeological evidence for the fourth century BC is not plentiful at some sites, and dating it sufficiently accurately to match it with the activities of individual regimes is not always possible—or even, from an archaeological point of view, methodologically advisable." In the last two decades, only Grant (1992, 49–52) has upheld the traditional

is no longer valid to say that "Archaeology has now confirmed the view of the ancient sources that from 405 to c. 340 much of southern Italy was ruined, undeveloped and under-populated,"[274] developments in Sicilian Greek settlement and territory during this time will need a generation of work before a clearer picture comes into focus.

We can begin by not treating Timoleon as an absolute watershed in Sicilian history, since this is both unhelpful and misleading. That Timoleon revived Sicily singlehandedly must today be set within a larger context of developments across Sicily and the Mediterranean in the first half of the fourth century BC that have emerged in the last generation. Within Sicily, the evidence is clearest in the island's western half, where systematic and topographic surveys have revealed an increase in small rural settlements, and presumably of intensification in the hinterland directed by nearby urban settlements, at the very time Carthage and Dionysius I were fighting over these areas.[275] Some of these western Sicilian farmsteads have been excavated, and what is most interesting about them is that similar farmsteads have also been excavated in Sicily's Greek eastern half, in the countryside of Akragas, Gela, and Kamarina (cf. Figure 42).[276] In size and design, all these farmsteads are essentially no different from the fifth-century examples discussed above. In fact, several of these earlier farmsteads continued to be used and renovated in the fourth and third centuries BC, including in the crucial two generations before Timoleon. What was then happening in Sicily's countryside also has parallels with other parts of the Carthaginian central Mediterranean and regions from Greece to Afghanistan.[277] That Sicilian developments started earlier than Timoleon and thus belong to bigger and longer-term phenomena seems undeniable. That admission should at least alert us to the probability that Timoleon either had nothing to do with some of the things he is credited with, or at least that he wisely latched on to these preexisting conditions and made the best of

---

reconstruction of Timoleon, against a growing tide of reassessments of the evidence and arguments, for which see most conveniently De Angelis 2001, 155, 164, 168, 176; 2007, 147, 155.

274. So Talbert 1974, 146 and, more recently, Hornblower 2011, 211, to be contrasted with Bonacasa, Braccesi, and De Miro 2002.

275. Conveniently summarized by van Dommelen 2006, 15–17. The numismatic evidence also supports this viewpoint (see Chapter 4 below).

276. A recent and thorough overview of all these farmsteads can be found in Di Stefano 2002.

277. For the Carthaginian central Mediterranean, see van Dommelen 2006, 8–14, 17–19; van Dommelen and Gómez Bellard 2008, 146, 204, 221, 232–39. For southern Italy, see Lombardo 1996, 215–18. For the eastern Mediterranean and beyond to central Asia, see Alcock 1994 and, more briefly, Shipley 2000, 29–31; Whitley 2001, 385–89.

them—a distinction that is extremely difficult to make, since it entangles us in the classic dilemma of great-man theorizing.[278]

All the same, it should not be denied altogether that Timoleon's arrival in Sicily brought some political, territorial, and urban changes, since he essentially favored a more decentralized and tyrant-free political landscape of independent polities, something which by extension must have put the focus on local settlement and territorial concerns in a way that had not been the case since Dionysius I's accession to power. The landscape must have reverted to the kinds of conditions that had characterized it in earlier times (see Tables 1 and 3). At Syracuse itself, the focus of Timoleon's attention, a moderate democracy was installed. He is said in the literary sources to have built law courts or a gymnasium (we are unsure which), but the archaeology is of no help in confirming or expanding on this, for the routine sorts of reasons.[279] This is unfortunate, since it therefore becomes even more difficult to assess the claims made by modern scholars for numerous other Sicilian cities, particularly Megara Hyblaia, Akragas, Gela, and Kamarina, that Timoleon brought them back to life.[280] In view of the evidence just discussed from the Sicilian countryside, a general fourth-century takeoff doubtless occurred, from which it can only follow that urban developments too belong to this century as a whole. Time will tell, and here the best we can do is to outline some of these fourth-century urban developments.

At Gela, a new city wall was constructed. Its best preserved stretch is at Capo Soprano, on which recent work argues that the wall was initially built entirely of stone and that the mud-brick superstructure, still visible today, was added later in the time of Agathokles (Figure 20).[281] On the acropolis, there are signs of activity in the sacred-domestic areas of earlier times, as well as the building of what have been identified as public baths.[282] Pottery production is also attested in the countryside. At Akragas, the preexisting city wall was restored, and in the settlement what the excavators have identified as a public assembly hall and a council chamber—the supposed hallmarks of the democratic government installed by Timoleon. These buildings took their place in the preexisting town plan, which was respected and used in

---

278. For a refreshing external perspective on this, see Diamond 1997, 420.

279. Talbert 1974, 147; Smarczyk 2003, 70–100; Evans 2009, 26, 126–27.

280. The longest list of candidates may be found in Talbert (1974, 148–60), but in its essentials much of it has been repeated more recently also by Di Vita (1996, 299–304; 2002, 143–46).

281. Milvia Morciano 2001; see also Panvini 1996, 117–20; Smarczyk 2003, 128–34.

282. Di Vita 1996, 300–01; Panvini 1996, 103–14.

FIGURE 20 View of Capo Soprano Fortifications at Gela.
© Author

the fourth century (Map 10).[283] Evidence for oil or wine production has been uncovered in the city. At Megara Hyblaia, abandoned since the early fifth century, life returned and is most prominently indicated by a new city wall, which enclosed a considerably smaller settlement than its Archaic predecessor.[284] Of all the Sicilian cities, the evidence is fullest at Kamarina (Map 13).[285] The preexisting city wall was restored, but the area that it enclosed, some 150 hectares, was now more densely settled than before. In general, the plan consisted of five north-south thoroughfares crossed by numerous east-west avenues, producing rectangular city blocks. The agora was surrounded by this street system, and the temple of Athena that had previously existed was refurbished with pedimental sculpture and an *in antis* plan. There also continues to be evidence for craft products in the city and countryside, as in the first half of the Classical period.

In summary, this second attempt at political centralization in Greek Sicily resulted in an even more simplified landscape, in which two main players, Syracuse and Carthage, dominated and vied for power. This led to their having even greater shares of territories, cities, and resources, both human and natural, than was the case in the early fifth century, during the first episode of political centralization in Sicily. By 340 BC, Syracuse, unlike Carthage, had lost its grip, resulting in a return to a politically fragmented Greek Sicily characteristic of earlier times. This was soon to lead to another showdown between Syracuse and Carthage under Agathokles, in which the independence of the Greek city-states was again undermined.

283. Di Vita 1996, 299–300; 2002, 143; Smarczyk 2003, 134–37. On Timoleon's political architecture, see Isler 2003.

284. Talbert 1974, 149.

285. Di Vita 1996, 301–04; 2002, 144–46; Smarczyk 2003, 125–28; Di Stefano 2006, 160–66.

To sum up this entire chapter, an attempt has been made to sketch out particular aspects of some four centuries of Sicilian Greek settlement and territory as a first way to study social and economic history. Greek Sicily experienced four phases of political, territorial, and urban development during this period, caused by the alteration of two basic types of states, city-states and territorial states, and driven by agents originating both inside and outside the island. Each attempt to centralize and decentralize state power was accompanied by different social and economic developments that added to the preceding base.

While our evidence for questions of politics, settlement, and territory is subject to the usual vagaries of discovery and preservation that can and cannot be rectified, it nevertheless is sufficient, as it currently stands, to allow us to raise a number of socially and economically relevant issues. The earliest town plans reveal the clear demarcation of private, public, and religious spheres on the ground from the very beginning. Patterns of building followed later, particularly during the hundred years spanning the mid-seventh to mid-sixth centuries (650–550 BC), bringing about the first transformation. At the beginning of this period, town plans which had been dominated mainly by open spaces and houses saw the establishment of religious architecture and, in some cases, city walls. At the end of this period, they were joined by more religious architecture, which became even more firmly established and sometimes took on monumental proportions, as well as by city walls and public architecture. Houses also developed further in this century, becoming more elaborate and larger than before. Both *polis* and individual identities would have literally materialized with these architectural developments. The economics that supported these physical developments were centered in both city and country. Various kinds of permanent and seasonal settlements in the countryside provided the backbone for the city. By the end of the Archaic period, it was these communities that were ripe for the taking by ambitious elites within Gela, Syracuse, and Akragas.

The elites who came out on top and set themselves up as tyrants in Classical Sicily managed to generate even greater levels of wealth than any one city-state could have previously done in order to support armies and navies on an unprecedented scale. With this wealth, they invested in the overall infrastructure of their cities, and they drew on the labor of locals and outsiders alike to support their projects. The success of Greek Sicily also continued outside of periods of tyranny, as indicated by similar developments in both city and country across the island in the mid-fifth and mid-fourth centuries (450–350 BC).

When viewed through the lens of social and economic history, the evidence for Sicilian Greek politics, settlement, and territory provides a revealing base from which to set out to investigate a further set of questions.

3

Societies

THE INCLUSION OF politics in the previous chapter inevitably highlighted elites and their actions. A social history of Archaic and Classical Greek Sicily must embed politics and elites in the broader societies to which they belonged. In doing so, we gain a clearer sense of the overall scale and organization of society, the parameters within which elites had to interact in pursuing their political goals. The aim of this chapter is to build on the last one by populating the urban and rural spaces of Archaic and Classical Greek Sicily as fully as we can.

Sicilian Greek Societies: Growth and Development

All societies are large, richly textured entities, whose study can be pursued in numerous different ways.[1] It tends to be easier to outline a theoretical agenda for social history than to achieve it in practice, since the evidence available for study is usually challenging. This is certainly the case with Sicilian Greek societies of the Archaic and Classical periods.

The written sources for Sicilian Greek societies follow particular ebbs and flows. Literary sources are usually available only for notable historical moments—foundations, civil strife, military affairs, and elite achievements being the most common. Surviving inscriptions are often associated with similar moments, as well as with burial and religious rituals. In general, as elsewhere in the study of Greek social history, written sources are less common

---

1. Note the recent balanced discussions of social history in Evans 1997, 161–90; Cartledge 2002; Burke 2005; Gallant 2012. Cf. also Austin and Vidal-Naquet 1977, 20–28; Weber 1978; Duplouy 2006.

the further back in time one goes. But in the case of Greek Sicily there are virtually no written sources relating to key social components, such as family structure, kinship, marriage, inheritance, and even, though to a lesser degree, dependent groups, at any period.[2]

This raises a crucial methodological issue. Given the ancient Greek world's regional nature, should the social history of Sicily be viewed through the lens of written sources that refer to and/or derive from authors living in the Greek homeland? For example, certain classic passages from the works of Thucydides and Plato (see below) recognize that differences existed between Athenian and Syracusan/Sicilian society in terms of elite power, citizenship, and ethnicity, and comment on them in rather pejorative terms.[3] The view taken here is that explanations for these differences must be grounded, first and foremost, in Sicily's cultural dynamics, and that the regional contexts in which Greek societies could develop need accordingly to be appreciated.[4]

Archaeology can help to a certain extent to make up for the deficiencies of the written sources. Inferences regarding, say, family, kinship, and demography can be made from material culture, especially given the relatively abundant data from burials and settlements in Sicily. However, archaeology is of limited use in relation to other areas of social history. To take one instance, despite what ancient written sources say about Sicilian demographic movements and the underlying issues they would have involved regarding, say, quality of life and the spread of disease, archaeology has had little curiosity in developing data that could test and expand on this information.[5] The data from Sicilian physical anthropology

---

2. For dependent populations, see Lombardo 1997a, 19–20, as well as Arafat and Morgan 1994, 130; Nash Briggs 2003, 248.

3. The status of these Thucydidean and Platonic passages as loci classici derives entirely from their use by ancient and modern scholars in discussing Sicilian Greek history, as observed by Mazzarino (1966, 1:223–24), Berger (1992, 4), and Fantasia (2003b, 467; 2006, 496–97). A good part of the force that they have had with modern scholars may be connected with the fact they survive as sources and that they have been handled in a positivistic manner. In other words, scholars have had little other source material to work with, and the material in their possession has been treated at face value. Those were the practices of previous generations of scholarship responsible for making these passages the best known and most authoritative ones of Sicilian Greek social history.

4. So, rightly, Lomas 2000, 174–76. Cf. also Vattuone 2002, 18 for similar comments made about the development of Western Greek historiography and, more generally, Momigliano 1979, 169; Vlassopoulos 2007a, 15–17 on regional historiographies.

5. On the plea for more archaeological work on these topics, see Lomas 2006, 116. A similar plea was made a generation ago: Pelagatti and Vallet 1980, 384–86. The underdevelopment of these topics is also reflected in the lack of attention given to them at major intellectual forums, like the annual Taranto conferences on Magna Graecia: Gras 2007, 19–21; see also Gras 2006–07, 10–11; D'Andria 2007.

have been collected only in fits and starts since the nineteenth century, and, for the most part, the great age of excavations in Greek cemeteries came and went with at best passing attention to skeletal remains.[6] To study Sicilian Greek demography requires generous amounts of guesswork and theoretical models. Therefore, while archaeology is certainly extremely useful in writing Sicilian Greek social history, it cannot fill all the existing gaps in the written sources.

The kind of social history that results from the foregoing limitations of the sources should be obvious. The surviving evidence imposes particular contours on the discussion. There are whole dimensions of Sicilian Greek societies about which we are poorly informed or not informed at all. Emphasis has to be placed not just on those topics that can be fruitfully discussed, but also on those of greatest relevance to understanding Sicilian Greek economic history. This means, therefore, limiting the discussion to demography (including kinship), social classes, status, wealth, constitutions, and citizenship—in other words, the societal structures of economies.[7]

1. From Foundation to Political Centralization

Demography. The excavators of Megara Hyblaia have recently observed that "Archaic society was no simple collection of individuals, but a complex structure of family groups about which we are badly informed."[8] The lack of evidence for the Sicilian Greek family has often led scholars to assume, not always cautiously,[9] that the better-documented situation of the Greek homeland, where the evidence suggests a nuclear family arrangement of four to six individuals, also held for Greek Sicily.[10] However plausible this may be, we should nevertheless be careful of not assuming a single family structure for the entire Archaic period and for all social groups. Theoretical and empirical arguments can be advanced to exclude this, demonstrating that the extended family was represented in the Archaic period.

---

6. Becker 1995–96; 2002. For recent theoretical discussions, see Chamberlain 2006; Sallares 2007; Scheidel 2007.

7. North 1981, 3. For such an approach to Classical antiquity, see Morris and Manning 2005b, 132; Scheidel, Morris, and Saller 2007; Engen 2010, 36. We will assume as read underlying social practices and institutions like marriage ritual, sexual and gender history, and the socialization of children.

8. "La société archaïque n'est pas une simple collection d'individus, mais une construction complexe de groupes familiaux que nous connaissons mal" (Gras, Tréziny, and Broise 2004, 541, cf. also 539–40, 565–66).

9. As in De Angelis 2003a, 41.

10. For a recent discussion, see Hansen 2006b, 59. Cf. also Gallant 1991, 11–33.

"The extended family," theorized Max Weber, "prevails where a large number of hands are required, hence where agriculture is intensive, and also where property is intended to remain concentrated in the interest of social and economic dominance, hence in aristocratic and plutocratic strata."[11] Trigger also noted that different types of family may exist in a single society through the development of civilization.[12] In such cases, differences between individual and collective land ownership can shape what kinds of family types emerge and survive. As discussed in Chapter 1, some natives and Greeks in Sicily had different systems of land ownership at the time of first contact. It will, moreover, be argued in this and the next chapter that the economic and social conditions highlighted by Weber and Trigger can also be found in Archaic Sicily. Thus, the necessary social terrain existed for extended families to plant themselves and thrive.

This is also supported by the empirical evidence for larger kinship groups claiming common descent in Archaic Greek Sicily. The evidence comes from Syracuse, Himera, Naxos, and Selinous, and it points to the existence of gentilicial groups or clans (the usual translation for the ancient Greek term *genos*).

Selinous has the richest evidence, and it is here that we must begin. Patrilineal corporate descent groups venerating a male ancestor, based in the sanctuary of Zeus Meilichios to the west of the city, can reasonably be envisaged.[13] Sacrifices, small altars, stelae (some inscribed), lead curse tablets, and a sacred law were all found here.[14] This material ranges in date between the seventh to fifth centuries BC and must be discussed together, since it forms part of, and helps to illuminate, the same social phenomenon.

The cult of Zeus Meilichios mediated between private and public interests, but it was not a cult whose festival calendar was organized by the city as a whole.[15] Instead, worship was primarily conducted by gentilicial groups, but in time the cult appears to have become significant for the wider community, while still providing social eminence for its founders.[16] A direct line between the seventh and fifth centuries BC may be established through a certain individual named Myskos. This name is found in a late-seventh-century

---

11. Weber 1978, 1:365. Cf. also Weber 2013, 148; Thompson 1973, 16–18.

12. Trigger 2003, 171, 270.

13. Bergquist 1992; Jameson et al. 1993; Robu 2009; Grotta 2010. For the terminology, see Trigger 2003, 168.

14. The sacred law is without context and, while it is logical to situate it in this sanctuary, it could in theory have come from elsewhere at Selinous (Rausch 2000, 40–41).

15. Jameson et al. 1993, 81–103; Antonetti and De Vido 2006b.

16. Rausch 2000, 42, 44; Dubois 2008, 47.

tombstone, and it is reasonable to associate this man with the individual of the same name mentioned in the sacred law of the mid-fifth century,[17] where it is stated that sacrifice is to occur "in the plot, or land, of Myskos."[18] Myskos later became a heroized ancestor and may have played an important role in the *polis'* formation, perhaps as one of the founders that the literary tradition did not pick up on.[19] The sacred law also mentions that sacrifice is also to take place "in [the plot, or land,] of Euthydamos," and a similar role and status can also be envisaged for him. "Myskos and Euthydamos would seem to be the names of men who had established important gentilicial groups"[20] who, to quote from the sacred law, were *homosepyoi* ("sharers of the same breadbasket or grain bin").[21]

Two other inscriptions from the same sanctuary help to support and fill out this reconstruction. The earlier one dates to the first quarter of the sixth century and speaks of "Meilichios of the Kleulidai."[22] This provides more direct evidence for the participation of a larger familial group descended from a male ancestor (here a certain Kleulidas) in this cult. The other inscription is of the mid-fifth century and refers to the "Meilichios of the daughters of Hermias and Eukleas."[23] This provides the only known evidence for the participation of women in the cult of Zeus Meilichios (perhaps in this case their initiation) and for the presence of a *patria*. To all appearances, the *patria* seems comparable to the phratry, or social division of a tribe, in that it likewise comprised a union of familial and pseudo-familial groups. However, the *patria* is distinct because of its gentilicial character.[24] The *patria*, like the phratry, presumably had corporate responsibilities, among which should be included the distribution and

---

17. Jameson et al. 1993, 5, 7, 28–29; Rausch 2000, 41–42. For the tombstone, see Arena 1989: no. 16.

18. Jameson et al. 1993, 15, 28–29 (plot); Robertson 2010, 17 (land). The Greek phrase consists of the particle *en* plus the name in the genitive, with the noun for plot or land implied.

19. So Jameson et al. 1993, 28–29; Dubois 2008, 47.

20. Jameson et al. 1993, 28; cf. also Dubois 2008, 47, 53.

21. For these translations, see respectively Jameson et al. 1993, 20 and Robertson 2010, 46–49. Cf. also Dubois 2008, 42; Grotta 2010, 134; Weber 2013, 148 (writing before the discovery of this inscription).

22. Grotta 2010, 101–03; Robertson 2010, 131.

23. For the most recent discussion, see Grotta 2010, 126–35.

24. Rausch 2000, 45; Ghinatti 2003, 704–05; Robu 2009, 283. The ambiguity of the relationship between the two is clearly seen in Grotta 2010, 128–29; cf. already Weber 2013, 152 for this problem.

administration of land allotments in general (and not just in the case of the sanctuary of Zeus Meilichios) from the time of Selinous' foundation.[25]

The evidence from Syracuse and Himera is intertwined, and they must be considered together. Clans certainly transferred themselves from Greece to Sicily when Corinth founded Syracuse, and then within Sicily from Syracuse to Himera during the latter's foundation. The Corinthian Arkhias, who directed Syracuse's foundation, was a member of the Bacchiads. They ruled as a group of two hundred and were known, among other things, for their strict endogamy.[26] This practice may have traveled westward, if the social inclusiveness at later Syracuse (see below) is anything to go by. At Himera, the founding party in the mid-seventh century also included an exiled clan from Syracuse, the so-called Myletidai.[27] This clan seems to have existed alongside other ones at Himera, since a union of familial groups is referred to in an inscription of the early fifth century.[28] Its duties there included distributing land and overseeing land ownership. Although evidence is lacking, we must imagine that Himera's clans also had associated religious activities, as seen at Selinous.[29]

Archaeological evidence also suggests broader kinship groups. Before the publication of Selinous' sacred law, Birgitta Bergquist had already defined the ritual practices at the sanctuary of Zeus Meilichios as gentilicial.[30] She detected the same practices at Naxos in Sicily and at Metapontion in southern Italy in contexts of the late seventh/early sixth century. The practices in question consisted of inscribed or uninscribed stelae crowning sacrificial deposits made up of the remains of ritual meals. The deposit from Naxos, found in what appears to be a sanctuary of Aphrodite, contains one of the earliest inscriptions from Greek Sicily, which makes this religious ritual stand out even further.[31]

---

25. Robu 2009, 288–89 makes the case.

26. Hdt. 5.92.1, in connection with the story concerning the lame Labda.

27. The clan's name may derive from Mylai in Zankle's territory, where presumably the exiles spent some time before going on to help found Himera (Cordano 1984b, 136–37), but that is not entirely certain (Arena 1994, 43 n. 1).

28. Brugnone 1997.

29. More evidence for Sicilian Greek clans dates to the third historical phase delineated in this book: the last two-thirds of the fifth century BC, in the interlude between the tyrants of Syracuse dominating Sicily. The evidence comes again from Selinous and Himera, as well as from Naxos, Kamarina, and Akragas. This evidence will not be pulled out of this historical context any more than it has been here, but it needs to be noted and the possibility raised that clans existed at other Sicilian Greek cities in the Archaic period.

30. Bergquist 1992; Morgan 1999, 129.

31. Cordano 1984a, 286. For the general picture of literacy, see W.V. Harris 1996.

All the finds discussed so far come from sanctuaries, but it seems likely that gentilicial cults also spread their tentacles into residential neighborhoods. Circular platforms discovered at Megara Hyblaia and Selinous have been interpreted as ritual areas bringing together several households for common worship.[32] A small temple at Megara Hyblaia mentioned in the previous chapter is also located in a residential neighborhood and may be another place where common worshippers came together. While it is likely that kindred households lived close to one another in the way required by such interpretations, it is less likely that the city wards postulated behind the different orientations of the town plans of Naxos and Megara Hyblaia discussed in the previous chapter, and again later in the present one, were self-contained kinship units.[33] Housing provides no convincing evidence of any materially discernible web of kinship relations across wider swathes of space.[34] Nor can any support be derived from the surviving written evidence for overarching kinships groups like the phratry and tribe (see immediately below for discussion).

Spatially segregated populations are more securely attested in cemeteries located just outside the living area proper. Perhaps it was easier to concentrate kin in death than in life. The evidence suggests that we are dealing not with large corporate descent groups,[35] but with cemeteries within a single city that are different from one another in their rituals.[36] Each cemetery had burial rituals with their own meaning and symbolism; the lack of ritual coherence across cemeteries in a single city marks them out as distinctive. This suggests some kind of kindred association in death as presumably in life.[37] Within each cemetery, the spatial configuration of the burials is not in itself unique, and belongs to a bigger pattern found in the early Greek world: burials are grouped together—in either groups belonging to individual households or generational groups of households.[38] They are not organized as large corporate descent groups per se, even though the overall effect of the cemetery itself may have suggested something of the sort.[39]

---

32. Gras, Tréziny, and Broise 2004, 541–44; Mertens 2010, 78–79; cf. also Robu 2009, 289.

33. Gras, Tréziny, and Broise 2004, 564–66. Cf. Trigger 2003, 171.

34. Varto 2009, 292–93.

35. Varto 2009; 2012; Gras 2011, 568.

36. Jackman 2005; cf. also Morris 2009b, 159–60.

37. Cf. recently Gras 2011, 568, who wondered whether the connection between life and death at Megara Hyblaia included the same people who attended the symposium together.

38. Varto 2009, 212; 2012, 214–15.

39. Cf. already Cébeillac-Gervasoni 1975, 32 on this problem.

The foregoing evidence for larger kinship groups should not be taken to imply extended families. We can define extended families as made up of the immediate family and near relatives living within the same household or whose members, if not living together, maintain close links in urban and even rural settings. The evidence does seem to support that idea of the spatial delineation of such larger familial groups in the cemeteries and sanctuaries of Archaic Sicily. By extension, the Sicilian Greek cities discussed above may have started their lives as a confraternity of clans.[40] These extended families were no doubt formed to support and promote their economic dominance through time and space. The countryside must also surely have been home to extended families, some as branches of their urban counterparts and some as legacies of the precontact situation which were incorporated into the territorial jurisdiction of the Sicilian Greek city. The possible evidence for this dates to the fifth century and is discussed in the appropriate section below. Yet it should not be seriously doubted that rural extended families would have first emerged in the Archaic period.

To sum up, both nuclear and extended families should be thought to have existed simultaneously in Greek Sicily, together acting as the basic building blocks in forming society.

Above their family structures Greeks usually had larger social groups, the phratry and tribe (the usual translation for the Greek term *phyle*). Quite apart from the difficulty encountered above in distinguishing between the *patria* and phratry at Selinous, the existence of this intermediate social grouping of several households claiming common descent is attested only later in the mid-fifth century BC in Sicily.[41] The evidence collected earlier, though, leaves little doubt of its presence more widely in Archaic Sicily. The same problem of evidence holds for the tribe. At Megara Hyblaia, where the evidence is strongest, the excavators have simply assumed that the first settlers, being of Dorian origin, came to Sicily in their three tribes and divided up the city's space among themselves.[42] Therefore, the Archaic phratry and tribe remain to be better documented, and only future discoveries hold the possibility of revealing how their dynamics played into the period's social history.

This gap can be offset somewhat for the time being by investigating the overall size of Archaic Greek Sicily's population. The best approach currently

---

40. For this notion, see Weber 1978, 2:1241–43. Cf. also Bintliff 2012, 242, and Gras and Tréziny 2012, 1143, the latter wondering whether the foundation of Selinous occurred because the clan could no longer occupy Megara Hyblaia's space coherently due to an absence of lots available close to the head of house of the first generation.

41. Cordano 1992a; Ghinatti 2000.

42. Gras, Tréziny, and Broise 2004, 565.

available is to use the degree of urbanization, as recently argued by Mogens Hansen, since no ancient written source preserves any information for the Archaic period.[43] As seen in the previous chapter, while it is possible to hypothesize the order of magnitude of Sicilian Greek territories, rural settlement within them still remains little and unsystematically addressed. Urban centers, by contrast, are usually much better known, and for that reason they offer the best way forward.[44] Hansen uses the following numerical variables to calculate population size: for cities, a population density of 150–200 people per hectare is envisioned; for territories between 200 and 500 square kilometers in size, population is divided equally between town and country; and for territories under 200 square kilometers or greater than 500 square kilometers in size, two-thirds of the population is placed in the countryside and one-third in the town.[45]

These variables help us advance rough and ready approximations of population size for Sicily's Archaic *poleis* (Table 5). Once calculated, they produce a grand total of 123,150–177,800 people living on a surface area of some 11,680–11,980 square kilometers, which works out to about 11–15 people per square kilometer.[46] As argued in Chapter 1, at the time of contact population density in native Sicily may have been about 3 people per square kilometer. However hypothetical these population estimates may be, it should not doubted that, with the arrival of Greeks in Sicily, landscapes became more densely populated, perhaps as much as four to five times greater than were initially encountered in settling the island. This resulted in the permanent transformation of Sicily's demographic history.

Even in the more secure cases where the population estimates are fairly firmly based, they reveal little in the way of the development of populations over time. The only site for which we can discern such information is Megara Hyblaia. The evidence unequivocally indicates that population grew steadily throughout the seventh century. From an estimated population size of 225–450 people at the end of the eighth century, the community more or less doubled in size every fifty years, reaching a high of some 1,375 to 2,075 people by century's end—or, put another way, a tenfold growth in one century.[47]

---

43. Hansen 2006b, 15. This approach is advocated in the context of arguing that previous methods of reconstructing ancient population are minimalistic. Cf. also Hansen 2008b.

44. The information from Sicilian Greek cemeteries is not sufficient to allow population estimates to be derived from them.

45. For the city densities, see Hansen 2006a, 75, and for the proportions of town-country population, see Hansen 2006b, 23–24.

46. In some cases (such as Zankle, Katane, and Akragas), our knowledge of urban settlement size is quite coarse, and thus the population estimates based on them are likely to be much too high.

47. See De Angelis 2003a, 49–52, 61–62. The excavators of Megara Hyblaia believe that my estimates are too low and favor instead Orsi's earlier estimates of 8,000 to 10,000 inhabitants at the city's height in the sixth century BC (Gras, Tréziny, and Broise 2004, 569–71). Hansen's

Table 5 A Summary of Population Estimates for Archaic Sicilian *Poleis.**

Polis	Urban Settlement Size in Ha.	People per Ha. Density for Urban Settlement Size	Estimated Total Population for *Polis*	Territory Size in Square Km for *Polis*	Urban/Rural Population Distribution
Zankle	50–88	150–200	7,500–17,600	1,000	2,498–5,861/ 5,002–11,739
Naxos	(10 to) 40	150–200	(1,500–2,000 to) 6,000–8,000	600	1,998–2,664/ 4,002–5,336
Leontinoi	40–60	150–200	6,000–12,000	830	1,998–3,996/ 4,002–8,004
Katane	50–100	150–200	7,500–20,000	830	2,498–6,660/ 5,002–13,340
Syracuse	50–100	150–200	7,500–20,000	1,670	2,498–6,660/ 5,002–13,340
Megara Hyblaia	61	150–200	9,150–12,200	400	3,047–4,063/ 6,103–8,137
Gela	200	150–200	15,000–20,000	1,350	4,995–6,660/ 10,005–13,340
Himera	120–130	150–200	18,000–26,000	1,000–1,300	5,994–8,658/ 12,006–17,342
Selinous	110	150–200	16,500–22,000	1,500	5,495–7,326/ 11,005–14,674
Akragas	200?	150–200	30,000–40,000	2,500	9,990–13,320/ 20,010–26,680
Total:			123,150–177,800		41,011–65,868/ 77,137–131,932

*For urban/ rural population distributions; note that fractional figures are rounded up and that the total is thus slightly higher than the total for estimated total population for the polis.

Considerable evidence exists for the construction of new houses in the seventh century. Some of them, as well as some eighth-century houses, were later renovated (Figure 13).[48] Underlying this development of new and renovated houses is not only the population growth just discussed but also changes in the standard of living. In only two cases do we have complete house plans to quantify these changes: the surface areas of house 14,17 + 23,11 grew from 19.35 square meters in the late eighth century to 34.35 square meters in the half century spanning 700–650 BC, and house 40,2a grew from 10.1 square meters in the quarter century spanning 700–675 BC to 52.98 square meters in that spanning 650–625 BC.[49] In the cases of renovated houses with fragmentary plans, we can at least note that they witnessed changes in their surface area of between at least seven and eighteen square meters.[50] Megara Hyblaia supplies valuable insights into a presumably much larger pattern of steady population growth throughout the seventh century—the first full century of a Sicilian Greek *polis*; from modest beginnings, it became home to a population of several thousand.

We know very little directly of the structure and health of Sicilian Greek populations in general, as discussed above, but the problem is most acute for the Archaic period, when written sources are less frequent. What direct evidence from physical anthropology exists, from Kamarina and in its native hinterland, reveals nothing truly exceptional for a preindustrial population.[51] The same holds for the demographic observations made by Ettore Gabrici on the high frequency of child burials in Himera's Pestavecchia cemetery.[52] He associated the numerous child deaths with malaria, which was still prevalent in his day in the Buonfornello plain. Not surprisingly, Gabrici did not submit the bone material he uncovered to physical anthropology.[53] More recent work has confirmed and refined his observation about the frequency of children's

---

more recent approach of estimating population size using the degree of urbanization would be more in line with these higher numbers. Nevertheless, my point holds: population grew steadily over time. The relative proportions over time can simply be multiplied by two or three to achieve higher absolute population estimates.

48. Cf. De Angelis 2003a, 20–29.

49. Compare the tables in De Angelis 2003a, 21, 23–24.

50. These are houses 47,11, 58,17, 22,6, 21,2, 58,10 + 49,9, and 58,17c. See tables in De Angelis 2003a, 20–29.

51. See Pelagatti 1976; Doro Garetto and Masali 1976; 1976–77; Pelagatti and Vallet 1980, 381–82; Facchini and Brasili Gualandi 1977–79; 1980; cf. G. Kron 2005.

52. Gabrici 1936–37, 35.

53. Even if he had chosen to do so, he would have found that soil conditions are adverse to the preservation of human bone, as demonstrated by more recent work in that cemetery (Fabbri, Schettino, and Vassallo 2006, 614).

burials, noting that the *enchytrismos* burials reserved for children made up about 50 percent of all inhumations.[54] But these numbers are what we would expect for a preindustrial population and represent nothing exceptional. High infant mortality for children on its own must be regarded as the primary cause for these deaths, aggravated no doubt by interaction with various diseases. Malaria is likely to have been one of these diseases, but it remains undocumented in the region in antiquity.[55] The fact that native Sicilian communities were generally living away from the coasts has also been invoked as indirect support for the existence of marshy conditions, for which evidence is now available from Gela, and perhaps by extension of malaria.[56] We can only hope for future work which has demography in its purview. We have every reason to be optimistic, given that research agendas have changed in recent years, as seen in the case of the recent excavations in the cemeteries of Himera.

The absence of direct demographic data can be counterbalanced somewhat by calling upon model life tables. In an earlier study, I suggested that the Princeton Model West, Males, mortality level 4, with an average life expectancy at birth of 25.26 years and an annual growth rate of 0.5 percent might be employed for sake of comparison with Athenian demography, where it had been used.[57] On this model, population is structured as follows: 46 percent of the population is under the age of nineteen, and 5 percent of the population above the age of sixty. The remaining 49 percent of the population was, therefore, between the ages of twenty and fifty-nine. About 10 percent of this group was aged 20–24, with each successive five-year age-group being about 1 percent smaller than its predecessor. The sex ratio favors male births slightly over those of females (105 to every 100); however, we have no way of knowing whether infanticide or other social practices were at play in Greek Sicily to alter this. For population to regenerate itself, this model also requires a woman to have had six births during her lifetime, half the offspring of which would not survive beyond their fifth birthday.

These and other possible descriptive statistics that could be derived from this demographic model represent at best guesswork for understanding the dynamics of Sicilian Greek demography. Nevertheless, they provide a possible indication of the demographic development of Greek Sicily in the absence of consolidated archaeological attention.

---

54. Fabbri, Schettino, and Vassallo 2006, 613, cf. also 618.

55. Sallares (2002) has made the general argument. On the interaction of malaria with other diseases, see Sallares 2002, 122–40.

56. De Angelis 2010, 39–40.

57. De Angelis 2003a, 46–47.

Social Classes, Status, and Wealth. Despite all the uncertainties that the study of Sicilian Greek demography contains, it is not in doubt that the various cities were of sufficient size for social differences to take root among the population at all stages of their Archaic development. This is supported by other contemporary evidence for social classes, status, and wealth.

As discussed in Chapter 1, when Greeks began settling Sicily in the eighth century BC, the societies from which they had come were being transformed, thanks to a doubling of population in Greece. Our best insights into this social transformation derive from the poems of Homer and Hesiod, which represent worlds grounded in enough reality to be intelligible to their audiences.[58] Anthropologically speaking, the term *basileus* (pl. *basileis*) found in these poems is most accurately translated as "big man" or "chief," not as "king."[59] *Basileis* won and lost their power over the masses (*demos*) through their charisma, prowess, and general achievements. The transition to statehood (*polis*) which followed resulted in a more stable power base for these individuals, unleashing social stratification to even greater heights. State formation also generally brought together different social groups into a single community, resulting in a sharing of power by the *basileis*.[60] It is wrong, as argued recently by Alain Duplouy, to describe the product of this social stratification as "aristocrats" and "nobles," since these terms conjure up images of the ancien régime inapplicable to ancient Greece.[61] Instead, the neutral term elite is to be preferred, and elitism must be viewed as requiring ongoing social recognition through such strategies as genealogy, marriage, death ritual, exotica, dedication, and originality. Elites, however formed, were always few in number, making up on one conservative estimate about 10 percent of the total population.[62] Thus we must imagine a few handfuls of powerful families (an idea supported in Sicily, as already seen above) dominating their societies and tilting affairs in their favor, as well as gradually but steadily accumulating power and control.

It is from this world that Sicilian Greek societies emerged and developed in the eighth century BC. Recent scholarship on the Homeric poems, especially the *Odyssey*, has argued that they were used to mediate and inform the cultural encounters and the building of civil society then happening in Italy.[63] Thus the

---

58. For recent discussions, see Hall 2007a, 25–27; Osborne 2009, 131–52.

59. Hall 2007a, 122–23; Mitchell 2013, 24–30.

60. Hall 2007a, 127–28.

61. Duplouy 2006, 11–35.

62. Hall 2007a, 128.

63. Malkin 1998; Dougherty 2001; McInerney 2010, 92–93.

names of the founders recorded in the ancient tradition should be regarded as elites. Their strategic capacities can be inferred by the sites they selected for settlement, and the duties that they performed afterward can be inferred from the opening verses of Book VI of the *Odyssey*, where the founder allocates land to his fellow settlers and their gods, as well as securing the settlement's safety by building a city wall.[64] Homeric *basileis* were also chief priests for the religious cults, and in general they were at the forefront of laying the groundwork for the newly established city, for which, as we have already seen, there is abundant archaeological evidence.

It is normally thought that founders laid down power on their death. Death marked both the end of the foundation period and the beginning of a cult venerating the founder.[65] No attempts are believed to have been made to establish royal lines. That view is ultimately based on a particular negative interpretation of the Syracusan *basileus* Pollis, who is mentioned in sources referring to a period before the mid-seventh century and who is said to be of Argive origin. Modern opinions concerning Pollis are more mixed, however. While one scholarly camp maintains that he is a fiction,[66] another scholarly camp believes in his authenticity, and so tries to explain him historically.[67] These positions occupy opposite ends of the spectrum. Even if Pollis' existence proves to be dubious, we are not compelled to accept Robert Drews' overall conclusion, that "none of the states of Western Greece was ruled by a monarch in the eighth century."[68]

More recent work has avoided the evolutionary schemes inherent in such a conclusion, arguing instead that the *basileus* emerged as a result of the overseas foundations and the dynamic sociopolitical world which begat them.[69] The *basileus* should thus be viewed as belonging to a larger phenomenon of singular individuals who, as founders, created a political system that centered power in their

---

64. Asheri 1966, 5. Osborne (2004b, 30–31) is right to observe that since the new community being founded in this passage represents a relocation of the entire previous community, it makes more sense to connect the passage with the relocation of entire communities such as Lefkandi and Zagora that were then occurring in Greece. He nevertheless thinks that similar duties were being undertaken by founders in southern Italy and Sicily.

65. Malkin 1987.

66. For example, see Dunbabin (1948, 94); Drews (1983, 38–40); Sartori (1997, 51), who is the least committed of these scholars.

67. For example, see Van Compernolle 1966; Manganaro 1979, 8 (who for no good reason puts Pollis in the late sixth century); Asheri 1980a, 121; Frolov 1995, 81–82; Coldstream 2003, 234; Gras, Tréziny, and Broise 2004. 549.

68. Drews 1983, 39.

69. Marcaccini 1999.

hands, or at least in those of their entourages.[70] In this system, moreover, power was transmitted to their descendants, and Pollis could be seen as simply a later successor. Whether or not we believe in Pollis' existence, there most certainly were attempts by individuals at Syracuse either to obtain power or to mediate later power struggles in a way that must have been reminiscent of the founders.[71] This would have been particularly true for those individuals connected with the founding families who either thought that they had, or were regarded by others as having, a special place in the overall functioning of their communities.

Founders and elites more generally could certainly have pretensions to status differences, whether or not there were any "royal lines." Association with mythological genealogies was one way to do so. Arkhias, founder of Syracuse, is described in the sources as connected with the elite Bacchiad clan at Corinth and a descendent of the heroic figure of Herakles and is said to have consulted the Delphic oracle.[72] As Lepore has observed, Arkhias' connection with this clan and hero would betoken a differentiated oligarchy in existence from Syracuse's foundation.[73] Other founders and elites also associated themselves with Herakles. Pentathlos, leader of Rhodian and Cnidian settlers attempting to settle in western Sicily between 580 and 576 BC, encountered and became entangled in a war between Egesta and Selinous, presumably over the Selinous' territorial expansion. This expansion may have already extended by this point as far as the environs of Poggioreale, where an inscription of this period records the existence of a cult of Herakles.[74] Another would-be founder in Sicily, the Spartan Dorieus, is also recorded as descended from Herakles. In general, cults of Herakles in Sicily are usually found at the margins, both within cities and between cities, a fitting connection with founders, who also often found themselves at the margins between cultures. Within a broadly similar logic

---

70. Marcaccini 1999, 411, 420. Frolov (1995, 82), therefore, may not be correct in saying that Arkhias or his descendants founded no royal line.

71. For Pollis as mediator, as in particular head of the prytany, see Frolov 1995, 81–82; Sartori 1997, 53.

72. Modern scholars usually view the oracle as invented, a commonly encountered folkloristic context created to explain Arkhias' departure (Salmon 1984, 65; Dougherty 1993b). By contrast, Frolov (1995, 75) finds the consultation entirely credible. For the otherwise general reliability of the ancient tradition on Arkhias, see Mele 2007, 46–51.

73. Lepore 1970, 50–53. This is something which in turn is presupposed by certain seventh-century developments discussed below.

74. The fullest source for Pentathlos is Diod. Sic. 5.9.2–3. Pentathlos and his group sided with Selinous. Pentathlos was killed in battle, and Rhodian and Cnidian settlers withdrew to the Aeolian Islands, where they successfully founded Lipari. For Herakles in western Sicily, see De Angelis 2003a, 153–54; Antonetti and De Vido 2006a, 143–48; De Angelis and Garstad 2006, 222; Malkin 2011, 121–29, 134.

one could situate the pirates who are memorialized as having founded Zankle. Such self-representation creates a genealogy that fits well for a trading city which occupied a highly strategic node in the web of maritime traffic.

Another way to stand out socially was through labels related to land and wealth more generally. These labels parallel practices found in other parts of the Greek world and likewise provide insights into the character and success of Sicily's elite. Thus, in sources referring to the Archaic period, we hear of the *gamoroi* (or "land-sharers") of Syracuse, the *pakheis* (or "thick ones") of Megara Hyblaia, the *hippeis* (or "cavalrymen") of Leontinoi, and the *periporphyra ekhein himatia* (or "wearers of purple") of Akragas.[75] The surviving literary sources contain other labels which denote/connote status and which refer to events of the fifth and fourth centuries BC.[76] Some of these labels, particularly *aristoi* and *agathoi* ("best" and "good"), were used to mark status elsewhere in the Greek world in the Archaic period. But one cannot simply assume that these and all the other labels just enumerated existed in Archaic Greek Sicily without first addressing a fundamental issue.

Finley argued that social classes only emerged in Greek Sicily in the second half of the sixth century, when elites became quite evident in wealthy burials.[77] On such a view, the status labels and mythological genealogies just discussed are to be regarded as inventions or exaggerated self-fashioning projected back to earlier times. Is it anachronistic, therefore, to talk of an elite social class in Sicily before the mid-sixth century? Did these later elites also consciously model their behavior on a Homeric lifestyle, since they had no previous history and identity and needed to be taken seriously by elites in the Greek homeland?[78] The answers to these questions are resoundingly negative. Inequality can be inferred from the start of Greek Sicily's history when we take a closer look at the archaeological evidence and combine it with the written evidence just discussed.

For the eighth century, let us begin with some basic observations. As argued in Chapter 1, the first settlers in Sicily had pretty much unfettered freedom to establish their societies, because coastal areas were generally thinly populated and needed land clearance. This afforded the settlers an unprecedented situation in which they could establish themselves however they thought fit.

---

75. For full ancient references and their discussion, see Cordano 1986a, 126–27; Nenci 1989; Collin Bouffier 1999a, 364–65.

76. Collin Bouffier 2010a, 293–94.

77. Finley 1979, 38, drawing on comments in Cébeillac-Gervasoni 1975, 33. Similar comments are also found in Collin Bouffier 1999a, 363–64. On the importance of class in the Archaic Greek world, see Redfield 2003, 154–56 and Rose 2012.

78. Collin Bouffier 1999a, 364–72. It is undeniable that Sicilian Greek elites could have Homeric overtones, but the rest of this thesis does not need to be accepted.

Thus it comes as no surprise, as shown in Chapter 2, that the settlers carefully separated, differentiated, and individualized their space from the beginning. Private and public spheres and their associated activities were demarcated, and the physical basis for society was laid. We can also be fairly certain that eighth-century communities must have contained several hundred people, if not more, as seen earlier in this chapter. So much should be clear and fairly indisputable. The challenges arise, however, in attempting to add details to this general picture, because the eighth century is the least documented and understood part of the entire Archaic period in Sicily.[79]

The situation at Megara Hyblaia, our best-known site, typifies these hurdles well: the evidence is insufficient in the case of burials, ambiguous in the case of house plots, and uniform in the case of house size.[80] Often, the uniformity and silence of the evidence has led scholars to conclude that an egalitarian community existed, but this approach is not sensitive enough to the nature of the evidence. The egalitarian reading of the similarly sized houses seems unfounded.[81] Three large subterranean silos were uncovered in the courtyards of three houses, which suggests not only the storage of large amounts of foodstuffs (most likely grain) but also status attached to their exchange.[82] In the next generation, these houses were the largest households in the material record of Megara Hyblaia; their elite status is not in doubt then and can only have logically begun to take root in the eighth century. Some

---

79. Collin Bouffier 1999a, 363–64, whose own statements regarding the evidence stand in need of revision.

80. Applying to both the burial and settlement data is the question of whether evidence of status and wealth can be extrapolated from their size, character, and associated goods (see in general Wason 1994). The answer will naturally depend on context. In general, the size and development of structures, and of the goods recovered within them, are indications of changes over time in the standards of living (Morris 2007); besides housing, von Reden (2007, 396–97) also includes clothing and heating, but, unfortunately, we know little about these indicators in Sicily. She also makes the general important point that burial changes could instead be due to changes in ritual and not standards of living. Moreover, such changes, if shown to be related to sociopolitical factors, can also reflect differences in status and wealth. The same holds for the burial data, which are not as homogeneous as those of the Aegean (see the still valuable comments of Pelagatti and Vallet 1980, 373–74; for a nuanced approach to Sicilian burial, see Marconi 2004, 29). For comparisons with the Aegean, see Jackman 2005. Nevertheless, the second half of the sixth century does seem to have been a time across the Greek world of greater investments in burial by the elite (Morris 1992b, 145–46; 1998, 31–32, 35–36, 75–79; Collin Bouffier 1999a, 364–65).

81. Shipley 2005, 347.

82. De Angelis 2002; 2003a, 51. Recent research has confirmed the importance of these silos, suggesting that they may belong to the period before the laying out of the settlement itself (Tréziny 2007, 184).

cremation tombs may have also been found near a major thoroughfare in the area of the Arenella depression, where the city's two parts seem to come together.[83] A similar, better-documented group of tombs has also been discovered in the middle of an urban area at Selinous, which Megara Hyblaia jointly established. The sole difference between these two related phenomena is that Megara Hyblaia's tombs appear to have been deposited later than the laying out of the town plan.

Still firmer evidence for eighth-century hierarchy comes from Naxos and Syracuse. At Naxos, as discussed in the previous chapter, houses and possibly plots of different sizes are attested from the eighth century. At Syracuse, we have both written and archaeological evidence. Archilochus recounts the story of Aithiops, who bartered his plot of land for a honey cake on his journey to Syracuse.[84] It would follow that Aithiops had been promised a plot of land before embarking ship,[85] but whether equality had been the guiding principle in distributing land remains an open matter.[86] In any case, there is reason to believe that land at Syracuse may have been alienable and society consequently susceptible to rapid change.[87] The most plausible cultural context for this story is Archilochus' satirizing of historical figures from the recent past and, in Aithiops' case, his greed and gluttony.[88] Therefore, such a story, which would have been performed at a public festival, served as a form of social control to keep the ambitions of some settlers in check. At Syracuse, this appears to have been a problem from the start, as implied by both this story and the burial data. At least two spatially distinct burying populations can be recognized in the Fusco cemetery, each practicing different symbolic systems and rituals.[89] Wealthy burials can also be identified in this cemetery, standing out for the large number of their metal objects (primarily jewelry), pottery, exotica, and receptacles (especially the sarcophagi).[90] These burials

---

83. Gras, Tréziny, and Broise 2004, 557–58, where the evidence consists of an old excavation photograph whose evidentiary significance is now better understood.

84. Archil. fr. 293W, quoted by Athen. 167d. How Archilochus came to acquire this story remains obscure: see Dougherty 1994, 41 n. 35.

85. Dunbabin 1948, 15; Asheri 1966, 19 n. 1; Salmon 1984, 63; Frolov 1995, 77.

86. Luraghi 1996.

87. Roebuck 1980, 1925; Frolov 1995, 80. For a contrary view, see Jackman 2005, 188.

88. Dougherty 1994, 41. Cf. also more generally Zurbach 2008, 92.

89. Jackman 2005, 27.

90. Jackman 2005, 36–38. Collin Bouffier (1999a, 370–71) also referred to this evidence and thought it was too minimal to document the existence of social hierarchy. The evidence in favor of the latter has grown steadily in recent years, as seen in this chapter.

are not restricted to a particular form, and this variety also suggests underlying competition.

The evidence becomes fuller and clearer for the seventh century, putting paid definitively to Finley's idea that no social classes existed until the mid-sixth century. As discussed in the previous chapter, the seventh century witnessed the development of Greek Sicily's physical spaces. New elements, particularly public architecture and city walls, were added, and previous elements, particularly houses, were filled out. This growth and development in physical space was an outward manifestation of society's own growth and development, and they deserve attention here alongside other relevant evidence.

Domestic architecture provides some indications of social differences.[91] At Naxos the appearance of a grand *pastas* house of three rooms and courtyard in the mid-seventh century BC adds another dimension to the city's architectural development. This house type was unique at Naxos on present evidence. At Megara Hyblaia only one *pastas* house is known, even after more extensive excavations have been undertaken, which reinforces the idea of uniqueness. The house faced out onto the agora and was located next to a building identified as the founder's shrine.[92] The connection is more than simply chance, and an interrelationship involving social class, status, and wealth must be envisaged.[93] Other seventh-century houses discussed above in connection with Megara Hyblaia's demographic growth also reveal differences in size and thus of variations in wealth when compared to others within the city. A similar cause and effect relationship between domestic architecture and religion also seems to hold for Gela during the second half of the seventh century, when the initial division of the urban space into blocks and house plots occurred.[94] The existence of possible houses near the sanctuaries on the acropolis might suggest an elite presence in close association with these religious cults and their running.[95] Throughout Greek Sicily, as seen in the previous chapter, the second half of the seventh century witnessed the architectural development of cities. While domestic and religious architectures developed on their own accord, the two could be connected and intertwined: both the community and

---

91. On the lack of such evidence from Greece, see Bintliff 2012, 262.

92. According to recent thinking, the shrine may have started its life as a house and was later converted into a shrine: Gras and Tréziny 2012, 1140–41.

93. De Angelis 2003a, 55.

94. Mertens 2006, 79; cf. Redfield 2003, 399–401 on religion and political authority in the Greek world.

95. For these possible houses, see De Miro 1996, 22; Mertens 2006, 79. For the elite monopolization of religion offices in the West, see Jackman 2005, 147–49.

individuals within it became more successful, and the process of forging collective and personal identities was afoot.

Cemeteries continued to be an arena for the display and establishment of class, status, and wealth. At Syracuse, greater consumption across society in general can be documented, as well as the entrenchment of previously existing social differences.[96] Most of the wealth was deposited in child burials, which may have been intended to emphasize the status of these children, which came with birth, and the traumatic impact their deaths had on issues of descent and inheritance.[97] At Leontinoi, in the Predio Pisano cemetery located about 1.5 kilometers to the northwest, a small concentration of wealthy tombs dates to the seventh and sixth centuries BC. They stand out, by comparison with other tombs from Leontinoi, for their spatial discreteness, size, and contents, especially jewelry and vases of gold, silver, and bronze.[98] These tombs may belong to a class of heroic Homeric-style burials also found at Eretria, Cumae, and Pontecagnano that formed a cross-cultural, interregional phenomenon of interacting elites.[99] The elite buried at Leontinoi were living the high life, and their pretensions to a Homeric lifestyle were not projected back, as discussed earlier, because of an apparent newfound elitism of the sixth century. At Selinous a group of seventh-century graves, enclosed by the sixth-century city wall, continued to be respected in later times.[100] The tombs precede the town plan. While this may mean that urban space had not been fully planned during Selinous' first generation or so, as noted in the previous chapter, an interpretation going beyond simply the haphazard may be needed, given that such intramural burial practice may also be found at Megara Hyblaia, as already seen. In both cases, a connection with elite groups perhaps connected with the city's foundation must be entertained.

Another development concerning the elite also emerged in the second half of the seventh century: figured polychrome pottery. Examples have been found at Megara Hyblaia, Syracuse, and Gela. The most abundant examples come from Megara Hyblaia because of the systematic excavations that could be undertaken.[101] All examples were found in settlement and votive deposits.

---

96. Frederiksen 1999; Shepherd 2007; Péré-Noguès 2008, 159–61.

97. Shepherd 2007.

98. Cavallari 1884; Orsi 1900, 82–88; cf. also Martin, Pelagatti, Vallet, and Voza 1980, 586–87; Frasca 2009, 14–16, 82. Cf. Frasca 2009, 17, 109 for the "poor" cemeteries at Leontinoi.

99. Frasca 2009, 82.

100. Rallo 2002.

101. De Angelis 2003a, 55–61.

Although it is hard to quantify what proportion polychrome pottery represents in Megara Hyblaia's overall material assemblage, it certainly was small and circulated in relatively restricted circles. Both mythological and real-life scenes can be identified, including the myth of the Argonauts and hoplite warfare, which was then spreading westward from Greece. Definite patterning in the shapes selected is also observable: various kinds of mixing bowls, cups, jugs, and plates predominate and presuppose functions of drinking and eating. The lifestyle of the symposium suggests itself.[102] This can be supported in part by setting polychrome pottery against the contemporary elite poetry of Theognis, who represents a figurehead for a larger poetic tradition that extended across the Megarian world, from Sicily through Greece to the Black Sea. This poetry embodied a strong oligarchic sentiment concerned with wealth, class, and the protection of an elite lifestyle, expressed through a didactic text aimed at a certain young Kyrnos.

The mid-seventh century also marked the first attested case of success in Panhellenic sport by a Sicilian Greek. It involves the Syracusan Lygdamis, said to have been the first ever victor in the pankration at the thirty-third Olympiad.[103] This victory, the first of many to come from Greek Sicily, is socially significant, for sport allowed the elite to demarcate differences in status, lifestyle, and wealth.[104] Simon Hornblower, talking about the mid-fifth-century victories of Psaumis of Kamarina in an equestrian event, makes comments equally applicable to earlier periods: "victors in the Greek Panhellenic Games, especially the equestrian victors among them, needed money to make a big splash at places like Delphi and Olympia."[105]

Sicilian Greek societies are even better documented in the sixth century. The evidence reveals a continuation of many of the same practices and trends of the seventh century, with the result that we have a clearer and fuller understanding of how these two centuries relate to each other in terms of social behavior.

Domestic architecture continued to be a venue for the display of status and wealth in Greek Sicily in both old and new ways. Two late-sixth-century *pastas* houses to the east of Selinous' agora stand out, in comparison with other known contemporary houses, for not just their unique floor plan but also for their luxurious nature.[106] Ornate mid-sixth-century houses have also

---

102. De Angelis 2003a, 25–29, 55–63.

103. Moretti 1959, 65 no. 51.

104. For this general line of argument, see Golden 1998; Mitchell 2013, 69–73.

105. Hornblower 2011, 54.

106. Mertens 2006, 179, 181.

been excavated on Katane's acropolis.[107] All these houses follow a pattern of elite behavior already seen at Megara Hyblaia and Naxos.

Alongside this older practice is a new one which blurred the lines between domestic and public architecture, especially in terms of masonry. Three sixth-century houses at Megara Hyblaia used the same masonry previously reserved for public monuments. Some interesting possible confirmation from elsewhere in Sicily comes from written sources referring to this same period. Diodorus Siculus records the story of a certain Agathokles charged with the building of a temple to Athena at Syracuse.[108] Agathokles is said to have used stone from this project to build himself a sumptuous home, for which the goddess struck him down. Agathokles' supporters claimed that he had paid for the stone out of his own pocket, yet this did not keep his property from being confiscated by the *gamoroi* and his home and land from being cursed forever. It may be that Agathokles was aiming for tyranny, and that the *gamoroi* took these measures to make an example of him.[109] The idea of using building to express political ambitions is certainly one that was not alien to Syracuse in the early sixth century, as revealed by the inscription on the eastern stylobate of the monumental temple of Apollo.[110] At Akragas, the connection between tyranny and public building is made for Phalaris, whose misappropriation of public building funds was used to establish himself as tyrant around 570 BC.[111]

Burials contain significant investments in wealth and status in the second half of the sixth century, as Finley rightly observed for Megara Hyblaia, but that evidence is not restricted just to that city (Figure 21). For Syracuse, the burials were so wealthy that they raised worries in the wider community. Diodorus Siculus notes that Gelon maintained the sumptuary laws he inherited, laws which were most certainly put into place in the sixth century before the *gamoroi* fell from power in the early fifth century.[112] These laws barred, among other things, luxurious personal adornment and ostentatious burial, which are indeed

107. For these houses, see the last chapter. We should not press this evidence, for we have no other such evidence from the site to act as a comparative yardstick.

108. Diod. Sic. 8.11. For these houses at Megara Hyblaia, see De Angelis 2003a, 65.

109. Frolov 1995, 86. Berger (1992, 35) does not go as far in his interpretation, but he does admit "a certain tension within the ruling class."

110. Mertens 2004, 29.

111. On the parallel with Phalaris, see Brugnone 1992, 23–24 and below in this chapter for discussion of his rise to power.

112. Diod. Sic. 11.38.2, with full analysis in Bindi (1980) and Brugnone (1992), who have noted parallels with the legislation of Zaleukos of Locri.

FIGURE 21 View of Monumental Tomb at Megara Hyblaia.
© Author

found at Syracuse in contexts dating to the second half of the sixth century.[113] At Akragas, the finds made in the contrada Mosè cemetery stand out for their structure and furnishings, especially in regard to the stone sarcophagi placed in large pits lined with ashlar blocks.[114] This cemetery was located, moreover, in a prominent position east of the city along the ancient road leading to Gela. Clemente Marconi has argued that tombs 1 and 2 in the cemetery are to be identified as a cenotaph, built around 510 BC and containing weapons and vases of a supposed elite warrior.[115] Several marble statues representing male figures also date to slightly later, and they help us to visualize the culture of competition and display to which these tombs belonged.[116] Wealthy Greek burials are also known in Akragas' hinterland at Terravecchia di Cuti, indicating also a connection between city and country.[117] Himera, further north on the coast, has, not

113. See De Angelis 2003a, 65, who discusses Syracuse in relation to nearby Megara Hyblaia.

114. De Miro 1980–81, 566–71; 1988b, 244–46. Excavations in the Pezzino cemetery have sometimes revealed tombs with more grave-goods, metal and pottery, than others, but on the whole the evidence is far from overwhelming to suggest that burial here was the arena for competition and displays of wealth (De Miro 1989, 34–35, 77).

115. Marconi 2004, 29–30.

116. See recent discussions, see Adornato 2003; 2007.

117. Belvedere 2001, 745.

surprisingly, also revealed some evidence (discussed immediately below). This trend toward wealthy burial is also attested in many other parts of the contemporary Greek world,[118] demonstrating the interaction of elites beyond Sicily.

Sicilian Greeks are known for several more victories in Panhellenic sporting events in the sixth century, even if details of the lives of these athletes are sparse. From Naxos are known the four Olympic victories in boxing by a certain Tisandros, son of Kleokritos, probably between 572 and 560 BC.[119] A success for Kamarina came via Parmenides' victory in the *stadion* during the sixty-third Olympiad (528 BC),[120] and in the same event by Ischyros of Himera at the sixty-sixth Olympiad (512 BC).[121] For Himera, tomb 5 from the Rocca d'Antoni cemetery may be that of an athlete. The tomb dates to the third quarter of the sixth century and comprises a large fossa burial covered with tiles and perhaps a grave-marker.[122] The tomb stood out spatially from others in the cemetery in terms of location and contents. Around the skeleton, which measured 1.8 meters in height, were placed arms and discs plausibly connected with the deceased's military and agonistic abilities. At least seventeen pots were uncovered outside the tomb, and nine inside it. This tomb stands in stark contrast to the more numerous ones with fewer or no goods at all and minimal attention to the grave itself.[123] Pantares of Gela won an Olympic victory, whose precise date and event are not known for certain. The victory was either in chariot racing or running and was probably gained in the sixty-eighth Olympiad (504 BC).[124] His son Kleander later established himself as Gela's tyrant, a detail which gives us a sense of what was happening in the background. The connection between Panhellenic sporting victories and tyranny is also encountered slightly later at Akragas. Xenocrates, the brother of Theron, later tyrant of Akragas, and relatives of the city's famed later philosopher, Empedocles, also brought victories and glory.[125] Although we do not hear of any Syracusans being victorious, the city issued its first coinage in the late sixth century on which the obverse depicts a chariot and charioteer, almost certainly to be connected with the horse interests of the *gamoroi* and equestrian

---

118. Morris 1992b, 128–55; 1998.

119. Moretti 1959, 69–71.

120. Moretti 1959, 74 no. 125.

121. Moretti 1959, 76 no. 137.

122. Allegro 1976a, 604–09; cf. Vassallo 2005b, 95–96, 140.

123. Allegro 1976a, 595–601; Fabbri, Schettino, and Vassallo 2006, 618–19.

124. Moretti 1959, 78, no. 151.

125. For full details, see Moretti 1959, 81 nos. 167, 170; Antonaccio 2007, 268.

FIGURE 22 View of Early Syracusan Tetradrachm showing Charioteer on Obverse.
© The Hunterian, University of Glasgow 2015

sport (Figure 22).[126] What all these Olympic victories reveal is that the individuals concerned had the necessary wherewithal and lifestyle to achieve these successes in Panhellenic sport, and in some cases, like those of Pantares and Xenocrates, this brought increased status to later generations of their families. Intergenerational lifestyle, status, and wealth doubtless lay behind all these sporting victories before and after they were achieved.

All of the foregoing individual features, once assembled, paint a clear picture of the crystallization of elite hierarchy and identity during the second half of the seventh century and into the sixth century. Elite difference manifested itself across the Archaic period in domestic architecture, burial, successes in Panhellenic sport, and lifestyle choices in general. The pattern that Finley observed for the second half of the sixth century was simply an intensification of this earlier development that became visible in literary

---

126. Rutter 1997, 114–15.

evidence.[127] Therefore, the associations and labels used by the later elite may be viewed as good guides to those of Archaic Sicilian society.

One way other new social elements could be added to a community was through the continued immigration of new settlers from the same homeland. The pirates that ancient tradition maintains were responsible for establishing Zankle were joined by a substantial second wave of settlers from Chalcis and Euboea. Factional discord ensued. Were the pirates operating unofficially and of their own accord before the settlers' arrival, which raised questions of priority and equity within the community, and presumably by extension in competing visions of trade versus agriculture?[128] A compromise seems to have been reached.[129] It may have been reached by establishing an emporium in block 224 and using administered trade, and by establishing a cult of founders, if that is how one is to interpret the recent discovery of a large ritual tumulus at Zankle.[130] In any case, both trade and agriculture give every appearance of flourishing at Zankle, and that the city grew wealthy from its hinterland and control of the strategic Straits of Messina. Thus both founding elements of Zankle's society came to be satisfied.

Settlers from Megaris joined in the foundation of Selinous by Megara Hyblaia, and, as seen earlier in this chapter, the founders give every appearance of having been organized as clans that later worshipped their male heads. The case of Selinous also highlights how migration from within Sicily forms another category of settlers from the homeland. Such intra-island inputs can be documented, as discussed in the previous chapter, for the foundation of Leontinoi (with settlers from Naxos), Himera (with settlers from Zankle and Syracuse), Kamarina (with settlers from Syracuse), and Akragas (with settlers from Gela).

Greeks from parts of Greece different from those from which the founders had come could add further elements to Sicilian Greek societies. Naxos' earliest town plan, as already noted, had various orientations. Each of these may have represented the city quarters for settlers of mixed origins, including possibly settlers from Naxos in the Cyclades. The foundation traditions for Megara Hyblaia speak of the participation of people from Boiotia and Euboia, but the details, while theoretically plausible, cannot be confirmed on the basis

---

127. As I have fully argued elsewhere: De Angelis 2012b; 2012c.

128. Although the sources are of much later date, Iannucci (1998) has recently argued for their faithful depiction of early sociopolitical tension at Zankle, restoring convincingly the word διχοστασίη in Callimachus' *Aetia* (2.43.73 Pf). A future list of staseis for Zankle-Messana should entertain this possibility, which does not appear in Berger (1992, 54–56). See Thuc. 6.4.5, who uses the word *plethos* to describe the second wave of settlers from the homeland (cf. Manganaro 1996d, 55).

129. The silence of the sources may not be deceptive on this issue. Cf. Asheri 1980a, 114.

130. Bacci et al. 2010–11; 2012. Cf. Greco 2012, 1174.

of any other form of evidence.[131] In all likelihood, they reflect a composite community that would have settled alongside the five Megarian villages participating in the foundation.[132] The different orientations in the town plan may reflect different social quarters for these various social groups.[133] If so, each quarter may have had its own sanctuaries.[134]

Euboeans from Chalcis may have preceded and/or participated in Syracuse's foundation, on the basis of local toponyms whose inspiration points to them. The case for Argos is more substantial, based on Argive pottery and individuals like Pollis, discussed earlier. In addition, Strabo claims that most of the settlers participating in Syracuse's foundation came from Tenea close to the border with Argos, and this in turn might have been an outlet for settlers from Argolis.[135] Attempts to detect Argive and Chalcidian elements in Syracuse's burials are difficult to confirm.[136]

The Teneans, whether or not they helped filter Argive settlers to Syracuse, are interesting in their own right. Were they simple farmers suffering from overpopulation and land hunger, in search of more substantial plots of land?[137] The Teneans may have been encouraged to help found Syracuse because of the agricultural insight and expertise they surely had thanks to cultivating flat arable land at home, and may have been selected also because the Herakleidai, to whom Syracuse's founder Arkhias belonged, had their family seat at Tenea, an important cult center for Herakles.[138] Were these Teneans of lowly ranks and dependent on some clan, but given the opportunity to rise up the ranks by taking part in Syracuse's foundation?

---

131. Asheri (1980a, 112) and Gras, Tréziny, and Broise (2004, 547–52) fully discuss this topic.

132. For which, see De Angelis 2003a, 48–49.

133. One of Megara Hyblaia's excavators has recently suggested that the settlement's laying out took account of a preexisting native topographical configuration. Earlier work had also suspected this in more general terms: Malkin 2002b, 221; De Angelis 2003b, 35. While there have been recent discoveries of BA material at Megara Hyblaia, EIA finds are still absent, which suggests that the site itself was uninhabited at the time of Megarian settlement (Tréziny 2007, 184, 187).

134. Note Mertens (2006, 65), who mentions both sides without taking a stand, and the idea that various village quarters may still be reflected in the town plan is maintained in the latest French work (Tréziny 2007, 185). See also de Polignac 2005, 55.

135. Str. 8.6.22. The veracity of this statement is hard to establish, but it is usually taken as a faithful account of Syracuse's foundation: Asheri 1980a, 116–17; Salmon 1984, 63; Coldstream 2003, 187.

136. Van Compernolle 1966, 93–96; Salmon 1984, 66; Coldstream 2003, 234.

137. As argued by Frolov 1995, 77.

138. Malkin 1994a, 3 n.9; C.K. Williams 1997, 41.

Gela may have drawn settlers from other parts of the southeastern Aegean than Rhodes and Crete.[139] Some of these settlers came from small islands poorly endowed with agricultural resources and would thus have jumped at the opportunity of improving their lot in life by settling on a very fertile Sicilian plain. Nevertheless a status of subordination may have existed among the various settler groups, even among the founders, Rhodes and Crete. The Cretans are always mentioned second in the ancient foundation tradition, and it is sometimes thought their material culture steadily disappeared and was finally extinguished by the arrival of a wave of fresh settlers from Rhodes in the mid-sixth century.[140]

These settlers arrived from Rhodes as part of a larger historical phenomenon connected with the Persian conquest of East Greece. They either sought to establish their own separate cities, as in the case of Pentathlos discussed earlier, or they integrated into preexisting ones. The immigrants were usually made up of highly skilled individuals, such as doctors and craftsmen. Only in the case of Leontinoi do we have a sense of how these immigrants were accommodated by their host cities. The quarter known as Phocaea that Thucydides mentions must have come into being in this context.[141]

Two main groups of non-Greeks could have contributed to populating Sicilian Greek societies: native Sicilians and other Italic peoples and Phoenicians. Of these, the native seem to have been the more prevalent group, since the Phoenicians themselves were immigrants to Sicily, which meant that their numbers started from a completely blank slate.[142] As discussed in Chapter 1, native Sicilians could have been recruited through situations

---

139. The Argive pottery found in the cemeteries and sanctuaries is usually not connected with Argive settlers at Gela: Raccuia 2000, 114–15.

140. Sammartano 1999, 481–83, 494–95; Perlman 2002, 200–02 (who notes the survival of Cretan names at the refoundation of Kamarina in 461 BC; see below for further discussion).

141. Thuc. 5.4.4, with Frasca 2009, 60, 65.

142. While there is no doubt that Sicily's *poleis* had mixed and fluid populations, it is more debated as to how to locate, if at all, these multicultural components and demographic shifts in the archaeological record. Scholars who work on southern Italy have optimistically used the usually abundant burial evidence for these purposes (cf. the revealing remarks at Lombardo 2004, 358), and such optimism has sometimes been carried over to Sicily, especially by scholars who work on both regions (for instance, de la Genière [1996, 169–71; 1999b; 2001] and Mercuri [2001] have sought to identify, respectively, Campanian mercenaries and natives in Sicilian cemeteries, while Rendeli [2005a, 178] has recently spoken generally of formal burial as being a feature of multiethnic communities). On the whole, however, the Sicilian burial data have been more critically handled, leading often to glaring differences in how they have been interpreted, notwithstanding the historical and scholarly connections between these two regions (thus in particular Hodos 1999; Shepherd 1999; 2005; Antonaccio 2003; 2005; see too Péré-Noguès 2008, 151–57). Such Sicilian reactions have provided laudable warnings against simplistic equations of ethnicity and identity with material culture, reminding us that

involving both conquest and the middle ground, and the Phoenicians appear to have been residents as enclaves of traders.

At Mylai, in Zankle's territory, the frequency of cremation burials has suggested a possible underlying native presence remaining due to social integration.[143] In general, the question of relations with the native population is one that remains poorly known, given the low level of fieldwork in Zankle's territory.[144] But if Metauros is included as part of Zankle's territory, evidence from the cemeteries there suggests a mixed community of Greeks and natives, making such integration possible also on the city's Sicilian mainland.[145]

A late-eighth-century tomb (number 72) at Naxos contained a newborn child of one to six months of age in an SOS amphora placed beside the well-preserved bones of a young woman, presumably her mother, of eighteen to twenty years of age.[146] The grave-goods accompanying this young woman have suggested to some scholars that she was of native origin.[147]

Our earliest knowledge of Leontinoi comprises literary and archaeological evidence, which suggests that both peaceful and violent integration occurred between native populations and Greek settlers. The abandonment of native settlements in the belt of ten or so kilometers around Leontinoi during the seventh century is in all likelihood to be related to these dual processes of demographic and cultural interaction.[148]

The site of Katane appears to have been unoccupied at the time of Greek settlement.[149] Social relations with native groups thus naturally leads us

---

the archaeological record is not a simple mirror. But these works are often divorced from their social and economic contexts, or at least have a more particular vision of them, and leave the impression that formal burial in cemeteries was only restricted to "Greeks" who just happened to exchange and use native artefacts and rituals. While this was, of course, sometimes the case, it was doubtless only one of a greater range of possibilities that needs to be admitted. In any case, instead of treating the burial data in isolation, we can often combine it with other forms of evidence to establish a wider context for ethnocultural mixing. Therefore, the answer must surely lie somewhere between overoptimistic acceptance and hypercritical denial of the burial data, and accordingly the hurdles and possibilities of recognizing materially Sicilian ethnicities and identities need not be exaggerated in one direction or the other.

143. Tigano 2002.

144. Bacci 1999b, 249.

145. Sabbione 2005, 245–46.

146. Pelagatti 1980–81, 699–700, 732–36.

147. Albanese Procelli 1997a, 519.

148. Procelli 1989, 682; Sammartano 1994, 61–62. Whether the natives entirely became an underclass (as in Frasca 2009, 96–97) that later formed a part of the *demos* that sought to overthrow the *hippeis* is only a possibility.

149. Frasca 2010. Thucydides (6.3.3) seems to be saying that the natives occupying the site at the time of settlement were driven out, but the earlier suspicion of Fischer-Hansen, Nielsen,

outside Katane to the surrounding native hinterland. At Valverde, to the north of Katane, this is thought to have entailed peaceful coexistence and integration, but that picture should not be pressed, let alone extended to Katane's remaining territory, where aggressiveness can be demonstrated.[150] At the same time, there existed native sites, like Mendolito di Adrano, located at what would have presumably been the edges of Katane's territory, that flourished economically, politically, and culturally throughout the Archaic period.[151] A variety of relationships, therefore, needs to be envisaged.

The largest increases in population growth at Megara Hyblaia seem to have come in the first half of the seventh century, which coincides with the appearance of an arguably native burial ritual at Megara Hyblaia and larger development in native and Greek settlement patterns in the Sicilian interior, involving the movement of people from there to the coast.[152]

It remains uncertain, as discussed in Chapter 1, whether native Sicilians occupied, either seasonally or permanently, the land that was later to become Syracuse. However, as Syracuse established Heloros and Kasmenai to the south and west of the city in the first half of the seventh century, direct contact with native communities occurred. The abandonment of such native sites as Pantalica and Monte Finnochito, whether forcefully, peacefully, or both, appears to have happened in and around this same time. The concentration and control of people and resources lend themselves, of necessity, to a nucleated settlement pattern that existed hereabouts down into the late sixth century, if not beyond.[153] The foundation of Heloros may have been a joint native-Greek venture intended to secure control and the exploitation of a fertile and strategic valley.[154] At the head of this valley stood a preexisting native settlement at Monte Finnochito that built a fortification, experienced population growth, and entertained relations with Greeks. Was the creation of a settlement at Heloros around 700 BC a challenge to Monte Finnochito, as traditionally believed, or a response to its successes? The same applies to the other Syracusan settlement, Kasmenai, founded slightly later in 664 BC. A new interpretation of Kasmenai calls into question the military nature and

and Ampolo (2004a, 206), who rightly talk about the tenuous nature of the archaeological evidence sometimes used to support this, seems well founded.

150. For full discussion, see Procelli 1989, 683–84.

151. Leighton 1999, 213, 215; Albanese Procelli 2003a, 132, 146, 223–24.

152. De Angelis 2003a, 51–54.

153. For a comparative perspective about nucleated settlement pattern as a form of social control, see Blok 1969; Blok and Driessen 1984. For the possibility in the Classical world, see Foxhall 1990, 108.

154. Copani 2005.

hostile relationship with nearby native populations suggested by earlier schol-arship.[155] Again, a positive synergistic scenario has been suggested.

This reconfiguration of the settlement also entailed population move-ments, some of which must have been directed to Syracuse itself. The iden-tification of native material culture and burial features in Syracuse's Fusco cemetery suggests some kind of exchanges, including in all likelihood the incorporation of natives into the community as equal members, as implied by their receipt of formal burial.[156] If true, such individuals must have repre-sented the more elite elements of their original communities

In the early fifth century BC, our sources talk about the revolt of the Killyrioi, Syracuse's serf class, attempting to acquire better political condi-tions for themselves.[157] We do not know when this class originated; how-ever, it is very possible it too should be situated in the first half of the seventh century.[158] Modern scholars regularly describe the Killyrioi as con-quered native Sicilians.[159] But, while possible, the conquering option prob-ably does not explain the full range of ways in which the Killyrioi came to Syracuse. As argued in Chapter 1, channels of middle-ground contact were also possible, in which case the native elite must have simply brought their dependents.[160]

Gela's interest in land took the settlers to the Sicilian interior in the sev-enth century, activities which brought them into direct contact with the native communities already in existence. Here, according to ancient tradition, we hear of the conquest of two native sites, Omphake and Ariaiton, and the estab-lishment of a new settlement called Maktorion.[161]

Conquest should not be viewed as the only route taken by Geloan settlers. Archaeological evidence suggests that Gela and the native communities in its

---

155. Melfi 2000.

156. Sammartano 1994, 91–93; Albanese Procelli 1997a, 519; 2003, 142; Leighton 1999, 235–36; De Angelis 2003b, 29–30.

157. For more details, see below. Frolov (1995, 79) has argued that the term Killyrioi derives from a native Sikel root borrowed by Greeks that may refer to the skin clothing they wore.

158. So Leighton 1999, 233.

159. Especially from Dunbabin (1948, 111–12, 400–01, 414–15) onward. So too in the two main discussion of Syracusan social structure: Lepore 1970, 53; Frolov 1995, 78.

160. Note the ancient saying when referring to large amounts: "more than the Kallikyrioi" (Zenobios 4.54; Souda, s.v. Καλλικύριοι). Cf. Frolov 1995, 78–79.

161. Omphake: Paus. 8.46.2 (often tentatively identified with Butera: Orlandini 1962, 82; Panvini 1996, 33; Fischer-Hansen, Nielsen, and Ampolo 2004a, 177); Ariaiton: FGrH 532 C25 (location unknown); Maktorion: Hdt. 7.155 (often tentatively identified with Monte Bubbonia: Panvini 1996, 33, 35; Fischer-Hansen, Nielsen, and Ampolo 2004a, 177).

hinterland reached a modus vivendi in which native communities adopted a veneer of Greek culture while maintaining their cultural core, and one in which all sides ultimately benefited.[162] Such mixing was already under way by the mid-seventh century, well exemplified by the "stratum II" burial evidence from Butera, which has native and Greek ritual and material culture alongside each other.[163] As Leighton has observed, "Butera resembles a provincial satellite with an indigenous substratum and an increasingly mixed population living within the orbit of Gela."[164]

This population mixing was not restricted to sites in the hinterland, however: it doubtless occurred at Gela itself.[165] There are two strands of evidence. The first derives from Gela's cemeteries, where native burial ritual and material culture have been recognized from the seventh century BC.[166] The second concerns the appearance of native names in late-sixth-century inscriptions from Gela's acropolis.[167] Certainly, at the very least, these inscriptions provide evidence of native individuals worshipping at Gela, as well as evidence of a bilingual environment.[168] But, when coupled with the burial evidence, we must entertain the strong possibility of native-Greek coexistence and integration of women and men.[169] As is only to be expected, the mixed and dynamic community taking shape in the seventh and sixth centuries created tension and conflict. Gela's first known stasis seems to have occurred between 625 and 575 BC, when a group of citizens sought refuge in Maktorion and were later coaxed back to the city by a certain Telines, said to be an ancestor of the Deinomenids.[170]

---

162. Fischer-Hansen 2002.

163. For overviews, see Orlandini 1962, 78–82; Panvini 1996, 33; Albanese Procelli 1997a, 520; 2003a, 168–71.

164. Leighton 1999, 251. Cf. also Fischer-Hansen 2002, 134–35.

165. Trombi 2002, 94–96.

166. Domínguez 1989, 327–32; Guglielmino 1994, 208–09; Albanese Procelli 1997a, 520; Leigthon 1999, 236; Mercuri 2001, 12.

167. Piraino Manni 1980; Lejeune 1980.

168. For joint worship, see Manni 1984–85, 177. For bilingualism, see Hall 2002, 115, who notes that "This level of linguistic interference between Greek and non-Greek idioms [at Gela and elsewhere in Sicily] requires more than casual intercourse and hints strongly at the existence of a bilingual environment on the island." See more fully Willi 2008, chs. 2 and 5; Tribulato 2012.

169. So too Di Vita 1999, 372; Fischer-Hansen 2002, 131, besides earlier references.

170. For the whole incident, see Berger 1992, 23–25; Raccuia 1999; Petruzzella 1999. There is no evidence for the sanctuary of Demeter at Bitalemi as having a direct connection with this civil strife (U. Kron 1992, 648–49).

The extensive votive offerings that have been recovered from the sanctuary of Demeter at Bitalemi provide unique insights into the life and roles of women at Gela, some of whom may well have been of native origin.[171] During the Archaic period, these offerings include weaving weights for textile production and hoes of various sizes that might suggest the tending of vegetable beds and/or the covering of seeds after broadcast, whereas offerings connected with plowing and harvesting are, revealingly, all but absent.

Relations between Himera and neighboring native peoples are already attested in the seventh century.[172] Thucydides mentions three oikists, Eukleides, Simos, and Sakon, the last two of whom are sometimes thought to be of native origin.[173] While that matter is open to discussion, it is undeniable that native and other Italic components made up Himera's population. The brother of the poet Stesichorus is said to have been named Mamertinos or Mamertios, but the evidence is not solely restricted to onomastics.[174] That some of Himera's burials contain people of native origin is a real possibility. But it is especially in the earlier sixth century, when the first permanent settlements in the territory came into being, that relations significantly increased. Native material culture and ritual has been found at Himera itself, while there is also mention of fighting in an inscription from Samos.[175] The variety of this evidence reflects a full range of relationships with native populations, from peaceful integration to outright conquest.[176]

Archaic Selinous seems also to have had a similar range of relationships with neighboring native populations. Selinous sought to secure a foothold for itself in western Sicily; this required the control of some preexisting native settlements, and presumably of the people within these settlements as labor for land clearance and agriculture. The widespread assumption by scholars that relations were initially peaceful, along the lines of Megara Hyblaia from where many of the settlers came, stands in need of revision.[177] Isolated native

---

171. U. Kron 1992, 630–31, 636–38, 649; Scheidel 1995, 216; 1996, 1. For terracotta statuettes in Sicily depicting women doing domestic work, see Pisani 2003.

172. Cf. De Angelis 2003a, 123.

173. Thuc. 6.5.1. On the onomastics, Cordano (1984b, 136) is noncommittal, while Knoepler (2007, 95) regards Sakon as being from the Myletidai, since the name is found in inscriptions from Selinous and near Gela.

174. Knoepfler 2007, 95.

175. Dunst 1972; cf. also Castellana 1980, 71; Allegro 1999, 281–82; Trombi 2002, 96–98; De Angelis 2003b, 30; Vassallo 2010c, 53.

176. Allegro 1999, 281–82.

177. De Angelis 2003a, 150–52.

objects are known from Archaic Selinous.[178] But there are also two tombstones containing revealing names: Lucania (dating to around 600 BC) and Latinos (dating to around 500 BC).[179] Names based on regional ethnics may mean that the bearer's family ultimately had hospitality and/or commercial links with these regions. The bulk of the clearest evidence of a multicultural community comes from epigraphic material dating to the first half of the fifth century.[180]

The Phoenicians are similarly documented in Sicilian Greek societies by written and archaeological sources. As mentioned already in Chapter 1, Phoenician presence in the early Greek *poleis* of eastern Sicily has been suspected on the basis of ceramic finds. But Phoenician presence has also been postulated for Gela in southern Sicily. An emporium may have existed prior to Gela's "official" foundation, to trade with Sicily and beyond and to serve as a stopping-point for east-west traffic.[181] Scholars point to a story in Zenobios of Phoenician pirates killing Gela's oikists.[182] It is, of course, plausible that Phoenicians could have frequented Gela, given their suspected presence in the early Greek *poleis* of eastern Sicily (see Chapter 1) and the importance of the Sicilian channel for their east-west movement. Rhodes and Crete, being strategically located islands, had been long visited by Phoenicians, stimulating an awareness of the possibilities of the wider world.[183] But the possibility of a tradition invented or exaggerated by Sicilian Greek propaganda of the fifth and fourth centuries BC also exists.[184]

The dynamics between elites and these other social elements within their communities and beyond can be documented sufficiently through only some Greek cities. For the seventh century, this means Syracuse and Leontinoi, and for the sixth century Selinous and Akragas.

The overthrow of the Bacchiad clan in Corinth by the tyrant Cypselus in the middle of the seventh century had reverberations that were also felt in

---

178. Trombi 2002, 98–102; Balco 2007.

179. Dubois 2008, 66–70 no. 20, 70–72 no. 24. The Latinos inscription came on the black market without provenance (of course), but its origins are unanimously placed in Selinous. Jameson and Malkin 1998; Nenci 1999.

180. De Angelis 2003a, 189–93; Antonetti and De Vido 2006a, 143, 159; 2006b, 421–23, 433, 438–39; Collin Bouffier 2010b.

181. Asheri 1980a, 124–25; Mafodda 1998, 21–22; Anello 1999, 392; Sammartano 1999, 475; Raccuia 2000, 46; cf. 70, 115, 127–28.

182. Zenobios 1.54.

183. See Coldstream 2003, 267, 384. Before Gela's foundation, there is a possible Rhodian presence at Pithekoussai and perhaps further west: Ridgway 1992, 111–13; Marton 1997; Raccuia 2000, 87–95; Coldstream 2003, 299–300.

184. Sammartano 1999, 477; Raccuia 2000, 111; 2008, 180–82. Cf. also Scheid and Svenbro 1985.

Syracuse.[185] This can be traced most visibly in the spread of Corinthian art and ideology through the migration of craftsmen and elites.[186] The Bacchiad exiles defined their place at Syracuse by promoting a horse culture with such symbols as the Gorgon and Pegasus, with their underlying social connotations of wealth and status, depicted in architectural terracottas.[187] These exiles took up residence in a community which had already had a sense of self and identity. A tumultuous second half century ensued, not only because of their arrival and but also because of the economic takeoff that Greek Sicily was experiencing at the time (for this takeoff, see Chapter 4 below).

The result was one, possibly two outbreaks of civil strife around 650 BC.[188] The more securely dated of these was the more significant, as it involved a change in government and the exile of the local Myletidai clan (discussed earlier), who, together with Zankle, founded Himera.[189] The cause seems to have been the need for "broadening the governments on an egalitarian basis, by the establishment of moderate oligarchies, more adapted to the conditions of the late seventh and sixth centuries, than by preserving the narrow aristocracies of the type prevalent in Greece in the eighth century when the colonies were founded."[190] On this reading, therefore, civil strife sought to share land and power more widely among the elite. The Parian Marble mentions that Sappho sought refuge in a Syracuse governed by the *gamoroi* ("landsharers").[191] It is very likely that this term, even if first known from events of the early fifth century, was adopted in common parlance in the second half of the seventh century, as a gesture of the new political reality. In the end, a political solution was reached, one that lasted throughout the sixth century, if the silence of the sources is anything to go by.

That does not mean that the political status quo went unchallenged or pleased everybody as the seventh century was coming to an end. Competition among

---

185. For the toppling of the Bacchiads and subsequent tyranny at Corinth, see Salmon 1984, 186–230.

186. See in detail Stazio and Ceccoli 1997.

187. Lubtchansky 2006, 224–26.

188. The second stasis, involving a love quarrel between two young men, is undated. Frolov (1995, 86–87) dates it to the third quarter of the sixth century BC, while Roebuck (1980, 24), followed by Berger (1992, 34–35), suggests a more plausible mid-seventh-century date. At any rate, details are few, and all that can be safely said about this stasis is that it "masks a more fundamental rift within the aristocracy" (Berger 1992, 35).

189. For analysis, see in particular Roebuck 1980, 1924–26; Berger 1992, 34–35.

190. Roebuck 1980, 1923.

191. *FGrH* 239 F36. Her exile is usually placed around 600 BC (Frolov 1995, 80–81). On the adoption of the *gamoroi* title, see also Roebuck 1980, 1927–28.

the elite continued, and may well be behind the foundation of Kamarina. While the creation of this city is usually regarded as the last strategic move in establishing Syracuse's Archaic territory, it is also possible that an unhappy exiled group may have been the driving force behind it. That suggestion might make better sense of Kamarina's later struggles to stay independent of Syracuse. It is interesting to observe that Kamarina's foundation occurred in a region witnessing social and economic success, judging from the recent discovery of the sculpted relief and burials at the native hilltop site at Castiglione, just outside Comiso.[192] There has been much speculation as to the historical context of the finds from Castiglione since their discovery, but at the very least they highlight a successful and attractive region, in which much cultural integration between Greeks and natives can be documented.[193] The foundation of Kamarina and the establishment of emporia (like Bosco Littorio at Gela and contrada Maestro between Syracuse and Kamarina) in southern Sicily indicate interest in interregional trade and in securing a stable spot along this coast in the sixth century, which resulted in the foundation of Akragas.[194]

Leontinoi represents the other seventh-century case of a community's internal social development about which we are fairly well informed.[195] The city wall and some sanctuaries in and around the city belong to this century. In the countryside, more territory was added to Leontinoi's possessions, whose control was solidified by the establishment of (sometimes fortified) settlements.[196] Monte San Mauro is one of the new sites established during this period of territorial expansion; it has reasonably been identified with Euboia of the ancient sources.[197]

Some of this archaeology has been connected with Panaetios' rise to tyranny in around 614 BC.[198] From what can be gleaned from the sources, Panaetios sought, with the support of the *demos*, to topple the *hippeis*, the elite horsemen

192. The sculpture is thoroughly discussed in Cordano and Di Salvatore 2002. For a succinct summary, see De Angelis 2007, 154; Dubois 2008, 101–02 no. 44.

193. Manni 1987; Cordano 1987; 1990; Holloway 1990; Pelagatti, Di Stefano, and De Lachenal 2006; Giangiulio 2010, 16–19. Cf. also Rubini, Bonafede, and Mogliazza 1999.

194. Anello (2002, 68 n. 51) also makes the connection with the wider Sicilian territorial and trade expansion intended to curb growing Phocaean influence in the western Mediterranean as a whole.

195. Frasca 2009.

196. Cordano 1988a, 54–55; Procelli 1989, 682–83; Frasca 2009, 39.

197. Frasca 2009, 40, 48–50.

198. Ancient sources date the beginning of his tyranny to 615–614 BC. There seems no good reason to deny this. See discussion in De Angelis 2003a, 62–63.

who held power.[199] Ideas about the activities of this elite can be conjured up by what ancient writers, like Herodotus and Aristotle, have to say about their Euboean counterparts in Greece.[200] It is undeniable that they were wealthy individuals who outwardly symbolized their status and position within society by their horses. Panaetios' tyranny implies unwillingness on their part to have others share in their successes six generations after Leontinoi's foundation, again during a period of economic takeoff.[201] Panaetios' motives may have been to seek status for himself and land for the unhappy *demos*, whose social and economic troubles were tackled by the tyrant perhaps through the foundation of sites like Monte San Mauro in the countryside. It can thus be presupposed that a greater range of Leontinoi's population entered a social and economic realm previously barred to them.

For sixth-century internal developments, we turn to Selinous and Akragas. Selinous' development played out inside the *polis* and in the wider region. In 580 BC, its territorial development was in full bloom, and Pentathlos, who allied himself with Selinous, was attempting to settle in western Sicily. These developments caused alarm in Egesta and Carthage. Carthage's response was to send its general Malchus in order to curb or at least control the growing tide of Selinous' development.[202] The events connected with Pentathlos and Malchus would naturally have elicited different positions within Selinous, and resorting to violence to resolve them is also spoken of in the same passage of Polyaenus. Factional fighting clearly was operating in the background, with the upper hand gained by the pro-Carthaginian and pro-Elymian factions as represented by the tyrant Theron, who is also reported by Polyaenus to have used 300 slaves to gain power. Whether or not Polyaenus is good evidence for the existence of slaves at Selinous in this period, and a possible rural uprising,[203] an insightful argument has recently hypothesized that the numerous iron dedications found in the earliest layers of the sanctuary of Demeter Malophoros could be explained as offerings of freed slaves.[204]

---

199. Berger 1992, 26; Luraghi 1994, 11–20. Braccesi 1998, viii mentions Panaetios in passing and starts his account of Sicily's Greek tyrants with Phalaris.

200. Cordano 1988a, 52–54; Lubtchansky 2006, 219–20, who argues, moreover, against Luraghi's (1994, 14) view that we are dealing with the existence of a true cavalry and not simply mounted hoplites.

201. Roebuck 1980, 1927–28.

202. Polyaen. 1.28.2. See also De Angelis 2003a, 155–57.

203. According to Mafodda (1998, 22–25), the appearance of slaves in this text may be a topos. For the rural uprising suggestion, see Antonetti 2009, 30.

204. Antonetti and De Vido 2006b, 434.

Another tyrant, Peithagoras, continued Theron's political policies, which survived beyond his own rule to the battle of Himera, thanks to the rise, in the interim, of Theron of Akragas as tyrant, whose territorial expansion included the conquest of parts of Selinous' eastern lands.[205] It should come as no surprise that the political stability that accompanied this pro-Carthaginian and pro-Elymian turn resulted in a remarkable urban flourishing, especially evident in the seven monumental peripteral temples constructed between 550 and 480 BC, discussed in the previous chapter.

Akragas' earliest sociopolitical developments are dominated by the tyrant Phalaris, who ruled for sixteen years with an iron fist in a reign of terror, and who never seems to have intended to establish a dynastic or hereditary line.[206] The ancient sources have much to say about how Phalaris established himself as tyrant, but, as is to be expected, they are virtually silent as to what motivated him in the first place. He may have been driven by issues arising from the mixed (Rhodian and Cretan) settlers and their relationship with Gela,[207] or he may have wanted to clear obstructive native populations in central southern Sicily.[208] These need not be mutually exclusive positions, nor should we view Phalaris' relations with Akragas' settlers and the natives in exclusively ethnic and monolithic terms, as a variety of relationships seems to be suggested by the written and archaeological sources.

While Polyaenus lists a number of stratagems Phalaris used against the natives, around these are embedded details about plausible economic and matrimonial exchanges that would indicate simultaneous policies of force and persuasion.[209] It is interesting to note in this connection the two inhumation burials in the first phase of the Pezzino cemetery that contained exclusively native pottery,[210] alongside other known native objects and a possible name from Akragas.[211] While, of course, none of this evidence necessarily means that the interred individuals or users of these artefacts were native Sicilians,

---

205. Cf. De Angelis 2003a, 159–63.

206. Braccesi and Millino 2000, 58.

207. Braccesi and Millino 2000, 55–56.

208. Berger 1992, 15.

209. See in particular Polyaen. 5.1.3–4. Manganaro (1992, 214, 222) points out the dual nature of this relationship in raising the possibility of intermarriage.

210. De Miro 1989, 27. This earliest phase of use is dated to 580–530 BC (De Miro 1989, 27–39).

211. Trombi 2002, 92–94; Dubois 2008, 150–52 no. 77. The possible onomastic evidence is found on a curse tablet of about 500 BC, in which the name *Rokes* may be a native name acting as a classification heading followed by Greek names.

the possibility of some equal integration within the *polis* is suggested by the round chthonic sanctuaries found in the urban heart of Akragas.[212]

Archaeology suggests, moreover, that native settlements in Akragas' hinterland now entered into a long-term relationship with the city that benefited both sides, as in the case of Gela.[213] This is most dramatically seen at Sant'Angelo Muxaro, where, already in the seventh century, wealthy burials with gold objects imply the existence of social and economic hierarchy as a result of exchange with Gela and later Akragas, as well as, more generally, with other Greeks and Phoenicians from various other points of the compass.[214] Whether this exchange included humans alongside the usually suspected regional mineral resources is notoriously difficult to confirm. Phalaris' use of slaves to rise to power, however, can only be hypothetically connected to the earlier acquisition and exploitation of labor resources from the native hinterland. It is possible that Phalaris' slaves came from exchange with this hinterland, although this part of his story may be nothing more than a topos.[215] Taken together, we have every right to think of native-Greek integration from the earliest years of Akragas' existence.

From the foregoing emerges a fairly consistent picture of Sicilian Greek societies being eclectic from their beginning. These societies were made up of people from various parts of the Greek homeland, from the Sicilian hinterland, from the Phoenician world, and from some other regions, especially Italy. It is impossible to quantify each of these social components,[216] though, as an educated guess, they must never have numbered more than one-half of the *polis* communities of which they were part. In the fifth and fourth centuries, Sicilian societies were known for their multifarious nature and their lack of civic cohesiveness; these characteristics certainly originated in the Archaic period. According to Morris, "The varied origins of settlers and the open frontier with native populations probably had a lot to do with this."[217] Society consisted of several fragments that challenged their coalescence into a

---

212. P. Marconi 1929a, 31–52, 59–68; 1933. For recent discussions, De Polignac 1995, 114–15; De Angelis 2003b, 30; De Angelis and Garstad 2006, 234.

213. Fischer-Hansen 2002.

214. On the sources of Sant'Angelo Muxaro's wealth, see De Angelis 2003a, 106. Other western Sicilian native sites have also revealed (less dramatic, but still significant) signs of wealth in this same period: Palermo 2004, 211–12.

215. Polyaen. 5.1.1. For the topos possibility, see Mafodda 1998, 22–25.

216. Albanese Procelli 2010; Allegro and Fiorentino 2010; Belvedere 2010; Mercuri 2010; Vassallo 2010.

217. Morris 2009b, 160; cf. also Jackman 2005, 1–10.

homogeneous body. In this respect, Archaic Greek Sicily parallels other immigrant societies.[218] Whether one thinks that the societal differences between Sicily and Greece are somehow a bad thing is ultimately a value judgment that has its origins in the racialized discourses of earlier generations of scholarship discussed in the Introduction.[219] The successes of Sicilian Greek societies cannot be doubted.

Constitutions and Citizenship. What constitutional and citizenship principles guided and organized these social groups, classes, statuses, and wealth between the eighth and sixth centuries BC?[220] Did constitutions and citizenship include only certain social classes and groups and their economic interests, what political rights were held by the various social classes and groups, and were constitutions and citizenships related in general to group, class, status, and wealth?

Democracy is sometimes thought to have existed in Archaic Greek Sicily. There is no shred of evidence for this. The regularly laid out town plans have been traditionally interpreted as containing socially inclusive and egalitarian communities, or, put another way, democracies in embryo, which sought to divide land and power on equal terms.[221] Town plans need not mean any such thing.[222] Echoes of the frontier thesis of Frederick Jackson Turner, the American historian who advanced it, continue to resonate in ancient Greek frontier history, despite its questioning in American history.[223] The ancient Greek frontier, like its modern counterpart, did indeed change people and their societies, but democracy is not a necessary corollary of this in antiquity. The ancient Greek frontier certainly created conditions in which greater rationality and cooperation came into being,[224] but a democracy of any kind was not one of their byproducts.

---

218. Thompson 1973, 5.

219. Cf. also recently Marconi 2012, 395–96.

220. For constitutions and citizenship as a phenomenon of social history, see Weber 2003, 315.

221. For example: Collin Bouffier 1999a, 364; McInerey 2004, 22–26.

222. A generation ago, the late David Asheri (1975, 12–13) reminded us that town plans can be produced in a variety of sociopolitical situations. Shipley (2005, 348–49) has laudably pursued Asheri's line and categorically argued that democracy has nothing to do with the earliest town planning. For similar arguments, see also Luraghi 1996; Menédez Varela 2003a, 226; Gras, Tréziny, and Broise 2004, 583; Gallo 2009; Bintliff 2012, 223. As with any piece of evidence, the best interpretations of town plans will be the ones that have recourse to the overall contexts to which they belong.

223. Cf. Finley 1968; Lepore 1968, 60–61.

224. De Angelis 2003b, 33.

An oligarchic form of government was the rule from the start in all the Greek cities of Archaic Sicily, and that included tyranny, which, as Greg Anderson puts it, was part of "mainstream oligarchic leadership in its most amplified form."[225] The case for oligarchic governments can be directly and indirectly established.

Our earliest direct evidence relates to the seventh century and concerns Kharondas of Katane's laws.[226] As is the case with a good many early Greek lawgivers, Kharondas' activities are enshrouded in later sources prone to embellishment and misinformation.[227] Nevertheless, the main lines of his activities can be reasonably sketched out.

Katane's economic development did not keep pace with social development within the community, as implied by the contents of Kharondas' laws.[228] He divided society into income classes, which in turn were used as the basis for the level of fine to be paid for offences. Kharondas, moreover, showed a concern for false testimony, contracts (to avoid the accumulation of credit), homicide, marriage, and inheritance. These areas represented symptoms of the underlying social and economic tensions over property at Katane that Kharondas sought to offset through legislation. A compromise between the wealthy and the poor was struck, and seems to have been effective, judging by the absence of any suggestion of tyranny there. The wealthy continued to exist unabated after Kharondas, who addressed just enough of the problems of, and requisite protection for, those less fortunate social classes.

Kharondas' legislation was in whole or in part adopted elsewhere in Sicily and beyond to help resolve similar situations of power struggles and state formation, a testimony to the effectiveness of his legislation. Twelve fragments of an inscription discovered during Orsi's excavations at Monte San Mauro belong to a copy of Kharondas of Katane's laws on homicide set up in a public building also used for storage.[229] It would follow that Kharondas' system of governance into income classes inside a moderate oligarchic constitution emerged in Leontinoi and its territory after Panaetios' tyranny, underlying which was greater legal attention to questions of power and intra-community

---

225. G. Anderson 2005, 173.

226. Martin, Pelagatti, Vallet, and Voza 1980, 688.

227. For Kharondas, see in particular Vallet 1958, 313–20; Cordano 1978; Roebuck 1980, 1928–30; Gagarin 1986, 64–75, 129–30; Camassa 1996; Hölkeskamp 1999, 130–44; Papakonstantinou 2008, 67; Willi 2008, 311–14. Cf. also Gagarin 2005, 91.

228. For this proposed date, see recently Thomas 2005, 44.

229. Cordano 1986b.

relations.[230] This constitution should not necessarily be seen as at variance with Panaetios and the *demos'* toppling of the elite. Those who had been barred from the land made their point by supporting Panaetios and received what they had sought. Society doubtless continued under its elite tenor, from Leontinoi to Monte San Mauro di Caltagirone, where wealthy burials stand out in the material record.

If Zankle and Naxos, two of the other Chalcidian cities of Sicily, also adopted Kharondas' laws, then ruling oligarchies in power in the sixth century are also presupposed.[231] In Naxos' case, evidence for religious ritual discussed earlier, as well as epigraphic evidence datable to the fifth century BC discussed below, supports that idea.

An oligarchy of some kind can also be supposed for the two Megarian cities of Sicily, Megara Hyblaia and Selinous, on the basis of a parallel culture in the Megarian world at large implied in the Theognidean poetic corpus. Unlike at other eastern Sicilian *poleis*, we hear of no civil strife at Megara Hyblaia in the second half of the seventh century caused by this dynamic social and economic environment. The silence of the sources here seems to be saying that the elite reached some sort of political equilibrium. The sixth century saw pretty much the same pattern repeating itself, with more public monuments and increased success across the board for the elite, who during the second half of the sixth century built for the community both a stone city wall and ornate tombs sometimes crowned by sculpture.[232] In general, they ruled the city's affairs until being moved in 483/82 BC to Syracuse during one of Gelon's population transfers and incorporated into the citizen body; the people over whom they ruled were sold into slavery.[233] A narrow oligarchy is the likeliest form of government, judging from parallels with contemporary Megarian constitutions elsewhere and from Selinous' own internal developments, which witnessed a turn to tyranny in the mid-sixth century BC.[234]

An oligarchic regime must have existed at Gela, on the assumption that oligarchic regimes preceded the tyrannies that emerged in about 505 BC. Tension within Gela would have arisen with the arrival of settlers from Lindos, then ruled by the tyrant Kleoboulos. The new settlers, who included craftsmen,

---

230. For this connection and its implications, see Cordano 1978, 94–98; 1986, 46; Roebuck 1980, 1927–28. For wealthy sixth-century burials at Monte San Mauro, see Frasca 1996b, 84; 2001b.

231. Cordano 1988b, 21.

232. De Angelis 2003a, 29–33, 63–67.

233. Hdt. 7.156.1–2.

234. For the date, see recently De Angelis 2003a, 157–59. More on the tyranny below.

are thought to have gone about rewriting their involvement in the original foundation and leaving their physical presence on the new home via the creation of their own fortified quarter on the acropolis at Gela, named Lindioi.[235] The newcomers wanted to leave their own imprint on Gela's foundation history, urban plan, and artistic traditions, and they certainly succeeded in doing so. This may have encouraged even further elite competition at Gela in the sixth century, which in turn may have led to our first evidence for permanent settlement in the countryside, as a way to intensify production to support the displays of wealth and status that went hand in hand with these activities. It is interesting to note that cremation practices disappeared altogether at Gela in the sixth century BC.[236] This may have had something to do with burials losing their status as an arena to display wealth and status. In any case, political competition certainly resulted in the seizure of power by the tyrant Kleander, son of Pantares, himself an Olympic victor, as discussed above.

While these developments should leave little doubt that oligarchic governments dominated Sicilian Greek societies in the Archaic period, we have practically no knowledge of political offices and magistrates.[237] Political institutions would have developed across Sicily in the seventh century, as elsewhere in the Greek world, as a way to share and control power. The evidence discussed above also demonstrates unequivocally that ruling elites only considered constitutional changes when forced by those lower down on the social spectrum seeking greater economic involvement and recognition. Political privilege was otherwise protected by the ruling social classes, and change came about from the lower classes aiming only at getting "one's just entitlement," which "was the limit of egalitarianism in early Greek society."[238] If the elite were responsible for founding the Sicilian Greek cities and controlled external trade, as they seem to have, then these structures reinforced their hold on wealth, status, and power, making their grip even harder to shake.[239]

Our sources are not sufficiently detailed to calculate the size of Greek Sicily's oligarchies and the wealth and resources they controlled for any moment of their history, let alone the Archaic period, as is possible for Classical Athens.[240]

---

235. Sammartano 1999, 486–99.

236. Panvini 1996, 71.

237. Berger 1992, 66–68; Sartori 1997, 43, 51–54; Cordano 1999, 149–52; Zelnick-Abramowitz 2004. On a theoretical note, Wallace (2013) argues that councils may not have existed in oligarchies, which, if true, would explain some of the sources' silences.

238. Shipley 2005, 350. But see already Luraghi (1996, 217) for the same point.

239. Tandy 1997.

240. Morris 2009b, 120.

However, all indications are that these oligarchies were always small and controlled most of the natural and human resources. In addition to the evidence just discussed, archaeology may also provide relevant insights. Cemeteries in particular contain extremes of material behavior that can only mean social differences. At Megara Hyblaia, of the 250 tombs excavated in an area of 800 square meters in the south cemetery, 75 percent (or 188 tombs) have been defined as "poor."[241] Of these, 42 percent (or 79 tombs) have no grave goods at all. Thirteen percent of other tombs (or 33) were bare earth, and a further 1.5 percent of tombs (or 4) were only very rudimentarily worked. Thus almost 90 percent (or 224 of 250 burials) stand in contrast to the remaining burials of monumental size and adornment. More recent discoveries at Himera supply a similar picture. Of the more than 2,400 burials known from the Pestavecchia cemetery, only 10 percent are made up of (mainly primary) cremations, which in turn also generally have more accompanying grave-goods.[242] Such quantifiable data are not available for Leontinoi, but here too there are stark differences with very modest burials in terms of structure, grave goods, and ritual, which are entirely made up of inhumations.[243] Again, these tombs stand in contrast to wealthier ones known elsewhere at Leontinoi and at Monte San Mauro in its hinterland, which have already been discussed.

It would be highly subjective to try to quantify the differences in wealth and status suggested by all these burial data. Perhaps a more objective measure can be achieved by looking at differences in house size from Megara Hyblaia. In the seventh century, as seen in the previous chapter, the uniformity of house size and plan disappears in the city. Houses could now consist of anywhere between one and four rooms and occupy surface areas of between twenty and eighty square meters.[244] This suggests a difference of wealth of at least four times, on the basis solely of house size. We know next to nothing of how a house's superstructure may have looked, but we can be certain that differences existed in features like masonry, such as the same stone work used in public and domestic architecture discussed earlier. In addition, the sample of excavated houses from Megara Hyblaia comes from around the agora, and it may be possible that the differences refer only to elites, and not to the full social spectrum. At any rate, the calculations suggest possible ratios of wealth differences from a segment of the population, and similar pictures can also

---

241. For this and what follows, see Cébeillac-Gervasoni 1975, 33–34.

242. Fabbri, Schettino, and Vassallo 2006, 613–14; Vassallo and Valentino 2009, 238–39.

243. Frasca 2009, 109–11.

244. De Angelis 2003a, 43.

be envisaged for other Sicilian Greek cities where the settlement evidence is known to some degree.

How far, therefore, were the other, non-elite social groups formally admitted to citizenship? Oligarchy by its nature will always mean rule by "some" or "a few," leaving which some and how few to the determination of a society's particular dynamics. There is every good reason to think that Sicilian Greek citizenship could be quite open when it came to citizenship at the level of the upper social classes, with Greeks and non-Greeks admitted to citizenship. This is the image that one gets in cemeteries, where the only distinction between some neighboring burials is the different methods of deposition, and not their elite or ethnic appearance.[245] Just as Greeks are known to have integrated into Archaic Etruscan society in burial, and Etruscans into Archaic Roman society as rulers, in a form of horizontal, territorial mobility without changing social class or status,[246] so too does it seem that Archaic Sicilian Greek societies behaved similarly. The existence of vertical social mobility may be documented by the Teneans at Syracuse, but, apart from this, direct evidence is harder to come by for the Archaic period, unless we make something of the differences between persons having gentilicial and non-gentilicial names associated with them.[247]

Emma Dench's recent observation that Greek citizen bodies were different from Roman ones is true when comparing central Italy with Aegean Greece.[248] However, Sicilian Greek citizen bodies, in both the Archaic and Classical periods, were closer in spirit to Roman ones than to those of the Greek homeland.[249] Communities across Archaic Italy are being seen more and more in recent scholarship as cooperative multiethnic endeavors in which citizenship could cut across the different social groups composing the community. That is because cultural and other barriers were poorly developed at this early stage of Mediterranean interaction, and because elites desired to achieve synergy for their community's long-term success.[250] Herein lay the origins of Greek Sicily's oft-observed multifarious society and frequent civil strife: society's heterogeneous base, encouraged by the frontier, created more intense conditions for factionalism.[251]

---

245. For discussion, see Leighton 1999, 236; Lomas 2000, 182; De Angelis 2003b, 29. The later onomastic evidence from Selinous suggests as much: Collin Bouffier 2010b, 101–02.

246. Ampolo 1976–77.

247. Cf. Ampolo 1976–77, 342–43.

248. Dench 2005, 93–94.

249. Gallo 1982; Torelli 1994; Lomas 2000; AA.VV. 2012.

250. Rendeli 2005a; 2005b; Giangiulio 2010.

251. Gallo 1982, 921; Berger 1992; cf. Thompson 1973, 16.

To sum up, the above discussion of Archaic Greek societies in Sicily, while containing inevitable gaps and uncertainties, nonetheless allows some firm conclusions to be drawn.

The groundwork for Sicilian Greek society was laid in the Archaic period. *Polis* populations were mixed from the start, with incomers drawn from 360 degrees and occupying places in society from the top down.[252] The basic reason for this is not far to seek. Between 30,000 and 60,000 adult male emigrants, or about 1 to 2 percent of all Greeks living in the Aegean, took part in all overseas Greek settlement.[253] From this initially small base, population could only grow as steadily and as large as it did from a combination of external migration and internal dynamics, as seen most clearly at seventh-century Megara Hyblaia. In general, situations of abundant land but limited labor tend to generate population growth.[254] Population mobility was inherent in and necessary for Greek Sicily's social and economic development, and it is a dynamic that can be documented at both the individual and group level from Archaic times onward.[255]

Social inequality characterized Greek Sicily from the eighth century. The only political equality that existed at this time was between the ruling elites sharing power.[256] Any social change was driven by the lower classes, leading to civil strife and, if successful, resolved by legislated compromise. The lower classes wanted a piece of the economic success and wealth that occurred from the seventh century onward and to recalibrate the control of Sicilian resources. In general, therefore, oligarchic governments, when not punctuated by tyrannies, were the order of the day and were opposed by the *demos* ("people").[257] From city-state to city-state this pattern dominated, facilitating the development of political centralization that followed.

---

252. To adopt and expand the wording used by Antonetti and De Vido (2006b, 433) in discussing the directions from which people came to Archaic Selinous.

253. Scheidel 2003, 133–34.

254. M.E. Smith 2004, 93.

255. See especially Gras (1991), who throws light on individual mobility, in the context of the larger group migrations out of Ionia in the sixth and fifth centuries BC, by tracing the steps in Xenophanes of Colophon's migration, which included stopovers in, among other places, Zankle, Katane, and Syracuse, emphasizing in doing so how migrants could set out without knowing exactly where they would end up.

256. A position long held by Lepore (1970, 43–54, 59; 2000, 64–66) and often taken up, both directly and indirectly, by later scholars (Sartori 1980–81, 265; Berger 1992, 63–64; Shipley 2005, 349–50).

257. So Cordano 1986a, 127.

2. The First Generation of Political Centralization

Gela's tyrants were the first in Sicily to create a centralized territorial state through conquest and coercion, eventually transferring their capital to Syracuse. Akragas also created a similar territorial state under its tyrants. While the relationship between Syracuse and Akragas is sometimes portrayed in the written sources as involving tension, with Syracuse having the upper hand,[258] both states were allied and followed some similar policies and trajectories.

Although Kleander, tyrant of Gela, formulated the basic plan for Greek Sicily's first centralized territorial state,[259] it was left to his brother and successor Hippokrates to execute it on the ground. The conquest of land and people was the essential and basic ingredient. Hippokrates attacked Kallipolis, Naxos, Zankle, Leontinoi, Syracuse, and many "barbarians" (presumably native towns), all of them, except for Syracuse, falling under his sway.[260] Syracuse was only saved through outside help and sued for peace with Hippokrates, who obtained Kamarina in exchange in about 493/92 BC.[261] Polyaenus adds Ergetion to Hippokrates' conquests,[262] and, although the sources are silent on other conquests, there must have been other cities in his sights, such as Katane. The result was a multiethnic state, which gathered together human and economic resources never before seen in Greek Sicily. This necessitated certain arrangements to control and exploit these resources.

Military might not only made these conquests possible but also ensured its continuing existence. Initially, Gela's manpower consisted of local troops, including its oft-mentioned cavalry, and hired mercenaries.[263] But, as with premodern territorial states elsewhere, it is possible that the conquered cities supplied troops to Gela as their tribute.[264] Troops and tribute required management, and Hippokrates installed regional governors in at least two of his captured cities—Skythes at Zankle and Enesidemos

---

258. Diod. Sic. 11.48.5–8; Bonanno 2010, 116–22.

259. Braccesi and Millino 2000, 59.

260. Hdt. 7.154.1.

261. For the date, see Sinatra 1998, 46, who discusses generally Hippokrates' involvement in Kamarina.

262. Polyaen. 5.6. Ergetion has not been identified on the ground, but it is likely to have lain to the north of Kamarina (Fischer-Hansen, Nielsen, and Ampolo 2004a, 176–77). Its conquest probably occurred around 491/90 BC (Sinatra 1998, 47).

263. Bettalli 1995, 92–93; Mafodda 1998, 26–28; Millino 2001, 129–30.

264. Morris 2009b, 111.

at Leontinoi—who would have kept an eye on these subject regions, protecting and promoting the tyrant's interests.[265] From Herodotus' account of Skythes' fall from power at Zankle, the governor's mandate seems to have included further territorial conquest.[266] This is known to us in the context of the seizure of Zankle by Samians, who acted while Skythes was deep in the hinterland on military campaign. The regional governors were, of course, beholden to the center, and the aura of the paramount ruler was promoted as a way to achieve this. In this connection, it is interesting to observe that the first material evidence for the worship of Gela's oikists dates to this very period, perhaps not a coincidence given how later tyrants fancied themselves as modern-day oikists.[267]

The exploitation of conquered peoples and territories occurred possibly through the levying of troops, as just mentioned, and certainly through tribute. We know of this in connection with the seizure of Zankle by the Samians, who assuaged any displeasure Hippokrates had with them by giving him one-half of the movable goods and slaves in the city and everything from the countryside. This appears to be an allusion to the extraction of tribute, which may have previously existed and which of course would have been an important source of revenue for Hippokrates, and perhaps was a much more widespread practice than our written sources indicate.[268] In support of this, it is usually believed that Hippokrates minted Gela's first coinage, with which he presumably exacted this tribute and paid his mercenaries.[269] With this tribute, Hippokrates funded his territorial state and managed to siphon wealth into his hands and into Gela, manifesting itself in his military successes and no doubt in the public building that dates to the early fifth century.[270]

The conquest of land and people continued after Hippokrates' death at the battle of Hybla in about 491/90 BC. Gelon, his cavalry commander, established himself as tyrant and continued in Hippokrates' footsteps.[271] During this transition, some of Hippokrates' territorial gains were lost, the most substantial

---

265. Vanotti 1995, 91–92; Mafodda 1998, 28.

266. Hdt. 6.23.1.

267. Antonaccio 1999, 120.

268. Cf. Cordano 1988a, 58.

269. Braccesi and Millino 2000, 61; Millino 2001, 130.

270. Millino 2001, 132.

271. For the date, see Berger 1992, 35 n. 172. This Hybla is usually identified with Ragusa (Fischer-Hansen, Nielsen, and Ampolo 2004a, 177).

being the seizure of Zankle by Anaxilas, tyrant of Rhegion, in around 488/ 87 BC.[272] Gelon quickly managed to consolidate his hold on affairs and added Syracuse, which helped to compensate for the loss of the Straits of Messina.[273] An excuse for Gelon to intervene in Syracuse's affairs came in connection with the civil strife that broke out in 491/90 BC.[274] The Killyrioi expelled the *gamoroi* and in their place established a democracy, in which they gave themselves citizenship. The *gamoroi* sought refuge at Kasmenai in Syracuse's territory, from where they harassed the democracy.[275] The democracy was chaotic and weak, according to Aristotle, and sought the support of Gelon, who then turned around and recalled the *gamoroi*.

This recalling of the old Syracusan elite can be seen as part of Gelon's wider strategy of strengthening the city and making it his new capital via population transfers of elites from conquered cities. The overall aim may have been not just to concentrate and keep an eye on the highest social classes for obvious reasons, but also to center their wealth on Syracuse in order to increase Gelon's tax base, required to fund his capital-intensive projects discussed in the previous chapter.[276] While Gelon is known from the ancient tradition to have sold the lower classes into slavery,[277] it is unlikely that Syracusan's conquered territories were cleared of their dependent populations. It has been suggested that, with Syracuse's ever-growing economic needs, farm workers in the neighboring conquered cities of Megara Hyblaia and Leontinoi were left on the land to avoid disrupting production.[278]

Social engineering was needed to bring together successfully these diverse groups in a common urban space. New city quarters were built. Gelon must have enacted institutional reforms of some kind to deal with his population transfers and their resultant deurbanization, although this

---

272. Braccesi and Millino 2000, 68.

273. On this urgency, see Braccesi and Millino 2000, 71.

274. Berger 1992, 35–36.

275. It remains uncertain, though possible, whether an inscription now in New York that is reputed to have been found at Monte Casale, usually identified with Kasmenai, and that mentions *gamoroi* and their obtaining of tax exemptions and land grants should be connected to this incident, not just because of the uncertainty of its find-spot but also because of the seemingly Megarian script it was written in. For full discussion, see Arena 1989, 79–80 no. 76; Dubois 1989, 275–76 no. 219; Berger 1992, 36 n. 178.

276. Morris 2009b, 161.

277. Hdt. 7.156.2.

278. Demand 1990, 48, although such an argument is difficult to support or deny on account of the customary problem of identifying movements of dependent labor, as noted earlier in this chapter.

is something that our sources are (not surprisingly) silent about.[279] The newcomers may have been distributed in these and the older city quarters, initially at least, according to their place of origin to respect their identity. In a general way, Kathryn Lomas has recently argued that, for all Sicilian population transfers of the fifth and fourth centuries BC, the identity and sense of self of incorporated communities were not destroyed.[280] We could also support this by recalling the residential segregation that existed in Archaic Sicily, as well as by the forms of commemoration, like the poetry of the transferred Megarian elite to Syracuse, that also later emerged as social identity markers.[281]

Regional governors continued, as under Hippokrates, to help maintain control across state territory. Insofar as we know, Gelon set up his brother Hieron at Gela and his friend Glaukos of Karystos at Kamarina.[282] Whether governors regularly collected tribute (beyond the lump sum paid by Carthage after being defeated at Himera[283]) and demanded troops from subject cities on behalf of Gelon remain issues that, as with Hippokrates, we cannot speak with much certainty. Gelon continued his predecessor's practice of extensively using mercenaries, perhaps upward of 10,000 of them. He gave them citizenship at some point between 485 and 480, so as to solidify their loyalty and his power over Syracuse.[284] The origin of these mercenaries, where known, can be traced to Arkadia, but they must have also come from other parts of Greece, and possibly too from the Italian mainland.[285]

The granting of citizenship to mercenaries is often thought to have broken new ground in the Greek world, causing a disruption of the "sacredness" of citizenship that would have a lasting effect on Sicilian politics and shape citizen

---

279. Braccesi and Millino 2000, 74.

280. Lomas 2006, 114.

281. For the Megarian elite at Syracuse, see De Angelis 2003a, 66. Cf. also the Megarian graffiti found on cups at Gela and Syracuse from this time, which have been linked to questions of population movement and identity (Arena 1989, 22 no. 10, 78 no. 75).

282. Fischer-Hansen, Nielsen, and Ampolo 2004a, 204; Adornato 2008, 52.

283. A sum of 2,000 talents, according to Diodorus Siculus (11.26.2). For the possibility that Selinous, Carthage's ally, also had to pay tribute, see De Angelis 2003a, 162–63.

284. Bettalli 1995, 94–98; Mafodda 1998, 30; Millino 2001, 143–47; Péré-Noguès 2004, 146.

285. For the Arkadian origins, see in particular Bettalli 1995, 98, 149–53. The tradition that includes Arkadians in Syracuse's Archaic foundation must surely be invented to justify the presence of these mercenaries. De la Genière (1996, 169, 171; 1999b; 2001) argues for mercenaries from the Italian mainland on the basis of particular graves in one of Gela's cemeteries, a suggestion which has both followers (Péré-Noguès 2006, 483) and detractors (Millino 2001, 157–60).

bodies in ways that would later receive comment by Thucydides and Plato.[286] However, this decision by Gelon, whose prime goal was to gain and hold on to power, can also be related to the ease of acquiring citizenship in Archaic Sicilian cities, rather than some kind of innovation. The type of imperial state Gelon was building demanded this measure, and any political ideals that may have existed among the Greeks were pushed aside to fulfil his goals.

An even greater cosmopolitan air must have characterized Syracuse with the arrival of these mercenaries and elites. While these population transfers (and later departures) created populations that fluctuated throughout the fifth century, such fluctuation should not put one off from making a first attempt at estimating Syracuse's overall population size.[287] One way to ground Syracusan population in reality is to follow Hansen in using the degree of urbanization, for which data exist. At 100–120 hectares in size, Syracuse under Gelon may have had a population on the order of 15,000–24,000.[288] Estimates of the total population within Deinomenid Syracuse's boundaries are even more difficult to make, given the sparseness of concrete data. But if, for the sake of argument, we put together all the estimates for the cities conquered (see Table 5) and the mercenaries employed, a guess of upward of 100,000 people should not be regarded as too far-fetched.[289]

Such a large population would have in itself presented challenges to Gelon, but this was compounded by the additional challenge of having to control a diverse and potentially very fractious array of social groups.[290] To all appearances, Gelon succeeded in massaging them into a workable whole by acting as a sort of mediator between them all and by adopting a careful middle-ground political approach that could range between elitism and democracy.[291] A passage of Diodorus Siculus depicts Gelon as a fair-minded and down-to-earth individual, a passage which, once shorn of its Hellenistic anachronisms, might well faithfully represent him.[292] Sumptuary

---

286. Bettalli 1995, 97–98; Péré-Noguès 1999, 106; 2004, 145–46. See below for these Athenian reactions.

287. As in Fischer-Hansen, Nielsen, and Ampolo 2004a, 225.

288. Compare with Drögemüller's (1969, 100) higher estimate of 40,000–45,000 people. Fischer-Hansen, Nielsen, and Ampolo (2004a, 226) also think this estimate is too high based on Syracuse's size, but they do not advance their own.

289. For an overview, cf. Fischer-Hansen, Nielsen, and Ampolo 2004a, 227; Morris 2013, 171–72, along with discussion in Chapter 2 and Table 5 here.

290. Demand 1990, 46–47.

291. See in particular Mafodda 1996; Consolo Langher 1997; and, more briefly, Brugnone 1992, 21.

292. Diod. Sic. 11.26.1–6. On the anachronisms, see Rutter (1993, 178–85).

laws concerned with luxurious burial and personal adornment were either reinstated or drawn up as part of this policy.[293] Syracusan burial forms and goods in the fifth century BC did indeed witness more uniformity and less investment.[294] These sumptuary laws were both economic and political in nature, aimed at curbing displays of wealth and status in order to strike the political balance Gelon sought for the community as a whole. In general, the sources are notable for their absence of emphasis on social hierarchy during Gelon's reign.

All this should not mask the fact that Gelon was himself elite, though from another city. It may be for this reason and the general balancing act Gelon attempted to maintain that Syracuse's old elite felt comfortable enough under his rule, since we hear of no challenges from them, despite the sumptuary laws clearly aimed at them.[295] It is possible that the tyrant may have nevertheless confiscated (or purchased?) land for himself and his entourage: a passing reference exists that his wife had a fortified estate, and that he himself had a garden at Hipponion.[296] Asheri was probably right to single out Deinomenid control of Syracuse as marking the beginning of radical land distribution, even though little can about be said about this and the whole question of resistance, as well as by extension of their social and economic ramifications.[297]

The attention Gelon devoted to making Syracuse a maritime power also impacted society, and not just the economy, as outlined in the previous chapter. The construction of a new port with arsenal, along with allusions to warships and merchant ships in the ancient sources, would imply a substantial navy and hence hefty expenditure.[298] Sadly, we know nothing of the number of their ships and the nature of their ownership (public versus private) in the period of the Deinomenids as a whole.[299] Thousands of rowers would have been needed to man these ships, and, as anywhere, problems of recruitment must have

---

293. Bindi 1980; Brugnone 1992.

294. Jackman 2005, 24; Shepherd 2007, 99. This coincides with a similar trend in the Aegean Greek world (Morris 1992b, 145–46).

295. So Mafodda 1998, 31; Rutter 2000, 141. See generally Braccesi and Millino 2000, 54.

296. For the estate: Diod. Sic. 11.38.4 (cf. Frederiksen 2011, 121); for the garden: Ath. 542a (cf. Redfield 2003, 217).

297. Asheri 1966, 39.

298. Corretti (2006, 419–21) is right, however, to point out the uncertainties of a navy for Gelon's reign. Instead, he argues that it is likelier that Hieron was responsible for establishing Syracuse's navy (see below).

299. Corretti 2006, 417.

ensued. At least for the warships, the bulk of the rowers presumably came from Syracuse's lower classes, empowering them and setting into motion social dynamics that Gelon, as a populist, marshaled to his advantage.[300]

Religion and dedications were other ways Gelon could foster social cohesion between all groups and classes. One of the first dedications he arguably made was in 485 BC, soon after he took the reins of power at Syracuse. It consisted of a tripod to Apollo at Delphi, an appropriate venue for a tyrant who was reasonably fancying himself as Syracuse's second founder in a similar time of state formation.[301] Other dedications at Panhellenic sanctuaries followed.[302] Gelon also used the cult of Demeter and Persephone, with its inclusive character for women of all standings and for its activities central to all human well-being, as a way to help bind people of different social classes and backgrounds together.[303] Whether or not Gelon constructed the temple of Athena on Ortygia, and whether or not its partner at Himera is also to be identified with Athena,[304] it would certainly have made sense to worship this goddess so closely connected with the military sphere in which Gelon sought to distinguish himself.

Sport also allowed Gelon and his entire Deinomenid court to elevate themselves above all other Syracusans in order to lay a legitimate claim to their rule and, equally important, to broadcast their status and achievements. Victory in sport was as effective as victory on the battlefield,[305] and the commissioning of poets, notably Pindar, let the world know about these victories.[306] Gelon won in the chariot competition during the seventy-third Olympiad while he was still at Gela and set a standard for others to follow. However even-handed and pragmatic Gelon is reputed to have been to all segments of society, he and his court still had to engage in status-seeking activities that secured their place at the head of Syracuse.

Gelon's death in 478 BC raised the question of the transference of power. Although Gelon himself could legitimately become tyrant because of the

---

300. Corretti 2006, 416, 421.

301. See Adornato 2005 and, in general, Mitchell 2013, 73–80.

302. See in particular Harrell 2002; 2006.

303. De Angelis 2006, 35–38.

304. So Gras 1990.

305. R.R.R. Smith 2007, 83.

306. Hornblower 2006; Hornblower and Morgan 2007. Hieron, however, seems to have been more interested than Gelon in commissioning poets and philosophers (cf. Demand 1990, 50–58).

important military command he held within Hippokrates' inner circle, the Deinomenids opted for a policy of inheritance within the immediate family. Power thus passed to Gelon's brother Hieron, who conspired against their brother Polyzelos to do so. Polyzelos may have been given Gela to govern as a consolation prize.[307] Hieron continued many of Gelon's policies, though he added some new ones, such as the patronage of poets and theater, to further his ideological schemes and to elevate his status.

Power was conceived of in ways both similar and different from before. Unlike Gelon, Hieron was not a supporter of the laws he had inherited at Syracuse and is said to have repealed Kharondas' laws.[308] Hieron established greater presence in Syracuse's extensive territorial holdings. Like his brother, he effected this by further population transfers; unlike his brother, he redesigned the urban look of those preexisting cities, like Naxos, which he decided to continue using. He also founded a new city, very much envisaging himself in doing so as an oikist (founder), though with a twist on tradition: he sought to be honored while still alive.[309] Clearly, the seeds of ruler ideology were being sown in this period, ones that gave rise to tools also used by later Sicilian tyrants (see below). The city's name was Aitna, a reference to its proximity to that great geographical feature that dominates the topography of eastern central Sicily. He settled his mercenary troops in Aitna and made it the seat of his governor Khromios. Hieron also established a temple of Demeter in the city.[310] This is a cult in which Gelon too had exhibited interest, but Hieron's planting of mercenary colonists there was interventionist and signaled a long-term agricultural interest in the region that must have worried its previous inhabitants.

Attention continued to be devoted to the development of Syracuse's maritime capabilities. This was a way not only to protect Hieron's domains and subjects, but also to project his power and extend his territorial reach. In fact,

---

307. Diod. Sic. 11.48.3–8. Associating the dedication at Delphi mentioning the ruler of Gela with Polyzelos is what is normally done (Arena 1998, 124–25 no. 68; Bonanno 2010, 55–69). Though, see now Adornato 2008, 52, who thinks that the dedication is likelier to refer to Hieron between 485 and 478 BC. Tension between Hieron and Polyzelos ensued whether or not this consolation prize was given.

308. Braccesi and Millino 2000, 51.

309. Bonanno 2010, 128–57. The ancient passage regarding Hieron's honors is Diodorus Siculus (11.49.2), which must be read in conjunction with modern analyses of it (Malkin 1987, 237–38; De Polignac 1995, 147; Antonaccio 1999, 121; cf. also De Angelis and Garstad 2006, 219–21).

310. Nothing is known archaeologically of this temple: Mertens 2006, 351.

according to a recent proposal, Hieron may have been chiefly responsible for creating Syracuse's navy.[311] This may explain why Hieron was able to break Anaxilas' hold on the Straits of Messina (though Messana itself remained out of his control)[312] and to establish Syracusan presence in the Tyrrhenian Sea after being victorious in 474 BC over the Etruscans in a battle off Cumae, with whose tyrant, Aristodemus, Hieron had allied.[313] The Syracusans dedicated two captured helmets (Etruscan and Corinthian) at Olympia, to mark their victory in an "international" forum.[314] Recently it has been argued, on good grounds, that Hieron built the monumental Temple of Athena at Syracuse from the spoils of this battle, thus also marking his victory at home.[315] If so, Hieron was deftly using the cult of Athena in the heart of the city to promote himself as a warrior and to cement his power over a population of disparate elements.

The sporting arena also provided opportunities to achieve success. Most of the Deinomenids' involvement in Panhellenic competitions occurred under Hieron.[316] Both he and members of his court earned a succession of victories in various competitions. The rivalry seems to have been not just between Syracusan and other Greek elites, but also between the Deinomenids themselves.[317] Some of these successes were commemorated by commissioning poets like Pindar. This move allowed for the satisfaction of both personal and state promotion.[318]

The patronage of poets was taken to new heights by actively supporting drama, both tragedy and comedy.[319] Such patronage required the necessary economic wherewithal. Syracusan tragedy and comedy also served similar social functions to their later, better-documented Athenian counterparts, allowing for the forging of local and Panhellenic identities.

---

311. Corretti 2006, 421.

312. Cf. Braccesi and Millino 2000, 83–84.

313. Bonanno 2010, 159–78. On Aristodemus, see generally Luraghi 1994, 79–118.

314. For the dedications, see Arena 1998, 122–23 nos. 67a–67b.

315. For discussion, see Chapter 2.

316. For full details of these victories, see Moretti 1959, 84–85 nos. 186–87, 87 nos. 196–98, 90 no. 221, 92 no. 234, 93 no. 246, 94 no. 248; Arena 1998, 119–20 nos. 64–65, 124 no. 68, R.R.R. Smith 2007; Antonaccio 2007; Bonanno 2010, 182–86.

317. Cf. Adornato 2008.

318. However, as Hornblower (2006) has argued in the case of Pindar, these poets should not be simply seen as the tyrant's slavish voices.

319. See Braccesi and Millino 2000, 89; Kowalzig 2008; Bonanno 2010, 199–209; and especially Bosher 2012a.

Any discussion of tragedy in this period must focus on the Athenian Aeschylus, who was invited to court to perform his play *The Persians*. It is generally thought, in the customary Athenocentric manner, that this play was a reperformance of the one originally staged in Athens. But a recent study convincingly revives a nineteenth-century view that *The Persians* was commissioned by Hieron and performed for the first time at Syracuse.[320] While it must remain a possibility for the time being that Syracusan initiative was behind his play, the overall effect and meaning of the play would have been largely the same for Hieron and Syracuse. Good leadership in a victory over one's opponents was being stressed.

The Sicilian theme and Hieronian initiative of Aeschylus' other play *Aetnaeae* have never been in doubt. The play can easily be connected with Hieron's foundation of the city of Aitna, discussed earlier. Its aim was not only to anchor this foundation to this conquered region, but also "to reconnect Xuthus to Sicily, where he properly belonged since Pentathlus [in 580–576 BC]" after he had been appropriated by Athens in the second half of the sixth century.[321]

Syracusan tragedy has been connected with Demeter and Persephone.[322] If so, this would provide a further indication of the Deinomenids' close association with these goddesses and their concern for the well-being of all social classes, from the populace to the elite. In other words, the tyrant and his people were not in opposition, but constituted a single whole. Some of Syracuse's economic success was deployed to broadcast this social message, as well as more simply to entertain.

Any discussion of comedy in this period must focus on another central figure, Epicharmus. A homegrown talent, his work survives in fragments, though enough can be gleaned from them to reconstruct the main outlines of his world.[323] Epicharmus preserves valuable information on Syracusan dialect in this period, and his fragments are notable for their significant number of Italic loan and hybrid words.[324] His work underlines, yet again, the cosmopolitan nature of Syracusan society at this time.[325] Although Epicharmus wrote numerous plays, sufficient fragments survive of only one of them—*Odysseus Automolos* (*Odysseus the Deserter*)—to say something of

---

320. Bosher 2012b.

321. Smith 2012, 133.

322. Kowalzig 2008.

323. See Willi 2008, 119–92; 2012 for excellent overviews of recent interpretations.

324. In general, see Tribulato 2012.

325. Hall 2012, 28.

its contents and aims. According to Andreas Willi, who has studied these fragments in detail:

> Epicharmus distances the normal discourse of his comedy from the high-flown discourse of epic, and his play becomes doubly subversive: firstly because Odysseus feels, thinks, and acts like an ordinary person, an anti-hero with whom an average Syracusan will identify more easily than an aristocrat dreaming of a heroic past; and secondly because heroic language is deflated, denounced as empty, pretentious, but ultimately ridiculous.[326]

As Willi goes on to argue, Syracusan comedy was similar to Aristophanes' two generations later, in that the elitism and authority of the characters are scrutinized and mocked for the audience. In this way, Syracusan comedy served the function required of it by Hieron and the Deinomenids in general: the populace was both entertained and made to feel comfortable in an otherwise authoritarian and ever-changing world.

The road taken by Hieron in his conception of power vis-à-vis his people charted new ground in maintaining his hold on power. To all appearances, he succeeded for eleven years until his death, by natural causes, in 467 BC. Thrasyboulos, Hieron's successor and the third Deinomenid tyrant, abused his power in an extreme way during his reign. Thrasyboulos acted against his fellow Syracusans in a harsh manner, killing and exiling many citizens, confiscating property, and using his mercenaries to support this behavior. Such actions resulted in the successful overthrow of Thrasyboulos within a year, and a change in government, whose character and nature will be discussed in the next section.

The Deinomenids were allied with Akragas, Sicily's other most powerful Greek state, then ruled by the Emmenid tyrants. Akragas' rise to power was similarly brought to fruition by a dynamic individual, Theron, who rose above his elite competition to become tyrant in 488/87 BC.

The conquest of land and people was also on Theron's agenda. He increased Akragas' territory considerably, particularly to the detriment of its northern and western neighbors Himera and Selinous (Figure 23). Both the latter cities had alliances of some kind with Carthage, and in the case of Himera Herodotus informs us that its tyrant Terillus had guest-friendship ties in Carthage that were so close they culminated in intervention in Sicily and prompted as a show of support the famous Battle of Himera.[327]

---

326. Willi 2012, 71.

327. Hdt. 7.165–66.

FIGURE 23 View of Didrachm Depicting Rooster and Crab Minted at Himera during Akragantine Occupation.
© The Hunterian, University of Glasgow 2015

The victory that ensued for Syracuse and Akragas marked a dramatic turning-point for all concerned, and at Akragas the influx of booty and prisoners, not to mention the enormous emotive boost it brought, helped to materialize Theron's earlier desire to leave his monumental stamp on the city and to secure his presence across his territorial domains. His building programs in the city would also have benefited the lower social classes financially and thereby garnered popular support for Theron.[328]

The existence of governors residing in Akragas' subject cities is attested via a passing mention in Diodorus Siculus of Theron's son, Thrasydaeus, in control of Himera.[329] Whether a system of regular tribute was imposed throughout or on parts of Akragas' territorial possessions, beyond any recompense received in connection with the victory at Himera, is completely unknown. Such a system presumably existed, but we have no details of tribute-paying cities and the amount of tribute extracted from them.[330]

We have no certain facts about the size and development of Akragas' population under tyranny, in both city and countryside. However, totals are unlikely to have exceeded those reached under democracy in the next historical period. A substantial population had to be managed, as well as social harmony sought between Akragas' Cretan and Rhodian components (Theron belonged to the

328. Braccesi and Millino 2000, 100.

329. Diod. Sic. 11.48.6.

330. Palermo (2004, 201), for example, has realistically suggested that Sant'Angelo Muxaro became a tribute-paying subject of Akragas during Theron's reign.

latter). According to ancient tradition, Theron had the bones of "Minos" returned to Crete from the Sicilian hinterland that, coincidentally, he had recently conquered.[331] Some possible archaeological confirmation for the "Cretanization" of sanctuaries at Akragas has emerged in recent years.[332] At the same time, there is also possible evidence for the suppression of Cretan elements in another sanctuary at Akragas. There seems to be something of a contradiction in these two types of evidence, which can only be clarified with future research.

Theron's son, Thrasydaeus, assumed power and acted outrageously against his fellow Akragantines, just like his Syracusan counterpart Thrasyboulos. Thrasydaeus also acted in a harsh manner by killing and exiling many citizens, confiscating their property and supporting himself with mercenaries. All this led to his expulsion, which occurred not long after his ascension to power in 472/71 BC.[333]

The tyrants of Syracuse and Akragas pursued similar policies, as just seen, in the sphere of social control before the last of each of them was ousted from power for abusing the fine balance their predecessors had sought. The Deinomenids and Emmenids created for themselves clans that intermarried and formed alliances.[334] By contrast, we hear nothing of the Archaic clans that had existed in the cities that these tyrants now controlled. The decline of extended families as royal power grows is a phenomenon encountered in other historical periods,[335] and in a similar fashion, the silence about clans during this period of Sicilian history may likewise reflect their suppression and discouragement by the tyrants, who saw them as a challenge to their own authority.

Something similar also appears to be at play with regard to the absence of strong administrative institutions during this period of Sicilian tyranny.[336] At best, we hear of the tyrants using family or supporters from the inner ruling circle to act as regional governors in their territorial states, but no mention is ever made of any bureaucracy or its constituent parts. While to some degree this may be the result of our scrappy written sources, at the same time it cannot be the whole explanation. Instead, the silence must surely reflect a real absence. Fiscal instability is one cause advanced for the collapse of

---

331. Braccesi and Millino 2000, 100; Perlman 2002, 193–99; Collin Bouffier 2010a, 297.

332. See conveniently De Angelis 2012a, 173 for this and the next point.

333. Berger 1992, 36–37; Collin Bouffier 2010a, 299.

334. See Vallet 1980 for full discussion. In general, see Mitchell 2013, 91–118.

335. Cf. Trigger 2003, 271; Weber 2003, 46. Therefore, the silence of the sources for Sicily seems significant.

336. Morris 2009b, 165–66.

Sicilian Greek tyrannies in the 460s, perhaps induced from this "light touch" approach to administration.[337]

Sicily was clearly transformed both socially and economically during the first phase of political centralization spearheaded by Gela/Syracuse and Akragas. While the tyrants followed activities inherited from their predecessors, such as monumental building projects, competitive displays, and mixed communities, they took them to new heights. At the same time, they steered their societies and economies in completely different directions. Sicilian Greek tyrants amassed extraordinary power and wealth that stood out to their fellow Greeks in the homeland.[338] Their territorial states were little different from most Old World ones, in that their rulers supplied ruthless leadership, and cities and people they conquered were treated as personal possessions.[339]

3. From the Collapse to the Return of Political Centralization

The collapse of these politically centralized states ushered in another phase of Sicilian Greek history, with its own social and economic outcomes. Out of a landscape dominated by territorial states, several city-states regained their independence for two generations, while the old imperial powers had to adapt themselves to their new realities. Aristotle and Diodorus Siculus claimed that democracies took root across the entire island in this period, and Thucydides makes some in-passing statements during Athens' invasion of Sicily that either mention democracies directly or contain details from which they have been inferred.[340] For these reasons Finley described this phase of history as a "democratic interlude."[341] This enchanting phrase has often been quoted in later scholarship.[342] Asheri, however, rightly urged caution and said to expect much local variety under such umbrella generalizations, owing to previous conditions and current circumstances in Sicily's cities.[343] The case for democracy, moreover, is sometimes made in isolation without considering the full

---

337. Morris 2009b, 162.

338. Note Thuc. 1.17; cf. also Morris 2009b, 120.

339. Morris 2009b, 166; cf. already Weber 2013, 176.

340. Arist., *Pol.* 1303a–b2; Diod. Sic. 11.72.2–73, 76.1–2; Thuc. 7.33.1; 55; 58.1.

341. Finley 1979, 58.

342. For a recent example, see Cartledge 2009, 124.

343. Asheri 1980b, 154. See Cordano (2003, 121) for a recent adoption of Asheri's stance.

material record and social history of a city by scholars more interested in the history of democracy than in Sicilian Greek democracy per se.

Demography. One of the reasons to be cautious in not labeling all of Sicily as democratic in this period concerns the presence of elite clans. These either re-emerged in cities previously ruled by tyrants or represented a continuation for cities outside their control.

The main instance of continuity involves Selinous. Three victims mentioned in a curse tablet dating to 475–450 BC are defined as Herakleidai.[344] Even if deriving from a private inscription, the existence of a gentilicial name and of individuals claiming heroic origins has stimulated further speculation. The Herakleidai may have associated themselves with the Spartan king Dorieus and his cultural framework, which remained a legacy in Sicily despite his failure at settling in western Sicily in the previous generation.[345] The adoption of a Spartan lifestyle may have been intended to oppose the isonomic and antisumptuary tendencies of the Greek world.[346] Another clan, the Tyndaridai ("descendants of the Dioscuri"), is mentioned in a public inscription from Temple G commemorating a victory in battle.[347] The young cavalrymen of this clan fell for their homeland and may have belonged to a Spartan form of ephebic organization adopted at Selinous.[348]

The re-emergence of the old clan order is attested at Naxos and Himera, which had become independent of tyrannical rule. The evidence from Naxos consists of two terracotta projectiles found in two different places within the city wall.[349] One of the projectiles dates to the first half of the fifth century and is probably connected with Hieron's assault on Naxos.[350] The name and patronymic on it are preceded by the word Pollidai. The second projectile dates to the end of the fifth century and is probably connected with Dionysius I's assault on Naxos.[351] On it the name and patronymic are also preceded by a similar identity marker, Hermondai. We can assume not only continuity in the clan's military function,

---

344. Arena 1989, 70–71 no. 69; Cordano 1997a, 403; Collin Bouffier 2010b, 94–95.

345. Antonetti and De Vido 2006a, 157.

346. Antonetti and De Vido 2006a, 161.

347. *IG* 14.268, line 4; cf. Arena 1989, 52–54 no. 53; De Angelis 2003a, 174–75.

348. Antonetti and De Vido 2006a, 157. The so-called "Ephebe" in bronze from Selinous of this period mentioned in the previous chapter may have been fortuitously labeled in light of this possible Spartan ephebic organization.

349. Cordano 1988b; Dubois 2008, 12–14 no. 4. Cf. also Cordano 1988a, 60; 2003, 124; Fischer-Hansen, Nielsen, and Ampolo 2004a, 219.

350. Cordano 1988b, 18–20.

351. Cordano 1988b, 18–20.

but also, more generally, the return of Naxos' exiles from forced confinement at Leontinoi by Hieron to their lifestyle and land as before their deportation.[352]

The evidence from Himera is found on a lead plaque dating to 475–450 BC that seems to record a message sent to a squadron commander (*lokhagos*).[353] Three names are involved: two are personal names, and the other Euopidas is usually regarded as gentilicial. The *lokhos* in question subdivided men for military purposes and was part of a larger whole, possibly the phratry attested in the late Archaic law on land redistribution discussed earlier.

Some interesting evidence is also known from Kamarina. It consists of an inscribed bronze cube mentioning a dedication by a certain Antandros to Apollo Patroios (or Apollo of the phratry).[354] This is the first attestation in Sicily of what seems to be a new cult, whose mandate was to protect the family and the descent group. The general context of this dedication was Kamarina's refoundation, which involved the distribution of plots of land to the settlers, who seem to have introduced a new cult to support the success of families and, presumably by extension, the succession and inheritance of these families with regard to their newly acquired land.

Important evidence for clans in rural contexts comes from Balate di Marianopoli in the territory of Akragas, where the names Chilaioi and Lykumnioi are inscribed on obelisk stelae in a religious precinct.[355]

Larger social subdivisions of the phratry and the tribe are much better documented in Classical Sicily, as mentioned above.[356] They are found in both literary and epigraphic sources and are generally documented in contexts referring to collective decisions or military actions. The single most important evidence derives from a cache of lead tablets found in the Temple of Athena at Kamarina.[357] These tablets provide evidence of a highly rational system of civic subdivisions into phratries, which served, among other things, as the basis of citizen membership and possibly military training.[358]

---

352. Cordano 2003, 124. Another clan, the Amphikleidai, is mentioned in Hellenistic temple inventories from Delos. The clan's origins have also been placed in this period (Rutherford 1998).

353. Dubois 1989, 13–14 no. 11; Arena 1994, 59–60 no. 51; Grotta 2008, 258–64. Cf. also Knoepler 2007, 97.

354. Manganaro 1995, 98–99; 1996, 77.

355. Cordano 1997a, 401–06; Ghinatti 2000, 37.

356. Cordano 1992a; Ghinatti 2000; 2003.

357. Cordano 1992b.

358. Helly 1997; Murray 1997; Robinson 2002; cf. Fischer-Hansen, Nielsen, and Ampolo 2004a, 204. Del Monaco (2004) suggests the military function. Any relationship with Kamarina's town plan is unknown (Mertens 2006, 354).

Estimating the overall size of Greek Sicily's population remains as much a challenge, even if we have a few more literary and epigraphic sources, as ever before. That is because many of the Classical cities occupied the same space as their Archaic predecessors. Evidence for contraction and densification is limited or nonexistent, which does not mean that they were absent. As a first step, the picture sketched out in Table 5 can be taken as a general benchmark in terms of population density and distribution. The cases in which this does not apply are discussed here.

For Himera, it looks possible that its fifth-century population was higher than the Archaic one. Asheri put this Classical population at 30,000 people for city and country, but that may still be on the low side according to a more recent consideration.[359]

The epigraphic evidence from Kamarina just discussed suggests a total of 5,400 citizens, which is then made to fit and corroborate earlier population estimates of 15,000–20,000 inhabitants.[360] If, however, one multiplies the total number of citizens by a factor of at least four, a slightly higher number of 21,600 inhabitants is produced. If Kamarina was indeed a city of 150 hectares—a figure requiring confirmation, as noted in the previous chapter—the figure might even be put higher, at 22,550–30,000 inhabitants when Hansen's multiplier of 150–200 people per hectare is used.

For Syracuse, by contrast, our current population estimates seem to be on the high side. Morris extends Hans-Peter Drögemüller's urban population of 40,000–45,000 to Syracuse during the Peloponnesian War, but, as argued above, Drögemüller's estimate, once grounded in current ideas of urbanization, suggest a total of 15,000–24,000 inhabitants. Similarly, Beloch's estimate of 250,000 people for Syracuse's whole territory may well be also too high.[361] More tempered guesswork is the best option. Did Syracuse's population surpass the 100,000 estimated above for the Deinomenid period?

Akragas' population size drew ancient attention in light of its temple building, discussed in the previous chapter, and the stories of wealthy individuals discussed below. Diogenes Laertius put the figure at 800,000 in the time of Empedocles, but modern scholars have rightly rejected this as "an obvious

---

359. Asheri (1973) based on the now outdated estimate of 80 hectares for Himera's urban size. For the higher but unspecified level of population: Fischer-Hansen, Nielsen, and Ampolo (2004a, 199).

360. For the number of citizens: Helly 1997. For the earlier population estimates: Beloch 1889, 51; Pelagatti and Vallet 1980, 383–84; Cordano 2003, 123.

361. Beloch 1886, 281; 1889, 60.

exaggeration."[362] At the time of the Carthaginian siege in 406 BC, Diodorus Siculus put the population of Akragas at 200,000 people, of whom 20,000 were citizens and the rest *xenoi* ("resident foreigners").[363]

Modern scholars have either followed this figure, or suggested somewhat smaller ones.[364] Jos de Waele regarded 200,000 inhabitants as an artificially high number and looked at the settlement evidence, arriving at an estimate of 16,000–18,000 citizens (still somewhat close to the ancient number).[365] While this approach is certainly laudable, our knowledge of Akragas' size is still best known for Hellenistic and Roman periods (200 hectares), and its extrapolation to the Archaic and Classical periods may be a wildly misleading assumption. Nevertheless, de Waele's estimate is probably closer to the truth than earlier estimates, because it includes a systematic look at the settlement data. If, simply for the sake of argument, we follow the same approach, but by again applying the 150–200 people per hectare multiplier to the 200 hectares, we arrive at a total population of some 30,000–40,000 inhabitants.

A slightly lower population can be estimated for Selinous. Diodorus Siculus, in narrating the Carthaginian sack of Selinous, gives various figures concerning deaths, military units, and refugees, alongside mentioning the city's obvious prosperity, but no overall figure for its total population.[366] Since the nineteenth century, scholars have turned to the archaeological evidence, sometimes combining it with these literary figures. The most recent example puts Selinous' fifth-century population at 14,000–19,000 inhabitants.[367] This would fall in the range of Hansen's urbanization procedure, and thus it may stand as a good guess.

The foregoing discussion should make clear that further work is needed if we want to estimate the number of people living in Sicily in the last two-thirds of the fifth century BC. For the sake of provoking thought, let us set this ancient period against the development of modern Sicilian population in the nineteenth century. In 1831, the population was about 1.9 million; in 1861, at

---

362. Fischer-Hansen, Nielsen, and Ampolo 2004a, 186. Cf. also De Waele 1980, 750, 752.

363. This information is given at 13.84.3, but at 13.90.3 he simply says 200,000 inhabitants. De Waele (1980, 751) regards these two passages as basically saying the same thing, noting that the *xenoi* here must mean non-citizen metics and slaves.

364. De Waele (1980, 752–56) provides an overview of modern estimates. Missing from his consideration is Waters (1974, 13), who supports Diodorus Siculus' figures of 200,000 inhabitants. As De Waele's overview has revealed, scholars have generally advanced estimates of greater than 100,000, including Beloch (1886, 281–85, 298; 1889, 15–17, 41–46, 60–61, 66), who put Akragas' late-fifth-century population at a grand total of 150,000 inhabitants.

365. De Waele 1980, 756–60.

366. Diod. Sic. xiii.44.3–4; 57.2–6; 58.3; cf. De Angelis 2003a, 146–49.

367. Zuchtriegel 2011, 121.

Italian unification, it had risen to 2.4 million; and by 1901 it had risen further to 3.5 million.[368] Ancient Greek Sicily's carrying capacity could certainly
support the first two of these population levels.[369] Sicily in the nineteenth
century, like many other parts of the world, was moving toward important
advances in political participation and health care, including the curbing of
diseases like malaria. The impacts that these developments had on modern
societies and economies are likewise well known. Did the democratic breeze
blowing through Sicily also result in the development of population size and
quality of life? Some indications to this effect exist for Classical Greek Sicily.

Disease is more attested in this period, simply because there are more surviving literary sources. These attestations are often referred by generic Greek
words, particularly *loimos* ("plague"), and thus need interpreting to reveal their
closest modern equivalent. Physical anthropology, as previously noted, has been
of little or no service in this regard, given the scant attention paid to the generally
well-preserved skeletal remains from cemeteries. Nevertheless, we can imagine a
population suffering from the usual sorts of ailments that affected preindustrial
standards of living, other than those that can be inferred from ancient literature.

Our knowledge is most detailed concerning Selinous. In about the mid-fifth
century, Empedocles, the distinguished philosopher from nearby Akragas, was
invited to rid the city of a disease, either malaria or typhus in all probability.[370]
Empedocles curbed it by blocking a mountain gorge carrying pestilential wind
to pregnant women and to the plain below.[371] An inscription mentioning victory and coins depicting Artemis and Apollo have often been used as evidence
commemorating this overcoming of disease at Selinous.[372] The victory, however, is usually connected with the border dispute that Selinous and Egesta
had in 454/53 BC, though that does not rule out a connection with this disease. The peace arrangement that followed must have included intermarriage
rights (*epigamia*) between the two cities, first attested otherwise in the later
fifth century.[373] These reciprocal marriage rights are sometimes connected

---

368. Aymard 1971, table 1; 1987, 8, 23.

369. Cf. De Angelis 2000a, 138–39.

370. Sallares 2002, 38, arguing against Collin Bouffier (1994, 330), who suggests typhus
was afflicting Selinous at the time of Empedocles' invitation. Note that Collin Bouffier
(1994) generally plays down the role of malaria in Greek Italy and sometimes advances other
interpretations.

371. Sallares 2002, 38, 73, to be contrasted with Collin Bouffier's (1994) more optimistic
outlook.

372. Brugnone 1999. For the coins, see Rutter 1997, 138–39.

373. Thuc. 6.6.2. Antonetti and De Vido (2006a, 159) have recently hypothesized that cavalrymen from the Tyndaridai could have been involved in the abduction of Egestan women in

with the Severe Style Heraion (Temple E3) and its metopes, especially those of Artemis and Aktaion, on Selinous' eastern hillside (Figure 24).[374] The ravages of disease would of course have impacted Selinous' population, which through these actions may have sought new lands and people away from the coast to replenish its demographic stocks.[375]

Two other possible cases of malaria are attested from this period. One involves Kamarina, not surprising given its well-watered surroundings, and the other Syracuse during the Athenian sieges of Syracuse in 415–413 BC.[376]

Social Classes, Status, and Wealth. The case for widespread democracy in this period has to be considered against a backdrop of abundant evidence for continuing elite classes, status, and wealth. Therefore, any discussion must begin with the broadest base possible, in order to assess properly the case for democracy in the next section.

As in earlier periods, houses were one arena for the display of elite class, status, and wealth. The fullest evidence comes from Selinous. Several sumptuous houses were constructed along the main north-south artery leading from the acropolis to the agora.[377] Apart from their central and prominent location, these houses employed isodomic masonry that resembled that in use in public buildings found close by. A second story can be made out for some of these houses, and in one case it could be ascertained that this stood on top of a first story rising to a height of 3.3 meters. These houses may have shared common walls, though it is clear that they shared a standard size and look that distinguished them from the humbler houses known elsewhere at the site. Moreover, the houses were built over older houses in an area previously densely settled, itself no mean feat financially.

Other evidence is known from other cities. Large atrium houses found at Naxos may date to this period or earlier to Hieron. For Himera, differences in house size and patterns of consumption have been suggested.[378] At Gela, four

the far reaches of the territory, thus leading to the conflict with Egesta and necessitating the marriage agreement in the first place.

374. For the fullest discussion of these metopes, see Marconi 1994. Junker (2003) is right to point out that no single narrative thread is being represented in these metopes. For a recent discussion of the temple, see Mertens 2006, 279–83.

375. Cf. Sallares 2002, 273.

376. See Collin Bouffier 1994; Villard 1994; Sallares 2002, 38. For the possibility that infant mortality was impacted, see Collin Bouffier 1994, 332.

377. Mertens 2006, 324–28.

378. Nevett 1999, 132–33.

FIGURE 24 View of Metope depicting Artemis and Aktaion from Temple E3 at Selinous.

© Author

houses from blocks I and II, although found in quite a fragmentary state, had relatively small courtyards and suggest a pattern of domestic life that differed from that current in Greece.[379]

Burials also seem to preserve their role as a venue for the display of elite class, status, and wealth.[380] Even though Gela's cemeteries have been heavily plundered, Michael Vickers' concentrated piecing together of various evidential strands also suggests that wealthy burials existed there in the 450s BC.[381] The same holds for Akragas, notwithstanding the extensive plundering its cemeteries have experienced since the Carthaginian sack of the city.[382] For the Pezzino cemetery, a general upsurge in the quality of grave goods over the previous Archaic phase has been noted.[383] Some of the tombs also had more material investment than others, both in terms of the tomb structure and furnishing.[384] In general, the difference between the Pezzino and the contrada Mosè cemeteries, as noted above, continued from Archaic to Classical times. Another marker of elite status in reverse, so to speak, is tomb 1771 in the Pezzino cemetery, which contained iron fetters, possibly belonging to a slave.[385]

Success in Panhellenic sport is known from this period, continuing a trend seen in earlier centuries. The earliest known case involves Ergoteles, who immigrated to Himera from Cnossos on Crete. He achieved two Olympic victories, one of which followed soon after Himera's regaining of independence.[386] Two other Olympic victors, Krison and Python, are attested at Himera in the 450s and 440s BC, earning between them a total of four victories.[387] At Kamarina, Psaumis won Olympic victories in 456 and 452 BC, both of them celebrated in odes by Pindar, for the chariot race with mules.[388]

---

379. De Miro 1996, 27, 29, with social analysis in Nevett 1999, 134.

380. Selinous' cemeteries, by contrast, show considerable variation within and between them, and, as in previous periods, do not appear to have been the place for displays of wealth: Meola 1996–98; Kustermann Graf 2002; Jackman 2005, 63–94.

381. Vickers 1996, 187.

382. For antiquity, see Diod. Sic. 13.86.1–4; for modern times, see De Miro 1980–81; 1988b; 1989.

383. De Miro 1989, 77; Torelli 1996.

384. De Miro 1989, 11–12, 17–26, 77.

385. De Miro 1989, 24, 70; Torelli 1996, 191, 193.

386. See Moretti (1959, 91 no. 224, 94 no. 251; 1987, 68 no. 224), as well as Silk (2007) for a recent analysis of Pindar's twelfth Olympian ode in honor of Ergoteles' first victory. For no obvious reason, Knoepfler (2007, 96) dates Ergoteles to the time of the Akragantine tyrant Theron.

387. Moretti 1959, 101 no. 294, 103 no. 306, 103–04 no. 312 (Krison), 101 no. 293 (Python).

388. Moretti 1959, 99 no. 280, 101 no. 292; Antonaccio 2007, 267. Note Lomiento (2006) who dates Pindar's fifth Olympian ode for Psaumis to 488 BC (or 73rd Olympiad).

Zankle produced two Olympic victors, Leontiskos and Symmakhos.[389] Leontiskos won twice in wrestling in 456 and 452 BC, and Symmakhos won at the *stadion* in 428 and 424 BC. Akragas produced an Olympic victor Exainetos, a relation of Empedocles, who won twice in the *stadion* in the ninety-first (416 BC) and ninety-second (412 BC) games, and who, on returning home after his second victory, led a procession of 300 chariots, each pulled by two white horses.[390] Different levels of status and wealth most certainly accompanied each of these categories, chariot racing being considerably more expensive and socially outstanding than a foot race. However, all these victories in Panhellenic competitions ranked their victors in the top social and economic tiers of their home communities.

Other miscellaneous indications of status and wealth are known from this period, and they suggest the continuation of two older elite practices and the emergence of a newer one.

The connection between religion and elite status may be the first continuity. A number of houses at Akragas near the Olympieion and gate V, in a very public location, may provide evidence of households associated with the nearby religious cults. The first possible evidence for a cult for Eukleides, one of Himera's seventh-century founders, comes from this period on a statue base (Figure 25).[391]

The second continuity concerns elite patronage of theater. A curse tablet from Gela mentions a *choragus*.[392]

The new practice (at least to us) concerns the acquisition of status and wealth for formerly non-elite individuals. In two long passages, Diodorus Siculus supplies numerous details of Akragas' wealth at both a collective and individual level in the years immediately before the Carthaginian sack of the city.[393] In them we hear of a certain Tellias. He is said to have been the city's richest man. He shared his wealth by employing an army of servants to throw lavish banquets for his guests. Tellias may have been one such new arrival, for, interestingly, in all the details about him room is found to depict him as a man of plain appearance and speech, whose lack of culture may be an allusion to his nouveau riche status.[394]

---

389. Moretti 1959, 98 no. 271, 100 no. 285 (Leontiskos), 106 no. 325, 106 no. 328 (Symmakhos).

390. For full details, see Moretti 1959, 81, 109 no. 341, 109–10 no. 346.

391. For the inscription, see Dubois 1989, 14 no. 12; Arena 1994, 55 no. 44.

392. Dubois 1989, 155–59 no. 134; Arena 1992, 28–30 no. 45. For a recent discussion of this tablet, see Eidinow 2007, 157–63.

393. Diod. Sic. 13.81–90.

394. Diod. Sic. 13.83.4–5.

FIGURE 25 Statue base for Eukleides, possibly the Oikist, from Himera. © Christine Lane

These passages, once stripped of the hubristic overtones required by the author's narrative,[395] suggest the emergence of new rich alongside the old elite. Diodorus Siculus' phrase "those cultivating the territory of Akragas" suggests that their newly acquired social status came about through cash crops (see Chapter 4). The new rich may have commemorated their success by building temple L in the mid-fifth century BC (possibly dedicated to Poseidon).[396]

---

395. De Miro (1998, 329) uses them in this way. Waters (1974), however, is so much swayed by their morality that he sees hubris as bringing on the Carthaginian offensive that ultimately led to the decline of Akragas and other Sicilian Greek cities.

396. Diod. Sic. 13.81.5, with De Miro 1998, 340.

Athens' political activities in Sicily led to the Congress of Gela in 424 BC, at which calls were made for an end to war in Sicily and independence for all. One of the ways to achieve this, as argued by Hermokrates, one of the speakers, was to promote a common Sicilian identity.[397] By this point, Athenian pressure encouraged Sicilian identity more powerfully than Carthage, the traditional opposition. Hermokrates could capitalize on the origins of this common Sicilian identity, going back ultimately to the mixed communities of Archaic period and their interaction with other communities across the island.[398] This long-standing phenomenon contributed, interestingly, to native material culture and the identities created out of it largely dying out by the late fifth century. To all appearances, native material culture never really caught on among the Greeks, and it was the latter's material culture that overwhelmingly replaced the native. Social and economic uniformity to some degree had also taken root in this period.

Constitutions and Citizenship. Since the ancient sources blanket this entire period of Sicilian history with the brush of democracy, it is best to proceed on a case-by-case basis before making any larger pronouncements.[399]

One of the first things the exiled citizens returning to Messana in 461 BC did was to restore the city's old name, Zankle. In that same year, Zankle was also designated as Sicily's mercenary city, but nothing more is known of the arrangements that followed.[400] Asheri has speculated that the old citizens lived alongside the new citizens, leaving the territory to the mercenaries in a perhaps an inferior metic-like status.[401] The issuing of coins may have been intended to pay these mercenaries,[402] but the rare issue of gold coins around 455 BC may instead reflect the demands of a military campaign, otherwise not known from the written record.[403]

---

397. Thuc. 4.59–64. Cf. Antonaccio 2001; Cardete 2008; Malkin 2011, 97–118; Vlassopoulos 2011, 19–23; Hall 2012, 31–32.

398. Antonaccio 2001, 122, 124, 127, 135; Galvagno 2006, 40–41; Malkin 2011, 108–09.

399. Naxos was allied in this period with Athens and minted tetradrachms on the Syracusan-Attic standard, but no democracy is implied by either this alliance (Cordano 2003, 124; Robinson 2011) or by these coins, which are a legacy of the previous period of tyrannical rule by Syracuse (for which see Chapter 4).

400. Braccesi and Millino 2000, 105–06.

401. Asheri 1980b, 153. Manganaro (1990, 426–27) adds that the mercenaries introduced the cults of Pan and Zeus Lykaios.

402. Braccesi and Millino 2000, 106.

403. Fischer-Hansen, Nielsen, and Ampolo 2004a, 236.

It was during the later years that Zankle became entangled in civic strife, thanks to the two political factions, one pro-Syracusan and the other pro-Athenian, that had developed. That struggle came to a head in 425 BC and again a decade later, and on both occasions the pro-Syracusan faction gained the upper hand.[404] Eric Robinson, while admitting that such civil strife did not necessarily have constitutional ramifications, argues that Zankle was democratic, judging from the city's reaction to larger political developments thereafter and its possession of a substantial navy.[405] This is as far as the discussion can be safely taken.

At Himera, the fall of the Akragantine tyranny encouraged the return of its exiled citizens, probably from Rhegion, where Terillus is said to have had guest-friendship ties.[406] Apart from Diodorus Siculus' blanket statement for democracy, the only other possible evidence consists of the introduction of the cult of Zeus Eleutherios cult in 466 BC, coinciding, according to Robinson, with its sudden appearance at a democratic Syracuse, and a bronze weight with the abbreviation ΔA on it, standing for ΔA(MOΣION) or "of the people," that can be dated to about 450 BC.[407]

Gela initiated Kamarina's refoundation in 461, which combined exiles from both cities and continued the old practice of intermarriage with native populations.[408] The clearest evidence for occupation comes from the countryside, as outlined in the previous chapter, with its articulated division of space and the proliferation of farmsteads, sometimes accompanied by nuclei of tombs. According to Diodorus Siculus, land was redistributed among the settlers, and this seems to be confirmed by these physical traces.[409] If so, Kamarina's refoundation was no mere restoration of the old citizen order.[410]

According to Robinson's recent discussion of the lead tablets from the city, earlier enthusiasm that they document a democracy in action needs

---

404. Berger 1992, 54–55.

405. Robinson 2011, 111–15.

406. Hdt. 7.165. Asheri (1980, 149) suggests the place of exile, as well as the length of exile between a minimum of four years and a maximum of ten years.

407. For the weight, see Arena 1994, 55 no. 44. It is missing from Robinson's (2011, 102–03) discussion. Of course, democracy need not be the only political context for such a weight, and one need to be careful of Robinson's circular argument: it is not certain that democracy existed at Syracuse in 466 BC.

408. Perlman 2002, 200–02; Cordano 2003, 123; Collin Bouffier 2010b.

409. Diod. Sic. 11.76.5; cf. Cordano 2003, 122.

410. Cordano 2003, 123.

dampening.[411] It remains at best only a possibility that democracy existed at Kamarina. This colors how we interpret Pindar's praise for Psaumis in the context of his second Olympic victory.[412] Psaumis used his wealth to build houses at Kamarina, acting for the public good. But his actions can be viewed in two ways: Psaumis may have been a democratic *leitourgos*, discharging public office at his own expense, or he could have been a would-be tyrant.[413] Moreover, whether we should be thinking of small landholders in a democracy interred in the rural tombs, becoming tied to the land in a way previously unknown to them, or the dependent labor of wealthy landowners buried on the land they were forced to work, or both, are still unresolved matters.

For Katane, all we know is that the old citizens returned home from their forced stay at Leontinoi, and that Thucydides mentions an *ekklesia* ("assembly") at the time of the Athenian invasion of Sicily in 415 BC.[414]

The development of oratory and rhetoric at Leontinoi in the 460s, as best known to us by Gorgias through his visit to Athens in 427 BC, is usually viewed as a symptom of political debate and consciousness that spread across Sicily and that was probably prompted by issues of citizenship and land ownership.[415] But a recent major study argues that the origins of rhetoric were part of the invention of drama in Athens in the late sixth century.[416] This view still allows for a Sicilian contribution to rhetoric that comprises "the extension of this form of argumentation about facts ... to a more creative and sophisticated form of argumentation about motives."[417] In this light, the associated hypothesis—that democracy may be another symptom of the growth and development of rhetoric in Sicily—could still hold, and it might perhaps be confirmed by political events at Leontinoi soon after it achieved independence following the Congress of Gela in 424 BC.[418] New citizens were enrolled at Leontinoi and the people contemplated a redistribution of land, whereupon civil strife broke out between them and the powerful citizens who certainly

---

411. Robinson 2002, 75; cf. also Robinson 2011, 96–100. Even Cordano (2003, 123), the tablets' original editor, seems recently to have moved in this direction.

412. Pind., *Olymp.* 5, with Hornblower 2011, 54; Nicholson 2011.

413. For Psaumis' connection to the tyrant Hieron, see Nicholson 2011.

414. Thuc. 6.51.2. Again, the city makes no appearance in Robinson's (2011) recent work.

415. Berger 1989, 313–14; Hofer 2000, 159–69; Robinson 2000, 203–04; 2011, 105; Willi 2008, 264–305; Hornblower 2011, 53, 151.

416. Sansone 2012, 117–224.

417. Sansone 2012, 161–62.

418. Berger 1989, 313–14 (against this view); Robinson 2011, 103–05 (for this view).

would lose under this "democratic" proposal.[419] The powerful citizens called in Syracuse's help, and in 422 BC Leontinoi once again became a dependency of Syracuse, where Leontinoï's powerful citizens also obtained citizen rights.

Syracuse naturally has the most evidence relating to constitutions and citizenship, but debate rages as to how far it documents democracy. One side, represented most recently by Robinson, sees democracy as having been established soon after Thrasyboulos' fall from power in 466 BC and the people as having exercised control of the state.[420] Scholars in this camp, moreover, tend to draw attention to the influence of Athens' democracy and to make comparisons with it. A more cautious line is taken by a second camp, whose minority stance is most fully represented by Keith Rutter.[421] Rutter demonstrates that it is not easy to say whether an oligarchic or democratic form of government existed in Syracuse during this period, reaching the conclusion, shared here, that some oligarchic and democratic elements combined, with oligarchic traditions remaining strong throughout the fifth century, and with democratic elements only introduced in the years immediately following Syracuse's successful fending off of Athens' invasion.[422] What this second position also has in its favor is the broader picture of Syracuse's sociopolitical developments over this sixty-year period, into which any discussion must be embedded.

The Syracusan citizens expelled by Thrasyboulos returned from exile after his tyranny was brought to an end. It is unlikely that Thrasyboulos had the time in power to assign what he had confiscated from them, so presumably they could have simply reclaimed their property.[423] Soon after, the Syracusan assembly met to discuss the grants of citizenship issued by the Deinomenids and the holding of public office. Mercenaries and elites from conquered cities came under scrutiny by the old citizens, who wanted the status of these newcomers revoked. As Shlomo Berger has well observed, "It was a bizarre coalition of ex-Gamoroi, demos and ex-Kyllirioi ... The express aim of the 'old citizens' to reduce the civic rights of the 'new' was in fundamental contradiction to the principles of a democratic regime and serves to illustrate the extent of aristocratic influence in the post-tyrannical polis."[424] Civil war

---

419. Berger 1992, 26.

420. Robinson 2000; 2011, 67–88. See also Berger 1989; 1992, 37–38; Braccesi and Millino 2000, 109; Hofer 2000, 146–59, 182–236; Fischer-Hansen, Nielsen, and Ampolo 2004a, 227.

421. Rutter 2000.

422. Rutter 2000, 150–51.

423. Asheri 1980b, 155.

424. Berger 1992, 38.

ensued, which the mercenaries lost. Eventually they left to join other mercenaries gathering in Zankle in 461 BC. It is doubtful whether all the conquered
elites left, as those from Megara Hyblaia no longer had a home to return to.
Class divisions at Syracuse seem to have been just as strong as the claims of
the old citizens.

The remaining Syracusan elite continued to exert influence in the years
that followed. Diodorus Siculus claims that by 463 BC Syracuse's population
had swelled through the importation of slaves, and the hand of the wealthier sectors of society was doubtless at work.[425] Then, in 454/53 BC, a certain
Tyndarides gained the support of the poor by giving them money and using
them to establish himself as tyrant.[426] "The best of the citizens"—an obvious
reference to the elite—slew Tyndarides because of his intention to redistribute
land and property to the poor. The divide that emerged between these various
groups led to the introduction of *petalismos*, a Syracusan version of ostracism,
which would have lasted for five years, if successfully applied. In consequence,
the elite removed itself from public life for fear of exile.

The people ran the city badly and asked for a return of the elite after the
law's repeal. As Berger has again so well observed, "This case demonstrates
the pervasive power of the aristocracy and its effect on the 'democratic' regime
in Syracuse. Although democratic institutions probably were introduced, they
were nevertheless overrun by aristocratic influence."[427] We hear of no more
civil strife at Syracuse until 412 BC.

Instead, the focus of the sources in these years is in connection with
Syracuse's external affairs, and especially its continued interest in imperialism and successful stopping of Ducetius' political and territorial expansion
(see previous chapter for discussion). It is possible that such activities may
have had a positive economic impact on Syracuse's poor, and thus in part may
account for this lack of political conflict. In particular, in 439 BC one hundred triremes were constructed, for which rowers were recruited for pay.[428]
As at Athens, imperialism could have had a trickle-down effect on the pock-
etbooks of the lower levels of society. Some dispersed farmsteads near Akrai,
discussed in the last chapter, may date as early as 450 BC. If so, they suggest
changes in settlement pattern, perhaps as a result of land redistribution to the

---

425. Diod. Sic. 11.72.

426. Berger 1992, 38–39.

427. Berger 1992, 39.

428. For the triremes, see Diod. Sic. 12.30.1. For payment to the poor at Syracuse for rowing
and other activities, see Morris 2006b, 45.

poor, although they could simply represent intensification of production by the elite.[429]

Athens' attempted takeover of Syracuse between 415 and 413 BC provides the next series of details into Syracusan society. A powerful passage in Thucydides has been instrumental in shaping ancient and modern perspectives of Syracusan and Sicilian Greek social development.[430] The passage forms part of a speech out of the mouth of Alcibiades, delivered on the eve of the Athenian invasion of Syracuse in 415 BC. In it Alcibiades describes the mixed populations of the Sicilian Greek cities as a rabble (*okhlos*) and how their frequent changeability created weak and unstable states with little or no social cohesiveness. This difference made for a vulnerable situation in his eyes and smacked of barbarization on the part of the Sicilian Greeks. Recent scholarship has read this passage with the necessary subtlety that Thucydides was employing. While his snapshot of Sicilian Greek society is realistic and valid, it says more about Thucydides and his view of Athens' resounding defeat by Syracuse than about condemning Sicilian Greeks for their social choices.[431]

Stasis resulted at Syracuse from victory over the Athenians, with the people, led by a certain Diokles, demanding a share in governing the city in return for their support during the invasion.[432] Diokles managed to get the constitution changed, overseen by the election of newly appointed lawgivers, and public offices filled by lot. This must be the moment in Syracuse's history when the term democracy legitimately applies and when elite power was successfully challenged.[433]

But it was not long before the first attempts to remove this democracy emerged. Hermocrates' role as naval commander went unquestioned at first by the democracy, but after a defeat in 409 BC he was removed. Hermocrates used funds from the Persian satrap Pharnabazus to hire a mercenary army and return to Syracuse, thinking that he would be welcomed home on the basis of his reputation alone. When he did not receive the welcome he expected, he

---

429. One should not assume that dispersed farmsteads at Syracuse emerged in the context of democracy, as at nearby Kamarina; different social and economic systems could be behind these similar settlement patterns. See Jameson 1994 for full discussion.

430. Thuc. 6.17.

431. For full discussion, see Seibert 1982–83, 34; Morris 1992a, 140; Lewis 1994, 124; Bettalli 1995, 98; Vanotti 1995, 89; Crane 1996, 226–27; D.G. Smith 2004, 56–61; Willi 2008, 36; Collin Bouffier 2010b, 103; Robinson 2011, 80 with n. 45. Jackman (2005, 61–62) and Funke (2006, 157–58) include the Archaic period in their discussion and consequently discuss this passage as part of the long-term social processes treated earlier in this chapter.

432. Berger 1992, 39.

433. Berger 1992, 39–40.

fled to Selinous to bolster further his reputation in Sicily. In 408/07 BC, he attempted to capitalize on this by taking Syracuse by storm, and in the ensuing battle both Hermocrates and Diokles fell. Although the democracy won the battle, one of the survivors on Hermocrates' side, Dionysius, would succeed in making himself tyrant of Syracuse in 405 BC.[434]

Elsewhere in Sicily, it can be inferred that Gela's citizens consisted of the one-half of the population which remained there during the Deinomenid tyranny plus the other deported half, now repatriated.[435] The mercenaries who garrisoned Gela appear to have retreated to the countryside to Omphake and Kakyron, from where they waged war on Gela.[436] Thucydides lists Gela as one of the democratic cities with a navy opposed to Athens during its invasion of Sicily. It may be much too generous to claim that this democracy existed between the 460s and 405, when Gela was again incorporated into Syracuse's territorial state, given the evidence for class, status, and wealth adduced earlier.[437] It is likelier that the old citizen order was restored at first, after the Deinomenids lost control of Gela. Calls for democracy came later in 406/05, when the people are reported as having exploited Carthage's imminent threat to attack the elite, calling in the help of Dionysius I of Syracuse.[438] Syracuse's democracy and Dionysius I's socially inclusive policies (see below) would have acted as the catalyst for this invitation, but it is clear that Dionysius I also seized the opportunity to advance his own social and economic needs. Some of the Geloan rich were found guilty and their property was confiscated, proceeds from whose sale were used by Dionysius I to pay his mercenaries and ensure their loyalty, helping to launch his installation as tyrant of Syracuse. Dionysius I also sent the message to non-elites elsewhere of his desire to champion their cause.

The end of tyranny at Akragas was followed by the establishment of a democracy, apart from three years of oligarchy around midcentury, and a great cultural and economic flourishing. Ancient tradition maintains that Empedocles, the city's famed philosopher, was involved in reformulating the political regime at Akragas.[439] While modern scholarship has sometimes embraced this tradition as truthful, there is another, rightly more skeptical

---

434. For the date, see discussion in Berger 1992, 41 n. 211.

435. Asheri 1980b, 147–48.

436. *P.Oxy.* 4.665, with Asheri 1980b, 148; Belvedere 2001, 732–33. Gela also sided with Himera against Akragas over Krastos.

437. Robinson 2011, 100–02.

438. Berger 1992, 25.

439. See especially Diog. Laert. 8.65–66. For full discussion, see recently Willi 2008, 193–263; Robinson 2011, 92–95.

school that rejects Empedocles' involvement but accepts the political developments connected with it.[440] In any case, the assembly of "The Thousand" that was established for three years was successfully abolished, and a regime of equality put into its place. Empedocles' supposed involvement in getting the council not to give land for the erection of a monument for the father of Akron, a physician and rival of the philosopher, might well be an indication of isonomic and antisumptuary forces at work in the city.[441] But, if anything, this detail reminds us that political competition lay beneath the surface, and that it could be channeled through public institutions. Politically, the trend for Akragas in the fifth century was toward a decline in its influence within the island in favor of Syracuse, due, according to one viewpoint, to the shifting between oligarchic and democratic forms of government.[442]

Akragas' onomastic record, though generally still quite poor, often has Greek and non-Greek names alongside one another, probably continuing the practice of a mixed community first formulated in the sixth century.[443] We know of that some of the outsiders came to Akragas as mercenaries at the time of the Carthaginian siege; mercenaries of Campanian origins are mentioned, as is the recruitment efforts of Dexippus, the Spartan, who must have done so in the Peloponnese.[444] Difficulties remain in identifying possible material remains of mercenaries in the service of Akragas.[445]

The situation regarding Selinous is somewhat similar to Gela's in that it is mentioned as one of the democratic cities with a navy opposing Athens during its invasion of Sicily. Again, it may be too generous to claim that this democracy existed continuously between the 460s and 409, when Carthage took over Selinous, given the evidence for class, status, and wealth adduced earlier.[446] Nevertheless the sacred law belonging to this period, and discussed earlier in this chapter for the evidence it provides of clans, has led one scholar to see in it a prominent role for the *damos* (or "people") that may well mirror

---

440. For an example of the first position, see De Miro 1998, 338–39, and for the second, see Berger 1992, 17, who thinks that Empedocles may simply have been too young.

441. So the reading of De Miro 1998, 338–39.

442. Braccesi and Millino 2000, 107–09.

443. The best example is Dubois 1989, 206–07 no. 180; Poccetti 2004. See also Dubois 1989, 198 no. 172, 199–200 no. 175, 202–204 no. 177; Arena 1992, 50–51 nos. 111–6.

444. Diod. Sic. 13.85.4. See also Trundle 2004, 156–57 on Spartan recruitment in the Peloponnese.

445. For a recent discussion, see Tagliamonte 2002, though compare with Couvenhes and Péré-Noguès 2005, 393.

446. Robinson 2011, 105–06.

the existence of democracy.[447] As noted above, Selinous continued to be characterized by a population of different ethnic and cultural origins.

Both continuities and changes to Sicily's social and economic structures can be documented during these two generations. Continuities can be seen in elite practices and lifestyle, along the lines first delineated in the Archaic period. At the same time, a democratic wind blew through Sicily. Redistribution of land and wealth occurred in some cases, and redistribution was called for unsuccessfully in others. We may even be witnessing in the case of Tellias of Akragas the emergence of new wealth buying status and class. So, on balance, the picture suggests the creation of new social and economic elements, but on top of an old elite base that continued to remain firmly in place. Hornblower has summed this up well: "Democracy, then, in Syracuse, Akragas and elsewhere, meant the rule of a prosperous agricultural class, which did not necessarily regard Carthage as an enemy, or benevolent co-existence with Carthage as a sin."[448]

4. Between Political Centralization and Independence

The independence of Greek Sicily's city-states was again taken away in the late fifth and early fourth centuries. There was a return to tyranny based out of Syracuse that lasted for almost two generations by the father-son duo Dionysius I and II. They raised Greek Sicily's social and economic development to greater heights, marking these developments as another important phase of state formation, the fourth and final one to be considered in this book.

The general context in which Dionysius I spearheaded his tyranny and state formation has been discussed in the previous chapter. While the springboard was the appearance of a Carthaginian army on Syracuse's doorstep in 405 BC, another major challenge came from within: the Syracusan elite stood in opposition to Dionysius I establishing himself as tyrant.[449] Internal social control initially dominated much of Dionysius I's attention. Elite opposition may have had its origins in Dionysius I's upbringing. One strand of ancient tradition claims he was a humble scribe, while another that he came from the old elite.[450] Whether or not his upbringing was a factor in the elite opposing him, Dionysius I set about to quell them and to centralize power into his

---

447. Rausch 2000, 46, 48–52 (missing in Robinson 2011).

448. Hornblower 2011, 53.

449. Berger 1992, 42; Collin Bouffier 2010a, 299–301.

450. Berve 1967: 1:222–27, 2:638–40.

hands. He either murdered his opponents or forced them into exile, confiscating their property in doing so.

In parallel with these tactics, Dionysius I adopted a policy of being more socially inclusive and rewarding this social expansion by economic means. Dionysius I sought the support of the people through an assembly and became their protector, adopting a classic format that tyrants had successfully earlier used in Syracuse and elsewhere.[451] It was with the people's support that he obtained the official title *strategos autokrator* ("commander-in-chief with full powers") which allowed him to deal with the Carthaginian threat and, conveniently, to keep the Syracusan elite in check. Dionysius I selected from the best land gifts for his friends and bureaucrats, giving the remainder in equal parts to resident foreigners and citizens.[452] He added to the citizen body by including freed slaves, who were designated as *neopolitai* ("new citizens") and who would naturally be eternally grateful to him. The spoils given to these newly freed slaves and other lower-class citizens also included houses and the wives of opponents.[453] While both of Diodorus Siculus' accounts of these matters are not entirely free of rhetoric, they can be taken as reliable concerning the policies of Dionysius I, whose actions and success can be explained by the differences in wealth and status that existed in Syracusan society and by his own desire to acquire mass support at Syracuse. His actions can be paralleled with those of other known tyrants, in whose cities similar circumstances appear to have obtained.[454] In addition, there are terracotta statuettes from slightly later in Dionysius I's reign whose iconography of the bridegroom unveiling his bride has been inserted into this social context.[455] While this is a plausible interpretation, it nevertheless remains likely that the tyrant made a concerted effort to promote marriage, so as to enlarge the civic body and to stimulate population growth for the needs of his new centralized state. Therefore, Dionysius I established mass loyalty to him by redistributing property and citizenship away from his rich challengers into the hands of his supporters.

---

451. Mitchell 2013, 131–32.

452. Diod. Sic. 14.7.2–5, with Asheri 1966, 86–88. Vinci (2004) connects two boundary stones found near Heloros with some of these confiscated lands redistributed to his supporters. We should not imagine any kind of egalitarian redistribution of land and wealth at Syracuse, judging from the civil unrest over these matters that occurred during Dion's reign (see below).

453. Diod. Sic. 14.66.5.

454. So Asheri 1977, 23–25, 36. See also Zahrnt 1997.

455. Pautasso 2008; cf. also Redfield 2003, 278–79.

The economic success of this social engineering may be seen in the archaeological record. In the previous chapter, changes in settlement pattern at Syracuse were noted. They involved dispersed farmsteads and presumably the intensification of production. While in general we do not know who owned these new farmsteads, it is likely that they belonged to the full spectrum of Syracusan society, from the newly made citizens to the old elite. Nevertheless Dionysius I's main financial aims must have been to secure economic prosperity within his entire realm, so that the various levels of society could in their own way benefit from his rule and, in turn, the tyrant had the necessary tax revenue and agricultural produce to support his state machinery (see next chapter for discussion).

The economic success of such policies may be reflected in burials and houses, which, as the fourth century wore on, again became arenas for investments of wealth and status—a trend which also finds parallels in the contemporary Aegean Greek world.[456] Practices to limit such social differentiation are not heard of in Sicily at this time, and individualism must have been socially acceptable as long as it did not challenge Syracuse's leadership.

Panhellenic sport continued to be an arena in which economic success was deployed to advance social status, but it is notable that victories are much fewer than under the Deinomenids. It may well be that wider elite involvement in Panhellenic sport was discouraged, if not socially restricted. This is suggested by the very close involvement of Dionysius I. The Olympic victor Dikon's first victory was in the children's *stadion* and took place in 392 BC when he was still living in Kaulonia, but he is stated as having come from Syracuse for his second victory in 384 BC, when he won again at the *stadion* and in another unknown competition (either the *diaulos* or hoplite race).[457] Dikon's case opens an interesting window onto not only Dionysius I's population relocations to Syracuse, but also onto the tyrant's supposed background arrangements for Dikon (and his family?) somehow to have the wherewithal to support his sporting activities.

To further cement his hold on power, Dionysius I resorted to four other tools, much in the same way as his Deinomenid predecessors had done, that united

456. For Sicilian burial in the fourth century, see recently Tigano 2001, 82–88. Most of the known Sicilian houses have been dated to the second half of the fourth century. There is some evidence from this period to suggest a pattern of development comparable to Greece (Nevett 1999, 135–44), but the possibility remains that the pattern could have also existed in the first half of the fourth century because of the chronological problems, already discussed, that plague this century as a whole. Nevett (1999, 169–70), unaware of these chronological problems, seeks to explain this apparent time-lag in historical circumstances that may or may not be true. For the burial and housing situation in Aegean Greece, see Morris 1992b, 145–55; Nevett 1999, 125–26.

457. Moretti 1959, 115–17 nos. 379, 388–389.

social and economic goals and policies. He first built up a navy of some two hundred ships, for which rowers would have been recruited from the citizen masses, who supported the tyrant politically and who benefited economically through their rowing. He secondly made heavy use of mercenaries, who probably made up around 30 percent of all his military forces.[458] Such use of mercenaries had not been seen in Sicily since the fall of the Deinomenid and Emmenid tyrants,[459] and in general the already very mixed population of Syracuse reached new dimensions with the incorporation of mercenaries from such places as Celtic Europe, Iberia, Italy, and Greece.[460] These mercenaries resided alongside Dionysius I and his court on Ortygia, which became their fortified and secluded stronghold, and formed a social and economic protective ring. Thirdly, Dionysius I is also likely to have established a cult of his own person during his reign, certainly as a way to project his image and power.[461] Lastly, he was a supporter of the theater and was himself a writer.[462] As has recently been argued, "Dionysius undertook a concerted campaign to present himself, both onstage and off, as a certain kind of tragic king; to that end, he wrote innovative historical and even autobiographical tragedies, as well as possibly a history of his own reign, and he adopted certain stage properties in his self-preservation."[463]

Dionysius I's state required enormous economic resources, as seen in the previous chapter and as discussed further in the next, that could only in part be fulfilled from those within Syracuse's boundaries. The expansion of his resource base was achieved to a substantial degree through wars of conquest, especially against Carthaginian holdings in Sicily, but also against other Greeks in Sicily and southern Italy. Such wars also ensured the tyrant, if successful, a fresh supply of status to solidify and maintain his power. Though Dionysius I's territorial holdings fluctuated during his reign, within a generation of seizing power he created the largest territorial state Europe had seen until then.

The overall social dimensions of this state are difficult to estimate at any one time, for reasons addressed above, but population must have numbered between one and two hundred thousand people. Like earlier Sicilian tyrants, he also relocated populations to Syracuse from Leontinoi, Kaulonia, and

458. Péré-Noguès 1999, 112; Millino 2001, 177. Contrast with Demand 1990, 99.

459. Cf. Bettalli 1995, 25.

460. Krasilnikoff 1995; Péré-Noguès 1999, 114; Millino 2001, 170–80; Zambon 2001, 261–66; Trundle 2004, 157.

461. For a recent discussion, see De Angelis and Garstad 2006, 224–25.

462. Duncan 2012.

463. Duncan 2012, 137.

Hipponion, making citizens out of those from at least the first two cities.[464] Whether Dionysius I's relocations failed because he did not have enough civilian population in them to secure their long-term success is a matter requiring further attention.[465]

Syracusan society under Dionysius I became even more highly mixed through the additions already discussed. It was the very mixed nature of this society that Plato felt compelled to comment on it in his *Seventh* and *Eighth Epistles*. These letters were written around the mid-fourth century BC by either the master himself or a well-informed pupil, though their authenticity remains debated.[466] These letters are addressed to the prominent Syracusan Dion and his associates. In them Plato, looking through the Athenians lens, frequently comments on the fluidity of Sicilian populations and of their risk of being overwhelmed by neighboring barbarians in northern Africa and southern Italy, especially Carthaginians, Phoenicians, and Opicians.[467] What can be best described as xenophobia pervades these two Platonic letters.

Again, as in the case of the Thucydides passage discussed earlier, we find ourselves today in a different scholarly environment as to the authoritative status of these passages. Recent scholarship has been more sensitive to the larger intellectual and political contexts to which these passages, and the works from which they have been plucked, belong. Their context and intentions have been better appreciated.[468] It is understood that Plato's voice is to be taken with a grain of salt, and that it has to be seen in its particular time and place. That Sicilian Greeks did not view their realities so negatively or even share these viewpoints at all must be remembered. Nevertheless, the passages in question still have an underlying value for the historian, in that they have been taken as realistic snapshots that Sicilian Greek societies were mixed, fragmented, and fluid in character in a way that amazed even an educated Athenian who had different values and specific purposes in his writings. This applies in more or less the same way, even if the letters are not by Plato himself.

---

464. Fischer-Hansen, Nielsen, and Ampolo 2004a, 225.

465. Demand 1990, 106.

466. Westlake 1994, 693; Monoson 2000, 119.

467. The Opicians are usually taken to have been Samnites or Campanian Oscans (see Sanders 1994, 76). It is sometimes believed that the entire Italic world is being referred to here (Fantasia 2003b, 483).

468. Sanders (1994), Fantasia (2003b; 2006), and De Angelis and Garstad (2006, 232, 235). In a similar vein, Monoson (2012) emphasizes that Plato's comments on Dionysius I's involvement in theater served as an exemplum to discuss the relationship between democracy and empire.

Dionysius II set out to follow the same paths laid down by his father as far as possible. He achieved power by being voted *strategos autokrator* by the people and supported selectively another Olympic victor, Arkhias of Hybla, who won three victories as herald in the second quarter of the fourth century, the first non-Elean ever to do so.[469] But, unlike his father, Dionysius II revealed himself as weak and vulnerable to meddling by Dion, who tried to effect policy changes and have him moderate his power, among other ways, by getting Plato invited to court. Plato's *Laws*, a product of the last five years of his life, takes both Sicilian and wider Greek developments into account.[470] Here, among other things, Plato singles out the proper organization of property as the basis of a healthy society and economy, enforced by the requisite legal and constitutional mechanisms.[471] Of course, if Plato's ideas had been adopted, they would have shaken Syracuse to its very core. But, not surprisingly, neither Plato nor Dion had their intended effects on Dionysius II, for that would have spelled the end to the state that he and his father had built up.

From Dion's later actions it would appear that his intentions to reform Syracusan society and economy were superficial, or never in fact intended. In 357 BC, Dion used his large mercenary force to topple Dionysius II from power, with partial success, since Dionysius II retained control of Ortygia. A tug of war ensued between Dionysius II and Dion. The people came to distrust Dion, because he showed himself to be no supporter of democracy, supporting instead traditional class divisions and their associated privileges. Dion upheld traditional elite rule and was suspected of wanting the tyranny for himself. His challenge to Dionysius II can be viewed as intra-elite factional fighting.

Matters became even messier with a third political trajectory led by Herakleides, Dion's naval commander, who wanted social equity and land redistribution for the people at large in the kind of ground-up manner that Plato espoused.[472] Dion had Herakleides murdered, but the tug of war between him and Dionysius II remained unresolved, and in fact ended when Kallipos, one his Athenian allies, turned on Dion and had him murdered in 354 BC. Kallipos ruled Syracuse for thirteen months, during which time he stopped an attempt by the elites favorable to Dion to take over the city.[473] A certain

---

469. Moretti 1959, 121–23 nos. 422, 429, 435.

470. Fuks 1984, 128.

471. Full discussion in Fuks 1984, 128–70.

472. For full discussion, see especially Fuks 1984, 213–29; Berger 1992, 46.

473. Berger 1992, 47.

Hipparinos, perhaps part of that same group, deposed Kallipos in 353/52 BC, who in turn was ousted by a certain Nissaios in 351 BC, and who in turn was ousted by Dionysius II, now in exile in Locri, in 347/46 BC.[474] Details about these individuals and events are meager, but we at least know that Dionysius II's seizure of Syracuse caused the elite who had been working against him to flee to Leontinoi, from where it plotted its return home.

In 345/44 BC, a certain Hiketas led a mercenary army from Leontinoi, eventually winning a victory over Dionysius II, who again sought refuge in Ortygia.[475] Hiketas tried to break the deadlock by asking Corinth, the metropolis of Syracuse, to send a new leader, which it agreed to do. Timoleon was selected, and while he made preparations to sail to Sicily, Hiketas and Dionysius II continued to wrangle for power.[476] The sources are not clear, moreover, as to what exactly transpired between Hiketas, Dionysius II, and Timoleon in Sicily. The end result, in any case, is that Dionysius II appears to have given in to Timoleon at some point, while Hiketas and Timoleon fought it out, with the latter victorious.

As discussed in the last chapter, Timoleon's revival of Sicily has been grossly exaggerated by ancient and modern scholars, particularly in connection with the dating of archaeological evidence. Nevertheless, a certain amount of credit cannot be denied to him, though it remains difficult to say just how much, and he dealt with several key social and economic issues. The ancient sources are not very helpful on this and other matters, including Timoleon's political and constitutional status and actions, since they are either vague or uninterested.[477]

At Syracuse, the most likely scenarios are that Timoleon, after having captured all of Syracuse, got himself elected as *strategos autokrator* and, in this capacity, seems to have introduced a moderate democracy.[478] He tore down the symbols of tyranny, starting with the fortress on Ortygia, where he established law courts on its ruins. Timoleon also removed the smaller tyrannies in other parts of Greek Sicily that had sprung up during the squabbles of Dionysius II and Dion. What kind of government replaced them is unknown, although it is possible that there were, like Syracuse, moderate democracies.

Timoleon also sought to restore Sicilian settlement and population via colonization from Greece. Ancient writers suggest that the concentration

---

474. Berger 1992, 47.

475. Berger 1992, 47–48.

476. Berger 1992, 48.

477. Cf. Talbert 1974, 122, 145.

478. Talbert 1974, 122–29, 130–43; Robinson 2011, 89–92.

of population in Syracuse weakened these other parts of the island,[479] and that to remedy the problem 60,000 colonists arrived from Greece.[480] Land was given and sold to these colonists. As outlined in the previous chapter, archaeological evidence exists to illustrate the infusion of new life into many Sicilian Greek cities at this time to support the scale and nature of the colonization program talked about in ancient sources.[481] While Timoleon aimed to create a federation headed by Syracuse, all the evidence indicates that Sicily's Greek cities were to remain independent in their internal and external affairs and not dominated by Syracuse, and the succeeding period in Sicily, and across much of the Mediterranean, was one of economic prosperity and social change.[482]

Within a decade of Timoleon's death in 336 BC, tensions within Syracuse are once again documented. By 317 BC, Agathokles, having acted as champion of the poor and democrats against the elite six hundred, had established himself as tyrant, and under his control the city returned to waging wars with Carthage for control of Sicily.[483] Syracuse was back to its old tricks, and this is the point where the present story ends.

To conclude this chapter, when one combines the results of this and the previous two chapters, it becomes undeniable that Greek Sicily's material and social development went hand in hand in the Archaic and Classical periods. This began as soon as Greeks started permanently settling Sicily, drawn there to exploit the unique mix of natural and human resources the island had to offer. Elite families, in at least some cases organized as clans, were the driving forces behind the establishment of these new societies and economies and so came to dominate Greek Sicily's early affairs. Once the elite took the reins of power into their hands, they were keen to protect their status and wealth in the long term and generally had to be fought with to relinquish any of it to other up-and-coming elites or to people further down the social scale.[484] Land

---

479. Diod. Sic. 14.66; Plut., *Tim.* 1.1–2.

480. Diod. Sic. 16.82; Plut., *Tim.* 23.3–4. Talbert (1974, 146) thinks that, if anything, this ancient figure could be an underestimate. Modern scholarly opinion believes generally in this ancient figure, as it is based on Athanis' contemporary account. As Talbert (1974, 116–21) also notes, it is not necessary to think that Timoleon carried out the recommendations in Plato's *Seventh* and *Eighth Epistles*.

481. Galvagno 2006, 39–40 connects this influx of settlers with the absorption of native Sicilian identity once and for all.

482. Talbert 1974, 143–45.

483. For full details, see Berger 1992, 49–50.

484. Collin Bouffier 2010a, 292–93.

ownership and property were forged from scratch by the elite before these secondary claims to access to the island's natural resources were ever made.

Sicilian Greek societies were never closed and could not develop in the same way as in the Aegean Greek world.[485] The island's frontier conditions were responsible for the difference. These conditions continued to prevail well after the initial foundation period, throughout the Archaic and Classical periods, and thus they continued to impact the nature and character of society in Greek Sicily.[486] Demographic influxes came from all over, both inside and outside Sicily, working with already present stocks to bring about population growth.[487] Greek Sicily could not have achieved its economic successes without people, but, at the same time, Greek Sicily clearly could not on its own meet its demographic needs.

It was labor in particular that was always desperately needed to make the economic difference, not just for the agricultural sector but also for the military, where manpower was essential to protect these societies and economies.[488] This is most clear in the extensive use of mercenaries. While it is often observed that mercenary service in Sicily, unlike in Greece, usually entailed permanent settlement encouraged by the tyrants who had recruited them,[489] current explanations fail to account completely for this difference in behavior. The reasons advanced include competition with Carthage and other powers for hiring mercenaries, tyrannical political and fiscal strategies, and the apparently more "unionized" mentality of the mercenaries themselves in Sicily.[490]

Disease and geography, broadly defined, are never evoked in explanations of the growth and development of Sicilian Greek societies. The easy accessibility of Sicily from all points of the compass and the need to control and build up demographic resources on thinly settled landscapes played crucial roles. Sicily was one of those steadily developing parts of ancient Italy which necessitated new and flexible forms of civic makeup and integration. Sicilian tyrants freely gave out citizenship and land because they could and had to, if they were

---

485. On social change in frontier situations, see R.C. Harris 1977; 1997, 253–74.

486. So recently Osborne 2009, 330: "The world of classical Greek Sicily was in many ways but the archaic world writ large. The same could not be said of the world of mainland Greece."

487. Gras 2006–07, 9–11.

488. For mercenaries as large-scale hired labor, see De Ste. Croix 1981, 182–88 (who first proposed the idea); Trundle 2004, 2; 2005, 2. On how the need for labor trumps ethnicity, see Webster 1990, Krasilnikoff 1995, and Bintliff 2012, 249.

489. Péré-Noguès 1999, 107.

490. Bettalli 1995, 97; Garlan 1989, 143–72; Péré-Noguès 1999, 115–17; Millino 2001, 125.

to successfully protect their social and economic achievements from internal and external threats. Mercenaries were in key ways no different from Archaic Greek settlers.[491]

Athenian writers in the fifth and fourth centuries BC were witnessing and commenting on the results of a process in Sicily that was grounded in the land and that had emerged long before, at the very beginning of Greek settlement. They were only vaguely aware of and cared little about the origins of this historical trajectory, which took a different turn from what they were accustomed to and had, as a result, different social outcomes. Much was at stake in exploiting to the fullest the excellent economic possibilities Sicily offered. It remains for us to consider these economic possibilities in the next and final chapter.

---

491. So, rightly, Moggi 2003, 980; cf. also Couvenhes and Péré-Nogùes 2005, 392.

4

Economics

THE FOCUS IN the previous chapter on societal structures highlighted features, such as factors affecting production and consumption, that provide insightful background for studying Sicilian Greek economics. The intention in this chapter is to build on this social base by tackling the full range of economic activities undertaken by these societies, a rarity in the study of Greek Sicily.[1] This chapter has two general goals. First, it adopts an inclusive approach and does not simply reduce Sicilian Greek economics to the items mentioned in the few surviving literary sources.[2] Second, it addresses economic growth and development and attempts to move beyond a static, one-dimensional view.[3] A broad-based approach, centered on the "holy trinity" of economics

---

1. As recently noted by Collin Bouffier 2012, 86. We will not discuss per se the technical aspects of production (such as how a pot was made), distribution (such as how a ship sailed from point A to point B), or food preparation (such as how wild boar was cooked and eaten); all of these and related topics (for which see Dark 1995; Mannoni and Giannichedda 1996) will be assumed.

2. De Angelis 2006; Rygorsky 2011. The suggestion made by M.E. Smith (2004, 82, 90, 94) that more archaeological attention has to be paid to lower-level economic issues, such as weight and measures, chimes well with this approach.

3. "Economic growth is defined ... as a sustained increase in the total output of goods and services produced by a given society. Growth in total output may occur either because the inputs of the factors of production (land, labor, and capital) increase or because equivalent quantities of the inputs are used more efficiently. Economic development ... means economic growth accompanied by a substantial structural or organizational change in the economy, such as a shift from local subsistence economy to markets and trade, or the growth of manufacturing and service outputs relative to agriculture. The structural or organizational change may be the "cause" of growth but not necessarily, sometimes the causal sequence moves in the opposite direction, or the two changes may be the joint product of still other changes within or outside the economy" (Cameron and Neal 2003, 8–9). This definition is applied to prehistory, where, even in the absence of quantifiable data and/or national income data, growth and development can be detected through indirect evidence (Cameron and Neal 2003, 8). For a similar definition of economic growth, see also Szostak 2009, 24, who specifies that art, the "artifacts or services produced primarily for their aesthetic value," should be included as part of economic output (47).

(production, distribution, and consumption[4]), will provide the framework to help achieve these goals. Within this framework, several key questions will be addressed. What cultivated and wild foodstuffs did Sicilian Greeks produce and consume? When did the manufacturing sector begin, and what were its products? How did agricultural and non-agricultural products get to market? Who distributed them? What was exported and imported?

Sicilian Greek Economies

It is necessary to begin by talking about the available sources and the underlying approaches to them, since they shape every discussion in fundamental ways.[5]

As noted in the previous chapters, written sources tend to become more common for the fifth and fourth centuries BC. This is also true in the study of Sicilian Greek economics: writing about economics became common only from the fourth century BC.[6] There is, however, an added twist to this problem. As in all economic history, there is an outright absence of written sources even for historical periods that are generally better documented.[7] This has two overall implications. First, whole areas of Sicilian Greek economic history will remain unknown and open only to speculation.[8] Second, any economically relevant information that the written sources contain tends to be isolated, oblique, or vague in character.[9]

---

4. For recent laudable examples worth emulation, see Davies 2007a; Möller 2007; von Reden 2007, although their accounts are largely based on Athenian evidence that is difficult to parallel elsewhere. See also a series of recent French publications: Baslez et al. 2007; Brunet and Collin Bouffier 2007; Bresson 2007–2008; Migeotte 2009.

5. Cipolla 1991, 14–16; Osborne 2004b, 52.

6. Foraboschi 1984, 78; Faraguna 1994; Fantasia 2003a, 102. For Sicily, two such works are known: one, written by the would-be Syracusan tyrant Dion, is now entirely lost; the other survives as the second book of Pseudo-Aristotle's *Oikonomika* and discusses the financial stratagems of Dionysius I (for the work and its date, see Foraboschi 1984, 77–87; von Reden 1997, 175–76; Aperghis 2004, 117, 128, 134–35; Osborne 2004b, 50–51).

7. Spedding 1975, 3–4; Cipolla 1991, 19. For a practical example of this sort of hurdle, see van Bath 1967, 29. On agricultural systems in general, see in particular Green 1980; Turner and Brush 1987; Stone 1991.

8. See Cartledge 1995, 131, who makes this realistic assessment for ancient Greek agriculture as a whole, and M.E. Smith 2004, 89, who notes our inability to identify commercial institutions and practices, like credit, banking, bills of exchange, and merchant partnerships, without written records. In general, we know the least about the distribution of goods in Archaic and Classical periods in the western Greek realm as compared to their production and consumption (Ampolo 1999, 452–53).

9. Regarding the lack of information, for instance, there are descriptions which simply name "Sicily" as a generic place in, say, the export of pigs to Polycrates of Samos or of Sicilian cheese to Athens in the fifth century BC.

The very partiality of the surviving written sources often results in a tendentious picture of Sicilian Greek economic activities focused on grain, fish, and luxury.[10] These sources derive from the moralizing perspectives of homeland Greeks and from the self-image of the Sicilian Greeks themselves; both consciously sought to project a distinctive identity and larger-than-life world.[11] Greek Sicily's food production and consumption were such that they could be used and commented on by islanders and outsiders alike to define the character and nature of this region in the ancient world, including into the Roman period.[12] While all these literary sources for Sicilian Greek economics are interesting and valuable in their own right, their limitations for the present purposes must also be appreciated.[13]

Material sources can remedy some of the foregoing challenges, as in other branches of economic history.[14] Sicilian Greek scholarship has followed the traditional trajectory in the creation and development of the material record for economic history: ancient sources and the more art historical and durable aspects of the material record, like coinage and pottery, have been privileged.[15] One of the upsides of the latter in the last generation has been the study of transport amphorae and tableware, as well as major advances in the study of coinage.[16] One of the downsides commonly encountered is the inadequate publication of material, as noted recently for the tool assemblages used in textile production.[17]

---

10. On grain: De Angelis 2006. On fish: Collin Bouffier 1999b, as well as Giacopini, Belelli Marchesini, and Rustico 1994; Horden and Purcell 2000, 191–94; Wilkins and Hill 2006, 154–55. On luxury: Collin Bouffier 1999a; 2000a; Wilkins and Hill 2006. Related to luxury is the development of cookbooks, which the Sicilian Greeks were among the first to use: Dalby 1996, 108–10, 152; Collin Bouffier 2000a, 195–98; Wilkins and Hill 2006, 29, 45–48, 245; Bats 2011, 352–54.

11. Greeks viewed their homeland as a receiver of more elaborate and sophisticated food from outsiders, given their generally poor agriculture; Sicily provided a contrast with their own practices and identity (Wilkins 2000, 194, 217). For homeland Greeks, luxury was also to be found in other cultures and in individuals veering from traditional codes of conduct.

12. De Angelis 2000a, 111–19; 2006; 2009b, 244–46. See also Foxhall 2007, 3 on the need to handle carefully Roman evidence in the study of earlier Greek agriculture.

13. Wilkins and Hill 2006, 194–95, 224, 245; cf. also Ober 2010. Contrast, for instance, the views of Plato on luxury with the surviving verses of the hexameter poem *Hedypatheia* by Archestratus of Gela, one of Plato's contemporaries, which opens an important window onto the elite luxury and pleasure against which Plato was reacting (on Archestratus, see Olson and Sens 2000, esp. xxi for his date in the first two-thirds of the fourth century BC and, more briefly, Montanari 1999; Wilkins and Hill 2006, 47–48, 52, 273–74).

14. Cf. Cipolla 1991, 23.

15. Morris 2002, 66–67; De Angelis 2006, 47; Rygorsky 2011.

16. Gras 1989, 402–07; Caccamo Caltabiano and Puglisi 2002; 2004.

17. Gleba 2008, 36.

These archaeological approaches have been joined by other less conventional ones in recent years. While we are still lacking projects that would make considerable scholarly sense in Greek Sicily, like those designed to detect surplus grain production[18] or urban-rural dependency and the extraction of agricultural surplus,[19] there are nevertheless some (usually small-scale) archaeological studies investigating ancient vegetation and zoology of particular sites and microregions that are invaluable for understanding ancient Sicilian economics.[20] Other newer avenues of inquiry, like underwater and landscape archaeology, while still not as common as they could be, also provide different and important dimensions to our economic reconstructions.

Even if we had more written and archaeological sources, we would still have to contend with certain economic activities that have left no material or textual trace. These include the widespread use of organic materials for activities connected with pastoralism, the presence of the poor in both city and countryside, the unlikelihood of some foodstuffs leaving recognizable remains or being picked up by our written sources, and the measuring of productivity.[21] As a result, we must have recourse to theoretical and comparative perspectives to fill out the discussion, thus helping to alleviate somewhat the inherent strengths and weaknesses of all our sources.

That the surviving sources provide material for only certain topics of discussion applies both to individual and larger issues. In the case of the latter, the single most notable issue concerns the gauging of continuity versus change in Greek Sicily's long-term economic history.[22] This will be particularly challenging given the state of our sources; nevertheless, an attempt must be made. The results of the previous chapters suggest that much continuity existed in social and material practices that favored the elite, thus implying continuity of the underlying economic ones. The evidence discussed below also suggests continuity in climate, diet, and technology throughout the Archaic and Classical periods. This conclusion stands in contrast to current generalizations concerning

---

18. Bakels 1996; see also Bakels 2001.

19. For a plea for more work of this kind in Sicily, see De Angelis 2000a, 141 and, in general, M.E. Smith 2004, 87; Small 2006, 328.

20. The study of wild and domesticated animals is still, however, known to us via written sources: Hodkinson 1988; Barker 1989; MacKinnon 2007, 491; Howe 2008, 52. For pastoralism in the ancient Greek context, see in particular Forbes 1995; Nixon and Price 2001; McInerney 2010, esp. 147. For the modern Mediterranean context, see Boyazoglu and Flamant 1990.

21. For these limitations, see, respectively, Barker 1989, 4; Jameson 1994 (cf. also M.E. Smith 2004, 92); Dalby 1996, 57; Osborne 1999, 329.

22. Cf. Anderson 1991.

Sicilian Greek production and consumption and establishes a yardstick against which to test them. The focus in what follows will be to emphasize the evidence for significant economic change against a backdrop of economic continuity.

1. From Foundation to Political Centralization
Agricultural Production and Wild Foodstuffs

There is enough ancient evidence to get a sense of the climate and landscapes encountered by the early Greek settlers in Sicily. This provides important background in assessing what Greeks had to work with in establishing their agricultural production and what wild foodstuffs were available.

The little work that has been done on Sicilian paleoclimatology fits into the larger pattern noted for the Mediterranean and temperate Europe in antiquity.[23] Cool, wet weather emerged in the years around 800 BC and gave way in the Hellenistic period to a warmer, drier phase. Greek settlement in Sicily coincided, therefore, with a favorable cycle of rainfall that lasted for five centuries. There would have been less interannual variability in rainfall, resulting in more predictable moisture for farmers. The agricultural systems and the populations they could support were reliably served.

While the evolution of the basic climatic framework for this period is not in doubt, we do not have any ancient descriptive statistics to quantify what we mean by "cool," "wet," "warm," or "dry." This is often the case with the study of premodern climates, and to help remedy the gap scholars have combined any surviving ancient information with later statistics and conditions thought to be broadly similar.[24] Thus it is legitimate to employ more recent statistics to get a glimpse of ancient conditions, be it levels of rainfall or temperatures, as an initial way out of this dilemma (Table 6a-b).

The monthly mean temperature for January is about 10–11 degrees centigrade on the coast, which declines gradually as one moves inland (Table 6a). In July, temperatures are usually above 26 degrees centigrade on the coast, this high decreasing further in the interior. These warm temperatures bring with them numerous hours of sunshine. Syracuse receives some 2,409 hours per annum, Catania some 2,558 hours, Messina some 2,400 hours, and Palermo some 2,200 hours.[25] About two-thirds to three-quarters of this sunshine occurs between April and September.

23. Belvedere 2001, 735; Belvedere, Bertini, Boschian, Burgio, Contino, Cucco, and Lauro 2002; Morris 2006a, 83; Collin Bouffier 2009, 66; De Angelis 2009b, 237.

24. So earlier De Angelis 2000a, 119.

25. Milone 1959, 53.

Table 6a The Dstribution of Temperatures (in degrees centigrade) within the Year for Six Sicilian Cities.

	JAN.	FEB.	MAR.	APR.	MAY	JUN.	JUL.	AUG.	SEP.	OCT.	NOV.	DEC.
Palermo	11.2	11.5	13.2	15.6	18.8	22.5	25.1	25.4	23.4	19.9	16.2	12.8
Messina	11.4	11.5	12.9	15.2	18.7	23.0	26.0	26.4	23.7	19.9	16.1	13.0
Catania	10.4	10.9	12.7	15.2	18.9	23.1	26.0	26.3	23.7	19.7	15.6	12.0
Caltanissetta	7.0	7.6	9.9	13.0	17.4	22.1	25.5	25.3	22.0	17.4	12.6	9.1
Agrigento	9.7	10.1	12.0	14.8	18.9	23.2	26.1	26.0	23.3	19.2	14.9	11.4
Trapani	11.0	11.2	12.8	15.1	18.3	22.1	24.9	25.3	23.6	20.1	16.2	12.7

Source: Milone (1959: 48, table 4), who calculates the monthly temperatureby averaging data mostly collected between 1924 and 1954

Table 6b The Distribution by Month of Rainfall (in millimeters) for Six Sicilian Cities (altitude in meters is given in parentheses)

	JAN.	FEB.	MAR.	APR.	MAY	JUN.	JUL.	AUG.	SEP.	OCT.	NOV.	DEC.	AVERAGE ANNUAL TOTAL
Palermo (31 m.)	109	95	64	42	31	14	6	16	44	90	90	130	731
Messina (54 m.)	135	97	82	60	37	25	10	25	66	99	156	146	938
Catania (65 m.)	106	60	63	32	16	6	3	8	39	56	101	112	602
Caltanisetta (570 m.)	80	57	59	39	27	18	5	9	38	70	87	92	581
Agrigento (313 m.)	59	53	44	25	16	5	1	4	20	65	81	90	463
Trapani (15 m.)	67	55	42	28	20	11	3	5	32	73	71	88	495

Source: Milone (1959: 47, table 3), who calculates the monthly temperature by averaging data mostly collected between 1921 and 1950

Abundant rainfall accompanies these favorable conditions of temperatures and sunshine: on average, between about 500 and 1,000 mm (Table 6b). About 95 percent of annual rainfall occurs in autumn, winter, and spring, particularly from October to May; summer, on the other hand, is virtually bone-dry, receiving between 20 and 50 mm of rain. The southern half of Sicily receives between 40 and 60 rain-days; this increases to 60 to 100 such days in the northern half, with high mountainous parts in the interior getting rain on over 100 days of the year. Today, as in antiquity, the Sicilian agricultural year adheres closely to the rainy season. Available statistics suggest that the degree of inter-annual variability was not great; in the majority of cases, the yearly average is more than enough, by a factor of two, for a suitable cereal crop. Sicily's good spring rain was recognized in antiquity as key to the richness of the island's agriculture.[26] Although we are uncertain whether irrigation and water management played a role in Sicilian Greek agriculture,[27] it is clear that dry farming was well supplied with moisture.

Written and archaeological sources also throw some light on the landscapes encountered by the early Greek settlers in Sicily, providing small, though invaluable, snapshots.

Literary sources are, not surprisingly, available only for Syracuse's territory.[28] One of the main differences between ancient Greek and recent landscapes is the existence of extensive marshlands and watercourses, which have now disappeared through human and natural processes, particularly the eradication of malaria in the later nineteenth and earlier twentieth centuries.[29] At Heloros, the river by the same name was Nile-like in that it overflowed its banks, and the wetlands that resulted attracted fish which the inhabitants readily exploited.[30] A similar picture existed at Kamarina, where abundant water resources created both marsh and attractive conditions for fish.[31] Lagoons were a common feature of the coastline of Syracuse's territory, and at least three lagoons are known to have been used as salt pans in

---

26. Thphr., *Enquiry into Plants* 8.6.6.

27. See in particular Collin Bouffier 2001; 2002; 2009 (the latter study rightly challenging the Romanocentric blinkers of Wilson 2000). Also relevant is Krasilnikoff 2002.

28. For a full collection for all ancient periods, see *BTCGI* 19.42–49. For some secondary accounts derived from them, see Hochholzer 1935; 1936; Mirisola and Polacco 1996.

29. For the evidence of human impact on the landscapes of the Mediterranean as a whole, see Bintliff 2002c.

30. For discussion, see Copani 2005, 246–47; Collin Bouffier 2009, 68.

31. Kamarina has been the best studied of the wetlands in Syracuse's territory. See in particular Cordano and Di Stefano 1997; Di Stefano 1998.

antiquity, one at Kamarina, another at Pachino, and the third near Vendicari.[32] Geomorphological research has also established that sandy and marshy coastlines existed when Gela and Himera were settled.[33] While it is easy enough to establish that early Greek Sicily had wetter environments than today,[34] and to locate the general areas of these ancient wet pockets, it is impossible to quantify their extent and development over time. Modern scholarship has in recent years come to appreciate the economic importance of marsh in general, and we should not let any modern notions of the "unproductiveness" or "badness" of such ancient wetlands negatively impact our view of them.[35]

The wetter climate and landscapes provided the necessary conditions for forests, for which there is both direct and indirect evidence. The direct evidence comes from Gela, Selinous, and Himera, thanks to recent paleoecological research. Gela's foundation caused an abrupt decline in the forests and a strong increase of agricultural activity and the first indications of local sweet chestnut and olive trees.[36] The landscape until Selinous' establishment consisted of undisturbed Mediterranean evergreen forest, which also declined abruptly and reduced the arboreal pollen sums from 80 percent to 20 percent.[37] The results of surface surveys and their associated geoarchaeological investigations suggest that some of the river valleys in the immediate interior of Himera's territory may have been cleared and under exploitation when Greek settlers arrived in the mid-seventh century.[38] At the same time, this same research has also shown that forests continued to exist in the Classical period close to some sites further into the interior. At Megara Hyblaia, the water table rose high enough to force the subterranean grain silos to be abandoned by the mid-seventh century. In turn, this indirectly suggests that the virgin site given to the settlers by the native leader Hyblon was forested and had to be cleared.[39] Therefore, Sicily at the time of early Greek settlement was still quite forested.

It was in these conditions that Sicilian Greeks established their agricultural production, which is documented by written and material evidence of

32. See, respectively, Traina 1992, 368; Manfredi 1992, 12–14; Guzzardi 2001, 105.

33. Belvedere 2001, 710, 734–35.

34. Collin Bouffier 1987; 2009, 73–74; Crouch 2004, 93–105.

35. For overviews, see Traina 1988; Fantasia 1999; Chatelain 2004.

36. Noti, van Leeuwen, Colombaroli, Vescovi, Pasta, La Mantia, and Tinner 2009, 384; cf. also Sadori and Narcisi 2001, 670.

37. Tinner et al., 2009, 1498–1510; cf. also Stika, Heiss, and Zach 2008, 139–48.

38. Belvedere, Bertini, Boschian, Burgio, Contino, Cucco, and Lauro 2002. On mixed farming at Himera, see De Angelis 2000a, 133; Belvedere 2001, 710–13; 2002, 386; Vassallo 2005b, 131.

39. De Angelis 2002, 301 n.8.

various kinds, whose evidentiary gaps can be filled in somewhat by comparative statistics.

In Chapter 2, we discussed Sicily's three geographical subregions and estimated the size of the territories the Greek cities carved out for themselves in the
Archaic and Classical periods (cf. Maps 4 and 12). No ancient information exists
for any of these territories from which to estimate their amount of arable land.
Modern statistics of the last century have been often called upon to fill this gap,[40]
since any discussion of agricultural geography would otherwise be meaningless.[41]
This is no easy decision, in view of the fact that Sicilian landscapes continue to
evolve because of modern industries and practices unknown in antiquity,[42] and
because of our inability to observe from antiquity the natural and human factors
that help to shape all agricultural output, such as soil fertility and the infiltration
and retention of rainfall in soil.[43] Even if we had ancient statistics, the amount of
arable land put under cultivation would have fluctuated from year to year. Instead,
our picture is necessarily static. The use of modern statistics can only provide food
for thought. The results of this exercise, as applied to Archaic and Classical Greek
Sicily, are summarized in Table 7. These statistics suggest that Greek Sicily was
between 57 and 95 percent arable, depending on the location of a city's territory.

Arable farming is documented at a general level by soil erosion, the
increase in fires that accompanied Greek settlement in Sicily, and agricultural tools.[44] Land clearance and the growing use of wood for everyday living
were behind these transformations. Iron tools employed for cereal cultivation and the clearing of undergrowth have been found at four Archaic
sites: Himera, Gela, Akragas, and Selinous. The finds from Himera consist
of a hoard of agricultural tools (four plowshares, two hoes, one hatchet,
and two double-headed axes) and can only be broadly dated to somewhere
between 648 and 409.[45] More securely dated to the first half of the sixth

---

40. Oliva 1948; Pollastri 1948–49; R.E. Dickinson 1955; Milone 1959; 1960; Antonietti and
Vanzetti 1961. The case is fully made in De Angelis 2000a, 117–18, but there is clearly room
for further study and corroboration (van Joolen 2003, 122–28).

41. For agricultural geography as an approach, see Symons 1978.

42. For a recent discussion, see Benedetto and Giordano 2008.

43. For these factors, see, respectively, Oertli 1979; Symons 1978, 22.

44. On soil erosion: Neboit 1984a, 1984b, 1984c; van Joolen 2003; cf. Collin Bouffier 2009,
66–67. On the increase of fires: Sadori and Giardini 2007, 179. For the iron tools, see next
five notes.

45. Allegro 2000; Belvedere 2001, 734–35; 2002, 386; Vassallo 2005b, 131. The broad date
for the hoard is due to the unfortunate circumstance that the tools came to light in a residential block in the upper city following plundering by illicit excavators, who left the tools
behind, but who had in the meantime destroyed their original context.

Table 7 A Summary of the Hypothesized Agricultural Productivity Capacities Calculated for Greek Sicily's Archaic City-states

	Estimated Territory Size in Km² (or Ha)	Estimated Percentage of Agricultural Land	Total Agricultural Land in Ha
Zankle	1,000 (100,000)	57	57,000
Naxos	600 (60,000)	59	35,400
Leontinoi	830 (83,000)	80	66,400
Katane	830 (83,000)	60	49,800
Syracuse	1,000 (100,000)	85–90	85,000–90,000
Kamarina	670 (67,000)	90	60,300
Megara Hyblaia	400 (40,000)	78	31,200
Gela	1,350 (135,000)	86	116,100
Himera	1,000–1,300 (100,000–130,000)	75	75,000–97,500
Selinous	1,500 (150,000)	70–95	105,000–142,500
Akragas	2,500 (250,000)	87	217,500
Total:	11,680–12,980 (1,168,000–1,298,000)		898,700–1,228,700

century are the iron tools dedicated at sanctuaries at Gela and Vassallaggi in its hinterland.[46] A hoe has been found in an Archaic tomb in the Pezzino cemetery at Akragas.[47] A still-unpublished foundation deposit of agricultural tools (hoe, plow, and shovel) has also been reported from Selinous, in what appears to be a seventh-century sanctuary near the well-known precinct of Demeter Malophoros.[48] While it is possible that iron tools may have been used in connection with arable farming from the seventh century, the evidence from Sicily and from across ancient Italy would suggest more common usage after 600 BC.[49] The introduction of iron

---

46. Orlandini 1965, 446–47. This evidence fits into a larger pattern in ancient Italy as a whole for a "revolution" in iron tools occurring from 600 BC onward (van Joolen 2003, 102).

47. De Miro 1989, 24, 26. Kelley (2012, 249–52) identifies the deposition of tools in burial as a native Italian practice.

48. Parisi Presicce 2003, 276–82.

49. Allegro 2000, 42; van Joolen 2003, 102–03.

tools would have cut down the number of hands and the amount of time involved in land clearance in an island in which population was sparse at first.[50] The mere existence of iron would have constituted the most important technological development, as opposed to any particular tool type.[51] Millstones of the saddle quern variety have been documented for Archaic Sicily in great numbers. It is likely that stones of this type formed the main technology used to process crops derived from arable farming, although they could have also been used to process a variety of other foodstuffs and inorganic materials.[52]

Cereals formed the cornerstone of the ancient Greek diet, constituting between 65 and 70 percent of daily consumption, and they thus represented the single largest activity in arable farming.[53] Although we might infer grain production in Archaic Greek Sicily from the indirect evidence just discussed, and indeed as being important from its very beginnings,[54] it is not until the sixth century that we have secure archaeological and epigraphic proof. Carbonized grain of some kind is known from two tombs at Megara Hyblaia and from Monte San Mauro di Caltagirone in Leontinoï's hinterland, where seeds recovered from two storage jars in a storeroom include barley and spelt, besides vetch and other harder-to-recognize plants.[55] An inscribed lead tablet of the second half of the sixth century BC, discovered in the emporium site at contrada Maestro in Syracuse's territory, records the sale of wheat (*spyros*

50. Morris 2013, 101. For recent overviews of the technological development of the ancient world, see Sallares 1991, passim; 2007; Schneider 2007. For the impact of technological change on agriculture, see in general Grigg 1983, and for the importance of technological change in newly settled regions for economic growth, see Baldwin 1956.

51. Amouretti 1986, 259; cf. also Gallo 1997, 429–30.

52. White 1963, 201–02, 204. The rotary mill is usually thought to have come to Sicily in Hellenistic times (White 1963, 206), but a recent study argues, on the basis of lava stone fragments found among the grave goods of a late-sixth-century tomb excavated on the Byrsa Hill at Carthage, that the manual rotary mill developed among the Phoenicians, who sought to add value to their grain cargoes by processing them into flour (Morel 2001). There is so far no evidence of rotary mills in Sicily in the either the Archaic or Classical periods, but of course that could change as a result of future archaeological investigations. Given the proximity of Carthage to Sicily, and to the overlapping between the Phoenician and Greek spheres in Sicily, the possibility exists that a transfer of technology could have occurred.

53. De Angelis 2000a, 118.

54. Leontinoi: Frasca 2009, 45. Gela: Panvini 1996, 5, 98. Selinous: De Angelis 2003a, 193–96. Akragas: Castellana 1985; 1989, who believes that the main aim of Phalaris' territorial acquisition was to secure the grain lands of Sicily's central interior.

55. Megara Hyblaia: De Angelis 2002, 302. Monte San Mauro di Caltagirone: Costantini 1979, who notes that because these seeds were found in a storeroom, they were probably intended for human consumption and not as animal fodder. For our purposes, this is irrelevant, as the production of these crops is firmly attested.

in the Doric dialect).[56] The tablet was presumably kept in the house in which it was found, perhaps by the trader. The exact quantity cannot be established, but the number three (followed by a gap) is attested in connection with the word *medimnoi*. There is mention also of a talent, which the tablet's editor suspects could be the Sicilian one weighing 209.28 grams and corresponding to 12 nomoi-tetradrachms.[57] The "mother" in the text probably refers to Demeter, the mother par excellence when it comes to grain.[58] Needless to say, this is an important inscription, which, if correctly interpreted, forms our earliest evidence for the production of grain under the aegis of the goddess Demeter in Sicily, a connection later well known in the island.

Arboriculture is also more fully attested beyond what has already been mentioned above in talking about the transformation of Sicily's landscapes by early Greek settlers. Arboriculture provided further products, which occupied about 10 percent of the diet.[59] The earliest possible evidence for the cultivation of the vine comes from three cities (Syracuse, Gela, and Naxos). The Argive Pollis is said to have introduced a wine to Syracuse, namely the variety Pollios (the equivalent of the Biblinos variety in Greece).[60] As discussed in the previous chapter, there is no good reason to deny the validity of the historical tradition surrounding Pollis, which dates him to before the mid-seventh century. By extension, the same holds for his contribution to Syracusan viticulture. The vine may have also been cultivated at Gela already from the seventh century, a suspicion fueled by two Archaic farmsteads, Manfria and Priorato, known for producing wine in Classical times.[61] Naxos' coins minted in the last quarter of the sixth century BC depict on the reverse the head of the god Dionysos and on the obverse a bunch of grapes (Figure 26).[62] Though the iconography on its own cannot be taken as evidence of wine production,[63] scholars who approach the matter from the point

---

56. For full details, see Cordano 1997, who notes that the tablet is fragmentary, made up of four separate pieces, and that two other rolls of lead tablets were also found in and around this and another house, although only one letter could be recorded from them both.

57. Cordano 1997, 352–53.

58. Cordano 1997, 352; Di Stefano 2008, 271.

59. Gallant 1991, 72.

60. Hyppis of Rhegion, *FGrH* 554 F4, to be read with the discussion of Vandermersch 1996, 161–62, 165.

61. Adamesteanu 1958, 300, 366–67 (the Manfria farmstead dates to the third quarter of the seventh century, and the Priorato to the second half of the sixth century); Vandermersch 1994, 36; Brun 2004, 168–69.

62. Lacroix 1965, 16–17.

63. Vandermersch 1994, 38–41. Gasparri (2008, 44 n. 32), for instance, believes that these images on Naxos' coins only have religious, and not economic, significance.

FIGURE 26 View of Naxian Drachm Showing Bunch of Grapes on Reverse.
© The Hunterian, University of Glasgow 2015

of view of viticulture draw attention to the existence of the necessary soil and climate at Naxos and the later, better-known Classical and Hellenistic production to argue for its existence in the Archaic period.[64] The identification of Western Greek transport amphorae dating to the late sixth century (discussed below) also generally supports the idea of Archaic production.

The evidence is less abundant for other areas of arboriculture. The cultivation of olive and chestnut can now be documented at Gela by the mid-seventh century, to within a generation of its foundation.[65] At Kamarina, finds from the Rifriscolaro cemetery indicate that the olive and olive wood, presumably

---

64. Vandermersch 1994, 55; 1996, 159, 166, 168; Brun 2004, 161, 165. The latter claims that the Naxians were producing their own amphorae to export this wine, but that is at best a presumption (Vandermersch 1996, 175–76). It is interesting to note, however, that few imported wine amphorae dating from the mid-seventh century and onward have been discovered during the years of excavation at the site (Albanese Procelli 1996b, 106–10; Pelagatti 1997, 411).

65. Noti, van Leeuwen, Colombaroli, Vescovi, Pasta, La Mantia, and Tinner 2009, 384.

deriving from local production, were in use.[66] Other finds from this cemetery consist of the remains of fir/spruce and yew trees that could have been growing in the region and that were used in burial rituals.[67]

Evidence demonstrates or suggests that a variety of domesticated and wild animals were exploited across Archaic Greek Sicily. For domesticated animals, Leontinoi provides us with the fullest evidence. The city had well-watered pasture lands, including marshland, highly suitable for the raising of livestock, mainly sheep, goat, pig, and cattle (Figures 7 and 27).[68] Two of Leontinoi's sanctuaries have revealed the bones of these animals. At the contrada Alaimo sanctuary, the evidence suggests that sheep and goat in particular were cooked and consumed, while at the Scala Portazza sanctuary, cattle were offered to Hera.[69] The same animals, as well as dogs, were offered at a sanctuary possibly of Artemis and Hekate at Syracuse in contexts dating to the seventh to fourth centuries BC. Sheep, goat, pig, and cattle have also been found in settlement and sanctuary contexts at Megara Hyblaia.[70] Earlier excavations at these and other cities sometimes refer to animal bones found in sacrificial deposits, but few details of the animals themselves are given, in line with the older archaeological practice of paying little attention to such finds.[71] A passing reference in Pindar's *Pythian* ode in honor of Midas' victory in 490 BC for flute-playing refers to "sheep grazing" (*melobrotes*) at Akragas, providing still useful, though less vivid, evidence of Greek Sicily's former pastoral landscapes.[72] Rooster bones have come to light from the sanctuary of Demeter Malaophoros at Selinous.[73] The cock represented on Himera's earliest coins is also thought to represent a wild variety that would have been indigenous to the area based on the animal's mention in the myths of Kokalos, but it is perhaps safer to think that the domesticated bird is being represented.[74] Horse raising is attested as a status symbol in connection with

---

66. Costantini 1983, 49.

67. Costantini 1983, 49–53.

68. Giuffrida 2002, 418; Frasca 2009, 45, 76–77.

69. For the connection between cattle and Hera (and other divinities), see recently McInerney 2010, 112–22.

70. Gras, Tréziny, and Broise 2004, 232–35.

71. Note the situation encountered by, for example, Bergquist 1992. See in general recently McInerney 2010, 10.

72. Pind., *Pythian* 12.4; cf. *BTCGI* 3.71; Nenci 1993, 2.

73. Collin Bouffier 2003, 54.

74. Manganaro 1996b, 221–22. Some other confirmation is ideally needed before this can be accepted as fact, since it is possible that the cock's appearance on Himera's coins is a pun on the word *hemera* (or "day"), which the animal would have announced (cf. Rutter 1997, 106).

FIGURE 27 View of Grazing Sheep in Eastern Central Sicily.
© Author

Panaetios' tyranny at Leontinoi against the elite, as seen in the previous chapter. Terracotta votives in the shape of horses are known from Megara Hyblaia and Selinous found in sanctuary and burial contexts.[75] At the former site, actual horse bones have been recovered in seventh- and sixth-century contexts.[76]

Domesticated animals would have provided other secondary products besides being used in religious and domestic contexts as, respectively, sacrifices and food. Wool from sheep is one possibility.[77] Needles, loom-weights, and *epinetra* (clay thigh protectors) have been found in domestic, burial, and sanctuary contexts at Leontinoi, Syracuse, Megara Hyblaia, Gela, Selinous, and Akragas; they can be connected with textile production using this suspected wool as its fiber.[78] Domesticated oxen in Greek Sicily were bigger compared to

75. De Angelis 2003a, 187.

76. Gras, Tréziny, and Broise 2004, 232–35.

77. Frasca 2009, 45–46.

78. De Angelis 2003a, 85–86; Mercati 2003, 73, 114, 118; Siracusano 2003; Balco 2007; Gleba 2008, 98, 132, 157, 166, 183. Two truncated pyramidal loom-weights have been found in the late Archaic and early Classical shipwrecks from coast off Gela; however, whether or not this ship was Geloan in some sense, the loom-weights were probably used on various cords on

their prehistoric predecessors, and they were butchered using metal tools as opposed to stone ones.[79] The hides and bones of cattle could have been used to fashion everyday products.[80] That the oxen were used for labor in various contexts can be presumed from both the extensive building projects undertaken in the island, for which they were the most likely beast of burden, and, more concretely, from age determinations of some faunal remains, which indicate that they were slaughtered at the end of their lives.[81] The integration of animal husbandry with cereal production is something that is well documented in Sicily for at least the late Medieval period. This is likely to have happened in Archaic Greek Sicily, for two reasons.[82] First, intensive agriculture, especially of wheat, will have quickly depleted soil quality, and regular high-yield harvests are unlikely to have occurred without cattle and their manure figuring into the equation.[83] Second, animals make agriculture practicable when the input from human labor is limited because of underpopulation of some kind.

Deer form the single largest known group of wild animals exploited on land. As discussed earlier, in several parts of Sicily the early Greek settlers encountered forested landscapes which they gradually cleared for arable farming. As also seen in Chapter 1, native Sicilians were avid deer hunters, incorporating the animal and the results of their hunt into their religious ritual. This provides further evidence of the existence of forests in EIA and Archaic Sicily.[84] Evidence from Archaic sanctuaries at Leontinoi and Syracuse also documents the use of wild deer in religious rituals on the part of later Greeks from the eighth century onward.[85]

---

board (Gleba 2008, 187). Similarly, there is uncertainty as to whether the faunal remains retrieved in connection with these shipwrecks—ox, horse, horse/ass, sheep/goat, and bird (Di Patti, Di Salvo, and Schimmenti 2001)—should be taken as evidence of livestock production at Gela itself, although it is worth noting here that an early Classical inscription from Gela, discussed below, does record the sale of livestock.

79. Villari 1987; 1989, 26; 1991a, 324, 327; 1992a, 115. Cf. also Kron 2002, who argues for the Romans introducing larger animals in parts of their empire, tracing the phenomenon back to Greek practices in Italy. McInerney 2010, 23–24 stands in need of revision on this point.

80. An offering found in Temple A at Himera dating to about 600 BC is made of unspecified worked bone (Vassallo 2005b, 126).

81. Villari 1991b, 111.

82. Halstead and Jones 1989, 49.

83. For the late Medieval evidence, see Epstein 1992, 290. I am grateful to my colleague Geoffrey Kron for discussion of the likelihood of such integration in Archaic Sicily.

84. Cf. Villari 1992c, 85.

85. Villari 1992c; Frasca 2009, 76–77, 79 n. 189. As noted earlier, an offering found in Temple A at Himera dating to about 600 BC is made of worked bone that is unspecified (Vassallo 2005b, 126).

Fish and mollusks were harvested from the sea. They are well documented among the faunal remains of the eighth and seventh centuries from the area of the Ionic temple at Syracuse.[86] The finds consist of large fish, perhaps tuna (the number is unspecified out of a total of 208 vertebrates), and 78 marine mollusks. Two other species of fish, the bonito and false albacore, are also known from a later deposit (late sixth through fifth centuries BC) from another of Syracuse's sanctuaries.[87] Some samples of mollusks and tuna, as well as fishhooks, have also been found in settlement and sanctuary contexts at Megara Hyblaia.[88] The so-called Ionic-Massaliot and pseudo-Chiot transport amphorae of western Greek manufacture may also have once carried salted fish and other items in brine.[89]

Most of the evidence for fishing in Sicily is usually thought to belong to the Classical period and later.[90] That and the fact that the Homeric poems have a very poor regard for fish have often led scholars to believe that the Archaic Sicilian Greeks did not consume fish.[91] But the evidence just discussed, limited as it still is, provides an important counterpoint to this reconstruction. The lack of evidence must have more to do with the absence of systematic research on the question, although fish acted at best as a supplement to the diet.[92]

Other wild animals from land and sea may have also been hunted and consumed, but they seem less certain and very occasional. A land turtle and reptile were found among the faunal remains from the area of the Ionic temple at Syracuse.[93] If a polychrome oinochoe from Megara Hyblaia is to be read literally, wild boar and panthers could have roamed the landscape (the former are still visible in protected parkland: Figure 28).[94] The region around Megara

---

86. Villari 1992c.

87. Chilardi 2006, 33.

88. De Angelis 2003a, 85–86; Gras, Tréziny, and Broise 2004, 232–35.

89. Albanese Procelli 1996b, 110–11; 1997b, 9–11.

90. Purpura 1982, 45; Trotta 1996, 230, 243–44; Collin Bouffier 1999b; cf. also Curtis 1991; Gianfrotta 1999.

91. Buccholz, Jöhrens, and Maull 1973; Wilkins 2000, 216–17. Animal husbandry and meat eating are instead featured prominently in these poems, though to take that picture at face value in whole or in part to mean that animal meat was the only or main source of protein consumed in the pre-Classical Greek world may be stretching the evidence too far (Graßl 1985, 77–78 moves along these lines). For the political choices behind the predominance of animal husbandry in the Homeric poems, see Hodkinson 1990–91, 142–45; McInerney 2010, 74–96, 171–72, 246.

92. For a recent plea for more research, see Boardman 2011. The classic work on fish in the ancient Greek diet remains Gallant 1985.

93. Villari 1992c.

94. De Angelis 2003a, 82–83.

FIGURE 28 View of Wild Boar in Monti Peloritani.
© Author

Hyblaia was known for its honey production in the Roman period, and it is possible that it was in the Archaic period as well.[95] Honey can be collected from bees living in the wild or from hives cultivated by humans, although we can say little about this from our limited evidence. Nevertheless, honey and other sweeteners like figs must have been much more common in the Archaic Greek Sicily than current evidence allows us to say, since they filled an important need in the diet that human societies are known to require.[96]

Non-agricultural Production

Non-agricultural production is attested most conspicuously for those activities with the most material traces in the archaeological record. Clay, stone, and metal products, because of their durability, form the bulk of what can be discussed, although other more perishable products can also be presumed on empirical and theoretical grounds.

The working of clay can be documented from earliest times in Archaic Greek Sicily via the production of various kinds of pottery, terracottas, and statuary. The necessary raw materials seem generally to have been obtained from local and regional sources. Although the location of clay beds has not

---

95. De Angelis 2003a, 86–88.

96. On the importance of honey as an ancient sweetener, see Balandier 2004.

been extensively studied, it can be presumed that suitable clays existed all across Greek Sicily for the variety of products produced. The matter has been particularly discussed at Himera, Zankle/Messana, and Gela.[97] At Naxos, the land provided ample supplies of lava stone to be used as temper in the preparation of clay, which must also have been locally extracted.[98] Water and fuel would also have come from local sources. The Sicilian Greeks were no doubt well equipped to create their own traditions of clay working.

As we saw in Chapter 2, spaces for craft production were delineated as part of Archaic town planning. Craft production occurred in a variety of settings and could be found in particular households or in specially designated quarters connected with sanctuaries or outside the city wall. Household industry, individual workshops, and nucleated workshops could be identified, supplying markets that were both internal and external to the city. Six Archaic cities have revealed evidence of these places of production, providing clues of the level and nature of their output. Only in the case of Gela does the earliest evidence of production date to the same general period as a discovered place of production.[99] Otherwise, although most of the places of production date later, generally to the sixth century, we can surmise from surviving exemplars that clay products began to be made locally during the eighth and seventh centuries, depending on when the city was founded. Therefore, the time-lag between the earliest known evidence for places of productions and the earliest known clay products is due to nothing more than to the happenstance of archaeological discovery.

The evidence is fullest for Himera. In the so-called Cancila quarter of the lower city, excavations in the rooms of houses uncovered tubs, water channels, and clay deposits that have been plausibly connected with potters' quarters.[100] In the countryside, at site 216 (briefly referred to already in Chapter 2), surface survey has revealed several wasters, as well as obsidian from Pantelleria, millstones, and powder (Map 4).[101] The existence of one or more kilns has been presupposed, something which seems well founded, given that site 216 is located close to clay sources whose exploitation may have started in prehistory, but can be

97. Zankle/Messana: Barone, Ioppolo, Majolino, Migliardo, Sannino, Spagnolo, and Tigano 2002. Himera: Vassallo 2005b, 81. Gela: Adamesteanu 1953, 244; 1956, 278. Pautasso 1996, 115 raises the possibility that Gela's greenish clay was created by the addition of salt and not due to the geology per se.

98. Pelagatti 1964, 158.

99. Adamesteanu 1953, 247.

100. Vassallo 2005b, 39, 60, 110.

101. Cucco 2002, 367–71.

more securely shown to have been used in the Greek period. These pottery kilns in the countryside may have sought to produce ceramic products in their own right, but it is also possible the placement of kilns here may have been intended to facilitate the collection of agricultural products from nearby fields.

The evidence for places of production from the five other Archaic cities is mainly restricted to kilns. At least eleven kilns have been uncovered at Naxos in all three spatial settings discussed above; the earliest usage can be securely placed in the mid-sixth century.[102] At Gela a partially uncovered circular kiln, dating to the late seventh/early sixth centuries, came to light in excavations.[103] The only known kiln at Leontinoi dates to the sixth century and is associated with a sanctuary, where it was used to produce tiles and architectural terracottas.[104] Three kilns of "Archaic/Classical" date have come to light in excavations at Akragas seemingly also associated with sanctuaries.[105]

Fine and coarse wares were produced from the eighth century for cities founded in that century. Local production at Zankle imitated widely circulating wares like Thapsos and Ionic cups.[106] Zankle became the specialist, on both sides of the straits, for "fornelli" (little stoves), found in its earliest archaeological layers, that belonged to a koine that embraced Etruria, Campania, and the Lipari Islands.[107] Naxos used prototypes of homeland Euboean origin, and the same holds for Leontinoï's earliest production, which was also influenced by Cycladic and Corinthian traditions.[108] Shapes included various kinds of cups, lekanai, craters, and hydriai. Leontinoï's local pottery can also be found at native sites in Leontinoï's hinterland.[109] At Megara Hyblaia and Syracuse, the earliest local pottery imitated Corinthian models.

Local pottery production also took root from early on at Sicilian Greek cities founded in the seventh and sixth centuries. Early Geloan potters made a variety of shapes (stamnoi, oinochoai, plates, pithoi, and amphorae). At first,

---

102. Pelagatti 1968–69, 351; Cuomo di Caprio 1971–72, 460; 1992, 73.

103. Adamesteanu 1956a, 277; Cuomo di Caprio 1971–72, 457–58; 1992, 72.

104. Frasca 2009, 79.

105. Cuomo di Caprio 1971–72, 457; 1992, 71.

106. Bacci and Coppolino 2002, 21–22; Tigano 2002, 42. Oinochoai were not among these first products. It is difficult to narrow down the extent of production, given the existence of a regional western Euboean *koine* with similarities in form and technique that suggest that various other production centers (Pithekoussai, Naxos, and Leontinoi) may have simultaneously been in operation (Bacci and Coppolino 2002, 24).

107. Coppolino 2002, 54–58.

108. Frasca 2009, 83–89.

109. Frasca 2009, 90.

the potters naturally followed decorative motifs that were in vogue in the set-tlers' Cretan and Rhodian homelands.[110] Himera's earliest pottery production dates to the seventh century and consists of small- and medium-sized pots (notably cups and lekanai) with simple decoration that is mainly inspired by the latest Geometric tradition of Euboea.[111] In the last decades of the sixth century, Himera began to produce its best-known and most widely distributed fine ware, the so-called Iato K480 cups (named after the native site in western Sicily and the excavators' inventory number) (Figure 29).[112] These cups are found at several sites in Sicily and beyond somewhat in southern Italy. Himera also produced some other fine wares (stamnoi, hydriai, and craters), as well as coarse wares (pithoi and chytrai) and other larger clay products, such as tiles, tubes, tubs, basins, sarcophagi, and rings for wells.[113] Selinous also produced from early on its own pottery, some of which traveled to destinations beyond the city's boundaries.[114] Pottery also began to be locally produced at Akragas in the sixth century.[115]

The seventh century also witnessed new developments in clay working in those cities founded in the eighth century. The most widespread phenom-enon involves a figured polychromatic style that appeared briefly during the second half of the seventh century at Megara Hyblaia, Syracuse, and Gela.[116] At Syracuse, the so-called Fusco craters, although manifesting strong connec-tions with Argive traditions, were locally made.[117] At Leontinoi, a local tradi-tion of figured pottery also emerged during the seventh century and lasted for a few decades at most. The figures, made up of both males and females, were surrounded by typical geometric motifs and appear on large shapes like craters and amphorae.[118]

---

110. Adamesteanu 1953; 1956a; Rizza and De Miro 1986, 152–54.

111. Vassallo 2005b, 81.

112. Vassallo 2005b, 84, who also notes that little pottery with figured decoration ever seems to have been produced at Himera.

113. Vassallo 2005b, 84, 138.

114. For a recent collection of the evidence, see De Angelis 2003a, 184–85. See also more recently Croissant 2007, 297–306.

115. Marconi 1929b, 173–224; Rizza and De Miro 1986, 197, 207–08; De Miro 1989, 32, 39; Pautasso 1996, 117, the latter drawing attention to the existence of molds for producing terracottas.

116. De Angelis 2003a, 84–85.

117. Rizza and De Miro 1986, 141–42; Spigo 1997, 559.

118. Frasca 2009, 83–89.

FIGURE 29 Iato K480 Cup Produced in Himera.
© Regione Siciliana, Dipartimento Regionale dei Beni Culturali e dell'Identità Siciliana, Parco archeologico di Himera

Terracottas, big and small, were produced from the seventh century onward in the various cities. One of the best-known producers was Naxos, the quality of whose terracottas has been compared to the famed output of Gela and Locri.[119] Quantity and quality also characterize the Silenos antefixes made at Naxos, which were exported to at least Syracuse and Kamarina.[120] Fine *pinakes* were produced at Naxos, and are also found in the hinterland at Francavilla di Sicilia.[121] Naxos doubtless had an active tradition of producing items out of clay, justifying the application of the term "school."[122]

At Leontinoi, architectural terracottas and tiles were being fabricated in the seventh century.[123] The production of architectural terracottas is also attested in Leontinoi's territory at Monte San Mauro di Caltagirone.[124] The

---

119. Pelagatti 1968–69, 352.

120. Pelagatti 1968–69, 351–52.

121. Spigo 2003.

122. Pautasso 1996, 120.

123. Frasca 2009, 73–75, 91.

124. Rizza and De Miro 1986, 187.

earliest terracotta statuettes date to the second half of the sixth century and derive from a votive deposit.[125] They consist of Ionic-inspired statuettes of women wearing a chiton and himation and holding a dove and flower. Two fragmentary terracottas depicting banqueting scenes have also been uncovered as well as protomai and standing female figures from cemetery contexts,[126] and a small household altar from Monte San Mauro di Caltagirone has Corinthian parallels.[127]

The existence of local coroplastic workshops at Syracuse in the seventh century can so far only be presumed.[128] Larger-scale architectural terracottas were made toward the end of this century and into the next.[129] Kamarina was best known for its antefixes, one of which, dating from the mid-sixth century, preserves a dipinto with the name Diopos on it.[130]

Gela also developed traditions of high-quality coroplastics and architectural terracottas from at least 630 BC.[131] Gela is thought to have created the uniquely Sicilian class of statuette of a seated Persephone (Kore) with pectoral decoration containing the symbols of fecundity.[132] It is uncertain whether the clay products that appear in Gela's hinterland were imported or locally manufactured using Geloan matrices.[133]

Himera has produced abundant evidence for the production of terracottas and architectural sculpture. The terracottas were initially made from East Greek models, but in the fifth century these were accompanied by models from Akragas and Athens, in which originality is also noticeable.[134] The architectural sculpture is heavily indebted to the Doric style of the western Mediterranean, while the antefixes are stylistically related to Campanian products (Figure 30).[135] At Selinous, production of terracottas also occurred from the seventh century

---

125. Frasca 2009, 90.

126. Frasca 2009, 91.

127. Spigo 1997, 571–72.

128. Rizza and De Miro 1986, 167; Spigo 1997, 562–63.

129. Rizza and De Miro 1986, 187, 194.

130. Rizza and De Miro 1986, 187. For the dipinto, see Arena 1998, 138, no. 81; Dubois 1989, 119 no. 112.

131. Rizza and De Miro 1986, 167–68, 187; Pautasso 1996, 115–17.

132. Pautasso 1996, 123–26, who notes that the issue is not conclusively resolved and that these statuettes are rarely, if at all, found at sites in eastern Sicily.

133. Pautasso 1996, 117.

134. Vassallo 2005b, 79, 126, 133.

135. Vassallo 2005b, 78, 127.

FIGURE 30 View of Antefix from Himera.
© Regione Siciliana, Dipartimento Regionale dei Beni Culturali e dell'Identità Siciliana,
Parco archeologico di Himera

and included Geloan and Attic-Ionic influences. At Akragas, to judge from the
surviving objects, terracottas and architectural sculpture were also produced
during the sixth century.[136]

Clay was also used to make statuary in some cities (cf. Figure 31, a speci-
men of Classical date). This statuary is especially known from Leontinoi and,
in the hinterland, from Grammichele and Monte San Mauro di Caltagirone.
At Megara Hyblaia, an exceptional Daedalic statue is also in evidence. The
so-called Biscari kore in Catania has also been attributed to a workshop in
Kamarina in the late sixth century.[137]

Other clays items were made for daily use, most notably loom-weights,
spindle whorls, and lamps.[138]

---

136. Marconi 1929b, 173–224; Rizza and De Miro 1986, 197, 207–08; De Miro 1989, 32,
39; Pautasso 1996, 117, the latter drawing attention to the existence of molds for producing
terracottas.

137. Pautasso 1996, 135.

138. The evidence is fullest from Megara Hyblaia because of the extensive settlement excavations (De Angelis 2003a, 85; Gras, Tréziny, and Broise 2004, 170–92), but similar products
are also attested at other Sicilian Greek cities. See also below.

FIGURE 31 View of Greek-style Statue (of Demeter?) from Terravecchia di Cuti.
© Regione Siciliana, Dipartimento Regionale dei Beni Culturali e dell'Identità Siciliana, Parco archeologico di Himera

From this overview, it is clear that Sicilian Greek cities established their own traditions of working clay within the first generation of their existence.[139] Several different pottery-shapes and object-types were produced, and output grew steadily to accompany building and other projects, most notably sanctuaries, in the seventh century. In the case of Himera, economic growth in the early sixth century can be related to its varied and extensive craft production, especially pottery, but such growth is also likely for other cities as they replaced or substituted their imports for local production.[140]

139. Denoyelle and Iozzo 2009, 27, 42–45, 53–65, 91–95.

140. Macaluso 2008a, 279. For the application of theories of import replacement or substitution to Archaic Greek Sicily, see De Angelis 2012a and 2012b.

The cities of Archaic Greek Sicily engaged heavily in building projects, particularly in the century spanning the mid-seventh to mid-sixth centuries, as just mentioned and as more fully seen in Chapter 2. The few instances in which the quantification of stone could be attempted for religious architecture and city walls revealed quantities measuring in the millions of cubic meters. The quarrying and working of stone thus formed a major component of non-agricultural production. The best known of Greek Sicily's Archaic quarries are those of Selinous' hinterland, most certainly because of the attraction and curiosity raised by its seven monumental temples.[141] Otherwise, most Archaic quarries remain to be documented in this way; even so, we should imagine local and regional sources of limestone being similarly available in them, and similarly lively activity at quarry sites for the extraction and transport of the stone. Given the scale of usage, the predominance of local masons has never been seriously doubted, at least as far as the rougher work of building projects is concerned.

Debate, however, is encountered over the finer pieces of stone work classifiable as "art," and especially those pieces executed in marble which required importation. Debate continues to follow for the most part the terms set out by Pace and Dunbabin before World War II, as discussed in the Introduction, with the former allowing for Sicilian production and the latter denying it altogether. Thus one still finds in the scholarly literature uncertainty as to whether the finished products were executed in whole or in part in Sicily, and how one should read any influences betraying a place of origin. Such is the case, for instance, with the late Archaic kouroi from Katane, Leontinoi, and Grammichele, but it also touches on marble sculpture from other cities.[142] The same debate applies to "art" fashioned out of limestone and clay. This can be best seen at Leontinoi and two satellite sites in its territory, Monte San Mauro di Caltagirone and Grammichele, as we are dealing with a single city-state over a single (sixth) century (Map 4). This debate rages regardless of site and product medium, whether it be a limestone head from Leontinoi, a limestone relief (heavily influenced by Corinthian art, depicting two sphinxes in heraldic pose) from Monte San Mauro di Caltagirone, or a limestone head of "indigenous" type and a large clay statuette of a seated divinity (usually identified with Demeter or Kore) from Grammichele. The latter site has earned the unique distinction of having had a school of sculpture, with Geloan influences.[143] But, despite all this variety and not insignificant output, it remains uncertain whether this

141. De Angelis 2003a, 183–84.

142. Rizza and De Miro 1986, 210, 223; De Angelis 2003a, 84, 184; Frasca 2009, 95.

143. Pautasso 1996, 131–32.

sculpture was produced locally or via imported talent.[144] The same problem is met with at Syracuse, Megara Hyblaia, Akragas, and Gela.[145]

Very recent work on the art of Archaic Greek Sicily by Marconi and Gianfranco Adornato has attempted to find a more nuanced solution to the dichotomous thinking that dominates interpretations.[146] While both scholars continue to follow external influences and skills alongside any imported materials, they prefer to look at them in the context of local developments and the formation of local artistic languages and styles that can rework and blend a variety of stimuli. Such thinking is more in line with the trends in the study of cultural history outlined in the Introduction, and appears to offer a more sensitive approach to the question than has ever been previously attempted.

The disentangling of local and external skills is a matter also encountered in discussing minerals and especially metals, as Sicily is not rich in these resources even by today's standards. With the exception of Zankle, the rest of Greek Sicily's cities had no naturally occurring metal resources of their own, which required importing and which thus raised the issue of local versus external skills in processing them. By contrast, deposits of alum, sulfur, and rock salt are more widely found in central southern Sicily, and if one includes sea salt under the heading of minerals, the island contained more kinds of other indigenous minerals.

Northeastern Sicily is home to deposits of iron, copper, and lead.[147] In the LBA, an increase in settlement in relation to these mineral deposits is noticeable. Some confirmation that the natural veins of ore were extracted near the surface derives from archaeometric work. The next known evidence for exploitation of these deposits comes from the late Archaic period. Pieces of chalcopyrite have been retrieved from archaeological deposits of the late sixth/early fifth centuries BC at Monte San Onofrio, located in the westernmost corner of Zankle's territory (Map 4).[148] This suggests the exploitation of the region's copper deposits. Recent excavations in an iron-smelting site at Zankle led to the recovery of thirty pieces of slag, archaeometric analyses of which have

144. Rizza and De Miro 1986, 171, 207, 210, 223; Frasca 2009, 94–96.

145. Syracuse: Rizza and De Miro 1986, 170–73. Megara Hyblaia: De Angelis 2003a, 83. Gela and its satellite site of Palma di Montechiaro: De Miro 1962, 128–35; Rizza and De Miro 1986, 169, 172–73; Panvini 1996, 43, 68. Akragas: Adornato 2011, 89–101, 121–37.

146. Marconi 2010; 2012; Adornato 2011, 147–58.

147. Villari 1981, 49–50; Giardino 1995, 134–39; 1996; 1997, 414; Leighton 1999, 207; Ingoglia 2012.

148. Genovese 1977a and 1977b.

confirmed their origin in the nearby Peloritani mountains.[149] The jury is out on whether the mineral deposits of Fiumedinisi to the south of Zankle were ever exploited in antiquity.[150]

Central southern Sicily, which was dominated by Akragas' territory, encompassed most of the island's deposits of alum, sulfur, and rock salt.[151] These resources were already seemingly exploited in prehistoric times. The rock salt in general probably supplied less of the salt consumed in antiquity and later, on account of its high production costs.[152] More recently, the suggestion has been made that ferrous minerals and red ochre, discovered at the native site of Rocca Ficarezze near Casteltermini, need to be added to list of available mineral resources known from the region.[153] Whether any of these were ever exploited in our period remains to be verified.

Given Sicily's favorable geography for sea salt, the island may have been able to supply its own needs. One has to imagine a much more widespread exploitation of salt in Archaic Sicily than our available sources currently allow us to see. Such must be the case with Gela, which had favorable conditions for the production of sea salt, of which later Classical sources speak, in light of the marshy nature of its coastline as established by recent geomorphological research.[154] Similar conditions in all likelihood existed along the coast of other Sicilian Greek cities, such as Syracuse, Megara Hyblaia, and Leontinoi, for the production of sea salt, which continues today in Sicily, though mainly in the area around the Phoenician city of Motya (Figure 32). Salt was required for a variety of daily human needs.[155] Salt, along with alum, could also bring together the world of agricultural and craft production. As a result of its importance, salt was probably controlled by the state.[156]

---

149. Ingoglia 2003 (actually published in 2009). This work responds to a long line of pleas for such work; see recently Gasparri 2008, 52 n. 69, who published her article one year before Ingoglia's results appeared.

150. Epstein 1992, 227–30; Mercuri 2004, 193–94; Gasparri 2008, 47 n. 47; Macaluso 2008b, 32; Ingoglia 2012, 254–55.

151. Caputo 1957; 1978; Vassallo 1990, 19–20; Manfredi 1992, 12–14; Traina 1992, 368; Gallo 2001b; in general, see Bergier 1982.

152. Epstein 1992, 226; Gallo 2001b, 461.

153. Gullì 2003, 389.

154. Manfredi 1992, 12–14; Traina 1992, 368.

155. On the uses of salt in Greek antiquity, see Gallo 2001b, 463–67; on the uses of alum and salt in late Medieval Sicily, where they are better documented, see Epstein 1992, 222–34.

156. Gallo 2001b, 467.

FIGURE 32 View of Sea-salt Production near Motya.
© Author

Worked, unworked metal, and places of production can be found all across Archaic Greek Sicily and provide insights into the origins and nature of this sector of non-agricultural production.

Lumps of "pre-monetary" bronze have been found in the sanctuaries of six different sites: Heloros, Monte San Mauro di Caltagirone, Gela, Himera, Selinous, and Akragas.[157] Where identifiable, the cults belong to chthonic divinities, usually Demeter. The single largest lump is the thirty-seven-kilogram one from Monte San Mauro di Caltagirone, and the single largest deposit consists of 150 kilograms found in a pithos in the Santa Anna sanctuary at Akragas. At Gela, the lumps consist of two varieties, *aes rude* (rough pieces of bronze of unequal weight) and *aes formatum* (pieces of bronze of a certain shape). For all the other sites, the lumps belong only to the *aes rude* variety. At Himera *aes rude* has also been found in the settlement. These lumps are thought to be dedications intended to give thanks to the earth which made wealth possible. They may have also been stored there for safekeeping. In any case, the lumps also document the circulation of metals, and in the case

---

157. Heloros: Hinz 1998, 112; De Miro 2008, 66–67. Monte San Mauro di Caltagirone: Frasca 1996b, 85. Gela: Orlandini 1965–67; U. Kron 1992, 633–35; Hinz 1998, 58–59; Verger 2003, 530–38. Himera: Macaluso 2008a; 2008b, 36–38. Selinous: Macaluso 2008b, 38. Akragas: Hinz 1998, 73; Verger 2003, 561–62; Macaluso 2008b, 34; De Miro 2008, 55.

of their appearance at Himera might also represent money, something to be discussed below.

Silver is also known to have circulated in bulk form. A silver ingot weighing 250 grams was discovered in the Punta Bracceto shipwreck off Kamarina.[158] The silver's provenience is unknown, but, given what we know about the importation of silver at Syracuse, as documented through its earliest coinage, it is likely to have come from the Greek homeland (see below). The existence of three silver ingots in a private collection from Palma di Montechiaro can be plausibly related to Archaic Akragas.[159] There are clues as to the origins of some of this metal. In the case of the silver ingots, two Phoenician letters (aleph and zayin) appear on them and could thus take us back ultimately to Spain.[160] Silver ingots are also known at Selinous from two coin hoards, one reputedly found in the city's territory and the other from Taranto.[161] Selinous' earliest coins, which date to 540–515 BC, may have required eight tons of silver to mint, a deduction which conjures up the kind of exchange networks to which Selinous belonged in this period.[162] Some of the silver may have come from Spain.

Finished objects are by far the most common source of metal finds. Many of them provide us with clues as to from where the hypothesized raw metals and workmanship may have ultimately come. Besides itinerant craftsmen, other mobile individuals from these regions may have brought these finished metal objects on dedicating and/or settling in Sicily.[163]

From Leontinoi come bronze pendants (which may have served as amulets) from the Balkans and a bronze situla from central Europe.[164] Two studded leg rings from Gaul, dating to the century spanning 650–550 BC, have been founded at Kasmenai in Syracuse's hinterland.[165] Two bronze pendants from Megara

---

158. For full discussion, see Parker 1992, 346 no. 915; Di Stefano 1993–94.

159. Manganaro 1990, 427 n. 77.

160. Note also a double shekel of Carcemish on a silver lingot found in 1913 at Agrigento (cf. Macaluso 2008b, 32). While of unknown context, it too probably came to Akragas via Phoenician channels.

161. The reputed hoard dates to the next historical period and is discussed below. For the bronze, see Macaluso 2008b, 38.

162. Lucchelli 2009, 181 n. 29. Worth noting here is the discovery of a rounded worked stone with the word *deka* written on it near temple D. The stone was found in a late-sixth-century context and may be a weight (Arena 1989, 55 no. 56). Sanctuaries are probably where precious metals were stored at Archaic Selinous (Lucchelli 2009. 184 n. 50).

163. Pingel 1980, 174; Bouzek 2000, 364; Verger 2003, 554–69.

164. See, respectively, Pingel 1980, 168; Frasca 2009, 93.

165. Verger 2003, 540.

Hyblaia can be traced to the Balkan Peninsula (and in particular in the area stretching from the former Yugoslavia through Albania to Macedonia).[166] Gallic and Balkan metal ornaments come from the sanctuary of Demeter Malophoros at Selinous.[167] Some of the finished metal objects found in Gela's sanctuaries can be traced back to Gaul, the central Mediterranean, the eastern Mediterranean, and the Black Sea, and it is likely that these regions provided not only the finished objects but possibly also the unfinished metal.[168] Two Etruscan funnels are known from the Gela area: one from a shipwreck and the other from Monte Bubbonia, deep in the countryside.[169] Some of the finished bronze objects found in the Santa Anna sanctuary point to an origin in southeastern France.[170]

Metal products are attested at Himera from the seventh century onward and include bronze for attachments, a mask, and the well-known statuette of Athena, the city's patron goddess.[171] A gold plaque with Gorgon decoration has also been found in Temple A.[172] More mundane bronze objects are also known from household contexts in the upper city, including a handle of some sort, nails, and an arrowhead.[173] Metals of any kind do not naturally occur in Himera's territory, and the discovery of worked and raw bronze there implies some form of exchange. Joseph Milne long ago suspected that the silver used in Himera's coins came from Spain.[174] This was before the discovery of the Bolognetta hoard in 1945,[175] which could indicate that Himera acted as an intermediary with the Phoenicio-Punic and Elymian cities of western Sicily, and with the Greek world as a whole.[176]

---

166. Pingel 1980, 170; Bouzek 2000, 364, 368.

167. Bouzek 2000, 364, 368; Verger 2003; Bellelli and Cultraro 2006, 209–10.

168. Verger 2003, 532, 545–46, 550–51, although for the Gallic material Verger speculates (554–69) whether women brought and dedicated the finished products at Gela and other Sicilian sites.

169. Naso 2006, 368–69, 391–92.

170. Verger 2003, 540.

171. Rizza and De Miro 1986, 168–69, 172.

172. Vassallo 2005b, 87, 124.

173. D'Esposito 2008.

174. Milne 1938, 45–48.

175. *IGCH* no. 2063.

176. Johnston 1993–94, 164 (who alone suggests that the Spanish silver could have traveled to the wider Greek world); Cutroni Tusa 2004, 384; Gasparri 2008, 49; Macaluso 2008b, 40–43. This may also explain why Zankle and Naxos, which minted on similar standards to Himera's, minted lighter coins, the thinking being that silver got more expensive as it moved from Himera through Zankle to Naxos (see most recently Gasparri 2008 for a discussion of

Syracuse's earliest coins also provide clues as to the origins of their silver. These coins depict on the obverse a horse-drawn chariot and charioteers and on the reverse a female head in the center of an incuse square (Figure 22).[177] They were minted, moreover, on the Euboic-Attic standard, and the standard coin was the tetradrachm. Syracuse's first coins were inspired by northern Aegean and Attic models, from where the silver may have come.[178]

Metalworking areas have so far been found in three, possibly four, Sicilian Greek sites. The earliest known comes from an eighth-century context at Megara Hyblaia and proves that local production occurred from the city's beginning.[179] At Selinous, evidence of metalworking is closely connected with a clay-working area on the city's acropolis and dates to as early as the last quarter of the seventh century.[180] At Zankle, a metalworking area dates to the very end of the Archaic period and appears to have been located inside the city wall.[181] The evidence consists of a water channel, tub, paved surfaces (often red in color because of burning), and several pits containing debris from the washing and smelting of ores found in situ. It is these ores that have been studied archaeometrically and have supplied, as mentioned above, definitive evidence of their extraction from the nearby mountains of northeastern Sicily. Many seashells recovered from this craftworking area may have been used in the reduction process. The fourth possible case concerns Himera, where the evidence is connected with textile production and is discussed below. While metalworking becomes most clearly attested among the western Greeks as a whole in the sixth century, the foregoing evidence nevertheless indicates production in the two previous centuries.[182]

At the same time, the problem of disentangling local production from import is endemic in several of the finished objects found in Archaic Greek

---

this thesis, which is regarded as plausible and which ultimately goes back to Vallet 1958). Note, by contrast, Rutter 1997, 105 who sees homeland Greek silver as the source of "much" of early Sicilian coinage. The case will ultimately be resolved via scientific methods, on which note Macaluso 2008b, 48 n. 24, who states that her two-decades-long plea for neutron activation analysis to determine the source of silver for early Sicilian coinage has now been approved on the coin collection of the Museo Archeologico Regionale "Antonino Salinas" in Palermo.

177. E. Boehringer 1929, 6–17; Cahn 1979; Rutter 1997, 114–16; Fischer-Hansen, Nielsen, and Ampolo 2004, 230; Fischer-Bossert 2012, 146.

178. Rutter 1997, 116.

179. De Angelis 2003a, 83–85; Gras, Tréziny, and Broise 2004, 170–92.

180. De Angelis 2003a, 184.

181. Ingoglia 2003. The area was occupied already from about 650 BC, and it is possible that the area may have used for craft production earlier than current evidence documents.

182. Rolley 2002, 51.

Sicily. This is encountered right from the earliest known bronze object in all Greek Sicily, a little bronze horse from Syracuse. Scholars are divided as to whether it was made locally or imported from Corinth.[183] The issue might be resolved if a local metalworking area were known from the eighth and seventh centuries.[184] A Corinthian helmet was also found in the Punta Bracceto shipwreck, but Corinthian helmets produced in Corinth and in the western Mediterranean are difficult to tell apart.[185] As in the case of stone work, a middle ground is opted for here, one that allows for local production alongside imported finished objects and blending of imported and local know-how, which is only to be expected from migrants establishing new life in a new land.

Some of the finished metal objects include needles and pins of various kinds. Along with the many loom-weights and spindle whorls known from Archaic Greek contexts in Sicily, all these items presuppose the raising of certain domesticated animals (not in doubt, as seen above) and the production of textiles, a basic human necessity that forms a crucial dimension of non-agricultural production for every society (considerably less documented in comparison). Of the fibers used, traces of hemp are attested at Himera and at the native site of Colle Madore in its hinterland.[186] At Kamarina, linen could have been growing in the region.[187] But other fibers, like wool, for which there is at present no direct evidence, were certainly also employed, judging from the keeping of sheep and must have been the most commonly used fiber. Production occurred in at least two possible ways: households and workshops. The discovery of loom-weights, spindle whorls, and needles in domestic, burial, and sanctuary contexts fits the traditional image and identity of Greek women spinning and weaving at home and in their public lives, in both life and death. At Himera, the production of textiles alongside metals was discovered in a workshop located in the eastern residential quarter of the upper city.[188] The telltale clues are the discovery of 19 loom-weights, two stone objects

---

183. For its being locally produced, see Spigo 1997, 551–52, and for its being imported, see Rolley 2002, 51. See Rizza and De Miro 1986, 154 on the difficulty of distinguishing between these two positions with regard to this piece and in general.

184. Spigo 1997, 575. For bronze working in Syracuse's native hinterland at this time, see Egg 1983; Melfi 2000.

185. Rolley 2002, 51.

186. Gleba 2008, 62.

187. Costantini 1983, 49–53. Northern Italy and Campania were ancient Italy's two main regions for the cultivation of flax and linen production (Gleba 2008, 69), but it is possible that these activities happened at Kamarina.

188. Allegro 1976b, 493–94, 557; Gleba 2008, 133, 166.

(possibly molds), and a terracotta stamp, all found in association with a roof collapse from the destruction of the city in 409 BC.

The production of textiles was surely much more widespread in Archaic Greek Sicily than can presently be documented.[189] As discussed in the previous chapter, Phalaris and other elites at sixth-century Akragas defined themselves by the purple garments they wore,[190] and in general textiles are still best known for Classical Greek Sicily on the basis of the ancient writings interested in their symbolic and social aspects. Much more remains to be done on textiles, including how the non-elite masses clothed themselves.

Trade and Exchange

The foregoing discussion has made passing reference to trade and exchange, and it is time to consider these topics more fully. Some related background on Sicily's geographic position and features was given in Chapters 1 and 2, the latter also including discussion of known and suspected spaces of Archaic exchange—ports, agoras, sanctuaries, and stand-alone emporia (cf. also Maps 4–13). These spaces were the conduits through which flowed goods, services, and more at an intra- and interregional level. It remains here to complement these previous discussions by considering distribution and merchants, imports and exports, and weights, measures, and coinage.

Some sunken cargoes and at least three shipwrecks from Sicilian waters can be dated to the Archaic period and provide valuable insights into the goods on board when they sank.[191] The so-called Plemmirio C shipwreck off Syracuse dates to the mid-sixth century.[192] Found at a depth of 35–50 meters, transport amphorae belonging to Corinthian A-B and "Graeco-Massaliot" types were recovered from it. Several Archaic cargoes in these waters also appear to be represented by finds of broken transport amphorae, including Corinthian A-B, "Ionian", and "Locrian" types.[193] The Punta Bracceto shipwreck discovered in the waters off Kamarina dates to about 500 BC. Fine wares and transport amphorae from mainly Aegean Greece were recovered in it. The fine wares consist mainly of Corinthian, East Greek, and Attic, while the transport amphorae are

---

189. On the problems of evidence, see Brugnone 2003b, 52–53.

190. Brugnone 2003b, 62–63.

191. The natural conditions affecting navigation to and from Sicily will be assumed here. For full details, see Arnaud 2005.

192. Parker 1992, 319–20, no. 835; not in Klug 2013.

193. Parker 1992, 293; Albanese Procelli 1996b, 99; 1997b, 4–5; not in Klug 2013. I assume that the descriptions "Ionian" and "Locrian" that appear in Parker refer to, respectively, transport amphorae from East and West Greece.

made up primarily of Corinthian A types, followed by Attic and non-Attic SOS amphorae, Chiot, Lesbian, Samian, Klazomenian, Milesian, and (for lack of identifiable details) "East Greek," as well as Ionic-Massaliot and pseudo-Chiot from the western Greek area.[194] A late Archaic shipwreck was discovered at a depth of five meters close to Gela's coast.[195] On the basis of the finds, the ship is thought to have originated in East Greece and sunk at Gela after having stopped in at least the Peloponnese, Athens, and perhaps Sicily.[196] Small quantities of the following transport amphorae were found in the wreck: Corinthian A-B, Attic SOS, Chiot, Lesbian, Samian, Klazomenian, Ionic Massaliot, Massaliot, and Punic.[197] The finds of transport amphorae on land include these and other types, including non-Attic SOS, Milesian, East Greek/Levantine, and pseudo-Chiot.[198] Hundreds of fragments of Corinthian A are known, and the earliest specimens date to the early seventh century.[199] Small quantities of late-sixth-century transport amphorae from Mende, Thasos, and the "Thasian Circle" have also been identified from among the land finds, and their arrival in Gela replete with wine is ascribed to Athenian intermediaries.[200] Fine pottery was also recovered from the shipwreck; it comprised BF kylikes, RF askoi and oino-choai, and BG cups. Corinthian A and western Greek transport amphorae have also been found on the seabed in the bay of Agnone, where presumably so many of these land finds originally came into Leontinoi.[201] Transport amphorae (Corinthian A, Attic SOS, Samian, and western Greek) have also been found in underwater contexts associated with Katane's port.[202]

These shipwrecks and cargoes are only the smallest glimpse of what must have been hundreds upon hundreds of ships and their cargoes coming and

---

194. Albanese Procelli 1996b, 96–108, 110–19; 1997b, 4–5; Pelagatti 1997, 413; Klug 2013, 152–53.

195. For brief accounts: Parker 1992, 188–89; Klug 2013, 144. For a full account from the pen of the excavator: Panvini 1996, 78–88; 2001.

196. See recently Naso 2006, 368, who thus suspects that the Etruscan funnels came to Gela via Greek intermediaries.

197. Albanese Procelli 1996b, 97, 103, 114, 116; 1997b, 4–5; Pelagatti 1997, 414.

198. Albanese Procelli 1996b, 103, 108, 114; 1997b, 4–5.

199. Pelagatti 1997, 414.

200. Spagnolo 2003.

201. La Fauci 2004. Leontinoi seems to have favored this bay over that at Punta Castelluzzo/ Brucoli, where the Megarian settlers landed before being invited to join in the settlement of Leontinoi, although the site continued to be used as a quarry by later Leontinoi and stone blocks were transported by river to the city (see Felici and Buscemi Felici 2004).

202. Albanese Procelli 1996b, 96, 100, 107, 114, 119; 1997, 5; Pelagatti 1997, 434–38.

going from Archaic Greek Sicily. While they provide valuable insights into exchange, they say little about the merchants who operated on these ships. For the merchants themselves we have some evidence, mostly indirect and mostly of individuals from Greece. The earliest comes from a seventh-century epitaph and graffito of two Corinthians from Selinous.[203] Corinthians are attested elsewhere in Archaic Italy via similar evidence. Even for the extensive Corinthian pottery trade, Corinthians can only have been partly behind the wide distribution of their products.[204] More direct evidence concerns the dedication made by Samian traders who frequented Himera from at least the early sixth century BC.[205] The dedication was discovered in the Heraion at Samos and mentions fighting between Himera and the native Sikans.[206] The dedication appears on a sculpted block whose front has a shield on it and the back a ship's stern. Phocaean traders were well known for their prowess on the seas and also frequented Sicily.[207] In the late sixth century, Massalia and Sicily were connected through imports of Sicilian wine and the influence of Sicilian coin types on Massalia's own issues.[208] The Phocaeans more generally may also be attested by the quarter named after them at Leontinoi, already discussed in Chapter 3, as well as possibly by the small quantities of Aeolic gray bucchero at Megara Hyblaia, Syracuse, Gela, Selinous, and Motya.[209] The Phocaeans may have also used Drepana (modern Trapani) as a port of call and thereby, through their exchange relations, helped to spread stories of the Trojan War in northwest Sicily.[210] The Phocaeans could have exchanged tin and other metals, as well as slaves, with the Sicilian Greeks.[211] In the later fourth century, Massalia's involvement in Sicilian trade is better documented (see below), but its origins are most certainly to be placed in the sixth century BC, if not slightly earlier.

---

203. De Angelis 2003a, 189.

204. Morgan 1997, 332.

205. Belvedere 2001, 742–43.

206. See Dunst 1972, 100–06 no. 2. For the wider evidence of Samian traders (and the poet Ibycus) in the western Mediterranean, see Dunst 1972, 156–59; Barron 2004, 63. It is also interesting to note that the earliest artistic depiction of the Himeran poet Stesichorus' Geryoneis is on a bronze plaque of the last third of the seventh century from Samos (Brize 1985).

207. Antonelli 2008.

208. Morel 1993–94, 351–53.

209. Antonelli 2008, 92–93.

210. Antonelli 2008, 51–59.

211. Morel 1993–94, 353; Nash Briggs 2003; Verger 2003.

Non-Greek merchants, especially Phoenicians, were also certainly involved in bringing and taking goods from Greek Sicily, as discussed in Chapters 1 and 2.

Something is also known of the exact exchange routes used by merchants. A close analysis of the fine wares imported to Katane suggests that they were carried over from Locri in southern Italy, passed through the port of Katane, and then shipped to Tocra and Naucratis in Africa.[212] Two other maritime routes with Sicily have also been distinguished.[213] The first connects Etruria with Corsica, Sardinia, western and southwestern Sicily, and Carthage; the other connects Etruria, Latium, and Campania with northern and eastern Sicily. It is easy to imagine the arrival of, say, Etruscan and Phoenician imports into Sicily through both these maritime routes, or to understand the emergence of connections in clay working between Himera, Zankle, and Campania through the second maritime route.

The evidence suggests that the Sicilian Greeks did not control this maritime traffic. No evidence exists for a merchant navy at Syracuse, our best-documented city.[214] We may be witnessing a precursor attested for late Medieval Sicily, when foreign navies dominated trade to and from the island.[215] Further work is needed to confirm or negate this impression.

Within Sicily, other intermediaries, including native Sicilians, must have played a role in distributing further these products once they arrived in the island and in moving products from the interior to the coast.[216] Whether economic relations involved the payment of tribute by these native hinterlands, as some scholars have suggested,[217] or a synergy that benefited both sides, or a combination of these two possibilities, is of course difficult to say given the nature of our sources. A reciprocal relationship is not in doubt. From the later seventh century onward, there is evidence for native pithoi at Gela and Himera and for Greek-influenced native amphorae in eastern central Sicily

---

212. Giudice 1996a, 101–02, 108; 1996b, 205, 207; cf. Mazza 1996, 296.

213. Tagliamonte 1994, 91–92.

214. Evans 2009, 29.

215. Epstein 1992, 311. For the related question of traders' commercial zones of influence, see most recently Vlassopoulos 2007a, 183.

216. For this whole question, see Graham 1984; Pancucci and Naro 1992; Leighton 1999; Gras 2000b, 601; Albanese Procelli 2003a, 176–83, 201–10; Fitzjohn 2007, 223–25.

217. Manganaro 1999; Rizza and Palermo 2004, 201; Copani 2005, 263. On gifts, tribute, and bribes in Greek-native relations, see now the overview by Tsetskhladze 2010. Whether the natives in Syracuse's territory were in a dependent tribute-paying relationship with Syracuse in the sixth century, as suggested by Manganaro, is doubtful. He bases his claim on a clever but not widely accepted reading of the word *skylon*, meaning "booty," in place of *Skylos*, a personal name, on the sculpted relief of a mounted warrior from Castiglione.

FIGURE 33 View of Imported Native Sicilian Transport Amphorae from Himera.
© Regione Siciliana, Dipartimento Regionale dei Beni Culturali e dell'Identità Siciliana,
Parco archeologico di Himera

(Figure 33).[218] The storage capacities of native settlements in the interior also increases in the sixth century, but this could have been due to a variety of factors.[219] Native sites began to import Greek fine-ware pottery from the eighth century and transport amphorae from the mid-seventh century, which may indicate a two-phase process of establishing social and economic relations between natives and Greeks, discussed in Chapter 1 (Figure 4).[220]

While no one carrier controlled the distribution of Sicilian and non-Sicilian goods to and within the island, no one form of economic transaction should necessarily be privileged over another. Written sources have practically nothing to say of these economic transactions and the goods and services that were at their heart. Strabo, for what he is worth, is the only ancient source to mention

218. Albanese Procelli 1996b, 125–26.

219. Albanese Procelli 2003a, 180.

220. Albanese Procelli 1997b, 13–14, who also notes that the situation could change with future research.

trade between Italy and Greece before 550 BC.[221] Therefore, it is hardly an exaggeration to say that the precise context of Sicilian Greek exchange is not clear, and that inference from archaeology is the best we have to go on. As elsewhere in Archaic Greece, various kinds of processes should be envisaged, from gift exchange, and socially embedded elite-controlled exchange in general, to professional, market-oriented exchange from especially the later sixth century BC onwards.[222] Let us begin by discussing the imports, since that topic both builds naturally from the discussion just had regarding shipwrecks and sunken cargoes and helpfully foregrounds the discussion on exports.

Pottery forms the largest and best-known group of imports.[223] The shipwrecks and sunken cargoes just discussed provide a comparable picture of shapes and producers encountered on land. As we saw in Chapter 2, archaeological conditions in Sicilian Greek cities and their territories are variable, resulting in some parts of settlements being better known than others. Nevertheless, imported pottery (fine and coarse wares) has been recovered from the same wide variety of spatial contexts; a consistent pattern of shapes and producers emerges and parallels developments noted elsewhere in the Greek Mediterranean.

Imported fine wares from the homelands from which the settlers originally came are usually found in the earliest layers of their newly founded cities. This is only natural and to be expected.[224] Such imports often disappeared in the course of the seventh century, when Corinthian imports, especially cups, craters, and aryballoi, came to dominate.[225] At Syracuse, a Corinthian foundation by tradition, the imports include not only the usual cups, aryballoi, and craters, but also a wider range of shapes than are encountered elsewhere in Greek Sicily—kyathoi, pyxides, kalathoi, oinochoai, and watering cans.[226] From 650 to 550 BC, a variety of East Greek imports can be found in Greek Sicily, especially cups, aryballoi, and plates.[227] From the mid-sixth

221. Str. 9.3–4; cf. van Compernolle 1992, 65; R.L. Smith 2009, 9.

222. For recent overviews, see Morris 2007; Osborne 2007; R.L. Smith 2009, 72–73. Modern debates about substantivist versus formalist economies, and primitive versus modernist economies, have run their course and are avoided here for their unhelpfulness in light of recent research (see Cohen 2001).

223. Cf. Fletcher 2007.

224. For Euboean imports: Vallet 1958, 140–53; Tigano 1999a, 108; 1999b, 125; 2002, 42–46; Bacci and Coppolino 2002 (Zankle); Lentini 1998 (Naxos); Frasca 2009, 76 (Leontinoi).

225. Dehl 1983; 1984, to be read with *BTCGI* 12.285; Giudice 1996a; 1996b (Katane); de Waele 1971, 88–97; De Miro 1989, 37–41 (Akragas).

226. Dehl 1984, 92–93, 189, 204–05, 223–24, 262–71.

227. Orlandini 1978.

century, Attic wares came to dominate. Cups, amphorae, and lekythoi were especially imported.[228] Laconian wares, especially craters, are known across Greek Sicily in the sixth century. Other finds are more sporadic and include what seem to be a LG Cycladic amphora and EPC Rhodian kotyle.[229] Of the non-Greek fine wares imported, red-slip Phoenician and Etruscan kantharoi are the most numerous.[230] As discussed in Chapters 1 and 3, the Phoenician material may have largely been brought by Phoenician traders frequenting and resident in Greek cities. The same may have held to some degree for the Etruscan material.

The coarse wares presently known are dominated by transport amphorae and some pithoi, and they are found in several different contexts, from settlements, sanctuaries, and burials, the latter to be regarded as secondary contexts. Corinthian A and B amphorae appear across the Archaic period and document city and country economic relations.[231] Corinthian *pithoi* are also mainly known from seventh-century contexts in eastern Sicily. Attic SOS and non-Attic amphorae have similarly been identified in city and country.[232] Chiot and Samian amphorae have been identified at Leontinoi, Monte San Mauro di Caltagirone, and Ramacca,[233] while Lesbian, Milesian, and (not more closely identifiable) East Greek transport amphorae are known from sites in the territory of Leontinoi and Syracuse.[234] Ramacca has also revealed small quantities of transport amphorae from Laconia, the northern Aegean (Mende), the

228. Frasca 1996b, 85.

229. Dehl 1984; Fletcher 2007.

230. Vallet 1958, 140–53; Dehl 1983; 1984; Tigano 1999a, 108; 1999b, 125; 2002, 42–46; Bacci and Coppolino 2002.

231. Zankle: Albanese Procelli 1996b; 1997b; Pelagatti 1997, 415; Spagnolo 2002; Tigano 2002, 42–46; Klug 2013, 60–61. Naxos: Albanese Procelli 1996b, 98; Pelagatti 1997, 403–04 n. 6. 410; Klug 2013, 61–62. Katane and territory: Albanese Procelli 1996b, 96, 100, 107, 114, 119; 1997, 5; Pelagatti 1997, 415, 434–38. Leontinoi and territory: Pelagatti 1997, 414–15; Albanese Procelli 1996b, 97; 1997b, 4–5; 2003b, 37–38. Syracuse and territory: Albanese Procelli 1996b, 99; 1997b, 4–5; Pelagatti 1997, 412–13; Klug 2013, 57–58. Himera and territory: Albanese Procelli 1996b, 96, 101, 103, 105–07, 109, 114, 119; 1997b, 4–5; Pelagatti 1997, 415; Vassallo 2005b, 136; Klug 2013, 53–56. Akragas' territory: Albanese Procelli 1996b, 98; Klug 2013, 47–49. See in general Sourisseau 2011, 173–226.

232. Zankle: Albanese Procelli 1996b; 1997b; Pelagatti 1997, 415; Spagnolo 2002; Tigano 2002, 42–46; Klug 2013, 60–61. Leontinoi and territory: Albanese Procelli 1996b, 101–02, 104; 1997b, 4–5. Syracuse and territory: Albanese Procelli 1996b, 100–03; 1997b, 4–5; Klug 2013, 57–58.

233. Albanese Procelli 1996b, 105–06, 108; 1997b, 4–5.

234. Albanese Procelli 1996b, 107–09; 1997b, 4–5.

Levant, Etruria, and the Punic world, and types similar to the amphorae from tomb 469 at Lipari.[235] From Himera's Pestavecchia cemetery come a possible Cypriot amphorae and some unidentified types that are a cross between Ionian, Corinthian, and western Greek.[236] Specimens of western Greek transport amphorae, the so-called Ionic-Massaliot types, are also known from all across Greek Sicily, from both urban and rural contexts.[237]

Megara Hyblaia provides a unique set of data for imports, both fine and coarse wares. Thousands of items have been recovered in controlled circumstances, making tentative quantification possible and helping to define the uses, contents, and proportions of these wares. The imports consist overwhelmingly of cups, craters, and other shapes used for wine services (which make up just under 91 percent of fine-ware imports), olive oil, and perfumed oil.[238] Oil and wine are presumed to have been the main commodities transported in the amphorae. From the late sixth century, western Greek transport amphorae, also thought to have contained regionally produced oil and wine, appear alongside their mainland Greek equivalents. The pattern revealed by Megara Hyblaia is one that seems to be extended to the rest of Greek Sicily.[239]

To help facilitate the exchange of imports and exports, and to help reduce the costs involved in establishing their weight and volume, standard forms of measurement would have been required. Recent work on Greek coinage has emphasized that weighed metals, particularly silver and bronze, were part of a moneyed economy long before the adoption of coinage.[240] Silver and bronze bullion overlap in their usage in Sicily and are frequently found, as seen earlier in this chapter, as dedications in sanctuaries in contexts as early as the seventh century. The overlap is best seen later at Himera, where silver and bronze coins were minted alongside each other in the sixth and fifth centuries BC.[241] The use of bronze as bullion has long been plausibly credited to native Sicilian

---

235. Albanese Procelli 2003b, 38–43.

236. Vassallo 1999.

237. Albanese Procelli 1996b, 107, 114–16, 119–20; 1997b, 4–5; Pelagatti 1997, 412.

238. De Angelis 2003a, 89–95.

239. Vallet 1958, 207; Gras 1995, 155; 1996, 124; Albanese Procelli 1996b, 102, 123; 1997b, 6, 9; Osborne 1996; Roller 1996; Pelagatti 1997, 410, 434–38; Dehl-von Kaenel 2001; Kustermann Graf 2002; De Angelis 2003a, 189–95; Johnston 2006, 30; Fletcher 2007; Lucchelli 2009, 181–82.

240. See especially Kim 2001; Kroll 2008; 2012; Macaluso 2008b. Among the Greeks, this may been preceded by iron spits (Seaford 2004, 102–09; Kroll 2008, 35–36).

241. Macaluso 2008b, 43.

practices, attested from the thirteenth century BC onward.[242] The introduction of weighed silver bullion was almost certainly due to the stimulus provided by the Phoenicians, who depended on it for their "international" economic activities well after the adoption of coinage.[243]

This helps to explain the mixed reaction to coinage in Archaic Greek Sicily (Table 8). Megara Hyblaia never minted coinage in the Archaic period, nor did it use the coins of other mints.[244] Therefore, barter is the only way in which these transactions could have been carried out.[245] A small insight into the system of weights and standards used at Megara Hyblaia is supplied by a mid-sixth-century inscription which mentions a fine of 16 litra for sacrificing against the priest's order.[246] The appearance of fines in litra from a late Archaic inscription from Megara Hyblaia must be an indication of how native Sicily's weights and measures had become a widespread standard of value in these coastal cities.[247] Similarly, Leontinoi did not mint coins until it was subjugated by the Deinomenid tyrants of Syracuse.[248] Gela did not mint coins until after it had spearheaded the conquest of eastern Sicily in the early fifth century.[249] Put another way, the minting of coinage required particular social and economic conditions.

Seven out of ten of Greek Sicily's Archaic cities fulfilled these conditions from the mid-sixth century (Table 8).[250] Their coinages coincided not only with the broader economic changes under way in the Mediterranean, but also with well-known developments within states, like building programs and

---

242. The most recent and fullest discussion can be found in Macaluso 2008b, 25–71. Cutroni Tusa (1979; 1997; 2004, 372) has also been a prominent advocate of this connection.

243. Kroll 2008, 31–32, 35–36, who connects this widespread Phoenician trade with a greater attention among the Greeks to their systems of weights and measures. See also Kim 2001, 17–18; Niemeyer 2004b.

244. De Angelis 2003a, 84.

245. On barter in general, see Humphrey and Hugh-Jones 1992.

246. Arena 1989, 25 no. 13; Dubois 1989, 25–27 no. 20; McInerney 2010, 198.

247. Thus recently Macaluso 2008b, 67.

248. Frasca 2009, 115.

249. For the start of Gela's coinage, see Rutter 1997, 118; Fischer-Hansen, Nielsen, and Ampolo 2004, 194. The earliest coins are discussed below in the section dealing with the second historical period.

250. Zankle: Rutter 1997, 108–10. Naxos: *BTCGI* 12.267–68; Rutter 1997, 110–13. Himera: Rutter 1997, 107–08. Macaluso (2008b, 43, cf. 54), by contrast, is content on placing this development more broadly in the second half of the sixth century. Selinous: Rutter 1997, 102–05; Lazzarini 2003; 2004; De Angelis 2003a, 185–86; Fischer-Hansen, Nielsen, and Ampolo 2004, 224; Macaluso 2008b, 52–53; Lucchelli, 2009. The possibility exists that fractions may have been minted as part of Selinous' first issue of coins (Lazzarini 2004; against this, see Macaluso 2008b, 50). Akragas: Manganaro 1996b, 220; Rutter 1997, 113–14; Fischer-Hansen, Nielsen, and Ampolo 2004, 189.

Table 8 Silver Coinages of Archaic Greek Sicily*

City	Date	Standard	Stater Weight	Fractions	Imagery on Obverse/Reverse
Zankle	525–500 BC	Euboeic	drachm	?	dolphin/harbor
Naxos	525–500 BC	Euboeic	drachm	obols or litrai?	Dionysos/grape bunches
Katane	—	—	—	—	—
Leontinoi	—	—	—	—	—
Megara Hyblaia	—	—	—	—	—
Syracuse	late 6th century	Euboeic-Attic	tetradrachm		charioteer/ female head in incuse square
Gela	—	—	—	—	—
Himera	540–520 BC	Euboeic	drachm 5.7–5.8 g	obols or litrai?	cock/windmill in incuse square (group 1) & cock/hen in incuse square (group 2)
Selinous	540–515 BC 515 BC–	Corinthian? Euboeic-Attic?	tridrachm? didrachm?	— fractions	parsley leaf/ incuse square
Akragas	520–510 BC	Attic	didrachm	—	eagle/crab

* Dashes indicate no information available for a particular entry.

the payment of wages and fines, that can be shown or hypothesized to have occurred in Sicily and elsewhere.[251] Moreover, the iconography chosen for the coins themselves is also significant. Milne argued that the Sicilian Greeks had to get their coins accepted to secure credit in the face of competition from native Sicilians using bronze and Carthage using silver:

> That meant advertisement: the mere use of city badges was not suf-
> ficient, as it had been in Greece, to secure credit for their silver: there
> had to be types chosen to emphasize the achievements or the products

251. On the needs for coinage, see, for instance, Martin 1996; Lombardo 1997b; von Reden 1995; 1997; 2002; Kurke 1999; Descat 2001, 78–81; Seaford 2004, 131–36. For Sicily, see De Angelis 2003a, 185; Lucchelli 2009, 183–86; Fischer-Bossert 2012, 145–46.

of the cities. This led to what may be called a medallic treatment of the types, which became more and more elaborate, abandoning the simplicity and directness that characterized the coinages of the homeland.[252]

The distribution of coins was not uniform in space or regular in minting.[253] The arrival of coinage in the Sicilian interior does not appear to have transformed economic relationships between Greeks and natives to any significant degree. While that does not preclude the possibility of a monetized economy, given the scarcity of fractional coinage at present, scholars are generally against the idea of a very monetized economy in the Archaic period.[254] In Archaic Sicily, coinage was by and large a Greek phenomenon that connected the island's *poleis* to other Greek *poleis* beyond.[255] That fact alone provides a small confirmation that the primary aim of the Sicilian Greeks was to trade with fellow Greeks, especially those of the homeland. The expanded study of Sicilian coinages has not shaken the fact they are rarely found in Greece, while those of Greece are widely found in Sicily, hardly surprising given that Sicily has no silver sources.[256]

This concludes our discussion of the evidence for the Archaic economies of Greek Sicily. While there is much that is known, there is much that we would still like to know. As discussed above, even if our written and archaeological sources were more plentiful, we would still need to combine them with economic theory to conjure up, so to speak, the possible economic scenarios that gave rise to our empirical evidence. That is the aim of what follows.

A recent characterization of the Roman economy applies equally well to Archaic Sicily: "symbiotic entrepreneurship with winner-take-all consequences, exercised in horizontal associations of networks rather than commercial companies, and with mostly aggrandizement strategies."[257] Property rights were essential for such economic systems to function and flourish, and, as argued in Chapters 1 and 3, conditions in Sicily at the time of permanent Greek settlement were conducive to the creation of property regimes

---

252. Milne 1950, 150. Some explanation for the appearance of Sicilian products on coins is needed, and this remains the best on offer. In a similar vein, see Descat (2001, 81), who has emphasized the connection between the need of cities to obtain credit and the minting of coinage.

253. Caccamo Caltabiano and Puglisi 2002.

254. Caccamo Caltabiano and Puglisi 2004, 340–41; Macaluso 2008b, 50. Parise 1999, 470 and Lucchelli 2009, 184–85 are more open to the idea.

255. Caccamo Caltabiano and Puglisi 2002, 34, 42–48; Lucchelli 2009, 186.

256. Milne 1950, 151; Finley 1979, 35; Fischer-Bossert 2012, 145.

257. Storey 2004, 126.

that favored the Greeks, and especially the Greek elite, who were the driving force behind these settlements and their state institutions.[258] Stability of kinship and families in and across households through clan formations is directly related to economic prosperity and developments and must have been a going concern of the elite, providing the necessary social foundations for the latter.[259] Dependent labor of all kinds was at the center of this economic success and represented the other side of Sicily's social spectrum in the Archaic and Classical periods.[260] The shots were called by elites at the head of such households, which, together, drove their states.[261]

Although our data are still insufficient to speak of economic growth in precise terms,[262] it remains clear that Archaic Greek Sicily witnessed two phases of economic prosperity. The first required a century or so to build, from about the mid-eighth to the mid-seventh centuries, and was followed by a half century or so of efflorescence. The second phase required another century or so to build, from about the mid-seventh to the mid-sixth centuries, and was similarly accompanied by another half century or so of efflorescence. Population growth appears to have gone hand in hand with and mirrored this economic prosperity, which can best be described as economic takeoff.

It can be argued that these economic takeoffs were driven by the export of a staple in high demand in homeland Greek markets and associated linkages which provided the necessary economic infrastructure for its export.[263] The main staple was most certainly grain, because of its importance to the diet of Sicilian Greeks and other peoples in the wider world. What percentage grain occupied in the local and export economy is, of course, difficult to estimate given the paucity of our sources, but, as a guess, agriculture as a whole would have probably occupied at least three-quarters of all economic activity, and exports perhaps about one-third of this total output.[264]

---

258. On the importance of property rights in general and in the context of Archaic Italy, see Kopytoff 1982, 219; Gilman 1998; Earle 2000; Nijboer 2001.

259. Varto 2009, 333. On the role of household production in Sicily, see De Angelis 2002; Pisani 2003.

260. On the importance of labor control for elite economic success, see in general Kopytoff 1982; Webster 1990; Osborne 1995; Hendon 1996.

261. On the overlap between elite and state interests, see Small 1994.

262. Cf. Morris 2013, 102. For the situation in Greece, see Morris 2004; Ober 2010.

263. For the full argument, including discussion of the theoretical literature, De Angelis 2012b and 2012c.

264. For comparative insight, see Allen 2011, 56, 68–71.

Some of this guesswork is owed to the fact that the jury is still out as to whether the "New Model of Classical Agriculture" delineated by scholars working on other parts of the Greek world for the years around 500 BC applies to Sicily.[265] This "New Model" would have entailed residence in dispersed rural settlements (which greatly reduced travel time), heavily fertilized fields (owing to the presence of domesticated animals), and no more fallowing of fields (because cereals were rotated with pulses). All of these advantages, concentrated as they were in one place, could be canceled out through the risk of climatic misfortune, but that was offset by increased productivity. Of the foregoing features of this proposed model, we can only be certain so far of the existence of dispersed rural settlements and the success of breeding domesticated animals. The model requires more data from Sicily—as well as, for that matter, from Greece, on the basis of whose data it was originally formulated—before being accepted.[266] Even if the model could be substantiated, Osborne is of the opinion that the change in settlement patterns was motivated by "politically induced social choices rather than major revolutions."[267] The current evidence from late Archaic Sicily inclines more toward this viewpoint: agriculture seems to have been practiced under fairly constant circumstances throughout the entire Archaic period.[268]

The associated linkages of staple exports impacted the economy in three particular ways, through the so-called backward, forward, and demand linkages.[269] In all cases, these linkages would have created a multi-sided synergy that fed off one another. The backward linkages would have involved any investments necessary to bring the staple to market. Here one thinks of the stimulus provided to infrastructure, such as craft production. The evidence from Greek Sicily is unequivocal that craft production occurred from earliest times. It is clearest for the sphere of pottery production,[270] but production in other clay products and materials can be established with almost the same degree of

265. Cartledge 1995, 134; Morris 1998, 78.

266. For Sicily, cf. De Angelis 2000a, 140–41.

267. Osborne 1999, 328.

268. The "New Model of Classical Agriculture" is better attested for the second half of the fifth century; whether this represents an intensification of a pre-existing phenomenon or something new altogether is difficult to ascertain.

269. Cf. De Angelis 2012b and 2012c.

270. Rizza and De Miro 1986, 140–41; Villard 1992; Siracusano 1994, 49; Fischer-Hansen 2000, 113. Perhaps the best discussion of the merits of Western Greek pottery production, in terms of originality and its relationship with art of the Greek homeland, is that of Siracusano 1994. This is not the place to discuss this highly interesting (though tangential for the present purposes) topic. See more fully Siracusano 2009; Marconi 2012.

certainty.[271] Some of this production was destined to service the agricultural sector, while the remaining production served other daily needs. The forward linkages would have entailed investments to prepare the staple for market, such as the processing of the crop and its preservation. The demand linkages would represent the generation of revenue for both individuals and the state (for which see further below). The wealth earned could have been deployed in any number of possible ways. For individuals, this may have involved the acquisition of luxuries and semi-luxuries, such as the commissioning of statues, for which there is abundant evidence in Archaic Greek Sicily.[272]

Olive oil and wine, the other two main agricultural staples, were certainly produced from the beginning.[273] To what degree they were locally produced is harder to know.[274] Without exception, all of the Sicilian Greek cities discussed earlier in this chapter have revealed imported transport amphorae which are presumed to have once contained olive oil and wine produced especially in the Greek homeland. That should not necessarily be taken to mean that the Sicilian Greeks relied exclusively on imports for these staples; as we have seen, evidence exists for the production and consumption of local and regional varieties of olive oil and wine.[275] The imports from Greece may have been because this Sicilian production was of insufficient quantity and even quality for local consumers. Clearly, more work on this question is justified and would do much to help delineate, among other things, the proportion of imports versus local production.

Evidence exists for the exploitation of mineral and sea resources, negated or played down in earlier scholarship. The two most notable cases regard fish and the metal deposits of northeastern Sicily. The evidence for the exploitation of other mineral and sea resources is either occasional or indirect, such as, in particular, salt, but given their importance to the daily diet and craft activities they can be presumed to have been produced, distributed, and consumed more than our current evidence allows us to deduce.

We know practically nothing directly about the financial systems established by the Sicilian Greek cities in the Archaic period. We may infer their presumed structure and workings on the basis of recent advances in the study of the finances of ancient Greek cities, which provide a solid theoretical basis

---

271. For terracottas, see Pautasso 1996, 113–48; for textiles, see Gleba 2008.

272. See further Foxhall 1998; 2005. Cf. also Pafumi 2004; Duplouy 2006.

273. Brun 2011, 99; Sourisseau 2011, 145–47. Cf. also Vandermersch 1996, 173.

274. On these crops and their redistribution, see the overview in Horden and Purcell 2000, 209–14, 372–75. See also the more recent discussions by J.-P. Brun 2004; 2011; Foxhall 2007; Vlassopoulos 2007a, 132–33; Sourisseau 2011.

275. Albanese Procelli 1996b, 110–11, 116–17; 1997b, 9–11.

for discussion.[276] The generation of revenue and the areas of expenditure are crucial economic issues to consider.

Revenues could have been generated by taxation and ad hoc euergetism. There is considerable evidence in Archaic Greek Sicily for both imports and exports, and this is one area which the various cities would have presumably taxed, with taxes being levied on such things as the use of harbors and custom dues at the most likely standard rate of 2 percent of the estimated value of the cargo.[277] The Greek communities of southern Italy and Sicily seem, unlike those in the Black Sea, to have allowed ships from states without formal commercial accords with them to land on their shores; thus the trade barriers were fewer and the situation more open.[278] Exports are another possible area which the city could have taxed to generate revenue.[279] Provisioning of visiting ships and crews should also not be forgotten, though through what hands (private versus public) this occurred is unknown. More difficult to establish is whether direct taxation on property and production was a general feature of life for citizens. The answer is part of a much larger debate for which arguments have been set forth on both sides.[280] Again, the matter cannot even be guessed at for Archaic Sicily, let alone resolved, but it must be a possibility of how the state financed itself. State revenues would presumably have also been built up through the leasing out of public land and mineral resources. Tapping into the elevated resources of the elite would have occurred via ad hoc euergetism in which fiscal resources deriving from the private sphere would have been deployed for public purposes, like sacred architecture. Archaic Sicily abounded in ambitious individuals and tyrants who sought to raise themselves to the forefront of their communities, and so it is easy to imagine the requisite politico-ideological conditions in existence to play a role in economics.

On the expenditures side, the state's primary commitments would have included religion; war and defense; urbanism; and administration of various kinds.[281] All of these areas are securely attested as having been going concerns

276. Good overviews can be found in Goldsmith 1987; Migeotte 1995; 1996; Salmon 1999.

277. Cf. Ampolo 1994, 31–32; Purcell 2005b, who both stress that such taxation was a feature from the Archaic period onwards.

278. Ampolo 1994, 33–34.

279. Thus Salmon 1999, 160: "No city is known to have discriminated between imports and exports when levying harbour taxes."

280. Migeotte 1995, 20; Gallo 2000, 25–26.

281. Migeotte 1996, 83–84; Salmon 1999, 156–60. The areas of war and defense are taken to another level in Sicily in the second major historical period delineated here, and they are therefore discussed below in more detail. For the connection between economics and religion (for Sicily and generally), see Martin 1973; Graßl 1985; Jameson 1988; Ampolo 2000; Davies 2001; Smith 2001; Horster 2003.

of the Archaic cities of Greek Sicily, and therefore areas which required the state to expend finances on a regular basis.

It was during the Archaic period that Greek Sicily established its economic profile within the larger ancient world. Exchange did much to shape all regional economic profiles. As Morris has recently summed up:

> If De Angelis [2002] is correct that grain trading tied Sicily and the Aegean together from the eighth century, colonization fundamentally changed the land: labor ratio in the Greek world, allowing Aegean Greeks to exploit comparative advantages in some agricultural goods (wine, oil) and in manufactures such as pottery, while Sicilian Greeks sold them grain. Rather than a developed Aegean core coupled with an underdeveloped periphery, as world-systems models would predict, gains from trade benefited all parties.[282]

It was common for Greek *poleis* to exploit their cultural geographical position within maritime networks and to specialize in cash-raising crops and other economic activities.[283] This regional specialization, however, should not cause us to lose sight of all the other economic activities that can be documented and inferred for Archaic Greek Sicily. Archaic Greek Sicily was not an agricultural, chiefly grain, monoculture. The evidence is overwhelmingly not in favor of this view and shows instead a wide variety of production activities aiming at both local and external needs. In other words, Greek Sicily's basic economic structures were laid in the Archaic period. The picture is much more complex and intertwined than previous accounts have allowed. When we turn to the subsequent Classical period, which has more written sources available for study, we must keep this point in mind in order to gauge continuity versus change in Greek Sicily's long-term economic history.

2. The First Generation of Political Centralization

Greek Sicily's economic prosperity in the second half of the sixth century was no doubt remarkable, occurring in a political landscape that was soon to be transformed. In the late sixth and early fifth centuries, as we have already seen, the tyrants of Gela initiated wars aimed at conquering other polities,

---

282. Morris 2007, 240. Moving in the same general direction, though in a less detailed and developed manner, see already Humphreys 1965, 427–28.

283. For a recent discussion, see Vlassopoulos 2007a, 138–39, 158–60. On the cash-raising possibilities, Bresson (2007–08, 2:221) observes that the price of grain was not the same everywhere, being cheaper in regions like the Black Sea and Sicily, where it was produced, than in regions where it was consumed.

both Greek and non-Greek. With the successful capture of Syracuse, Gelon transferred his seat of power to there and made it the capital of his territorial state (Map 6). Arguably, what may have spurred the creation of this state in the first place was the economic prosperity that Sicily was experiencing in the second half of the sixth century. The tyrants of Gela perhaps sought to capture and bring together under their control the successes and energies of the various city-states in eastern Sicily. Once these tyrants had set that process into motion, their Sicilian neighbors, near and far, were forever changed. Some, like Akragas, reacted with a parallel development; others, like Selinous, sought an alliance with a more powerful neighbor, Carthage (Map 12a). The remaining succumbed to one of the larger powers.

For the economic historian, this is in some regards a better-documented period, in that more literary evidence is available than ever before. But, interestingly, the archaeological evidence is not as abundant for this period as for the Archaic period, and in part this must be because Syracuse, the chief center of power in the island, has continuously been inhabited from then until today (see Chapter 2), but in part it must also have to do something with the scholarly practice of not being as keen to develop the archaeological record when literary sources become more abundant, as noted above.

Gela is the most logical place to begin this discussion. Hippokrates' wars of conquest in eastern Sicily set into motion several economic developments at home and wherever he took his campaigns.[284] Sufficient manpower for these military ambitions was a central concern for the tyrant. Cavalry made up of individuals close to the tyrant is mentioned in various ancient sources referring to this period, especially Herodotus.[285] As discussed in the previous chapter, alongside locally raised troops Hippokrates employed mercenaries, and both are likely to have been a major cause for the minting of Gela's first coins.[286] These consisted of didrachms on the Attic standard; the obverse depicts a naked rider wielding a spear and the reverse the local river god Gelas represented as a man-faced bull (Figure 34). This is the first time a local river god was represented on Sicilian coinage, but its legacy survived long after the collapse of the Deinomenid territorial state, the iconography being adopted by

---

284. On the connection between warfare and economic development, see the discussions in Garlan 1989; Wasowicz 1994; Corvisier 1999; Prost 1999; Couvenhes and Péré-Noguès 2005; Wilkins and Hill 2006, 61–62; Morley 2007, 51–52, which contain frequent reference to Sicily.

285. For all these sources, see *BTCGI* 8.8.

286. Rutter 1997, 118 ascribes these coins later to Gelon; nevertheless, his account of them remains very useful.

FIGURE 34 View of Tetradrachm from Gela with Forepart of Man-faced Bull on Reverse.

© The Hunterian, University of Glasgow 2015

former subjects.[287] At Gela, the river fertilizes the coastal plain and brought fecundity to the city, something rightly deemed worthy of commemoration on coinage.[288]

Military pay enabled the local and foreign troops to purchase food while on campaign, as well as any other services they required. Some of this food could have been supplied from Gela's own territory, and thus local markets aimed at supplying the troops can be safely assumed. It may not be a coincidence that the second half of the sixth century witnessed the establishment of more rural farmsteads, some possibly specializing in viticulture (see above). That more wine was produced among the western Greeks as a whole in the early

---

287. Collin Bouffier 2003, 50.

288. Collin Bouffier 2003, 60.

fifth century is the impression given by the transport amphorae, particularly the consistent appearance of pseudo-Chiot imitations.[289] It is reasonable to suspect that demand increased for staples as a result of Hippokrates' military ambitions, because soldiers on campaign usually consumed more calories, probably twice the daily standard of 2,000 calories for males.[290] Increased demand would certainly have resulted in agricultural intensification at Gela. These needs will have continued outside of Gela's territory while on campaign. The troops would presumably have obtained in whole or in part (nothing is known of Geloan supply lines) their food from the enemy's land, with their service train presumably accompanying them. Whether these items were by payment or plunder, or both, is also unknown.

We must also imagine that such demand increased Gela's imports in general. Metals for coins and other objects, especially of war, would have been on the rise and thus imported in ever greater quantities. The regions that supplied the city in the Archaic period may have continued to do so (the uncertainty is due to the absence of deposits with metal finds), but it is also possible that new regions were tapped into. A business-as-usual impression is given for pottery imports: the regions from which fine and coarse wares came remain unchanged from the Archaic period, even if we cannot speak of a noticeable increase.[291]

Something had to be offered in exchange for these imports, and grain seems to have been one of the prime exports in these transactions.[292] Greek and Roman sources from the Imperial period talk about Rome receiving grain from Gela during Gelon's tyranny.[293] Earlier generations of scholars tended to dismiss such claims as fabricated, as a way to give a longer (pre-Mid-Republican pedigree) to the Rome-Sicily relationship. But in recent years the scholarly tide has turned, in large part because of the lifting of skepticism with the sources for early Roman history.[294]

Wars of conquest and the general working of the economy created wealth that manifested itself at Gela through the building and cultural programs undertaken by its tyrants and their associates. Aeschylus' stay at Gela implies the existence of a theater, and by extension a supportive local audience.[295] Such

---

289. Albanese Procelli 1996b, 124.

290. For a recent discussion, see Wilkins and Hill 2006, 61–62.

291. Giudice 1985; Albanese Procelli 1996b, 103, 106–07, 114, 116; 1997b, 4–5; Pelagatti 1997, 414; Spagnolo 2003.

292. So, for example, Panvini 1996, 81–82.

293. The ancient sources are conveniently collected in Fantasia 1993, 9–11.

294. For full discussion, see Fantasia 1993, 9–11; Mafodda 2000; Purcell 2003b, 334–35.

295. Fischer-Hansen, Nielsen, and Ampolo 2004, 194; Kowalzig 2008.

investments were not restricted to the city. A temple, with nearby cemetery, has been uncovered at Fiume di Mallo (Butera), at a strategic communication point leading to the interior, and dates to the first half of the fifth century BC.[296]

Gela took a back seat to Syracuse once Gelon captured it in 485 BC. He then proceeded to lavish attention on Syracuse, so as to make it a suitable capital for his territorial state. This entailed, as seen in the previous two chapters, enhancing the urban infrastructure for symbolic, military, and practical reasons, the latter primarily on account of the migration of individuals, forcible or otherwise, into the new capital.

Syracuse minted coinage under the Deinomenid tyrants, in large part, no doubt, to pay for its military personnel and urban infrastructure.[297] The relative sequence of Syracuse's coins established by Eric Boehringer's 1929 study has stood the test of time; his Groups II (subdivided into Series 3–5) and III (subdivided into Series 6–12) were minted on the Euboic-Attic standard.[298] Boehringer's chronology, however, has come under scrutiny.[299] Boehringer baptized Series 8–11 of his Group III the "Massenprägung" (or "mass minting") and assigned its decadrachms, tetradrachms, and obols to Gelon (Figure 35).[300] The publication of the Randazzo Hoard 1980 led to further refinement.[301] The "Massenprägung" must date to after the orthographic change from koppa to kappa introduced by Hieron I, which is likely to have happened in 478 BC.[302] Thus, the most plausible scenario is that Hieron I minted these coins in large quantities because of his building up of Syracuse's navy in the years before the Battle of Cumae against the Etruscans in 474 BC.[303]

Regional coinages were also minted on the Euboic-Attic standard across the Deinomenid territorial state. While the new chronology renders improbable Boehringer's claim that a die was borrowed from Leontinoi to execute the "Massenprägung,"[304] he was certainly correct in identifying a close numismatic

---

296. Adamesteanu 1958, 380. Given the latitude in date, the temple is placed in this period, although it could in theory date later.

297. On Syracusan coinage in this period, see in particular E. Boehringer 1929; Arnold-Biucchi 1990; Knoepfler 1992; Rutter 1993, 1997, 1998.

298. Boehringer 1929, 17–41, with Rutter 1998, 307 on its lasting validity.

299. The matter is fully reviewed in Rutter 1998, 308, 315.

300. Boehringer 1929, 17, 29, 74–75.

301. Arnold-Biucchi 1990, 46.

302. Knoepfler 1992, 12–27.

303. For this dating from Knoepfler onward, see Luraghi 1994, 303–04; Rutter 1998, 311–14; Corretti 2006, 420.

304. Boehringer 1929, 74–75.

FIGURE 35 View of Syracusan Tetradrachm Depicting Head of Arethusa and Dolphins Minted under the Deinomenids.

© Trustees of the British Museum

relationship between Syracuse and Leontinoi, in which Leontinoï's first coins were minted under Syracusan control.[305] The largest denomination in Leontinoï's issues consisted of a silver drachma weighing 4.37 grams. These have a chariot with Nike flying overhead on the reverse, and the head of a lion surrounded by four ears of barley on the observe. The arrival of Polyzelos in Gela is also thought to have entailed a numismatic development: the minting of tetradrachms, which depict, similarly to Leontinoi, a chariot on the obverse and, similarly to Gela's earliest coins, the foreparts of a man-faced bull on the reverse.[306] Coins were also issued at Katane, now renamed Aitna by Hieron I as discussed in the previous chapter.

In minting these regional coinages, the Syracusan state wanted to serve their respective economies, and especially the garrisons now installed in them.

---

305. C. Boehringer 1998, 44; Frasca 2009, 115–17.

306. Rutter 1997, 131.

Deinomenid numismatic policy respected regionalism and at the same time sought uniformity through the adoption of the Euboic-Attic standard across its territory.[307] This standard would have created a kind of common market not only within the domains of Syracuse but also in those of Akragas and Zankle/Messana, the island's other major tyrannies, which also minted on this standard.[308] This postulated common market may have had as its foundation the lack of restriction beforehand in coins moving beyond the boundaries of their respective *poleis*. Numismatic uniformity would doubtless also have served ideological purposes.

It is unfortunate that little else is known of the financial arrangements of Greek Sicily's Deinomenid and other tyrants.[309] Nevertheless, we can be certain that political and military developments affected Greek Sicily's numismatic and economic trajectories in other ways. For the Chalcidian cities of northeast Sicily, this was part of a process of the "de-Chalcidianization" imposed by the tyrants, which included not only disruptive population transfers but also economic changes that brought to an end their earlier numismatic practices (as in the case, for instance, of Naxos) and imposed new ones on the subject cities.[310] It remains to be seen whether centralized policies in weight and measures were adopted more generally across the entire Syracusan state. Two bronze weights from early-fifth-century Gela inscribed with the words *damosia* ("public") and *ton Geloion emi* ("I belong to the Geloans") may support the idea of centralization.[311] But these two weights currently represent the extent of the available evidence, and of course much more evidence is needed in general from the Archaic period too before one can say anything further on the subject.

A centralized system of weights and measures would make sense given the Syracusan tyrants' attention to agriculture and grain across their domains. This attention extended to Gelon being an avid supporter of the cult of Demeter and Persephone. He placed himself at the forefront of the patronage of these goddesses.[312] Gelon thus mediated between the immortal and mortal worlds and their chief economic activity, agriculture, which was actively

307. See the recent discussion in Caccamo Caltabiano and Puglisi 2004, 337–38; Fischer-Bossert 2012, 145–46.

308. After about 480 BC, the Attic standard was generally used for Sicilian silver coinages (Rutter 1997, 120). See further below in this chapter for discussion.

309. Rutter 1993, 185–86.

310. Fischer-Hansen, Nielsen, and Ampolo 2004, 220; Gasparri 2008, 53; Fischer-Bossert 2012, 143.

311. Dubois 1989, 174 nos. 152–53; Arena 1992, 25 no. 16, 26 no. 26.

312. See L. Martin 1990, 256–58; De Angelis 2006, 35–38. On the impact Deinomenid devotion had on the production of terracottas, see Pautasso 1996, 135.

promoted.[313] The close relationship between agriculture, especially grain, and intra- and interstate affairs as depicted in the ancient sources leaves little doubt of the centralization of agricultural surpluses under the Deinomenids.[314] The minting of coins at Gela and Leontinoi, and with them the creation of governorships there, seem also to underline that centralization even further, when one considers how these two cities were known for the agricultural richness in general and for their prowess in grain production at this very period, and later for that matter (see next section). Syracuse would seem to belong to that class of imperial states that finance themselves via staples.[315] If Sicilian agriculture was dominated by wealthy landowners and their estates, as we have every reason to believe after the discussion in the previous chapter, this would have been a more reliable basis for such a financial system.

Staple finance required not only a configuration of internal developments, but also an eye on external developments. Gelon provided shipments of grain to Rome while his capital was still Gela and also, a few years later, made an offer to the Athenian and Spartan ambassadors to feed the entire Greek army fighting the Persians.[316] In doing so, Gelon reproached the ambassadors because he had not received help from Greece in freeing the emporia.[317] Much ink has been spilled on trying to identify these emporia as associated with particular cities, like Himera and Selinous, but that is a futile exercise according to Michel Gras, who argues that they are to be viewed as trade routes, and Gelon was in a dispute with Carthage over the trade routes in the Sicilian Channel.[318] We know that Rome was denied access to this area by a treaty of 509 BC, and it is likely that Gelon and his Sicilian Greeks were also locked out. Carthage's blockade might explain, Gras observes, why Rome had grain shortages between 491 and 485 BC.[319] It would follow that if Gelon could supply grain to Rome, his ships were not blocked in going through the Straits of Messina, despite Anaxilas taking control of Zankle from the Samians at roughly the midpoint of these years of shortage at Rome. It has been suggested that the

---

313. See especially Colum., *Rust.* 1.1.8; Plut., Mor. 175a, 552a. Cf. also *BTCGI* 19.42; De Angelis 2006; Kowalzig 2008.

314. Fantasia 1993, 11.

315. For discussion in the context of Greek and Roman economies, see M.E. Smith 2004, 86–87 and Storey 2004, 116–17.

316. Hdt. 7.158.4.

317. Hdt. 7.158.2.

318. Gras 2000.

319. Gras 2000, 132.

Deinomenids eventually had their own blockade in the Straits of Messina, causing Athens to find new ways (up through the Adriatic Sea) to supply the hungry Etruscan market with its fine pottery.[320] It is interesting to observe that two well-known Archaic emporia, Bosco Littorio at Gela and the Cardillo Property at Himera, went out of use during this period. Their excavators have argued that they were abandoned respectively because of earthquake and the transference of commercial activities to the agora.[321] As argued in Chapter 2, the Sicilian Greek agora may have started to be commercialized in the seventh century, while a postulated earthquake, for which no evidence exists, seems to hold little explanatory power. Were these emporia abandoned for reasons caused by Sicily's Greek and non-Greek territorial states to reorganize, secure, and control previous economic landscapes and trade routes?

Apart from centralizing grain surpluses, Gelon is known to have resorted to other revenue-generating activities. He is said to have sold into slavery those elements of the population that he did not want transferred to Syracuse. If true, we have to envisage the sale of thousands of people, but that can be at best only a guess, given the uncertainties in our information regarding the demographic size of the various conquered cities and whether or not some people remained behind as agricultural laborers. Revenue could also be made through war against particularly Carthage, a non-subject state, both in regard to the revenue generated from its spoils and to the economic stimulation caused by waging it.

Symbolic capital, revenue of another sort, is something that we see Sicilian tyrants engaged in during the Hellenistic period in a big way, but the acquisition of gifts from other rulers is first attested in early Classical Sicily, if we are to believe Athenaeus' testimony that Theron gave Gelon a big pool for the raising of fish.[322] To engage in pure speculation, this gift may have been a

---

320. Giudice 1985. G. Giudice (2007, 416) repeats the hypothesis, while Hannestad (1996, 213), though sounding a note of caution, finds the idea tempting. The cemeteries of Mylai, to the west of Zankle/Messana, provide another sequence of local and imported pottery during late Archaic and early Classical times that can be taken into account (Tigano 2002, 44–46). While the grave goods are less varied than before, the imports continue to come from the same sources. The only class of artefact that is missing is Attic RF at Mylai and at Zankle/Messana. Conditions of excavation could explain this absence, but it could also be, as Giudice suggests, because the Straits of Messina were blocked to Athenian products. The evidence could be read in this way and can also be made to suggest that, by and large, the pattern of pottery imports otherwise indicates little disruption in economic patterns during the period in which Zankle changed hands and name.

321. Personal communication.

322. Ath. 12.541–42, quoting Diodorus Siculus, who actually makes no mention of Gelon (11.25.4; cf. also 13.82.5). Collin Bouffier (1999b, 39–41) has discussed the issue in detail, concluding that Athenaeus is probably wrong in saying that Gelon was the beneficiary, and that such a fish pool is unlikely on various other grounds (cf. also Collin Bouffier 2000b). Nevertheless, perhaps we should not reject a connection between tyrants and their patronage

symptom of a greater cultural turn toward fish in the fifth century among the western Greeks.[323]

If this incident represented the creation of a new dimension in the eco-nomics of Greek Sicily, or at least an amplification of an existing one, all other indications are that everything else in Syracuse's economy, and those of its dependent territories, seem to have been business as usual. No changes in, say, agricultural technology or new crops can be detected, other than the inten-sification of certain staples surmised above.

By the time Gelon had consolidated his power in Syracuse the strate-gic port city of Zankle had changed hands twice: the first time by refugees from Samos and Miletos, invited by Zankle before its capture, who seized it from Hippokrates' governor Skythes in 493/92, and then in about 488/87 by Anaxilas, the tyrant of Rhegion. Hippokrates came to terms with the Samians, allowing them to continue to occupy Zankle so long as they paid him off with one-half of the movable goods and slaves from the city and countryside. A trib-utary relationship may be envisaged.

The Samians were quick to identify their occupation of Zankle with coins,[324] whose ship iconography has certainly done much to shape the view that Samians brought technical expertise that helped in the establishment of Sicily's later navies.[325] It would be almost a century before Zankle returned into Syracuse's hands, but it must be imagined that the loss of this port city deprived Syracuse of a lucrative income-generation source.

The numismatic evidence, nevertheless, suggests that northeastern Sicily played a vital role in the economics of Rhegion from Anaxilas onward, since Rhegion's coinage gravitated towards Sicily in the fifth century.[326] This is, for instance, evident in the iconography. Anaxilas used the coins types of Samian Zankle at both Messana and Rhegion down to 480 BC. He then introduced his

---

and consumption of fish, for, as Collin Bouffier (2000a) has noted elsewhere, it was wealthy western Greeks who were the patrons behind their sophisticated food culture in this very period. Theron's gift should not be seen as some kind of offering from a subservient state but as intra-elite exchange between rulers (cf. Bringmann 2001 for the Hellenistic period).

323. Trotta 1996, 242; cf. also Collin Bouffier 2009, 73–74, on water in Deinomenid Syracuse.

324. On the Samians minting these coins while at Zankle, see especially E.S.G. Robinson 1946, 14–15. Cf. also Rutter 1997, 119; Fischer-Hansen, Nielsen, and Ampolo 2004, 235.

325. Corretti 2006, 419. As seen earlier, Samians are attested at Himera in the mid-sixth century. The frequent interchanges that can be documented between East Greece and Sicily would have also served as an earlier conduit for ideas. On the related issues of the movement of people, ideas, and technologies, including discussion of this historical episode at Zankle, see Vlassopoulos 2007b, 98–104.

326. Carbè 2002, 80.

famous types with the mule-cart on the obverse and a hare on the reverse.[327] There are other iconographic overlaps between the coinages of these two cities on the Straits of Messina, and taken together it is tempting to think, among other things, of close economic relations, such as harbor dues on incoming and outgoing goods and vessels.

Theron and his sons ruled Akragas, the third power bloc in Sicily, in a way rather similar to Syracuse. This happened both socially, as seen in the previous chapter, and economically. Theron engaged in territorial expansion and left his numismatic imprint on Himera, the only other city in his domain with a prior history of minting coins (Map 12a).[328] The cock emblem of these earlier coins was joined on the reverse by a crab, the symbol of Akragas, and now struck on the Attic standard, also in use at Akragas (Figure 23). As at Syracuse, the unity of standard created a common market throughout the territorial state of Akragas.

While a relationship of dependency can be demonstrated to have existed to some extent between Himera and Akragas, the evidence elsewhere in Akragas' domains is scant. That has not stopped scholars from speculating about possible tribute-paying subjects of Akragas, as recently with Sant'Angelo Muxaro, the impressive native site.[329] Whether the Emmenids also practiced staple financing, as presumed for Syracuse, is even less certain, given the paucity of written sources for the subject of grain or other crops as a whole.[330] That grain also perhaps had a role similar to the role it played in the Deinomenids' domain is suggested by the expansion of Demeter cults at Akragas and its territory during Theron's rule (Figure 31).[331] For other crops, the only indication we have is that the vine and (unspecified) trees of all kinds were planted around the *kolymbethra*, and that great revenues were generated from them.[332] Nonetheless, some form of extraction from Akragas' subjects has to be imagined, besides the booty earned through Akragas' military successes.

The numismatic evidence may reflect that, as argued by Vassallo in his excellent little study on the bronze coinage in Akragas' hinterland between 480

327. For a discussion of these hares as evidence for fauna in Messana's territory, see Manganaro 1996b, 220. Their presence on these coins must doubtless symbolize the animal's agility.

328. For these developments, see Chapters 2 and 3. On this numismatic development, see Rutter 1997, 120; Stazio 1999, 414.

329. Rizza and Palermo 2004, 201.

330. For full discussion, see Nenci 1993; Fantasia 1993.

331. Fiorentini 2005, 162–63.

332. Diod. Sic. 11.25.4–5. Cf. Brun 2004, 165.

and 406 BC.[333] He connects their wide distribution with the establishment of a medium of exchange between agricultural and mineral producers and the *polis* center on the coast, and reasons that bronze coinage was created to control this hinterland both economically and politically: there seemingly existed a cause-and-effect relationship between the appearance of this bronze coinage and the creation of Akragas' immense wealth in the fifth century. While, as just mentioned, we can only guess at what Akragas exported in this period, it is probably a good guess that the state and individuals within it generated revenue in much the same way as they did in the Archaic period. Despite the patchiness of the written sources, the financial situation of Akragas under Theron was clearly healthy, as indicated by the attention the tyrant lavished on the material development of his capital city, as seen in Chapter 2.

We can be certain about what was imported. The largest and most obvious group of evidence belongs to fine wares produced in Athens.[334] Scholars have been struck by the large number of high-quality Athenian vases found at Akragas in the fifth century as a whole, arguing, moreover, that Athenian potters were commissioned and took into account the particular tastes of their clients. The main shapes are made up of different kinds of cups, craters, lekythoi, and pelikai.

Selinous was the only independent Greek city-state left standing in early Classical Sicily, and that is only because it had aligned itself politically with Carthage (Map 12a). The Archaic coinage of Selinous discussed earlier continued into this period, but scholars see it dropping off in the years immediately following 480 BC, perhaps because of an economic downturn associated with the alliance with Carthage.[335] Foreign coins and ingots continued to be imported, but the evidence provides more support for the hypotheses discussed earlier for the sources of Archaic silver and merchants.[336] Pottery

---

333. Vassallo 1983. See more recently Sole 2012.

334. See especially de la Genière 1995; 2006; De Miro 1989, 59–80; Torelli 1996.

335. Rutter 1997, 138; Cutroni Tusa 2004, 391.

336. Arnold-Biucchi, Beer-Tobey, and Waggoner 1988. Manganaro (1990, 427 n. 77) challenges the hoard's find spot, on the basis of a local collector's report that it came from Palma di Montechiaro. Even if true, the hoard would nevertheless document mainland Greek trade (via especially Corinth and Aegina) with central southern Sicily, to which circuits Selinous also belonged (Bresson 1993, 179; Johnston 2006, 32; Kroll 2008, 32–33). Lead isotope analysis has revealed a Spanish origin for at least some of this silver (Beer-Tobey, Gale, Kim, and Stos-Gale 1998). Rutter (1997, 105) believes that the single coin from Abdera in the hoard would indicate a Thracian origin of the silver. As we have already seen, this is part of his view that much of the silver used by the Archaic Sicilian Greeks came from the Aegean. Clearly, the range of possible silver sources needs to be widened.

imports also continued in much the same way as before and provide another indication of underlying economic stability.[337]

In summary, the archaeology of this generation in Sicily is still underdeveloped, and the problem is only somewhat alleviated by the surviving written record. In spite of this, there are sufficient indications to allow us to imagine that warfare and the accumulation of resources heavily directed economies in a way never before seen in Greek Sicily. This would have heightened demand for money, goods, and services needed to maintain armies, and to help fund these needs tyrants turned to centralizing economic surpluses through a system of provincial governors extracting tribute. Reconfigurations of space and forced population movements helped to achieve this. Militarization and imperial control had a lasting legacy on Sicily.

3. The Collapse and Return of Political Centralization

Agricultural Production and Wild Foodstuffs

In this two-generation-long interlude between territorial states, political autonomy and the city-state once again characterized the Sicilian Greek landscape (Map 12b). Economic continuity and change are discernible. The latter is in part due to the democratic wind that blew through Sicily, as seen in the previous chapter, which appears to have entailed a change in land distribution and ownership. The existence of small, medium, and large properties at Himera and Syracuse can be inferred from archaeological evidence (discussed in Chapter 2), and such variety of land ownership can also be inferred from literary evidence referring to Syracuse and Akragas.[338] While a direct one-to-one correlation between this evidence and a particular social group or social problem discussed in the previous chapter is difficult to draw, the broader social and economic implications seem easier to make.

---

337. Commercial marks in Greek letters not of the Selinountine alphabet have also been identified on cups deposited as grave goods in the Manicalunga cemetery (Johnston 2006, 257, drawing on Kustermann Graf 2002). It is in this and the Buffa cemetery that the largest number of pottery imports have been retrieved. Imported pottery tends to be more frequent than local wares. In the Manicalunga cemetery, local wares make up no more than 30 percent of 155 pottery items, and in the Buffa cemetery they make up about 50 percent of 59 pottery items (Meola 1996–98, 1.301; Kustermann Graf 2002, 34). The matter is a bit more complicated to work out for the Buffa cemetery, given the broad range within which material can often be dated. While the range of shapes and sizes was doubtless conditioned by their burial contexts, the trends are still informative, indicating that Attic, Corinthian, and East Greek cups predominated (Meola 1996–98, 1.301; Kustermann Graf 2002, 34).

338. For a large estate mentioned during the Athenian invasion of Syracuse, see Thuc. 7.81.4; Plut., *Nic.* 27.1 (for possible archaeological evidence for large estates in Syracuse's territory, see Guzzardi 2001, 104–05 and, more generally, Vandermersch 1994, 99). The evidence from Akragas is intimately connected with wine and olive oil production and is discussed immediately below.

Material well-being for a wide range of social groups is suggested, some of it certainly new. A change in economic strategy—perhaps the so-called "New Model of Classical Agriculture"—can also be associated with the isolated farmsteads, which facilitated the constant work required for the more intensive cultivation of olive trees and the vine which now occurred.[339] This change would have complemented other agricultural activities in the economic calendar and spread the use of labor throughout the year to autumn and early winter, when grapes and olives were, respectively, usually harvested.[340] The evidence for these is not necessarily any greater than for the Archaic period,[341] but the existing literary and archaeological evidence suggests some notable changes in the production of wine and olive oil in this period.

The archaeological evidence comes from Kamarina. Legumes appear in the archaeobotanical record for the first time in Greek Sicily.[342] While it has to be conceded that their "newness" could be due to the silence of the sources, it is equally possible that legumes were new to the Sicilian Greeks and employed, besides as food, for their nitrogen-fixing qualities to help offset soil exhaustion caused by residence on the land in the isolated farmsteads that seem to have emerged in this period. A second apparent novelty concerns burnt olive pits, with no parallel in Italy, recovered from the Iurato farmstead.[343] These olive pits are small, short, and of elliptical-ovoid shape and resemble specimens from Salamis in Cyprus, and may betoken the introduction of a new variety into Sicily. Excavations in the Capodicasa farmstead also revealed a wine press, the earliest known one from Greek Sicily.[344]

---

339. Cf. Osanna 2001, 213. Fifth-century Greek agriculture witnessed two technological changes, the dikella (the hoe with two prongs) and the so-called Olynthus or hopper rubber mill, that may have also played a part in the success of the period (Amouretti 1986, 140–47; Gallo 1997, 429; Frankel 2003, who maintains [p. 18] that this mill type came to Sicily in the fourth century BC, although the Marzamemi shipwreck discussed earlier, and absent in Frenkel's study, seems to put this innovation, at least in the waters off Sicily, in the late fifth century). Neither innovation has yet been documented on Sicily. In any case, even had they been documented, they would not have in and of themselves produced a technological revolution of any sort.

340. In the idealized scenarios discussed below, we must never lose sight of factors that we know little about: the time stress that accompanied harvests (Halstead and Jones 1989) and the labor fluctuations caused by family life cycles and general availability (Gallant 1991).

341. Images on the coins of Naxos supply evidence for the continued production of wine production and are joined by coins from Katane with Silenes that may also provide evidence for wine production (Vandermersch 1994, 21, 38–41; Brun 2004, 165).

342. Di Vita 1959, 350; Costantini 1983, 56; Di Stefano 2001, 700. Whether the famed lentils of Gela of which Athenaeus (2.67b) talks, citing Amphis, the comic poet of the fourth century BC, ultimately go back to this period must remain at best a tantalizing possibility. Amphis, cited by Diogenes Laertius (3.27), also talks about flax at Gela, which, besides being used for linen, is an excellent companion crop to help establish legumes.

343. Costantini 1983, 55 (the finds consist of twenty-five whole and nineteen fragmentary pits).

344. Di Stefano 2001, 694.

The literary evidence comes from Diodorus Siculus's long account of how Akragas acquired wealth by exchanging locally produced wine and olive oil with Carthage.[345] Implied are high levels of production for both items and their novelty. Diodorus Siculus gives figures only for the amount of wine produced by the wealthy citizen Tellias, citing Polykleitos' eyewitness account of the fourth century BC of this individual's still-visible wine cellar.[346] Diodorus Siculus' narrative required exemplification of the wealth that Akragantines could generate, and Tellias' wine cellar provided an appropriate illustration of it. This account contains enough information to allow some detailed hypothetical quantification that will provide insights into these economic activities.

Polykleitos saw three hundred casks hewn into the rock, each capable of holding one hundred amphorae, and a stuccoed wine vat with a capacity of one thousand amphorae feeding these casks. If we take these figures at face value and assume that the cellar contained only a year's production (we know nothing of Tellias' marketing strategy and whether these figures represented an accumulated production of a number of years), the casks work out to a volume of 6,000 hectoliters (or 600,000 liters), a calculation which led its formulator to remark that such volumes were rarely attained even in the Roman Empire.[347] The amount of land needed by Tellias to produce these quantities has been estimated at between 70 and 105 hectares.[348] Comparative data from Greece and Italy suggest that a hectare of land planted with vines would have required 147 man-days of labor per annum.[349] Assuming a work year of 250 workdays would result in a workforce of between about 41 and 62 full-time laborers for Tellias' estate. In addition to the necessary skilled labor and environmental conditions, still evident today (Figures 36 and 37), Akragas would have had locally available sulfur, known in antiquity for acting as a fungicide to stop infestations of mildew and mold on grapes.[350] Akragas' territory, if it were planted exclusively with the vine, could have supported a total of between 2,071 and 3,071 estates similar to Tellias' in size.[351]

---

345. Diod. Sic. 13.81.4–5.

346. Diod. Sic. 13.83.2–4, esp. 3. Timaeus later also mentions Tellias. For a discussion of these ancient sources, see Vandermersch 1994, 28.

347. Brun 2004, 166; 2011, 109. This calculation is to be preferred over the exaggerated one found in Hochholzer 1935, 92.

348. Vandermersch 1994, 99. Again, this estimate is to be preferred to the overly generous one in Hochholzer 1935, 92.

349. Gallant 1991, 76.

350. Vandermersch 1994, 50.

351. Recalling, as estimated earlier in this chapter, that Akragas' territory may have consisted of 217,500 hectares of arable land. If each estate also produced 6,000 hectoliters of wine, that would mean a grand total of 12,426,000 to 18,642,000 hectoliters produced by a workforce of between 84,911 and 190,402 laborers.

FIGURE 36 View of Olive Grove near Poggioreale in Central Western Sicily.
© Author

FIGURE 37 View of Vine Intercropped in the Background with Olive Trees near Poggioreale in Central Western Sicily.
© Author

This imaginary scenario is advanced here simply to conjure up hypothetical parameters. Such a scenario in fact did not and could not exist, given that Diodorus Siculus, besides mentioning the production of grain in passing by the Akragantines, states that in the time of Tellias "the greater part of their territory was planted in olive trees."[352] Unfortunately, Diodorus Siculus does not provide specifics on this occasion; nevertheless, some hypothetical quantification is possible and just as illuminating. Assuming a population of 30,000–40,000 people for Akragas in this period (as calculated in the preceding chapter), a wealthy household would have required between 200 and 330 kg of olive oil per annum.[353] If we assume that each household consisted of, say, six people, and consumed the same range of olive oil, then we could expect that local demand would have amounted to between 1 and 2.2 million kg.

This figure allows us, in turn, to estimate the number of trees and the amount of land planted. If we assume that each tree produced 2.16 kg every two years, then we can imagine somewhere between 384,615 and 846,154 olive trees planted in Akragas' territory.[354] Olive trees require, depending on the level of moisture available, a particular spacing in order to thrive.[355] At ancient Akragas, rainfall would probably have averaged between 400 and 600 mm per annum, placing its soils in the thin-permeable category, and so a figure of about 150 trees per hectare seems a reasonable guess based on the parameters derived from comparative data. Therefore, between 2,564 and 5,641 hectares of land would have been required, and, as already seen, Akragas had ample land available in its territory to meet these needs. What about labor, however? Each hectare planted with olives would have required about 125 man-days per annum.[356] Assuming again a work year made up of 250 days, and no time stress at harvest or other constraints, would mean that between 2,564 and 5,641 hectares of land required a labor force of roughly between 1,282 and 2,821 full-time workers. The point of this exercise has been to establish the consumption needs of Akragas in the first instance. It obviously would follow that if Akragas was in a position to export to Carthage, the city would presumably have had to produce above and beyond what it itself needed.[357]

---

352. Diod. Sic. 13.81.4.

353. Foxhall 2007, 86.

354. Foxhall 2007, 216. Elsewhere (p. 79) she cites a figure of 3.4 kg per tree, which would yield a range of 294,118 to 647,059 olive trees planted.

355. For full details, see Amouretti 1986, 26; Foxhall 2007, 6, 116.

356. Gallant 1991, 76; cf. also Amouretti 1986, 203.

357. It is also possible, though perhaps unlikely, that Akragas could have acted as an intermediary and obtained some of the wine and olive oil it exported to Carthage from other sources.

While scholars have long accepted the historical validity of these passages concerning wine and olive oil production at Akragas,[358] new evidence can be adduced to help back them up: western Greek transport amphorae that may have once contained such liquid contents are increasingly being recognized in Carthage and elsewhere in Punic Africa.[359] If we join the dots provided by Diodorus Siculus' testimony, the tyrant Theron may have started, or at least taken to another level, the cultivation of the vine and olive at Akragas, which continued to grow and develop as sectors of the agricultural economy here and perhaps elsewhere in Sicily.

The cultivation of grain is better attested via literary, numismatic, and archaeological sources for this period, due to the greater abundance of source material for the Classical period and the single-minded focus of outsiders interested in this one dimension of Greek Sicily's economy.[360] The same crops—wheat, barley, and oats—show continuity of production from the Archaic period to this one.[361] What may be new in this period is that some cities were branded as grain producers, as with Gela, described in the epitaph of the Athenian playwright Aeschylus, who died in 456 BC, as *pyrophoroios* ("wheat bearing").[362] In the fourth century, Theophrastus mentioned a famed variety of Selinountine wheat (something repeated by Pliny the Elder in the first century AD), which can be extended back into the mid-fifth century on the basis of tetradrachms whose reverses are adorned with ears and sheaves of grain held by the local river god Selinous.[363] Similarly, the imagery on Zankle's coins can be an indication of the importance of grain to the economy at the time. It seems likely that this branding represented a new economic change, given that tyrants had previously invested much effort in promoting Sicilian grain.

The pattern of wild and domesticated animals was established in the Archaic period. Though the evidence is more abundant for that period than the current one, we have every reason to imagine the same sorts of economic and cultural uses as before, including their uses in agricultural production,[364] as well as

---

358. For example, Hochholzer 1935, 92; Dunbabin 1948, 221; Pace 1958, 403.

359. Albanese Procelli 1996a, 124–25; 1997b, 13; Sourisseau 2011, 216–17. Cf. also De Angelis 2006, 46.

360. Fantasia 1993; Nenci 1993.

361. For the archaeological evidence, see Di Vita 1959, 350; Costantini 1983, 56; Di Stefano 2001, 700.

362. Page 1972, 332.

363. Theophr., *Caus. pl.* 3.21.2; Plin., *HN* 18.12.64; cf. De Angelis 2003a, 186.

364. This is shown from the faunal remains found in wells of Classical date at Zankle (Martinelli, Bacci, Paglialunga, and Mangano 1999; cf. also Tigano, Martinelli, Ingoglia,

the same sort of environmental conditions.[365] Even so, the surviving evidence throws light on three issues that appear to be new.

First, literary sources speak of Sicilian and Syracusan cheese, fish, and livestock. Attic comedy from the mid-fifth century to the early third century BC contains a few handfuls of references to Sicilian cheese and tuna.[366] "Sicilian" is not of course synonymous with "Syracusan," but since two other fifth-century Attic comedians, Eupolis and Hermippus, talk of the excellence of Syracusan cheese and swine, there can be little doubt that Sicilian must have sometimes been shorthand for Syracuse, given the city's political and culinary importance.[367] This does not preclude other places outside Syracuse producing cheese. Economic historians, even taking into account this and other issues raised by the comic context in which these references are made, have had no hesitation in seeing them as realistic reflections of interregional exchange.[368] That Punic-prepared fish from Gades was imported to Corinth is certain, given the discovery of the so-called Punic Amphora Building of mid-fifth-century date.[369] Imported transport amphorae are also known from contemporary Athens.[370] But this evidence is far from being confirmation of

---

Sannino, Paglialunga, Severini, Bartoli, and Mangano 1999, 188–89, on late Hellenistic faunal remains from a cemetery context): 1,021 vertebrate fragments of sheep/goat and pig were recovered, many of them preserving signs of butchering and cooking. The sheep/goat were slaughtered in adulthood and thus presumably used for milk, wool, and meat; the pigs were slaughtered at a young age for their meat. Dog remains (at least five of small-medium adults) were also recovered; they too may have been eaten. There are also 212 mollusk shells in this deposit. The sacrificing of animals must have continued as before, although it took on new dimensions with the 450 bulls sacrificed annually to Zeus Eleutherios at Syracuse, a practice instituted to commemorate the end of Thrasyboulos' tyranny in 466 BC; see Diod. Sic. 11.72.2, and cf. Scramuzza 1937, 278; Habermann 1987, 101.

365. The border areas disputed by Selinous and Egesta in 454 BC (discussed in the previous two chapters) may have consisted of forest. That could be presumed if we work backward from a possible restoration (in lines 7–8) of a golden deer being dedicated to commemorate the victory mentioned in *IG* XIV 268 (Manganaro 1996b, 218). This region preserves signs of deer and forest in the preceding Archaic period and in the fourth century BC (De Angelis 2003a, 183), and so it is plausible to assume similar conditions for the century in between.

366. Most of this material dates from the fifth and fourth centuries and is to be found in the fragmentary works of the Attic comedians. All of these references are considered together here, given their similar nature and the issues that they raise. See Ar., *Vesp.* 838, 909–10; Edmonds 1957–61, 1:866–67; 2:288–89, 353–53; 3:470–71, 478–79. Cf. also Habermann 1987, 99–100.

367. For Eupolis, see Edmonds 1957–61, 1:304–05; for Hermippus, see Ath. 1.27f.

368. Curtis 1991, 114; Dalby 1996, 68, 112.

369. For a recent discussion, see Zimmerman Munn 2003.

370. Lawall 2006, 269.

a trade in fish between Sicily and Athens. We face an even greater paucity of information for the cheese, including which animal milk was used to produce it.

Second, the working of animal hides mentioned in *IG* I³ 386–87 lists the dedication of *byrsai Sikelikai* ("Sicilian animal hides") during the Decelean War.[371] The hides may have formed part of a ship's accessories and arrived in Athens as war booty from one of the Syracusan ships sent to aid the Spartans in the Aegean.[372] The hides could have originally been used on board as some kind of protective/resistant material. Similar uses could be found on land for the leather industry that presumably existed behind this dedication in an Athenian sanctuary.

Third, a fragmentary inscription said to be from Gela dates broadly to the fifth century and involves the sale of oxen.[373] The text's general sense can be understood: someone arrived with the sum of money for an unspecified number of oxen, but decided not to purchase them. In any case, these were presumably locally raised oxen, given that Gela's territory contained the necessary environmental conditions and salt, as discussed above.

Non-agricultural Production

Clay working is not as well attested as it was for the Archaic period. The vagaries of archaeological research must be borne in mind, as discussed in Chapter 2, but the absence of evidence can also be partly explained by a decline in output, as argued for Leontinoi.[374] The available evidence indicates considerable continuity in clay-working practices. It is most evident in the places of production and their products. The location of workshops follows the pattern delineated for the Archaic period, being found in residential quarters, sanctuaries, outside the city wall, and in the countryside.[375] The kilns also belong to previously known shapes (rectangular and round/elliptical) and designs, and the materials used in their construction are also the same (stone and clay). The

---

371. Habermann 1987, esp. 99–100.

372. Habermann 1987, 111.

373. For full discussion, see Dubois 1989, 152–59 no. 134; Arena 1992, 28–30 no. 45, 35–36 no. 79 (who prefers a slightly more precise date in the first half of the fifth century).

374. Frasca 2009, 112–13, 117, 120.

375. Akragas: Adamesteanu 1956b, 123; Cuomo di Caprio 1971–72, 457; 1992, 71; A. Calderone 1984–85, 536; Fischer-Hansen 2000, 94; 2002, 150–51; Fischer-Hansen, Nielsen, and Ampolo 2004, 180 (in city and countryside). Kamarina: Cuomo di Caprio 1971–72, 458; 1992, 72; Pautasso 1996, 141; Di Stefano 2001, 702 (in city and countryside). Selinous: Albers et al. 2011; 2012 (near the city wall; an earlier Archaic usage is possible).

clay products continued pretty much as before and included pottery, terracottas, architectural sculpture, and small altars.[376]

Alongside these continuities are some developments attested for the first time. With regard to the tools and processes, it is unlikely that they represent a technological change of some kind; they are instead due to the nature of archaeological research, often targeted at settlement and production contexts. Numerous spacers, nine-tenths of them being of the wedge-shaped type, were discovered in Selinous' workshops, located just outside the city wall.[377] One of them has a kind of letter "H" on it, another a small circle, and yet another a kind of diagonal slash. These marks could represent the brand of the workshop or stages in the production process. An inscribed kiln spacer (of probably the fifth century) is known from a house in Himera's upper city and may have been used in pottery production.[378]

Regional interaction between clay-working traditions is well attested in this period, and this is likely to represent a newfound interest in looking for inspiration for products not just with the top clay producers of the Greek homeland, as primarily done in the Archaic period, but with the top regional producers that had since emerged in Sicily and southern Italy.[379] The production of terracottas was reinvigorated in Gela in about the mid-fifth century, thanks in large part to the stimuli provided by nearby Akragas.[380] A single product could combine stimuli from Sicily, southern Italy, and Greece, as in the case of Kamarina's antefixes (mainly of the Silenos and pentagonal palmette varieties), which can be traced to Naxos, Kaulonia, and Corinth.[381] New appears to be the production of fired clay bricks, not previously known at Selinous or Sicily for that matter. Before this discovery, fired bricks were only known from the Near East in late Classical and Hellenistic times.[382] Perhaps a new regional connection via Carthage could explain their appearance.

---

376. Akragas: Rizza and De Miro 1986, 233–34, 239; Pautasso 1996, 139. Gela: Pautasso 1996, 138–39. Kamarina: Pautasso 1996, 143; Pelagatti 2003. Leontinoi: Frasca 2009, 112–13, 117, 120. Naxos: Gentili 1956, 331; Cuomo di Caprio 1971–72, 460; 1992, 73.

377. Albers et al. 2012, 109.

378. Grotta 2008, 266 no. 8.

379. Influences from Greece alone continued, as in the Attic influences on the clay busts of female divinities produced at Akragas (Pautasso 1996, 140; Croissant 2007, 297–306) and on the well-established class of terracottas depicting Demeter holding a piglet in her arms at Syracuse (Rizza and De Miro 1986, 239–40; Pautasso 1996, 144–45).

380. Pautasso 1996, 138–39.

381. Pelagatti 2003.

382. Albers et al. 2012, 108.

There are indications that other areas of non-agricultural production documented for the Archaic period also continued into this period. However, the
evidence is so exiguous as to preclude any attempt to gauge continuity versus change. In the case of quarrying and stone working, little public building
occurred in this period, as discussed in Chapter 2. This may be because the cities
had established their architectural backbone in Archaic times, which obviated
the need for new building. Instead, some renovations are known. Quarrying
and stone working certainly did decline in intensity in some cities as a result.
In other cities, by contrast, building is abundantly attested, as most dramatically
at Akragas with its impressive monumental temples, but also in other media
(Figure 38). Such new building seems to have exploited the same quarries as
previously used. Metalworking is little known in any direct way, despite the abundant coinage produced in this period (see below). The location of production in
workshops in sanctuaries and residential quarters is attested as before,[383] as is
the problem of disentangling local versus external skills.[384] There is little or no
archaeological evidence for the production of textiles in this period, apart from
some ambiguous evidence from Himera, discussed earlier. Literary sources provide the only evidence; it pertains only to two cites, Syracuse and Akragas, and is
included for the ideological overtones luxury served.[385] More attention needs to
be paid in future work to non-agricultural production in this period.

Trade and Exchange

The export of agricultural products was discussed in passing earlier, and this
provides a backdrop against which to address trade and exchange more fully.
Various shipwrecks and their cargoes date to the period, and they provide
both new and expected details.[386] The Porticello wreck found in the waters
of Zankle contained, among other things, bronze statues and two lead ingots
from Laurium in Attica, besides the expected transport amphorae. Two shipwrecks in the waters off Syracuse also had cargoes containing western Greek
and Corinthian A and B transport amphorae, but volcanic millstones were also
recovered.[387] A second shipwreck, dating to the third quarter of the fifth century

---

383. Fischer Hansen 2002, 94.

384. As in Kamarina's bronzes: Rizza and De Miro 1986, 208.

385. Brugnone 2003b, 54, 66 and discussion in Chapter 3.

386. Parker 1992, 332–34; Gianfrotta 2005, 149–50.

387. Parker 1992, 269 no. 677 (from Marzamemi, south along the coast from Syracuse),
405–06 no. 1091 (the "Siracusa A" site in shallow waters in the city's harbor). The latter's
status as a shipwreck is less certain, but scholars are inclined to indentify it as such. The
millstones are from the Marzamemi site and comprise two hopper-type levers belonging
probably to a much larger consignment.

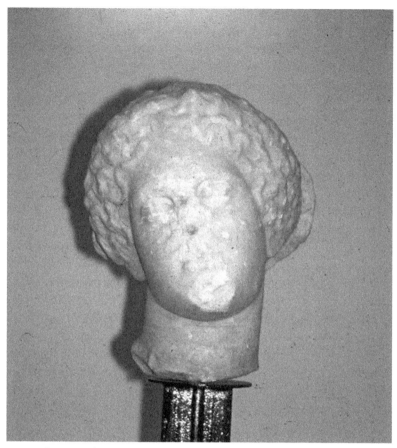

FIGURE 38 View of Sculpted Head of Demeter from Akragas.
© Author

BC, was discovered in the waters off Gela, with finds consisting primarily of Attic fine wares and transport amphorae.[388] These shipwrecks fit the already established picture of exchange with Greece and the central Mediterranean, but add new evidence for the goods transported for exchange.

The existence of Sicilian Greek ships can be documented, though just barely, for the first time in this period in connection with war and defense. Thucydides records that five Geloan ships were sent to aid the Syracusans during Athens' invasion, but we are in the dark about the overall number and type of ships Gela maintained.[389] The only direct evidence for shipping in

388. See Panvini 2001. On the Attic fine wares, see Vickers 1996; G. Giudice 2007, 243–76, 355–67. For the transport amphorae, see Pelagatti 1997; Spagnolo 2003.

389. Thuc. 7.33.1; cf. Moggi 1999, 529.

Sicily is provided by ship sheds from Naxos, first constructed in the mid-fifth century.[390] While it would be rash to read too much into the general silence of the sources, or into these meager details, it is worth observing that Sicilian merchants are known to have been involved in regional and extra-regional exchange for the later Classical period (see below).

On land, some inscriptions document distribution and merchants in the deep interior of Sicily for the first time. A lead tablet, perhaps from Terravecchia di Cuti in Akragas' territory, dates to the second half of the fifth century and contains the first known reference to a banking transaction in Sicily.[391] The debtors are a certain Arkhon, his unnamed sister, and his daughters or nieces Kypara and Saiso, who owe money to an unspecified goddess.[392] The amount owed with interest is expressed in both Sicilian talents and Euboic-Attic minae (8,720 grams), but after that the poor ancient editing in the central part of the inscription leaves much unclear. From Vassallaggi come two other inscriptions. The first is a possible shopping list containing the word *hekaton* ("one hundred"), leading Alan Johnston to speculate from this inscription and what is generally known of Vassallaggi (a commercial graffito on an Attic pelike is also dated to the same period[393]) that it may have served as an emporium.[394] This suggestion would fit with John Bintliff's predictive model for the location of markets in a city's territory.[395] Another graffito of a commercial character is known from a small Attic RF pelike of about 420 BC imported to Kamarina.[396] All this evidence supplies snapshots of fifth-century exchange from coast to interior only suspected previously.

---

390. For a convenient overview, see De Angelis 2007, 157.

391. Dubois 1989, 202–04 no. 177; Arena 1992, 54–55 no. 119. The precise find spot is unknown, and consequently scholars, like Arena, think that it may come from Terravecchia di Cuti or Montagna di Marzo, the latter lying outside Akragas' territory. The onomastic parallels between this and an inscribed loomweight from Terravecchia di Cuti lead to Dubois' attribution to this site, which, although far from certain, has the most going for it so far. Also to be noted here is the transaction recorded in an inscription on bronze of the first half of the fifth century from Selinous' agora which mentions a certain Nikon paying back eight heptalitra of silver (Mertens 2012, 165–68).

392. It is interesting to note that ten inscribed clay weights, with native names like Kypara on them, also belong to the same site and time period (Dubois 1989, 199–200 nos. 175a–d; Arena 1992, 50–51 nos. 111–15, 117). An eleventh inscribed loom-weight dates to about 500 BC (Arena 1992, 51 no. 116).

393. Dubois 1989, 195–97 no. 169; Arena 1992, 61 no. 152.

394. Johnston 1993–94, 157–58; cf. also Johnston 1996; 1999; 2006.

395. Bintliff 2002b; cf. also Bintliff 2002a.

396. Arena 1992, 61 no. 152.

The appearance of these Attic vases with possible commercial graffiti deep in the Sicilian interior was part of a wider and continuing habit of importing Attic fine-ware pottery. This continued in much the same way as before.[397] The same holds for transport amphorae, with pretty much the same types transporting the same products (wine, oil, and fish) imported in this period.[398]

Scholars usually propose that Sicilian grain was offered in exchange for these imports from Greece. For Syracuse, evidence for its export (and even production) is circumstantial. Athens' failure in Egypt in 454/53 BC is thought to have caused the city to turn to Sicily and other regions for its imports of grain.[399] Overall, it is improbable that Syracusan grain and other exports (like fish, cheese, and livestock, discussed earlier) arrived in Athens the closer we get to the Peloponnesian War, as Thucydides tells us that Syracuse was shipping grain to the Peloponnese in 427 BC at the time of Athens' first expedition to Sicily, leaving the distinct impression that Athens was receiving none.[400] In any case, the Peloponnesian market for Syracusan grain will surely have predated this mention, and we can be certain that it originated in the Archaic period because of Corinth's role in founding Syracuse. It is not too difficult to imagine Leontinoi also exporting grain to Athens, as Syracuse's blockades of Leontinoi by land and sea in especially the 420s BC were perhaps intended to stop grain exports to Athens.[401] Akragas remained neutral during the Peloponnesian War, and it is possible that grain was exported to Athens as it would be later in the fourth century BC.

The Adriatic Sea opened up to Syracusan imports and exports in the fifth century BC as a result of the breaking up of Etruscan maritime control.[402] The

---

397. For full details of the painters and shapes, see G. Giudice 2007, 243–76, 355–67 (Zankle, Naxos, Katane, Syracuse, Kamarina, Himera, Gela, Akragas, and Selinous). For Akragas, see also De Miro 1989; de la Genière 1995; Torelli 1996.

398. Tigano 2002, 45–46 (Mylai); Lentini, Savelli, and Blackman 2005–06 (Naxos, where their discovery in connection with the slipways means that they were being used for secondary functions as water pitchers and containers to hold materials for maintaining the ships, after having served their primary purpose as wine amphorae).

399. On grain for pottery, see recently G. Giudice 2007, 243–76, 355–67, 412–13 n. 7. See also Lepore 1990, 292–95; Ampolo 1992a; Davies 2007b; Cataldi 2007, as well as, more generally, Migeotte 1998; Greco and Lombardo 2007.

400. Thuc. 3.86.4.

401. As recorded by Thucydides (3.86.3) for 427 BC (cf. also Diod. Sic. 12.54.1). For full discussion, see Vattuone 1994, 86 with n. 15; Vanotti 1995, 97–98. Cf., however, Fantasia 1993, 11–23, who is quite doubtful, with Raviola 1999, 54.

402. See in particular Raviola 1999; Harari 2002, esp. 23. Athenian involvement, as is well known, also coincided with this and can be ascribed to strategic and economic motives (cf. Thuc. 1.36.2 on Corcyra with Ampolo 1992a).

most tangible manifestation of this so far comes in the form of Syracusan influences on local terracotta production at, among other places, Spina.[403] Ionic-Massaliot transport amphorae have also been found at Spina, though their contents and carriers are harder to distinguish.[404] In return, the list of possible hypothesized items emanating out of the Adriatic region includes grain, bronze, slaves, horses, and timber.[405]

Two new developments in weights, measures, and coinage certainly facilitated and secured exchange in unprecedented ways. The first concerns bronze coinage, which all Sicilian Greek cities minted and which was fiduciary in them all (Table 9; Figures 39 and 40).[406] Bronze coins may have been used for market exchange transactions with the hinterland for goods and services and as a response to the heightened military activity that characterized the end of this period.[407] The distribution of Syracusan bronze coins in its hinterland can also be related in part to the collection of the tribute and tithes discussed below.[408] The appearance of gold coins is the other new development. At Zankle, the minting of gold coins as tetradrachms around 455 BC may have been stimulated by military developments not otherwise attested in our surviving written sources.[409] Syracuse also issued gold drachms, probably during the Carthaginian threat that emerged between 408 and 406 BC (cf. Figure 41), in order to secure goods and services, the ratio of silver to gold being 1:13.

Three old developments continued, sometimes with slight variations on previous practices that need to be noted. The first concerns the continuing use of *aes rude*.[410] The second concerns how previous imperial subjects (Leontinoi,

---

403. Pautasso 1996, 148.

404. Raviola 1999, 56–57, by contrast, believes that they contained wine and were made somewhere in northeastern Sicily, while admitting that they may have arrived through Athenian intermediaries.

405. Raviola 1999, 59–60.

406. Selinous: Price 1979a, 85, wondered whether the cast pieces were initially issued by private individuals and then taken up by the state. There is no definitive way to make this distinction. Akragas: Vassallo 1983; Cutroni Tusa 2004, 389–90; Fischer-Bossert 2012, 148. Gela: Jenkins 1979, 186. Himera: Kraay 1979; Rutter 1997, 142. Kamarina: Jenkins 1979; Rutter 1997, 148–49. Katane: C. Boehringer 1979; Manganaro 1996a, 311; Rutter 1997, 148; Fischer-Hansen, Nielsen, and Ampolo 2004, 207. It is possible that some of these coins were minted for the garrison later installed in the city after its capture by Dionysius I (see below). The matter is complex, and absolute certainty is impossible at present. Syracuse: *IGCH* 2091; Rutter 1997, 147; Morcom 1998.

407. Rutter 1979; Belvedere 2001, 746.

408. Cf. Rutter 1997, 141; Galvagno 2000, 97–98; Morris 2006b, 46.

409. Rutter 1997, 134; Fischer-Hansen, Nielsen, and Ampolo 2004, 236.

410. Macaluso 2008a, 2008b, 36–38.

Table 9 Coinages of Classical Greek Sicily*

City	Metal Type (Date)	Standard	Stater Weight	Fractions	Imagery on Obverse/ Reverse
Zankle	silver (ca. 460 BC)	Euboeic	tetradrachm	?	
	bronze (late 5th BC)	"	tetradrachm		mule-Victory/ hare-grain
	gold (455 BC)	"			
Naxos	silver (ca. 460 BC)	Syracusan-Attic	tetradrachm	?	Dionysos/Silene
Katane	silver (460–50 BC)	Syracusan-Attic "	tetradrachm	?	Victory/river god
	silver (450–40 BC)	"	"	?	chariot/Apollo
	silver (ca. 402 BC)	"	"	☑	Apollo/chariot
	bronze (ca. 405 BC–)			?	river god/Silene-bull
Leontinoi	silver (ca. 460–22 BC)	Syracusan-Attic "	tetradrachm	—	—
	bronze				
Syracuse	Silver (ca. 460–BC)	Syracusan-Attic	tetradrachm		charioteer/female head in incuse square
	Bronze (ca. 460–BC)				Athena-Leukaspis hero
	Gold (late 5th and 380 BC)				
Kamarina	silver (ca. 460–BC)	?	litrai	—	Nymph-Victory/Athena
	bronze (ca. 420–BC)		"	—	river god/chariot/ Herakles
Gela	silver (ca. 460)	Syracusan-Attic	tetradrachms	—	Horseman/
	bronze	"	litrai	triantes, onkiaia	man-faced bull "
Himera	silver (BC)	Euboeic	didrachm	?	Nike/river god (group 1) &
	bronze (BC)				Pelops/nymph (group 2)
Selinous	silver (ca. 460 BC)	Euboeic-Attic	tetradrachm	fractions	river god/grain
	bronze (ca. 420 BC)				
Akragas	silver (ca. 460–BC)	Attic	didrachm	—	eagle/crab
	bronze (ca. 450–BC)				

* Dashes indicate no information available for a particular entry.

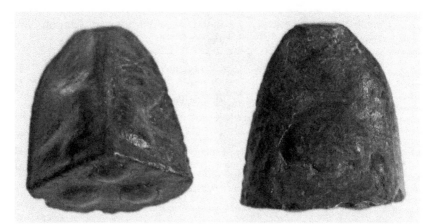

FIGURE 39 View of Cast Three-unica Bronze Cone from Akragas.
© Trustees of the British Museum

FIGURE 40 View of Cast Three-unica Bronze Coin from Himera.
© Trustees of the British Museum

Gela, Naxos, and Himera) continued to orient themselves to Syracuse, their previous master, by adopting the same weight standard and similarly replacing the didrachm with the tetradrachm as the main denomination.[411] The third and main older development concerns silver coins, minted by all the Sicilian Greek cities in this period soon after they had regained their independence

---

411. Rutter 1997, 136–37; Fischer-Bossert 2012, 145–46.

FIGURE 41 View of Gold Coin Minted by Dionysius I.
© Trustees of the British Museum

(Table 9).[412] Some fractional silver coinage is known among these issues, but standards and stater weights appear to have remained constant from before. Many of the images on the coins also highlight local landscapes, resources, and divinities, often depicted for the first time.[413]

Coinage, as just mentioned, helped to collect and generate revenues and to pay for expenditures. The military continued to be a significant sphere of military expenditure in this period, especially for Syracuse, which maintained its imperial ambitions and which, accordingly, generated revenues to support them. The ancient sources make reference to Syracuse's infantry, cavalry, and navy. Nothing is known of the size of the infantry and cavalry, but they were certainly smaller than under the Deinomenids, if only because of the departure of several thousand unwanted mercenaries after their downfall. In 439 BC, we hear of 100 triremes being built and equipped, and, as we did earlier, we can estimate the cost the state incurred to maintain each at 1 talent per month.[414] Thus 100 triremes would have cost 100 talents per month, or 1,200 talents per annum.

412. Zankle: Lacroix 1965, 111–12; Rutter 1997, 134. Naxos: Rutter 1997, 137. Katane: Manganaro 1996a, 305–06; Rutter 1997, 136–37; Fischer-Hansen, Nielsen, and Ampolo 2004, 207. Gela: Rutter 1997, 133–34. Leontinoi: Rutter 1997, 135; C. Boehringer 1979a; 1998. Syracuse: E. Boehringer 1929, 45–68; Rutter 1997, 144–47. Kamarina: Rutter 1997, 137–38.

413. Collin Bouffier 2003, 52–53.

414. Diod. Sic. 12.30.1. Also relevant to note, for the recurring expenditure that they entailed, are the Syracusan ships that took part in the Decelean War (see Thuc. 8.61.2; 84.2; 91.2 with Moggi 1999, 529).

While state revenues will have been generated by the usual means, such as a tax on imports and exports, larger sources of revenue would have been needed to fund this navy. Diodorus Siculus tells us that in the same year as this navy was built, the Syracusans imposed even heavier tribute.[415] This implies that the levying of such tribute existed before then, and Carmine Ampolo is inclined to place its beginning between 451 and 440 BC.[416] Diodorus Siculus also adds that Syracuse had under its subjugation all the Sikel cities, with the exception of Trinakie.[417] The most likely reading of a passage of Thucydides with textual problems also documents the payment of tribute by the Sikels to Syracuse.[418] Sikels contributed at least 160 talents to Athens' first expedition to Sicily in 427 BC, alongside Greek cities to be discussed immediately below.[419] So the existence of a "counter-tribute" reinforces what Diodorus Siculus records.[420] The Syracusans were proverbial for a tithe that can be traced back at least to the fourth century to a mention by Demon of Athens, who explains that the Syracusans used the tithe for the upkeep of their temples, votive offerings, and religious festivals.[421] It is usually held that the tithe dates to the period of Syracusan history under discussion here, and that it was of an extraordinary nature and most likely levied on agricultural holdings.[422] The tithe is thought to have generated 20 talents per annum, on the basis of comparisons with Athens, and thus presupposes an overall level of agricultural revenue of 200 talents.[423]

Some Sicilian Greek cities openly supported Athens as leverage to Syracuse and made financial contributions to Athens in 427 BC, at the time of its first

---

415. Diod. Sic. 12.30.1.

416. Ampolo 1984, 31. It is worth mentioning that we know of an inscribed official state weight from these very years, 450 BC (Arena 1998, 136 no. 79; Dubois 1989, 113 no. 108). It weighs about 17.4–5 grams, the equivalent to an Attic tetradrachm.

417. Diod. Sic. 12.29.2.

418. Thuc. 6.18–23, esp. 20.2–4, with Ampolo 1984, 31–32.

419. Ampolo 1987, 11. Galvagno 2000, 98–105 restores Si[gesta] or Se[gesta]. This restoration is very unlikely, because Segesta is the name the Romans gave the city (for a recent discussion, see De Angelis 2006, 39). Egesta is what one would expect in this period.

420. It does not follow, however, that all Sikels were pro-Athenian (Galvagno 2000, 91).

421. Demon, FGrH 327 F14; Str. 6.2.3. Ampolo 1984, 32–34 is essential reading on this tithe.

422. Ampolo 1984, 33 thinks that tithe was extraordinary, simply because he followed the scholarly line of his day that the Greeks were not regularly and directly taxed. However, as we have seen earlier in this chapter, this line of thinking is currently undergoing reconsideration. For a regular agricultural tithe, see E. Boehringer 1929, 76. For the possibilities that Syracuse had for generating revenue, see also the statements Thucydides (6.90.4; 6.91.3) put into Alcibiades' mouth in 415 BC.

423. See E. Boehringer 1929, 76 for full discussion.

expedition to the island. The evidence is both literary and epigraphic. For one city, only the letters *kappa* and *alpha* survive, and that can either mean Kamarina or Katane.[424] In any case, the amount contributed also does not survive. However, a grand total of at least 240 talents can be accounted for, and the amount contributed by either Kamarina or Katane will not have been insubstantial. In Thucydides, Naxos is also recorded as having contributed to Athens' first expedition to Sicily in 427 BC and to have sided with Athens in its attack on Syracuse, supplying cavalry at the Battle of Epipolae in 414 BC.[425] It is interesting to note the close stylistic affiliations between the coinages of Katane and Naxos, which may reflect some kind of political and economic dependency and cooperation.[426] Given the uncertain political climate in eastern Sicily, it is possible that Naxos and Katane could have felt the need to stay close for mutual protection. Only Zankle is not on record as having contributed to Athens' first expedition in Sicily in 427 BC, but that may be because the city was divided between a pro-Syracusan and a pro-Athenian faction, not because it did not possess the economic wherewithal to do so.

To sum up, the second half of the fifth century was a time of prosperity across a good part of Sicily, from what we can gather. Diodorus Siculus says as much for Sicily as a whole, underlining how peace permitted this.[427] The widespread appearance of the water divinities and other symbols of agriculture and fertility on coins in this period has been taken as another sign of this success. At Selinous, Akragas, and Kamarina, as we have seen in the previous two chapters, domestic and sacred architecture exists to support these ancient accounts and indicates that the cities and the individuals within them prospered. Olympic victories were also brought home, and made possible at home in the first place, by athletes from Himera, Kamarina, Zankle, and Akragas.

Although old social and economic practices remained strong, as seen in the reinvigoration of the elite and the reversion to numismatic behavior first introduced by tyrants, social and economic changes also occurred. The democratic undertow of this period may have resulted in a greater number of people having access to land that was previously barred to them. The economic changes are clearer. An important innovation of the period was bronze fiduciary coinage.[428] Its introduction can be connected with payment for daily goods and

---

424. *IG* I³ 291, col. II, line 15, with Ampolo 1987.

425. Thuc. 6.98.1; 7.14.2; Ampolo 1987.

426. Fischer-Hansen, Nielsen, and Ampolo 2004, 207. On the stylistic affiliations: Manganaro 1996a; Rutter 1997, 137.

427. Diod. Sic. 11.72.1. Cf. also Descat 1995, 964; G. Giudice 2007, 270.

428. Holloway 1979; Price 1979b; Lombardo 1997b, 704–05; Seaford 2004, 136–46.

services at a new and much wider level. That bronze coins were also widely minted by "native" communities in the interior is, so to speak, the other side of the coin in this development.[429] As in other parts of the Greek world, there may have been a turn to a profit-oriented economy.[430] Although some technological developments in agriculture occurred, what arguably had a greater impact was a change in rural settlement pattern, with increased residence on the land and a turn to a more diversified agricultural economy involving olive oil and wine, which helped to contribute to another economic takeoff in the mid-fifth century similar to the one that had occurred a century before. Was the throwing off of Sicily's tyrannies that ushered in this period due to the onset of an economic cycle that brought prosperity? Was the reemergence of Syracusan imperialism and tyranny in the late fifth century an attempt to claw it back, after a decade of political maneuvering by political players both inside and outside the island? The timing of the next political and military turbulence in the island may not have been mere coincidence.

4. Between Political Centralization and Independence

The economics of this period are characterized by both continuities and changes. The tyrant Dionysius I introduced some innovations and variations that were unavailable to his predecessors. The driving force was the development of warfare throughout the fifth century. To be "cutting edge," Dionysius I invested heavily in research and development, resulting in new weaponry like the catapult, and succeeded in attracting highly skilled labor to Syracuse, from the philosopher Plato to mercenaries, and in creating a culture of ingenuity and innovation from the very start of his reign.[431]

We are slightly better informed than about earlier historical periods, thanks in large part to a series of stories about Dionysius I's fiscal schemes and Timoleon's revival of Sicily preserved in the literary sources.[432] While the stories concerning Timoleon's revival have traditionally been believed, as we have already seen, the historicity of the stories concerning Dionysius I has been more questioned because some of these stories are shaped by clichés associated with tyrants. Caution in approaching them is in order, and,

---

429. For a convenient and quick overview, see Rutter 1997, 139–42.

430. Belvedere 2001, 731–32.

431. Cf. Diod. Sic. 14.41.3–6; 42.1.

432. The stories concerning Dionysius I are collected in Andreades 1933 and Berve 1967, 2:645–46. Cf. also *BTCGI* 19.42–49.

although it is admittedly challenging to disentangle with absolute certainty fact from fabrication, the skepticism characteristic especially of earlier generations of scholarship has given way to approaches seeking to gauge their plausibility by looking at the wider economic context to which they purportedly belong.[433]

While the political upheavals that dominated Syracuse in and around the mid-fourth century certainly caused economic disruptions, most visible in the minting of coins, where a generation-long gap can be noted,[434] what remains debated is the depth of these disruptions. On the one hand, adherents of the traditional picture of gloom and doom are still occasionally met with.[435] On the other hand, this position is steadily losing ground to scholars, usually with economic interests, who point out its unlikelihood in three ways. First, Diodorus Siculus and Plutarch take one (tendentious) side of a polarized argument that favors Timoleon to the detriment of Dionysius I and the other Syracusan tyrants.[436] Second, numismatists have also refined our picture of this period, revealing how the downfall of the Dionysian tyrants saw their mercenaries in northeastern Sicily taking matters into their own hands and minting their own bronze coins.[437] This activity doubled the number of mints in existence in Sicily and no doubt preserved the underlying regional economic structures. Third, soil erosion caused by agriculture can be documented for the later fourth century BC around Morgantina in Sicily's eastern central interior.[438] While it could be argued that these numismatic and geomorphological developments occurred outside Syracuse's sphere, Syracuse was part of the same larger economic phenomena to which these developments belong. As the leading specialist in western Greek viticulture has observed regarding the agricultural situation presented in the ancient sources, "La réalité apparaît cependant plus nuancée et plusieurs remarques s'imposent ... En ce qui concerne l'état des campagnes siciliennes vers 350, il semble difficile d'imaginer qu'elles étaient totalement désertes: on

---

433. See in particular C. Boehringer 1979b; Ampolo 1984, 31; Foraboschi 1984, 82–87; Mele 1993; Austin 2000, 21; Archibald, Davies, Gabrielsen, and Oliver 2001, passim; Caccamo Caltabiano 2002.

434. Rutter 1997, 165.

435. Talbert 1974. See more recently, for instance, Manganaro 1996b, 218; Rutter 1997, 165.

436. Diod. Sic. 16.65.9; 83; Plut., *Tim.* 1.1–3; 22.4–5; 35.1–2. Cf. Castellana 1984, 382; Gallo 1989, 45–46; Fantasia 1993, 29–30.

437. Cutroni Tusa 1993, 267–68; Castrizio 2000; Caccamo Caltabiano and Puglisi 2002, 35–36; 2004, 336.

438. Judson 1963; Neboit 1984a, 1984b, 1984c; Collin Bouffier 2009, 66–67.

s'expliquerait mal la rapidité avec laquelle Timoléon a pu faire redémarrer le secteur agricole."[439] Even so, as with so many of the literary sources, the stories concerning the economic behavior of Dionysius I and Timoleon generally contain oblique information that is supplemented only occasionally by the still largely underdeveloped archaeological sources.

Agricultural Production and Wild Foodstuffs

At the height of Dionysius I's power, the domains under Syracuse's control consisted of about 18,500 square kilometers and a population estimated at between 100,000 and 200,000 in Sicily, southern Italy, and the Adriatic (see Chapters 2 and 3 for full discussion; cf. Map 12c). The dimensions of this territorial state necessitated that close attention be paid to food supply, and in particular to grain, which formed the cornerstone of the daily diet.

Dionysius I, like the Deinomenids before him, conquered Leontinoi, which had briefly gained its independence in the treaty concluded by Carthage and Syracuse in 405 BC.[440] Between 403 and 398 BC, the recapture of Leontinoi was part of Dionysius I's strategy of gaining control of all the Chalcidian cities of Sicily and their hinterlands.[441] Starting with Katane and Naxos, so as to control the flanks around Mt. Etna, he turned his attention last to Leontinoi, which surrendered without resistance. Dionysius I, after destroying the Archaic city wall with which the inhabitants of Leontinoi attempted to defend themselves, refortified the acropolis and built grain silos.[442] Mercenaries garrisoned the city and protected the very lucrative grain fields, and Leontinoi reverted back to its role as grain belt for the Syracusan tyranny.[443]

The literary sources tell us a little more about grain production under Dionysius I.[444] Aelian records that the tyrant had one million *medimnoi* (or

---

439. Vandermersch 1994, 149–50. "The reality seems, however, more nuanced, and several remarks are called for . . . As for the state of the Sicilian countryside around 350, it is difficult to imagine that it was completely deserted; that would explain poorly the speed with which Timoleon was able to restart the agricultural sector."

440. Giuffrida 2002, 421.

441. Giuffrida 2002, 422.

442. Diod. Sic. 14.58.1 is the main source for these statements, but archaeology confirms the renewed attention to the fortifications in this period (Rizza 2002; Frasca 2009, 121–31), and the agricultural potential of Leontinoi has been established earlier in this chapter.

443. Giuffrida 2002, 417. Some evidence exists for the development of the domestic settlement in this period (Frasca 2009, 132–36), so a larger community beyond the troops can be imagined.

444. On the limitations of the evidence for grain for the Classical period as a whole, see Fantasia 1993, 31.

52,500,000 liters) in reserve grain.[445] It is difficult to verify this figure, though no scholar has challenged the view that Syracuse harvested and stored large amounts of grain in this era of empire. Mercenaries received payment in grain, and its consumption is also presupposed in the stories concerning the luxury and opulence of Syracuse under Dionysius I.[446]

Little Syracusan grain probably left Sicily during the reign of Dionysius I's reign, given that it formed such a crucial foundation in his imperial system. But that seems to have changed by the 350s, perhaps after Dion challenged Dionysius II for control of Syracuse. For we see Athens returning as a destination for Syracusan grain, and Dion, with his Athenian connections, would make perfect sense as marking this turn.[447] Akragas, which had also been pro-Athenian since the fifth century, is also on record as having supplied grain to Athens, according to an honorary inscription, dating to 331–324 BC, for its citizen Sopratos.[448]

Material evidence of two kinds has been used to expand the discussion in default of written sources. The first consists of the concurrent development of ceramic workshops producing proto-Siceliot wares for export, which mirrored the tyrant's interest in grain lands elsewhere in Sicily, Italy, and the Adriatic Sea region.[449] Proto-Siceliot pottery was intended to supplant the role that Attic fine-ware imports had traditionally occupied: luxury items exchanged for

---

445. Ael., *VH* 6.12; cf. Mele 1993, 6.

446. Mele 1993, 4–5. References to Syracusan luxury and opulence are collected in *BTCGI* 19.42–44.

447. Xen., *Oec.* 20.27, referring to 355 BC (Fantasia 1993, 26, who is right to assume Sicilian exports); Dem., *Against Zenothemis* (32), perhaps dating to the last third of the century (Talbert 1974, 165–66; Garnsey 1988, 151–52; Habicht 1997, 26–27, 69; see also P. Brun 1993; Descat 2004; the precise date of Demosthenes' speech is unknown, but it could be even a little earlier than indicated); *IG* II² 499 and Diod. Sic. 19.103, referring to the reign of Agathokles. For Athenian involvement in Sicily in these years, see Whitehead 2008. One should not read too much into Dion's difficulties in obtaining grain supplies for his troops around this time (Diod. Sic. 16.13.3; 18.2). These may have to do with his opponents' success in starving out his troops, rather than indicating a decline in production.

448. Camp 1973; cf. Gallo 1984, 112–13 n. 148, 116 n. 40; 1989, 40; Reed 2003, 82, 127 no. 55; Engen 2010, 108, 253–55, 296. A topographic survey in the area of Palma di Montechiaro has brought to light a silo and workshop, throwing a little light on the rural production and storage that underpinned Akragas' agriculture (Castellana 1983, 121). It is worth noting here the proxeny decree for all Akragantines from Dodona, probably to be dated to the years 338–317 BC and in connection with Alexander I the Molossian (Dubois 1989, 209–10 no. 184), and Samos' granting of the proxeny to an individual from Herakleia Minoa (Fischer-Hansen, Nielsen, and Ampolo 2004, 196). The forging of connections through this institution are abundantly clear in this period.

449. Scerra 2004. Cf. Trendall 1989, 29–30; Denoyelle and Iozzo 2009, 166–71; Todisco 2012.

grain. If so, Dionysius I succeeded insofar as Sicily is concerned; Attic imports during his reign are practically nonexistent. This idea is reasonable and believable; the later Classical farmstead at Manfria near Gela had alongside its agricultural vocation producing grain (presumably long-standing, going back as far as the Archaic period) a second function as a workshop producing RF pottery.[450] The second kind of material evidence relates to the circulation of so many Corinthian coins, which have been connected with the trade in agricultural products which Diodorus Siculus, shorn of his polemical slant, may nevertheless be taken to document.[451]

Even though the evidence for production of the vine and olive is equally poor for this period, it suggests further growth and development of these sectors of the agricultural economy. The study of transport amphorae and archaeological data in general has done much to reveal the production side of this phenomenon in the fourth and third centuries BC.[452] While there is no evidence from fourth-century Syracuse itself,[453] we have evidence from other Sicilian sites which at one time or another in that century were under Syracuse's control. This evidence consists of empty wine amphorae found in the west stoa at Kamarina,[454] channels cut into the soil for the planting of the vine from Megara Hyblaia,[455] and the production of wine in quantity and quality at Messana.[456] If, as one specialist has observed, we range more widely in cobbling together all the available evidence, what emerges is Syracuse producing a sweet wine on the karst limestone plateaus and calcareous tuff of southeastern Sicily.[457] Moreover, the production of wine involved both small and large establishments (Figure 42).[458] A recent survey of historical topography in the area of Licata (roughly midway between Gela and Akragas) suspects that wine production may have expanded in the second

450. Adamesteanu 1958, 300–33. On the identification of the so-called Lentini-Manfria RF Group that resulted from these discoveries, see Trendall 1989, 235–38; Denoyelle and Iozzo 2009, 174; Todisco 2012.

451. Diod. Sic. 16.83.1.

452. Vandermersch 1994, 59–92; Sourisseau 2011, 145–46, 215–17.

453. Apart from the literary sources' mention of an annual wine festival involving competitions and prizes from the time of Dionysius II (Vandermersch 1994, 29).

454. Vandermersch 1994, 86, 123.

455. De Angelis 2003a, 86; Brun 2004, 165; Boissinot 2009.

456. Vandermersch 1994, 48; Botte 2009, 82–83.

457. Vandermersch 1994, 48–49.

458. Vandermersch 1994, 98, 152.

FIGURE 42 View of Reconstructed Model of the Iurato Farmstead at Kamarina (note tombs in lower left corner).
© Author

half of the fourth century, on the basis of the appearance of farmsteads and their associated vats dug into the rock.[459] The increase in wine production among the western Greeks in the fourth and third centuries BC seems to have been substantial enough to have impacted the Aegean producers who traditionally supplied these markets.[460]

Even less can be said about olive production in this period. The few insights we have might be pressed to suggest that it was business as usual, though clearly more work is needed.[461]

The little evidence for wild and domesticated animals gives us a better sense of the scale and nature of production than ever before. The involvement of animals in Dionysius I's economy is documented in two literary sources, one recounting that 6,000 pairs of oxen were used in the building of Syracuse's fortifications and the other his taxation scheme to raise revenues from

---

459. Amato 2012, 340–43.

460. Vlassopoulos 2007a, 174; Sourisseau 2011, 224–26. Cf. also Lawall 2006.

461. Diogenes Laertius (6.25) records the story of Plato not eating olives in Athens with the same gusto as he had in Syracuse. One certain and one possible olive oil press are known from the Cancelliere farmstead in Kamarina's territory (Di Stefano 2001, 698; Brun 2004, 169) and Akragas (Brun 2004, 170; for the possibility that it is a wine press, see Vandermersch 1994, 91–94).

livestock.[462] These statements imply that livestock were readily available in significant numbers inside the territory controlled by Syracuse, and that they were owned by a high enough proportion of the population to be deemed worthwhile as a source of taxation. This scale of livestock raising is also suggested by the evidence of secondary usage, namely worked animal bone.[463] About 300 bone fragments (not horn, teeth, or ivory) have been retrieved mostly in excavations from the first half of the twentieth century, when techniques of recovery may have favored certain bone types over others. Even so, a remarkably consistent pattern has emerged: ox and horse make up 100 percent of the identifiable fragments, and within this group ox bones comprise 90 percent of the total. Some of the bone fragments are easily recognizable by their worked shapes and perforations. The concentration of this material in Syracuse's Acradina quarter suggests the existence of one or more workshops. Thus, all this information, though limited, opens a window onto bigger issues relating to the scale and nature of livestock production and consumption in this period.

Moving from land to sea, we are very well informed of fish, mollusks, and lobster thanks to literary and archaeological sources, which supply new dimensions of seafood exploitation that previous scholars thought represented the beginning of production, distribution, and consumption. What is new is the degree of the literary, archaeological, and iconographical evidence (Figure 43).

Most of the literary evidence derives from the work of Archestratus of Gela, dating to the first two-thirds of the fourth century. Most of the locations he mentions as providing the best products concern the central northern and northeastern parts of Sicily.[464] The fish include eels, sea-bream, tuna, swordfish, grey mullet, sea-bass, and small sturgeon (sterlet), and the mollusks include clams. We should not conclude from Archestratus' silences, or from the silences of the generally poor written record, that no other species were exploited. For example, the silver scabbard fish is today the most commonly consumed fish in Sicily (Figure 44).[465]

---

462. Diod. Sic. 14.18.5; Ps.-Arist., Oec. 1349b.7–10. For secondary discussions, see Scramuzza 1937, 278; Habermann 1987, 101; McInerney 2010, 179–80. See also further below.

463. Chilardi 2005, who claims that this is the first known evidence from the entire Western Greek area. Note, however, the offering of unspecified worked bone found in Temple A at Himera dating to about 600 BC, mentioned earlier (Vassallo 2005b, 126).

464. For the mentions in question, see Olson and Sens 2000, 39–44 (fr. 7, lines 4–5), 48–53 (fr. 10, lines 1–4), 61–64 (fr. 12), 85–87 (fr. 17, lines 1–3), 87–88 (fr. 18, lines 1–3), 96–99 (fr. 22, lines 1–3), 114–17 (fr. 35, lines 6–7), 162–68 (fr. 39, lines 1–2), 170–72 (fr. 41, lines 2–3), 179–90 (fr. 46, lines 10–18), 199–200 (fr. 52, lines 1–2). For modern discussions, see Scramuzza 1937, 283–85; Trotta 1996, 230–31; Davidson 2002; Gianfrotta 2005, 156; Botte 2009, 53–60.

465. Cf. Davidson 2002, 117, 119, 225, to be read in conjunction with Gallant 1985 on ancient fishing technology.

FIGURE 43 RF Vase with Scene of Tuna Butchering from Lipari.
© Fondazione Culturale Mandralisca

The archaeological evidence confirms and expands on the insights supplied by Archestratus.[466] From Lipari comes a RF vase depicting the butchering of tuna (Figure 43). This represents the earliest known iconographical representation of one aspect of the processing process, for which on the Sicilian mainland, and from this same date, there is abundant archaeological evidence for tuna processing and salting. Two such facilities have been excavated. One is located

---

466. Salted fish and fish sauce are also more abundantly attested across non-Greek Sicily in the fourth century than ever before: Purpura 1982, 45; 1985, 60–62, 77–78; Botte 2009, 72–82, 105–14.

FIGURE 44 View of Freshly Caught Silver Scabbard Fish in Waters off Northern Sicily.

© Author

at Portopalo near Cape Pachino on Syracuse's southeast coast (Map 12c).[467] In all, fifty-five rectangular and circular basins have been uncovered, with a minimum capacity of just under 250 cubic meters.[468] Layers of fish remains, especially bones, were found nearby. Many of the bones revealed signs of burning that has been connected with regular cleaning up for reasons of hygiene, and this, together with the evidence of production capacities from similar sites of later date, suggests that large volumes of fish were once processed here.[469] The other facility is located at Vendicari, about 20 kilometers north of Portopalo.[470] Its first use was in the last third of the fourth century BC (and continued until the middle of the next century). Two sectors to the site have been distinguished, one devoted to

467. Bacci 1982–83; 1984–85; Botte 2009, 86–88, is tempted to date the site's beginning to as early as the fifth century in light of the presence of Corinthian A-like transport amphorae. Giovanna Bacci, the excavator, instead placed it in the early Hellenistic period. As Botte (2009, 103–04) has emphasized, his dating also fits in well with the rise of mentions of Sicilian fish in the literary sources of the late fifth and early fourth centuries BC. For other discussions of the Portopalo site, see Purpura 1982, 45; 1989; Curtis 1991, 99–101, 143; Guzzardi and Basile 1996, 202.

468. For the figure, see Botte 2009, 99.

469. Botte 2009, 88, 100.

470. Purpura 1989, 30–31; Basile 1992; Botte 2009, 83–86.

salting basins and the other to pre- and post-salting activities. At least 25 basins have been identified, with a minimum capacity of about 97 cubic meters.[471] Both of these excavated facilities were located in regions with abundant salt-pans, discussed earlier in this chapter. The nature of ownership has been guessed at: scholars agree on hypothesizing small and large establishments existing side by side.[472] More difficult to establish are the volumes produced here and in Greek Sicily, which will require future work to be clarified. Was consumption mainly for local or export markets, or for a bit of both? Some of this fish was certainly consumed at Syracuse. Excavations in the Nymphaeum on the terrace above Syracuse's theater brought to light remains of 19 gastropods and 182 bivalves in layers of the fourth and third centuries BC.[473] The level of export will remain elusive so long as it is difficult to identify the containers in which salted fish products could have been transported.[474]

Non-agricultural Production

Non-agricultural production is scantily documented. The absence of evidence must in part be the result of the chronological difficulties discussed in Chapter 2 and earlier in this chapter. But that cannot provide the entire explanation— the underdevelopment of the archaeological record is also at play. Merely a handful of isolated facts relating to clay working, quarrying and stone working, timber and pitch, metalworking, and luxury textiles is all that we presently know.[475] For both pottery and luxuries, the output of finished products appears to have grown, given, respectively, the replacement of Athenian imports and the rewards provided by Dionysius I and II to their supporters.

---

471. Botte 2009, 99.

472. Trotta 1996, 242; Botte 2009, 103.

473. Villari 1992b, 73.

474. Botte 2009, 116, 170.

475. Pottery (especially the Lentini-Manfria Group): Trendall 1989, 235–38; Pautasso 1996; Frasca 2009, 140, 146. Terracottas: Pautasso 1996, 145; 2008; Uhlenbrock 2002, 337; Frasca 2009. Amphorae and pithoi: Di Stefano 2001, 702; cf. also *BTCGI* 4.297. Quarrying and stone working: De Angelis 2003a, 75–76, 83; Mertens 2004. Timber and pitch: Diod. Sic. 14.42.4; cf. Corvisier 1999, 154. Metalworking (especially the breaking up of the monopoly of an iron-seller by Dionysios I): Arist. *Pol.* 1.1259a. Cf. also Mele 1993, 33–34; Austin 2000, 21, who notes that "This limited control [by Greek cities] is one of the implications of the many fiscal and other stratagems mentioned in Book 2 of the Aristotelian *Oeconomica*, which paints a picture of numerous local crises that could only be met by strictly local action." Textiles and luxuries: the sources are collected in *BTCGI* 19.44–45, 47–48; Mele 1993, 25–28, 30; Gleba 2008, 31, 80–81. In this connection, we should not read too much into the story that Dionysius I plundered a splendid cloak made by Alkisthenes of Sybaris from the temple of Hera at Kroton and resold it to Carthaginians as illustrating the first of these scenarios (Ps.-Arist., *Mir. ausc.* 96.838a; Ath. 12.541b; Tzetz., *Chil.*, 1.821–23).

Trade and Exchange

The items exchanged to and from Classical Greek Sicily were distributed by new and old carriers. Continuing Corinthian involvement in moving grain and other products can be suspected on the basis of the influx of Corinthian coins from the time of Timoleon, as discussed earlier, and on a shipwreck of broadly fourth-century date in the waters off Marzamemi on Syracuse's southeast coast, from which were recovered mainly Corinthian B transport amphorae.[476] The Phocaeans operating out of Massalia seem also to have played a continuing role, judging from Demosthenes' speech involving Zenothemis of Massalia, who borrowed money at Syracuse.[477]

The new distributors included merchants from the eastern Mediterranean and Greek Sicily itself. Athenians are attested in various bits of information. As seen above, Athenian merchant ships entered Syracuse's harbor during the reign of Agathokles to transport grain shipments homeward. Pseudo-Demosthenes' expression *Sikelikos kataplous* (or "Sicilian sailing back"), found in the speech *Against Dionysodoros* (56), also implies a regular event from Athens.[478] Athenian connections to Sicily and Sicilian grain also emerge from *IG* II² 283, mentioning a certain Cypriot (Ph-. . .) who ransomed Athenians captured in Sicily,[479] and from *IG* II² 408 mentioning Mnemon and another Herakleot (. . .-ias) selling Sicilian wheat and barley at Athens.[480]

A role for Sicilian Greeks is also attested in distributing grain regionally and interregionally. From Katane we hear of fishing boats from the city used to transport grain in Timoleon's time, and, interestingly, though difficult to know if related to the grain trade, two individuals were made *proxenoi* by Athens.[481] Some grain may have been brought directly from Akragas to Athens, according to Darrel Tai Engen: "it is clear that Sopratos brought grain to Athens personally, since he is honored with xenia in the Prytaneion and a seat at the

---

476. Parker 1992, 268 no. 674. This is in addition to another wreck from Marzamemi discussed earlier. For other shipwreck and cargo sites in and around Sicily at this date, see Parker 1992, 160 no. 355 (Dattilo), 292–93 no. 756 (Ognina D, OG-2, OG-3), 352 no. 936 (Punta di San Francesco), 402–03 no. 1081 (Sicilian Channel).

477. Dem., *Against Zenothemis* (32).

478. Talbert 1974, 165; Gallo 1984, 113 n. 148; Garnsey 1988, 151–52; Fantasia 1993, 26–27.

479. Reed 2003, 30, 100–01 no. 4, 126 no. 50; Whitehead 2008; Engen 2010, 252, 292–94, who all date the inscription to the first half of the 330s.

480. Engen 2010, 108, 258–59.

481. Plut., *Tim.* 18.1; Fischer-Hansen, Nielsen, and Ampolo 2004, 206. Cyrene was another major grain producer, and it is interesting to note that one of the region's cities, Euesperides, honored two Syracusan citizens, Eubios and Hegestratos, for having acted as their *proxenoi* in the second half of the fourth century (cf. *SEG* 18.772 with Gill 2004, 391).

Great Dionysia, which would require his presence in Athens to enjoy. Thus, it is likely that Sopratos was a common professional trader who simply imported grain into Athens and sold it at the going rate during a time of great need in Athens."[482] It is very possible that Sicilian Greeks were involved in such activities in earlier periods, but that we are prevented from seeing them because of the silence of our sources.

The need for materials and labor was absolutely crucial to Dionysius I's success, and much effort was expended on expanding and protecting the land and sea routes to and from Syracuse, so that imports and exports could be safely transmitted.[483] Some of these materials could be imported from conquered regions rich in resources, such as the forests around Mt. Etna and in the toe of southern Italy, or by practicing import replacement or substitution in the case of RF pottery for regions beyond his grasp. Even despite the extent of Syracuse's territorial state and connections in the time of Dionysius I and II, we can be certain that imports did not altogether disappear. Syracusan coins from the reigns of Dionysius I and his son are also often found throughout the Adriatic, not just in regions known to have been colonized by them.[484] The same holds for Corinthian B transport amphorae, which dominate finds from the Adriatic (at last count there are 241 find spots with material dating to the fourth and third centuries BC).[485] An interregional trading relationship, in the same kinds of goods and services enumerated earlier for the fifth century, can be envisaged, but to what extent this was in the hands of Syracuse remains to be defined.[486]

As Syracuse's centralized control over eastern Sicily weakened in the second half of the fourth century, it is perhaps no surprise that we hear again of grain exports, as the demand and control exercised by Syracusan militarism had certainly slackened. Exports of fish, cheese, and livestock from Sicily had been raised earlier, and they may have been accompanied by wine in this period.[487] These meager details obviously do not do justice to the complexities of exchange in Classical Greek Sicily. That can be partly rectified when we turn to fourth-century developments in weights, measures, and coinage.

---

482. Engen 2010, 296.

483. On land and sea travel during the reign of Dionysius I, see Uggeri 2002, esp. 303, 305, 316–17.

484. Lamboley 1993, 232–33; D'Andria 2002; Visonà 2007.

485. Lamboley 1993, 234; D'Andria 2002, 133 (for the number of sites).

486. Cf. Lamboley 1993, 237; D'Andria 2002, 123–29.

487. For discussion, see Vandermersch 1994, 23–24.

Dionysius I' fiscal schemes have done much to color modern views of his coinage policies as a whole. But a clearer picture has emerged in recent years as a result of new research. The result, as Rutter has summed up, is that "it has become generally recognized that Dionysius' coinage matched the scope and ambition of his military plans and was minted in a range of denominations in all three metals, gold, silver and bronze."[488] In general, unity and interchangeability were other underlying motivations for his numismatic policies, as in the case of Himera, which, under Syracuse's control, reintroduced a new coinage with its principal denomination based on the Syracusan tetradrachm.[489]

The gold coins pick up on a recent phenomenon that appeared, as we have already seen, in response to the renewed hostilities between Carthage and the Sicilian Greek cities (Figure 41). The coins were at first struck as tetradrachms of 1.16 grams and didrachms of 0.58 grams.[490] These first gold coins seem to have been issued in limited quantities, and thus give every impression of being an emergency response. The next series of gold coins, by contrast, were minted in larger quantities and were used for a longer period of time, perhaps until about 380 BC.[491] A new and enduring policy concerning gold coinage was in play. This second series is also heavier than the previous one, with one denomination weighing 5.82 grams and the other 2.91 grams. The denominations and their weights are idiosyncratic to Syracuse, but they adhere to a gold to silver ratio of 1:15; that is, 100 silver litrai or 20 silver drachms for the heavier denomination and, of course, half these equivalents for the lighter denomination.

The silver tetradrachms issued from before Dionysius I continued for a handful of years after his rise to power.[492] His own silver issues were struck as decadrachms, last seen under the Deinomenids. There are two main groups, each signed by an artist (Kimon and Euainetos), with the first group appearing around 404 BC and the other a little later. It is not clear how long these issues were in circulation, but they were minted in large quantities and may have been in use, particularly in the case of those signed by Euainetos, for much of Dionysius I's reign.

Dionysius I's preference for large denominations of 10 to 20 drachmas for his gold and silver coinage is clear, as is his abandonment of tetradrachms

488. Rutter 1997, 153–54, though he later notes the many still unresolved issues connected with this coinage (Rutter 1997, 158–59; cf. also C. Boehringer 1993; Fischer-Bossert 2012, 151–52).

489. Fischer-Hansen, Nielsen, and Ampolo 2004, 200–01.

490. For discussion, see C. Boehringer 1979b, 15–18; Bérend 1993; Rutter 1997, 154.

491. See C. Boehringer 1979b, 15–18; Rutter 1997, 154–55.

492. Rutter 1997, 155.

(a traditional staple of Syracusan coinage) and lower denominations.[493] His decision has been rightly connected with signaling his pay commitments to his hired labor.[494] Two coin hoards from Avola in Syracuse's immediate territory, buried respectively around 370 and 360 BC, contain Persian darics and East Greek coins alongside Syracusan 50 and 100 litra gold coins, which are equivalent to a daric and half daric.[495] It would follow that mercenaries were recruited from these eastern parts at a pay scale to which they were accustomed.

The bronze coinage minted by Dionysius I provided the denominations of lower value, most probably in the form of a litra and a drachma, and sought to fulfill other ends, which included the needs of these mercenaries.[496] The bronze coinage was intended as fiduciary money, in very much the same way as previously established in Greek Sicily. Because there was a competitive international market for precious metals, bronze was used in local markets to avoid being affected by the prices of precious metals, an advantage to, say, citizens and mercenaries in their purchasing of goods and services.[497] Syracuse's bronze coinage followed Dionysius I's military activities into western Sicily and the garrisons he established, and presumably served a similar function there too.[498]

For the remainder of the Classical period, at first the coins in circulation were either minted previously or, more commonly, Punic and especially Corinthian imports, the so-called pegasi.[499] Soon alongside these imports appeared almost identical Syracusan copies struck as drachms and hemidrachms.[500] Timoleon's precious metal issues are probably to be related to the battle of Crimisus, which took place between 341 and 339 BC, to pay for this campaign.[501] Other issues of silver and bronze are known from Syracuse and

---

493. On the tetradrachms in circulation, including those of Punic and Corinthian mints, see Cutroni Tusa 1993, 246–47.

494. Mele 1993, 18; Rutter 1997, 157.

495. *IGCH* nos. 2122 and 2124. Their full implications are discussed in Mele 1993, 7–9; Cutroni Tusa 1993, 253.

496. See in general Mele 1993, 23–25; Cutroni Tusa 1993, 254, 266–67; Rutter 1997, 157–58; Morcom 1998; Puglisi 2005, 286–87.

497. Mele 1993, 23–25; Fischer-Bossert 2012, 151. On the value of bronze to silver, see the discussions by Bérend 1979; Lacroix 1979.

498. Puglisi 2005, 286–87. On the question of function, see Caccamo Caltabiano and Puglisi 2004, 336.

499. Cf. Talbert 1974, 161–78; Rutter 1997, 165–67.

500. Rutter 1997, 166–67.

501. Rutter 1997, 166; Castrizio 2000, 67.

other Sicilian cities (Messana, Gela, Akragas, and Kamarina).[502] All these coinages sought to help restore the normal functioning of the state and individuals
within it.[503]

Evidence exists for a bureaucracy under Dionysius I and II in the form
of treasurers to help manage their finances and in particular to ensure that
revenue, particularly taxes, flowed into state coffers.[504] As we have seen in the
previous chapters, the tyrants incurred large expenditures through infrastructure and other projects to support their imperial ambitions. It is commonly
believed that Dionysius I and his successors taxed all agricultural holdings
in some way; one story mentions a tax on cattle (mentioned earlier) and
the wheeling and dealing Dionysius I engaged in to ensure its payment.[505]
Aristotle also mentions the levying of taxes in general by Dionysius I, whereby
those taxed contributed all of their worth in five years.[506] And there is the
already mentioned tithe, whose institution was situated earlier in the decades
before Dionysius I's coming to power. All of this evidence is largely indirect
and inferential, but it tends on the whole to point to Dionysius having taxed
agriculture and general wealth.[507]

Dionysius I employed three other ways to obtain revenues. First, he made
money through the selling and ransoming of the spoils captured in war, as in
the case of the people of Rhegion, whom Dionysius I first tricked into revealing their wealth on the promise of setting them free in return for recoup-
ing the costs incurred in capturing their city.[508] This was a kind of indemnity
imposed on Rhegion, but the practice of requesting indemnities of conquered
territories was common.[509] Second, Dionysius I also attacked convoys and
plundered sanctuaries, such as those at Kroton and Pyrgi, which filled his coffers to the tune of, respectively, 1,500 talents and at least 120 talents.[510] Cities,

---

502. Rutter 1997, 168–72; Castrizio 2000, 65–74; Puglisi 2005, 287–88.

503. Castrizio 2000, 78.

504. Plut., *Dio.* 4.2; Diog. Laert. 2.75. Cf. also Mele 1993, 32–33.

505. Ps.-Arist., *Oec.* 1349b.7–10. Cf. Habermann 1987, 101.

506. Arist., *Pol.* 5.1313b, which Ampolo 1984, 33 finds suspect. Nevertheless, other stories outline the schemes by Dionysius I to tax the household and personal possessions of
Syracusans (Ps.-Arist., *Oec.* 1349a-b), and so the possibility remains that total worth, and not
just that derived from agriculture, was under scrutiny.

507. A conclusion also reached by, for example, Vandermersch 1994, 109 with n. 179.

508. Ps.-Arist. *Oec.* 1349b.18–27

509. Mele 1993, 23.

510. Mele 1993, 10; Corvisier 1999, 149.

territories, land, and possessions of the enemy were confiscated in part or in whole for the benefit of his mercenaries and other supporters.[511] Finally, Dionysius I is also said to have generated revenue by manipulating coinage in two ways: by repaying borrowed money by restriking drachma coins as two-drachma coins, and by minting tin coins that he forced the citizenry to accept as the equivalent of silver.[512]

In summary, the remaining decades of the Classical period in Sicily that comprise the fourth and final historical period distinguished in this book witnessed the addition of some new economic elements to the previously laid foundations. Changes in the scale and nature of warfare led to greater competition for hired specialists, including mercenaries,[513] and the creation of even more infrastructure. Perhaps not unconnected to these changes in warfare are two other developments at Syracuse, and in Sicily more widely, involving increased production of two particular foodstuffs, fish and wine.[514]

To conclude this chapter, the aim throughout has been to collect and analyze the evidence for the Sicilian Greek economy in the Archaic and Classical periods against a backdrop of economic changes versus long-term continuities. The picture over these more than four hundred years contains many certainties and uncertainties, owing to the nature of our source material. Nevertheless, the general direction in which the Sicilian Greek economy evolved is beyond doubt.

Greeks came to Sicily to seek agricultural and trade opportunities. That grain was the cornerstone of the agricultural economy may be safely assumed, for two reasons. First, newly settled regions often make their initial living through the export of a particular staple, and that this happened in Sicily is suggested by the abundant evidence of homeland Greek transport amphorae once containing wine and olive oil imported by the thousands upon thousands of liters. This is all in keeping with our new and emerging vision of the Archaic Mediterranean, where mobility was normal, knowledge was plentiful, and bulk goods moved over long distances.

But the Archaic economies of Greek Sicily also grew by the spin-off industries associated with its staple exports and by import replacement of items used daily, such as textiles, fine-ware pottery, and votive terracottas, not to

---

511. Mele 1993, 23.

512. Arist., *Oec.* 1349a.33–37; 1349b.28–32. On countermarks and restrikes by Dionysius I, see Garraffo 1993. Mele 1993, 20–21 argues in favor of the existence of the tin coinage.

513. Trundle 2005, 8.

514. So Vandermersch 1994, 130 for wine. On the importance of salted fish as a source of protein in general, see Curtis 1991, 22–23.

mention because of their joint roles as port and capital cities. The Greeks brought new products (like the cultivated olive, vine, and chestnut) or took preexisting ones to new levels (like bigger domesticated animals and greater metallurgical activity). It may have also been in the Archaic period that the Sicilian Greeks took the exploitation of mollusks and fish to another level.

All of these factors and activities fed into one another to bring about island-wide prosperity, which came to a head in the middle of both the seventh and sixth centuries. Each wave of prosperity was accompanied by growth and development in population and in legal and logistical infrastructure, as well as by weighed bullion and coinage and by outlays in wealth like monumental buildings and tombs. The second economic cycle coincided with intense elite competition, which resulted in some cases in tyrannies and, from within these regimes, inter-polity warfare.

The onset of the Classical period witnessed a continuation of these economic trajectories, as well as the addition of others. Mercenaries, fleets, and other defensive and offensive mechanisms of war developed as a result of the imperial and territorial conquests of the tyrannies based in Gela/Syracuse and Akragas. At about the midway point of the Classical period, with the accession of Dionysius I at Syracuse, Sicilian Greeks and Carthaginians became even more militarized. The Classical period also witnessed the ever more intensive use of land and sea resources, especially olive oil, wine, and fish, which included greater residence on the land and possibly a trickle-down of economic opportunities to non-elites.

This pattern waxed and waned until the Romans succeeded in ending it and thus in inheriting it, ensuring that the economic systems the Sicilian Greeks created from the eighth century BC onward both continued and evolved to meet the needs of another master at the dawn of a new era in Mediterranean economic history.

Conclusions

WHILE CONCLUSIONS WERE summarized in each of the preceding chapters, fitting them all together and inserting them into the big picture is the purpose of this final chapter. The overall aim is to relate my conclusions to previous ones and to tell a new story about Greek Sicily. The chapter will end by considering the general role that social and economic questions can have in future studies of Greek Sicily.

The Introduction outlined modern approaches to Greek Sicily from the sixteenth century to the present, and how they have been influenced by a combination of regional, national, and international developments. Given Sicily's position as a place of cultural encounter and its frequent political dependence on a capital located outside the island, two main themes emerged. The first concerns the roles of natives and outsiders in making ancient Sicily, which have been contrasted as either backward colonial offshoots or as quite the opposite. The second theme is related and involves theory and method. The full spectrum of theoretical and methodological approaches to Greek Sicily has been developed and applied to historical interpretations since the nineteenth century. Although balanced approaches using different disciplines and incorporating various ancient cultures have appeared from time to time, the study of Greek Sicily remains polarized between two extremes. On the one hand, Sicily is studied by a school of Sicilian-dominated scholarship that discusses the island's multiethnic and overlapping cultural history, but often in isolation vis-à-vis other regions. On the other hand, Sicily is studied by a school of foreign-dominated scholars that treats it as being on the colonial periphery of modern narratives of ancient Greece. Both schools of scholarship are similarly characterized by strong disciplinary divides and regional specializations that base their accounts either on written or archaeological sources or on a particular cultural group, such as Greeks, Phoenicians, or natives.

I argued in the Introduction, after reviewing these developments, that one-sided and isolationist approaches cannot do proper justice to Greek Sicily's social and economic complexities. That is because the Mediterranean's micro-regionalism has recently been appreciated, resulting in a view of the ancient world that is now characterized by mobility, connectivity, and decentering. To understand this interconnectedness, a more comprehensive approach is needed that takes into account both regional and global factors and views ancient Greek Sicily as simultaneously part of frontier and world history. Interdisciplinary theories and methods are also required. These entail not only the combination of texts and material culture, as well as classical and prehistoric studies, but also theories and methods derived from postcolonialism and Marxism that seek to give a ground-up and multi-sided perspective to Sicilian Greek society and economy. Moreover, a social and economic history of Archaic and Classical Greek Sicily also has to complement the numerous political, military, and culture histories, in order to establish, among other things, the integrated nature of all these histories. This approach produces the following new vision of Archaic and Classical Greek Sicily, which brings us into the twenty-first century and thus goes beyond Moses Finley's single-volume history (second edition, 1979).

Chapter 1 was devoted to ancient Sicily's geographical and historical settings at the time of Greek settlement. There it was shown that Sicily's place in the wider Mediterranean had changed in the transition from the Bronze to the Iron Age. Etruria and Sardinia became the center of interregional exchange because of their metal resources and developed into powerful polities, in all likelihood states and chiefdoms of some kind. This occurred to Sicily's detriment and involved a deflation of social and economic complexity. Sicily was being left behind.

It would be wrong to pretend that Sicily's native populations are for that reason not worth any attention in our social and economic history of Greek Sicily, as colonialist Hellenocentric approaches once did. My research has shown that Sicily's deflation in this period is still of interest and importance in that the historical and geographical conditions that the early Greek settlers were attracted to and encountered had an impact on their own societies and economies. As seen in Chapters 1 and 4, paleoecological research now documents that land clearance and the introduction of large-scale agricultural regimes coincided with the permanent settlement of Greeks in Sicily. Greece was experiencing rapid development in the eighth and seventh centuries as state formation took root, and Sicily could help satisfy these social and economic pressures at home. The traditional image of Sicily's landscapes at the time of Greek settlement, of extensively cultivated and established fields, must now be revised. This helps to explain how Greeks could successfully establish their societies and economies—little impediment existed on the coastal plains, because natives avoided pirates by living in the safety of the interior—and how they could both collaborate with and coopt natives, either forcefully or voluntarily. Opportunities existed in the form of ecological and institutional differences between natives and Greeks, and both sides either took advantage of them or were taken advantage of in the pursuit of success.

For this success to happen, Greeks had to establish settlements and delineate territories, a subject fully discussed in Chapter 2. My approach adopts two new directions. First, it combines the political, territorial, and urban trajectories of Greek Sicily's cities, in line with recent work on Greek state formation which has emphasized their intimate connection. Second, it arranges the discussion diachronically and subdivides it into four chronological phases, each representing a major episode in Sicilian Greek state formation: 1) from the *poleis'* foundation between the eighth and sixth centuries BC to their initial overwhelming by a fewer larger states beginning in about 500 BC; 2) the generation covering this first attempt at political centralization (ca. 500–465 BC); 3) the two generations that followed, which saw the collapse and return of political centralization at the hands of Syracuse and Carthage in particular (ca. 465-405 BC); and 4) the remainder of the Classical period, which again witnessed a reinvigorated Syracuse wrestling against Carthage and various other smaller states (ca. 405 to 320 BC). These four phases witness an alternation between the two basic state types, city-states and territorial states. This all makes my approach unique and results in new conclusions.

The evolution of Greek Sicily's identities and institutions can be documented throughout all four chronological phases and their associated types of state. The idea, going back at least to Karl Julius Beloch in the nineteenth century, that Greek Sicily's settlement pattern was always nucleated is no longer valid. Evidence exists today for Archaic and Classical farmsteads from survey and excavation data. To the well-known phenomenon of Sicilian Greek town planning we can now also add the possibilities of commercialized agoras from the seventh century and craft production in the countryside. Four important phases of building can also be documented, all starting at the midpoint of each century, after a city's foundation: hence 650 BC, 550 BC, 450 BC, and 350 BC. While these phases were previously noted to some degree, discussion tended to be descriptive rather than explanatory. These phases must be related to economic factors (for which see below). The lack of public building in many cities in the fifth century and the generation of wealth even in periods of apparent "crisis" are also conclusions emerging from this chapter. Sicilian Greek imperialism also caused new configurations of the island's landscapes, ranging from the abandonment of entire cities and emporia to the systematic centralized exploitation of agriculture and the creation of consumer cities supporting non-agricultural populations.

This chapter on politics and settlement provides the physical base for Chapter 3, on Sicilian Greek societies. Here I set out to find explanations for the development of these societies instead of judging or condemning them as some kind of aberration of normalized ancient Greek behavior derived from the Greek homeland, as has often been done. Sicilian Greek societies must be embedded in their frontier circumstances, so as to understand why these societies attracted attention for their differences in the eyes of Classical Athenian writers.

Several fresh conclusions emerge from this chapter. In light of recent advances in Greek demography, it seems that both Adolph Holm and Beloch's population estimates from the nineteenth century are still much too high. Greek Sicily's population almost certainly numbered in the lower hundreds of thousands and never reached a million. Various social groups, both Greeks and non-Greeks, made up these communities and seem to have been integrated through horizontal territorial mobility. The mixed nature of Greek Sicily's communities, although known since antiquity, can be explained by the need to build up demographic stocks to satisfy their labor requirements in conditions of land abundance, to ensure the communities' long-term economic success. Flexible forms of civic makeup were needed throughout Sicilian Greek history for these reasons. There are also many indications that Sicilian Greek societies were unequal and organized in oligarchic clans from their beginnings, contrary to what Finley had maintained. This would better explain certain seventh-century developments: factionalism and civil strife (also doubtless due to the mixed communities) and the appearance of Olympic victors (who embody elitism at their very core). Property rights and the distribution of land were also established in favor of the elite, and were controlled by these clans from the beginning. These societies also provided fertile ground for the emergence of tyrants and their imperial ambitions, both of which were taken to a new level in the late sixth/early fifth centuries BC. The tyrants seem to have suppressed clans and avoided bureaucracies in ruling their domains. They also played down their elitism and supported themselves by appealing to the lower classes and using foreign mercenaries. The so-called "democratic interlude" that followed appears to have been more interlude than democratic. The continuation of elite practices, including the return of clan organization, can be better appreciated for the last two-thirds of the fifth century, and later in the later fourth century following the tyrannies of Dionysius I–II of Syracuse.

Chapter 4 set out to discuss the full range of economic activities under-taken by these societies. The study of Sicilian Greek economics has mirrored and been mired by the ancient written sources' strong focus on agriculture and grain. Therefore, Chapter 4 broke new ground by adopting an inclusive approach that aimed at discussing production, consumption, and distribution as much as possible. This laid the groundwork for assessing modern claims about the nature of Sicilian Greek economics, and especially whether or not they were monocultures engaged in a colonial-like relationship with the Greek homeland.

The background to Sicilian Greek agriculture can today be greatly appreci-ated, thanks to recent paleoecological research. This suggests not only that landscapes were more vegetated at the time of first Greek settlement, but also that the estimates of agricultural potential advanced in the nineteenth century by Holm and Beloch are too low. Land abundance and the need for labor, as already noted, were certainly driving determinants for some aspects of Greek Sicily's earliest economic growth and development. Moreover, given Sicily's excellent natural resources and climate, grain made considerable sense as the main planted crop: it requires the least amount of labor to grow, and thus can be cultivated from nucleated settlements, and it was in high demand because of its role in the diet (two-thirds to three-quarters of daily caloric intake) and of Greece's rapid population growth, which created a demand and market for Sicilian grain. Staple theory helps to explain which economic decisions were taken and which dynamics propelled its engine. However, one must not go the extreme conclusion and imagine agricultural monoculture. The theoreti-cal and especially empirical evidence is simply against this. The Greek world's interconnected economies did not abandon producing and consuming other items, and in the case of Greek Sicily, local sources of fish, the olive, and the vine can be documented in the Archaic period, and for the first two items from earliest times within it. The Archaic Greek world certainly developed regional economic profiles and specialist emphases, but underneath them they sup-plied themselves with the basics from local sources as far as this was feasi-bly possible. This also applies to craft production. The evidence in Archaic Greek Sicily is greater than previously imagined, putting paid to the colonialist mindset of some earlier generations of scholars who thought that manufac-tured goods were exchanged for agricultural commodities, meaning that no manufactured goods were produced in Sicily. When this evidence is placed in the theoretical framework of import replacement or substitution, it not only provides another dimension to our understanding, but it also fits in well with human expectations in similar situations.

Therefore, one has to envisage Sicilian Greek economies firing on several different cylinders from the start, so to speak, with some cylinders hotter than others depending on local environmental, social, and economic conditions and possibilities. Economic staple theory demands such a view, and it is one supported by growing empirical evidence in Greek Sicily. Approaching Sicilian Greek economies in this way also helps to explain the building booms that occurred at the midpoint of each successive century of the Archaic and Classical periods. These booms are best described as economic takeoffs and can be paralleled in later periods of human history, whether on frontiers or in industrializing societies. The development of systems of weights, measures, coinage, and administrative institutions aimed at managing exchange (such as emporia) were also offshoots of these booms from the sixth century onward. Warfare and militarization also went hand in hand with these economic successes. The expenditures and economic stimuli from warfare and militarization are well known from other historical periods, and these played similar roles, of the periods considered in this book, in the fifth and fourth centuries BC. The impact was not just economic but also social, as observed above, with the incorporation of various Greek and non-Greek peoples, like mercenaries, into Sicilian Greek societies.

All these results allow us to return to the more general question of the role of Greeks in the making of ancient Sicily. In the late nineteenth century, Edward Freeman argued for Greeks having created our current image of ancient Sicily:

> It is the joint presence of Greek and Phoenician which gives the elder Sicilian history its highest interest and its deepest instruction. But it is the presence of the Greek, not that of the Phoenician, which gives Sicilian history its special and abiding charm. It was the coming of the Greek which made Sicily all that we understand by Sicily. Of a Sicily in which the Phoenicians held the mastery over Sikels, we cannot divine what the fate might have been. But we know that it could never have been the Sicily which holds so brilliant a place in the world's history. The Roman might still have overcome the Phoenician, the Norman might still have overcome the Saracen, but the element which in either case was the true life of the island would have been lacking. The true Sicily is the Hellenic Sicily and none other. It is the settlements from Greece, the great cities which their founders planted, the mighty monuments which they have left behind them, the contributions of Sicily to the art, the literature, and the philosophy of the common Hellenic stock—it is the thrilling interest of the internal stories of her Greek

cities—it is the constant connexion between them and the history of the elder Hellas, the tale of attack by the Athenian and of deliverance by the Corinthian—it is all this that gives Sicily its earliest right to rank among the most historic regions of the earth.[1]

The intellectual context of Freeman's statements needs to be recalled: his words come from the pen of a comparative world historian interested in challenging traditional disciplinary boundaries. And yet it is telling that such an open-minded historian singles out the ancient Greeks alone as having been behind Sicily's success and character. That is what makes his statements about the role of Hellenism in making ancient Sicily the attractive model to test. Freeman's view raises two important questions. Was Freeman correct about the role of the Greeks? On what did his view rest?

Freeman did not explicitly spell out his reasoning. Two Sicilian geographers have recently provided a plausible answer to the second question: "The island's fertile land has historically been exploited for agriculture following the pattern set by the Greeks and later the Romans who introduced large-scale agriculture."[2] As discussed above, paleoecological research, unavailable to Freeman and not cited by the two geographers, is beginning to confirm this: land clearance and the introduction of large-scale agricultural regimes coincided with the permanent settlement of Greeks in Sicily. While the Romans rejigged the island's agriculture for their purposes,[3] they no doubt continued to practice large-scale agriculture there and to find challenging the recruitment of enough labor to work the land in the same way as their Greek predecessors and their post-antique successors (up to the present day, in fact, though migrant laborers from Africa have now largely replaced a once-dependent Sicilian peasantry). In the case of ancient Greek Sicily, elite domination of society and economy ensued, and the result was the hierarchical division of natural and human resources. Once this domination took root, as it did and could from earliest times (since such large-scale agriculture was an innovation), elite domination proved hard to shake, as the history of the Archaic and Classical periods in Sicily attests. The structures of Sicilian Greek society and economy thus played the determining role in shaping political, military, and cultural history at home and abroad. Although not spelled out by Freeman in this way, there are nevertheless elements of truth in saying that

---

1. Freeman 1891–94, 1:10. A century later Holloway (1991, 47) expressed rather similar sentiments: "To most of us ancient Sicily means Greek Sicily."

2. Benedetto and Giordano 2008, 118, cf. 127.

3. De Angelis 2009b, 244–46.

the ancient Greeks have indeed given Sicily "its special and abiding charm," if that statement is today first qualified and supported empirically, and also includes the collaboration of native and other peoples. The Greeks' personality was the strongest stamp on the island.[4]

Scholars working on other parts of ancient Italy have already explicitly recognized the importance of social and economic questions to the development of ethnicity, identity, multiculturalism, mobility, and other areas of life from the Archaic period onward.[5] I have myself made some initial stabs at this in the chapters above and elsewhere.[6] But the interconnections could be further developed, as can the interconnections between social and economic questions and political, military, and cultural questions. All of these questions must move in tandem and not be treated as distinct separate spheres.

There is much more at stake than usually realized. The "Greek miracle" was built on regions like Sicily, from which flowed foodstuffs, ideas, and challenges vital for the development of Greece itself.[7] Sicily was an integral and important part of the ancient Greek world. As the editors of the recent *The Cambridge Economic History of the Greco-Roman World* have observed, "The Greco-Roman world generated a distinct Iron Age economics, involving much larger movements of staples through markets, concentration of people in cities, extensive monetization, and investment in the stock of knowledge."[8] To these we might also add the spread of malaria and other diseases.[9] We are talking about nothing less than the basis of the Mediterranean's Classical, Hellenistic, and Roman civilizations. However, non-specialists in general know very little of what is happening in the field of economics.[10] The risk exists, therefore, for the just discussed interconnections not to develop and become part of "mainstream" practice, given current disciplinary divisions. Much, therefore, is at stake in understanding the pre-Classical Mediterranean. The onus rests on the specialists to point out the significance and future directions of their research.

---

4. For similar thinking applied to the entire Mediterranean and Near East, see recently Vlassopoulos 2013, 322.

5. Torelli 1994; Corcella 1999, 79–80, 82; Morgan 1999, 86–87; Purcell 1999, 575.

6. See also De Angelis 2003b.

7. Vlassopoulos 2007a, 188–89 has recently made a similar point.

8. Morris, Saller, and Scheidel 2007, 10.

9. Sallares 2002, 103.

10. Morris, Saller, and Scheidel 2007, 1.

The study of the pre-Classical Mediterranean presents its own set of challenges. Given the geographical scope and interconnected nature of this world and the character of the sources available for study, it is necessary to move outside academic boundaries, to become interdisciplinary by combining different sources and regional specialties, as done in this book.[11] Courage and the willingness to experiment are needed. If ever there were a period of human history for the bold and energetic to study, this would be it. These same challenges exist at both the macro and micro levels and apply simultaneously to the Mediterranean as a whole and to individual regions within it.

Sicily is no exception. This book has sought to collect and analyze the available evidence and to provide a framework for future discussions of Sicilian Greek social and economic history. It is hoped that this book will act as a springboard. While we can always wish for the discovery of new literary and epigraphic material, archaeology will be the main provider of new material in the future. Archaeology's importance for social and economic questions cannot be overstated.[12] We need the retrieval and analysis of more archaeological data via excavations and surface surveys, which seek not only to accumulate more data but to acquire and interpret them using theoretical frameworks like "the archaeology of imperialism" to do so.[13] It will also involve coordinating contributions from a wide variety of disciplines. Archaeobotany, faunal studies, settlement and survey archaeology, literary criticism, numismatics, anthropology, sociology, geography, demography, and theoretical economics, to name the most prominent ones, must be included, as I have done here. The efforts will prove worthwhile, enabling the writing of a richer history, and key to understanding a wider range of issues that go beyond the social and economic realm for both Sicily and the outside world with which it interacted.

---

11. Gras 1995, 5; 2000c. See too now Vlassopoulos 2007a, 222–23; 2007b.

12. For a recent case study emphasizing the decisive role archaeology has played, for a rather similar, though later time period, see Wells 2008. See also M.E. Smith et al. 2012.

13. Cf. Given 2004, 49–68.

References

AA.VV. 1969. *La circolazione della moneta ateniese in Sicilia e in Magna Grecia: Atti del I. convegno del Centro Internazionale di Studi Numismatici, Napoli 5–8 aprile 1967.* Supplement to *AIIN* vols. 12–14. Rome.

AA.VV. 1990–91. Processo storico e metodologia nel pensiero di Eugenio Manni. *Kokalos* 36–37: 3–50.

AA.VV. 1991. *Atti del convegno Paolo Orsi e l'archeologia del '900, Rovereto 12–13 maggio 1990.* Annali dei Musei Civici di Rovereto, no. 6. Rovereto.

AA.VV. 1994. Scritti in memoria di Emanuele Ciaceri. *Sileno* 20: 8–116.

AA.VV. 2003. Cento anni dopo. La figura e l'opera di Adolfo Holm (3/VI 2000). *Kokalos* 49: 133–302.

AA.VV. 2004. *Atti della XXXVII Riunione Scientifica dell'Istituto Italiano di Preistoria e Protostoria della Calabria. Scalea, Papasidero, Praia a Mare, Tortora 29 settembre–4 ottobre.* Florence.

AA.VV. 2012. *Atti della XLI Riunione Scientifica dell'Istituto Italiano di Preistoria e Protostoria della Sicilia: Dai Ciclopi agli Ecisti. Società e territorio nella Sicilia preistorica e protostorica, San Cipirello (PA), 16–19 novembre 2006.* Florence.

Adamesteanu, D. 1953. Vasi gelesi arcaici di produzione locale. *ArchClass* 5: 244–47.

———. 1956a. Via Dalmazia, scoperta di una fornace greca arcaica. *NSc* 10: 277–81.

———. 1956b. Monte Saraceno ed il problema della penetrazione rodio-cretese nella Sicilia meridionale. *ArchClass* 8: 121–46.

———. 1958. Scavi e scoperte nella provincia di Caltanisetta dal 1951 al 1957. *NSc* 12: 288–408.

Adornato, G. 2003. I guerrieri di Agrigento. *Prospettiva* 110–111: 2–17.

———. 2005. Il tripode di Gelone a Delphi. *RAL* 16: 395–420.

———. 2006. Monumenti per una vittoria. Agrigento e Siracusa tra alleanze e rivalità. In *Guerra e pace in Sicilia e nel Mediterraneo antico (VIII–III sec. a.C.): Arte, prassi e teoria della pace e della guerra. Atti delle quinte giornate internazionali di studi sull'area elima e la Sicilia Occidentale nel contesto Mediterraneo, Erice, 12–15 ottobre 2003*, ed. M.A. Vaggioli and C. Michelini, 447–60. Pisa.

———. 2007. L'Efebo di Agrigento: Cultura figurativa e linguaggi artistici ad Akragas in età tardoantica e protoclassica. *Prospettiva* 128: 2–25.

———. 2008. Delphic Enigmas? The Γέλας ἀνάσσων, Polyzalos, and the Charioteer Statue. *AJA* 112: 29–55.

———. 2011. *Akragas arcaica: Modelli culturali e linguaggi artistici di una città greca d'Occidente.* Milan.

Aiosa, S. 2001. Un palazzo dimenticato: I tyranneia di Dionisio I ad Ortigia. *QuadMess* 2: 91–110.

Albanese Procelli, R.M. 1988–89. Calascibetta (Enna): Le necropoli di Malpasso, Carcarella e Valle Coniglio. *NSc* 42–43, I Supplemento: 161–398.

———. 1992. "La necropoli di Madonna del Piano presso Grammichele: Osservazioni sul rituale funerario," *Kokalos* 38: 33–68.

———. 1995. Contacts and Exchanges in Protohistoric Sicily. *Acta Hyperborea* 6: 33–49.

———. 1996a. Greek and Indigenous People in Eastern Sicily: Forms of Interaction and Acculturation. In *Early Societies in Sicily: New Developments in Archaeological Research*, ed. R. Leighton, 167–76. Accordia Specialist Studies on Italy, Vol. 5. London.

———. 1996b. Appunti sulla distribuzione delle anfore commerciali nella Sicilia arcaica. *Kokalos* 42: 91–137.

———. 1997a. Le etnie dell'età del ferro e le prime fondazioni coloniali. In *Prima Sicilia: Alle origini della società siciliana*, ed. S. Tusa, 511–22. Palermo.

———. 1997b. Échanges dans la Sicile archaïque: Amphores commerciales, inter-médiaires et redistribution en milieu indigène. *RA*: 3–25.

———. 1999. Identità e confini etnico-culturali: La Sicilia centro-orientale. In *Confini e frontiera nella grecità d'Occidente: Atti del trentasettesimo convegno di studi sulla Magna Grecia, Taranto, 3–6 ottobre 1997*, ed. A. Stazio and S. Ceccoli, 327–59. Taranto.

———. 2000. Necropoli e società coloniali: Pratiche funerarie 'aristocratiche' a Siracusa in età arcaica. In *Demarato: Studi di antichità classica offerti a Paola Pelagatti*, ed. I. Berlingò, H. Blanck, F. Cordano, P.G. Guzzo, and M.C. Lentini, 32–38. Milan.

———. 2001a. L'introduzione della siderugia in Sicilia. In *Studi di preistoria e protostoria in onore di Luigi Bernabò Brea*, ed. M.C. Martinelli and U. Spigo, 241–59.

———. 2001b. L'agro netino nella protostoria: Economia e organizzazione sociale. In *Contributi alla geografia storica dell'agro netino: Atti delle giornate di studio, Noto, Palazzo Trigona, 29–30–31 maggio 1998*, ed. F. Balsamo and V. La Rosa, 55–72. Noto.

———. 2001c. Gli Etruschi in Sicilia. In *Gli Etruschi fuori d'Etruria*, ed. G. Camporeale, 292–314. San Giovanni Lupatoio.

————. 2003a. *Sicani, Siculi, Elimi: Forme di identità, modi di contatto e processi di trasformazione.* Biblioteca di Archeologia, no. 33. Milan.

————. 2003b. Anfore commerciali dal centro indigeno della Montagna di Ramacca (Catania). In *Archeologia del Mediterraneo: Studi in onore di Ernesto De Miro,* ed. G. Fiorentini, M. Caltabiano, and A. Calderone, 37–50. Rome.

————. 2005a. Fasi e facies della prima età del Ferro in Sicilia: Dati e problemi interpretative. In *Oriente e Occidente: Metodi e discipline a confronto; Riflessioni sulla cronologia dell'età del ferro in Italia. Atti dell'incontro di studi, Roma, 30–31 ottobre 2003,* ed. G. Bartoloni and F. Delpino, 517–25. Pisa.

————. 2005b. Pratiche alimentari nella Sicilia protostorica a arcaica tra tradizione e innovazione. In *Papers in Italian Archaeology VI: Communities and Settlements from the Neolithic to the Early Medieval Period,* ed. P. Attema, A. Nijboer, and A. Zifferero, 358–66. BAR International Series Vol. 1452. Oxford.

————. 2010. Presenze indigene in contesti coloniali sicelioti: Sul problema degli indicatori archeologici. In *Grecs et indigènes de la Catalogne à la mer Noire: Actes des rencontres du programme européen Ramses² (2006–2008),* ed. H. Tréziny, 501–08. Aix-en-Provence.

Albanese Procelli, R.M., and F. Lo Schiavo. 2004. La comunità di Madonna del Piano presso Grammichele (Catania): Rapporti con l'area calabra. In *Atti della XXXVII Riunione Scientifica dell'Istituto Italiano di Preistoria e Protostoria della Calabria. Scalea, Papasidero, Praia a Mare, Tortora 29 settembre–4 ottobre,* 403–20. Florence.

Albers, J., M. Bentz, J.M. Müller, and G. Zuchtriegel. 2011. Werkstätten in Selinunt: Ein neues Forschungsprojekt. *Kölner und Bonner Archaeologica* 1: 45–48.

————. 2012. Werkstätten in Selinunt—Vorbericht zur Kampagne 2011. *Kölner und Bonner Archaeologica* 2: 105–11.

Albertocchi, M. 2009. Daedalica Selinuntia II: Osservazioni sulla coroplastica selinuntina d'età tardo-orientalizzante. In *Temi selinuntini,* ed. C. Antonetti and S. De Vido, 9–27. Pisa.

Alcock, S.E. 1994. Breaking up the Hellenistic World: Survey and Society. In *Classical Greece: Ancient Histories and Modern Archaeologies,* ed. I. Morris, 171–90. Cambridge.

Alcock, S.E., and R. Osborne, eds. 2007. *Classical Archaeology.* Oxford.

Allegro, N. 1976a. Le necropoli orientale. In *Himera.* Vol. 2: *Campagne di scavo 1966–1973,* ed. N. Allegro, O. Belvedere, N. Bonacasa, R.M. Bonacasa Carra, C.A. Di Stefano, E. Epifanio, E. Joly, M.T. Manni Piraino, A. Tullio, and A. Tusa Cutroni, 595–625. Rome.

————. 1976b. Il Quartiere Est. In *Himera.* Vol. 2: *Campagne di scavo 1966–1973,* ed. N. Allegro, O. Belvedere, N. Bonacasa, R.M. Bonacasa Carra, C.A. Di Stefano, E. Epifanio, E. Joly, M.T. Manni Piraino, A. Tullio, and A. Tusa Cutroni, 471–573. Rome.

————. 1997. Le fasi dell'abitato di Himera. In *Wohnbauforschung in Zentral—und Westsizilien: Sicilia occidentale e centro-meridionale; ricerche archeologiche nell'abitato*

(*Zürich, 28. Februar–3. März 1996*). *Akten der Forschungstagung/Atti delle giornate di studio sul tema*, eds. H.P. Isler, D. Käch, and O. Stefani, 65–80. Zürich.

———. 1999. Imera. In *La città greca antica: Istituzioni, società e forme urbane*, ed. E. Greco, 269–301. Rome.

———. 2000. Un ripostiglio di attrezzi agricoli da Himera. In *Demarato: Studi di antichità classica offerti a Paola Pelagatti*, ed. I. Berlingò, H. Blanck, F. Cordano, P.G. Guzzo, and M.C. Lentini, 39–49. Milan.

———. 2008a. L'abitato di Himera. In *Himera*. Vol. 5, *L'abitato: Isolato II. I blocchi 1–4 della Zona 1*, ed. N. Allegro, 4–16. Palermo.

———. 2008b. I blocchi 1–4. Considerazioni generali. In *Himera*. Vol. 5, *L'abitato: Isolato II. I blocchi 1–4 della Zona 1*, ed. N. Allegro, 209–20. Palermo.

Allegro, N., and S. Fiorentino. 2010. Ceramica indigena dall'abitato di Himera. In *Grecs et indigènes de la Catalogne à la mer Noire : Actes des rencontres du programme européen Ramses² (2006–2008)*, ed. H. Tréziny, 511–19. Aix-en-Provence.

Allen, R.C. 1997. Agriculture and the Origins of the State in Ancient Egypt. *Explorations in Economic History* 34: 135–54.

———. 2011. *Global Economic History: A Very Short Introduction*. Oxford.

Alliata, V., O. Belvedere, A. Cantoni, G. Cusimano, P. Marescalchi, and S. Vassallo. 1988. *Himera*. Vol. 3.1, *Prospezione archeologica nel territorio*. Rome.

Alram-Stern, E., and G. Nightingale, eds. 2007. *KEIMELION: Elitenbildung und elitärer Konsum von der mykenischen Palastzeit bis zur homerischen Epoche/The Formation of Elites and Elitist Lifestyles from Mycenaean Palatial Times to the Homeric Period. Akten des internationalen Kongresses vom 3. bis 5. Februar 2005 in Salzburg*. Vienna.

Altekamp, S. 2000. *Rückkehr nach Afrika: Italienische Kolonialarchäologie in Libyen, 1911–1943*. Cologne.

Amari, S. 2004. Tipologia dei materiali. In *La necropoli di Sant'Angelo Muxaro: Scavi Orsi-Zanotti Bianco 1931–1932*, ed. G. Rizza and D. Palermo, 129–78. CdA 24–25, 1985–1986. Catania.

Amato, F. 2012. Prospettive di ricerca sulla produzione vitivincola antica a Licata (Agrigento). In *Archeologia della vite e del vino in Toscana e nel Lazio*, ed. A. Ciacci, P. Rendini, and A. Zifferero, 307–48. Florence.

Amico, A. 2008. Il blocco 2. In *Himera*. Vol. 5, *L'abitato: Isolato II. I blocchi 1–4 della Zona 1*, ed. N. Allegro, 75–130. Palermo.

Amouretti, M.-C. 1986. *Le pain et l'huile dans la Grèce antique : De l'araire au moulin*. Paris.

———. 1994. L'agriculture de la Grèce antique: Bilan des recherches de la dernière décennie. *Topoi* 4: 69–94.

———. 2000. L'artisanat indispensable au fonctionnement de l'agriculture. In *L'artisanat en Grèce ancienne : Les productions, les diffusions*, ed. F. Blondé and A. Muller, 147–64. Villaneuve d'Ascq.

Amouretti, M.-C., and J.-P. Brun, eds. 1993. *La production de vin et de l'huile en Méditerranée/Oil and Wine Production in the Mediterranean Area.* BCH Suppl. Vol. 26. Paris.

Ampolo, C. 1976–77. Demarato: Osservazioni sulla mobilità sociale arcaica. *DdA* 9–10: 333–45.

———. 1984. Tributi e decime dei Siracusani. *Opus* 3: 31–36.

———. 1987. I contributi alla prima spedizione ateniese in Sicilia (427–424 a.C.). *PdP* 42: 5–11.

———. 1992a. Gli Ateniesi e la Sicilia nel V secolo: Politica e diplomazia, economia e guerra. *Opus* 11: 25–35.

———. 1992b. The Economics of the Sanctuaries in Southern Italy and Sicily. In *Economics of Cult in the Ancient Greek World: Proceedings of the Uppsala Symposium,* ed. T. Linders and B. Alroth, 25–28. Uppsala.

———. 1994. Tra empòria ed emporìa: Note sul commercio greco in età arcaica e classica. In AΠΟΙΚΙΑ: *I più antichi insediamenti greci in Occidente; funzioni e modi dell'organizzazione politica e sociale. Scritti in onore di Giorgio Buchner,* ed. B. D'Agostino and D. Ridgway, 29–36. AION n.s. 1. Naples.

———. 1997. *Storie greche: La formazione della moderna storiografia sugli antichi Greci.* Biblioteca Einandi, no. 11. Torino.

———. 1999. La frontiera dei Greci come luogo del rapporto e dello scambio: I mercati di frontiera fino al V secolo a.C. In *Confini e frontiera nella grecità d'Occidente: Atti del trentasettesimo convegno di studi sulla Magna Grecia, Taranto, 3–6 ottobre 1997,* ed. A. Stazio and S. Ceccoli, 451–64. Taranto.

———. 2000. I terreni sacri nel mondo greco in età arcaica e classica. In *Production and Public Powers in Classical Antiquity,* ed. E. Lo Cascio and D.W. Rathbone, 14–19. Cambridge.

———. ed. 2010. *Immagine e immagini della Sicilia e di altre isole del Mediterraneano antico: Atti delle seste giornate internazionale di studi sull'area elima e la Sicilia occidentale nel contesto mediterraneo, Erice 12–16 ottobre 2006.* Pisa.

Anderson, G. 2005. Before *Turannoi* were Tyrants: Rethinking a Chapter of Early Greek History. *Classical Antiquity* 24: 173–222.

Anderson, J.L. 1991. *Explaining Long-Term Economic Change.* Houndmills, UK.

Andreades, A.M. 1933. *A History of Greek Public Finance.* Cambridge, MA.

Anello, P. 1990–91. Rapporti dei Punici con Elimi, Sicani e Greci. *Kokalos* 36–37: 175–213.

———. 1997. Le popolazioni epicorie della Sicilia nella tradizione letteraria. In *Prima Sicilia: Alle origini della società siciliana,* ed. S. Tusa, 539–57. Palermo.

———. 1999. La storia di Gela antica. *Kokalos* 45: 385–408.

———. 2002. L'ambiente greco. In *Il Guerriero di Castiglione di Ragusa: Greci e Siculi nella Sicilia sud-orientale. Atti del Seminario—Milano, 15 maggio 2000,* ed. F. Cordano and M. Di Salvatore, 59–76. Hesperìa Vol. 16. Rome.

———. 2005. Cittadini e barbari in Sicilia. In *Il cittadino, lo straniero, il barbaro, fra integrazione ed emarginazione nell'antichità*, ed. M.G. Angeli Bertinelli and A. Donati, 143–76. Rome.

Antonaccio, C. 1999. Colonization and the Origins of Hero Cult. In *Ancient Greek Hero Cult*, ed. R. Hägg, 109–21. Stockholm.

———. 2001. Ethnicity and Colonization. In *Ancient Perceptions of Greek Ethnicity*, ed. I. Malkin, 113–57. Cambridge, MA.

———. 2003. Hybridity and the Cultures within Greek Culture. In *The Cultures within Ancient Greek Culture: Contact, Conflict, Collaboration*, ed. C. Dougherty and L. Kurke, 57–74. Cambridge.

———. 2005. Excavating Colonization. In *Ancient Colonizations: Analogy, Similarity and Difference*, ed. H. Hurst and S. Owen, 97–113. London.

———. 2007. Elite Mobility in the West. In *Pindar's Poetry, Patrons, and Festivals: From Archaic Greece to the Roman Empire*, ed. S. Hornblower and C. Morgan, 265–85. Oxford.

Antonelli, L. 1996. La falce di Crono. Considerazioni sulla prima fondazione di Zancle. *Kokalos* 42: 315–25.

———. 2008. *Traffici focei di età arcaica: Dalla scoperta dell'Occidente alla battaglia del mare Sardonio*. Hesperìa, vol. 25. Rome.

Antonetti, C. 2009. Riflessioni zu Zeus Agoraios a Selinunte. In *Temi selinuntini*, ed. C. Antonetti and S. De Vido, 29–51. Pisa.

Antonetti, C., and S. De Vido. 2006a. Conflitti locali e integrazione culturale a Selinunte: Il nuovo profilo della *polis* nell'iscrizione della vittoria. In *Guerra e pace in Sicilia e nel Mediterraneo antico (VIII–III sec. a.C.): Arte, prassi e teoria della pace e della guerra. Atti delle quinte giornate internazionali di studi sull'area elima e la Sicilia Occidentale nel contesto Mediterraneo, Erice, 12–15 ottobre 2003*, ed. M.A. Vaggioli and C. Michelini, 143–80. Pisa.

———. 2006b. Cittadini, non cittadini e stranieri nei santuari della Malophoros e del Meilichios di Selinunte. In *Stranieri e non cittadini nei santuari del Mediterraneo antico*, ed. A. Naso, 410–51. Florence.

Antonietti, A., and C. Vanzetti. 1961. *Carta della utilizzazione del suolo d'Italia*. Milan.

Antonini, F. 1996. Problemi dell'urbanizzazione e del rapporto città-campagna in Sicilia dall'età arcaica all'età di Agatocle. *Seia* n.s. 1: 87–98.

Aperghis, G.G. 2004. *The Seleukid Royal Economy: The Finances and Financial Administration of the Seleukid Empire*. Cambridge.

Arafat, K., and C. Morgan. 1994. Athens, Etruria and the Heuneburg: Mutual Misconceptions in the Study of Greek-Barbarian Relations. In *Classical Greece: Ancient Histories and Modern Archaeologies*, ed. I. Morris, 108–34. Cambridge.

Archibald, Z.H., J. Davies, V. Gabrielsen, and G.J. Oliver, eds. 2001. *Hellenistic Economies*. London.

Arena, R. 1989. *Iscrizioni greche arcaiche di Sicilia e Magna Grecia: Iscrizioni di Sicilia*. Vol. 1, *Iscrizioni di Megara Iblea e Selinunte*. Milan.

———. 1992. *Iscrizioni greche arcaiche di Sicilia e Magna Grecia*. Vol. 2, *Iscrizioni di Gela e Agrigento*. Milan.

———. 1994. *Iscrizioni greche arcaiche di Sicilia e Magna Grecia*. Vol. 3, *Iscrizioni delle colonie euboiche*. Milan.

———. 1998. *Iscrizioni greche arcaiche di Sicilia e Magna Grecia*. Vol. 5, *Iscrizioni di Taranto, Locri Epizefiri, Velia e Siracusa*. Alessandria.

Arias, P.E. 1976. *Quattro archeologi del nostro secolo: Paolo Orsi, Biagio Pace, Alessandro Della Seta, Ranuccio Bianchi-Bandinelli*. Università degli studi di Pisa Istituti per le scienze dell'antichità, Biblioteca degli Studi Classici e Orientali, no. 5. Pisa.

———. 1987. Biagio Pace: un'esperienza di costante ricerca della Sicilia antica. *Kokalos* 33: 213–21.

Arnaud, P. 2005. *Les routes de la navigation antique. Itinéraires en Méditerranée*. Paris.

Arnold-Biucchi, C. 1990. *The Randazzo Hoard 1980 and Sicilian Chronology in the Early Fifth Century B.C*. New York.

Arnold-Biucchi, C., L. Beer-Tobey, and N.M. Waggoner. 1988. A Greek Archaic Silver Hoard from Selinus. *American Numismatic Society Museum Notes* 33: 1–35.

Ashcroft, B., G. Griffiths, and H. Tiffin. 1998. *Post-colonial Studies: The Key Concepts*. London.

Asheri, D. 1966. *Distribuzioni di terre nell'antica Grecia*. Turin.

———. 1973. La popolazione di Imera nel V secolo a.C. *RFIC* 101: 457–65.

———. 1975. Osservazioni sulle origini dell'urbanistica ippodamea. *Rivista Storica Italiana* 87: 5–16.

———. 1977. Tyrannie et mariage forcé: Essai d'histoire sociale grecque. *AnnalesESC* 32: 21–48.

———. 1980a. La colonizzazione greca. In *La Sicilia antica*, ed. E. Gabba and G. Vallet, Vol. 1, pt. 2, 89–142. Naples.

———. 1980b. Rimpatrio di esuli e ridistribuzione di terra nella città siciliote, ca. 466–461 a.C. In Φιλίας χάριν: *Miscellanea di studi classici in onore di Eugenio Manni*, 143–58. Rome.

Aubet, M.E. 2001. *The Phoenicians and the West: Politics, Colonies, and Trade*. 2nd ed. Cambridge.

Austin, M.M. 1986. Hellenistic Kings, War, and the Economy. *CQ* 36: 450–66.

———. 1988. Greek Trade, Industry, and Labor. In *Civilization of the Ancient Mediterranean: Greece and Rome*, ed. M. Grant and R. Kitzinger, 723–51. New York.

———. 2000. Ancient Greece: Some General Points. In *Production and Public Powers in Classical Antiquity*, ed. E. Lo Cascio and D.W. Rathbone, 20–26. Cambridge.

Austin, M.M., and P. Vidal Naquet. 1977. *Economic and Social History of Greece: An Introduction*. Trans. and rev. M.M. Austin. London.

Avery, H.C. 1973. Themes in Thucydides' Account of the Sicilian Expedition. *Hermes* 101: 1–13.

Avram, A. 2006. The Territories of Istros and Kallatis. In *Surveying the Greek Chora: The Black Sea Region in a Comparative Perspective*, ed. P.G. Bilde and V.F. Stolba, 59–80. Aarhus.

Aymard, M. 1971. In Sicilia: Sviluppo demografico e sue differenziazioni geografiche. *Quaderni Storici* 17: 417–46.

———. 1987. Economia e società: Uno sguardo d'insieme. In *Storia d'Italia Regioni dall'unità a oggi: La Sicilia*, ed. M. Aymard and G. Giarrizzo, 3–37. Turin.

Bacci, G.M. 1982–83. Antico stabilimento per la pesca e la lavorazione del tonno presso Portopalo. *Kokalos* 28–29: 345–47.

———. 1984–85. Scavi e ricerche a Avola, Grammichele, Portopalo, Taormina. *Kokalos* 30–31: 711–25.

———. 1999a. Alcuni elementi di topografia antica. In *Da Zancle a Messina: Un percorso archeologico attraverso gli scavi*, ed. G.M. Bacci and G. Tigano, 1.51–57. Palermo.

———. 1999b. Siti e insediamenti nell'area peloritana e nella cuspide nord orientale della Sicilia. In *Magna Grecia e Sicilia: Stato degli studi e prospettive di ricerca; atti dell'incontro di studi, Messina, 2–4 dicembre 1996*, ed. M. Barra Bagnasco, E. De Miro, and A. Pinzone, 249–58. Messina.

Bacci, G.M., and P. Coppolino. 2002. Ceramica protoarcaica di Zancle: Aspetti e problemi. In *Da Zancle a Messina: Un percorso archeologico attraverso gli scavi*, ed. G.M. Bacci and G. Tigano, 2/2.21–30. Palermo.

Bacci, G.M., E. D'Amico, and M. Ravesi. 2002. La carta archeologica. In *Da Zancle a Messina: Un percorso archeologico attraverso gli scavi*, ed. G.M. Bacci and G. Tigano, 2/2.9–20. Palermo.

Bacci, G.M., G. Pavia, and M.C. Martinelli. 2001. Isolato 145. Via dei Mille. In *Da Zancle a Messina: Un percorso archeologico attraverso gli scavi*, ed. G.M. Bacci and G. Tigano, 2/1.9–48. Palermo.

Bacci, G.M., M.L. Lazzarini, A.M. Mastelloni, et al. 2001. Archeologia subacquea. In *Da Zancle a Messina: Un percorso archeologico attraverso gli scavi*, ed. G.M. Bacci and G. Tigano, 2/1.269–301. Palermo.

Bacci, G.M., and G. Tigano, eds. 1999–2002. *Da Zancle a Messina: Un percorso archeologico attraverso gli scavi*. 3 vols. Palermo.

Bacci, G.M., G. Tigano, M. Ravesi, and G. Zavettieri. 2010–11. Prime considerazioni su una nuova area sacra arcaica di Messina. *Archivio Storico Messinese* 91–92: 45–66.

———. 2012. L'area sacra dell'isolato Z a Messina e la *ktisis* di Zancle. In *Alle origini della Magna Grecia: Mobilità, migrazioni, fondazioni; Atti del cinquantesimo Convegno di Studi sulla Magna Grecia, Taranto 1—4 ottobre 2010*, ed. M. Lombardo et al., 927–45. Taranto.

Badagliacca, F. 2008. Il blocco 3. In *Himera*. Vol. 5, *L'abitato: Isolato II. I blocchi 1–4 della Zona 1*, ed. N. Allegro, 131–169. Palermo.

Bairoch, P. 1988. *Cities and Economic Development: From the Dawn of History to the Present*. Chicago.

———. 1989. Urbanization and the Economy in Pre-industrial Societies: The Findings of Two Decades of Research. *Journal of European Economic History* 18: 239–90.

Bakels, C. 1996. Growing Grain for Others or How to Detect Surplus Production. *Journal of European Archaeology* 4: 329–36.

———. 2001. Producers and Consumers in Archaebotany: Comment on "When Method meets Theory: The Use and Misuse of Cereal Producer/Consumer Models in Archaeobotany." In *Environmental Archaeology: Meaning and Purpose*, ed. U. Albarella, 299–301. Dordrecht.

Balandier, C. 2004. L'importance de la production du miel dans l'économie gréco-romaine. *Pallas* 64: 183–96.

Balco, W.M. 2007. A Material Culture Analysis of Eighth to Fourth Century BC Loomweights recovered in Western Sicily. MA thesis, Northern Illinois University.

Baldwin, R.E. 1956. Patterns of Development in Newly Settled Regions. *Manchester School of Economic and Social Studies* 24: 161–79.

Barbanera, M. 1998. *L'archeologia degli italiani: Storia, metodi e orientamenti dell'archeologia classica in Italia*. Rome.

Barceló, J.A., G. Pelfer, and A. Mandolesi. 2002. The Origins of the City from Social Theory to Archaeological Description. *Archeologia e Calcolatori* 13: 41–63.

Barker, G. 1989. The Archaeology of the Italian Shepherd. *PCPhS* n.s. 35: 1–19.

———. 1995. *A Mediterranean Valley: Landscape Archaeology and Annales History in the Biferno Valley*. Leicester.

———. 2005. Agriculture, Pastoralism, and Mediterranean Landscapes in Prehistory. In *The Archaeology of Mediterranean Prehistory*, ed. E. Blake and A.B. Knapp, 46–76. Oxford.

Barker, G., and T. Rasmussen. 1998. *The Etruscans*. Oxford.

Barletta, B.A. 2001. *The Origins of the Greek Architectural Orders*. Cambridge.

Barlow, F. 2004. Freeman, Edward Augustus (1823–1892). In *Oxford Dictionary of National Biography: From the Earliest Times to the Year 2000*, 20: 920–24.

Barone, G., S. Ioppolo, D. Majolino, P. Migliardo, L. Sannino, G. Spagnolo, and G. Tigano. 2002. Contributo delle analisi archeometriche allo studio delle ceramiche provenienti dagli scavi di Messina: Risultati preliminari. In *Da Zancle a Messina: Un percorso archeologico attraverso gli scavi*, ed. G.M. Bacci and G. Tigano, 2/2.87–117. Palermo.

Barra Bagnasco, M. 1996. Housing and Workshop Construction in the City. In *The Western Greeks*, ed. G. Pugliese Carratelli, 353–60. Milan.

Barron, J. 2004. Go West, Go Native. In *Greek Identity in the Western Mediterranean: Papers in Honour of Brian Shefton*, ed. K. Lomas, 259–66. Mnemosyne Suppl. Vol. 246. Leiden.

Basile, B. 1992. Stabilimenti per la lavorazione del pesce lungo le coste siracusane: Vendicari e Portopalo. In *Vᵃ Rassegna di Archeologia Subacquea, V premio Franco Papò, Giardini Naxos, 19–21 ottobre 1990*, 55–86. Messina.

Baslez, M.-F., A. Avram, M.-C. Marcellesi, I. Pernin, E. Perrin-Saminadayar. 2007. *Économies et sociétés en Grèce ancienne: 478–88*. Paris.

Bats, M. 2011. De la cuisine à la table du banquet entre Grecs et indigenes de Grande Grèce: Aspects de l'usage et de la consummation du vin (Ve–IIIe s. av. J.-C.). In *La vigna di Dionisio: Vite, vino e culti in Magna Grecia. Atti del quarantanovesimo Convegno di Studi sulla Magna Grecia, Taranto, 24–28 settembre 2009*, ed. M. Lombardo et al., 349–73. Taranto.

Battaglia, G., and V. Alliata. 1991. Modelli di insediamento in Sicilia nel bronzo finale. *SicArch* xxiv.75: 7–30.

Battaglia, S. 1964. Colonialismo. *Grande dizionario della lingua italiana* 3: 308. Turin.

Becker, M.J. 1995–96. Skeletal Studies of Sicilian Populations: A Survey. *The Accordia Research Papers* 6: 83–117.

———. 2002. The People of Sicily: Studies of Human Skeletal Remains and of Human Biology from the Paleolithic to Modern Times. *Rivista di Antropologia (Rome)* 80: 1–120.

Beer-Tobey, L., N.H. Gale, H.S. Kim, and Z.A. Stos-Gale. 1998. Lead Isotope Analysis of Four Late Archaic Silver Ingots from the Selinus Hoard. In *Metallurgy in Numismatics*. Vol. 4, ed. A. Oddy and M.R. Cowell, 385–92. London.

Bejor, G. 1991. Spunti diodorei e problematiche dell'archeologia siciliana. In *Mito, storia, tradizione: Diodoro Siculo e la storiografia classica. Atti del convegno internazionale Catania-Agira 7–8 dicembre 1984*, ed. E. Galvagno and C. Molè Ventura, 255–69. Catania.

Bekker-Nielsen, T. 2002. Fish in the Ancient Economy. In *Ancient History Matters: Studies Presented to Jens Erik Skydsgaard on his Seventieth Birthday*, ed. K. Ascani, V. Gabrielsen, K. Kvist, and A.H. Rasmussen, 29–38. Rome.

Belich, J. 2010. Exploding Wests: Boom and Bust in Nineteenth-Century Settler Societies. In *Natural Experiments of History*, ed. J. Diamond and J.A. Robinson, 53–87. Oxford.

Bell, M., III. 1997. Unequal Block Division in Orthogonal Planning. *AJA* 101: 382.

———. 2000. Camarina e Morgantina al Congresso di Gela. In *Un ponte fra l'Italia e la Grecia: Atti del simposio in onore di Antonino Di Vita, Ragusa, 13–15 febbraio 1998*, 291–97. Padua.

Bellelli, V., and M. Cultraro. 2006. Etruria, penisola balcanica ed Egeo settentrionale. In *Gli Etruschi e il Mediterraneo: Commerci e politica*, ed. G.M. Della Fina, 197–251. Rome.

Beloch, K.J. 1874. Sulla popolazione dell'antica Sicilia. *RFIC* 2: 545–62.

———. 1886. *Die Bevölkerung der griechisch-roemischen Welt*. Leipzig.

———. 1889. La popolazione antica della Sicilia. *ArchStorSic* 14: 1–83.

———. 1895. Nuove osservazioni sulla popolazione antica della Sicilia. *ArchStorSic* 20: 63–70.

———. 1912–27. *Griechische Geschichte*. 2nd ed. 4 vols. Strassburg and Berlin.

Belozerskaya, M., and K. Lapatin. 2004. *Ancient Greece: Art, Architecture, and History*. Los Angeles.

Belvedere, O. 2001. Il territorio di Himera e il problema della *chora* coloniale in Sicilia. In *Problemi della chora coloniale dall'Occidente al Mar Nero: Atti del quarantesimo convegno di studi sulla Magna Grecia, Taranto, 29 settembre–3 ottobre 2000*, ed. A. Stazio, 707–55. Taranto.

———. 2002. L'evoluzione storica del territorio imerese dalla fondazione della colonia al periodo tardo-antico. In *Himera*. Vol. 3.2, *Prospezione archeologica nel territorio*, ed. O. Belvedere, A. Bertini, G. Boschian, A. Burgio, A. Contino, R.M. Cucco, and D. Lauro, 377–97. Rome.

Belvedere, O., A. Bertini, G. Boschian, A. Burgio, A. Contino, R.M. Cucco, and D. Lauro, eds. 2002. *Himera*. Vol. 3.2, *Prospezione archeologica nel territorio*. Rome.

Benedetto, G., and A. Giordano. 2008. Sicily. In *Mediterranean Island Landscapes*, ed. I.N. Vogiatzakis, G. Pungetti, and A.M. Mannion, 117–42. Berlin.

Bérard, J. 1937. Review of Pace 1935. *REG* 50: 259–60.

———. 1939. Review of Pace 1938. *REG* 52: 544–45.

Bérend, D. 1979. Le monnayage de bronze de Segeste. In *Le origini della monetazione di bronzo in Sicilia e in Magna Grecia: Atti del VI Convegno del Centro Internazionale di Studi Numismatici—Napoli 17–22 aprile 1977*, ed. A. Stazio, 53–76. Rome.

———. 1993. Le monnayage d'or de Syracuse sous Denys I. In *La monetazione dell'età dionigiana: Atti dell'VIII Convegno Internazionale di Studi Numismatici—Napoli 29 maggio–1 giugno 1983*, ed. A. Stazio, M. Taliercio Mensiteri, and S. Ceccoli, 104–43. Rome.

Bergemann, J., and U. Gans. 2004. Der Bochumer Gela-Survey: Vorbericht über die Kampagnen von 2002 bis 2004. *MDAI(R)* 111: 437–76.

Berger, S. 1989. Democracy in the Greek West and the Athenian Example. *Hermes* 117: 303–14.

———. 1992. *Revolution and Society in Greek Sicily and Southern Italy*. Historia Suppl. Vol. 71. Stuttgart.

Bergier, J.-F. 1982. *Une histoire du sel*. Fribourg.

Bergquist, B. 1992. A Particular, Western Greek Cult Practice? *Opuscula Atheniensia* 19: 41–47.

Bernabò Brea, L. 1957. *Sicily before the Greeks*. Ancient Peoples and Places Series Vol. 3. London.

———. 1964–65. Leggenda e archeologia nella protostoria siciliana. *Kokalos* 10–11: 1–33.

———. 1968. Il crepuscolo del re Hyblon: Considerazioni sulla cronologia delle fondazioni di Leontinoi, Megara e Siracusa e sulla topografia della Megaride di Sicilia. *PdP* 23: 161–86.

————. 1971. Xuthia e Hybla e la formazione della facies culturale di Cassibile. In *Atti della XIII Riunione Scientifica dell'Istituto Italiano di Preistoria e Protostoria, Siracusa-Malta 22–26 ottobre 1968*, 11–28. Florence.

————. 1990. *Pantalica : Ricerche intorno all'anaktoron*. Cahiers du Centre Jean Bérard. Vol. 14. Naples.

Bernal, M. 1987. *Black Athena*. Vol. 1, *The Fabrication of Ancient Greece*. New Brunswick, NJ.

Bernardini, P. 2000. I Phoinikes verso Occidente: Una riflessione. *RSF* 28: 13–33.

Bernstein, F. 2004. *Konflikt und Migration: Studien zu griechischen Fluchtbewegungen im Zeitalter der sogenannten Großen Kolonisation*. St. Katharinen.

Bertesago, S.M. 2009. Figurine fittili da Bitalemi (Gela) e dalla Malophoros (Selinunte): Appunti per uno studio comparato di alcune classi della coroplastica votive. In *Temi selinuntini*, ed. C. Antonetti and S. De Vido, 53–69. Pisa.

Bertesago, S.M., and A. Sanavia. 2009. Omaggio veneziano a Ettore Gabrici. In *Temi selinuntini*, ed. C. Antonetti and S. De Vido, 71–92. Pisa.

Berve, H. 1967. *Die Tyrannis bei den Griechen*. 2 vols. Munich.

Bethemont, J., and J. Pelletier. 1983. *Italy: A Geographical Introduction*. Trans. and ed. E. Kofman and R. King. London.

Bettalli, M. 1995. *I mercenari nel mondo greco*. Vol. 1, *Dalle origini alla fine del V sec. a.C.* Pisa.

Bianchi, R., et al.. 1998. *Selinunte*. Vol. 4. Rome.

Biers, W.R. 1987. *The Archeology of Greece: An Introduction*. 2nd ed. Ithaca, NY.

Bietti Sestieri, A.M. 1979. I processi storici nella Sicilia orientale fra la tarda Età del Bronzo e gli inizi dell'Età del Ferro sulla base dei dati archeologici. In *Atti della XXI Riunione Scientifica dell'Instituto Italiano di Preistoria e Protostoria, Firenze 21–23 ottobre 1977*, 599–628. Florence.

————. 1981. Economy and Society in Italy between the Late Bronze Age and Early Iron Age. In *Archaeology and Italian Society: Prehistoric, Roman and Medieval Studies*, ed. G. Barker and R. Hodges, 133–55. Papers in Italian Archaeology II; BAR International Series 102. Oxford.

————. 1985. Contact, Exchange and Conflict in the Italian Bronze Age: The Mycenaeans on the Tyrrhenian Coasts and Islands. In *Papers in Italian Archaeology* IV: *The Cambridge Conference*, ed. C. Malone and S. Stoddart, 305–37. BAR International Series 243–46. Oxford.

————. 1988. The "Mycenaean Connection" and its Impact on the Central Mediterranean Societies. *DdA* 6: 23–51.

————. 1997a. Italy in Europe in the Early Iron Age. *Proceedings of the Prehistoric Society* 63: 371–402.

————. 1997b. Sviluppi culturali e socio-politici differenziati nella tarda età del bronzo della Sicilia. In *Prima Sicilia: Alle origini della società siciliana*, ed. S. Tusa, 473–91. Palermo.

———. 2003. Un modello per l'interazione tra Oriente e Occidente Mediterranei nel secondo millennio a.C.: Il ruolo delle grandi isole. In *Atti della XXXV riunione scientifica Istituto Italiano di preistoria e protostoria a Lipari*, 557–86. Firenze.

———. 2005. A Reconstruction of Historical Processes in Bronze and Early Iron Age Italy Based on Recent Archaeological Research. In *Papers in Italian Archaeology VI: Communities and Settlements from the Neolithic to the Early Medieval Period*, ed. P. Attema, A. Nijboer, and A. Zifferero, 9–24. BAR International Series Vol. 1452. Oxford.

Bietti Sestieri, A.M., A. Cazzella and A. Schnapp. 2002. The Mediterranean. In *Archeology: The Widening Debate*, ed. B. Cunliffe, W. Davies and C. Renfrew, 411–38. Oxford.

Bindi, M.P. 1980. Osservazioni sulla legislazione arcaica di Siracusa. *Annali della Facoltà di Lettere e Filosofia dell'Università di Siena* 1: 15–17.

Bintliff, J. 1982. Settlement Patterns, Land Tenure and Social Structure: A Diachronic Model. In *Ranking, Resource and Exchange: Aspects of the Archaeology of Early European Society*, ed. A.C. Renfrew and S. Shennan, 106–11. Cambridge.

———. 1999. Settlement and Territory. In *Companion Encyclopedia of Archaeology*, G. Barker, 505–45. London.

———. 2002a. Rethinking Early Mediterranean Urbanism. In *Mauerschau: Festschrift für Manfred Korfmann*, ed. R. Aslan, S.W. Blum, G. Kastl, F. Schweizer, and D. Thumm, 153–77. Tübingen.

———. 2002b. Going to Market in Antiquity. In *Stuttgarter Kolloquium zur historischen Geographie des Altertums 7, 1999: Zu Wasser und zu Land; Verkehrswege in der antiken Welt*, ed. E. Olshausen and H. Sonnabend, 209–30. Stuttgart.

———. 2002c. Time, Process and Catastrophism in the Study of Mediterranean Alluvial History: A Review. *World Archaeology* 33: 417–35.

———. 2012. *The Complete Archaeology of Greece: From Hunter-Gatherers to the 20th Century A.D.* Malden, MA.

Black, J. 2003. *Italy and the Grand Tour*. New Haven, CT.

Blake, E., and A.B. Knapp, eds. 2005. *The Archaeology of Mediterranean Prehistory*. Oxford.

Blake, E. 2005. The Material Expression of Cult, Ritual, and Feasting. In *The Archaeology of Mediterranean Prehistory*, ed. E. Blake and A.B. Knapp, 102–29. Oxford.

Blok, A. 1969. South Italian Agro-Towns. *Comparative Studies in Society and History* 11: 121–35.

Blok, A., and H. Driessen. 1984. Mediterranean Agro-Towns as a Form of Cultural Dominance: With Special Reference to Sicily and Andalusia. *Ethnologia Europaea* 14: 111–24.

Blondé, F., and A. Muller, eds. 2000. *L'artisanat en Grèce ancienne : Les productions, les diffusions*. Villaneuve d'Ascq.

Boardman, J. 1999a. *The Greeks Overseas: Their Early Colonies and Trade.* 4th ed. London.

———. 1999b. Greek Colonization: The Eastern Contribution. In *La colonisation grecque en Méditerraanée occidentale: Actes de la reconte scientifique en hommage à Georges Vallet organisée par le Centre Jean-Bérard, l'École Française de Rome, l'Istituto universitario orientale et l'Università degli studi di Napoli «Federico II» (Rome-Naples, 15–18 novembre 1995),* 39–50. Collection de l'École Française de Rome Vol. 251. Rome.

———. 2001. Aspects of Colonization. *Bulletin of the American Schools of Oriental Research* 322: 33–42.

———. 2006. Early Euboean Settlements in the Carthage Area. *OJA* 25: 195–200.

———. 2011. Fish and the Mediterranean: The Nourishing Sea. *AWE* 10: 1–9.

Boehringer, C. 1979a. Die frühen Bronzemünzen von Leontinoi und Katane. In *Le origini della monetazione di bronzo in Sicilia e in Magna Grecia: Atti del VI Convegno del Centro Internazionale di Studi Numismatici—Napoli 17–22 aprile 1977,* ed. A. Stazio, 145–76. Rome.

———. 1979b. Zu Finanzpolitik und Münzprägung des Dionysios von Syrakus. In *Greek Numismatics and Archaeology: Essays in Honor of Margaret Thompson,* ed. O. Mørkholm and N.M. Waggoner, 9–32. Wetteren.

———. 1998. Zur Münzgeschichte von Leontinoi in Klassischer Zeit. In *Studies in Greek Numismatics in Memory of Martin Jessop Price,* ed. R. Ashton, S. Hurter, G. Le Rider, and R. Bland, 43–53. London.

Boehringer, E. 1929. *Die Münzen von Syrakus.* Berlin.

Boissinot, P. 2009. Les vignobles des environs de Mégara Hyblaea et les traces de la viticulture italienne durant l'Antiquité. *MEFRA* 121: 83–132.

Bonacasa, N. 1977. Orientamenti della cultura archeologica in Sicilia. In *La presenza della Sicilia nella cultura degli ultimi cento anni,* 676–84. Palermo.

———. 1992. Da Agrigento a Himera: La proiezione culturale. In *Agrigento e la Sicilia greca: Atti della settimana di studio, Agrigento 2–8 maggio 1988,* ed. L. Braccesi and E. De Miro, 133–50. Rome.

———. 1997. Il progetto Himera nel prossimo futuro. In *Wohnbauforschung in Zentral- und Westsizilien: Sicilia Occidentale e centro-meridionale; Ricerche archeologiche nell'abitato,* ed. H.P. Isler et al., 55–64. Zurich.

Bonacasa, N., L. Braccesi, and E. De Miro, eds. 2002. *La Sicilia dei due Dionisî: Atti della settimana di studio, Agrigento, 24–28 febbraio 1999.* Rome.

Bonanno, A. 1988. Evidence of Greek, Carthaginian and Etruscan Maritime Commerce South of the Tyrrhenian: The Maltese Case. In *Navies and Commerce of the Greeks, the Carthaginians and the Etruscans in the Tyrrhenian Sea: Proceedings of the European Symposium held at Ravello, January 1987,* ed. T. Hackens, 417–28. Strasbourg.

Bonanno, D. 2010. *Ierone il Dinomenide: Storia e rappresentazione. Kokalos* Suppl. 21. Pisa.

Bondì, S.F. 2001. Aspetti della politica cartaginese in Sicilia. *Daidalos* 3: 27–35.

———. 2002. Dalle città ai comprensori prospettive recenti sulla Sicilia fenicia e punica. In *Fra Cartagine e Roma: Seminario di studi italo-tunisino, Bologna, 23 febbraio 2001*, ed. P. Donati Giacomini and M.L. Uberti, 87–94. Faenza.

———. 2005. Interazioni culturali nel Mediterraneo fenicio. In *Greci, Fenici, Romani: Interazioni culturali nel Mediterraneo antico*, ed. S.F. Bondì and M. Vallozza, 17–26. Viterbo.

Bonfante, L., and V. Karageorghis, eds. 2001. *Italy and Cyprus in Antiquity: 1500–450 BC*. Nicosia.

Bonfiglio, L. 1999. La distribuzione dei siti archeologici, il contesto stratigrafico e la ricostruzione paleoambientale. In *Da Zancle a Messina: Un percorso archeologico attraverso gli scavi*, ed. G.M. Bacci and G. Tigano, 1.9–17. Palermo.

Bonnet, C. 2009. Appréhender les Phéniciens en Sicile: Pour une relecture de l'"archéologie sicilienne" de Thucydide (VI, I, 1–2). *Pallas* 79: 27–40.

Bookidis, N. 2008. The Sanctuary of Demeter and Kore at Corinth and Colonization. In *Demetra: La divinità, i santuari, il culto, la leggenda. Atti del I Congresso Internazionale, Enna, 1–4 luglio 2004*, ed. C.A. Di Stefano, 99–105. Pisa and Rome.

Bosher, K., ed. 2012a. *Theater outside Athens: Drama in Greek Sicily and South Italy*. Cambridge.

———. 2012b. Hieron's Aeschylus. In *Theater Outside Athens: Drama in Greek Sicily and South Italy*, ed. K. Bosher, 97–111. Cambridge.

Botte, E. 2009. *Salaisons et sauces de poissons en Italie du sud et en Sicile durant l'antiquité*. Collection du Centre Jean Bérard Vol. 31. Naples.

Bouzek, J. 2000. Makedonische Bronzen in Italien. In *Akten des Symposions Die Ägäis und das westliche Mittelmeer: Beziehungen und Wechselwirkungen 8. bis 5. Jh. v. Chr., Wien, 24. bis 27 März 1999*, ed. F. Krinzinger, 363–69. Vienna.

Boyazoglu, J., and J.-C. Flamant. 1990. Mediterranean Systems of Animal Production. In *The World of Pastoralism: Herding Systems in Comparative Perspective*, ed. J.G. Galaty and D.L. Johnson, 353–93. New York.

Boyd, T.D., and M. Jameson. 1981. Urban and Rural Land Division in Ancient Greece. *Hesperia* 50: 327–42.

Braccesi, L. 1998. *I tiranni di Sicilia*. Rome.

Braccesi, L., and E. De Miro, eds. 1992. *Agrigento e la Sicilia greca: Atti della settimana di studio, Agrigento 2–8 maggio 1988*. Rome.

Braccesi, L., and G. Millino. 2000. *La Sicilia greca*. Rome.

Brancato, F. 1973. *Storiografia e politica nella Sicilia dell'Ottocento*. Collana di Saggi e Monografie, n.s., no. 33. Palermo.

Branciforti, M.G., and S. Amari. 2005. Gli scavi archeologici nell'ex Reclusorio della Purità di Catania. In Μεγάλαι νῆσοι: *Studi dedicati a Giovanni Rizza per il suo ottantesimo compleanno*, ed. R. Gigli, 2.47–77. Catania.

Brandherm, D. 2006. Zur Datierung der ältesten griechischen und phönizischen Importkeramik auf der iberischen Halbinsel. *MDAI(M)* 47: 1–23.

Brandherm, D., and M. Trachsel, eds. 2008. *A New Dawn for the Dark Age? Shifting Paradigms in Mediterranean Iron Age Chronology.* BAR International Series 1871. Oxford.

Braudel, F. 1972. *The Mediterranean and the Mediterranean World in the Age of Philip II.* 2 vols. 2nd ed. Trans. S. Reynolds. London.

———. 2001. *The Mediterranean in the Ancient World.* Trans. S. Reynolds. London.

Bresson, A. 1993. Les cités grecques et leurs *emporia.* In *L'emporion,* ed. A. Bresson and P. Rouillard, 163–226. Paris.

———. 2005. Ecology and Beyond: The Mediterranean Paradigm. In *Rethinking the Mediterranean,* ed. W.V. Harris, 94–114. Oxford.

———. 2007. La construction d'un espace d'approvisionnement: Les cités égéennes et le grain de la mer Noire. In *Une koinè pontique : Cités grecques, sociétés indigènes et empires mondiaux sur le littoral nord de la mer Noire (VIIe s. a.C.–IIIe s. p.C.),* ed. A. Bresson, A. Ivantchik, and J.L. Ferrare, 49–68. Bordeaux.

———. 2007–08. *L'économie de la Grèce des cites (fin VIe–Ier siècle a.C.).* 2 vols. Paris.

Bringmann, K. 2001. Grain, Timber and Money: Hellenistic Kings, Finance, Buildings and Foundations in Greek Cities. In *Hellenistic Economies,* ed. Z.H. Archibald, J. Davies, V. Gabrielsen, and G.J. Oliver, 205–14. London.

Brize, P. 1985. Samos und Stesichoros: Zu einem früharchaischen Bronzeblech. *MDAI(A)* 100: 53–90.

Brock, R., and S. Hodkinson, eds. 2000. *Alternatives to Athens: Varieties of Political Organization and Community in Ancient Greece.* Oxford.

Brodersen, K. 1994. Männer, Frauen und Kinder in Grossgriechenland: Quellen und Modelle zur frühen Siedler-Identität. *Mnemosyne* 47: 47–63.

Broodbank, C. 2000. *An Island Archaeology of the Early Cyclades.* Cambridge.

———. 2013. *The Making of the Middle Sea: A History of the Mediterranean from the Beginning to the Emergence of the Classical World.* Oxford.

Brugnone, A. 1992. Le leggi suntuarie di Siracusa. *PdP* 47: 5–24.

———. 1997. Legge di Himera sulla ridistribuzione della terra. *PdP* 52: 262–305.

———. 1999. L'iscrizione del tempio G di Selinunte e le tradizioni sui responsi oracolari delfici. In *Sicilia epigraphica: Atti del convegno internazionale, Erice, 15–18 ottobre 1998,* ed. M.I. Gulletta, 129–39. ASNP Quaderni 7–8. Pisa.

———. 2003a. *Nomima Chalkidikia*: Una laminetta iscritta da Himera. In *Quarte giornate internazionali di studi sull'area elima (Erice, 1–4 dicembre 2000): Atti,* ed. A. Corretti, 75–89. Pisa.

———. 2003b. Tessuti costumi e mode nella Sicilia antica. *Kokalos* 49: 51–85.

Brun, J.-P. 2004. *Archéologie du vin et de l'huile: De la Préhistoire à l'époque hellénistique.* Paris.

———. 2011. La produzione del vino in Magna Grecia e in Sicilia. In *La vigna di Dionisio: Vite, vino e culti in Magna Grecia. Atti del quarantanovesimo Convegno di Studi sulla Magna Grecia, Taranto, 24–28 settembre 2009,* ed. M. Lombardo et al., 95–142. Taranto.

Brun, P. 1993. La stèle des céréales de Cyrène et le commerce du grain en Égée au IVᵉ s. av. J.C. *ZPE* 99: 185–96.

Brunet, M., and S. Collin Bouffier. 2007. *Économies et sociétés en Grèce ancienne, 478–88 av. J.-C.: Grèce contientale, îles de la mer Égée, cites cotières d'Asie Mineure*. Paris.

Bruno Sunseri, G. 1994. Giulio Beloch a Palermo. *QS* 40: 85–140.

Buchholz, H.G., G. Jöhrens, and I. Maull. 1973. *Jagd und Fischfang*. Archaeologica Homerica, no. 2J. Göttingen.

Burford, A. 1993. *Land and Labor in the Greek World*. Baltimore.

Burgers, G.-J. 2004. Western Greeks in their Regional Setting: Rethinking Early Greek-Indigenous Encounters in Southern Italy. *AWE* 3: 252–82.

Burgio, A. 2002. *Resuttano (IGM 260 III SO)*. Forma Italiae, Vol. 42. Florence.

Burke, P. 2004. *What is Cultural History?* Cambridge.

———. 2005. *History and Social Theory*. 2nd ed. Ithaca, NY.

Caccamo Caltabiano, M. 1999. Identità e peculiarità dell'esperienza monetale siciliana. In *Magna Grecia e Sicilia: Stato degli studi e prospettive di ricerca; atti dell'incontro di studi, Messina, 2–4 dicembre 1996*, ed. M. Barra Bagnasco, E. De Miro, and A. Pinzone, 295–311. Messina.

———. 2002. La monetazione di Dionisio I fra economia e propaganda. In *La Sicilia dei due Dionisî: Atti della settimana di studio, Agrigento, 24–28 febbraio 1999*, ed. N. Bonacasa, L. Braccesi, and E. De Miro, 33–45. Rome.

———. 2003. Holm numismatico. *Kokalos* 49: 285–302.

Caccamo Caltabiano, M., and M. Puglisi. 2002. La funzione della moneta nella Sicilia antica. In *Ritrovamenti monetali nel mondo antico: Problemi e metodi. Atti del congresso internazionale, Padova 31 marzo–2 aprile 2000*, ed. G. Gorini, 31–49. Padua.

———. 2004. Presenza e funzioni della moneta nelle chorai delle colonie greche della Sicilia: Età arcaica e classica. In *Presenza e funzioni della moneta nelle chorai delle colonie greche dall'Iberia al Mar Nero*, 333–70. Rome.

Caccamo Caltabiano, M., L. Campagna and A. Pinzone, eds. 2004. *Nuove prospettive della ricerca sulla Sicilia del III sec. a.C.: Archeologia, numismatica, storia. Atti dell'incontro di studio (Messina 4–5 luglio 2002*. Messina 2004.

Caccamo Caltabiano, M., Castrizio, D., and M. Puglisi. 2006. Dinamiche economiche in Sicilia tra guerre e controllo del territorio. In *Guerra e pace in Sicilia e nel Mediterraneo antico (VIII–III sec. a.C.): Arte, prassi e teoria della pace e della guerra. Atti delle quinte giornate internazionali di studi sull'area elima e la Sicilia Occidentale nel contesto Mediterraneo, Erice, 12–15 ottobre 2003*, ed. M.A. Vaggioli and C. Michelini, 655–73. Pisa.

Caffi, M. 2004. Il porto fluviale di Lentini. In *Leontini: Il mare, il fiume, la città. Atti della giornata di studio, Lentini, 4 maggio 2002*, ed. M. Frasca, 71–77. Catania.

Cagnetta, M. 1994. Pais e il nazionalismo. *QS* 39: 209–25.

Cahn, H.A. 1979. "Olynthus" and Syracuse. In *Greek Numismatics and Archaeology: Essays in Honor of Margaret Thompson*, ed. O. Mørkholm and N.M. Waggoner, 47–52. Wetteren.

Calafato, B., S. Tusa, and G. Mammina. 2001. *Uomo e ambiente nella storia di Mazara del Vallo: Indagine topografica nell'agro mazarese.* Palermo.

Calder, W.M., III. 2004. Freeman, Edward Augustus (1823–92). In *The Dictionary of British Classicists,* ed. R. Todd, 342–43. Bristol.

Calderone, A. 1984–85. Monte Saraceno di Ravanusa: Abitato del terrazzo inferiore. *Kokalos* 30–31: 535–38.

Calderone, S. 1978. Problemi storici relativi alle «Apoikiai» siceliote in età proto-arcaica. In *Insediamenti coloniali greci in Sicilia nell'VIII e VII secolo a.C.,* ed. G. Rizza, 11–20. Catania.

———. [1994] 1997. Sicilia greca e Mediterraneo. *Messana* 19: 5–22.

Camassa, G. 1996. Leggi orali e leggi scritte: I legislatori. In *I Greci: Storia, cultura, arte, società,* Vol. 2, pt. 1, ed. S. Settis, 561–76. Turin.

Cambi, N. 2002. Urbanistica e architettura del IV secolo a.C. ad oriente dell'Adriatico. In *La Sicilia dei due Dionisî: Atti della settimana di studio, Agrigento, 24–28 febbraio 1999,* ed. N. Bonacasa, L. Braccesi, and E. De Miro, 47–75. Rome.

Cameron, R.E., and L. Neal. 2003. *A Concise Economic History of the World: From Paleolithic Times to the Present.* 4th ed. Oxford.

Camp, J. McK., II. 1973. Greek Inscriptions. *Hesperia* 43: 314–24.

Campagna, B. 2003. Recenti ricognizioni nel territorio di Rodì Milici. In *Archeologia del Mediterraneo: Studi in onore di Ernesto De Miro,* ed. G. Fiorentini, M. Caltabiano, and A. Calderone, 151–66. Rome.

Campanella, L., and A.M. Niveau de Villedary y Mariñas. 2005. Il consume del pescato nel Mediterraneo fenicio e punico: Fonti letterarie, contesti archeologici, vasellame ceramico. In *Greci, Fenici, Romani: Interazioni culturali nel Mediterraneo antico,* ed. S.F. Bondì and M. Vallozza, 27–67. Viterbo.

Cancio, S. 1980. *Siracusa e provincia: Topografia storica e archeologica.* Catania.

Caputo, G. 1955. Il pensiero di Bagio Pace e l'archeologia italiana. *Dioniso* 18: 83–121.

———. 1957. Il fiume Halykos, via del sale e centro della Sikania. *PdP* 12: 439–41.

———. 1978. Sale, zolfo, grano: Tre sicane risorse. *SicArch* xi,37: 7–9.

Carbè, A. 2002. Considerazioni sulla circolazione monetale a Messina alla luce dei materiali degli scavi recenti. In *Da Zancle a Messina: Un percorso archeologico attraverso gli scavi,* ed. G.M. Bacci and G. Tigano, 2/2.71–85. Palermo.

———. 2003. Ritrovamenti monetari a Francavilla di Sicilia (ME). In *Archeologia del Mediterraneo: Studi in onore di Ernesto De Miro,* ed. G. Fiorentini, M. Caltabiano, and A. Calderone, 181–202. Rome.

Cardete, C. 2008. De griegos a siciliotas: La dimensión étnica del Congreso de Gela. *ASAA* 86 (8³): 153–67.

Cardosa, M. 2002. Il dono di armi nei santuari della divinità femminili in Magna Grecia. In *Le arti di Efesto: Capolavori in metallo dalla Magna Grecia; catalogo della mostra (Trieste, 8 marzo–28 luglio 2002),* 99–103. Milan.

Carroccio, B. 2004. *Dal basileus Agatocle a Roma: Le monetazioni siciliane d'età ellenistica; cronologia, iconografia, metrologia.* Messina.

Carter, J.C. 1996. Agricultural Settlements. In *The Western Greeks*, ed. G. Pugliese Carratelli, 361–68. Milan.

Carter, S.B., and S. Cullenberg. 1996. Labor Economics and the Historian. In *Economics and the Historian*, ed. T. Rawski, 85–121. Berkeley.

Cartledge, P. 1993. Classical Greek Agriculture: Recent Work and Alternative Views. *Journal of Peasant Studies* 21: 127–36.

———. 1995. Classical Greek Agriculture II: Two More Alternative Views. *Journal of Peasant Studies* 23: 131–39.

———, ed. 1998. *The Cambridge Illustrated History of Ancient Greece*. Cambridge.

———. 2002. What is Social History Now? In *What is History Now?*, ed. D. Cannadine, 19–35. Houndmills.

———. 2009. *Ancient Greece: History in Eleven Cities*. Oxford.

Casevitz, M. 2002. Sur les fragments des historiens grecs, particulièrement Diodore de Sicile. In *Fragments d'historiens grecs: Autour de Denys d'Halicarnasse*, ed. S. Pittia, 449–60. Collection de l'École Française de Rome, no. 298. Rome.

Castellana, G. 1980. Indigeni ad Himera? *SicArch* xiii,44: 71–76.

———. 1983. Nuove ricognizioni nel territorio di Palma di Montechiaro (Agrigento). Seconda parte. *SicArch* xvi,52–53: 119–46.

———. 1984. La Neapolis nella chora acragantina e la colonizzazione dionisiana della Sicilia. *PdP* 39: 375–83.

———. 1985. Note sul bacino del Salso (Himera) e il surplus di grano dall'antichità ai nostri caricatori marittimi. *SicArch* xviii,57–58: 87–90.

———. 1989. La produzione del grano nel bacino della valle dell'Himera meridionale nell'antichità. In *Homo edens*, ed. O. Longo and P. Scarpi, 131–40. Verona.

———. 2002. *La Sicilia nel II millennio a.C.*. Caltanisetta.

Castrizio, D. 2000. *La monetazione mercenariale in Sicilia: Strategie economiche e territoriale fra Dione e Timoleonte*. Soveria Mannelli.

Cataldi, S. 2003. Alcuni considerazioni su eparchia ed epicrazia cartaginese nella Sicilia occidentale. In *Quarte giornate internazionali di studi sull'area elima (Erice, 1–4 dicembre 2000): Atti*, ed. A. Corretti, 217–52. Pisa.

———. 2007. Atene e l'Occidente: Trattati e alleanze dal 433 al 424. In *Atene e l'Occidente: I grandi temi, le premesse, i protagonisti, le forme della communicazione e dell'interazione, i modi dell'intervento ateniese in Occidente. Atti del Convegno Internazionale, Atene 25–27 maggio 2006*, ed. E. Greco and M. Lombardo, 421–70. Athens.

Cavallari, F.S. 1884. Lentini. *NSc*: 252–54.

Caven, B. 1990. *Dionysius I: War-lord of Sicily*. New Haven.

Cébeillac-Gervasoni, M. 1975. Les nécropoles de Mégara Hyblaea. *Kokalos* 21: 3–36.

———. 1976–77. Une étude systématique sur les nécropoles de Mégara Hyblaea: L'example d'une partie de la nécropole méridionale. *Kokalos* 22–23: 587–97.

Ceka, N. 2002. I riflessi della politica di Dionisio il Grande nel territorio dell'attuale Albania. In *La Sicilia dei due Dionisî: Atti della settimana di studio, Agrigento, 24–28 febbraio 1999*, ed. N. Bonacasa, L. Braccesi, and E. De Miro, 77–80. Rome.

Ceserani, G. 2000. The Charm of the Siren: The Place of Classical Sicily in Historiography. In *Sicily from Aeneas to Augustus: New Approaches in Archaeology and History*, ed. C.J. Smith and J. Serrati, 174–93. Edinburgh.

———. 2012. *Italy's Lost Greece: Magna Graecia and the Making of Modern Archaeology*. Oxford.

Challis, D. 2010. 'The Ablest Race': The Ancient Greeks in Victorian Racial Theory. In *Classics and Imperialism in the British Empire*, ed. M. Bradley, 94–120. Oxford.

Chamberlain, A. 2006. *Demography in Archaeology*. Cambridge.

Chamoux, F. 2003. *Hellenistic Civilization*. Trans. M. Roussel. Oxford.

Chandezon, C. 1999. L'économie rurale et la guerre. In *Armées et sociétés de la Grèce classique: Aspects sociaux et politiques de la guerre aux Ve et IVe s. av. J.-C.*, ed. F. Prost, 195–208. Paris.

Chao, K. 1983. *The Economic Development of Manchuria: The Rise of a Frontier Economy*. Ann Arbor.

Chapman, R. 2005. Changing Social Relations in the Mediterrancean Copper and Bronze Ages. In *The Archaeology of Mediterranean Prehistory*, ed. E. Blake and A.B. Knapp, 77–101. Oxford.

Chatelain, T. 2004. Entre terre et eau : L'exploitation des marais en Grèce ancienne; une pratique aux marges de l'agriculture? *Pallas* 64: 211–20.

Chiai, G.F. 2002. Il nome della Sardegna e della Sicilia sulle rotte dei Fenici e dei Greci in età arcaica: Analisi di una tradizione storico-letteraria. *RSF* 30: 125–46.

Chilardi, S. 2005. Botteghe artigiane per la lavorazione dell'osso di Siracusa antica. In *Atti del 3° Convegno Nazionale di Archeozoologia, Siracusa 3–5 novembre 2005*, ed. I. Fiore, G. Malerba, and S. Chilardi, 371–78. Rome.

———. 2006. Artemis Pit? Dog Remains from a Well in the Ancient Town of Siracusa (Sicily). In *Dogs and People in Social, Working, Economic or Symbolic Interaction: Proceedings of the Ninth Conference of the International Council of Archaeozoology, Durham, August 2002*, ed. L.M. Snyder and E.A. Moore, 32–37. Oxford.

Chisholm, M. 1979. *Rural Settlement and Land Use: An Essay in Location*, 3rd ed. London.

Christ, K. 1996. *Griechische Geschichte und Wissenschaftsgeschichte*. Historia Suppl. Vol. 106. Stuttgart.

Ciasca, A. 1988–89. Fenici. *Kokalos* 34–35: 75–88.

Cipolla, C.M. 1991. *Between History and Economics: An Introduction to Economic History*. Trans. C. Woodall. Oxford.

Clavel-Lévêque, M. 1994. Conclusions I. In *Structures rurales et sociétés antiques: Actes du colloque de Corfou (14–16 mai 1992)*, ed. P.N. Doukellis and L.G. Mendoni, 477–81. Paris.

Cleuziou, S., A. Coudart, J.-P. Demoule, and A. Schnapp. 1991. The Use of Theory in French Archaeology. In *Archaeological Theory in Europe: The Last Three Decades*, ed. I. Hodder, 91–128. London.

Coarelli, F., and M. Torelli. 1984. *Sicilia*. Guide archeologiche Laterza, no. 13. Rome.

Cohen, E.E. 2001. A New Balance Sheet for the Ancient Economy. *AJA* 105: 313–15.

Coldstream, J.N. 2003. *Geometric Greece: 900–700 BC*. 2nd ed. London.

Collin Bouffier, S. 1987. L'alimentation en eau de la colonie grecque de Syracuse. *MEFRA* 99: 661–91.

———. 1994. Marais et paludisme en occident grec. In *L'eau, la santé et la maladie dans le monde grec*, ed. R. Ginouvès, A.-M. Guimier-Sorbets, J. Jouanna, and L. Villard, 321–36. BCH Suppl. Vol. 28. Paris.

———. 1999a. Les elites urbaines en Sicile grecque du VIIe au Ve siècle av. J.-C. ou la reproduction d'un modèle homerique. In *Construction, reproduction et representation des patriciats urbains de l'Antiquité au XXe siècle: Actes du colloque des 7, 8, 9 septembre 1998 tenu à Tours*, ed. C. Petitfrère, 363–73. Tours.

———. 1999b. La pisciculture dans le monde grec: État de la question. *MEFRA* 111: 37–50.

———. 2000a. La cuisine des Grecs d'Occident, symbole d'une vie de tryphé? *Pallas* 52: 195–208.

———. 2000b. Quelles fonctions pour la kolymbethra d'Agrigente? In *Cura aquarum in Sicilia: Proceedings of the Tenth International Congress on the History of Water Management and Hydraulic Engineering in the Mediterranean Region, Syracuse, May 16–22, 1998*, ed. G.C.M. Jansen, 37–43. Leiden.

———. 2001. Les adductions hydrauliques des villes grecques de Sicile: Des ouvrages techniques méconnus. In *Techniques et sociétés en Méditerranée: Hommage à Marie-Claire Amouretti*, ed. J.-P. Brun and P. Jockey, 513–27. Paris.

———. 2002. Eau et campagne en Sicilie grecque: Observations préliminaires à l'étude. *In Binos Actus Lumina: Rivista di Studi e Ricerche sull'Idraulica Storica e la Storia della Tecnica* 1: 27–35.

———. 2003. Il culto delle acque in Sicilia greca: Mito o realtà? In *Storia dell'acqua: Mondi materiali e universi simbolici*, ed. V. Teti, 43–66. Rome.

———. 2009. La gestion de l'eau en Sicile grecque: État de la question. *Pallas* 79: 65–79.

———. 2010a. Les élites face au tyran en Sicilie grecque à l'époque classique. In *La cité et ses élites: Pratique et représentation des formes de domination et de contrôle social dans les cités grecques. Actes du colloque de Potiers, 19–20 octobre 2006*, ed. L. Capdetrey and Y. Lafond, 291–305. Pessac.

———. 2010b. Parentés et spécificités culturelles en Sicile grecque à travers les tablettes de malédiction. In *Alleanze e parentele: Le "affinità elettive" nella storiografia sulla Sicilia antica. Convegno internazionale Palermo 14–15 aprile 2010*, ed. D. Bonanno et al., 89–112. Caltanissetta.

———. 2012. Diasporas grecques en Sicile. In *Les diasporas grecques: Du détroit de Gibraltar à l'Indus (VIII* s. Av. J.-C. à la fin du III* s. av. J.-C.)*, ed. S. Bouffier, 53–97. Paris.

Columba, G.M. [1906] 1991. *I porti della Sicilia*. Reprint, Palermo.

Consolo Langher, S.N. 1997. *Un imperialismo tra democrazia e tirannide: Siracusa nei secoli V e IV a.C. Kokalos* Suppl. 12. Rome.

———. 2000. *Agatocle: Da capoparte a monarca fondatore di un regno tra Cartagine e i Diadochi*. Messina.

Copani, F. 2005. Alle origini di Eloro: L'espansione meridionale di Siracusa arcaica. *Acme* 58: 245–63.

Coppolino, P. 2002. La ceramica comune «da fuoco» a Messina tra VII e IV sec. a.C.: Una nota preliminare. In *Da Zancle a Messina: Un percorso archeologico attraverso gli scavi*, ed. G.M. Bacci and G. Tigano, 2/2.47–58. Palermo.

Corcella, A. 1999. La frontiera nella storiografia sul mondo antico. In *Confini e frontiera nella grecità d'Occidente: Atti del trentasettesimo convegno di studi sulla Magna Grecia, Taranto, 3–6 ottobre 1997*, ed. A. Stazio and S. Ceccoli, 43–82. Taranto.

Cordano, F. 1978. Leggi e legislatori calcidesi. *Miscellanea Greca e Romana* 6: 89–98.

———. 1984a. L'uso della scrittura in Italia meridionale e Sicilia nei secoli VIII e VII a.C. *Opus* 3: 281–302.

———. 1984b. *Sakon*, un antroponimo importante nella Sicilia antica. *PdP* 39: 136–39.

———. 1986a. *Antiche fondazioni greche: Sicilia e Italia meridionale*. Palermo.

———. 1986b. Le leggi calcidesi di Monte S. Mauro di Caltagirone. *Miscellanea Greca e Romana* 10: 33–60.

———. 1987. Contributo onomastico alla storia di Camarina arcaica. *Kokalos* 33: 121–27.

———. 1988a. L'evoluzione sociale dei Calcidesi di Sicilia. *Miscellanea Greca e Romana* 13: 51–62.

———. 1988b. Naxos IV: Gruppi gentilizi presso i Nassii di Sicilia. *BdA* 73: 18–22.

———. 1990. Alcuni aspetti dell'onomastica personale di Camarina. *PdP* 45: 442–46.

———. 1992a. Note sui gruppi civici sicelioti. *Miscellanea Grece e Romana* 17: 135–44.

———. 1992b. *Le tessere pubbliche dal tempio di Atena a Camarina*. Rome.

———. 1997a. Considerazioni sull'uso greco del terzo nome in Sicilia. In *Seconde giornate internazionali di studi sull'area elima (Gibellina, 22–26 ottobre 1994): atti*, ed. S. De Vido, 401–13. Pisa and Gibellina.

———. 1997b. Un documento arcaico da contrada Maestro (Camarina). *PdP* 52: 349–54.

———. 1999. Le istituzioni della città greche di Sicilia nelle fonti epigrafiche. In *Sicilia epigraphica. Atti del convegno internazionale, Erice, 15–18 ottobre 1998*, ed. M.I. Gulletta, 149–58. ASNP Quaderni 7–8. Pisa.

————. 2003. Fondazioni repubblicane e fondazioni tiranniche nella Sicilia del V sec. a.C. In *La naissance de la ville dans l'antiquité: De l'archéologie à l'histoire*, ed. M. Reddé, L. Dubois, D. Briquel, H. Lavagne, and F. Queyrel, 121–25. Paris.

————. 2006. A Project of Greek Colonisation from Sicily to Etruria? *ASAA* 6: 465–80.

Cordano, F., and M. Di Salvatore, eds. 2002. *Il Guerriero di Castiglione di Ragusa: Greci e Siculi nella Sicilia sud-orientale. Atti del Seminario—Milano, 15 maggio 2000.* Hesperìa Vol. 16. Rome.

Cordano, F., and G. Di Stefano. 1997. Il fiume e la città nella Sicilia meridionale: Il caso di Camarina. In *Uomo, acqua e paesaggio*, ed. S. Quilici Gigli, 289–300. Rome.

Cordiano, G. 1996. Aspects du problème de l'expansion territoriale d'une πόλις en domaine coloniale: Le case de Ῥήγιον. In *Les moyens d'expression du pouvoir dans les sociétés anciennes*, ed. M. Broze, P.-J. Dehon, P. Talon, T. Van Compernolle, and E. Warmenbol, 221–36. Leuven.

Corretti, A. 1988. Contributo alla discussione sulle strutture del commercio arcaico: le navi. In *Navies and Commerce of the Greeks, the Carthaginians and the Etruscans in the Tyrrhenian Sea: Proceedings of the European Symposium Held at Ravello, January 1987*, ed. T. Hackens, 243–56. Strasbourg.

————. 2006. «Fornirò 200 triremi ...» (Hdt., 7,158,4): Per un riesame della tradizione antiche sulla marineria siceliota. In *Guerra e pace in Sicilia e nel Mediterraneo antico (VIII–III sec. a.C.): Arte, prassi e teoria della pace e della guerra. Atti delle quinte giornate internazionali di studi sull'area elima e la Sicilia Occidentale nel contesto Mediterraneo, Erice, 12–15 ottobre 2003*, ed. M.A. Vaggioli and C. Michelini, 415–30. Pisa.

Corvisier, J.-N. 1999. *Guerre et société dans les mondes grecs (490–322 av. J.-C.).* Paris.

Costantini, L. 1979. Monte San Mauro di Caltagirone: Analisi paleoetnobotaniche dei semi contenuti nei pithoi 4 e 6. *BdA* 64: 43–4.

————. 1983. Analisi paleoetnobotaniche nel comprensorio di Camarina. *BdA* 68: 49–56.

Couvenhes, J.-C., and S. Péré-Noguès. 2005. «Quoi de neuf sur la guerre?» Perspectives de recherche et données nouvelles sur la guerre dans le monde méditerranéen aux époques archaïque, classique et hellénistique (à partir de quelques publications récentes). *Pallas* 67: 379–99.

Cracco, G. 1981. Edward Augustus Freeman (1823–1892), un medievista senza Medioevo. *ASNP* 11: 341–61.

Crane, G. 1996. *The Blinded Eye: Thucydides and the New Written Word.* Lanham, MD.

Crielaard, J.P. 2009. Cities. In *A Companion to Archaic Greece*, ed. K.A. Raaflaub and H. van Wees, 349–72. Oxford.

Crippa, S., and M. De Simon. 2009. Sulla valenza pubblica dei rituali defissori a Selinunte. In *Temi selinuntini*, ed. C. Antonetti and S. De Vido, 93–104. Pisa.

Croissant, F. 2007. Les échos de la sculpture attique. In *Atene e l'Occidente: I grandi temi, le premesse, i protagonisti, le forme della communicazione e dell'interazione, i modi dell'intervento ateniese in Occidente. Atti del Convegno Internazionale, Atene 25–27 maggio 2006,* ed. E. Greco and M. Lombardo, 295–324. Athens.

Crouch, D.P. 2004. *Geology and Settlement: Greco-Roman Patterns.* Oxford.

Cucco, R.M. 2002. Il territorio tra il fiume Imera e il territorio Roccella. In *Himera.* Vol. 3.2: *Prospezione archeologica nel territorio,* ed. O. Belvedere, A. Bertini, G. Boschian, A. Burgio, A. Contino, R.M. Cucco, and D. Lauro, 231–375. Rome.

Cumin, G. 1944. *La Sicilia: Profilo geografico-economico.* Catania.

Cunliffe, B., W. Davies, and C. Renfrew, eds. 2002. *Archaeology: The Widening Debate.* Oxford.

Cuomo di Caprio, N. 1971–72. Proposta di classificazione delle fornaci per ceramica e laterizi nell'area italiana: Dalla preistoria a tutta l'epoca romana. *Sibrium* 11: 371–461.

———. 1992. *Morgantina.* Vol. 3, *Fornaci e officine da vasaio tardo-ellenistiche.* Princeton.

Curbera, J. 2009. Note di onomastica selinuntina e siceliota. In *Temi selinuntini,* ed. C. Antonetti and S. De Vido, 105–10. Pisa.

Curcio, A. 1979. Resti di fattorie antiche nella vallata del Tellaro. *SicArch* xii,41: 79–90.

Curcio, G. 1966. Tombe greche e tracce di edificio di epoca romana in contrada Fùrmica. *BdA* 51: 92–93.

Curtis, R.I. 1991. *Garum and Salsamenta: Production and Commerce in Materia Medica.* Leiden.

Cusumano, N. 1994. *Una terra splendida e facile di possedere: I Greci e la Sicilia. Kokalos* Suppl. 10. Rome.

———. 2009. Mots pour dire les mots : Interactions, acculturations et relations inter-culturelles dans la Sicile antique (V^e–Ier siècle avant J.-C.). *Pallas* 79: 41–63.

Cutroni Tusa, A. 1979. La circolazione della moneta bronzea in Sicilia. In *Le origini della monetazione di bronzo in Sicilia e in Magna Grecia: Atti del VI Convegno del Centro Internazionale di Studi Numismatici—Napoli 17–22 aprile 1977,* ed. A. Stazio, 225–57. Rome.

———. 1980. La monetazione di Siracusa sotto Dionisio I. In Φιλίας χάριν: *Miscellanea di studi classici in onore di Eugenio Manni,* 629–47. Rome.

———. 1993. La circolazione in Sicilia. In *La monetazione dell'età dionigiana: Atti dell'VIII Convegno Internazionale di Studi Numismatici—Napoli 29 maggio–1 giugno 1983,* ed. A. Stazio, M. Taliercio Mensiteri, and S. Ceccoli, 245–69. Rome.

———. 1997. I ripostigli di bronzo e la loro funzione pre o paramonetale. In *Prima Sicilia: Alle origini della società siciliana,* ed. S. Tusa, 567–78. Palermo.

———. 1999. Considerazioni numismatiche. *Kokalos* 45: 413–26.

———. 2004. Presenza e funzioni della moneta nelle *chorai* delle colonie greche della Sicilia occidentale. In *Presenza e funzioni della moneta nelle* chorai *delle colonie greche dall'Iberia al Mar Nero,* 371–95. Rome.

D'Agostino, B. 1973. Appunti sulla funzione dell'artigianato nell'Occidente greco dall'VIII al IV sec. a.C. In *Economia e società nella Magna Grecia: Atti del dodicesimo convegno di studi sulla Magna Grecia, Taranto, 8–14 ottobre 1972,* ed. P. Romanelli, 207–36. Naples.

————. 1991. The Italian Perspective on Theoretical Archaeology. In *Archaeological Theory in Europe: The Last Three Decades*, ed. I. Hodder, 52–64. London.

————. 2006. The First Greeks in Italy. In *Greek Colonisation: An Account of Greek Colonies and Other Settlements Overseas*, ed. G. Tsetskhladze, 201–37. Leiden.

D'Agostino, B., and P. Gastaldi. 1988. *Pontecagnano*. Vol. 2, *La necropoli del Picentino 1: Le tombe della Prima Età del Ferro*. AION Quaderno 5. Naples.

Dalby, A. 1996. *Siren Feasts: A History of Food and Gastronomy in Greece*. London.

D'Andria, F. 2002. L'Adriatico. I rapporti tra le due sponde: Stato della questione. In *La Sicilia dei due Dionisî: Atti della settimana di studio, Agrigento, 24–28 febbraio 1999*, ed. N. Bonacasa, L. Braccesi, and E. De Miro, 117–37. Rome.

————. 2007. Nuove prospettive di metodo nella ricerca: Osservazioni e proposte. In *Passato e futuro dei convegni di Taranto: Atti del quarantaseiesimo convegno di studi sulla Magna Grecia, Taranto 29 settembre–1 ottobre 2006*, ed. A. Stazio and S. Ceccoli, 117–68. Taranto.

Danile, L. 2008. Il blocco 1. In *Himera*. Vol. 5, *L'abitato: Isolato II. I blocchi 1–4 della Zona 1*, ed. N. Allegro, 17–74. Palermo.

Dark, K.R. 1995. *Theoretical Archaeology*. London.

Davidson, A. 2002. *Mediterranean Seafood: A Comprehensive Guide with Recipes*. 3rd ed. Berkeley.

Davies, J.K. 1998. Ancient Economies: Models and Muddles. In *Trade, Traders and the Ancient City*, ed. H. Parkins and C. Smith, 225–56. London.

————. 2001. Temples, Credit, and the Circulation of Money. In *Money and its Uses in the Ancient Greek World*, ed. A. Meadows and K. Shipton, 117–28. Oxford.

————. 2002. The Strategies of Mr Theopompos. In *Money, Labour and Land: Approaches to the Economies of Ancient Greece*, ed. P. Cartledge, E.E. Cohen, and L. Foxhall, 200–08. London.

————. 2007a. Classical Greece: Production. In *The Cambridge Economic History of the Greco-Roman World*, ed. W. Scheidel, I. Morris, and R. Saller, 333–61. Cambridge.

————. 2007b. The Legacy of Xerxes: The Growth of Athenian Naval Power. In *Atene e l'Occidente: I grandi temi, le premesse, i protagonisti, le forme della communicazione e dell'interazione, i modi dell'intervento ateniese in Occidente. Atti del Convegno Internazionale, Atene 25–27 maggio 2006*, ed. E. Greco and M. Lombardo, 71–98. Athens.

D'Esposito, L. 2008. Il blocco 4. In *Himera*. Vol. 5, *L'abitato: Isolato II. I blocchi 1–4 della Zona 1*, ed. N. Allegro, 171–207. Palermo.

De Angelis, F. 1998. Ancient Past, Imperial Present: The British Empire in T.J. Dunbabin's *The Western Greeks. Antiquity* 72: 539–49.

————. 2000a. Estimating the Agricultural Base of Greek Sicily. *PBSR* 68: 111–48.

————. 2000b. The Agricultural Capacity of Archaic Syracuse. In *Akten des Symposions Die Ägäis und das westliche Mittelmeer: Beziehungen und Wechselwirkungen 8. bis 5. Jh. v. Chr., Wien, 24. bis. 27 März 1999*, ed. F. Krinzinger, 109–15. Vienna.

————. 2001. Archaeology in Sicily, 1996–2000. *AR* 47: 145–201.

————. 2002. Trade and Agriculture at Megara Hyblaia. *OJA* 21: 299–310.

————. 2003a. *Megara Hyblaia and Selinous: The Development of Two Greek City-states in Archaic Sicily.* Oxford University School of Archaeology Monograph, no. 57. Oxford.

————. 2003b. Equations of Culture: The Meeting of Natives and Greeks in Sicily (*ca.* 750–450 BC). *AWE* 2: 19–50.

————. 2006. Going against the Grain in Sicilian Greek Economics. *G&R* 53.1: 29–47.

————. 2007. Archaeology in Sicily, 2001–2005. *AR* 53: 123–90.

————. 2009a. Colonies and Colonization. In *The Oxford Handbook of Hellenic Studies,* ed. G. Boys-Stones, B. Graziosi, and P. Vasunia, 48–64. Oxford.

————. 2009b. Ancient Sicily: The Development of a Microregional Tessera in the Mediterranean Mosaic. In *Société et climats dans l'empire romain,* ed. E. Hermon, 235–50. Naples.

————. 2010. Re-assessing the Earliest Social and Economic Developments in Greek Sicily. *MDAI(R)* 116: 21–53.

————. 2012a. Archaeology in Sicily 2006–2010. *AR* 58: 123–95.

————. 2012b. Art and Power in Archaic Greek Sicily: Investigating the Economic Substratum. In *Arte—Potere: Forme artistiche, istituzioni, paradigmi interpretativi. Atti del Convegno di studio tenuto a Pisa Scuola Normale Superiore, 25–27 Novembre 2010,* ed. M. Castiglione and A. Poggio, 173–84. Milan.

————. 2012c. Teorizzando l'economie arcaiche della Sicilia greca. In *Griechen in Übersee und der historische Raum,* ed. J. Bergemann, 27–28. Rahden.

De Angelis, F., and B. Garstad. 2006. Euhemerus in Context. *Classical Antiquity* 25: 211–42.

De Cesare, M., and M. Gargini. 1997. Monte Finestrelle di Gibellina: Nota preliminare sulla prima campagna di scavo. In *Seconde giornate internazionali di studi sull'area elima (Gibellina, 22–26 ottobre 1994): Atti,* ed. S. De Vido, 371–74. Pisa and Gibellina.

De Francesco, A. 2013. *The Antiquity of the Italian Nation: The Cultural Origins of a Political Myth in Modern Italy, 1796–1943.* Oxford.

Dehl, C. 1983. Cronologia e diffusione della ceramica corinzia dell'VIII s. a.C. in Italia. *ArchClass* 35: 186–211.

————. 1984. *Die korinthische Keramik des 8. und frühen 7. Jhs. v. Chr. in Italien: Untersuchungen zu ihrer Chronologie und Ausbreitung.* MDAI(A) Suppl. Vol. 11. Berlin.

Dehl-von Kaenel, C. 1994. Keramik als Handelsware: Zum Vertrieb korinthischer Keramik in das Malophoros Heiligtum in Selinunt. *Münstersche Beiträge zur Antiken Handelsgeschichte* 13.1: 55–82.

————. 1995. *Die archaische Keramik aus dem Malophoros-Heiligtum in Selinunt.* Berlin.

————. 1997. Le importazioni corinzie nel santuario della Malophoros di Selinunte e le strutture della distribuzione della ceramica corinzia in Sicilia e in Magna

Grecia. In *Corinto e l'Occidente: Atti del trentaquattresimo convegno di studi sulla Magna Grecia, Taranto, 7–11 ottobre 1994*, ed. A. Stazio and S. Ceccoli, 345–66. Taranto.

——. 2001. Eine Gruppe archaischer Transportamphoren aus der 'Ladenzeile' an der Agora von Selinunt. In *Zona archeologica: Festschrift für Hans Peter Isler zum 60. Geburtstag*, ed. S. Buzzi, 101–10. Bonn.

De Juliis, E.M. 2000. *I fondamenti dell'arte italica*. Rome.

De la Genière, J. 1978. C'è un 'modello' Amendolara? *ASNP* 8: 335–54.

——, ed. 1994. *Nécropoles et sociétés antiques (Grèce, Italie, Languedoc)*. Cahiers du Centre Jean Bérard Vol. 18. Naples.

——. 1995. Vases attiques à Agrigente au temps de Bacchylide et de Pindare. *CRAI*: 1005–21.

——. 1996. Quelques observations sur les céramiques grecques présentes dans les nécropoles de Gela. In *I vasi attici ed altre ceramiche coeve in Sicilia: Atti del convegno internazionale Catania, Camarina, Gela, Vittoria, 28 marzo–1 aprile 1990*, ed. G. Rizza and F. Giudice, Vol. 2, 167–72. CdA 30 (1991). Catania.

——. 1999a. Μεταξύ Ἑλλήνων καὶ Βαρβάρων. In *Confini e frontiera nella grecità d'Occidente: Atti del trentasettesimo convegno di studi sulla Magna Grecia, Taranto, 3–6 ottobre 1997*, ed. A. Stazio and S. Ceccoli, 503–18. Taranto.

——. 1999b. De la céramique pour les mercenaires. In *La colonisation grecque en Méditerraanée occidentale : Actes de la recontre scientifique en hommage à Georges Vallet organisée par le Centre Jean-Bérard, l'École française de Rome, l'Istituto universitario orientale et l'Università degli studi di Napoli «Federico II» (Rome-Naples, 15–18 novembre 1995)*, 121–30. Collection de l'École Française de Rome Vol. 251. Rome.

——. 2001. *Xenoi* en Sicile dans la première moitié du Ve siècle (Diod. XI, 72,3). *REG* 114: 24–36.

——. 2006. Clients, potiers et peintres. In *Les clients de la céramique grecque: Actes du colloque de l'Académie des Inscriptions et Belles-Lettres, Paris, 30–31 janvier 2004*, ed. J. de la Genière, 9–15. Paris.

Del Monaco, L. 2004. Le fatrie di Camarina e gli strateghi di Siracusa. *Mediterraneo Antico* 7: 597–613.

Demand, N. 1990. *Urban Relocation in Archaic and Classical Greece: Flight and Consolidation*. Norman.

——. 2004. Models in Greek History and the Question of the Origins of the Polis. *AHB* 18.1–2: 61–86.

——. 2006. *A History of Ancient Greece in its Mediterranean Context*. 2nd ed. Cornwall-on-Hudson, NY.

De Miro, E. 1956. Agrigento arcaica e la politica di Falaride. *PdP* 11: 263–73.

——. 1962. La fondazione di Agrigento e l'ellenizzazione del territorio fra il Salso e il Platani. *Kokalos* 8: 122–52.

———. 1980. La casa greca in Sicilia: Testimonianze nella Sicilia centrale dal VI al III sec. a.C. In Φιλίας χάριν: *Miscellanea di studi classici in onore di Eugenio Manni*, 709–37. Rome.

———. 1980–81. Ricerche archeologiche nella Sicilia centro-meridionale. *Kokalos* 26–27: 561–80.

———. 1988a Polizzello, centro della Sicania. *QuadMess* 3: 25–42.

———. 1988b. Akragas, città e necropoli nei recenti scavi. In *Veder greco: Le necropoli di Agrigento. Mostra internazionale, Agrigento, 2 maggio–31 luglio 1988*, 235–52. Rome.

———. 1989. *Agrigento: La necropoli greca di Pezzino*. Messina.

———. 1992. L'urbanistica e i monumenti pubblici. In *Agrigento e la Sicilia greca: Atti della settimana di studio, Agrigento 2–8 maggio 1988*, ed. L. Braccesi and E. De Miro, 151–56. Rome.

———. 1996. La casa greca in Sicilia. In *Ricerche sulla casa in Magna Grecia e in Sicilia: Atti del colloquio, Lecce, 23–24 giugno 1992*, ed. F. D'Andria and K. Mannino, 17–40. Galatina.

———. 1998. Società e arte nell'età di Empedocle. *Elenchos* 19: 325–44.

———. 2008. Thesmophoria di Sicilia. In *Demetra: La divinità, i santuari, il culto, la leggenda. Atti del I Congresso Internazionale, Enna, 1–4 luglio 2004*, ed. C.A. Di Stefano, 47–92. Pisa and Rome.

Dench, E. 1995. *From Barbarians to New Men: Greek, Roman, and Modern Perceptions of Peoples from the Central Apennines*. Oxford.

———. 2003. Beyond Greeks and Barbarians: Italy and Sicily in the Hellenistic Age. In *A Companion to the Hellenistic World*, ed. A. Erskine, 294–310. Oxford.

———. 2005. *Romulus' Asylum: Roman Identities from the Age of Alexander to the Age of Hadrian*. Oxford.

Denoyelle, M., and M. Iozzo. 2009. *La céramique grecque d'Italie méridionale et de Sicile: Productions coloniales et apparentées du VIIIe au IIIe siècle av. J.-C.* Paris.

Denti, M. 1999. Per una fenomenologia storico-culturale del linguaggio figurativo dei Greci d'Occidente in età arcaica. In *KOINA: Miscellanea di studi archeologici in onore di Piero Orlandini*, ed. M. Castoldi, 205–21. Milan.

Descat, R. 1995. *L'Économie antique* et la cité grecque: Un modèle en question. *AnnalesESC* 50: 961–89.

———. 2001. Monnaie multiple et monnaie frappée en Grèce archaïque. *Revue Numismatique* 157: 69–81.

———. 2004. Les années 330–325 av. J.-C. et la politique athénienne du blé. *Pallas* 64: 267–80.

Descoeudres, J.-P., ed. 1990. *Greek Colonists and Native Populations*. Oxford.

———. 2008. Central Greece on the Eve of the Colonisation Movement. In *Greek Colonisation. Vol. 2, An Account of Greek Colonies and Other Settlements Overseas*, ed. G. Tsetskhladze, 289–382. Leiden.

De Sensi Sestito, G. 2002. La Magna Grecia nell'età dei Dionisî. In *La Sicilia dei due Dionisî: Atti della settimana di studio, Agrigento, 24–28 febbraio 1999*, ed. N. Bonacasa, L. Braccesi, and E. De Miro, 389–403. Rome.

De Souza, P. 1998. Towards Thalassocracy? Archaic Greek Naval Developments. In *Archaic Greece: New Approaches and New Evidence*, ed. N. Fisher and H. Van Wees, 271–93. London.

De Ste. Croix, G.E.M. 1981. *The Class Struggle in the Ancient Greek World: From the Archaic Age to the Arab Conquests*. London.

De Vido, S. 2009. Selinunte: Gli ultimi anni. In *Temi selinuntini*, ed. C. Antonetti and S. De Vido, 111–28. Pisa.

———. 2013. *Le guerre di Sicilia*. Rome.

Devoto, G. 1957. Biagio Pace e gli studi sull'antica Sicilia. *SE* 25: 3–12.

De Waele, J.A. 1971. *Acragas Graeca: Die historische topographie des griechischen Akragas auf Sizilien*. Gravenhagen.

———. 1980. La popolazione di Akragas antica. In Φιλίας χάριν: *Miscellanea di studi classici in onore di Eugenio Manni*, 747–60. Rome.

———. 1992. I grandi templi. In *Agrigento e la Sicilia greca: Atti della settimana di studio, Agrigento 2–8 maggio 1988*, ed. L. Braccesi and E. De Miro, 157–205. Rome.

Diamond, J. 1997. *Guns, Germs, and Steel: The Fate of Human Societies*. New York.

Di Bella, V., and F. Santagati. 1998. Prospezione archeologica nel territorio costiero tra Agrigento e Siculiana. *SicArch* xxxi,96: 71–104.

Dickinson, E.R. 1955. *The Population Problem of Southern Italy: An Essay in Social Geography*. Syracuse, NY.

Dickinson, O. 2006. *The Aegean from Bronze Age to Iron Age: Continuity and Change between the Twelfth and Eighth Centuries BC*. London.

Dietler, M. 2007. The Iron Age in the Western Mediterranean. In *The Cambridge Economic History of the Greco-Roman World*, ed. W. Scheidel, I. Morris, and R. Saller, 242–76. Cambridge.

Di Gennaro, F. 1997. Collegamenti tra Eolie e coste tirreniche nell'età del bronzo. In *Prima Sicilia: Alle origini della società siciliana*, ed. S. Tusa, 421–28. Palermo.

Dinsmoor, W. 1927. *Architecture of Ancient Greece*. London.

Di Patti, C., R. Di Salvo, and V. Schimmenti. 2001. I reperti faunistici rinvenuti nei relitti di Gela. *Quaderni del Museo Archeologico Regionale 'Antonino Salinas'* 7: 121–24.

Di Stefano, C.A., ed. 1998. *Palermo punica*. Palermo.

Di Stefano, G. 1987a. Camarina VIII: L'emporio greco arcaico di contrada Maestro sull'Irminio; Rapporto preliminare della prima campagna di scavi. *BdA* 72: 129–40.

———. 1987b. Il territorio di Camarina in età arcaica. *Kokalos* 33: 129–201.

———. 1988–89. Indigeni e Greci nell'entroterra di Camarina. *Kokalos* 34–35: 89–105.

———. 1993–94. Il relitto di Punta Braccetto (Camarina), gli *emporia* e i relitti di età arcaica lungo la costa meridionale della Sicilia. *Kokalos* 39–40: 111–33.

———. 1998. La bonifica di Camarina: Un esempio della Sicilia classica. In *Bonifiche e drenaggi con anfore in epoca romana: Aspetti tecnici e topografici*, ed. S. Pesavento Mattioli, 265–73. Modena.

———. 2001. La *chora* di Camarina. In *Problemi della* chora *coloniale dall'Occidente al Mar Nero: Atti del quarantesimo convegno di studi sulla Magna Grecia, Taranto, 29 settembre–3 ottobre 2000*, ed. A. Stazio, 689–705. Taranto.

———. 2002. La casa greca nel IV secolo a.C. nella Sicilia sud-orientale: Il caso della Chora di Camarina. In *La Sicilia dei due Dionisî: Atti della settimana di studio, Agrigento, 24–28 febbraio 1999*, ed. N. Bonacasa, L. Braccesi, and E. De Miro, 93–115. Rome.

———. 2006. Aspetti urbanistici e topografici per la storia di Camarina. In *Camarina: 2600 anni dopo la fondazione. Atti del Convegno Internazionale*, ed. P. Pelagatti, G. Di Stefano, and L. De Lachenal, 157–176. Rome.

———. 2008. Demetra a Camarina: Note di topografia; Revisioni e novità. In *Demetra: La divinità, i santuari, il culto, la leggenda. Atti del I Congresso Internazionale, Enna, 1–4 luglio 2004*, ed. C.A. Di Stefano, 261–71. Pisa and Rome.

Di Vita, A. 1956. La penetrazione siracusana nella Sicilia sud-orientale alla luce delle più recenti scoperte archeologiche. *Kokalos* 2: 177–205.

———. 1959. Breve rassegna degli scavi archeologici condotti in provincia di Ragusa nel quadriennio 1955–1959. *BdA* 44: 347–64.

———. 1987. Tucidide VI 5 e l'epicrazia siracusana Acre, Casmene, Camarina. *Kokalos* 33: 77–86.

———. 1996. Urban Planning in Ancient Sicily. In *The Western Greeks*, ed. G. Pugliese Carratelli, 263–308. Milan.

———. 1999. Siracusa, Camarina, Selinunte: Quale frontiera? In *Confini e frontiera nella grecità d'Occidente: Atti del trentasettesimo convegno di studi sulla Magna Grecia, Taranto, 3–6 ottobre 1997*, ed. A. Stazio and S. Ceccoli, 361–79. Taranto.

———. 2002. L'urbanistica nella Sicilia del IV secolo a.C. In *La Sicilia dei due Dionisî: Atti della settimana di studio, Agrigento, 24–28 febbraio 1999*, ed. N. Bonacasa, L. Braccesi, and E. De Miro, 139–46. Rome.

Docter, R.F., H.G. Niemeyer, A.J. Nijboer, and J. van der Plicht. 2005. Radiocarbon Dates of Animal Bones in the Earliest Levels of Carthage. In *Oriente e Occidente: Metodi e discipline a confronto; Riflessioni sulla cronologia dell'età del ferro in Italia. Atti dell'incontro di studi, Roma, 30–31 ottobre 2003*, ed. G. Bartoloni and F. Delpino, 557–77. Pisa.

Domínguez, A.J. 1989. *La Colonización griega en Sicilia: Griegos, indígenas y púnicos en la Sicilia arcaica; Interacción*. BAR International Series 549.i–ii. Oxford.

———. 2006. Greeks in Sicily. In *Greek Colonisation: An Account of Greek Colonies and Other Settlements Overseas*, ed. G. Tsetskhladze, 253–357. Leiden.

Doro Garetto, T., and M. Masali. 1976. I tre inciniti della tomba 497 di Kamarina-Rifriscolaro (VI sec. a.C.): Note antropologiche. *SicArch* ix,30: 51–60.

———. 1976–77. Prime osservazioni antropologiche sui reperti scheletrici della necropoli di Kamarina. *Kokalos* 22–23: 598–606.

Dougherty, C. 1993a. *The Poetics of Colonization: From City to Text in Archaic Greece.* Oxford.

———. 1993b. It's Murder to Found a Colony. In *Cultural Poetics in Archaic Greece: Cult, Performance, Politics,* ed. C. Dougherty and L. Kurke, 178–98. Cambridge.

———. 1994. Archaic Greek Foundation Poetry: Questions of Genre and Occasion. *JHS* 114: 35–46.

———. 2001. *The Raft of Odysseus: The Ethnographic Imagination of Homer's* Odyssey. Oxford.

Dougherty, C., and L. Kurke, eds. 2003. *The Cultures within Ancient Greek Culture: Contact, Conflict, Collaboration.* Cambridge.

———. 2003. Introduction: The Cultures within the Greek Culture. In *The Cultures within Ancient Greek Culture: Contact, Conflict, Collaboration,* ed. C. Dougherty and L. Kurke, 1–19. Cambridge.

Drakidès, D., E. Nantet, M. Gras, and A. Esposito. 2010. Échanges et circulations. In *La Méditerranée au VIIᵉ siècle av. J.-C.: Essais d'analyses archéologique,* ed. R. Étienne and A. Esposito, 91–146. Paris.

Drennan, R.D., and C.E. Peterson. 2006. Patterned Variation in Prehistoric Chiefdoms. *Proceedings of the National Academy of Sciences of the United States of America* 103.11: 3960–67.

Drews, R. 1983. *Basileus: The Evidence for Kingship in Geometric Greece.* New Haven, CT.

Drögemüller, H.-P. 1969. *Syrakus: Zur Topographie und Geschichte einer griechischen Stadt.* Heidelberg.

Dubois, L. 1989. *Inscriptions grecques dialectales de Sicile: Contribution à l'étude du vocabulaire grec colonial.* Vol. 1. Collection de l'École française de Rome Vol. 119. Rome.

———. 2008. *Inscriptions grecques dialectales de Sicile.* Vol. 2. Hautes Études du monde gréco-romain, Vol. 40. Geneva.

Dunbabin, T.J. 1938. Review of Pace 1938. *JHS* 58: 271–73.

———. 1948. *The Western Greeks: The History of Sicily from the Foundation of the Greek Colonies to 480 BC.* Oxford.

———. 1951. Review of Pace 1945. *JRS* 41: 179–81.

Duncan, A. 2012. A Thesues outside Athens: Dionysius I of Syracuse and the Tragic Self-representation. In *Theater Outside Athens: Drama in Greek Sicily and South Italy,* ed. K. Bosher, 137–55. Cambridge.

Dunst, G. 1972. Archaische Inschriften und Dokumente der Pentekontaetie aus Samos. *MDAI(A)* 87: 99–163.

Duplouy, A. 2002. L'aristocratie et la circulation des richesses: Apport de l'histoire économique à la définition des élites grecques. *Revue Belge de Philologie et d'Histoire* 80: 5–24.

———. 2006. *Le prestige des élites: Recherches sur les modes de reconnaissance sociale en Grèce entre les Xe e Ve siècles avant J.-C.* Paris.

Dyson, S.L. 2006. *In Pursuit of Ancient Pasts: A History of Classical Archaeology in the Nineteenth and Twentieth Centuries.* New Haven, CT.

Dyson, S.L., and R.J. Rowland, Jr. 2007. *Archaeology and History in Sardinia from the Stone Age to the Middle Ages: Shepherds, Sailors, and Conquerors.* Philadelphia.

Earle, T. 2000. Archaeology, Property, and Prehistory. *Annual Review of Anthropology* 29: 39–60.

Eckstein, F. 1974. *Handwerk: Die Aussagen des frühgriechischen Epos.* Vol. 1. Archaeologica Homerica, no. 2L. Göttingen.

Edmonds, J.M. 1957–61. *The Fragments of Attic Comedy after Meineke, Bergk, and Kock.* 4 vols. Leiden.

Egg, M. 1983. Ein eisenzeitlicher Weihefund aus Sizilien. *Jahrbuch des Römisch-Germanischen Zentralmuseums, Mainz* 30: 195–205.

Eidinow, E. 2007. *Oracles, Curses and Risk among the Ancient Greeks.* Oxford.

Elkins, C., and S. Pedersen. 2005. Introduction: Settler Colonialism; A Concept and Its Uses. In *Settler Colonialism in the Twentieth Century: Project, Practices, Legacies,* ed. C. Elkins and S. Pedersen, 1–20. New York.

Engen, D.T. 2010. *Honor and Profit: Athenian Trade Policy and the Economy and Society of Greece, 415–307 B.C.E.* Ann Arbor.

Epstein, S.R. 1992. *An Island for Itself: Economic Development and Social Change in Late Medieval Sicily.* Cambridge.

Erskine, A., ed. 2003. *A Companion to the Hellenistic World.* Oxford.

Etienne, R., C. Müller, and F. Prost. 2000. *Archéologie historique de la Grèce antique.* Paris.

Étienne, R., and A. Esposito, eds. 2010. *La Méditerranée au VIIe siècle av. J.-C. Essais d'analyses archéologique.* Paris.

Evans, R.J. 1997. *In Defence of History.* London.

Evans, R.J. 2009. *Syracuse in Antiquity: History and Topography.* Pretoria.

Fabbri, P.F. 2006. Appendice: Gli scheletri da due tombe della necropoli A di Entella (Palermo). In *Guerra e pace in Sicilia e nel Mediterraneo antico (VIII–III sec. a.C.): Arte, prassi e teoria della pace e della guerra. Atti delle quinte giornate internazionali di studi sull'area elima e la Sicilia Occidentale nel contesto Mediterraneo, Erice, 12–15 ottobre 2003,* ed. M.A. Vaggioli and C. Michelini, 515–20. Pisa.

Fabbri, P.F., R. Schettino, and S. Vassallo. 2006. Lo scavo delle sepolture della necropoli di Himera Pestavecchia (Palermo). In *Guerra e pace in Sicilia e nel Mediterraneo antico (VIII–III sec. a.C.): Arte, prassi e teoria della pace e della guerra. Atti delle quinte giornate internazionali di studi sull'area elima e la Sicilia Occidentale nel contesto Mediterraneo, Erice, 12–15 ottobre 2003,* ed. M.A. Vaggioli and C. Michelini, 613–20. Pisa.

Facchini, F., and P. Brasili Gualandi. 1977–79. I reperti scheletrici di età arcaica dalla necropoli di Castiglione (Ragusa) VII–VI sec. a.C. *Rivista di Antropologia (Rome)* 60: 113–158.

———. 1980. Reperti scheletrici della necropoli arcaica di Monte Casasia (Ragusa) (VII–VI sec. a.C.). *SE* 48: 253–75.

Falsone, G. 1994. Sicile. In *La civilization phénicienne et punique: Manuel de recherche*, ed. V. Krings, 674–97. Leiden.

Falsone, G., and G. Mannino. 1997. Le Finestrelle di Gibellina e di Poggioreale: Due necropoli rupestri nella valle del Belice. In *Seconde giornate internazionali di studi sull'area elima (Gibellina, 22–26 ottobre 1994): Atti*, ed. S. De Vido, 613–41. Pisa and Gibellina.

Fantasia, U. 1993. Grano siciliano in Grecia nel V e IV secolo. *ASNP* 23: 9–31.

———. 1999. Aree marginali nella Grecia antica: Paludi e bonifiche. In *Demografia, sistemi agrari, regimi alimentari nel mondo antico*, ed. D. Vera, 65–116. Bari.

———. 2003a. Per una storia degli studi sull'agricoltura e la storia agraria della Grecia antica. *QS* 57: 101–45.

———. 2003b. Entella, Etna, Galaria: Greci e non Greci in Sicilia fra Dionisio I e Timoleonte. In *Quarte giornate internazionali di studi sull'area elima (Erice, 1–4 dicembre 2000): Atti*, ed. A. Corretti, 467–95. Pisa.

———. 2006. Gli inizi della presenza campana in Sicilia. In *Guerra e pace in Sicilia e nel Mediterraneo antico (VIII–III sec. a.C.): Arte, prassi e teoria della pace e della guerra. Atti delle quinte giornate internazionali di studi sull'area elima e la Sicilia Occidentale nel contesto Mediterraneo, Erice, 12–15 ottobre 2003*, ed. M.A. Vaggioli and C. Michelini, 491–501. Pisa.

Faraguna, M. 1994. Alle origini dell'*oikonomia*: Dall'anonimo di Giamblico ad Aristotele. *RAL* 5: 551–89.

———. 2000. A proposito degli archivi nel mondo greco: Terra e registrazioni fondiarie. *Chiron* 30: 65–115.

Farris, W.W. 2004. *Japan to 1600: A Social and Economic History*. Honolulu.

Felici, E., and G. Buscemi Felici. 2004. Cave costiere nel territorio di Leontini. In *Leontini: Il mare, il fiume, la città. Atti della giornata di studio, Lentini, 4 maggio 2002*, ed. M. Frasca, 27–48. Catania.

Feyel, C. 1999. Aperçu sur le financement de la guerre dans la cité classique. In *Armées et sociétés de la Grèce classique: Aspects sociaux et politiques de la guerre aux Ve et IVe s. av. J.-C.*, ed. F. Prost, 209–21. Paris.

Finley, M.I. 1968. Il dibattito. In *La città e il suo territorio: Atti del settimo convegno di studi sulla Magna Grecia, Taranto 8–12 ottobre 1967*, ed. P. Romanelli, 186. Naples.

———. 1976. Colonies—An Attempt at a Typology. *Transactions of the Royal Historical Society* 26: 167–88.

———. 1979. *Ancient Sicily*. 2nd ed. London.

———. 1980. *Ancient Slavery and Modern Ideology*. London.

————. 1985a. *The Ancient Economy*. 2nd ed. Berkeley.

————. 1985b. *Ancient History: Evidence and Models*. London.

Fiorentini, G. 2005. Agrigento: La nuova area sacra sulle pendici dell'Acropoli. In Μεγάλαι νῆσοι: *Studi dedicati a Giovanni Rizza per il suo ottantesimo compleanno*, ed. R. Gigli, 2.147–65. Catania.

————. 2006. Le fortificazioni di Agrigento alla luce dei recent scavi. *Sicilia Antiqua* 3: 67–125.

————. 2009a. *Agrigento V: Le fortificazioni*. Rome.

————. 2009b. Il Ginnasio di Agrigento. *Sicilia Antiqua* 6: 71–109.

Fischer-Bossert, W. 2012. The Coinage of Sicily. In *The Oxford Handbook of Greek and Roman Coinage*, ed. W.E. Metcalf, 142–56. Oxford.

Fischer-Hansen, T. 1996. The Earliest Town Planning of the Western Greek Colonies, with Special Regard to Sicily. In *Introduction to an Inventory of Poleis: Symposium August 23–26 1995*, ed. M.H. Hansen, 317–73. Copenhagen.

————. 2000. *Ergasteria* in the Western Greek World. In *Polis & Politics: Studies in Ancient Greek History presented to Mogens Herman Hansen on his Sixtieth Birthday, August 20, 2000*, ed. P. Flensted-Jensen, T.H. Nielsen, and L. Rubinstein, 91–120. Copenhagen.

————. 2002. Reflections on Native Settlements in the Dominions of Gela and Akragas—as Seen from the Perspective of the Copenhagen Polis Centre. In *Even More Studies in the Ancient Greek Polis*, ed. T.H. Nielsen, 125–86. Stuttgart.

Fischer-Hansen, T., T.H. Nielsen, and C. Ampolo. 2004a. Sikelia. In *An Inventory of Archaic and Classical Poleis: An Investigation Conducted by the Copenhagen Polis Centre for the Danish National Research Foundation*, ed. M.H. Hansen and T.H. Nielsen, 172–248. Oxford.

Fischer-Hansen, T., T.H. Nielsen, and C. Ampolo. 2004b. Italia and Kampania. In *An Inventory of Archaic and Classical Poleis: An Investigation Conducted by the Copenhagen Polis Centre for the Danish National Research Foundation*, ed. M.H. Hansen and T.H. Nielsen, 249–320. Oxford.

Fitzjohn, M. 2007. Equality in the Colonies: Concepts of Equality in Sicily during the Eighth to Six [sic] Centuries BC. *World Archaeology* 39: 215–28.

Fletcher, R.N. 2004. Sidonians, Tyrians and Greeks in the Mediterranean: The Evidence from Egyptianising Amulets. *AWE* 3: 51–77.

————. 2007. *Patterns of Imports in Iron Age Italy*. BAR International Series, no. 1732. Oxford.

————. 2012. Opening the Mediterranean: Assyria, the Levant and the Transformation of Early Iron Age Trade. *Antiquity* 86: 211–20.

Foraboschi, D. 1984. Archeologia della cultura economica: Ricerche economiche ellenistiche. In *Studi ellenistici*. Vol. 1, ed. B. Virgilio, 75–105. Pisa.

Forbes, H. 1995. The Identification of Pastoralist Sites within the Context of Estate-based Agriculture in Ancient Greece: Beyond the 'Transhumance versus Agro-pastoralism' Debate. *BSA* 90: 325–38.

Forbes, H., and L. Foxhall. 2002. *Anonyma Therina*: Summer Crops in Theophrastus and in Modern Greece. In *Ancient History Matters: Studies Presented to Jens Erik Skydsgaard on his Seventieth Birthday*, ed. K. Ascani, V. Gabrielsen, K. Kvist, and A.H. Rasmussen, 87–100. Rome.

Fortunelli, S., and C. Masseria, eds. 2009. *Ceramica attica da santuari della Grecia, della Ionia e dell'Italia (Atti del Convegno Internazionale Perugia 14–17 marzo 2007)*. Venosa.

Fourmont, M.H. 1992. Les ateliers de Sélinonte (Sicile). In *Les ateliers de potiers dans le monde grecque aux époques géométrique, archaïque et classique*, ed. F. Blondé and J.Y. Perreault, 57–68. BCH Suppl. Vol. 23. Paris.

———. 1993. Un moule pour le travail du bronze à Selinonte. In *Studi sulla Sicilia Occidentale in onore di Vincenzo Tusa*, ed. J. de la Genière, M.L. Famà, G. Gullini, H.P. Isler, G. Nenci, and A. Spanò, 57–60. Padua.

Foxhall, L. 1990. The Dependent Tenant: Land Leasing and Labour in Italy and Greece. *JRS* 80: 97–114.

———. 1998. Cargoes of the Heart's Desire: The Character of Trade in the Archaic Mediterranean World. In *Archaic Greece: New Approaches and New Evidence*, ed. N. Fisher and H. Van Wees, 295–309. London.

———. 2002. Access to Resources in Classical Greece: The Egalitarianism of the Polis in Practice. In *Money, Labour and Land: Approaches to the Economies of Ancient Greece*, ed. P. Cartledge, E.E. Cohen, and L. Foxhall, 209–20. London.

———. 2003. Cultures, Landscapes, and Identities in the Mediterranean World. *MHR* 18.2: 56–74.

———. 2005. Village to City: Staples and Luxuries? Exchange Networks and Urbanization. In *Mediterranean Urbanization 800–600 BC*, ed. R. Osborne and B. Cunliffe, 233–48. Proceedings of the British Academy Vol. 126. Oxford.

———. 2007. *Olive Cultivation in Ancient Greece: Seeking the Ancient Economy*. Oxford.

Fracchia, H. 2005. Wine Production in Pre-Roman Italy: A Case Study. In *Geografia dell'alimentazione: Atti dell'Ottavo Seminario Internazionale di Geografia Medica (Roma, 16–18 dicembre 2004)*, ed. C. Palagiano and G. De Santis, 33–43. Perugia.

Frankel, R. 2003. The Olynthus Mill, Its Origin, and Diffusion: Typology and Distribution. *AJA* 107: 1–21.

Frasca, M. 1981. La necropoli di Monte Finocchito. *CdA* 20: 13–102.

———. 1983. Una nuova capanna «sicula» a Siracusa, in Ortigia: Tipologia dei materiali. *MEFRA* 95: 565–98.

———. 1996a. Iron Age Settlements and Cemeteries in Southeastern Sicily: An Introductory Survey. In *Early Societies in Sicily: New Developments in Archaeological Research*, ed. R. Leighton, 139–45. Accordia Specialist Studies on Italy, Vol. 5. London.

———. 1996b. *La necropoli greca di Monte S. Mauro di Caltagirone: Necropoli Saita e Primitivo*. Catania.

———. 2000a. Sull'urbanistica di Catania in età greca. In *Demarato: Studi di antichità classica offerti a Paola Pelagatti*, ed. I. Berlingò, H. Blanck, F. Cordano, P.G. Guzzo, and M.C. Lentini, 119–25. Milan.

————. 2000b. Monte Casasia: Un villaggio indigeno prima di Camarina. In *Un ponte fra l'Italia e la Grecia: Atti del simposio in onore di Antonino Di Vita, Ragusa, 13–15 febbraio 1998*, 143–47. Padua.

————. 2001a. L'agro netino nella protostoria: Insediamenti e distribuzione territoriale. In *Contributi alla geografia storica dell'agro netino: Atti delle giornate di studio, Noto, Palazzo Trigona, 29–30–31 maggio 1998*, ed. F. Balsamo and V. La Rosa, 47–54. Noto.

————. 2001b. Monte San Mauro di Caltagirone: Quattro tombe di un nucleo aristocratico nel VI secolo a.C. *BdA* 117: 1–26.

————. ed. 2004. *Leontini: Il mare, il fiume, la città. Atti della giornata di studio, Lentini, 4 maggio 2002*. Catania.

————. 2009. *Leontinoi: Archeologia di una colonia greca*. Rome.

————. 2010. Katáne: Il period protostorico e le prime fasi della colonia. In *Tra lava e mare: Contributi all'archaiologhia di Catania. Atti del Convegno, Catania, ex Monastero dei Benedettini, novembre 2007*, ed. M.G. Branciforti and V. La Rosa, 101–08. Catania.

Frederiksen, M.W. 1968. Campania Cavalry: A Question of Origins. *DdA* 2: 3–31.

Frederiksen, R. 1999. From Death to Life: The Cemetery of Fusco and the Reconstruction of Early Colonial Sicily. In *Ancient Greeks West and East*, ed. G.R. Tsetskhladze, 229–65. Leiden.

————. 2011. *Greek City Walls of the Archaic Period, 900–480 BC*. Oxford.

Freeman, E.A. 1891–94. *The History of Sicily: from the Earliest Times*. 4 vols. Oxford.

Frolov, E.D. 1986. Greki v Sitsilii [The Greeks in Sicily]. *Vestnik Leningradskogo gosudarstvennogo universiteta. Istoriia, Iazyk, i Literatura* 2: 18–26 (in Russian with English summary).

————. 1995. Gamoroi et Killyrioi. In *Esclavage et dépendance dans l'historiographie soviétique récente*, ed. M.M. Mactoux and E. Geny, 73–91. Besançon.

Frost, F.J. 1992. Staying Alive on the Ancient Greek Farm. *AHB* 6: 187–95.

————. 1999. Sausage and Meat Preservation in Antiquity. *GRBS* 40: 241–52.

Fuks, A. 1984. *Social Conflict in Ancient Greece*. Jerusalem.

Funke, P. 2006. Western Greece (Magna Graecia). In *A Companion to the Classical Greek World*, ed. K. Kinzl, 153–73. Oxford.

Gabba, E. 1981. E.A. Freeman e il federalismo antico. *ASNP* 11: 323–40.

Gabrici, E. 1927. Il santuario della Malophoros a Selinunte. *MAL* 32: 1–419.

————. 1936–37. Un lembo della necropoli di Imera. *Atti della Reale Accademia di Scienze, Lettere e Arti di Palermo* 20: 33–37.

Gaebel, R.E. 2002. *Cavalry Operations in the Ancient Greek World*. Norman.

Gagarin, M. 1986. *Early Greek Law*. Berkeley.

————. 2005. Early Greek Law. In *The Cambridge Companion to Ancient Greek Law*, ed. M. Gagarin and D. Cohen, 82–94. Cambridge.

Galaty, M.L., and C. Watkinson, eds. 2004. *Archaeology under Dictatorship*. New York.

Gallant, T. 1985. *A Fisherman's Tale: An Analysis of the Potential Productivity of Fishing in the Ancient World.* Gent.

——. 1991. *Risk and Survival in Ancient Greece: Reconstructing the Rural Domestic Economy.* Cambridge.

——. 2012. Long Time Coming, Long Time Gone: The Past, Present and Future of Social History. *Historein* 12: 9–20.

Gallo, L. 1982. Polyanthropia, eremia e mescolanza etnica in Sicilia: Il caso di Entella. *ASNP* 12: 917–44.

——. 1984. *Alimentazione e demografia della Grecia antica.* Salerno.

——. 1989. Produzione cerealicola e demografia siciliana. *AION* 11: 31–53.

——. 1992. La Sicilia occidentale e l'approvvigionamento cerealicolo di Roma. *ASNP* 22: 365–98.

——. 1997. Lo sfruttamento delle risorse. In *I greci: Storia, cultura, arte, società,* Vol. 2, pt. 2, ed. S. Settis, 423–52. Turin.

——. 2000. Le imposte dirette nelle poleis greche: un istituto tirannico? *Minima Epigraphica et Papyrologica* 3: 17–36.

——. 2001a. Le fonti letterarie sulle *chorai* coloniali. In *Problemi della chora coloniale dall'Occidente al Mar Nero: Atti del quarantesimo convegno di studi sulla Magna Grecia, Taranto, 29 settembre–3 ottobre 2000,* ed. A. Stazio, 49–71. Taranto.

——. 2001b. Appunti per una storia del sale nel mondo greco. In ΠΟΙΚΙΛΜΑ: *Studi in onore di Michele R. Cataudella in occasione del 60° compleanno,* ed. S. Bianchetti, E. Galvagno, A. Magnelli, G. Marasco, G. Mariotta, and I. Mastrorosa, 459–71. La Spezia.

——. 2009. L'*isomoiria*: Realtà o mito? In *Temi selinuntini,* ed. C. Antonetti and S. De Vido, 129–36. Pisa.

Galvagno, E. 2000. *Politica ed economia nella Sicilia greca.* Rome.

——. 2003. Diodoro e il territorio ibleo. *Quaderni Catanesi di Studi Antichi e Medievale* n.s. 2: 259–88.

——. 2005. I Sicelioti tra Cartagine e Roma. In *Greci, Fenici, Romani: Interazioni culturali nel Mediterraneo antico,* ed. S.F. Bondì and M. Vallozza, 97–125. Viterbo.

——. 2006. I Siculi: Fine di un ethnos. In *Diodoro Siculo e la Sicilia indigena: Atti del Convegno di studi, Caltanissetta, 21–22 maggio 2005,* ed. C. Miccichè, S. Modeo, and L. Santagati, 34–50. Palermo.

Garfinkle, S.J. 2007. The Assyrians: A New Look at an Ancient Power. In *Current Issues and the Study of the Ancient Near East,* ed. M.W. Chavalas, 53–96. Publications of the Association of Ancient Historians, no. 8. Claremont, CA.

Garlan, Y. 1989. *Guerre et économie en Grèce ancienne.* Paris.

Garnsey, P. 1988. *Famine and Food Supply in the Graeco-Roman World: Responses to Risk and Crisis.* Cambridge.

Garraffo, S. 1984. *Le riconiazioni in Magna Grecia e in Sicilia: Emissioni argentee dal VI al IV secolo a.C.* Catania.

———. 1993. La monetazione dell'età dionigiana: Contromarche e riconiazioni. In *La monetazione dell'età dionigiana: Atti dell'VIII Convegno Internazionale di Studi Numismatici—Napoli 29 maggio–1 giugno 1983*, ed. A. Stazio, M. Taliercio Mensiteri, and S. Ceccoli, 191–242. Rome.

Gasparri, L. 2008. Considerazioni sull'inizio della monetazione calcidese in Sicilia. *NAC* 37: 39–58.

———. 2009. Greci e non Greci in Sicilia: Note sulla coroplastica greca arcaica nelle necropoli indigene e puniche. In *Obeloi: Contatti, scambi e valori nel Mediterraneo antico; Studi offerti a Nicola Parise*, ed. F. Camia and S. Privitera, 153–74. Paestum and Athens.

Genovese, P. 1977a. Testimonianze archeologiche e paletnologiche nel bacino del Longano. *SicArch* x,33: 9–37.

———. 1977b. Il centro fortificato (sicano-greco) di M.te S. Onofrio. *SicArch* x,33: 39–54.

Gentili, G.V. 1956. Naxos alla luce dei primi scavi. *BdA* 41: 326–33.

Ghedini, F., J. Bonetto, A.R. Ghiotto, and F. Rinaldi, eds. 2005. *Lo stretto di Messina nell'antichità*. Rome.

Ghinatti, F. 2000. Le organizzazioni civiche siceliote. *Kokalos* 46: 31–73.

———. 2003. Per un comprensione delle feste della Sicilia occidentale. In *Quarte giornate internazionali di studi sull'area elima (Erice, 1–4 dicembre 2000): Atti*, ed. A. Corretti, 693–718. Pisa.

Giacopini, L., B. Belelli Marchesini, and L. Rustico. 1994. *L'itticoltura nell'antichità*. Rome.

Gianfrotta, P.A. 1999. Archeologia subacquea e testimonianze di pesca. *MEFRA* 111: 9–36.

———. 2005. I rinvenimenti subacquei. In *Lo stretto di Messina nell'antichità*, ed. F. Ghedini, J. Bonetto, A.R. Ghiotto, and F. Rinaldi, 143–57. Rome.

Giangiulio, M. 2001. L'*eschatia*. Prospettive critiche su rappresentazioni antiche e modelli moderni. In *Problemi della chora coloniale dall'Occidente al Mar Nero: Atti del quarantesimo convegno di studi sulla Magna Grecia, Taranto, 29 settembre–3 ottobre 2000*, ed. A. Stazio, 333–61. Taranto.

———. 2010. Deconstructing Ethnicities: Multiple Identities in Archaic and Classical Greek Sicily. *BABesch* 85: 13–23.

Giannitrapani, E. 1997. Rapporti tra la Sicilia e Malta durante l'età del bronzo. In *Prima Sicilia: Alle origini della società siciliana*, ed. S. Tusa, 429–44. Palermo.

———. 1998. Public Archaeology and Prehistory in Sicily. *Antiquity* 72: 739–43.

Giardino, G. 1995. *Il Mediterraneo Occidentale fra XIV ed VIII secolo a.C.: Cerchie minerarie e metallurgiche*. BAR International Series Vol. 612. Oxford.

———. 1996. Miniere e techniche metallurgiche nella Sicilia protostorica: Nuove linee di ricerca. In *Early Societies in Sicily: New Developments in Archaeological Research*, ed. R. Leighton, 129–38. Accordia Specialist Studies on Italy, Vol. 5. London.

—. 1997. La metallotecnica nella Sicilia pre-protostorica. In *Prima Sicilia: Alle origini della società siciliana*, ed. S. Tusa, 405–14. Palermo.

—. 2005. Metallurgy in Italy between the Late Bronze Age and the Early Iron Age: The Coming of Iron. In *Papers in Italian Archaeology VI: Communities and Settlements from the Neolithic to the Early Medieval Period*, ed. P. Attema, Λ. Nijboer, and A. Zifferero, 491–505. BAR International Series Vol. 1452. Oxford.

Gibson, M. 1998. Biology or Environment? Race and Southern "Deviancy" in the Writings of the Italian Criminologists, 1880–1920. In *Italy's "Southern Question": Orientalism in One Country*, ed. J. Schneider, 99–115. Oxford.

Gill, D.W.J. 2004. Euesperides: Cyrenaica and its Contacts with the Greek World. In *Greek Identity in the Western Mediterranean: Papers in Honour of Brian Shefton*, ed. K. Lomas, 391–409. Mnemosyne Suppl. Vol. 246. Leiden.

Gilman, A. 1998. Reconstructing Property Systems from Archaeological Evidence. In *Property in Economic Context*, ed. R.C. Hunt and A. Gilman, 215–33. Lanham, MD.

Giudice, F. 1985. Gela e il commercio attico verso l'Etruria nel primo quarto del V sec. a.C. *SE* 53: 115–39.

—. 1996a. Il ruolo di Catania nella rete dei traffici commerciali del Mediterraneo. In *Catania antica*, ed. B. Gentili, 97–148. Pisa.

—. 1996b. La ceramografia attica in Sicilia nel VI sec. a.C.: Problemi e metodologie. In *I vasi attici ed altre ceramiche coeve in Sicilia: Atti del convegno internazionale Catania, Camarina, Gela, Vittoria, 28 marzo–1 aprile 1990*, ed. G. Rizza and F. Giudice, Vol. 2, 199–210. CdA 30 (1991). Catania.

—. 2002. La ceramica attica del IV secolo a.C. in Sicilia ed il problema della formazione delle officine locali. In *La Sicilia dei due Dionisî: Atti della settimana di studio, Agrigento, 24–28 febbraio 1999*, ed. N. Bonacasa, L. Braccesi, and E. De Miro, 169–201. Rome.

—. 2006. La ceramica attica del IV secolo e i clienti delle due Sicilie. In *Les clients de la céramique grecque : Actes du colloque de l'Académie des Inscriptions et Belles-Lettres, Paris, 30–31 janvier 2004*, ed. J. de la Genière, 93–95. Paris.

Giudice, F., and V.G. Rizzone. 2000. Le importazioni attiche a Camarina: Considerazioni preliminari. In *Demarato: Studi di antichità classica offerti a Paola Pelagatti*, ed. I. Berlingò, H. Blanck, F. Cordano, P.G. Guzzo, and M.C. Lentini, 301–14. Milan.

Giudice, G. 2007. *Il tornio, la nave e le terre lontane: Ceramografici attici in Magna Grecia nella seconda metà del V sec. a.C.; Rotte e vie di distribuzione*. Rome.

Giuffrida, M. 2002. I Dionisî e l'area calcidese. In *La Sicilia dei due Dionisî: Atti della settimana di studio, Agrigento, 24–28 febbraio 1999*, ed. N. Bonacasa, L. Braccesi, and E. De Miro, 417–26. Rome.

Giuliani, A. 1995. Le migrazioni forzate in Sicilia e in Magna Grecia sotto Dionigi I di Siracusa. In *Coercizione e mobilità umana nel mondo antico*, ed. M. Sordi, 107–24. Milan.

Given, M. 2004. *The Archaeology of the Colonized*. London.

Gleba, M. 2008. *Textile Production in Pre-Roman Italy*. Oxford.

Golden, M. 1998. *Sport and Society in Ancient Greece*. Cambridge.

Goldsmith, R.W. 1987. *Premodern Financial Systems: A Historical Comparative Study*. Cambridge.

González de Canales, F., L. Serrano, and J. Llompart. 2006. The Pre-colonial Phoenician Emporium of Huelva ca 900–770 BC. *BABesch* 81: 13–29.

González-Ruibal, A. 2004. Facing Two Seas: Mediterranean and Atlantic Contacts in the North-west of Iberia in the First Millennium BC. *OJA* 23: 287–317.

Gorini, G. 2002. La monetazione dionigiana in Adriatico: Sue sopravvivenze e implicazioni sociali. In *La Sicilia dei due Dionisî: Atti della settimana di studio, Agrigento, 24–28 febbraio 1999*, ed. N. Bonacasa, L. Braccesi, and E. De Miro, 203–15. Rome.

Gorton, A.F. 1996. *Egyptian and Egyptianising Scarabs: A Typology of Steatite, Faience and Paste Scarabs from Punic and other Mediterranean Sites*. Oxford University Committee for Archaeology Vol. 44. Oxford.

Gosden, C. 2004. *Archaeology and Colonialism: Culture Contact from 5000 BC to the Present*. Cambridge.

Graham, A.J. 1984. Commercial Interchanges between Greeks and Natives. *The Ancient World* 10: 3–10.

———. 1988. Megara Hyblaea and the Sicels. In *Mestnye etno-političeskie ob"edinenija Pričernomor'ja v VII–IV vv. do n.e.: Materialy IV Vsesojuznogo simpoziuma po drevnej istorii Pričernomor'ja, Cchaltubo-Vani, 1985* [(reprinted in *Collected Papers on Greek Colonization* [Leiden, 2001] 149-64). *Local Ethno-Political Entities of the Black Sea Area in the 7th–4th Centuries BC: Materials of the 4th All-Union Symposium Dedicated to the Problems of the Ancient History of the Black Sea Littoral Tsqaltubo-Vani—1985*], ed. O. Lordkipanidze, 304–21. Tbilisi.

Grande Dizionario della Lingua Italiana Moderna. 1998. Colonialismo. In Vol. 1, *A–D*, 656. Cernusco sul Naviglio.

Grant, M. 1992. *The Visible Past: Greek and Roman History from Archaeology 1960–1990*. New York.

Gras, M. 1985. *Trafics tyrrhéniens archaïques*. BEFAR Vol. 258. Rome.

———. 1989. L'economia. In *Un secolo di ricerche in Magna Grecia: Atti del ventottesimo convegno di studi sulla Magna Grecia, Taranto, 7–12 ottobre 1998*, ed. G. Pugliese Carratelli, 395–420. Taranto.

———. 1991. Occidentalia : Le concept d'émigration ionienne. *ArchClass* 43: 269–78.

———. 1993. Pour une Méditerranée des *emporia*. In *L'emporion*, ed. A. Bresson and P. Rouillard, 103–12. Paris.

———. 1995. *La Méditerranée archaïque*. Paris.

———. 1996. Les grands courants commerciaux : Époques archaïque et classique. In *La Magna Grecia e il mare: Studi di storia marittima*, ed. F. Prontera, 121–44. Taranto.

———. 2000a. La Sicile, l'Afrique et les ἐμπόρια. In *Demarato: Studi di antichità classica offerti a Paola Pelagatti*, ed. I. Berlingò, H. Blanck, F. Cordano, P.G. Guzzo, and M.C. Lentini, 130–34. Milan.

————. 2000b. Donner du sens à l'objet: Archéologie, technologie culturelle et anthropologie. *AnnalesESC* 55: 601–14.

————. 2000c. Fra storia greca e storia dei Greci. *QS* 51: 227–31.

————. 2002a. Périples culturels entre Carthage, la Grèce et la Sicile au VIIIe siècle av. J.-C. In *Identités et cultures dans le monde méditerranéen antique en l'honneur de Francis Croissant*, ed. C. Müller and F. Prost, 183–98. Paris.

————. 2002b. L'urbanisme de Zancle. In *Messina e Reggio nell'antichità: Storia, società, cultura. Atti del Convegno della S.I.S.A.C. (Messina–Reggio Calabria 24–26 maggio 1999)*, ed. B. Gentili and A. Pinzone, 13–24. Messina.

————. 2005. Il commercio in età arcaica e classica. In *Lo stretto di Messina nell'antichità*, ed. F. Ghedini, J. Bonetto, A.R. Ghiotto, and F. Rinaldi, 159–63. Rome.

————. 2006–07. Mégara Hyblaea et la naissance de l'urbanisme grec en Occident. *Rendiconti della Pontifica Accademia Romana di Archeologia* 79: 3–11.

————. 2007. Guardare al passato pensando al futuro. In *Passato e futuro dei convegni di Taranto: Atti del quarantaseiesimo convegno di studi sulla Magna Grecia, Taranto 29 settembre–1 ottobre 2006*, ed. A. Stazio and S. Ceccoli, 15–36. Taranto.

————. 2011. Conclusioni. In *La vigna di Dionisio: Vite, vino e culti in Magna Grecia. Atti del quarantanovesimo Convegno di Studi sulla Magna Grecia, Taranto, 24–28 settembre 2009*, ed. M. Lombardo et al., 563–68. Taranto.

Gras, M., E. Greco, and P.G. Guzzo, eds. 2000. *Nel cuore del Mediterraneo antico: Reggio, Messina e le colonie calcidesi dell'area dello Stretto*. Corigliano Calabro.

Gras, M., P. Rouillard, and J. Teixidor. 1995. *L'univers phénicien*. 2nd ed. Paris.

Gras, M., and H. Tréziny. 2012. Mégara Hyblaea: Le domande e le risposte. In *Alle origini della Magna Grecia: Mobilità, migrazioni, fondazioni. Atti del cinquantesimo Convegno di Studi sulla Magna Grecia, Taranto 1–4 ottobre 2010*, ed. M. Lombardo et al., 1131–47. Taranto.

Gras, M., H. Tréziny, and H. Broise. 2004. *Mégara Hyblaea 5: La ville archaïque: L'espace urbain d'une cité grecque de Sicile orientale*. Mélanges d'Archéologie et d'Histoire, Suppl. 1/5. Rome.

Graßl, H. 1985. Zur Geschichte des Viehhandels im klassichen Griechenland. *Münsterische Beiträge zur antiken Handelsgeschichte* 4: 77–88.

Gray, D. 1974. *Seewesen*. Archaeologica Homerica, no. 1G. Göttingen.

Greco, C. 1997. Nuovi elementi per l'identificazione di Solunto arcaica. In *Wohnbauforschung in Zentral- und Westsizilien: Sicilia occidentale e centro-meridionale; ricerche archeologiche nell'abitato (Zürich, 28. Februar–3. März 1996). Akten der Forschungstagung/Atti delle giornate di studio sul tema*, ed. H.P. Isler, D. Käch, and O. Stefani, 97–111. Zürich.

Greco, E. 1998. Agora eumeghetes: L'espace public dans les *poleis* d'Occident. *Ktema* 23: 153–58.

————. 2001. Abitare in campagna. In *Problemi della chora coloniale dall'Occidente al Mar Nero: Atti del quarantesimo convegno di studi sulla Magna Grecia, Taranto, 29 settembre–3 ottobre 2000*, ed. A. Stazio, 171–201. Taranto.

————. 2006. Greek Colonisation in Southern Italy: A Methodological Essay. In *Greek Colonisation: An Account of Greek Colonies and Other Settlements Overseas*, ed. G. Tsetskhladze, 169–200. Leiden.

————. 2007. Dialogo tra storici ed archeologi: Spunti per una discussione. In *Passato e futuro dei convegni di Taranto: Atti del quarantaseiesimo convegno di studi sulla Magna Grecia, Taranto 29 settembre–1 ottobre 2006*, ed. A. Stazio and S. Ceccoli, 61–77. Taranto.

————. 2012. Il dibattito. In *Alle origini della Magna Grecia: Mobilità, migrazioni, fondazioni. Atti del cinquantesimo Convegno di Studi sulla Magna Grecia, Taranto 1–4 ottobre 2010*, ed. M. Lombardo et al., 1174. Taranto.

Greco, E., and M. Lombardo, eds. 2007. *Atene e l'Occidente: I grandi temi, le premesse, i protagonisti, le forme della communicazione e dell'interazione, i modi dell'intervento ateniese in Occidente. Atti del Convegno Internazionale, Atene 25–27 maggio 2006*. Athens.

Green, S.W. 1980. Towards a General Model of Agricultural Systems. In *Advances in Archaeological Method and Theory*. Vol. 3, ed. M.B. Schiffer, 311–55. New York.

Griffo, P. 1964–65. Recenti scavi archeologici in Sicilia: Problemi e risultati. *Kokalos* 10–11: 135–68.

Grigg, D.B. 1983. *The Dynamics of Agricultural Change: The Historical Experience.* New York.

Grote, G. 1846–56. *A History of Greece*. 12 vols. London.

Grotta, C. 2008. Le iscrizioni. In *Himera*. Vol. 5, *L'abitato: Isolato II. I blocchi 1–4 della Zona 1*, ed. N. Allegro, 255–72. Palermo.

————. 2010. *Zeus Meilichios a Selinunte*. Rome.

Gruzinski, S., and A. Rouveret. 1976. «Ellos son como niños»: Histoire et acculturation dans le monde Mexique colonial et l'Italie méridionale avant la romanisation *MEFRA* 88: 159–219.

Guglielmino, R. 1994. La necropoli di Entella. In *Nécropoles et sociétés antiques (Grèce, Italie, Languedoc)*, ed. J. de la Genière, 203–19. Naples.

————. 2006. Corredi tombali di tipo italico da Entella. In *Guerra e pace in Sicilia e nel Mediterraneo antico (VIII–III sec. a.C.): Arte, prassi e teoria della pace e della guerra. Atti delle quinte giornate internazionali di studi sull'area elima e la Sicilia Occidentale nel contesto Mediterraneo, Erice, 12–15 ottobre 2003*, ed. M.A. Vaggioli and C. Michelini, 503–13. Pisa.

Guidi, A. 1988. *Storia della paletnologia*. Rome.

————. 1998. The Emergence of the State in Central and Northern Italy. *Acta Archaeologica* 69: 139–61.

————. 2002. An Italian Perspective. In *Archäologien Europas: Geschichte, Methoden und Theorien/Archaeologies of Europe: History, Methods and Theories*, ed. P.F. Biehl, A. Gramsch, and A. Marciniak, 353–60. Münster.

Gula, C. 1995. *Storia di Leontinoi: Dalle origini alla conquista romana*. Catania.

Gulletta, M.I. 2006. Kamikos/Lykos/Halykos: Da 'via del sale' a 'confine' tra le due eparchie (note di geografia storica nella Sicilia centro-occidentale). In *"Troianer sind wir gewesen"—Migrationen in der antiken Welt: Stuttgarter Kolloquium zur Historischen Geographie des Altertums 8, 2002*, ed. E. Olshausen and H. Sonnabend, 402–19. Stuttgart.

Gullì, D. 2000. Nuove indagini e nuove scoperte nella media e bassa valle del Platani. *QuadMess* 1: 139–77.

———. 2003. Recenti scavi a Monte Roveto e Rocca Ficarazze di Casteltermini (AG). In *Archeologia del Mediterraneo: Studi in onore di Ernesto De Miro*, ed. G. Fiorentini, M. Caltabiano, and A. Calderone, 375–99. Rome.

Guzzardi, L. 1991. Importazioni dal Vicino Oriente in Sicilia fino all'età orientalizzante. In *Atti del II Congresso Internazionale di Studi Fenici e Punici, Roma, 9–14 novembre 1987*. Vol.3, ed. E. Acquaro et al., 941–54. Rome.

———. 2001. Il territorio di Noto nel periodo greco. In *Contributi alla geografia storica dell'agro netino: Atti delle giornate di studio, Noto, Palazzo Trigona, 29–30–31 maggio 1998*, ed. F. Balsamo and V. La Rosa, 97–109. Noto.

Guzzardi, L., and B. Basile. 1996. Il Capo Pachino nell'antichità. In *La Magna Grecia e il mare: Studi di storia marittima*, ed. F. Prontera, 189–226. Taranto.

Guzzo, P.G. 2003. Sul mito di Sibari. *BABesch* 78: 221–23.

Haagsma, M., P. den Boer, and E.M. Moormann, eds. 2003. *The Impact of Classical Greece on European and National Identities: Proceedings of an International Colloquium, Held at the Netherlands Institute at Athens, 2–4 October 2000*. Amsterdam.

Habermann, W. 1987. IG I^3 386/387, sizilische Häute und die athenisch-sizilischen Handelsbeziehungen im 5. Jahrh. v. Chr. *Münsterische Beiträge zur antiken Handelsgeschichte* 6: 89–113.

Habicht, C. 1997. *Athens from Alexander to Antony*. Trans. D. Lucas Schneider. Cambridge, MA.

Hall, J.M. 2002. *Hellenicity: Between Ethnicity and Culture*. Chicago.

———. 2003. 'Culture' or 'Cultures'? Hellenism in the Late Sixth Century. In *The Cultures within Ancient Greek Culture: Contact, Conflict, Collaboration*, ed. C. Dougherty and L. Kurke, 23–34. Cambridge.

———. 2004. Culture, Cultures and Acculturation. In *Griechische Archaik: Interne Entwicklungen—Externe Impulse*, ed. R. Rollinger and C. Ulf, 33–50. Innsbruck.

———. 2007a. The Creation and Expression of Identity. In *Classical Archaeology*, ed. S.E. Alcock and R. Osborne, 337–59. Oxford.

———. 2007b. *A History of the Archaic Greek World ca. 1200–479 BCE*. Oxford.

———. 2012. Early Greek Settlement in the West: The Limits of Colonialism. In *Theater Outside Athens: Drama in Greek Sicily and South Italy*, ed. K. Bosher, 19–34. Cambridge.

Halstead, P. 1987. Traditional and Ancient Rural Economy in Mediterranean Europe: Plus ça Change? *JHS* 107: 77–87. Reprinted in Scheidel and von Reden 2002, 53–70.

Halstead, P., and G. Jones. 1989. Agrarian Ecology in the Greek Islands: Time Stress, Scale, and Risk. *JHS* 109: 41–55.

Hannestad, L. 1996. Athenian Pottery in Italy c. 550–470: Beazley and Quantitative Studies. In *I vasi attici ed altre ceramiche coeve in Sicilia: Atti del convegno internazionale Catania, Camarina, Gela, Vittoria, 28 marzo–1 aprile 1990*, ed. G. Rizza and F. Giudice, Vol. 2, 211–16. CdA 30 (1991). Catania.

Hans, L.-M. 1983. *Karthago und Sizilien*. Hildesheim.

Hansen, M.H. 2003. 95 Theses about the Greek Polis in the Archaic and Classical Periods: A Report on the Results Obtained by the Copenhagen Polis Centre in the Period 1993–2003. *Historia* 52: 257–82.

———. 2006a. *Polis: An Introduction to the Ancient Greek City-state*. Oxford.

———. 2006b. *The Shotgun Method: The Demography of the Ancient Greek City-state Culture*. Columbia, MO.

———. 2008a. Analyzing Cities. In *The Ancient City: New Perspectives on Urbanism in the Old and New Worlds*, ed. J. Marcus and J.A. Sabloff, 67–76. Santa Fe.

———. 2008b. An Update on the Shotgun Method. *GRBS* 48: 259–86.

Hansen, M.H., and T.H. Nielsen, eds. 2004. *An Inventory of Archaic and Classical Poleis: An Investigation Conducted by the Copenhagen Polis Centre for the Danish National Research Foundation*. Oxford.

Hanson, V.D. 1995. *The Other Greeks: The Family Farm and the Agrarian Roots of Western Civilization*. New York.

Harari, M. 2002. Tirreno e Adriatico: Mari paralleli. *Padusa* 38: 19–27.

Härke, H. 1991. All Quiet of the Western Front? Paradigms, Methods, and Approaches in West German Archaeology. In *Archaeological Theory in Europe: The Last Three Decades*, ed. I. Hodder, 187–222. London.

Harrell, S.E. 2002. King or Private Citizen: Fifth-century Sicilian Tyrants at Olympia and Delphi. *Mnemosyne* 55: 439–64.

———. 2006. Synchronicity: The Local and the Panhellenic within Sicilian Tyranny. In *Ancient Tyranny*, ed. S. Lewis, 119–34. Edinburgh.

Harris, R.C. 1977. The Simplification of Europe Overseas. *Annals of the Association of American Geographers* 67: 469–83.

———. 1997. *The Resettlement of British Columbia: Essays on Colonialism and Geographical Change*. Vancouver.

Harris, W.V. 1996. Writing and Literacy in the Archaic Greek City. In ΕΝΕΡΓΕΙΑ: *Studies on Ancient History and Epigraphy presented to H.W. Pleket*, ed. J.H.M. Strubbe, R.A. Tybout, and H.S. Versnel, 57–77. Amsterdam.

———, ed. 2005. *Rethinking the Mediterranean*. Oxford.

Hawke, G.R. 1980. *Economics for Historians*. Cambridge.

Helas, S. 2011. Der politische Anspruch Karthagos auf Westsizilien. Mittel und Wege der Machtsicherung. In *Krise und Wandel: Süditalien im 4. und 3. Jahrhundert v. Chr.*, ed R. Neudecker, 175–91. Wiesbaden.

Helly, B. 1997. Sur les fratrai de Camarina. *PdP* 52: 365–406.

Hendon, J.A. 1996. Archaeological Approaches to the Organization of Domestic Labor: Household Practices and Domestic Relations. *Annual Review of Anthropology* 25: 45–61.

Herring, E. 1998. *Explaining Change in the Matt-Painted Pottery of Southern Italy*. BAR International Series Vol. 722. Oxford.

Hinz, V. 1998. *Der Kult von Demeter und Kore auf Sizilien und in der Magna Graecia*. Wiesbaden.

Hobson, J.M. 2004. *The Eastern Origins of Western Civilisation*. Cambridge.

Hochholzer, H. 1935. Historische Kulturgeographie des großgriechischen Sizilien. *Klio* 28: 85–107.

———. 1936. Zur Geographie des antiken Syrakus. *Klio* 29: 164–72.

Höcker, C. 1985–86. Die klassichen Ringhallentempel von Agrigent: Überlegungen zu Bauplanung und Arbeitsorganisation bei der Errichtung dorischer Tempel in Bauwesen Westgriechenlands im 5. Jh. v. Chr. *Hephaistos* 7–8: 233–47.

———. 1993. *Planung und Konzeption der klassischen Ringhallentempel von Agrigent: Überlegungen zur Rekonstruktion von Bauentwurfen des 5. Jhs. v. Chr.* Frankfurt am Main.

———. 1996. Architekur als Metapher: Überlegung zur Bedeutung des dorischen Ringhallentempels. *Hephaistos* 14: 45–79.

Höckmann, O. 2001. Etruskische Schiffahrt. *Jahrbuch des Römisch-Germanischen Zentralmuseums, Mainz* 48: 227–308.

Hodder, I. 1991. Archaeological Theory in Contemporary European Societies: The Emergence of Competing Traditions. In *Archaeological Theory in Europe: The Last Three Decades*, ed. I. Hodder, 1–24. London.

Hodkinson, S. 1988. Animal Husbandry in the Greek Polis. In *Pastoral Economies in Classical Antiquity*, ed. C.R. Whittaker, 35–74. PCPhS Suppl. Vol. 14. Cambridge.

———. 1990–91. Politics as a Determinant of Pastoralism: The Case of Southern Greece, ca. 800–300 B.C. *Rivista di Studi Liguri* 56: 139–63.

Hodos, T. 1999. Intermarriage in the Western Greek Colonies. *OJA* 18: 61–78.

———. 2000. Wine Wares in Protohistoric Eastern Sicily. In *Sicily from Aeneas to Augustus: New Approaches in Archaeology and History*, ed. C.J. Smith and J. Serrati, 41–54. Edinburgh.

———. 2005. Changing Communities in Iron Age Sicily. In *Papers in Italian Archaeology VI: Communities and Settlements from the Neolithic to the Early Medieval Period*, ed. P. Attema, A. Nijboer, and A. Zifferero, 103–08. BAR International Series Vol. 1452. Oxford.

———. 2006. *Local Responses to Colonization in the Iron Age Mediterranean*. London.

Hofer, M. 2000. *Tyrannen, Aristokraten, Demokraten: Untersuchungen zu Staat und Herrschaft im griechischen Sizilien von Phalaris bis zum Aufstieg von Dionysios I.* Frankfurt am Main.

Hölkeskamp, K.-J. 1999. *Schiedsrichter, Gesetzgeber und Gesetzgebung im archaischen Griechenland*. Historia Suppl. Vol. 131. Stuttgart.

Holloway, R.R. 1979. L'inizio della monetazione in bronzo siracusana. In *Le origini della monetazione di bronzo in Sicilia e in Magna Grecia: Atti del VI Convegno del Centro Internazionale di Studi Numismatici—Napoli 17–22 aprile 1977*, ed. A. Stazio, 123–41. Rome.

———. 1990. The Geography of the Southern Sicels. In EYMOYΣIA: *Ceramic and Iconographic Studies in Honour of Alexander Cambitoglou*, ed. J.-P. Descoeudres, 147–53. Sydney.

———. 1991. *The Archaeology of Ancient Sicily*. London.

Holm, A. 1871. *Geografia antica della Sicilia*. Trans. P.M. Latino. Palermo.

———. 1896–1906. *Storia della Sicilia nell'antichità*. 3 vols. Trans. G. Kirner. Turin.

———. 1906. *Storia della moneta siciliana fino all'età di Augusto*. Trans. G. Kirner. Turin.

———. 1925. *Catania antica*. Trans. G. Libertini. Catania.

Hölscher, T. 2007. Urban Spaces and Central Spaces. In *Classical Archaeology*, ed. S.E. Alcock and R. Osborne, 164–81. Oxford.

Hornblower, S. 2006. Pindar and Kingship Theory. In *Ancient Tyranny*, ed. S. Lewis, 151–63. Edinburgh.

———. 2011. *The Greek World 479–323 BC*. 4th ed. London.

Hornblower, S., and C. Morgan. 2007. Introduction. In *Pindar's Poetry, Patrons, and Festivals: From Archaic Greece to the Roman Empire*, ed. S. Hornblower and C. Morgan, 1–43. Oxford.

Hornig, K. 2005–06. Zu Amphoren aus Unterwasser-Fundkontexten—Entwurf eines Funddatenblattes. *Skyllis* 7: 116–25.

Horster, M. 2003. *Landbesitz griechischer Heiligtuemer in archaischer und klassischer Zeit*. Berlin.

Horden P., and N. Purcell. 2000. *The Corrupting Sea: A Study of Mediterranean History*. Oxford.

———. 2005. Four Years of Corruption: A Response to Critics. In *Rethinking the Mediterranean*, ed. W.V. Harris, 348–75. Oxford.

Howe, T. 2008. *Pastoral Politics: Animals, Agriculture and Society in Ancient Greece*. Publications of the Association of Ancient Historians, no. 9. Claremont, CA.

Humphrey, G., and S. Hugh-Jones, eds. 1992. *Barter, Exchange and Value: An Anthropological Approach*. Cambridge.

Humphreys, S.C. 1965. Il commercio in quanto motivo della colonizzazione greca dell'Italia e della Sicilia. *Rivista Storica Italiana* 77: 421–33.

Hurst, H., and S. Owen, eds. 2005. *Ancient Colonizations: Analogy, Similarity and Difference*. London.

Iacovou, M. 2008. Cyprus: From Migration to Hellenisation. In *Greek Colonisation*. Vol. 2, *An Account of Greek Colonies and Other Settlements Overseas*, ed. G. Tsetskhladze, 219–88. Leiden.

Iannucci, A. 1998. Callimaco e la "discordia" degli ecisti di Zancle (Call. *Aet.* 2.43.73 Pf = *P.Oxy.* 2080 col. 2.73). *Sileno* 24: 173–79.

Inglieri, R.U. 1957. Casmene ritrovata? *ArchClass* 9: 223–33.

Ingoglia, C. 2003. Archeologia urbana a Messina: lo scavo dell'isolato "P" in Via La Farina—Via Oddo delle Colonne (rapporto preliminare). *QuadMess* 4: 83–105.

———. 2012. La Valle del Patrì: Un corridoio obbligato tra Tirreno e Ionio? In *Cultura e religione delle acque*, ed. A. Calderone, 247–69. Rome.

Isager, S., and J.E. Skydsgaard. 1992. *Ancient Greek Agriculture: An Introduction.* London.

Isler, H. 2003. *Bouleuteria* di Sicilia. In *Archeologia del Mediterraneo: Studi in onore di Ernesto De Miro,* ed. G. Fiorentini, M. Caltabiano, and A. Calderone, 429–33. Rome.

Isserlin, B.S.J. 1982. Motya: Urban Features. In *Phönizier im Westen,* ed. II.G. Niemeyer, 113–27. Madrider Beiträge 8. Mainz.

Isserlin, B.S.J., and J. Du Plat Taylor. 1974. *Motya: A Phoenician and Carthaginian City in Sicily.* Vol. 1. Leiden.

Jackman, T. 2005. Political Communities in the Greek Colonies of Sicily and Southern Italy. PhD thesis, Stanford University.

———. 2006. Ducetius and Fifth-century Sicilian Tyranny. In *Ancient Tyranny,* ed. S. Lewis, 33–48. Edinburgh.

Jacobs, J. 1969. *The Economy of Cities.* New York.

———. 1984. *Cities and the Wealth of Nations: Principles of Economic Life.* New York.

Jacquemin, A. 1993. Oikiste et tyran: Fondateur-monarque et monarque-fondateur dans l'Occident grec. *Ktema* 18: 19–27.

Jameson, M. 1988. Sacrifice and Animal Husbandry in Classical Greece. In *Pastoral Economies in Classical Antiquity,* ed. C.R. Whittaker, 87–119. PCPhS Suppl. Vol. 14. Cambridge.

———. 1994. Class in the Ancient Greek Countryside. In *Structures rurales et sociétés antiques: Actes du colloque de Corfou (14–16 mai 1992),* ed. P.N. Doukellis and L.G. Mendoni, 55–63. Paris.

Jameson, M.H., and I. Malkin. 1998. Latinos and the Greeks. *Athenaeum* 86: 477–85.

Jameson, M.H., D.R. Jordan, and R.D. Kotansky. 1993. *A Lex Sacra from Selinous.* GRBS monograph 11. Durham, NC.

Jenkins, G.K. 1976. *Coins of Greek Sicily.* 2nd ed. London.

———. 1979. The Fifth Century Bronze Coins of Gela and Kamarina. In *Le origini della monetazione di bronzo in Sicilia e in Magna Grecia: Atti del VI Convegno del Centro Internazionale di Studi Numismatici—Napoli 17–22 aprile 1977,* ed. A. Stazio, 181–89. Rome.

Johnson, M. 1999. *Archaeological Theory: An Introduction.* Oxford.

Johnston, A.W. 1993–94. Emporia, Emporoi and Sicilians: Some Epigraphical Aspects. *Kokalos* 39–40: 155–69.

———. 1996. Fifth Century Prices. In *I vasi attici ed altre ceramiche coeve in Sicilia: Atti del convegno internazionale Catania, Camarina, Gela, Vittoria, 28 marzo–1 aprile 1990,* ed. G. Rizza and F. Giudice, Vol. 2, 81–87. CdA 30 (1991). Catania.

———. 1999. Ceramic Texts, Archaic to Hellenistic. In *Sicilia epigraphica: Atti del convegno internazionale, Erice, 15–18 ottobre 1998,* ed. M.I. Gulletta, 407–15. ASNP Quaderni 7–8. Pisa.

———. 2006. *Trademarks on Greek Vases: Addenda.* Oxford.

Judson, S. 1963. Stream Changes during Historic Time in East-central Sicily. *AJA* 67: 287–89.

Junker, K. 2003. Die Reliefmetopen des Heratempels in Selinunt: Mythoskritik und der Wandel des Sagenbildes im 5. Jh. v. Chr. *MDAI(R)* 110: 227–61.

Karlsson, L. 1989. Some Notes on the Fortifications of Greek Sicily. *Opuscula Romana* 17: 77–89.

———. 1992. *Fortification Towers and Masonry Techniques in the Hegemony of Syracuse, 405–211 BC.* Skrifter utgivna av Svenska Institutet i Rom, Vol. 49. Stockholm.

Kassianidou, V. 2001. Cypriot Copper in Sardinia: Yet Another Case of Bringing Coals to Newcastle? In *Italy and Cyprus in Antiquity: 1500–450 BC*, ed. L. Bonfante and V. Karageorghis, 97–119. Nicosia.

Kassianidou, V., and A.B. Knapp. 2005. Archaeometallurgy in the Mediterranean: The Social Context of Mining, Technology, and Trade. In *The Archaeology of Mediterranean Prehistory*, ed. E. Blake and A.B. Knapp, 215–51. Oxford.

Kelley, O. 2012. Beyond Intermarriage: The Role of the Indigenous Italic Population at Pithekoussai. *OJA* 31: 245–60.

Kenzler, U. 1999. *Studien zur Entwicklung und Struktur der griechischen Agora in archäischer und klassischer Zeit.* Frankfurt am Main.

Kilian, K. 1975. Trachtzubehör der Eisenzeit zwischen Ägäis und Adria. *Prähistorische Zeitschrift* 50: 9–140.

———. 1983. Oggetti dell'ornamento personale caratteristici in Bosnia e Macedonia, loro divulgazione in Grecia ed in Italia durante l'età del Ferro. In *L'Adriatico tra Mediterraneo e penisola balcanica nell'antichità: Atti del Congresso dell'Associazione Internazionale di Studi del Sud-Est Europeo, Lecce-Matera 21-27 ottobre 1973*, 61–65. Taranto.

Kim, H.S. 2001. Archaic Coinage as Evidence for the Use of Money. In *Money and Its Uses in the Ancient Greek World*, ed. A. Meadows and K. Shipton, 7–21. Oxford.

King. R. 1973. *Sicily.* The Islands Series. Newton Abbot.

———. 1975. *Sardinia.* The Islands Series. Newton Abbot.

Kleibrink, M. 2001. The Search for Sybaris: An Evaluation of Historical and Archaeological Evidence. *BABesch* 76: 33–70.

Klug, R.D. 2013. *Griechische Transportamphoren im regionalen und überregionalen Handel: Untersuchungen in griechischen und nicht-griechischen Kontexten in Unteritalien und Sizilien vom 8. bis zum 5. Jh. v. Chr.* Rahden.

Knapp, A.B. 2008. *Prehistoric and Protohistoric Cyprus: Identity, Insularity, and Connectivity.* Oxford.

Knapp, A.B., and E. Blake. 2005. Prehistory in the Mediterranean: The Connecting and Corrupting Sea. In *The Archaeology of Mediterranean Prehistory*, ed. E. Blake and A.B. Knapp, 1–23. Oxford.

Knoepfler, D. 1992. La chronologie du monnayage de Syracuse sous les Deinomènides: Nouvelles données et critères méconnus. *SNR* 71: 5–41.

———. 2007. Was There an Anthroponymy of Euboian Origin in the Chalkido-Eretrian Colonies of the West and of Thrace? *PBA* 148: 87–119.

Kolb, M.J. 2005. The Genesis of Monuments among the Mediterranean Islands. In *The Archaeology of Mediterranean Prehistory*, ed. E. Blake and A.B. Knapp, 156–79. Oxford.

Kopytoff, I. 1982. Slavery. *Annual Review of Anthropology* 11: 207–30.

Kotsakis, K. 1991. The Powerful Past: Theoretical Trends in Greek Archaeology. In *Archaeological Theory in Europe: The Last Three Decades*, ed. I. Hodder, 65–90. London.

Kowalzig, B. 2008. Nothing to do with Demeter? Something to do with Sicily! Theatre and Society in the Early Fifth-century West. In *Performance, Iconography, Reception: Studies in Honour of Oliver Taplin*, ed. M. Revermann and P. Wilson, 128–57. Oxford.

Kraay, C.M. 1979. The Bronze Coinage of Himera and 'Himera.' In *Le origini della monetazione di bronzo in Sicilia e in Magna Grecia: Atti del VI Convegno del Centro Internazionale di Studi Numismatici—Napoli 17–22 aprile 1977*, ed. A. Stazio, 27–47. Rome.

Krasilnikoff, J.A. 1995. The Power Base of Sicilian Tyrants. In *Ancient Sicily*, ed. T. Fischer-Hansen, 171–84. Acta Hyperborea Vol. 6. Copenhagen.

———. 2002. Water and Farming in Classical Greece: Evidence, Method and Perspective. In *Ancient History Matters: Studies Presented to Jens Erik Skydsgaard on His Seventieth Birthday*, ed. K. Ascani, V. Gabrielsen, K. Kvist, and A.H. Rasmussen, 48–62. Rome.

Krings, V., ed. 1994. *La civilisation phénicienne et punique: Manuel de recherche.* Leiden.

Kristiansen, K., and T.B. Larsson. 2005. *The Rise of Bronze Age Society: Travels, Transmissions and Transformations.* Cambridge.

Kroll, J.H. 2008. The Monetary Use of Weighed Bullion in Archaic Greece. In *The Monetary Systems of the Greeks and Romans*, ed. W.V. Harris, 12–37. Oxford.

———. 2012. The Monetary Background of Early Coinage. In *The Oxford Handbook of Greek and Roman Coinage*, ed. W.E. Metcalf, 33–42. Oxford.

Kron, G. 2002. Archaeozoological Evidence for the Productivity of Roman Livestock Farming. *Münstersche Beiträge zur Antiken Handelsgeschichte* 21.2: 53–73.

———. 2005. Anthropometry, Physical Anthropology, and the Reconstruction of Ancient Health, Nutrition, and Living Standards. *Historia* 54: 68–83.

Kron, U. 1992. Frauenfeste in Demeterheiligtümern: Das Thesmophorion von Bitalemi. Eine archäologische Fallstudie. *AA*: 611–50.

———. 1998. Sickles in Greek Sanctuaries: Votives and Cultic Instruments. In *Ancient Greek Cult Practice from the Archaeological Evidence: Proceedings of the Fourth International Seminar on Ancient Greek Cult, Organized by the Swedish Institute at Athens, 22–24 October 1993*, ed. R. Hägg, 187–216. Stockholm.

Kurke, L. 1999. *Coins, Bodies, Games, and Gold: The Politics of Meaning in Archaic Greece.* Princeton.

Kustermann Graf, A. 2002. *Selinunte: Necropoli di Manicalunga; le tombe della contrada Gaggera.* Soveria Mannelli.

Lacroix, L. 1965. *Monnaies et colonisation dans l'Occident grec.* Brussels.

———. 1979. La typologie du bronze par rapport a celle de l'argent. In *Le origini della monetazione di bronzo in Sicilia e in Magna Grecia: Atti del VI Convegno del Centro*

Internazionale di Studi Numismatici—Napoli 17–22 aprile 1977, ed. A. Stazio, 265–86. Rome.

La Fauci, F. 2004. Rinvenimenti archeologici sottomarini ad Agnone e Punta Castelluccio. In *Leontini: Il mare, il fiume, la città. Atti della giornata di studio, Lentini, 4 maggio 2002*, ed. M. Frasca, 21–26. Catania.

Lagona, S. 1996. Catania: Il problema del porto antico. In *Catania antica*, ed. B. Gentili, 223–30. Pisa.

Lamboley, J.-L. 1993. Etat de la recherche sur les relations sud-adriatiques: Bilan et perspectives. In *L'Illyrie méridionale et l'Epire dans l'antiquité, 2. Actes du IIe Colloque International de Clermont-Ferrand, 25–27 octobre 1990*, ed. P. Cabanes, 231–37. Paris.

———. 1996. *Les Grecs d'Occident: La période archaïque*. Paris.

Lancel, S. 1995. *Carthage: A History*. Trans. A. Nevill. Oxford.

Lane Fox, R. 2008. *Travelling Heroes: Greeks and their Myths in the Epic Age of Homer*. London.

Lang, F. 2002. Housing and Settlement in Archaic Greece. *Pallas* 58: 13–32.

La Rosa, V., ed. 1986. *L'archeologia italiana nel Mediterraneo fino alla seconda Guerra mondiale*. Catania.

———. 1987. "Archaiologhia" e storiografia: Quale Sicilia? In *Storia d'Italia Regioni dall'unità a oggi: La Sicilia*, ed. M. Aymard and G. Giarrizzo, 701–31. Turin.

———. 1989. Le popolazioni della Sicilia: Sicani, Siculi, Elimi. In *Italia omnium terrarum parens: La civiltà degli Enotri, Choni, Ausoni, Sanniti, Lucani, Bretti, Sicani, Siculi, Elimi*, ed. G. Pugliese Carratelli, 1–110. Milan.

———. 1993–94. Influenze di tipo egeo e paleogreco in Sicilia. *Kokalos* 39–40: 9–47.

———. 1996. Il Monte Saraceno di Ravanusa. *ArchStorSicO* 92: 193–97.

———. 1997. Per una storia degli studi. In *Prima Sicilia: Alle origini della società siciliana*, ed. S. Tusa, 7–30. Palermo.

La Torre, G.F. 2004. Il processo di «romanizzazione» della Sicilia: Il caso di Tindari. *Sicilia Antiqua* 1: 111–46.

Lauro, D. 1999. Il complesso collinare di Montagnola della Borrania (TP): (F. 257 IV SE, Borgo Fazio). *Kokalos* 45: 157–271.

Lawall, M. 2006. Consuming the West in the East: Amphoras of the western Mediterranean in Athens before 86. In *Old Pottery in a New Century: Innovating Perspectives on Roman Pottery Studies, Catania 22–24 April, Catania*, ed. D. Malfitana, J. Poblome, and J. Lund, 265–86. Rome.

Lazzarini, L. 2003. Monete arcaiche inedite di Selinunte e nuove considerazioni sul tipo della foglia. *NAC* 32: 11–22.

———. 2004. I primi oboli di Selinunte arcaica. *SNR* 83: 17–26.

———. 2009. Nota sull'*aes grave* di Selinunte. In *Temi selinuntini*, ed. C. Antonetti and S. De Vido, 159–75. Pisa.

Lehmler, C. 2005. *Syrakus unter Agathokles und Hieron II: Die Verbindung von Kultur und Macht in einer hellenistischen Metropole*. Frankfurt am Main.

Leighton, R. 1985. Evidence, Extent and Effects of Mycenaean Contacts with Southeast Sicily during the late Bronze Age. In *Papers in Italian Archaeology* IV: *The Cambridge Conference*, ed. C. Malone and S. Stoddart, 399–412. BAR International Series. Oxford.

———. 1986. Paolo Orsi (1859–1935) and the Prehistory of Sicily. *Antiquity* 60: 15–20.

———. 1993. Sicily during the Centuries of Darkness. *CAJ* 3: 271–76.

———. ed., 1996a. *Early Societies in Sicily: New Developments in Archaeological Research*. Accordia Specialist Studies on Italy, Vol. 5. London.

———. 1996b. Research Traditions, Chronology and Current Issues: An Introduction. In *Early Societies in Sicily: New Developments in Archaeological Research*, ed. R. Leighton, 1–19. Accordia Specialist Studies on Italy, Vol. 5. London.

———. 1996c. From Chiefdom to Tribe? Social Organisation and Change in Later Prehistory. In *Early Societies in Sicily: New Developments in Archaeological Research*, ed. R. Leighton, 101–16. Accordia Specialist Studies on Italy, Vol. 5. London.

———. 1999. *Sicily before History*. London.

———. 2000a. Indigenous Society between the Ninth and Sixth Centuries BC: Territorial, Urban and Social Evolution. In *Sicily from Aeneas to Augustus: New Approaches in Archaeology and History*, ed. C.J. Smith and J. Serrati, 15–40. Edinburgh.

———. 2000b. Time versus Tradition: Iron Age Chronologies in Sicily and Southern Italy. In *Ancient Italy in Its Mediterranean Setting: Studies in Honour of Ellen Macnamara*, ed. D. Ridgway et al., 33–48. Accordia Specialist Studies on the Mediterranean Vol. 4. London.

———. 2005. Later Prehistoric Settlement in Sicily: Old Paradigms and New Surveys. *European Journal of Archaeology* 8.3: 261–87.

———. 2011. Pantalica (Sicily) from the Late Bronze Age to the Middle Ages: A New Survey and Interpretation of Rock-cut Monuments. *AJA* 115: 447–64.

Lejeune, M. 1980. Observations linguistiques sur le nouveau matériel épigraphique de Géla. In Φιλίας χάριν: *Miscellanea di studi classici in onore di Eugenio Manni*, 1309–15. Rome.

Lemon, M.C. 2003. *Philosophy of History: A Guide for Students*. London.

Lemos, I.S. 2002. *The Protogeometric Aegean: The Archaeology of the Late Eleventh and Tenth Centuries BC*. Oxford.

Lentini, M.C. 1998. Nuovi rinvenimenti di ceramica euboica a Naxos di Sicilia. In *Euboica: L'Eubea e la presenza euboica in Calcidica e in Occidente*, ed. M. Bats and B. D'Agostino, 377–86. Naples.

———. 2010. Naxos tra Egeo e Sicilia: Ricerche nel più antico abitato coloniale (scavi 2003–2006). In *Immagine e immagini della Sicilia e di altre isole del Mediterraneano antico: Atti delle seste giornate internazionale di studi sull'area elima e la Sicilia occidentale nel contesto mediterraneo, Erice 12–16 ottobre 2006*, ed. C. Ampolo, 519–28. Pisa.

Lentini, M.C., S. Savelli, and D.J. Blackman. 2005–06. Amphorae from the Slipways of the Ancient Dockyard of Naxos in Sicily. *Skyllis* 7: 94–102.

Lentini, M.C., M.G. Vanaria, and M.C. Martinelli. 2008–09. Messina: Stratigrafia di una città; Resti dell'antico tessuto urbano in Piazza Duomo (campagna di scavi 2005–2006). *NSc* 19–20: 359–420.

Lepore, E. 1968. Per una fenomenologia storica del rapporto città-territorio in Magna Grecia. In *La città e il suo territorio: Atti del settimo convegno di studi sulla Magna Grecia, Taranto 8–12 ottobre 1967*, ed. P. Romanelli, 29–66. Naples.

———. 1970. Classi e ordini in Magna Grecia. In *Recherches sur les structures sociales dans l'antiquité classique, Caen 25–26 avril 1969*, ed. C. Nicolet, 43–62. Paris.

———. 1973. Problemi dell'organizzazione della chora coloniale. In *Problèmes de la terre en Grèce ancienne*, ed. M.I. Finley, 15–47. Paris.

———. 1990. Parallelismi, riflessi e incidenza degli avvenimenti del contesto mediterraneo in Italia. In *Crise et transformation des sociétés archaïques de l'Italie antique au V⁰ siècle av. J.-C.*, ed. F.-H. Massa-Pairault, 289–97. Rome.

———. 2000. *La Grande Grèce: Aspects et problèmes d'une «colonisation» ancienne. Quatre conférences au Collège de France (1982)*. Naples.

Lewis, D.M. 1994. Sicily, 413–368 B.C. In *The Cambridge Ancient History*. Vol. 6, *The Fourth Century B.C.*, ed. D.M. Lewis, J. Boardman, S. Hornblower, and M. Ostwald, 120–55. 2nd ed. Cambridge.

Lewis, S., ed. 2006. *Ancient Tyranny*. Edinburgh.

Lightfoot, K.G., and A. Martinez. 1995. Frontiers and Boundaries in Archaeological Perspective. *Annual Review of Anthropology* 24: 471–92.

Lomas, K. 2000. The Polis in Italy: Ethnicity, Colonization, and Citizenship in the Western Mediterranean. In *Alternatives to Athens: Varieties of Political Organization and Community in Ancient Greece*, ed. R. Brock and S. Hodkinson, 167–85. Oxford.

———. 2006. Tyrants and the *Polis*: Migration, Identity and Urban Development in Sicily. In *Ancient Tyranny*, ed. S. Lewis, 95–118. Edinburgh.

Lombardo, M. 1996. Greci e 'indigeni' in Italia meridionale nel IV secolo a.C. In *Le IV⁰ siècle av. J.-C.: Approches historiographiques*, ed. P. Carlier, 205–22. Nancy.

———. 1997a. Schiavitù e «oikos» nella società coloniali magnogreche da Smindiride ad Archita. In *Schiavi e dipendenti nell'ambito dell'«oikos» e della «familia»: Atti del XXII Colloquio GIREA Pontignano (Siena) 19–20 novembre 1995*, ed. M. Moggi and G. Cordiano, 19–43. Pisa.

———. 1997b. Circolazione monetaria e attività tra VI e IV secolo. In *I greci: Storia, cultura, arte, società*, Vol 2, pt. 2, ed. S. Settis, 681–706. Turin.

———. 2002. La colonizzazione adriatica in età dionigiana. In *La Sicilia dei due Dionisî: Atti della settimana di studio, Agrigento, 24–28 febbraio 1999*, ed. N. Bonacasa, L. Braccesi, and E. De Miro, 427–42. Rome.

———. 2004. Poleis e politeiai nel mondo 'coloniale'. In *Poleis e politeiai: Esperienze politiche, tradizioni letterarie, progetti constituzionali*, ed. S. Cataldi, 351–68. Turin.

———. 2009. Da apoikiai a metropoleis: Dal progetto al convegno. In *Colonie di colonie: Le fondazioni sub-coloniali tra colonizzazione e colonialismo. Atti del convegno internazionale, Lecce, 22–24 giugno 2006*, ed. M. Lombardo and F. Frisone, 17–30. Galatina.

Lombardo, M., F. Aversa, and F. Frisone. 2001. La documentazione epigrafica. In *Problemi della chora coloniale dall'Occidente al Mar Nero: Atti del quarantesimo convegno di studi sulla Magna Grecia, Taranto, 29 settembre–3 ottobre 2000*, ed. A. Stazio, 73–152. Taranto.

Lombardo, M. et al., eds. 2012. *Alle origini della Magna Grecia: Mobilità, migrazioni, fondazioni. Atti del cinquantesimo Convegno di Studi sulla Magna Grecia, Taranto 1–4 ottobre 2010*. Taranto.

Lomiento, L. 2006. Pindaro Olimpica V e Camarina: Una nuova proposta di datazione. In *Camarina: 2600 anni dopo la fondazione. Atti del Convegno Internazionale*, ed. P. Pelagatti, G. Di Stefano, and L. De Lachenal, 285–93. Rome.

López Castro, J.L. 2000. Carthage and Mediterranean Trade in the Far West (800–200 B.C.). *Rivista di Studi Punici* 1: 123–44.

———. 2006. Colonials, Merchants and Alabaster Vases: The Western Phoenician Aristocracy. *Antiquity* 80: 74–88.

Lo Presti, L.G. 2000. Gela e l'entroterra tra il VII e VI secolo a.C. *Kokalos* 46: 365–80.

Lo Schiavo, F. 2000. Sea and Sardinia: Nuragic Bronze Boats. In *Ancient Italy in its Mediterranean Setting: Studies in Honour of Ellen Macnamara*, ed. D. Ridgway et al., 141–58. Accordia Specialist Studies on the Mediterranean Vol. 4. London.

———. 2001. Late Cypriot Bronzework and Bronzeworkers in Sardinia, Italy and elsewhere in the West. In *Italy and Cyprus in Antiquity: 1500–450 BC*, ed. L. Bonfante and V. Karageorghis, 131–52. Nicosia.

Lo Schiavo, F., E. Macnamara, and L. Vagnetti. 1985. Late Cypriot Imports to Italy and their Influence on Local Bronzework. *PBSR* 53: 1–71.

Lubtchansky, N. 2006. Cavaliers siciliens : Contribution à l'étude sur la formation des traditions équestres dans la Sicile archaïque. In *Les équidés dans le monde méditerranéen antiques : Actes du colloque organisé par l'École Française d'Athènes, le Centre Camille Julien, et l'UMR 5140 du CNRS, 26–28 novembre 2003*, ed. A. Gardeisen, 219–31. Paris.

Lucchelli, T. 2009. L'adozione della moneta a Selinunte: Contesti e interazioni. In *Temi selinuntini*, ed. C. Antonetti and S. De Vido, 177–91. Pisa.

Luraghi, N. 1994. *Tirannidi arcaiche in Sicilia e Magna Grecia: Da Panezio di Leontini alla caduta dei Dinomenidi*. Florence.

———. 1995. Review of Dougherty 1993. *Storia della Storiografia* 27: 147–52.

———. 1996. Partage du sol et occupation de territoire dans les colonies grecques d'Occident au VIIIe siècle. In *Les moyens d'expression du pouvoir dans les sociétés anciennes*, ed. M. Broze, P.-J. Dehon, P. Talon, T. Van Compernolle, and E. Warmenbol, 213–19. Leuven.

———. 2006. Traders, Pirates, Warriors: The Proto-History of Greek Mercenary Soldiers in the Eastern Mediterranean. *Phoenix* 60: 21–47.

Ma, J. 2009. Afterword: Whither the Athenian Empire? In *Interpreting the Athenian Empire*, ed. J. Ma, N. Papazarkadas, and R. Parker, 223–31. London.

Macaluso, R. 2008a. Note sull'uso del bronzo scambiato a peso e sulla circolazione monetaria a Himera. In *Himera*. Vol. 5, *L'abitato: Isolato II. I blocchi 1–4 della Zona 1*, ed. N. Allegro, 273–81. Palermo.

———. 2008b. *La Sicilia e la moneta: Dai mezzi di scambio premonetari alla coniazione in argento dell'unità ponderale indigena*. Kokalos Suppl. Vol. 20. Pisa.

Macgregor Morris, I. 2008. Navigating the *Grotesque*; or, Rethinking Greek Historiography. In *Reinventing History: The Enlightenment Origins of Ancient History*, ed. J. Moore, I. Macgregor Morris, and A.J. Bayliss, 247–90. London.

Mack Smith, D. 1968. *Modern Sicily: After 1713*. London.

MacKinnon, M. 2007. State of the Discipline: Osteological Research in Classical Archaeology. *AJA* 111: 473–504.

Maddoli, G. 1980. Il VI e V secolo a.C. In *La Sicilia antica*, ed. E. Gabba and G. Vallet, Vol. 2, pt.1, 1–102. Naples.

Mafodda, G. 1996. *La monarchia di Gelone tra pragmatismo, ideologia e propaganda*. Messina.

———. 1998. Tiranni ed indigeni di Sicilia in età arcaica tra schiavitù, guerra e mercenariato. In *Hesperìa: Studi sulla grecità di occidente*, ed. L. Braccesi, Vol. 9, 19–31. Rome.

———. 1999. Tiranni sicelioti ed indigeni in età arcaica. In *Magna Grecia e Sicilia: Stato degli studi e prospettive di ricerca; atti dell'incontro di studi, Messina, 2–4 dicembre 1996*, ed. M. Barra Bagnasco, E. De Miro, and A. Pinzone, 313–19. Messina.

———. 2000. Transazioni economiche e relazioni diplomatiche tra Roma e Gela al tempo della tirannide di Gelone. *Kokalos* 46: 253–59.

Malkin, I. 1987. *Religion and Colonization in Ancient Greece*. Leiden.

———. 1994. Inside and Outside: Colonisation and the Formation of the Mother City. In *AΠOIKIA: I più antichi insediamenti greci in Occidente; funzioni e modi dell'organizzazione politica e sociale. Scritti in onore di Giorgio Buchner*, ed. B. D'Agostino and D. Ridgway, 1–9. AION ns 1. Naples.

———. 1998. *The Returns of Odysseus: Colonization and Ethnicity*. Berkeley.

———. 2002a. A Colonial Middle Ground: Greek, Etruscan, and Local Elites in the Bay of Naples. In *The Archaeology of Colonialism*, ed. C.L. Lyons and J.K. Papadopoulos, 151–81. Malibu,CA.

———. 2002b. Exploring the Validity of the Concept of "Foundation": A Visit to Megara Hyblaia. In *Oikistes: Studies in Constitutions, Colonies, and Military Power in the Ancient World, Offered in Honor of A.J. Graham*, ed. V.B. Gorman and E.W. Robinson, 195–225. Leiden.

———. 2004. Postcolonial Concepts and Ancient Greek Colonization. *Modern Language Quarterly* 65.3: 341–64.

———. 2009. Foundations. In *A Companion to Archaic Greece*, ed. K.A. Raaflaub and H. van Wees, 373–94. Oxford.

————. 2011. *A Small Greek World: Networks in the Ancient Mediterranean*. Oxford.

Malone, C., and S. Stoddart. 2004. Towards an Island of Mind? In *Explaining Social Change: Studies in Honour of Colin Renfrew*, ed. J. Cherry, C. Scarre, and S. Shennan, 93–102. Cambridge.

Malone, C., S. Stoddart, and R. Whitehouse. 1994. The Bronze Age of Southern Italy Sicily and Malta *c*. 2000–800 B.C. In *Development and Decline in the Mediterranean Bronze Age*, ed. C. Mathers and S. Stoddart, 167–94. Sheffield.

Manfredi, L.I. 1992. Le saline e il sale nel mondo punico. *RSF* 20: 3–14.

Manganaro, G. 1965. Ricerche di antichità e di epigrafia siceliote. *ArchClass* 17: 183–210.

————. 1979. L'età greca. In *La Sicilia nella storiografia dell'ultimo tretennio: Atti del Congresso di Mazara*, ed. G. Di Stefano, 3–22. Mazara del Vallo.

————. 1990. Due studi di numismatica greca. *ASNP* 20: 409–27.

————. 1992. Istituzioni pubbliche e culti religiosi. In *Agrigento e la Sicilia greca: Atti della settimana di studio, Agrigento 2–8 maggio 1988*, ed. L. Braccesi and E. De Miro, 207–18. Rome.

————. 1995. *Sikelika* I. *QUCC* 49: 93–109.

————. 1996a. La monetazione di Katane dal V al I sec. a.C. In *Catania antica*, ed. B. Gentili, 303–29. Pisa.

————. 1996b. Raffigurazioni di fauna e flora nella monetazione, in bronzetti e su anelli della Sicilia greca. In *Stuttgarter Kolloquium zur historischen Geographie des Altertums 5,1993: "Gebirgsland als Lebensraum,"* ed. E. Olshausen and H. Sonnabend, 215–22. Amsterdam.

————. 1996c. Figurazioni e dediche religiose della Sicilia greca e romana. *ZPE* 113: 77–81.

————. 1996d. Una nota su chora e polis in Sicilia. In *Atti delle giornate di studio sugli insediamenti rurali nella Sicilia, Caltagirone 1992*, ed. S. Lagona, 53–55. Aitna: Quaderni di Topografia Vol. 2. Catania.

————. 1999. La Syrakosion Dekate, Camarina e Morgantina nel 424 a.C. *ZPE* 128: 115–23.

————. 2000. Revisione di un'iscrizione di Segesta e di un decreto frammentario di Himera. In *Terze giornate internazionali di studi sull'area elima (Gibellina, Erice, Contessa Entellina, 23–26 ottobre 1997): Atti*, ed. S. De Vido, 747–53. Pisa.

Manni, E. 1969. La Sicile à la veille de la colonisation grecque. *REA* 71: 5–22.

————. 1977. La Sicilia antica nella storiografia straniera degli ultimi cento anni. In *La presenza della Sicilia nella cultura degli ultimi cento anni*, 19–31. Palermo.

————. 1981. *Geografia fisica e politica della Sicilia antica*. Kokalos Suppl. Vol. 4. Rome.

————. 1984–85. La Sicilia e il mondo greco arcaico fino alla fine del VI secolo a.C.: L'apporto della ierologia. *Kokalos* 30–31: 165–87.

————. 1987. Brani di storia di Camarina arcaica. *Kokalos* 33: 67–76.

Manning, S.W., and L. Hulin. 2005. Maritime Commerce and Geographies of Mobility in the Late Bronze Age of the Eastern Mediterranean: Problematizations. In *The

Archaeology of Mediterranean Prehistory, ed. E. Blake and A.B. Knapp, 270–302. Oxford.

Mannoni, T., and E. Giannichedda. 1996. *Archeologia della produzione*. Turin.

Marcaccini, C. 1999. Spunti per una nuova interpretazione della figura del basileus in Grecia arcaica. *Athenaeum* 87: 395–424.

Marchiandi, D. 2007. Kallipos di Axione, un Ateniese tiranno di Siracusa e la tomba della sua famiglia al Pireo. In *Atene e l'Occidente: I grandi temi, le premesse, i protagonisti, le forme della communicazione e dell'interazione, i modi dell'intervento ateniese in Occidente. Atti del Convegno Internazionale, Atene 25–27 maggio 2006*, ed. E. Greco and M. Lombardo, 481–509. Athens.

Marcone, A. 2010. L'agricoltura antica: Progresso antico, sviluppo economico e letteratura scientifica. *Technai* 1: 13–21.

Marconi, C. 1994. *Selinunte: Le metope dell'Heraion*. Modena.

———. 2004. Images for a Warrior: On a Group of Athenian Vases and their Public. In *Greek Vases: Images, Contexts and Controversies*, ed. C. Marconi, 27–40. Leiden.

———. 2010. Orgoglio e pregiudizio: La connoisseurship della scultura in marmo dell'Italia meridionale e della Sicilia. In *Scolpire il marmo: Importazioni, artisti itineranti, scuole artistiche nel Mediterraneo antico. Atti del Convegno di studio tenuto a Pisa Scuola Normale Superiore, 9–11 novembre 2009*, ed. G. Adornato, 339–59. Pisa.

———. 2012. Sicily and South Italy. In *A Companion to Greek Art*, ed. T.J. Smith and D. Plantzos, Vol. 1, 369–96. Oxford.

Marconi, P. 1929a. Studi agrigentini. *RIA* 1: 29–68, 185–231, 293–324.

———. 1929b. *Agrigento: Topografia ed arte*. Florence.

———. 1933. *Agrigento arcaica: Il santuario delle divinità chtonie e il tempio detto di Vulcano*. Rome.

Marincola, J. 2001. *Greek Historians*. Oxford.

Markoe, G.E. 2000. *Phoenicians*. London.

Marazzi, M. 1997. I contatti transmarine nella preistoria siciliana. In *Prima Sicilia: Alle origini della società siciliana*, ed. S. Tusa, 365–74. Palermo.

Marilli, E. 2004. Il bacino del fiume San Leonardo: Il paesaggio fluviale. In *Leontini: Il mare, il fiume, la città. Atti della giornata di studio, Lentini, 4 maggio 2002*, ed. M. Frasca, 55–70. Catania.

Martin, L. 1990. Greek Godesses and Grain: The Sicilian Connection. *Helios* 17: 251–61.

Martin, R. 1973. Aspects financiers et sociaux des programmes de construction dans les villes grecques de Grand Grèce et de Sicile. In *Economia e società nella Magna Grecia: Atti del dodicesimo convegno di studi sulla Magna Grecia, Taranto, 8–14 ottobre 1972*, ed. P. Romanelli, 185–205. Naples.

Martin, R., P. Pelagatti, G. Vallet, and G. Voza. 1980. Le città greche. In *La Sicilia antica*, ed. E. Gabba and G. Vallet, Vol. 1, pt. 3, 483–705. Naples.

Martin, R., P. Pelagatti, and G. Vallet. 1980. Alcune osservazioni sulla cultura materiale. In *La Sicilia antica*, ed. E. Gabba and G. Vallet, Vol. 1, pt. 2, 397–447. Naples.

Martin, T.R. 1996. Why Did the Greek *polis* Originally Need Coins? *Historia* 45: 257–83.

Martinelli, M.C., G.M. Bacci, L. Paglialunga, and G. Mangano. 1999. Isolato 158. Via La Farina—ex mercato coperto. In *Da Zancle a Messina: Un percorso archeologico attraverso gli scavi*, ed. G.M. Bacci and G. Tigano, 1.61–100. Palermo.

Marton, L. 1997. Le tradizioni sui Rodii in Occidente in età pre-olimpiadica: Tra realtà storica e propaganda. In *Il dinamismo della colonizzazione greca*, ed. C. Antonetti, 135–44. Naples.

Mattaliano, F. 2012. *Atene e Siracusa: poleis homoiotropoi.* Palermo.

Matthäus, H. 2001. Studies on the Interrelations of Cyprus and Italy during the 11th to 9th Centuries B.C.: A Pan-Mediterranean Perspective. In *Italy and Cyprus in Antiquity: 1500–450 BC*, ed. L. Bonfante and V. Karageorghis, 153–214. Nicosia.

Mattingly, D.J., and J. Salmon. 2001. The Productive Past: Economics beyond Agriculture. In *Economies beyond Agriculture in the Classical World*, ed. D.J. Mattingly and J. Salmon, 3–14. London.

Maurici, F. 2001. Le difese costiere della Sicilia (secoli VI–XV). In *Zones côtières littorales dans le monde méditerranéen au Moyen Âge*, ed. J.-M. Martin, 177–204. Collection de l'École Française de Rome Vol. 105.7; Collection de la Casa de Velázquez Vol. 76. Rome and Madrid.

Mazarakis Ainian, A. 1997. *From Rulers' Dwellings to Temples: Architecture, Religion and Society in Early Iron Age Greece (1100–700 B.C.).* Jonsered.

Mazza, M. 1996. Qualche considerazione finale. In *Catania antica*, ed. B. Gentili, 293–302. Pisa.

Mazzarino, S. 1966. *Il pensiero storico classico.* 2 vols. Bari.

———. 1977. La presenza della Sicilia nel pensiero storico dopo l'Unità: Premesse originarie e problemi generali. In *La presenza della Sicilia nella cultura degli ultimi cento anni*, 3–18. Palermo.

McInerney, J. 2004. Nereids, Colonies and the Origin of *Isêgoria*. In *Free Speech in Classical Antiquity*, ed. I. Sluiter and R.M. Rosen, 21–40. Mnemosyne Suppl. Vol. 254. Leiden.

———. 2010. *The Cattle of the Sun: Cows and Culture in the World of the Ancient Greeks.* Princeton.

McNeal, R.A. 1991. Archaeology and the Destruction of the Later Athenian Acropolis. *Antiquity* 65: 49–63.

Mederos Martín, A. 1996. La conexión Levantino-Chipriota: Indices de comercio Atlántico con el Mediterráneo Oriental durante el Bronce Final (1150–950 A.C.). *Trabajos de Prehistoria* 53: 95–115.

Mele, A. 1993. Arché e Basileia: La politica economica di Dionisio I. In *La monetazione dell'età dionigiana: Atti dell'VIII Convegno Internazionale di Studi Numismatici— Napoli 29 maggio–1 giugno 1983*, ed. A. Stazio, M. Taliercio Mensiteri, and S. Ceccoli, 3–38. Rome.

————. 2007. La colonizzazione greca arcaica: Modi e forme. In *Passato e futuro dei convegni di Taranto: Atti del quarantaseiesimo convegno di studi sulla Magna Grecia, Taranto 29 settembre–1 ottobre 2006*, ed. A. Stazio and S. Ceccoli, 39–60. Taranto.

Melfi, M. 2000. Alcune osservazioni sul cosidetto Tempio di Ares a Monte Casale-Kasmenai. *Geo-Archeologia* 2: 39–48.

Menédez Varela, J.L. 2003a. *Consideraciones acerca del origen y la naturaleza de la ciudad planificada en las colonias griegas de Occidente*. BAR International Series Vol. 1104. Oxford.

————. 2003b. Griegos e indígenas en la colonización de occidente: Algunas reflexiones sobre la afirmación de la polis en los nuevos territories. *AHB* 17.1–4: 48–84.

Meola, E. 1996–98. *Necropoli di Selinunte*. Vol. 1: *Buffa*. Palermo.

Mercati, C. 2003. *Epinetron: Storia di una forma ceramica fra archeologia e cultura*. Perugia.

Mercuri, L. 2001. Tête sans corps, corps sans tête: De certains pratiques funéraires en Italie méridionale et en Sicile (VIIIe–Ve siècle avant J.-C.). *MEFRA* 113: 7–31.

————. 2004. *Eubéens en Calabre à l'époque archaïque: Formes de contacts et d'implantation*. BEFAR Vol. 321. Rome.

————. 2010a. Archéologie des pratiques funéraires en Grèce d'Occident au premier âge du Fer: De quelques idées reçues. In *Grecs et indigènes de la Catalogne à la mer Noire: Actes des rencontres du programme européen Ramses² (2006–2008)*, ed. H. Tréziny, 521–27. Aix-en-Provence.

————. 2010b. Monte San Mauro di Caltagirone: Histoire des interprétations d'un site du premier âge du Fer. In *Grecs et indigènes de la Catalogne à la mer Noire: Actes des rencontres du programme européen Ramses² (2006–2008)*, ed. H. Tréziny, 695–700. Aix-en-Provence.

Mertens, D. 2003. *Selinus I : Die Stadt und ihre Mauern*. 2 vols. Mainz.

————. 2004. Siracusa e l'architettura del potere: Uno schizzo. *Sicilia Antiqua* 1: 29–34.

————. 2006. *Città e monumenti dei Greci d'Occidente: Dalla colonizzazione alla crisi del V secolo a.C.* Rome.

————. 2010. Von Megara nach Selinunt: Raumordnung und Baukunst als Mittel zur Identitätsbildung griechischer Poleis während der Großen Kolonisation. *MDAI(R)* 116: 55–103.

————. 2012. Die Agora von Selinunt: Der Platz und die Hallen. *MDAI(R)* 118: 51–178.

Mertens, D., and E. Greco. 1996. Urban Planning in Magna Graecia. In *The Western Greeks*, ed. G. Pugliese Carratelli, 243–62. Milan.

Migeotte, L. 1995. Les finances publiques des cités grecques: Bilan et perspectives de recherches. *Topoi* 5: 7–32.

————. 1996. Les finances des cités grecques au-delà du primitivisme et du modernisme. In ΕΝΕΡΓΕΙΑ: *Studies on Ancient History and Epigraphy Presented to H.W. Pleket*, ed. J.H.M. Strubbe, R.A. Tybout, and H.S. Versnel, 79–96. Amsterdam.

———. 1998. Les ventes de grain public dans les cités grecques aux périodes classique et hellénistique. In *La mémoire perdue: Recherches sur l'administration romaine*, 229–46. Rome.

———. 2006. Les cités grecques: Une économie à plusieurs niveaux. In *L'économie antique, une économie de marché? Actes des deux tables rondes tenues à Lyon les 4 février et 30 novembre 2004*, ed. Y. Roman and J. Dalaison, 69–86. Paris.

———. 2009. *The Economy of the Greek Cities: From the Archaic Period to the Early Roman Empire*. Trans. J. Lloyd. Berkeley.

Millino, G. 2001. Mercenariato e tirannide in Sicilia tra V e IV secolo. *Anemos* 2: 125–88.

Milne, J.G. 1938. The Early Coinages of Sicily. *Numismatic Chronicle* 18: 36–52.

———. 1950. Review of *Masterpieces of Greek Coinage*, by Charles Seltman. *CR* 64.3–4: 149–51.

Milone, F. 1959. *Memoria illustrativa della utilizzazione del suolo della Sicilia*. Rome.

———. 1960. *Sicilia: La natura e l'uomo*. Turin.

Milvia Morciano, M. 2001. Gela: Osservazioni sulla tecnica costruttiva delle fortificazioni di Capo Soprano. *JAT/RTA* 11: 115–54.

Minà, P., ed. 2005. *Urbanistica e architettura nella Sicilia greca*. Palermo.

Mirisola, R., and L. Polacco. 1996. *Contributi alla paleogeografia di Siracusa e del territorio siracusano (VIII–V sec. a.C.)*. Istituto Veneto di Scienze, Lettere ed Arti. Memorie: Classe di Scienze Morali, Lettere ed Arti, no. 66. Venice.

Mitchell, L. 2013. *The Heroic Rulers of Archaic and Classical Greece*. London.

Moggi, M. 1995. Emigrazioni forzate e divieti di ritorno nella colonizzazione greca dei secoli VIII–VII a.C. In *Coercizione e mobilità umana nel mondo antico*, ed. M. Sordi, 27–49. Milan.

———. 1999. Guerra e diplomazia. In *Confini e frontiera nella grecità d'Occidente: Atti del trentasettesimo convegno di studi sulla Magna Grecia, Taranto, 3–6 ottobre 1997*, ed. A. Stazio and S. Ceccoli, 519–45. Taranto.

———. 2003. I campani: Da mercenari a cittadini. In *Quarte giornate internazionali di studi sull'area elima (Erice, 1–4 dicembre 2000): Atti*, ed. A. Corretti, 973–86. Pisa.

———. 2006. Peculiarità della guerra in Sicilia? In *Guerra e pace in Sicilia e nel Mediterraneo antico (VIII–III sec. a.C.): Arte, prassi e teoria della pace e della guerra. Atti delle quinte giornate internazionali di studi sull'area elima e la Sicilia Occidentale nel contesto Mediterraneo, Erice, 12–15 ottobre 2003*, ed. M.A. Vaggioli and C. Michelini, 67–89. Pisa.

Möller, A. 2007. Classical Greece: Distribution. In *The Cambridge Economic History of the Greco-Roman World*, ed. W. Scheidel, I. Morris, and R. Saller, 362–84. Cambridge.

Momigliano, A. 1966. Beloch, Karl Julius. In *Dizionario biografico degli italiani*. Vol. 8, 32–45. Rome.

———. 1968. Prospettiva 1967 della storia greca. *Rivista Storica Italiana* 80: 5–19.

———. 1979. The Rediscovery of Greek History in the Eighteenth Century: The Case of Sicily. In *Studies in Eighteenth Century Culture*, ed. R. Runte, 9.167–87. Madison.

———. 1980. La riscoperta della Sicilia da T. Fazello a P. Orsi. In *La Sicilia antica*, ed. E. Gabba and G. Vallet, Vol. 1, pt. 3, 767–80. Naples.

———. 1981. Uno storico liberale fautore del Sacro Romano Impero: E.A. Freeman. *ASNP* 11: 309–22.

———. 1987. *Ottavo contributo alla storia degli studi classici e del mondo antico*. Rome.

Monoson, S.S. 2000. *Plato's Democratic Entanglements: Athenian Politics and the Practice of Philosophy*. Princeton.

———. 2012. Dionysius I and Sicilian Theatrical Traditions in Plato's Republic: Representing Continuities between Democracy and Tyranny. In *Theater Outside Athens: Drama in Greek Sicily and South Italy*, ed. K. Bosher, 157–72. Cambridge.

Montanari, O. 1999. I pesci di pregio nella "Vita di delizie" di Archestrato di Gela. *MEFRA* 111: 67–77.

Morakis, A. 2011. Thucydides and the Character of Greek Colonisation in Sicily. *CQ* 61: 460–92.

Morcom, J. 1998. Syracusan Bronze Coinage in the Fifth and Early Fourth Centuries BC. In *Studies in Greek Numismatics in Memory of Martin Jessop Price*, ed. R. Ashton, S. Hurter, G. Le Rider, and R. Bland, 287–92. London.

Morel, J.-P. 1983. Les relations économiques dans l'Occident grec. In *Modes de contacts et processus de transformation dans les sociétés anciennes : Actes du colloque de Cortone (24–30 mai 1981)*, 549–76. Rome and Pisa.

———. 1984. Greek Colonization in Italy and the West (Problems of Evidence and Interpretation). In *Crossroads of the Mediterranean*, ed. T. Hackens, N.D. Holloway, and R.R. Holloway, 123–61. Providence.

———. 1993–94. Les rapports entre la Sicile et la Gaule jusqu'au VIème siècle av. J.-C. *Kokalos* 39–40: 333–61.

———. 2000. La céramique attique à vernis noir du IVe siècle: Position des problèmes. In *La céramique attique du 4e siècle en Méditerranée occidentale*, ed. B. Sabattini, 11–21. Naples.

———. 2001. Aux origines de Moulin rotatif? Une meule circulaire de la fin du 6eme siècle avant notre ère à Carthage. In *Techniques et sociétés en Méditerranée: Hommage à Marie-Claire Amouretti*, ed. J.-P. Brun and P. Jockey, 241–50. Paris.

———. 2007. Early Rome and Italy. In *The Cambridge Economic History of the Greco-Roman World*, ed. W. Scheidel, I. Morris, and R. Saller, 487–510. Cambridge.

Moretti, L. 1959. Olympionikai, i vincitori negli antichi agoni olimpici. *Accademia Nazionale dei Lincei, Memorie della Classe di Scienze Morali, Storiche e Filologiche* 8: 55–198.

———. 1987. Nuovo supplemento al catalogo degli Olympionikai. *Miscellanea Greca e Romana* 12: 67–91.

Morgan, C. 1997. Problems and Prospects in the Study of Corinthian Pottery Production. In *Corinto e l'Occidente: Atti del trentaquattresimo convegno di studi sulla Magna Grecia, Taranto, 7–11 ottobre 1994*, ed. A. Stazio and S. Ceccoli, 313–44. Taranto.

———. 1999. The Archaeology of Ethnicity in the Colonial World of the Eighth to Sixth Centuries B.C.: Approaches and Prospects. In *Confini e frontiera nella grecità d'Occidente: Atti del trentasettesimo convegno di studi sulla Magna Grecia, Taranto, 3–6 ottobre 1997*, ed. A. Stazio and S. Ceccoli, 85–145. Taranto.

Morley, N. 2004. *Theories, Models, and Concepts in Ancient History*. London.

———. 2007. *Trade in Classical Antiquity*. Cambridge.

Morris, I. 1986. Gift and Commodity in Archaic Greece. *Man* 21.1: 1–17.

———. 1987. *Burial and Ancient Society: The Rise of the Greek City-State*. Cambridge.

———. 1991. The Early Polis as City and State. In *City and Country in the Ancient World*, ed. J. Rich and A. Wallace-Hadrill, 24–57. Leicester-Nottingham Studies in Ancient Society Vol. 2. London.

———. 1992a. Greeks on the Move. *AHB* 6.3: 137–45.

———. 1992b. *Death-Ritual and Social Structure in Classical Antiquity*. Cambridge.

———, ed. 1994. *Classical Greece: Ancient Histories and Modern Archaeologies*. Cambridge.

———. 1994. Archaeologies of Greece. In *Classical Greece: Ancient Histories and Modern Archaeologies*, ed. I. Morris, 8–47. Cambridge.

———. 1998. Archaeology and Archaic Greek History. In *Archaic Greece: New Approaches and New Evidence*, ed. N. Fisher and H. Van Wees, 1–91. London.

———. 1999. The Social and Economic Archaeology of Greece: An Overview. In *Proceedings of the XVth International Congress of Classical Archaeology, Amsterdam, July 12–17, 1998*, ed. R.F. Docter and E.M. Moormann, 27–33. Amsterdam.

———. 2000. *Archaeology as Cultural History: Words and Things in Iron Age Greece*. Oxford.

———. 2002. Archaeology and Ancient Greek History. In *Current Issues and the Study of Ancient History*: 45–67. Publications of the Association of Ancient Historians 7. Claremont, CA.

———. 2003. Mediterraneanization. *MHR* 18.2: 30–55 (reprinted with same pagination in I. Malkin [ed.], *Mediterranean Paradigms and Classical Antiquity* [London, 2005]).

———. 2004. Economic Growth in Ancient Greece. *Journal of Institutional and Theoretical Economics/Zeitschrift für die gesamte Staatswissenschaft* 160.4: 709–42.

———. 2005. Archaeology, Standards of Living, and Greek Economic History. In *The Ancient Economy: Evidence and Models*, ed. J. Manning and I. Morris, 91–126. Stanford.

———. 2006a. The Collapse and Regeneration of Complex Society in Greece, 1500–500 BC. In *After Collapse: The Regeneration of Complex Societies*, ed. G.M. Schwartz and J.J. Nichols, 72–84. Tuscon.

———. 2006b. The Growth of Greek Cities in the First Millennium BC. In *Urbanism in the Preindustrial World: Cross-cultural Approaches*, ed. G.R. Storey, 27–51. Tuscaloosa.

———. 2007. Early Iron Age Greece. In *The Cambridge Economic History of the Greco-Roman World*, ed. W. Scheidel, I. Morris, and R. Saller, 211–41. Cambridge.

———. 2009a. The Eighth-century Revolution. In *A Companion to Archaic Greece*, ed. K.A. Raaflaub and H. van Wees, 64–80. Oxford.

———. 2009b. The Greater Athenian State. In *The Dynamics of Ancient Empires: State Power from Assyria to Byzantium*, ed. I. Morris and W. Scheidel, 99–177. Oxford.

———. 2013. *The Measure of Civilization: How Social Development Decides the Fate of Nations*. Princeton.

Morris, I., T. Jackman, E. Blake, and S. Tusa. 2002. Stanford University Excavations on the Acropolis of Monte Polizzo, Sicily, II: Preliminary Report of the 2001 Season. *MAAR* 47: 153–98.

Morris, I., T. Jackman, E. Blake, B. Garnand, and S. Tusa. 2003. Stanford University Excavations on the Acropolis of Monte Polizzo, Sicily, III: Preliminary Report of the 2002 Season. *MAAR* 48: 243–315.

Morris, I., and J. Manning. 2005a. "Introduction." In *The Ancient Economy: Evidence and Models*, ed. J. Manning and I. Morris, 1–44. Stanford.

———. 2005b. The Economic Sociology of the Ancient Mediterranean World. In *The Handbook of Economic Sociology*, ed. N.J. Smelser and R. Swedberg, 131–59. 2nd ed. Princeton.

Morris, I., and B.B. Powell. 2006. *The Greeks: History, Culture, and Society*. Upper Saddle River, NJ.

Morris, I., R. Saller, and W. Scheidel. 2007. Introduction. In *The Cambridge Economic History of the Greco-Roman World*, ed. W. Scheidel, I. Morris, and R. Saller, 1–12. Cambridge.

Morris, S.P. 2007. Greeks and "Barbarians." In *Classical Archaeology*, ed. S.E. Alcock and R. Osborne, 383–400. Oxford.

Morris, S.P., and J. Papadopoulos. 2005. Greek Towers and Slaves: An Archaeology of Exploitation. *AJA* 109: 155–225.

Mossé, C. 2006. Plutarch and the Sicilian Tyrants. In *Ancient Tyranny*, ed. S. Lewis, 188–96. Edinburgh.

Muccioli, F. 1999. *Dionisio II: Storia e tradizione letteraria*. Bologna.

Muggia, A. 1997. *L'area di rispetto nelle colonie magno-greche e siceliote: Studio di antropologia della forma urbana*. Palermo.

Murray, O. 1997. Rationality and the Greek City: The Evidence from Kamarina. In *The Polis as an Urban Centre and as a Political Community: Symposium August 29–31, 1996*, ed. M.H. Hansen, 493–504. Copenhagen.

Musti, D. 1990–91. Processi storici e metodologia. *Kokalos* 36–37: 10–16.

———. 2004. "La μεγίστη δυναστεία di Dionisio I e la centralità della Sicilia: Struttura e immagine." *Sicilia Antiqua* 1: 35–39.

———. 2005. Tindari. La città dei gemelli. *Sicilia Antiqua* 2: 141–43.

Myres, J.L. 1937. Review of Pace 1935. *CR* 51: 128–29.

Näf, B., ed. 2001. *Antike und Altertumswissenschaft in der Zeit von Faschismus und Nationalsozialismus: Kolloquium Universität Zürich 14.–17. Oktober 1998.* Mandelbachtal.

Nash Briggs, D. 2003. Metals, Salt, and Slaves: Economic Links between Gaul and Italy from the Eighth to the Late Sixth Centuries BC. *OJA* 22: 243–59.

Naso, A. 2000. Etruscan and Italic Artefacts from the Aegean. In *Ancient Italy in its Mediterranean Setting: Studies in Honour of Ellen Macnamara*, ed. D. Ridgway et al., 193–207. Accordia Specialist Studies on the Mediterranean Vol. 4. London.

———. 2006. Anathemata etruschi nel Mediterraneo orientale. In *Gli Etruschi e il Mediterraneo: Commerci e politica*, ed. G.M. Della Fina, 351–416. Rome.

Neboit, R. 1984a. Erosion des sols et colonisation grecque en Sicile et en Grande Grèce. *Bulletin de l'Association des Géographes Français* 499: 5–13.

———. 1984b. Genèse des terrasses fluviales holocènes en Sicile et en Italie méridionale. *Bulletin de l'Association Française pour l'Étude de Quaternaire* 21.1–3: 157–60.

———. 1984c. À propos des terrasses fluviales récentes en Sicile. *Physio-Géo* 11: 129–36.

Nenci, G. 1988. Pentatlo e i Capi Lilibeo e Pachino in Antioco (Paus., 5,25,5; 10,11,3). *ASNP* 18: 317–23.

———. 1989. Pratiche alimentari e forme di definizione sociale nella Grecia arcaica. In *Homo edens*, ed. O. Longo and P. Scarpi, 25–30. Verona (also published in *ASNP* 18 [1988] 1–10).

———. 1993. Agrigento e la Sicilia nel quadro dei rifornimenti granari del mondo greco. *ASNP* 23: 1–7.

———. 1999. Un'altra iscrizione siciliana finita al Getty Museum. *Kokalos* 45: 3–9.

Nevett, L. 1999. *House and Society in the Ancient Greek World.* Cambridge.

Neville, A. 2007. *Mountains of Silvers & Rivers of Gold: The Phoenicians in Iberia.* Oxford.

Nicholson, N. 2007. Pindar, History, and Historicism. *CPh* 102: 208–27.

———. 2011. Pindar's *Olympian* 4: Psaumis and Camarina after the Deinomenids. *CPh* 106: 93–114.

Nicoletti, F. 1997. Tradizione ed innovazione negli apporti transmarine alle produzioni indigene. In *Prima Sicilia: Alle origini della società siciliana*, ed. S. Tusa, 527–29. Palermo.

Niemeyer, H.G. 1990. The Phoenicians in the Mediterranean: A Non-Greek Model for Expansion and Settlement in Antiquity. In *Greek Colonists and Native Populations*, ed. J.P. Descoeudres, 469–89. Oxford

———. 2004a. Phoenician or Greek: Is There a Reasonable Way out of the Al Mina Debate? *AWE* 3: 38–49.

———. 2004b. The Phoenicians and the Birth of a Multinational Mediterranean Society. In *Commerce and Monetary Systems in the Ancient World: Means of Transmission and Cultural Interaction*, ed. R. Rollinger and C. Ulf, 245–56. Stuttgart.

————. 2006. The Phoenicians in the Mediterranean. Between Expansion and Colonisation: A Non-Greek Model of Overseas Settlement and Presence. In *Greek Colonisation: An Account of Greek Colonies and Other Settlements Overseas*, ed. G. Tsetskhladze, 143–68. Leiden.

Nijboer, A.J. 2001. Regimes of Hoarding. In *Caeculus IV: Interpreting Deposits; Linking Ritual with Economy*, ed. A.J. Nijboer, 35–44. Groningen.

————. 2005a. La cronologia assoluta dell'età del Ferro nel Mediterraneo, dibattito sui metodi e sui risultati. In *Oriente e Occidente: Metodi e discipline a confronto; Riflessioni sulla cronologia dell'età del ferro in Italia. Atti dell'incontro di studi, Roma, 30–31 ottobre 2003*, ed. G. Bartoloni and F. Delpino, 527–56. Pisa.

————. 2005b. The Iron Age in the Mediterranean: A Chronological Mess or "Trade before the Flag," Part II. *AWE* 4: 255–77.

Nijboer, A.J., and J. van der Plicht. 2006. An Interpretation of the Radiocarbon Determination of the Oldest Indigenous-Phoenician Stratum Thus Far, Excavated at Huelva, Tartessos (South-west Spain). *BABesch* 81: 31–36.

Nixon, L., and S. Price. 2001. The Diachronic Analaysis of Pastoralism through Comparative Variables. *BSA* 96: 395–424.

North, D.C. 1981. *Structure and Change in Economic History*. New York.

Noti, R., J.F.N. Leeuwen, D. Colombaroli, E. Vescovi, S. Pasta, T. La Mantia, and W. Tinner. 2009. Mid- and Late-Holocene Vegetation and Fire History at Biviere di Gela, A Coastal Lake in Southern Sicily, Italy. *Vegetation History and Archaeobotany* 18.5: 371–87.

Nuss, A. 2010. Dionysios I. und die Gründung von Tyndaris—ein Beleg für die Etablierung der Territorialherrschaft auf Sizilien im 4. Jahrhundert v. Chr. In *Militärsiedlungen und Territorialherrschaft in der Antike*, ed. F. Daubner, 19–40. Berlin.

Ober, J. 2010. Wealthy Hellas. *TAPhA* 140: 241–86.

Oertli, J.J. 1979. Soil Fertility. In *The Encyclopedia of Soil Science*, ed. R.W. Fairbridge and C.W. Finkl Jnr., 453–62. Stroudsburg, PA.

Oliva, A. 1948. *Le sistemazioni dei terreni*. 2nd ed. Bologna.

Olson, S.D., and A. Sens. 2000. *Archestratos of Gela: Greek Culture and Cuisine in the Fourth Century BCE: Text, Translation, and Commentary*. Oxford.

Oppermann, M. 2005. Wesenszüge der griechischen Kolonisation am Westpontos. *Eurasia Antiqua* 11: 3–14.

Orlandini, P. 1962. L'espansione di Gela nella Sicilia centro-meridionale. *Kokalos* 8: 69–121.

————. 1965. Attrezzi da lavoro in ferro del periodo arcaico e classico nella Sicilia greca. *Economia e Storia* 12: 445–47.

————. 1965–67. Gela: Depositi votivi di bronzo premonetale nel santuario di Demetra Thesmophoros a Bitalemi. *AIIN* 12–14: 1–20.

————. 1968. Gela—topografia dei santuari e documentazione archeologica dei culti. *RIA* 15: 20–66.

————. 1978. Ceramiche della Grecia dell'Est a Gela. In *Les céramiques de la Grèce de l'Est et leur diffusion en Occident. Centre Jean Bérard. Institut Français de Naples 6–9 juillet 1976*, ed. G. Vallet, 93–98. Naples.

————. 2008. Demetra a Gela. In *Demetra: La divinità, i santuari, il culto, la leggenda. Atti del I Congresso Internazionale, Enna, 1–4 luglio 2004*, ed. C.A. Di Stefano, 173–86. Pisa and Rome.

Orlandini, P., and D. Adamesteanu. 1962. IV. Gela. L'acropoli di Gela. *NSc* 16: 340–408.

Orsi, P. 1893. Di due sepolcreti siculi nel territorio di Siracusa. *ArchStorSic* 18: 308–25.

————. 1895. Thapsos. *MAL* 6: 89–150.

————. 1899. Pantalica e Cassibile. *MAL* 9: 33–146.

————. 1900. Siculi e Greci in Leontinoi. *MDAI(R)* 15: 62–98.

————. 1904. Caltagirone: Siculi e Greci a Caltagirone. *NSc*: 65–98, 132–41, 373.

————. 1909. Sepolcri di transizione dalla civiltà sicula alla greca. *MDAI(R)* 24: 59–99.

————. 1912. La necropoli sicula di Pantalica, e la necropoli sicula di M. Dessueri. *MAL* 21: 301–408.

Osanna, M. 2001. Fattorie e villaggi in Magna Grecia. In *Problemi della chora coloniale dall'Occidente al Mar Nero: Atti del quarantesimo convegno di studi sulla Magna Grecia, Taranto, 29 settembre–3 ottobre 2000*, ed. A. Stazio, 203–20. Taranto.

Osanna, M., and M. Torelli, eds. 2006. *Sicilia ellenistica, consuetudo italica: Alle origini dell'architettura ellenistica d'Occidente; Spoleto, Complesso monumentale di S. Nicolò, 5–7 novembre 2004*. Biblioteca di Sicilia Antiqua Vol. 1. Rome.

Osborne, R. 1995. The Economics and Politics of Slavery at Athens. In *The Greek World*, ed. A. Powell, 27–43. London.

————. 1996. Pots, Trade and the Archaic Greek Economy. *Antiquity* 70: 31–44.

————. 1998. Early Greek Colonization? The Nature of Greek Settlement in the West. In *Archaic Greece: New Approaches and New Evidence*, ed. N. Fisher and H. Van Wees, 251–69. London.

————. 1999. Archaeology and the Athenian Empire. *TAPhA* 129: 319–32.

————. 2004a. Greek Archaeology: A Survey of Recent Work. *AJA* 108: 87–102.

————. 2004b. *Greek History*. London.

————. 2007. Archaic Greece. In *The Cambridge Economic History of the Greco-Roman World*, ed. W. Scheidel, I. Morris, and R. Saller, 277–301. Cambridge.

————. 2009. *Greece in the Making, 1200–479 BC*. 2nd ed. London.

Osborne, R., and B. Cunliffe, eds. 2005. *Mediterranean Urbanization 800–600 BC*. Proceedings of the British Academy, Vol. 126. Oxford.

Owen, S. 2003. Of Dogs and Men: Archilochos, Archaeology and the Greek Settlement of Thasos. *PCPhS* 49: 1–18.

Pacciarelli, M. 1999. *Torre Galli: La necropoli della prima età del ferro (scavi Paolo Orsi 1922–23)*. Soveria Mannelli.

————. 2000. *Dal villaggio alla città: La svolta protourbana del 1000 a.C. nell'Italia tir-renica.* Florence.

————. 2004. La prima età del Ferro in Calabria. In *Atti della XXXVII Riunione Scientifica dell'Istituto Italiano di Preistoria e Protostoria della Calabria: Scalea, Papasidero, Praia a Mare, Tortora 29 settembre–4 ottobre,* 447–75 Florence.

Pace, B. 1935–49. *Arte e civiltà nella Sicilia antica.* 4 vols. Milan.

————. 1958. *Arte e civiltà nella Sicilia antica.* Vol. 1, 2nd ed. Milan.

Pafumi, S. 2004. Scultura e committenza in Occidente: Contesto e ruolo sociale della scultura a tuttotondo in Sicilia tra la fine del VI e la prima metà del V secolo a.C. *NAC* 33: 41–96.

Page, D. L., ed. 1972. *Aeschyli septem quae supersunt tragoedias.* Oxford.

Pais, E. 1894. *Storia della Sicilia e della Magna Grecia.* Turin.

————. 1934. Romanità e ellenismo. *Historia* 8: 3–16.

Palazzo, S. 2009. Selinunte e gli altri 'invisibili' protagonisti della battaglia di Imera. In *Temi selinuntini,* ed. C. Antonetti and S. De Vido, 211–28. Pisa.

Palermo, D. 1996. Tradizione indigena e apporti greci nelle culture della Sicilia centro-meridionale: Il caso di Sant'Angelo Muxaro. In *Early Societies in Sicily: New Developments in Archaeological Research,* ed. R. Leighton, 147–54. Accordia Specialist Studies on Italy, Vol. 5. London.

————. 2004. Caratteri e sviluppo della necropoli e del centro antico di Sant'Angelo Muxaro. In *La necropoli di Sant'Angelo Muxaro. Scavi Orsi-Zanotti Bianco 1931–1932,* ed. G. Rizza and D. Palermo, 179–220. CdA 24–25,1985–1986. Catania.

Pancucci, D. 1997. Genti e culture nella Sicilia preclassica. In *Prima Sicilia: Alle origini della società siciliana,* ed. S. Tusa, 559–65. Palermo.

Pancucci, D., and M.C. Naro. 1992. *Monte Bubbonia. Campagne di scavo 1905, 1906, 1955.* Rome.

Pandolfi, M. 1998. Two Italies: Rhetorical Figures of Failed Nationhood. In *Italy's "Southern Question": Orientalism in One Country,* ed. J. Schneider, 285–289. Oxford.

Panvini, R. 1993–94. L'attività della Soprintendenza di Caltanissetta tra gli anni 1992–93. *Kokalos* 39–40: 783–823.

————. 1996. Γέλας: *Storia e archeologia dell'antica Gela.* Turin.

————. 1997. Osservazioni sulle dinamiche formative socio-culturali a Dessueri. In *Prima Sicilia: Alle origini della società siciliana,* ed. S. Tusa, 493–501. Palermo.

————. 2001. *La nave greca arcaica di Gela: E primi dati sul secondo relitto greco.* Caltanissetta.

————. 2003. Monte Dessueri. In *Butera dalla preistoria all'età medievale,* ed. R. Panvini, 41–50. Caltanissetta.

————. 2006. Ceramica attica per i Sicani. In *Les clients de la céramique grecque: Actes du colloque de l'Académie des Inscriptions et Belles-Lettres, Paris, 30–31 janvier 2004,* ed. J. de la Genière, 85–91. Paris.

Panvini, R., and L. Sole. 2005. *L'acropoli di Gela: Stipi, depositi o scarichi*. Corpus delle stipi votive in Italia Vol. xviii. Rome.

Papadopoulos, J.K. 2001. Magna Achaea: Akhaian Late Geometric and Archaic Pottery in South Italy and Sicily. *Hesperia* 70: 373–460.

Papakonstantinou, Z. 2008. *Lawmaking and Adjudication in Archaic Greece*. London.

Pappa, E. 2013. *Early Iron Age Exchange in the West: Phoenicians in the Mediterranean and the Atlantic*. Ancient Near Eastern Studies Vol. 43. Leuven.

Pare, C. 1997. La dimension européenne du commerce grec à la fin de la periode archaïque et pendant le début de la periode classique. In *Vix et les éphèmères principautés celtiques: Les VIe et Ve siècles avant J.-C. en Europe centre-occidentale*, ed. P. Brun and B. Chaume, 261–86. Paris.

Parise, N.F. 1979. Il sistema della litra nella Sicilia antica tra V e IV secolo a.C. In *Le origini della monetazione di bronzo in Sicilia e in Magna Grecia: Atti del VI Convegno del Centro Internazionale di Studi Numismatici—Napoli 17–22 aprile 1977*, ed. A. Stazio, 293–304. Rome.

———. 1993. Il sistema della litra tra Siracusa e Locri nel IV secolo a.C. In *La monetazione dell'età dionigiana: Atti dell'VIII Convegno Internazionale di Studi Numismatici—Napoli 29 maggio–1 giugno 1983*, ed. A. Stazio, M. Taliercio Mensiteri, and S. Ceccoli, 271–75. Rome.

———. 1999. Modi e mezzi dello scambio. In *Confini e frontiera nella grecità d'Occidente: Atti del trentasettesimo convegno di studi sulla Magna Grecia, Taranto, 3–6 ottobre 1997*, ed. A. Stazio and S. Ceccoli, 465–73. Taranto.

Parisi Presicce, C. 1984. La funzione delle aree sacre nell'organizzazione urbanistica primitiva delle colonie greche alla luce della scoperta di un nuovo santuario periferico di Selinunte. *ArchClass* 36: 19–132.

———. 2003. Selinunte dalla scelta del sito alle prime fasi di vita. *MDAI(R)* 110: 263–84.

Parker, A.J. 1992. *Ancient Shipwrecks of the Mediterranean and Roman Provinces*. BAR International Series Vol. 580. Oxford.

Pastore, M. 1997. Taxation, Coercion, Trade and Development in a Frontier Economy: Early and Mid Colonial Paraguay. *Journal of Latin American Studies* 29: 329–54.

Pautasso, A. 1996. *Terrecotte arcaiche e classiche del Museo Civico di Castello Ursino a Catania*. Catania.

———. 2008. *Anakalypsis* e *Anakalypteria*: Iconografie votive e culto nella Sicilia dionigiana. In *Demetra: La divinità, i santuari, il culto, la leggenda. Atti del I Congresso Internazionale, Enna, 1–4 luglio 2004*, ed. C.A. Di Stefano, 285–91. Pisa and Rome.

Pedley, J.G. 2002. *Greek Art and Archaeology*. 3rd ed. Upper Saddle River, NJ.

Pelagatti, P. 1964. Naxos. Relazione preliminare delle campagne di scavo 1961–1964. *BdA* 49: 149–65.

———. 1968–69. L'attività della Soprintendenza alle Antichità della Sicilia Orientale tra il 1965 e il 1968. *Kokalos* 14–15: 344–57.

———. 1976. Ricerche antropologiche per una miglior conoscenza del mondo greco coloniale: Nuovi dati sui riti funebri a Camarina. *SicArch* ix,30: 37–49.

———. 1980–81. L'attività della Soprintendenza alle Antichità della Sicilia orientale, parte II. *Kokalos* 26–27: 694–731.

———. 1997. Le anfore commerciali. In *Corinto e l'Occidente: Atti del trentaquattresimo convegno di studi sulla Magna Grecia, Taranto, 7–11 ottobre 1994*, ed. A. Stazio and S. Ceccoli, 403–16. Taranto.

———. 2003. Antefisse di provenienza camarinese certa o presunta. In *Archeologia del Mediterraneo: Studi in onore di Ernesto De Miro*, ed. G. Fiorentini, M. Caltabiano, and A. Calderone, 515–32. Rome.

Pelagatti, P., and G. Vallet. 1980. Le necropoli. In *La Sicilia antica*, ed. E. Gabba and G. Vallet, Vol. 1, pt. 2, 355–96. Naples.

Pelagatti, P., and G. Spadea, eds. 2004. *Dalle Arene candide a Lipari: Scritti in onore di Luigi Bernabò Brea. Atti del convegno di Genova, 3–5 febbraio 2001*. Rome.

Pelagatti, P., G. Di Stefano, and L. De Lachenal, eds. 2006. *Camarina: 2600 anni dopo la fondazione. Atti del Convegno Internazionale*. Rome.

Pelling, C.B.R. 2000. *Literary Texts and the Greek Historian*. London.

Perale, M. 2009. Μαλοφόρος: Etimologia di teonimo. In *Temi selinuntini*, ed. C. Antonetti and S. De Vido, 229–44. Pisa.

Péré-Noguès, S. 1999. Mercenaires et mercenariat d'Occident: Réflexions sur le développement du mercenariat en Sicile. *Pallas* 51: 105–27.

———. 2004. Citoyenneté et mercenariat en Sicile à l'époque classique. *Pallas* 66: 145–55.

———. 2006. Mercenaires et mercenariat en Sicile: L'exemple campanien et ses enseignements. In *Guerra e pace in Sicilia e nel Mediterraneo antico (VIII–III sec. a.C.): Arte, prassi e teoria della pace e della guerra. Atti delle quinte giornate internazionali di studi sull'area elima e la Sicilia Occidentale nel contesto Mediterraneo, Erice, 12–15 ottobre 2003*, ed. M.A. Vaggioli and C. Michelini, 483–90. Pisa.

———. 2008. Recherches autour des «marqueurs funéraires» à travers l'exemple de quelques sépultures féminines de la nécropole du Fusco (Syracuse). *Pallas* 76: 151–71.

———. 2009. Les enseignements d'un récit: L'exemple des débuts politiques de Denys l'Ancien selon Diodore de Sicile. *Pallas* 79: 105–18.

Perlman, P.J. 2002. The Cretan Colonists of Sicily: Prosopography, Onomastics, and Myths of Colonization. *Cretan Studies* 7: 177–211.

Petruzzella, M. 1999. La *stasis* a Gela in età arcaica e la figura dello ierofante *Telines*. *Kokalos* 45: 501–07.

Philippson, A. 1934. Die Landschaften Siziliens. *Zeitschrift der Gesellschaft für Erdkunde zu Berlin* 9–10: 321–43.

Pingel, V. 1980. "Balkanische" Bronzen der älteren Eisenzeit in Sizilien und Unteritalien. In *Zbornik Posvečen Stanetu Gabrovcu ob šestdesetletnici*, 165–75. Situla 20–21. Ljubljana.

Pinzone, A. 2000. Adolf Holm nel contesto della cultura siciliana. *Mediterraneo Antico* 3: 113–40.

Piraino Manni, M.T. 1980. Nuove iscrizioni dall'acropoli di Gela. In Φιλίας χάριν: *Miscellanea di studi classici in onore di Eugenio Manni*, 1765–832. Rome.

Pisani, M. 2003. Vita quotidiana nel mondo greco tra il VI e il V secolo a.C.: Un contributo per la classificazione delle rappresentazioni fittili. *BdA* 123: 3–24.

Pisano, G. 1999. Remarks on Trade in Luxury Goods in the Western Mediterranean. In *Phoenicians and Carthaginians in the Western Mediter*ranean, ed. G. Pisano, 15–30. Rome.

Pizzo, M. 1999. Sulla ceramica più antica di Gela e la topografia della città. In *KOINA: Miscellanea di studi archeologici in onore di Piero Orlandini*, ed. M. Castoldi, 157–68. Milan.

Poccetti, P. 1999. Frontiere della scrittura e scritture di "frontiera" tra colonizzazione occidentale e culture indigene. In *Confini e frontiera nella grecità d'Occidente: Atti del trentasettesimo convegno di studi sulla Magna Grecia, Taranto, 3–6 ottobre 1997*, ed. A. Stazio and S. Ceccoli, 609–56. Taranto.

———. 2004. Intorno a due laminette plumbee della Sicilia del V secolo a.C. *Mediterraneo Antico* 7: 615–72.

Polignac, F. de. 1995. *Cults, Territory and the Origins of the Greek City-state*. Trans. J. Lloyd. Chicago.

———. 2005. Forms and Processes: Some Thoughts on the Meaning of Urbanization in Early Archaic Greece. In *Mediterranean Urbanization 800–600 BC*, ed. R. Osborne and B. Cunliffe, 45–69. Proceedings of the British Academy Vol. 126. Oxford.

Pollastri, F. 1948–49. *Sicilia: Notizie e commenti ecologici di agricoltura siciliana*. 3 vols. Palermo.

Polverini, L., ed. 1990. *Aspetti della storiografia di Giulio Beloch*. Incontri perugini di storia della storiografia antica e sul mondo antico, no. 1. Naples.

———, ed. 2002. *Aspetti della storiografia di Ettore Pais*. Rome.

———. 2009. La storia economica nell'insegnamento di Giulio Beloch. *Rivista Storica Italiana* 121: 1232–45.

Pomeroy, S.B., S.M. Burstein, W. Dolan, and J. Tolbert Roberts. 2008. *Ancient Greece: A Political, Social, and Cultural History*. 2nd ed. New York.

Ponting, C. 2000. *World History: A New Perspective*. London.

Pontrandolfo, A. 1989. Greci e indigeni. In *Un secolo di ricerche in Magna Grecia: Atti del ventottesimo convegno di studi sulla Magna Grecia, Taranto, 7–12 ottobre 1998*, ed. G. Pugliese Carratelli, 329–50. Taranto.

Portale, E.C. 2008. Cultura materiale e organizzazione degli spazi domestici. In *Himera*. Vol. 5, *L'abitato: Isolato II. I blocchi 1–4 della Zona 1*, ed. N. Allegro, 221–53. Palermo.

Potter, D.S. 1999. *Literary Texts and the Roman Historian*. London.

Powelson, J.P. 1988. *The Story of Land: A World History of Land Tenure and Agrarian Reform*. Cambridge, MA.

Prag, J. 2009. Republican Sicily at the Start of the 21st Century: The Rise of the Optimists? *Pallas* 79: 131–44.

Prag, J.R.W., and J. Crowley Quinn, eds. 2013. *The Hellenistic West: Rethinking the Ancient Mediterranean*. Cambridge.

Prestianni Giallombardo, A.M. 2006. Il ruolo dei mercenari nelle dinamiche di guerra e di pace in Sicilia tra fine V e metà del III sec. a.C. In *Guerra e pace in Sicilia e nel Mediterraneo antico (VIII–III sec. a.C.): Arte, prassi e teoria della pace e della guerra. Atti delle quinte giornate internazionali di studi sull'area elima e la Sicilia Occidentale nel contesto Mediterraneo, Erice, 12–15 ottobre 2003*, ed. M.A. Vaggioli and C. Michelini, 107–29. Pisa.

———. 2009. Zancle e le colonie zanclei. In *Colonie di colonie: Le fondazioni sub-coloniali tra colonizzazione e colonialismo. Atti del convegno internazionale, Lecce, 22–24 giugno 2006*, ed. M. Lombardo and F. Frisone, 267–76. Galatina.

Price, M.J. 1979a. Selinus. In *Le origini della monetazione di bronzo in Sicilia e in Magna Grecia: Atti del VI Convegno del Centro Internazionale di Studi Numismatici—Napoli 17–22 aprile 1977*, ed. A. Stazio, 79–86. Rome.

———. 1979b. The Function of Early Greek Bronze Coinage. In *Le origini della monetazione di bronzo in Sicilia e in Magna Grecia: Atti del VI Convegno del Centro Internazionale di Studi Numismatici—Napoli 17–22 aprile 1977*, ed. A. Stazio, 351–58. Rome.

Privitera, F. 1988–89. Valverde: Saggi di scavo in contrada Casalrosato. *Beni Culturali ed Ambientali, Sicilia* 9–10: 80–83.

Procelli, E. 1989. Aspetti e problemi dell'ellenizzazione calcidese nella Sicilia orientale. *MEFRA* 101: 679–89.

Procelli, E., and R.M. Albanese Procelli. 2003. Riti funerari dell'età del Bronzo in Sicilia. In *Atti della XXXV Riunione Scientifica dell'Istituto Italiano di Preistoria e Protostoria a Lipari "Le comunità della preistoria italiana: Studi e ricerche sul Neolitico e le età dei metalli" in memoria di Luigi Bernabò Brea (Lipari, 2–7.6.2000)*, 323–41. Florence.

Prost, F., ed. 1999. *Armées et sociétés de la Grèce classique: Aspects sociaux et politiques de la guerre aux Ve et IVe s. av. J.-C.* Paris.

Pugliese Carratelli, G. [1980] 1994. La Sicilia nel VI secolo a.C. In *Architettura e urbanistica nella Sicilia greca arcaica*, ed. G. Rizza, 13–19. Siracusa.

———. ed. 1989. *Un secolo di ricerche in Magna Grecia: Atti del ventottesimo convegno di studi sulla Magna Grecia, Taranto, 7–12 ottobre 1998*. Taranto.

Puglisi, M. 2005. Distribuzione e funzione della moneta bronzea in Sicilia dalla metà del V sec. a.C. all'età ellenistica. In *XIII Congreso Internacional de Numismática, Madrid, 15–19 septiembre 2003: Actas, Proceedings, Actes*, ed. C. Alfaro, C. Marcos, and P. Otero, 285–94. Madrid.

———. 2009. *La Sicilia da Dionsio I a Sesto Pompeo: Circolazione e funzione della moneta*. Messina.

Pulvirenti, F. 2004. Evidenze archeologiche di Masseria Castellana. In *Leontini: Il mare, il fiume, la città. Atti della giornata di studio, Lentini, 4 maggio 2002*, ed. M. Frasca, 139–44. Catania.

Purcell, N. 1999. Mobilità e Magna Grecia. In *Confini e frontiera nella grecità d'Occidente: Atti del trentasettesimo convegno di studi sulla Magna Grecia, Taranto, 3–6 ottobre 1997*, ed. A. Stazio and S. Ceccoli, 573–80. Taranto.

———. 2003a. The Boundless Sea of Unlikeness? On Defining the Mediterranean. *MHR* 18.2: 9–29 (reprinted with same pagination in I. Malkin [ed.], *Mediterranean Paradigms and Classical Antiquity* [London, 2005]).

———. 2003b. The Way We Used to Eat: Diet, Community, and History at Rome. *AJPh* 124: 329–58.

———. 2005a. Colonization and Mediterranean History. In *Ancient Colonizations: Analogy, Similarity and Difference*, ed. H. Hurst and S. Owen, 115–39. London.

———. 2005b. The Ancient Mediterranean: The View from the Customs House. In *Rethinking the Mediterranean*, ed. W.V. Harris, 200–32. Oxford.

———. 2005c. Statics and Dynamics: Ancient Mediterranean Urbanism. In *Mediterranean Urbanization 800–600 BC*, ed. R. Osborne and B. Cunliffe, 249–72. Proceedings of the British Academy Vol. 126. Oxford.

Purpura, G. 1982. Pesca e stabilimenti antichi per la lavorazione del pesce in Sicilia: I—S. Vito (Trapani), Cala Minnola (Levanzo). *SicArch* xv,48: 45–60.

———. 1985. Pesca e stabilimenti antichi per la lavorazione del pesce in Sicilia: II— Isola delle Femmine (Palermo), Punta Molinazzo (Punta Rais), Tonnara del Cofano (Trapani), S. Nicola (Favignana). *SicArch* xviiii,57–58: 59–86.

———. 1989. Pesca e stabilimenti antichi per la lavorazione del pesce in Sicilia: III— Torre Vindicari (Noto), Capo Ognina (Siracusa). *SicArch* xxii,69–70: 25–37.

Raccuia, C. 1999. La secessione in *Maktorion. Kokalos* 45: 457–69.

———. 2000. *Gela antica: Storia, economia, istituzioni; le origini*. Messina.

———. 2008. Pirati e Barbari: Rappresentazioni di fenicio-punici nella Sicilia greca. In *Greci e Punici in Sicilia tra V e IV secolo a.C.*, ed. M. Congiu, C. Miccichè, L. Modeo, and L. Santagati, 173–91. Caltanissetta.

Rallo, A. 1978. Le importazioni greco-orientali a Selinunte a seguito dei più recenti scavi. In *Les céramiques de la Grèce de l'Est et leur diffusion en Occident: Centre Jean Bérard. Institut Français de Naples 6–9 juillet 1976*, ed. G. Vallet, 99–103. Naples.

———. 2002. Considérations sur les fouilles récentes de Sélinonte. *RA*: 194–98.

Rausch, M. 2000. *Damos*, gruppi e individui in una *lex sacra* di Selinunte. *Minima Epigraphica et Papyrologica* III.3: 39–52.

Raviola, F. 1999. Atene in Occidente e Atene in Adriatico. In *La Dalmazia e l'altra sponda: Problemi di* archaiologhía *adriatica*, ed. L. Braccesi and S. Graciotti, 41–70. Florence.

Redfield, J.M. 2003. *The Locrian Maidens: Love and Death in Greek Italy*. Princeton.

Reed, C. 2003. *Maritime Traders in the Ancient Greek World*. Cambridge.

Reese, D.S. 1993. Animal Bones. In *Morgantina Studies IV: The Protohistoric Settlement on the Cittadella*, ed. R. Leighton, 91–95. Princeton.

Reitz, E.J., and E.S. Wing. 2008. *Zooarchaeology*. 2nd ed. Cambridge.

Rendeli, M. 2005a. Condivisioni tirreniche - I. In *Greci, Fenici, Romani: Interazioni culturali nel Mediterraneo antico*, ed. S.F. Bondì and M. Vallozza, 173–83. Viterbo.

———. 2005b. La Sardegna e gli Eubei. In *Il Mediterraneo di Herakles: Studi e ricerche*, ed. P. Bernardini and R. Zucca, ed. 91–124. Rome.

Rengakos, A., and A. Tsakmakis, eds. 2006. *Brill's Companion to Thucydides*. Leiden.

Ridgway, D. 1983. David Randall-MacIver 1873–1945. *PBA* 69: 559–77.

———. 1990. The First Western Greeks and their Neighbours, 1935–1985. In *Greek Colonists and Native Populations*, ed. J.P. Descoeudres, 61–72. Oxford.

———. 1992. *The First Western Greeks*. Cambridge.

———. 2004. Euboeans and Others along the Tyrrhenian Seabord in the 8th Century B.C. In *Greek Identity in the Western Mediterranean: Papers in Honour of Brian Shefton*, ed. K. Lomas, 15–33. Mnemosyne Suppl. Vol. 246. Leiden.

———. 2006a. Aspects of the 'Italian Connection.' In *Ancient Greece: From the Mycenaean Palaces to the Age of Homer*, ed. S. Deger-Jalkotzy and I.S. Lemos, 299–313. Edinburgh.

———. 2006b. Early Greek Imports in Sardinia. In *Greek Colonisation: An Account of Greek Colonies and Other Settlements Overseas*, ed. G. Tsetskhladze, 239–52. Leiden.

Ridley, R.T. 1975–76. Ettore Pais. *Helikon* 15–16: 500–33.

Ritter, H. 1986. *Dictionary of Historical Concepts in History*. Reference Sources for the Social Sciences and Humanities, no. 3. Westport, CT.

Riva, C. 2010. *The Urbanisation of Etruria: Funerary Practices and Social Change, 700–600 BC*. Cambridge.

Riva, C., and N.C. Vella. 2006. Introduction. In *Debating Orientalization: Multidisciplinary Approaches to Change in the Ancient Mediterranean*, ed. C. Riva and N.C. Vella, 1–20. London.

Rizza, G. 1971. Ricordo di Biagio Pace. *ArchStorSicO* 67: 345–55.

———. 1996. Catania in età greca: L'evidenza archeologica. In *Catania antica*, ed. B. Gentili, 11–18. Pisa.

———. 2002. Dionigi a Leontini. In *La Sicilia dei due Dionisî: Atti della settimana di studio, Agrigento, 24–28 febbraio 1999*, ed. N. Bonacasa, L. Braccesi, and E. De Miro, 339–41. Rome.

———. 2004. La ricerca archeologica a Lentini: Contributi e prospettive. In *Leontini: Il mare, il fiume, la città. Atti della giornata di studio, Lentini, 4 maggio 2002*, ed. M. Frasca, 81–86. Catania.

———. 2008. Demetra a Catania. In *Demetra: La divinità, i santuari, il culto, la leggenda. Atti del I Congresso Internazionale, Enna, 1–4 luglio 2004*, ed. C.A. Di Stefano, 187–91. Pisa and Rome.

Rizza, G., and E. De Miro. 1986. Le arti figurative dalle origini al V secolo a.C. In *Sikanie: Storia e civiltà della Sicilia greca*, ed. G. Pugliese Carratelli, 125–242. 2nd ed. Milan.

Rizza, G., and D. Palermo, eds. 2004. *La necropoli di Sant'Angelo Muxaro: Scavi Orsi-Zanotti Bianco 1931–1932*. CdA 24–25,1985–1986. Catania.

Rizza, S. 2000. *Studi sulle fortificazioni greche di Leontinoi*. 2 vols. Catania.

Robertson, N. 2010. *Religion and Reconciliation in Greek Cities: The Sacred Laws of Selinus and Cyrene*. American Philological Association American Classical Studies vol. 54. Oxford.

Robinson, E. 2000. Democracy in Syracuse, 466–412 B.C. *Harvard Studies in Classical Philology* 100: 189–205.

———. 2002. Lead Plates and the Case for Democracy in Fifth-Century BC Camarina. In *Oikistes: Studies in Constitutions, Colonies, and Military Power in the Ancient World, Offered in Honor of A.J. Graham*, ed. V.B. Gorman and E.W. Robinson, 61–77. Leiden.

———. 2011. *Democracy beyond Athens: Popular Government in the Greek Classical Age*. Cambridge.

Robinson, E.S.G. 1946. Rhegion, Zankle-Messana and the Samians. *JHS* 66: 13–20.

Robu, A. 2009. Le culte de Zeus Meilichios à Sélinonte et la place des groupements familiaux et pseudo-familiaux dans la colonisation mégarienne. In *La norme en matière religieuse en Grèce ancienne: Actes du XIIe colloque international du CIERGA (Rennes, septembre 2007)*, ed. P. Brulé, 277–91. Kernos Suppl. Vol. 21. Liège.

———. 2014. *Mégare et les établissements mégariens de Sicile, de la Propontide et du Pont-Euxin: Histoire et institutions*. Bern.

Rocca, G. 2009. Due inediti da Selinunte. In *Temi selinuntini*, ed. C. Antonetti and S. De Vido, 269–76. Pisa.

Roebuck, C. 1980. Stasis in Sicily in the Seventh Century B.C. In Φιλίας χάριν: *Miscellanea di studi classici in onore di Eugenio Manni*, 1921–30. Rome.

Roller, L. 1996. East Greek Pottery in Sicily: Evidence for Forms of Contact. In *I vasi attici ed altre ceramiche coeve in Sicilia: Atti del convegno internazionale Catania, Camarina, Gela, Vittoria, 28 marzo–1 aprile 1990*, ed. G. Rizza and F. Giudice, Vol. 2, 89–95. CdA 30 (1991). Catania.

Rolley, C. 2002. Produzione e circolazione dei bronzi nella Magna Grecia. In *Le arti di Efesto: Capolavori in metallo dalla Magna Grecia*, ed. A. Giumlia-Mair and M. Rubinich, 51–57. Cinisello Balsamo.

Rose, P.W. 2012. *Class in Archaic Greece*. Cambridge.

Rosengarten, F. 1998. Homo Siculus: Essentialism in the Writing of Giovanni Verga, Giuseppe Tomasi Di Lampedusa, and Leonardo Sciascia. In *Italy's "Southern Question": Orientalism in One Country*, ed. J. Schneider, 117–31. Oxford.

Rostow, W.W. 1956. The Take-off into Self-sustained Growth. *The Economic Journal* 66: 25–48.

————. 1990. *The Stages of Economic Growth: A Non-Communist Manifesto*. 3rd ed. Cambridge.

Rowland, R.J., Jr. 1975. The Biggest Island in the World. *Classical World* 68: 438–39.

Rubini, M., E. Bonafede, and S. Mogliazza. 1999. The Population of East Sicily during the Second and First Millennium BC: The Problem of the Greek Colonies. *International Journal of Osteoarchaeology* 9.1: 8–17.

Ruby, P. 2006. Peuples, fictions? Ethnicité, identité ethnique et sociétés anciennes. *REA* 108: 25–60.

Ruschenbusch, E. 1985. Die Zahl der griechischen Staaten und Arealgrösse und Bürgerzahl der 'Normalpolis'. *ZPE* 59: 253–63.

Russell, A. 2011. In the Middle of the Corrupting Sea: Cultural Encounters in Sicily and Sardinia between 1450–900 BC. PhD thesis, University of Glasgow.

Russell, J.W. 1989. *Modes of Production in World History*. London.

Russo, I., P. Gianino, and R. Lanteri. 1996. *Augusta e territori limitrofi, I: Preistoria; dal paleolitico superiore alla precolonizzazione*. ArchStorSir Suppl. Vol. 5. Siracusa.

Rutherford, I. 1998. The Amphikleidai of Sicilian Naxos: Pilgrimage and Genos in the Temple Inventories of Delos. *ZPE* 122: 81–89.

Rutter, N.K. 1979. South Italy and Messana. In *Le origini della monetazione di bronzo in Sicilia e in Magna Grecia: Atti del VI Convegno del Centro Internazionale di Studi Numismatici—Napoli 17–22 aprile 1977*, ed. A. Stazio, 193–218. Rome.

————. 1993. The Myth of the "Damareteion." *Chiron* 23: 171–88.

————. 1997. *Greek Coinages of Southern Italy and Sicily*. London.

————. 1998. The Coinage of Syracuse in the Early Fifth Century BC. In *Studies in Greek Numismatics in Memory of Martin Jessop Price*, ed. R. Ashton, S. Hurter, G. Le Rider, and R. Bland, 307–16. London.

————. 2000. Syracusan Democracy: 'Most Like the Athenian'? In *Alternatives to Athens: Varieties of Political Organization and Community in Ancient Greece*, ed. R. Brock and S. Hodkinson, 137–51. Oxford.

Rygorsky, J.M. 2011. Economies of Archaic Sicily: The Archaeological Evidence from the Northeastern Euboian Settlements. PhD dissertation, University of California Berkeley.

Sabbione, C. 2005. Le testimonianze di *Metauros* a Gioia Tauro. In *Lo stretto di Messina nell'antichità*, ed. F. Ghedini, J. Bonetto, A.R. Ghiotto, and F. Rinaldi, 241–52. Rome.

Sadori, L., and B. Narcisi. 2001. The Postglacial Record of Environmental History from Lago di Pergusa, Sicily. *The Holocene* 11.6: 655–70.

Sadori, L., and M. Giardini. 2007. Charcoal Analysis, a Method to study Vegetation and Climate of the Holocene: The Case of Lago di Pergusa (Sicily, Italy). *Geobios* 40.2: 173–180.

Said, E.W. 1978. *Orientalism*. New York.

Salinas, A. 1976–77. *Scritti scelti*. 2 vols. Palermo.

Sallares, R. 1991. *The Ecology of the Ancient Greek World*. London.

———. 2000. Ancient Greece: Some General Considerations. In *Production and Public Powers in Classical Antiquity*, ed. E. Lo Cascio and D.W. Rathbone, 5–13. Cambridge.

———. 2002. *Malaria and Rome: A History of Malaria in Ancient Italy*. Oxford.

———. 2007. Ecology. In *The Cambridge Economic History of the Greco-Roman World*, ed. W. Scheidel, I. Morris, and R. Saller, 15–37. Cambridge.

Salmeri, G. 1991. Grecia vs Roma nella cultura siciliana dal XVII al XX secolo. In *Römische Geschichte und Zeitgeschichte in der deutschen und italienischen Altertumswissenschaft während des 19 und 20 Jahrhunderts*. Vol. 1, *Caesar und Augustus*, ed. K. Christ and E. Gabba, 275–97. Biblioteca di Athenaeum no. 12. Como.

———. 1992. *Sicilia romana: Storia e storiografia*. Catania.

———. 1993. L'antiquaria italiana dell'ottocento. In *Lo studio storico del mondo antico nella cultura italiana dell-Ottocento*, ed. L. Polverini, 265–98. Incontri Perugini di storia della storiografia Antica e sul Mondo Antico, no. 3. Naples.

———. 1996. Gli studi di geografia antica di Gaetano Maria Columba. *Geographia Antiqua* 5: 87–95.

Salmon, J.B. 1984. *Wealthy Corinth: A History of the City to 338 B.C.* Oxford.

———. 1999. The Economic Role of the Greek City. *G&R* 46: 147–67.

Sammartano, R. 1994. Tradizioni ecistiche e rapporti greco-siculi: Le fondazioni di Leontini e di Megara Hyblaea. *SEIA* 11: 47–93.

———. 1999. Le tradizioni letterarie sulla fondazione di Gela e il problema di *Lindioi*. *Kokalos* 45: 471–99.

Sanders, L. 1994. Nationalistic Recommendations and Policies in the Seventh and Eighth Platonic Epistles. *AHB* 8.3: 76–85.

———. 2002. The Relations of Syracuse and Magna Grecia in the Era of the Dionysii. In *La Sicilia dei due Dionisî: Atti della settimana di studio, Agrigento, 24–28 febbraio 1999*, ed. N. Bonacasa, L. Braccesi, and E. De Miro, 473–92. Rome.

Sansone, D. 2012. *Greek Drama and the Invention of Rhetoric*. Malden, MA.

Sapuppo, L. 1998. *Alle origini: La presenza umana nel territorio di Palagonia*. Palagonia.

Sartori, F. 1980–81. Storia costituzionale della Sicilia antica. *Kokalos* 26–27: 263–91.

———. 1997. Schemi costituzionali nell'Occidente greco. In *Il dinamismo della colonizzazione greca*, ed. C. Antonetti, 43–57. Naples.

Scerra, S. 2004. Leontinoi: La città, il grano e i vasi nella prima metà del IV secolo a.C. In *Leontini: Il mare, il fiume, la città. Atti della giornata di studio, Lentini, 4 maggio 2002*, ed. M. Frasca, 145–47. Catania.

Schaps, D.M. 2004. *The Invention of Coinage and the Monetization of Ancient Greece*. Ann Arbor.

Scheid, J., and J. Svenbro. 1985. Byrsa: La ruse d'Élissa et la foundation de Carthage. *AnnalesESC* 40: 328–42.

Scheidel, W. 1995. The Most Silent Women of Greece and Rome: Rural Labour and Women's Life in the Ancient World (I). *G&R* 42: 202–17.

————. 1996. The Most Silent Women of Greece and Rome: Rural Labour and Women's Life in the Ancient World (I). *G&R* 43: 1–10.

————. 2003. The Greek Demographic Expansion: Models and Comparisons. *JHS* 123: 122–40.

————. 2007. Demography. In *The Cambridge Economic History of the Greco-Roman World*, ed. W. Scheidel, I. Morris, and R. Saller, 38–86. Cambridge.

Scheidel, W., I. Morris, and R. Saller, eds. 2007. *The Cambridge Economic History of the Greco-Roman World*. Cambridge.

Scheidel, W., and S. von Reden, eds. 2002. *The Ancient Economy*. Edinburgh.

Schnapp-Gourbeillon, A. 2002. *Aux origines de la Grèce: XIIIe–VIIIe siècles avant notre ère, la genèse du politique*. Paris.

Schneider, H. 2007. Technology. In *The Cambridge Economic History of the Greco-Roman World*, ed. W. Scheidel, I. Morris, and R. Saller, 144–71. Cambridge.

Schneider, J., ed. 1998. *Italy's "Southern Question": Orientalism in One Country*. Oxford.

Schortman, E.M., and P.A. Urban. 2004. Modeling the Roles of Craft Production in Ancient Political Economies. *Journal of Archaeological Research* 12: 185–226.

Schulz, R. 2008. *Kleine Geschichte des antiken Griechenland*. Stuttgart.

Scramuzza, V. 1937. Roman Sicily. In *An Economic Survey of Ancient Rome*, Vol. 3, ed. T. Frank, 225–377. Baltimore.

————. 1938. Review of Pace 1935. *CPh* 33: 335–38.

Seaford, R. 2004. *Money and the Early Greek Mind: Homer, Philosophy, Tragedy*. Cambridge.

Seibert, J. 1982–83. Die Bevölkerungsfluktuation in den Griechenstädten Siziliens. *Ancient Society* 13–14: 33–65.

Settis, S. 1993. Da centro a periferia: L'archeologia degli italiani nel secolo XIX. In *Lo studio storico del mondo antico nella cultura italiana dell'Ottocento*, ed. L. Polverini, 299–334. Incontri Perugini di storia della storiografia Antica e sul Mondo Antico, no. 3. Naples.

Shapiro, H.A. 1996. Tradizioni regionali, botteghe e stili d'arte. In *I greci: Storia, cultura, arte, società*, Vol. 2, pt. 1, ed. S. Settis, 1181–1207. Turin.

Shavit, Y. 1994. Mediterranean History and the History of the Mediterranean: Further Reflections. *Journal of Mediterranean Studies* 4: 313–29.

Shaw, B. 2003. A Peculiar Island: Maghrib and Mediterranean. *MHR* 18: 93–125.

Shepherd, G.B. 1995. The Pride of Most Colonials: Burial and Religion in the Sicilian Colonies. *Acta Hyperborea* 6: 51–82.

————. 1999. Fibulae and Females: Intermarriage in the Western Greek Colonies and the Evidence from Cemeteries. In *Ancient Greeks West and East*, ed. G.R. Tsetskhladze, 267–300. Leiden.

————. 2005a. The Advance of the Greek: Greece, Great Britain and Archaeological Empires. In *Ancient Colonizations: Analogy, Similarity and Difference*, ed. H. Hurst and S. Owen, 23–44. London.

————. 2005b. Dead Men Tell No Tales: Ethnic Diversity in Sicilian Colonies and the Evidence of Cemeteries. *OJA* 24: 115–36.

————. 2007. Poor Little Rich Kids? Status and Selection in Archaic Western Greece. In *Children, Childhood and Society*, ed. S. Crawford and G. Shepherd, 93–106. Oxford.

————. 2009. Greek Colonisation in Sicily and the West: Problems of Evidence and Interpretation Twenty-five Years on. *Pallas* 79: 15–25.

Sherratt, S., and A. Sherratt. 1993. The Growth of the Mediterranean Economy in the Early First Millennium BC. *World Archaeology* 24: 361–78.

Shipley, G. 2000. *The Greek World after Alexander, 323–30 BC*. London.

————. 2005. Little Boxes on the Hillside: Greek Town Planning, Hippodamos and Polis Ideology. In *The Imaginary Polis*, ed. M.H. Hansen, 335–403. Acts of the Copenhagen Polis Centre, Vol. 7. Copenhagen.

Shrimpton, G. 1990. Review of B. Caven 1999. *AHB* 4.5: 101–03.

Silk, M. 2007. Pindar's Poetry as Poetry: A Literary Commentary on *Olympian* 12. In *Pindar's Poetry, Patrons, and Festivals: From Archaic Greece to the Roman Empire*, ed. S. Hornblower and C. Morgan, 177–97. Oxford.

Sinatra, D. 1998. Camarina: Città di frontiera? In *Hesperìa: Studi sulla grecità di occidente*, ed. L. Braccesi, 9.41–52. Rome.

Siracusano, A. 1994. Ceramica di produzione coloniale nell'VIII e nel VII sec. a.C. *QuadMess* 9: 49–61.

————. 2003. A proposito di due oscilla figurati da Monte Saraceno. In *Archeologia del Mediterraneo: Studi in onore di Ernesto De Miro*, ed. G. Fiorentini, M. Caltabiano, and A. Calderone, 605–17. Rome.

————. 2009. *Arte greca: Un'interpretazione*. Messina.

Skeates, R. 2005. Museum Archaeology and the Mediterranean Cultural Heritage. In *The Archaeology of Mediterranean Prehistory*, ed. E. Blake and A.B. Knapp, 303–20. Oxford.

Small, D.B. 1994. A Different Distinction: The Case of Ancient Greece. In *The Economic Anthropology of the State*, ed. E.M. Brumfiel, 287–313. Lanham, MD.

————. 2006. Factoring the Countryside into Urban Populations. In *Urbanism in the Preindustrial World: Cross-cultural Approaches*, ed. G.R. Storey, 317–29. Tuscaloosa.

Smarczyk, B. 2003. *Timoleon und die Neugründung von Syrakus*. Abhandlungen der Akademie der Wissenschaften in Göttingen, Philologisch-Historische Klasse, Vol. 251. Göttingen.

Smith, C.J. 1999. Medea in Italy: Barter and Exchange in the Archaic Mediterranean. In *Ancient Greeks West and East*, ed. G.R. Tsetskhladze, 179–206. Leiden.

————. 2000. Introduction. In *Sicily from Aeneas to Augustus: New Approaches in Archaeology and History*, ed. C.J. Smith and J. Serrati, 1–6. Edinburgh.

————. 2001. Ritualising the Economy. In *Caeculus IV: Interpreting Deposits; Linking Ritual with Economy*, ed. A.J. Nijboer, 17–23. Groningen.

Smith, D.G. 2004. Thucydides' Ignorant Athenians and the Drama of the Sicilian Expedition. *Syllecta Classica* 15: 33–70.

———. 2011. Colonisation in Sicily and North America. *AWE* 10: 309–28.

Smith, M.E. 2004. The Archaeology of Ancient State Economies. *Annual Review of Anthropology* 33: 73–102.

Smith, M.E., G.M. Feinman, R.D. Drennan, T. Earle, and I. Morris. 2012. Archaeology as a Social Science. *Proceedings of the National Academy of Sciences* 109.20: 7617–21.

Smith, R.L. 2009. *Premodern Trade in World History.* London.

Smith, R.R.R. 2007. Pindar, Athletes, and the Early Greek Statue Habit. In *Pindar's Poetry, Patrons, and Festivals: From Archaic Greece to the Roman Empire*, ed. S. Hornblower and C. Morgan, 83–139. Oxford.

Snell, D.C. 2007. Syria-Palestine in Recent Research. In *Current Issues and the Study of the Ancient Near East*, ed. M.W. Chavalas, 113–49. Publications of the Association of Ancient Historians, no. 8. Claremont, CA.

Snodgrass, A. 1983. Heavy Freight in Archaic Greece. In *Trade in the Ancient Economy*, ed. P. Garnsey, K. Hopkins, and C.R. Whittaker, 16–26. London.

———. 1993. The Rise of the *Polis*: The Archaeological Evidence. In *The Ancient Greek City-State*, ed. M. Hansen, 30–40. Copenhagen.

———. 1994a. The Nature and Standing of the Early Western Colonies. In *The Archaeology of Greek Colonisation: Essays Dedicated to Sir John Boardman*, ed. G.R. Tsetskhladze and F. De Angelis, 1–10. Oxford University Committee for Archaeology, monograph 40. Oxford.

———. 1994b. Conclusions II. In *Structures rurales et sociétés antiques: Actes du colloque de Corfou (14–16 mai 1992)*, ed. P.N. Doukellis and L.G. Mendoni, 483–84. Paris.

———. 1998. Rural Burial in the World of Cities. In *Nécropole et pouvoir: Pratiques et interprétations. Actes du colloque Théories de la nécropole antique, Lyon 21–25 janvier 1995*, ed. S. Marchegay, M-T. Le Dinahet, and J.-F. Salles, 37–42. Lyon. Reprinted in Snodgrass 2006, 468–78.

———. 2002. A Paradigm Shift in Classical Archaeology? *CAJ* 12: 179–94.

———. 2006. *Archaeology and the Emergence of Greece.* Ithaca, NY.

———. 2007. What is Classical Archaeology? Greek Archaeology. In *Classical Archaeology*, ed. S.E. Alcock and R. Osborne, 13–29. Oxford.

Sole, L. 2012. *Gli indigeni e la moneta: Rinvenimenti monetali e associazioni contestuali dai centri dell'entroterra siciliano.* Caltanissetta.

Sollars, L. 2005. Settlement in the Prehistoric Mediterranean. In *The Archaeology of Mediterranean Prehistory*, ed. E. Blake and A.B. Knapp, 252–69. Oxford.

Sourisseau, J.-C. 2011. La diffusion des vins grecs d'Occident du VIIIe au IVe s. av. J.-C., sources écrites et documents archéologiques. In *La vigna di Dionisio: Vite, vino e culti in Magna Grecia. Atti del quarantanovesimo Convegno di Studi sulla Magna Grecia, Taranto, 24–28 settembre 2009*, ed. M. Lombardo et al., 143–252. Taranto.

Spagnolo, G. 2002. Le anfore da trasporto arcaiche e classiche nell'occidente greco: Nuove acquisizioni da recenti rinvenimenti a Messina. In *Da Zancle a Messina: Un percorso archeologico attraverso gli scavi*, ed. G.M. Bacci and G. Tigano, 2/2.31–46. Palermo.

————. 2003. Anfore da trasporto nord-Egee in occidente nel periodo arcaico e classico: L'esempio di Gela. In *Archeologia del Mediterraneo: Studi in onore di Ernesto De Miro*, ed. G. Fiorentini, M. Caltabiano, and A. Calderone, 619–41. Rome.

Spanò Giammellaro, A. 2000a. I fenici in Sicilia: Modalità insediamentali e rapporti con l'entroterra, problematiche e prospettive di ricerca. In *Fenicios y territorio: Actas del II Seminario Internacional sobre Temas Fenicios, Guardamar del Segura, 9–11 de abril de 1999*, ed. A. González Prats, 295–335. Alicante.

————. 2000b. Pappe, vino e pesce salato: Appunti per uno studio della cultura alimentare fenicia e punica. *Kokalos* 46: 417–64.

————. 2001. Osservazioni sulle più antiche fasi della presenza fenicia in Sicilia. In *Architettura, arte e artigianato nel Mediterraneo dalla Preistoria all'Alto Medioevo: Atti della Tavola Rotonda Internazionale in memoria di Giovanni Tore, Cagliari, 17–19 dicembre 1999*, ed. Associazione Culturale "Filippo Nissardi," 183–204. Oristano.

Sparkes, B.A., ed. 1998. *Greek Civilization: An Introduction*. Oxford.

Spatafora, F. 2001. La Sicilia occidentale tra l'Età del Bronzo Recente e la Prima Età del Ferro. In *Architettura, arte e artigianato nel Mediterraneo dalla Preistoria all'Alto Medioevo: Atti della Tavola Rotonda Internazionale in memoria di Giovanni Tore, Cagliari, 17–19 dicembre 1999*, ed. Associazione Culturale "Filippo Nissardi," 143–59. Oristano.

————. 2006. Vincitori e vinti: Sulla deposizione di armi e armature nella Sicilia di età arcaica. In *Guerra e pace in Sicilia e nel Mediterraneo antico (VIII–III sec. a.C.): Arte, prassi e teoria della pace e della guerra. Atti delle quinte giornate internazionali di studi sull'area elima e la Sicilia Occidentale nel contesto Mediterraneo, Erice, 12–15 ottobre 2003*, ed. M.A. Vaggioli and C. Michelini, 215–26. Pisa.

Spedding, C.R.W. 1975. The Study of Agricultural Systems. In *Study of Agricultural Systems*, ed. G.E. Dalton, 3–19. London.

Spence, I.G. 1993. *The Cavalry of Classical Greece*. Oxford.

Spencer, C.S. 1998. A Mathematical Model of Primary State Formation. *Cultural Dynamics* 10.1: 5–20.

Spigo, U. 1997. Corinto e la Sicilia: Gli influssi dell'arte corinzia nella cultura figurativa dell'arcaismo siceliota: alcuni aspetti. In *Corinto e l'Occidente: Atti del trentaquattresimo convegno di studi sulla Magna Grecia, Taranto, 7–11 ottobre 1994*, ed. A. Stazio and S. Ceccoli, 551–84. Taranto.

————. 2000. Rapporti della pittura vascolare siceliota con la ceramic attica dello stile di Kerč per un approccio al problema. In *La céramique attique du 4ᵉ siècle en Méditerranée occidentale*, ed. B. Sabattini, 111–20. Naples.

————. 2003. Un ventennio di ricerche a Francavilla di Sicilia. In *Archeologia del Mediterraneo: Studi in onore di Ernesto De Miro*, ed. G. Fiorentini, M. Caltabiano, and A. Calderone, 643–63. Rome.

Stanier, R.S. 1953. The Cost of the Parthenon. *JHS* 73: 68–76.

Starr, C.G. 1977. *The Economic and Social Growth of Early Greece 800–500 B.C.* New York.

Stazio, A. 1992. Moneta, economia e società. In *Agrigento e la Sicilia greca: Atti della settimana di studio, Agrigento 2–8 maggio 1988*, ed. L. Braccesi and E. De Miro, 219–29. Rome.

———, ed. 1993. *La monetazione corinzia in Occidente: Atti del IX convegno del Centro Internazionale di Studi Numismatici, Napoli 27–28 ottobre 1986*. 2 vols. Rome.

———. 1999. Modelli di gestione del territorio della *poleis* italiote e siceliote nella documentazione numismatica. In *La colonisation grecque en Méditerraanée occidentale: Actes de la recontre scientifique en hommage à Georges Vallet organisée par le Centre Jean-Bérard, l'École française de Rome, l'Istituto universitario orientale et l'Università degli studi di Napoli «Federico II» (Rome-Naples, 15–18 novembre 1995)*, 411–18. Collection de l'École Française de Rome Vol. 251. Rome.

———. 2001. La documentazione numismatica. In *Problemi della chora coloniale dall'Occidente al Mar Nero: Atti del quarantesimo convegno di studi sulla Magna Grecia, Taranto, 29 settembre–3 ottobre 2000*, ed. A. Stazio, 153–56. Taranto.

Stazio, A., and S. Ceccoli, eds. 1997. *Corinto e l'Occidente: Atti del trentaquattresimo convegno di studi sulla Magna Grecia, Taranto, 7–11 ottobre 1994*. Taranto.

———. 1999. *Confini e frontiera nella grecità d'Occidente: Atti del trentasettesimo convegno di studi sulla Magna Grecia, Taranto, 3–6 ottobre 1997*. Taranto.

Stein, G. 2002. From Passive Periphery to Active Agents: Emerging Perspectives in the Archaeology of Interregional Interaction. *American Anthropologist* 104: 903–16.

Stika, H.-P., A.G. Heiss, and B. Zach. 2008. Plant Remains from the Early Iron Age in Western Sicily: Differences in Subsistence Strategies of Greek and Elymian Sites. *Vegetation History and Archaeobotany* 17 (Suppl. 1): 139–48.

Stone, G.D. 1991. Agricultural Territories in a Dispersed Settlement System. *Current Anthropology* 32: 343–53.

Storey, G.R. 2004. Roman Economies: A Paradigm of their Own. In *Archaeological Perspectives on Political Economies*, ed. G.M. Feinman and L.M. Nicholas, 105–28. Salt Lake City.

———. ed. 2006. *Urbanism in the Preindustrial World: Cross-cultural Approaches*. Tuscaloosa.

Stroheker, K. F. 1958. *Dionysios I: Gestalt und Geschichte des Tyrannen von Syrakus*. Wiesbaden.

Symons, L. 1978. *Agricultural Geography*. 2nd ed. Boulder.

Szostak, R. 2009. *The Causes of Economic Growth: Interdisciplinary Perspectives*. Berlin.

Tagliamonte, G. 1994. *I figli di Marte: Mobilità, mercenari e mercenariato italici in Magna Grecia e Sicilia*. Rome.

———. 1999. Rapporti tra società di immigrazione e mercenari italici nella Sicilia greca del IV secolo a.C. In *Confini e frontiera nella grecità d'Occidente: Atti del trentasettesimo convegno di studi sulla Magna Grecia, Taranto, 3–6 ottobre 1997*, ed. A. Stazio and S. Ceccoli, 547–72. Taranto.

———. 2002. Mercenari italici ad Agrigento. In *La Sicilia dei due Dionisî: Atti della settimana di studio, Agrigento, 24–28 febbraio 1999*, ed. N. Bonacasa, L. Braccesi, and E. De Miro, 501–17. Rome.

Talalay, L.E. 2005. The Gendered Sea: Iconography, Gender, and Mediterranean Prehistory. In *The Archaeology of Mediterranean Prehistory*, ed. E. Blake and A.B. Knapp, 130–55. Oxford.

Talbert, R. 1974. *Timoleon and the Revival of Greek Sicily, 344–317 B.C.* Cambridge. Reprinted without modification in a paperback edition in 2006.

———. 1992. Review of B. Caven 1990. *AJPh* 113: 455–57.

Tamburello, I. 1977. Palermo antica. *SicArch* x,35: 33–41.

Tandy, D.W. 1997. *Warriors into Traders: The Power of the Market in Early Greece.* Berkeley.

Tanner, J. 1999. Culture, Social Structure and the Status of Visual Artists in Classical Greece. *PCPhS* 45: 136–75.

Thomas, R. 2005. Writing, Law, and Written Law. In *The Cambridge Companion to Ancient Greek Law*, ed. M. Gagarin and D. Cohen, 41–60. Cambridge.

Thompson, F.H. 2003. *The Archaeology of Greek and Roman Slavery.* London.

Thompson, S.I. 1973. *Pioneer Colonization: A Cross-cultural View.* Addison-Wesley Module in Anthropology, no. 33. Reading, MA.

Thompson, S.M. 1999. A Central Sicilian Landscape: Settlement and Society of Ancient Morgantina (5000 BC–AD 50) Italy. PhD dissertation, University of Virginia.

Thomson de Grummond, N. ed. 1996. *An Encyclopedia of the History of Classical Archaeology.* 2 vols. Westport, CT.

Tigano, G. 1999a. Isolato 2–via Torino. In *Da Zancle a Messina: Un percorso archeologico attraverso gli scavi*, ed. G.M. Bacci and G. Tigano, 1.101–19. Palermo.

———. 1999b. Isolato S. Via Industriale. In *Da Zancle a Messina: Un percorso archeologico attraverso gli scavi*, ed. G.M. Bacci and G. Tigano, 1.121–55. Palermo.

———. 2001. Isolati 83 and 96. Via Cesare Battisti. In *Da Zancle a Messina: Un percorso archeologico attraverso gli scavi*, ed. G.M. Bacci and G. Tigano, 2/1.77–97. Palermo.

———., ed. 2002. *Le necropoli di Mylai (VIII–I sec. a.C.). Catalogo.* Milazzo.

Tigano, G., M.C. Martinelli, C. Ingoglia, L. Sannino, L. Paglialunga, F. Severini, F. Bartoli, and G. Mangano. 1999. Isolato 141. Via Cesare Battisti. In *Da Zancle a Messina: Un percorso archeologico attraverso gli scavi*, ed. G.M. Bacci and G. Tigano, 1.157–210. Palermo.

Tinner, W., J.F.N. Leeuwen, D. Colombaroli, E. Vescovi, W.O. van der Knaap, P.D. Henne, S. Pasta, S. D'Angelo, and T. La Mantia. 2009. Holocene Environmental and Climatic Changes at Gorgo Basso, a Coastal Lake in Southern Sicily, Italy. *Quaternary Science Reviews* 28: 1498–510.

Tirnetta, P. 1978. Sciacca. Insediamenti rurali di età greca e romana nel territorio. *Kokalos* 24: 156–74.

Tisseyre, P. 1998. Armi. In *Palermo punica*, ed. C.A. Di Stefano, 360–70. Palermo.

Todisco, L. 2012. *La ceramica a figure rosse della Magna Grecia e della Sicilia.* 3 vols. Rome.

Torelli, M. 1994. Le forme dell'integrazione: Colonizzazione, integrazione economica e politica, stati etnici e stati interetnici. In *Storia d'Europa*. Vol. 2, *Preistoria e antichità*, ed. J. Guilaine and S. Settis, 843–90. Turin.

———. 1996. Riflessi dell'*eudaimonia* agrigentina nelle ceramiche attiche importate. In *I vasi attici ed altre ceramiche coeve in Sicilia: Atti del convegno internazionale Catania, Camarina, Gela, Vittoria, 28 marzo–1 aprile 1990*, ed. G. Rizza and F. Giudice, Vol. 2, 189–98. CdA 30 (1991). Catania.

———. 1999. Santuari, offerte e sacrifici nella Magna Grecia della frontiera. In *Confini e frontiera nella grecità d'Occidente: Atti del trentasettesimo convegno di studi sulla Magna Grecia, Taranto, 3–6 ottobre 1997*, ed. A. Stazio and S. Ceccoli, 685–705. Taranto.

———. 2003. I culti di Imera tra storia e archeologia. In *Archeologia del Mediterraneo: Studi in onore di Ernesto De Miro*, ed. G. Fiorentini, M. Caltabiano, and A. Calderone, 671–83. Rome.

Tosi, M. 1984. The Notion of Craft Specialization and its Representation in the Archaeological Record of Early States in the Turanian Basin. In *Marxist Perspectives in Archaeology*, ed. M. Spriggs, 22–52. Cambridge.

Touring Club Italiano. 1989. *Sicilia*. 6th ed. Milan.

Traina, G. 1988. *Paludi e bonifiche del mondo antico: Saggio di archeologia geografica*. Rome.

———. 1992. Sale e saline nel Mediterraneo antico. *PdP* 47: 363–78.

Trendall, A.D. 1989. *Red Figure Vases of South Italy and Sicily: A Handbook*. London.

Treves, P. 1982. Columba, Gaetano Mario. In *Dizionario biografica degli italiani*. Vol. 27, 501–03. Rome.

Tréziny, H. 1999. Les fortifications grecques en Occident à l'époque classique (491–322 av. J.-C.). *Pallas* 51: 241–82.

———. 2001. Le prix des murailles. In *Techniques et sociétés en Méditerranée: Hommage à Marie-Claire Amouretti*, ed. J.-P. Brun and P. Jockey, 367–80. Paris.

———. 2002. Urbanisme et voirie dans les colonies grecque archaïques de Sicile Orientale. *Pallas* 58: 267–82.

———. 2006. Les fortifications archaïques dans le monde grec colonial d'Occident. In *Guerra e pace in Sicilia e nel Mediterraneo antico (VIII–III sec. a.C.): Arte, prassi e teoria della pace e della guerra. Atti delle quinte giornate internazionali di studi sull'area elima e la Sicilia Occidentale nel contesto Mediterraneo, Erice, 12–15 ottobre 2003*, ed. M.A. Vaggioli and C. Michelini, 255–66. Pisa.

———. 2007. Nouvelles recherches à Mégara Hyblaea. *RA*: 183–88.

———. 2008. Mégara Hyblaea. *MEFRA* 120: 256–60.

Tribulato, O., ed. 2012. *Language and Linguistic Contact in Ancient Sicily*. Cambridge.

Trigger, B.G. 1972. Determinants of Urban Growth in Pre-industrial Societies. In *Man, Settlement and Urbanism*, ed. P.J. Ucko, R. Tringham, and G.W. Dimbleby, 575–99. London.

———. 2003. *Understanding Early Civilizations: A Comparative Study*. Cambridge.

———. 2006. *A History of Archaeological Thought*. 2nd ed. Cambridge.

Trombi, C. 2002. Il materiale indigeno presente nelle colonie greche di Sicilia: La parte occidentale. Parte I. *QuadMess* 3: 91–118.

Trotta, F. 1996. La pesca nel mare di Magna Grecia e Sicilia. In *La Magna Grecia e il mare: Studi di storia marittima*, ed. F. Prontera, 227–50. Taranto.

Trundle, M. 2004. *Greek Mercenaries: From the Late Archaic Period to Alexander*. London.

———. 2005. Ancient Greek Mercenaries (664–250 BCE). *History Compass* 3.1 (online journal:www.blackwell-synergy.com/doi/full/10.1111/j.1478–0542.2005.00116.x).

———. 2006. Money and the Great Man in the Fourth Century BC: Military Power, Aristocratic Connections and Mercenary Service. In *Ancient Tyranny*, ed. S. Lewis, 65–76. Edinburgh.

Tsetskhladze, G. 2006. Revisiting Ancient Greek Colonisation. In *Greek Colonisation*. Vol. 1, *An Account of Greek Colonies and Other Settlements Overseas*, ed. G. Tsetskhladze, xxiii–lxxxiii. Leiden.

———. 2010. "Beware of Greeks Bearing Gifts": Gifts, Tribute, Bribery and Cultural Contacts in the Greek Colonial World. In *Interkulturalität in der Alten Welt: Vorderasien, Hellas, Ägypten und die vielfältigen Ebenen des Kontakts*, ed. R. Rollinger, B. Gufler, M. Lang, and I. Madreiter, 41–61. Wiesbaden.

Turco, M. 2000. *La necropoli di Cassibile (Scavi Paolo Orsi 1897 e 1923)*. Cahiers du Centre Jean Bérard. Vol. 21. Naples.

Turner, B.L., II, and S.B. Brush, eds. 1987. *Comparative Farming Systems*. New York.

Tusa, S. 1992. *La Sicilia nella preistoria*. 2nd ed. Palermo.

———. ed., 1997. *Prima Sicilia: Alle origini della società siciliana*. Palermo.

Tusa, V. 1972. La necropoli arcaica ed adiacenze. Lo scavo del 1970. In *Mozia*. Vol. 7, *Rapporto preliminare della Missione congiunta con la Soprintendenza alle Antichità della Sicilia Occidentale*, ed. F. Bevilacqua et al., 5–82. Rome.

Uggeri, G. 2000. Adolfo Holm e la geografia della Sicilia antica. *RTA/JAT* 10: 277–86.

———. 2002. Dalla Sicilia all'Adriatico: Rotte maritime e vie terrestri nell'età dei due Dionigi (405–344). In *La Sicilia dei due Dionisî: Atti della settimana di studio, Agrigento, 24–28 febbraio 1999*, ed. N. Bonacasa, L. Braccesi, and E. De Miro, 295–320. Rome.

Uhlenbrock, J. 2002. La coroplastica nella Sicilia orientale e meridionale nell'età dei due Dionisî: Problemi di stile e di cronologia archeologica. In *La Sicilia dei due Dionisî: Atti della settimana di studio, Agrigento, 24–28 febbraio 1999*, ed. N. Bonacasa, L. Braccesi, and E. De Miro, 321–37. Rome.

Ulf, C. 2007. Elite oder Eliten in den Dark Ages und der Archaik: Realitäten und Modelle. In *KEIMELION: Elitenbildung und elitärer Konsum von der mykenischen Palastzeit bis zur homerischen Epoche/The Formation of Elites and Elitist Lifestyles from Mycenaean Palatial Times to the Homeric Period. Akten des internationalen Kongresses vom 3. bis 5. Februar 2005 in Salzburg*, ed. E. Alram-Stern and G. Nightingale, 317–24. Vienna.

Urquhart, L.M. forthcoming. English-Speaking Traditions in Studies of the Greeks outside their Homelands. In *A Companion to Greeks across the Ancient World*, ed. F. De Angelis. Malden, MA.

Vallet, G. 1958. *Rhégion et Zancle: Histoire, commerce et civilisation des cités chalcidiennes du détroit de Messine.* BEFAR Vol. 189. Paris.

———. 1980. Note sure la «maison» des Deinoménides. In Φιλίας χάριν: *Miscellanea di studi classici in onore di Eugenio Manni,* 2139–56. Rome.

Valsecchi, M.C. 2008. Ancient Mass Graves of Soldiers, Babies Found in Italy. *National Geographic News* (Dec. 17, 2008). http://news.nationalgeographic.com/news/pf/43325893.html.

van Bath, B.H.S. 1967. The Yields of Different Crops (Mainly Cereals) in Relation to the Seed c. 810–1820. *Acta Historiae Neerlandica* 2: 26–106.

Vanbremeersch, N. 1987. Représentation de la terre et du travail agricole chez Pindare. *QS* 13: 73–95.

Van Compernolle, R. 1966. Syracuse, colonie d'Argos? *Kokalos* 12: 75–101.

———. 1992. La signoria di Terone. In *Agrigento e la Sicilia greca: Atti della settimana di studio, Agrigento 2–8 maggio 1988,* ed. L. Braccesi and E. De Miro, 61–75. Rome.

Vandermersch, C. 1994. *Vins et amphores de Grand Grèce et de Sicile IVe–IIIe s. avant J.-C.* Naples.

———. 1996. Vigne, vin et économie dans l'Italie du sud grecque à l'époque archaïque. *Ostraka* 5: 155–185.

Van Dommelen, P. 2006. Punic Farms and Carthaginian Colonists: Surveying Punic Rural Settlement in the Central Mediterranean. *JRA* 19: 7–28.

Van Dommelen, P., and C. Gómez Bellard, eds. 2008. *Rural Landscapes of the Punic World.* London.

van Joolen, E. 2003. Archaeological Land Evaluation: A Reconstruction of the Suitability of Ancient Landscapes for Various Land Uses in Italy Focused on the First Millennium BC. PhD thesis, University of Groningen.

Vanotti, G. 1995. Leontini nel V secolo, città di profughi. In *Coercizione e mobilità umana nel mondo antico,* ed. M. Sordi, 89–106. Milan.

———. 2004. I rapporti fra la Persia e Siracusa: Il V secolo. In *In Limine: Ricerche su marginalità e periferia nel mondo antico,* ed. G. Vanotti and C. Perassi, 59–104. Milan.

Vanschoonwinkel, J. 2006. Mycenaean Expansion. In *Greek Colonisation: An Account of Greek Colonies and Other Settlements Overseas,* ed. G. Tsetskhladze, 41–113. Leiden.

Van Wees, H. 1995. Review of Dougherty 1993. *G&R* 42: 89–90.

———. 2000. Megara's Mafiosi: Timocracy and Violence in Theognis. In *Alternatives to Athens: Varieties of Political Organization and Community in Ancient Greece,* ed. R. Brock and S. Hodkinson, 52–67. Oxford.

———. 2003. Conquerors and Serfs: Wars of Conquest and Forced Labour in Archaic Greece. In *Helots and their Masters in Laconia and Messenia: Histories, Ideologies, Structures,* ed. N. Luraghi and S.E. Alcock, 33–80. Cambridge, MA.

Varto, E. 2009. Early Greek Kinship. PhD thesis, University of British Columbia, Vancouver.

——. 2012. Interacting Ideas of Kinship and the Nature of Greek Influence on Orientalizing Pontecagnano. In *Griechen in Übersee und der historische Raum*, ed. J. Bergemann, 213–17. Göttinger Studien zur Mediterranen Archäologie vol. 3. Rahden.

Vassallo, S. 1983. La circolazione della moneta bronzea di Agrigento nel V sec. a.C. *RIN* 85: 17–34.

——. 1990. *S. Caterina Villarmosa*. Forma Italiae, Vol. 34. Florence.

——. 1993–94. Ricerche nella necropoli orientale di Himera in località Pestavecchia (1990–93). *Kokalos* 39–40: 1243–55.

——. 1997–98. Himera—indagini a Pestavecchia 1994–1996. *Kokalos* 43–44: 731–43.

——. 1999. Himera, necropoli di Pestavecchia: Un primo bilancio sulle anfore da trasporto. *Kokalos* 45: 329–79.

——., ed. 1999. *Colle Madore: Un caso di ellenizzazione in terra Sicana*. Palermo.

——. 2000. Abitati indigeni ellenizzati della Sicilia centro-occidentale dalla vitalità tardo-arcaica alla crisi del V sec. a.C. In *Terze giornate internazionali di studi sull'area elima (Gibellina, Erice, Contessa Entellina, 23–26 ottobre 1997): Atti*, ed. S. De Vido, 983–1008. Pisa.

——. 2003. Ceramica indigena arcaica ad Himera. In *Quarte giornate internazionali di studi sull'area elima (Erice, 1–4 dicembre 2000): Atti*, ed. A. Corretti, 1343–56. Pisa.

——. 2005a. Nuovi dati sull'urbanistica e sulle fortificazioni di Himera. In *Papers in Italian Archaeology VI: Communities and Settlements from the Neolithic to the Early Medieval Period*, ed. P. Attema, A. Nijboer, and A. Zifferero, 325–33. BAR International Series Vol. 1452. Oxford.

——. 2005b. *Himera: Città greca; Guida alla storia e ai monumenti*. Palermo.

——. 2005c. Anfore da trasporto fenicio-puniche a Himera. In *Atti del V Congresso Internazionale di Studi Fenici e Punici, Marsala-Palermo, 2–8 ottobre 2000*, ed. A. Spanò Giammellaro, 829–35. Palermo.

——. 2006. La guerra ad Himera: Il sistema difensivo della città e del territorio. In *Guerra e pace in Sicilia e nel Mediterraneo antico (VIII–III sec. a.C.): Arte, prassi e teoria della pace e della guerra. Atti delle quinte giornate internazionali di studi sull'area elima e la Sicilia Occidentale nel contesto Mediterraneo, Erice, 12–15 ottobre 2003*, ed. M.A. Vaggioli and C. Michelini, 315–25. Pisa.

——. 2010a. L'incontro tra indigeni e Greci di Himera nella Sicilia centro-settentrionale (VII–V sec. a.C.). In *Grecs et indigènes de la Catalogne à la mer Noire: Actes des rencontres du programme européen Ramses² (2006–2008)*, ed. H. Tréziny, 41–54. Aix-en-Provence.

——. 2010b. Le battaglie di Himera alla luce degli scavi nella necropoli occidentale e alle fortificazioni: I luoghi, i protagonisti. *Sicilia Antiqua* 7: 17–38.

——. 2010c. Himera alla luce delle recenti indagini nella città e nelle necropoli. *Mare Internum* 2: 45–56.

————. 2012. Nuovi dati per la localizzazione dell'agora di Himera. In *Agora greca e agorai di Sicilia: Atti delle settime giornate internazionali di studi sull'area elima e la Sicilia occidentale nel contesto mediterraneo Erice, 12–15 ottobre 2009*, ed. C. Ampolo, 201–10. Pisa.

Vassallo, S., and M. Valentino. 2009. Himera: Indagini nelle necropoli. In *Tra Etruria, Lazio e Magna Grecia: Indagini sulle necropoli. Atti dell'Incontro di Studio, Fisciano, 5–6 marzo 2009*, ed. R. Bonaudo, L. Cerchiai, and C. Pellegrino, 233–60. Paestum.

Vassilaki, E. 2007. L'éloge des dieux, de la terre et des hommes dans les odes siciliennes de Pindare: Le cas de Déméter et Persephone. In *L'hymne antique et son public*, ed. Y. Lehman, 205–23. Turnhout.

Vattuone, R. 1994. 'Metoikesis': Trapianti di popolazione nella Sicilia greca fra VI e IV sec. a.C. In *Emigrazione e immigrazione nel mondo antico*, ed. M. Sordi, 81–113. Milan.

————, ed. 2002. *Storici greci d'Occidente*. Bologna.

Verger, S. 2003. Des objets gaulois dans les sanctuaires archaïques de Grèce, de Sicile et d'Italie. *CRAI*: 525–73.

Veronese, F. 2000. Poleis, santuari e «paesaggi di potere» nella Sicilia greca di età arcaica. In *Paesaggi di potere: Problemi e prospettive*, ed. G. Camassa, A. De Guio, and F. Veronese, 239–83. Rome.

————. 2006. *Lo spazio e la dimensione del sacro: Santuari greci e territorio nella arcaica*. Padua.

Vickers, M. 1996. The Greek Pottery Vases from Gela in Oxford: Their Place in History and in the History of Art. In *I vasi attici ed altre ceramiche coeve in Sicilia: Atti del convegno internazionale Catania, Camarina, Gela, Vittoria, 28 marzo–1 aprile 1990*, ed. G. Rizza and F. Giudice, Vol. 2, 181–89. CdA 29 (1990). Catania.

Villard, F. 1992. Les céramiques locales: Problèmes généraux. In *Les ateliers de potiers dans le monde grecque aux époques géométrique, archaïque et classique*, ed. F. Blondé and J.Y. Perreault, 3–9. BCH Suppl. Vol. 23. Paris.

————. 1994. Les sièges de Syracuse et leurs pestilences. In *L'eau, la santé et la maladie dans le monde grec*, ed. R. Ginouvès, A.-M. Guimier-Sorbets, J. Jouanna, and L. Villard, 337–44. BCH Suppl. Vol. 28. Paris.

————. 2000. La place de l'Occident dans les exportations attiques à figures rouges au IVe siècle. In *La céramique attique du 4e siècle en Méditerranée occidentale*, ed. B. Sabattini, 7–10. Naples.

Villari, P. 1981. *Monte di Giove e Fiumedinisi*. Verona.

————. 1987. Nota preliminare allo studio delle faune della tarda preistoria della Sicilia Orientale. *Studi per l'Ecologia del Quaternario* 8: 169–76.

————. 1989. Nature des offrandes animales du puits de Piazza della Vittoria à Syracuse (milieu du IIe siècle av. J.-C.): Étude archéozoologique. *Anthropozoologica* 11: 9–30.

————. 1991a. Appendice V: Le faune del villaggio di Capo Graziano nel contesto archeozoologico eoliano e siciliano dell'età del Bronzo. In *Meligunìs Lipára*

VI: Filicudi insediamenti dell'età del Bronzo, ed. L. Bernabò Brea and M. Cavalier, 315–30. Palermo.

———. 1991b. The Faunal Remains in the Bothros at Eolo (Lipari). *Archaeozoologia* 4: 109–26.

———. 1992a. Faunal Remains from Thapsos Pits 1–2 (Syracuse, Sicily). *Bulletin du Musée d'Anthropologie Préhistorique de Monaco* 34: 109–24.

———. 1992b. I molluschi marini nell'alimentazione preistorica e nei culti d'età greca e romana della Sicilia orientale: I dati archeozoologici. *Animalia* 19: 67–77.

———. 1992c. I resti animali di una fossa votiva del Tempio Ionico di Siracusa. *Animalia* 19: 79–89.

———. 1995. *Le faune della tarda preistoria della Sicilia orientale*. Siracusa.

Vinci, M. 2004. Horoi: Due nuovi cippi confinari nella Sicilia sud orientale. *ArchStorSir* 18: 83–104.

Visonà, P. 2007. Greek Coinage in Dalmatia and Trans-Adriatic Relations in the 4th Century B.C. *Chiron* 37: 479–94.

Vlassopoulos, K. 2007a. *Unthinking the Greek Polis: Ancient Greek History beyond Eurocentrism*. Cambridge.

———. 2007b. Between East and West: The Greek *Poleis* as Part of a World-System. *AWE* 6: 91–111.

———. 2007c. Beyond and Below the *Polis*: Networks, Associations, and the Writing of Greek History. *MHR* 22.1: 11–22.

———. 2011. Regional Perspectives and the Study of Greek History. *Incidenza dell'Antico* 9: 9–31.

———. 2013. *Greeks and Barbarians*. Cambridge.

Von Reden, S. 1995. *Exchange in Ancient Greece*. London.

———. 1997. Money, Law and Exchange: Coinage in the Greek Polis. *JHS* 117: 154–76.

———. 2002. Money in the Ancient Economy: A Survey of Recent Research. *Klio* 84: 141–74.

———. 2007. Classical Greece: Consumption. In *The Cambridge Economic History of the Greco-Roman World*, ed. W. Scheidel, I. Morris, and R. Saller, 385–406. Cambridge.

Voza, G. 1980–81. L'attività della Soprintendenza alle Antichità della Sicilia Orientale. *Kokalos* 26–27: 674–93.

———. 1999. *Nel segno dell'antico: Archeologia nel territorio di Siracusa*. Palermo.

Walker, D.S. 1967. *A Geography of Italy*. 2nd ed. London.

Wallace, R.W. 2013. Councils in Greek Oligarchies and Democracies. In *A Companion to Ancient Greek Government*, ed. H. Beck, 191–204. Malden, MA.

Wallinga, H.T. 1993. *Ships and Sea-power before the Great Persian War: The Ancestry of the Ancient Trireme*. Mnemosyne Suppl. Vol. 121. Leiden.

———. 1995. The Ancestry of the Trireme 1200–525. In *The Age of the Galley: Mediterranean Oared Vessels since Pre-Classical Times*, ed. R. Gardiner, 36–48. London.

Wason, P.K. 1994. *The Archaeology of Rank*. Cambridge.

Wasowicz, A. 1994. Vin, salaison et guerre dans le Bosphore aux confins des ères. In *Structures rurales et sociétés antiques: Actes du colloque de Corfou (14–16 mai 1992)*, ed. P.N. Doukellis and L.G. Mendoni, 227–35. Paris.

———. 2001. Trentatrè anni dopo il convegno "La città e il suo territorio." In *Problemi della chora coloniale dall'Occidente al Mar Nero: Atti del quarantesimo convegno di studi sulla Magna Grecia, Taranto, 29 settembre–3 ottobre 2000*, ed. A. Stazio, 9–26. Taranto.

Waters, K.H. 1974. The Rise and Decline of Some Greek Colonies in Sicily. *Ancient Society* 5: 1–19.

Watkins, M.H. 1963. A Staple Theory of Economic Growth. *Canadian Journal of Economics and Political Science* 29.2: 141–58.

Weber, M. 1978. *Economy and Society: An Outline of Interpretive Sociology*, ed. G. Roth and C. Wittich. 2 vols. Berkeley.

———. 2003. *General Economic History*. Trans. F.H. Knight. Mineola, NY.

———. 2013. *The Agrarian Sociology of Ancient Civilizations*. Trans. R.I. Frank. London.

Webster, G.S. 1990. Labor Control and Emergent Stratification in Prehistoric Europe. *Current Anthropology* 31.4: 337–66.

———. 1996. *A Prehistory of Sardinia 2300–500 BC*. Sheffield.

Wegner, M. 1964. *Sizilien, von Einheimischen und Fremden erlebt: Charakter-studie einer Weltinsel*. Berlin.

Wells, P.S. 2008. *Barbarians to Angels: The Dark Ages Reconsidered*. New York.

Westermark, U. 1979. The Fifth Century Bronze Coinage of Akragas. In *Le origini della monetazione di bronzo in Sicilia e in Magna Grecia: Atti del VI Convegno del Centro Internazionale di Studi Numismatici—Napoli 17–22 aprile 1977*, ed. A. Stazio, 3–17. Rome.

Westlake, H.D. 1994. Dion and Timoleon. In *The Cambridge Ancient History*. Vol. 6, *The Fourth Century B.C.*, ed. D.M. Lewis, J. Boardman, S. Hornblower, and M. Ostwald, 693–722. 2nd ed. Cambridge.

White, D. 1963. A Survey of Millstones from Morgantina. *AJA* 67: 199–206.

Whitehead, D. 2008. Athenians in Sicily in the Fourth Century BC. In *Epigraphy and the Greek Historian*, ed. C. Cooper, 57–67. Phoenix Suppl. Vol. 47. Toronto.

Whitley, J. 2001. *The Archaeology of Ancient Greece*. Cambridge World Archaeology Series. Cambridge.

———. 2004. Cycles of Collapse in Greek Prehistory: The House of the Tiles at Lerna and the 'Heroon' at Lefkandi. In *Explaining Social Change: Studies in Honour of Colin Renfrew*, ed. J. Cherry, C. Scarre, and S. Shennan, 193–201. Cambridge.

Wilkes, J., and T. Fischer-Hansen. 2004. The Adriatic. In *An Inventory of Archaic and Classical Poleis: An Investigation Conducted by the Copenhagen Polis Centre for the*

Danish National Research Foundation, ed. M.H. Hansen and T.H. Nielsen, 321–37. Oxford.

Wilkins, J.M. 2000. Food, Culture, and People Moving. *Journal of Mediterranean Studies* 10.1–2: 213–22.

Wilkins, J.M., and S. Hill. 2006. *Food in the Ancient World*. Oxford.

Willi, A. 2008. *Sikelismos: Sprache, Literatur und Gesellschaft im griechischen Sizilien (8.–5. Jh. v. Chr.)*. Basel.

———. 2012. Challenging Authority: Epicharmus between Epic and Rhetoric. In *Theater Outside Athens: Drama in Greek Sicily and South Italy*, ed. K. Bosher, 56–75. Cambridge.

Williams, C.K. 1997. Archaic and Classical Corinth. In *Corinto e l'Occidente: Atti del trentaquattresimo convegno di studi sulla Magna Grecia, Taranto, 7–11 ottobre 1994*, ed. A. Stazio and S. Ceccoli, 31–45. Taranto.

Wilson, R. J. A. 1990. *Sicily under the Roman Empire: The Archaeology of a Roman Province, 36 BC–AD 535*. Warminster.

———. 2000. Aqueducts and Water Supply in Greek and Roman Sicily: The Present *status quaestionis*. In *Cura aquarum in Sicilia: Proceedings of the Tenth International Congress on the History of Water Management and Hydraulic Engineering in the Mediterranean Region, Syracuse, May 16–22, 1998*, ed. G.C.M. Jansen, 5–36. Leiden.

Woodhead, A.G. 1962. *The Greeks in the West*. London.

Woolf, G. 2004. The Present State and Future Scope of Roman Archaeology: A Comment. *AJA* 108: 417–28.

Yntema, D. 2000. Mental Landscapes of Colonization: The Ancient Written Sources and the Archaeology of Early Colonial-Greek Southeastern Sicily. *BABesch* 75: 1–50.

Zahrnt, M. 1997. Der Demos von Syrakus im Zeitalter der Dionysioi. In *Volk und Verfassung im vorhellenistischen Griechenland: Beiträge auf dem Symposium zu Ehren von Karl-Wilhelm Welwei in Bochum, 1.–2. März 1996*, ed. W. Eder and K.-J. Hölkeskamp, 153–75. Stuttgart.

———. 2006. Sicily and Southern Italy in Thucydides. In *Brill's Companion to Thucydides*, ed. A. Rengakos and A. Tsakmakis, 629–55. Leiden.

Zambon, E. 2001. Esperienze europee di mercenariato in area italico-siceliota e nel Mediterraneo occidentale tra IV e III secolo. *Anemos* 2: 229–77.

———. 2008. *Tradition and Innnovation: Sicily between Hellenism and Rome*. Historia Suppl. Vol. 205. Stuttgart.

Zarmati, L. 2004. Dunbabin, Thomas James (1911–55). In *The Dictionary of British Classicists*, ed. R. Todd, 266–67. Bristol.

Zelnick-Abramowitz, R. 2004. The Proxenoi of Western Greece. *ZPE* 147: 93–106.

Zimmerman Munn, M.L. 2003. Corinthian Trade with the Punic West in the Classical Period. In *Corinth: The Centenary 1896–1996*, ed. C.K. Williams II and N. Bookidis, 195–217. Princeton.

Zoepffel, R. 1993. Le fonti scritte su Dionigi I di Siracusa. In *La monetazione dell'età dionigiana: Atti dell'VIII Convegno Internazionale di Studi Numismatici—Napoli 29 maggio–1 giugno 1983*, ed. A. Stazio, M. Taliercio Mensiteri, and S. Ceccoli, 39–56. Rome.

Zuchtriegel, G. 2011. Zur Bevölkerungszahl Selinunts im 5 Jh. v. Chr. *Historia* 60: 115–21.

Zurbach, J. 2008. Question foncière et departs coloniaux: À propos des *apoikiai* archaïques. *ASAA* 86 (8³): 87–103.

Index

fibula, 31, 42

fiduciary, 296, 301, 315

fig, 240

finances and revenue, 88, 112, 115, 129, 181, 214, 269–71, 278–82, 299–300, 307, 316–17

fine, legal, 174, 264–65

Finley, M.I., 23–24, 53, 149, 152, 155, 158, 193, 320, 322

fir, 236

fish/fishing, 4, 224, 229, 239, 269, 279–80, 289–90, 295, 308–13, 317–18, 323

Fiumedinisi, 215

flax, 255n.187, 284n.342

flour, 233n.52

fodder, animal, 233n.55

food (cultivated and wild), 47, 59, 105, 126, 150, 222n.1, 223–40, 273–74, 280n.322, 283–311, 317, 326 *See also* meals, ritual

forest, 65, 230, 238, 289n.365, 313

fortifications, 45, 71, 88n.85, 117, 124–25, 127–28, 163, 169, 175, 185, 215, 304, 307

foundation (of settlement), 17, 33, 36–37, 47, 63, 66–74, 76, 93n.107, 106, 112, 118, 126n.262, 127, 134, 139, 141n.40, 147–48, 153, 159–63, 167, 169–70, 176, 183n.285, 189, 195, 205, 220, 230, 235, 261, 321

founder, 33, 137–38, 147–48, 152, 159–61, 186–87, 202, 324 *See also* oikist

Francavilla di Sicilia, 95, 244

France, French, 19, 49, 160n.134, 233n.4

Freeman, E.A., 8–9, 13, 17, 18n.73, 324–25

frontier, xv, 3–4, 13, 17, 20, 22, 24, 26, 56, 98n.131, 172–73, 178, 220, 320, 322, 324

fuel, 241

funerary evidence, 35, 41, 43, 47, 50, 83, 97, 120–21, 134–35, 140, 144–45, 149–51, 153, 155–58, 160–66, 169, 171–72, 175–78, 185, 201, 214, 232, 236–37, 255, 262, 283n.337

fungicide, 285

fusion, cultural, 6, 219

Gabrici, E., 144

Gades, 36, 289

gamoroi (of Syracuse), 149, 155, 157, 168, 182, 207

garden, 185

garrison, 122, 124, 210, 276, 296n.406, 304, 315

gastropod, 311

Gaul, 252–53

Gela, 33, 50, 51n.142, 71–73, 75–76, 82–85, 87, 89, 93, 95n.115, 96–97, 100–101, 104, 112, 114, 117, 121, 130–33, 143, 145, 152–53, 156–57, 159, 161, 164–67, 169, 171–72, 175–76, 180–83, 186–87, 193, 199, 202, 204–6, 210, 224n.13, 230–35, 237–38, 241–45, 249–51, 253, 257–59, 264–65, 271–78, 284n.342, 288, 290–91, 293, 295n.397, 296n.406, 297–99, 306, 308, 316, 318

Gelon, 101–6, 112, 125, 155, 181–87, 272, 275, 277–80

gender, 136n.7, 166

genealogy, 146, 148–49

genos, see clan

gentilicial, 137–40, 178, 194–95

geography, 28–61, 62–66, 68n.18, 71, 94, 187, 220, 231, 250, 256, 271, 320, 325, 327

geology, 62–66, 241n.97

geomorphology, 230, 250, 303

Geometric, 31, 38–39, 243, 262

Germany, German, 9–13, 15

private, 60, 62, 64, 66, 83, 86, 88–89, 92, 99, 133, 137, 150, 185, 194, 270, 296n.406

production, 35–36, 42, 46–48, 84–85, 97, 120, 226–56, 273–74, 283–92, 304–11, 317–18, 321–25

productivity, 225, 232, 268

professionalization (of scholarship), 8–13

propaganda, 167

property, property rights, 48, 53, 56, 86, 88, 119, 137, 155, 174, 190, 192, 207–8, 210, 213, 217, 220, 266–67, 270, 322

protohistory, 33

provisions, provisioning, 270

proxenos, proxenoi, proxeny (consular agent), 305n.448, 312

prytaneion, 92, 312

Psaumis, 154, 201, 206

public, 62, 64, 83–84, 88–89, 92–94, 99, 103, 110, 112–17, 122, 131, 133, 137, 150–52, 155, 174–75, 177, 181, 185, 194, 199, 202, 206–9, 211, 255, 270, 277, 292, 321

pulses, 268

Punic, 1n.1, 46–48, 50n.132, 51n.140, 125, 253, 257, 263, 288–89, 315

Punta Bracceto, 252, 255–56

Punta Castelluzzo, 55n.153, 257n.201

Pyrgi, 316

Pystilos, 73

Pythagoras, Pythagorean, 114

quarry, 89, 124, 248, 257n.201, 292, 311

quern, 233

Quellenforschung ("source research"), 10
See also sources

race, racial theory, 6, 8–20, 173

rainfall, 65–66, 226, 228–29, 231, 287

Ramacca, 262

ranking, social, 160

ransom(ing), 312, 316

region(al) (-ism), 22, 46, 277, 320

religion, 16, 19, 60, 62, 84, 88–93, 98–99, 112, 133–34, 139, 147, 152, 175, 186, 195, 202, 234n.63, 237–38, 248, 270, 300

renovation, 87, 292

reptile, 239

resistance, 20, 185, 304

Resuttano, 98

Rhegion, 95n.119, 105, 110, 114, 126–27, 182, 205, 280, 316

rhetoric, 206, 213

Rhodes, 33, 71, 73n.39, 148, 161, 167, 171, 191, 243, 262

Ridgway, D., 36

roads, 47, 156

Rocca d'Antoni, 84, 157

Robinson, E., 205–7

Rodì, 97

Romanitas, Romanocentrism, 14, 19, 229n.27

Rome, Roman, 1, 5, 7, 11–12, 14–16, 26, 33, 35, 42n.82, 103n.155, 120, 178, 197, 224, 240, 266, 274, 278, 285, 324, 326

roofing, 41, 45, 86, 103, 256

Rosolini, 97

Rutter, N.K., 207, 314

Sakon, 166

Salamis (Attica and Cyprus), 104, 284

Salinas, A., 7–10, 15–16

Salso river (ancient Himeras), 65, 74

salt, rock and sea, 46, 65, 216, 229, 241n.97, 249–51, 269, 290, 311

Samos, 166, 181, 223n.9, 257–58, 262, 278, 280, 305n.448

sanctuary, 30, 45, 47, 51, 62n.2, 84, 88, 90–92, 95–96, 98, 105, 114, 116, 137–41, 152, 160–61, 165n.170, 166, 169–70, 172, 186, 192, 232, 236–39, 241–42, 247, 251–53, 255–56, 262–63, 290, 292, 316